FOURTH EDITION

ETHICS AND TECHNOLOGY

Controversies, Questions, and Strategies for Ethical Computing

HERMAN T. TAVANI

Rivier University

WILEY

VP & Executive Publisher:	*Donald Fowley*
Executive Editor:	*Beth Lang Golub*
Editorial Assistant:	*Katherine Willis*
Marketing Manager:	*Chris Ruel*
Marketing Assistant:	*Marissa Carroll*
Associate Production Manager:	*Joyce Poh*
Production Editor:	*Jolene Ling*
Designer:	*Kenji Ngieng*
Cover Photo Credit:	*Bernhard Lang/Getty Images, Inc.*
Production Management Services:	*Thomson Digital*

This book was set in 10/12 TimesTenLTStd-Roman by Thomson Digital, and printed and bound by Edwards Brothers Malloy. The cover was printed by Edwards Brothers Malloy.

This book is printed on acid free paper.

Founded in 1807, John Wiley & Sons, Inc. has been a valued source of knowledge and understanding for more than 200 years, helping people around the world meet their needs and fulfill their aspirations. Our company is built on a foundation of principles that include responsibility to the communities we serve and where we live and work. In 2008, we launched a Corporate Citizenship Initiative, a global effort to address the environmental, social, economic, and ethical challenges we face in our business. Among the issues we are addressing are carbon impact, paper specifications and procurement, ethical conduct within our business and among our vendors, and community and charitable support. For more information, please visit our website: www.wiley.com/go/citizenship.

Library of Congress Cataloging-in-Publication Data

Tavani, Herman T.
    Ethics and technology : controversies, questions, and strategies for ethical computing / Herman T. Tavani, Rivier University—Fourth edition.
        pages cm
    Includes bibliographical references and index.
    ISBN 978-1-118-28172-7 (pbk.)
    1.   Computer networks—Moral and ethical aspects.   I. Title.
    TK5105.5.T385 2013
    175—dc23

                                    2012028589

Printed in the United States of America

10 9 8 7 6 5 4 3 2 1

In memory of my grandparents,
Leon and Marian (Roberts) Hutton,
and Antonio and Clelia (Giamberardino) Tavani

CONTENTS AT A GLANCE

TABLE OF CONTENTS

▶ **CHAPTER 2**

ETHICAL CONCEPTS AND ETHICAL THEORIES: ESTABLISHING AND JUSTIFYING A MORAL SYSTEM 33

▶ **CHAPTER 7**

CYBERCRIME AND CYBER-RELATED CRIMES 201

▶ **CHAPTER 8**

INTELLECTUAL PROPERTY DISPUTES IN CYBERSPACE   230

► **CHAPTER 10**

THE DIGITAL DIVIDE, DEMOCRACY, AND WORK   303

► **CHAPTER 11**

ONLINE COMMUNITIES, CYBER IDENTITIES, AND SOCIAL NETWORKS   337

PREFACE

As the digital landscape continues to evolve at a rapid pace, new variations of moral, legal, and social concerns arise along with it. Not surprisingly, then, an additional cluster of cyberethics issues has emerged since the publication of the previous edition of *Ethics and Technology* in late 2009. Consider, for example, the ways in which Cloud-based storage threatens the privacy and security of our personal data. Also consider the increasing amount of personal data that social networking sites such as Facebook and major search engine companies such as Google now collect. Should we worry about how that information can be subsequently used? Should we also worry about the filtering techniques that leading search engines now use to tailor or "personalize" the results of our search queries based on profiles derived from information about our previous search requests? Some analysts note that the current information-gathering/profiling practices and techniques used in the commercial sector can also be adopted by governments, and they point out that these practices could not only support the surveillance initiatives of totalitarian governments but could also threaten the privacy of citizens in democratic countries as well.

Also consider the impact that recent cyberwarfare activities, including the clandestine cyberattacks allegedly launched by some nation sates, could have for our national infrastructure. Additionally, consider the national-security-related concerns raised by the WikiLeaks controversy, which has also exacerbated an ongoing tension between free speech on the Internet vs. standards for "responsible reporting" on the part of investigative journalists. And the recent debate about "network neutrality" causes us to revisit questions about the extent to which the service providers responsible for delivering online content should also be able to control the content that they deliver.

Other kinds of concerns now arise because of developments in a relatively new subfield of cyberethics called "machine ethics" (sometimes referred to as "robo-ethics"). For example, should we develop autonomous machines that are capable of making decisions that have moral implications? Some semiautonomous robots, which serve as companions and caregivers for the elderly and as "babysitters" for young children, are already available. Recent and continued developments in robotics and autonomous machines may provide many conveniences and services, but they can also cause us to question our conventional notions of autonomy, moral agency, and trust. For example, can/should these machines be fully autonomous? Can they qualify as (artificial) moral agents? Also, will humans be able to trust machines that they will increasingly rely on to carry out critical tasks? If we do not yet know the answers to these questions, and if no clear and explicit policies are in place to guide research in this area, should we continue to develop autonomous machines? These and related questions in the emerging field of machine ethics are but a few of the many new questions we examine in the fourth edition of *Ethics and Technology*.

Although new technologies emerge, and existing technologies continue to mature and evolve, many of the ethical issues associated with them are basically variations of existing ethical problems. At bottom, these issues reduce to traditional ethical concerns having to do with dignity, respect, fairness, obligations to assist others in need, and so forth. So, we should not infer that the moral landscape itself has been altered because of behaviors made possible by these technologies. We will see that, for the most part, the new issues examined in this edition of *Ethics and Technology* are similar in relevant respects to the kinds of ethical issues we examined in the book's previous editions. However, many emerging technologies present us with challenges that, initially at least, do not seem to fit easily into our conventional ethical categories. So, a major objective of this textbook is to show how those controversies can be analyzed from the perspective of standard ethical concepts and theories.

The purpose of *Ethics and Technology*, as stated in the prefaces to the three previous editions of this book, is to introduce students to issues and controversies that comprise the relatively new field of cyberethics. The term "cyberethics" is used in this textbook to refer to the field of study that examines moral, legal, and social issues involving cybertechnology. *Cybertechnology*, in turn, refers to a broad spectrum of computing/ information and communication technologies that range from stand-alone computers to the current cluster of networked devices and technologies. Many of these technologies include devices and applications that are connected to privately owned computer networks as well as to the Internet itself.

This textbook examines a wide range of cyberethics issues—from specific issues of moral responsibility that directly affect computer and information technology (IT) professionals to broader social and ethical concerns that affect each of us in our day-to-day lives. Questions about the roles and responsibilities of computer/IT professionals in developing safe and reliable computer systems are examined under the category of professional ethics. Broader social and ethical concerns associated with cybertechnology are examined under topics such as privacy, security, crime, intellectual property, Internet regulation, and so forth.

▶ NEW TO THE *FOURTH EDITION*

New pedagogical material includes

- a newly designed set of end-of-chapter exercises called "Scenarios for Analysis," which can be used for either in-class analysis or group projects;
- new and/or updated (in-chapter) *scenarios*, illustrating both actual cases and hypothetical situations, which enable students to apply methodological concepts/ frameworks and ethical theories covered in Chapters 1 and 2;
- new *sample arguments* in some chapters, which enable students to apply the tools for argument analysis covered in Chapter 3;
- updated "review questions," "discussion questions," and "essay/presentation questions" at the end of chapters;

- an updated and revised glossary of key terms used in the book;
- an updated *Ethics and Technology* Companion Site with new resources and materials for students and instructors.

New issues examined and analyzed include

- ethical and social aspects of Cloud computing, including concerns about the privacy and security of users' data that is increasingly being stored in "the Cloud";
- concerns about the "personalization filters" that search engine companies use to tailor our search results to conform to their perceptions of what we want.
- questions about Google's (2012) privacy policy vis-à-vis the amount of user data that can be collected via the search engine company's suite of applications;
- concerns about cyberwarfare activities involving nation states and their alleged launching of the Stuxnet worm and Flame virus;
- controversies surrounding WikiLeaks and the tension it creates between free speech and responsible journalism, as well as for concerns involving national security;
- concerns affecting "network neutrality" and whether regulation may be required to ensure that Internet service providers do not gain too much control over the content they deliver;
- controversies in "machine ethics," including the development of autonomous machines capable of making decisions that have moral impacts;
- questions about whether we can trust artificial agents to act in ways that will always be in the best interests of humans.

In revising the book, I have also eliminated some older, now out-of-date, material. Additionally, I have streamlined some of the material that originally appeared in previous editions of the book but still needs to be carried over into the present edition.

▶ AUDIENCE AND SCOPE

Because cyberethics is an interdisciplinary field, this textbook aims at reaching several audiences and thus easily runs the risk of failing to meet the needs of any one audience. I have nonetheless attempted to compose a textbook that addresses the needs of computer science, philosophy, social/behavioral science, and library/information science students. Computer science students need a clear understanding of the ethical challenges they will face as computer professionals when they enter the workforce. Philosophy students, on the contrary, should understand how moral issues affecting cybertechnology can be situated in the field of applied ethics in general and then analyzed from the perspective of ethical theory. Social science and behavioral science students will likely want to assess the sociological impact of cybertechnology on our social and political institutions (government, commerce, and education) and sociodemographic groups (affecting gender, race, ethnicity, and social class). And library science and information science students should be aware of the complexities and nuances of current intellectual property laws that threaten unfettered access to electronic information, and should be informed about recent regulatory schemes that threaten to censor certain forms of electronic speech.

Students from other academic disciplines should also find many issues covered in this textbook pertinent to their personal and professional lives; some undergraduates may elect to take a course in social and ethical aspects of technology to satisfy one of their general education requirements. Although *Ethics and Technology* is intended mainly for undergraduate students, it could be used, in conjunction with other texts, in graduate courses as well.

We examine ethical controversies using *scenarios* that include both actual cases and hypothetical examples, wherever appropriate. In some instances I have deliberately constructed provocative scenarios and selected controversial cases to convey the severity of the ethical issues we consider. Some readers may be uncomfortable with, and possibly even offended by, these scenarios and cases—for example, those illustrating unethical practices that negatively affect children and minorities. Although it might have been politically expedient to skip over issues and scenarios that could unintentionally offend certain individuals, I believe that no textbook in applied ethics would do justice to its topic if it failed to expose and examine issues that adversely affect vulnerable groups in society.

Also included in most chapters are *sample arguments* that are intended to illustrate some of the rationales that have been put forth by various interest groups to defend policies and laws affecting privacy, security, property, and so forth, in cyberspace. Instructors and students can evaluate these arguments via the rules and criteria established in Chapter 3 to see how well, or how poorly, the premises in these arguments succeed in establishing their conclusions.

Exercise questions are included at the end of each chapter. First, basic "review questions" quiz the reader's comprehension of key concepts, themes, issues, and scenarios covered in that chapter. These are followed by higher level "discussion questions" designed to encourage students to reflect more deeply on some of the controversial issues examined in the chapter. In addition to "essay/presentation questions" that are also included in each chapter, a new set of "Scenarios for Analysis" have been added in response to instructors who requested the addition of some *unanalyzed* scenarios for classroom use. Building on the higher level nature of the discussion questions and essay/presentation questions, these scenarios are intended to provide students and instructors with additional resources for analyzing important controversies introduced in the various chapters. As such, these scenarios can function as in-class resources for group projects.

Some essay/presentation questions and end-of-chapter scenarios ask students to compare and contrast arguments and topics that span multiple chapters; for example, students are asked to relate arguments used to defend intellectual property rights, considered in Chapter 8, to arguments for protecting privacy rights, examined in Chapter 5. Other questions and scenarios ask students to apply foundational concepts and frameworks, such as ethical theory and critical thinking techniques introduced in Chapters 2 and 3, to the analysis of specific cyberethics issues examined in subsequent chapters. In some cases, these end-of-chapter questions and scenarios may generate lively debate in the classroom; in other cases, they can serve as a point of departure for various class assignments and group projects. Although no final "solutions" to the issues and dilemmas raised in these questions and scenarios are provided in the text, some "strategies" for analyzing them are included in the section of the book's Web site (www.wiley.com/college/tavani) entitled "Strategies for Discussion Questions."

▶ ORGANIZATION AND STRUCTURE OF THE BOOK

Ethics and Technology is organized into 12 chapters. Chapter 1, "Introduction to Cyberethics: Concepts, Perspectives, and Methodological Frameworks," defines key concepts and terms that will appear throughout the book. For example, definitions of terms such as *cyberethics* and *cybertechnology* are introduced in this chapter. We then examine whether any ethical issues involving cybertechnology are unique ethical issues. We also consider how we can approach cyberethics issues from three different perspectives: professional ethics, philosophical ethics, and sociological/descriptive ethics, each of which represents the approach generally taken by a computer scientist, a philosopher, and a social/behavioral scientist. Chapter 1 concludes with a proposal for a comprehensive and interdisciplinary methodological scheme for analyzing cyberethics issues from these perspectives.

In Chapter 2, "Ethical Concepts and Ethical Theories: Establishing and Justifying a Moral System," we examine some of the basic concepts that make up a moral system. We draw a distinction between "ethics" and "morality" by defining ethics as "the study of morality." "Morality," or a moral system, is defined as an informal, public system comprising rules of conduct and principles for evaluating those rules. We then examine consequence-based, duty-based, character-based, and contract-based ethical theories. Chapter 2 concludes with a model that integrates elements of competing ethical theories into one comprehensive and unified theory.

Chapter 3, "Critical Reasoning Skills for Evaluating Disputes in Cyberethics," includes a brief overview of basic concepts and strategies that are essential for debating moral issues in a structured and rational manner. We begin by describing the structure of a logical argument and show how arguments can be constructed and analyzed. Next, we examine a technique for distinguishing between arguments that are valid and invalid, sound and unsound, and inductive and fallacious. We illustrate examples of each type with topics affecting cybertechnology and cyberethics. Finally, we identify some strategies for spotting and labeling "informal" logical fallacies that frequently occur in everyday discourse.

Chapter 4, "Professional Ethics, Codes of Conduct, and Moral Responsibility," examines issues related to professional responsibility for computer/IT professionals. We consider whether there are any special moral responsibilities that computer/IT professionals have *as* professionals. We then examine some professional codes of conducted that have been adopted by computer organizations. We also ask: To what extent are software engineers responsible for the reliability of the computer systems they design and develop, especially applications that include "life-critical" and "safety-critical" software? Are computer/IT professionals ever permitted, or perhaps even required, to "blow the whistle" when they have reasonable evidence to suggest that a computer system is unreliable? Finally, we examine some schemes for analyzing risks associated with the development of safety-critical software.

We discuss privacy issues involving cybertechnology in Chapter 5. First, we examine the concept of privacy as well as some arguments for why privacy is considered an important human value. We then look at how personal privacy is threatened by the kinds of surveillance techniques and data-collection schemes made possible by cybertechnology. Specific data-gathering and data-exchanging techniques are examined in detail. We next consider some challenges that data mining and Web mining pose for protecting personal privacy in public space. In Chapter 5, we also consider whether technology itself, in the form of privacy-enhancing technologies (or PETs), can provide an adequate solution to some privacy issues generated by cybertechnology.

Chapter 6, "Security in Cyberspace," examines security threats in the context of computers and cybertechnology. Initially, we differentiate three distinct senses of "security": data security, system security, and network security. We then examine the concepts of "hacker" and "hacker ethic," and we ask whether computer break-ins can ever be morally justified. Next, we differentiate acts of "hacktivism," cyberterrorism, and information warfare. Chapter 6 concludes with a brief examination of risk analysis in the context of cybersecurity.

We begin our analysis of cybercrime, in Chapter 7, by considering whether we can construct a profile of a "typical" cybercriminal. We then propose a definition of cybercrime that enables us to distinguish between "cyberspecific" and "cyber-related" crimes to see whether such a distinction would aid in the formulation of more coherent cybercrime laws. We also consider the notion of legal jurisdiction in cyberspace, especially with respect to the prosecution of cybercrimes that involve interstate and international venues. In addition, we examine technological efforts to combat cyber-crime, such as controversial uses of biometric technologies.

Chapters 8 and 9 examine legal issues involving intellectual property and free speech, respectively, as they relate to cyberspace. One objective of Chapter 8, "Intellectual Property Disputes in Cyberspace," is to show why an understanding of the concept of intellectual property is important in an era of digital information. We consider three theories of property rights and make important distinctions among legal concepts such as copyright law, patent protection, and trademarks. Additionally, we consider specific scenarios involving intellectual property disputes, including the original Napster contro-versy as well as some recent peer-to-peer (P2P) networks that have been used for file sharing. We also examine the Free Software and the Open Source Software initiatives. Finally, we consider a compromise solution that supports and encourages the sharing of digital information in an era when strong copyright legislation seems to discourage that practice.

Chapter 9, "Regulating Commerce and Speech in Cyberspace," looks at additional legal issues, especially as they involve regulatory concerns in cyberspace. We draw distinctions between two different senses of "regulation" as it applies to cyberspace, and we also consider whether the Internet should be understood as a medium or as a "place." We also examine controversies surrounding e-mail spam, which some believe can be viewed as a form of "speech" in cyberspace. We then ask whether all forms of online speech should be granted legal protection; for example, should child pornography, hate speech, and speech that can cause physical harm to others be tolerated in online forums?

Chapter 10 examines a wide range of equity-and-access issues from the perspective of cybertechnology's impact for sociodemographic groups (affecting class, race, and gender). The chapter begins with an analysis of global aspects of the "digital divide." We then examine specific equity-and-access issues affecting disabled persons, racial minor-ities, and women. Next, we explore the relationship between cybertechnology and democracy, and we consider whether the Internet facilitates democracy or threatens it. We then examine some social and ethical issues affecting employment in the contemporary workplace, and we ask whether the use of cybertechnology has trans-formed work and has affected the overall quality of work life.

In Chapter 11, we examine issues pertaining to online communities, virtual-reality (VR) environments, and artificial intelligence (AI) developments in terms of two broad themes: *community* and *personal identity* in cyberspace. We begin by analyzing the impact that cybertechnology has for our traditional understanding of the concept of community. In particular, we ask whether online communities, such as Facebook and Twitter, raise any special ethical or social issues. Next, we examine some implications that behaviors made possible by virtual environments and virtual-reality applications have for our conventional understanding of personal identity. The final section of Chapter 11 examines the impact that developments in AI have for our sense of self and for what it means to be human.

Chapter 12, the final chapter of *Ethics and Technology*, examines some ethical challenges that arise in connection with emerging and converging technologies. We note that cybertechnology is *converging* with noncybertechnologies, including biotechnology and nanotechnology, generating new fields such as bioinformatics and nanocomputing that, in turn, introduce ethical concerns. Chapter 12 also includes a brief examination of some issues in the emerging (sub)field of machine ethics. Among the questions considered are whether we should develop autonomous machines that are capable of making moral decisions and whether we could trust those machines to always act in our best interests.

A Glossary that defines terms commonly used in the context of computer ethics and cyberethics is also included. However, the glossary is by no means intended as an exhaustive list of such terms. Additional material for this text is available on the book's Web site: www.wiley.com/college.tavani.

▶ THE WEB SITE FOR *ETHICS AND TECHNOLOGY*

Seven appendices for *Ethics and Technology* are available only in online format. Appendices A through E include the full text of five professional codes of ethics: the ACM Code of Ethics and Professional Conduct, the Australian Computer Society Code of Ethics, the British Computer Society Code of Conduct, the IEEE Code of Ethics, and the IEEE-CS/ACM Software Engineering Code of Ethics and Professional Practice, respectively. Specific sections of these codes are included in hardcopy format as well, in relevant sections of Chapter 4. Two appendices, F and G, are also available online. Appendix F contains the section of the *IEEE-CS/ACM Computing Curricula 2001 Final Report* that describes the social, professional, and ethical units of instruction mandated in their computer science curriculum. Appendix G provides some additional critical reasoning techniques that expand on the strategies introduced in Chapter 3.

The Web site for *Ethics and Technology* also contains additional resources for instructors and students. Presentation slides in PowerPoint format for Chapters 1–12, as well as graphics (for tables and figures in each chapter), are available in the "Instructor" and "Student" sections of the site. As noted earlier, a section on "Strategies," which includes some techniques for answering the discussion questions and unanalyzed scenarios included at the end of each of the book's 12 chapters, is also included on this site.

The book's Web site is intended as an additional resource for both instructors and students. It also enables me to "update the book," in between editions, with new issues and scenarios in cyberethics, as they arise. For example, a section entitled "Recent

Controversies" is included on the book's Web site. I invite your feedback as to how this site can be continually improved.

▶ A NOTE TO STUDENTS

If you are taking an ethics course for the first time, you might feel uncomfortable with the prospect of embarking on a study of moral issues and controversial topics that might initially cause you discomfort because ethics is sometimes perceived to be preachy, and its subject matter is sometimes viewed as essentially personal and private in nature. Because these are common concerns, I address them early in the textbook. I draw a distinction between an ethicist, who studies morality or a "moral system," and a moralist who may assume to have the correct answers to all of the questions; note that a primary objective of this book is to examine and analyze ethical issues, not to presume that any of us already has *the* correct answer to any of the questions I consider.

To accomplish this objective, I introduce three types of conceptual frameworks early in the textbook. In Chapter 1, I provide a methodological scheme that enables you to identify controversial problems and issues involving cybertechnology *as* ethical issues. The conceptual scheme included in Chapter 2, based on ethical theory, provides some general principles that guide your analysis of specific cases as well as your deliberations about which kinds of solutions to problems should be proposed. A third, and final, conceptual framework is introduced in Chapter 3 in the form of critical reasoning techniques, which provides rules and standards that you can use for evaluating the strengths of competing arguments and for defending a particular position that you reach on a certain issue.

This textbook was designed and written for you, the student! Whether or not it succeeds in helping you to meet the objectives of a course in cyberethics is very important to me, so I welcome your feedback on this textbook; and I would sincerely appreciate hearing your ideas on how this textbook could be improved. Please feel free to write to me with your suggestions, comments, and so forth. My email address is htavani@rivier .edu. I look forward to hearing from you!

▶ NOTE TO INSTRUCTORS: A ROADMAP FOR USING THIS BOOK

The chapters that make up *Ethics and Technology* are sequenced so that readers are exposed to foundational issues and conceptual frameworks before they examine specific problems in cyberethics. In some cases, it may not be possible for instructors to cover all of the material in Chapters 1–3. It is strongly recommended, however, that before students are assigned material in Chapter 4, they at least read Sections 1.1, 1.4–1.5, 2.4–2.8, and 3.1. Instructors using this textbook can determine which chapters best accommodate their specific course objectives. Computer science instructors, for example, will likely want to assign Chapter 4, on professional ethics and responsibility, early in the term. Social science instructors, on the other hand, will likely examine issues discussed in Chapters 10 and 11 early in their course. Philosophy instructors may wish to structure their courses beginning with a thorough examination of the material on ethical concepts and ethical theory in Chapter 2 and techniques for evaluating logical arguments in Chapter 3. Issues discussed in Chapter 12 may be of particular interest to CS instructors teaching advanced undergraduate students.

Many textbooks in applied ethics include a requisite chapter on ethical concepts/theory at the beginning of the book. Unfortunately, they often treat them in a cursory manner; furthermore, these ethical concepts and theories are seldom developed and reinforced in the remaining chapters. Thus, readers often experience a "disconnect" between the material included in the book's opening chapter and the content of the specific cases and issues discussed in subsequent chapters. By incorporating elements of ethical theory into my discussion and analysis of the specific cyberethics issues I examine, I have tried to avoid the "disconnect" between theory and practice that is commonplace in many applied ethics textbooks.

▶ A NOTE TO COMPUTER SCIENCE INSTRUCTORS

Ethics and Technology can be used as the main text in a course dedicated to ethical and social issues in computing, or it can be used as a supplementary textbook for computer science courses in which one or more ethics modules are included. As I suggested in the preceding section, instructors may find it difficult to cover all of the material included in this book in the course of a single semester. And as I also previously suggested, computer science instructors will likely want to ensure that they allocate sufficient course time to the professional ethical issues discussed in Chapter 4. Also of special interest to computer science instructors and their students will be the sections on computer security and risk analysis in Chapter 6; open source code and intellectual property issues in Chapter 8; and regulatory issues affecting software code in Chapter 9. Because computer science instructors may need to limit the amount of class time they devote to covering foundational concepts included in the earlier chapters, I recommend covering at least the critical sections of Chapters 1–3 described previously. This should provide computer science students with some of the tools they will need as professionals to deliberate on ethical issues and to justify the positions they reach.

In designing this textbook, I took into account the guidelines on ethical instruction included in the *Computing Curricula 2001 Final Report*, issued in December 2001 by the IEEE-CS/ACM Joint Task Force on Computing Curricula, which recommends the inclusion of 16 core hours of instruction on social, ethical, and professional topics in the curriculum for undergraduate computer science students. [See the online Appendix F at www.wiley.com/college.tavani for detailed information about the social/professional (SP) units in the Computing Curricula 2001.] Each topic prefaced with an SP designation defines one "knowledge area" or a CS "body of knowledge." They are distributed among the following 10 units:

SP1: History of computing (e.g., history of computer hardware, software, and networking)

SP2: Social context of computing (e.g., social implications of networked computing, gender-related issues, and international issues)

SP3: Methods and tools of analysis (e.g., identifying assumptions and values, making and evaluating ethical arguments)

SP4: Professional and ethical responsibilities (e.g., the nature of professionalism, codes of ethics, ethical dissent, and whistle-blowing)

SP5: Risks and liabilities of computer-based systems (e.g., historical examples of software risks)

SP6: Intellectual property (e.g., foundations of intellectual property, copyrights, patents, and software piracy)

SP7: Privacy and civil liberties (e.g., ethical and legal basis for privacy protection, technological strategies for privacy protection)

SP8: Computer crime (e.g., history and examples of computer crime, hacking, viruses, and crime prevention strategies)

SP9: Economic issues in computing (e.g., monopolies and their economic implications; effect of skilled labor supply)

SP10: Philosophical frameworks (e.g., ethical theory, utilitarianism, relativism)

All 10 SP units are covered in this textbook. Topics described in SP1 are examined in Chapters 1 and 10, and topics included in SP2 are discussed in Chapters 1 and 11. The methods and analytical tools mentioned in SP3 are described at length in Chapters 2 and 3, whereas professional issues involving codes of conduct and professional responsibility described in SP4 are included in Chapters 4 and 12. Also discussed in Chapter 4, as well as in Chapter 6, are issues involving risks and liabilities (SP5). Intellectual property issues (SP6) are discussed in detail in Chapter 8 and in certain sections of Chapter 9, whereas privacy and civil liberty concerns (SP7) are discussed mainly in Chapters 5 and 12. Chapters 6 and 7 examine topics described in SP8. Economic issues (SP9) are considered in Chapters 9 and 10. And philosophical frameworks of ethics, including ethical theory (SP10), are discussed in Chapters 1 and 2.

Table 1 illustrates the corresponding connection between SP units and the chapters of this book.

TABLE 1 SP ("Knowledge") Units and Corresponding Book Chapters

SP unit	1	2	3	4	5	6	7	8	9	10
Chapter(s)	1, 10	1, 11	2, 3	4, 12	4, 6	8, 9	5, 12	6, 7	9, 10	1, 2

ACKNOWLEDGMENTS

In revising *Ethics and Technology* for a fourth edition, I have once again drawn from several of my previously published works. Chapters 1–4, on foundational and professional issues in cyberethics, incorporate material from four articles: "The State of Computer Ethics as a Philosophical Field of Inquiry," *Ethics and Information Technology* 3, no. 2 (2001); "Applying an Interdisciplinary Approach to Teaching Computer Ethics," *IEEE Technology and Society Magazine* 21, no. 3 (2002); "The Uniqueness Debate in Computer Ethics," *Ethics and Information Technology* 4, no. 1 (2002); and "Search Engines and Ethics," *Stanford Encyclopedia of Philosophy* (2012).

Chapter 5, on privacy in cyberspace, also draws from material in four works: "Computer Matching and Personal Privacy," *Proceedings of the Symposium on Computers and the Quality of Life* (ACM Press, 1996); "Informational Privacy, Data Mining, and the Internet," *Ethics and Information Technology* 1, no. 2 (1999); "Privacy Enhancing Technologies as a Panacea for Online Privacy Concerns: Some Ethical Considerations," *Journal of Information Ethics* 9, no. 2 (2000); and "Applying the 'Contextual Integrity' Model of Privacy to Personal Blogs in the Blogosphere" (coauthored with Frances Grodzinsky), *International Journal of Internet Research Ethics* 3 (2010). Chapters 6 and 7, on security and crime in cyberspace, draw from material in three sources: "Privacy and Security" in Duncan Langford's book *Internet Ethics* (Macmillan/St. Martins, 2000); "Defining the Boundaries of Computer Crime: Piracy, Trespass, and Vandalism in Cyberspace" in *Readings in CyberEthics* 2nd ed. (Jones and Bartlett, 2004); and "Privacy in 'the Cloud'" (coauthored with Frances Grodzinsky), *Computers and Society* 41, no. 1 (2011).

In Chapters 8 and 9, on intellectual property and Internet regulation, I drew from material in "Information Wants to be Shared: An Alternative Approach for Analyzing Intellectual Property Disputes in the Information Age," *Catholic Library World* 73, no. 2 (2002); and two papers coauthored with Frances Grodzinsky: "P2P Networks and the *Verizon v. RIAA* Case," *Ethics and Information Technology* 7, no. 4 (2005) and "Online File Sharing: Resolving the Tensions between Privacy and Property" *Computers and Society* 38, no. 4 (2008). Chapters 10 and 11, on the digital divide, democracy, and online communities, draw from material from two papers: "Ethical Reflections on the Digital Divide," *Journal of Information, Communication and Ethics in Society* 1, no. 2 (2003) and "Online Communities, Democratic Ideals, and the Digital Divide" (coauthored with Frances Grodzinsky) in Soraj Hongladarom and Charles Ess's book *Information Technology Ethics: Cultural Perspectives* (IGI Global, 2007).

Chapter 12, on emerging and converging technologies, incorporates material from my book *Ethics, Computing, and Genomics* (Jones and Bartlett, 2006), and from three recently published papers: "Can We Develop Artificial Agents Capable of Making Good

Moral Decisions?" *Minds and Machines* 21, no. 3 (2011); "Trust and Multi-Agent Systems" (coauthored with Jeff Buechner), *Ethics and Information Technology* 13, no. 1 (2011); and "Ethical Aspects of Autonomous Systems" in Michael Decker and Mathias Gutmann's book *Robo- and Information-Ethics* (Berlin: Verlag LIT, 2012).

The fourth edition of *Ethics and Technology* has benefited from suggestions and comments I received from many anonymous reviewers, as well as from the following colleagues: Jeff Buechner, Lloyd Carr, Jerry Dolan, Frances Grodzinsky, Kenneth Himma, James Moor, Martin Menke, Wayne Pauley, Mark Rosenbaum, Regina Tavani, and John Weckert. I am especially grateful to Fran Grodzinsky (Sacred Heart University), with whom I have coauthored several papers, for permitting me to incorporate elements of our joint research into relevant sections of this book. And I am most grateful to Lloyd Carr (Rivier University) for his invaluable feedback on several chapters and sections of this edition of the book, which he was willing to review multiple times; his astute comments and suggestions have helped me to refine many of the positions I defend in this book.

The new edition of the book has also benefited from some helpful comments that I received from many students who have used previous editions of the text. I am also grateful to the numerous reviewers and colleagues who commented on the previous editions of this book; many of their helpful suggestions have been carried over to the present edition.

I also wish to thank the editorial and production staffs at Wiley and Thomson Digital, especially Beth Golub, Elizabeth Mills, Katherine Willis, Jolene Ling, and Sanchari Sil, for their support during the various stages of the revision process for the fourth edition of *Ethics and Technology*.

Finally, I must once again thank the two most important people in my life: my wife Joanne, and our daughter Regina. Without their continued support and extraordinary patience, the fourth edition of this book could not have been completed.

This edition of *Ethics and Technology* is dedicated to the memory of my grandparents: Leon and Marian (Roberts) Hutton, and Antonio and Clelia (Giamberardino) Tavani.

Herman T. Tavani
Nashua, NH

FOREWORD

The computer/information revolution is shaping our world in ways it has been difficult to predict and to appreciate. When mainframe computers were developed in the 1940s and 1950s, some thought only a few computers would ever be needed in society. When personal computers were introduced in the 1980s, they were considered fascinating toys for hobbyists but not something serious businesses would ever use. When Web tools were initially created in the 1990s to enhance the Internet, they were a curiosity. Using the Web to observe the level of a coffee pot across an ocean was intriguing, at least for a few moments, but not of much practical use. Today, armed with the wisdom of hindsight, the impact of such computing advancements seems obvious, if not inevitable, to all of us. What government claims that it does not need computers? What major business does not have a Web address? How many people, even in the poorest of countries, are not aware of the use of cell phones?

The computer/information revolution has changed our lives and has brought with it significant ethical, social, and professional issues; consider the area of privacy as but one example. Today, surveillance cameras are abundant, and facial recognition systems are effective even under less than ideal observing conditions. Information about buying habits, medical conditions, and human movements can be mined and correlated relentlessly using powerful computers. Individuals' DNA information can easily be collected, stored, and transmitted throughout the world in seconds. This computer/information revolution has brought about unexpected capabilities and possibilities. The revolution is not only technological but also ethical, social, and professional. Our computerized world is perhaps not the world we expected, and, even to the extent that we expected it, it is not a world for which we have well-analyzed policies about how to behave. Now more than ever we need to take cyberethics seriously.

Herman Tavani has written an excellent introduction to the field of cyberethics. His text differs from others in at least three important respects: First, the book is extraordinarily comprehensive and up to date in its subject matter. The text covers all of the standard topics such as codes of conduct, privacy, security, crime, intellectual property, and free speech, and also discusses sometimes overlooked subjects such as democracy, employment, access, and the digital divide. Tavani more than anyone else has tracked and published the bibliographical development of cyberethics over many years, and his expertise with this vast literature shines through in this volume. Second, the book approaches the subject matter of cyberethics from diverse points of view. Tavani examines issues from a social science perspective, from a philosophical perspective, and from a computing professional perspective, and then he suggests ways to integrate these diverse approaches. If the task of cyberethics is multidisciplinary, as many of us believe, then such a diverse but integrated methodology is crucial to accomplishing the task. His book is one of the few that constructs such a methodology. Third, the book is unusually helpful to students and teachers because it contains an entire chapter discussing critical thinking skills and is filled with review and discussion questions.

The cyberage is going to evolve. The future details and applications are, as always, difficult to predict. But it is likely that computing power and bandwidth will continue to grow while computing devices themselves will shrink in size to the nanometer scale. More and more information devices will be inserted into our environment, our cars, our houses, our clothing, and us. Computers will become smarter. They will be made out of new materials, possibly biological. They will operate in new ways, possibly using quantum properties. The distinction between the virtual world and the real world will blur more and more. We need a good book in cyberethics to deal with the present and prepare us for this uncertain future. Tavani's *Ethics and Technology* is such a book.

James H. Moor
Dartmouth College

CHAPTER

1

Introduction to Cyberethics: Concepts, Perspectives, and Methodological Frameworks

Our primary objective in Chapter 1 is to introduce some foundational concepts and methodological frameworks that will be used in our analysis of specific cyberethics issues in subsequent chapters of this textbook. To accomplish this objective, we

- define key terms such as *cyberethics* and *cybertechnology*;
- describe key developmental phases in cybertechnology that influenced the evolution of cyberethics as a distinct field of applied ethics;
- consider whether there is anything unique or special about cyberethics issues;
- examine three distinct perspectives for identifying and approaching cyberethics issues;
- propose a comprehensive methodological scheme for analyzing cyberethics issues.

We begin by reflecting briefly on three scenarios, each illustrating a cluster of ethical issues that will be examined in detail in later chapters of this book.

▶ **SCENARIO 1–1:** A Fatal Cyberbullying Incident on MySpace

Megan Meier, a 13-year-old resident of Dardenne Prairie, Missouri, had an account on MySpace where she received a "friend" request from a user named Josh Evans. Evans, who claimed to be a 16-year-old boy, told Meier that he lived near her and was being home-schooled by his parents. At first, Evans sent flattering e-mails to Meier, which also suggested that he might be romantically interested in her. Soon, however, Evans's remarks turned from compliments to insults, and Evans informed Meier that he was no longer sure that he wanted to be friends with her because he heard that she "wasn't very nice to her friends." Next, Meier noticed that some highly derogatory posts about her—e.g., "Megan Meier is a slut" and "Megan Meier is fat"—began to appear on MySpace. Meier, who was reported to have suffered from low self-esteem and depression, became increasingly distressed by the online harassment (cyberbullying) being directed at her—i.e., from both the insulting MySpace postings and hurtful e-mail messages she continued to receive from Evans. On October 17, 2006, Meier decided to end her life by hanging herself in her bedroom. An investigation of this incident, following Meier's death, revealed that Josh Evans was not a teenage boy; she was Lori Drew, the 49-year-old mother of a former friend of Meier's.[1] ■

▶ **SCENARIO 1–2:** Contesting the Ownership of a Twitter Account

Noah Kravitz was employed by PhoneDog Media, a mobile phone company, for nearly four years. PhoneDog had two divisions: an e-commerce site (phonedog.com) that sold mobile phones, and a blog that enabled customers to interact with the company. Kravitz created a blog on Twitter (called Phonedog_Noah) while employed at PhoneDog, and his blog attracted 17,000 followers by the time he left the company in October 2010. However, Kravitz informed PhoneDog that he wanted to keep his Twitter blog, with all of his followers; in return, Kravitz agreed that he would still "tweet" occasionally on behalf of his former company, under a new (Twitter) "handle," or account name, NoahKravitz. Initially, PhoneDog seemed to have no problem with this arrangement. In July 2011, however, PhoneDog sued Kravitz, arguing that his list of Twitter followers was, in fact, a company list. PhoneDog also argued that it had invested a substantial amount of money in growing its customer list, which it considered to be the property of PhoneDog Media. The company (as of early 2012) is seeking $340,000 in damages—the amount that PhoneDog estimated it had lost based on 17,000 customers at $2.50 per customer over an eight-month period (following Kravitz's departure from the company).[2] ■

▶ **SCENARIO 1–3:** "The Washingtonienne" Blogger

Jessica Cutler, a former staff assistant to U.S. Senator Michael DeWine (R-Ohio), authored an online diary (on blogger.com) under the pseudonym "The Washingtonienne." In May 2004, she was fired when the contents of her diary appeared in *Wonkette: The DC Gossip*, a popular blog in the Washington D.C. area. Until her diary was discovered and published in *Wonkette*, Cutler assumed that it had been viewed by only a few of her fellow "staffers" (Washington D.C. staff assistants) who were interested in reading about the details of her romantic relationships and sexual encounters. In her diary, Cutler disclosed that she earned an annual salary of only $25,000 as a staffer and that most of her living expenses were "thankfully subsidized by a few generous older gentlemen." She also described some details of her sexual relationships with these men, one of whom was married and an official in the George W. Bush administration. (Cutler did not use the real names of these men but instead referred to them via initials that could easily be linked to their actual identities.) Following her termination as a staffer, in response to the political fallout and the media attention resulting from the publication of her diary, Cutler was offered a book contract with a major publisher. She was also subsequently sued by one of the men implicated in her blog.[3] ■

First, consider some ethical concerns that arise in the Megan Meier cyberbullying scenario. These include worries affecting anonymity and pseudonymity, deception, crime, legal liability, and moral responsibility. Should Lori Drew, as well as any other MySpace user, have been permitted to open an account on that social networking site (SNS) under an alias or pseudonym that also included a fictitious profile? Should MySpace, or any SNS, tolerate members who deceive, intimidate, or harass other users? Should users who create accounts on SNSs with the intention to deceive or harass others be subject to criminal prosecution? Should MySpace have been held legally liable, at least in some contributory sense, for Meier's death? Also, do ordinary users of an SNS who discover that someone is being bullied in that online forum have a moral responsibility to inform the SNS? Do they also have a moral responsibility to inform that SNS if they discover that someone has created a fraudulent account on their forum, which could be used to deceive and harass other members? These and similar questions are examined in detail in Chapters 7 and 11.

Next, consider the scenario involving Twitter. Here, several important ethical, legal, and policy issues also arise—especially with respect to intellectual property rights and ownership of information. For example, can an employer's customer list constitute a "trade secret," as PhoneDog claimed? Should an employee be authorized to create a single Twitter account in which the followers are simultaneously interested both in the employer's product and in the employee's (private) blog? Should employees be allowed to post to their private accounts on SNSs, such as Twitter or Facebook, during work hours or, for that matter, whenever/wherever they are using an employer's computing resources? If so, who has legal ownership rights to that information? A different, but somewhat related, question has to do with whether ordinary users should be able to post on their private SNS accounts anything they wish to say about their current or former employers, without first getting explicit permission to do so. Questions pertaining to these and related issues are examined in Chapters 8 and 9.

Third, consider "The Washingtonienne" scenario, where a wide range of ethical and legal issues also arise. These include concerns affecting privacy, confidentiality, anonymity, free speech, defamation, and so forth. For example, did Cutler violate the privacy and confidentiality of her romantic partners through the remarks she made about them in her online diary? Should she be held liable for defamation because of the nature of her remarks about these individuals, or was she merely exercising her right to free speech? Was Cutler's expectation of anonymity violated when she was eventually "outed" by *Wonkette*, or were the circumstances surrounding this incident no different from that of any author or journalist who writes under a pseudonym but whose real identity is eventually discovered and made public? Should Cutler's online diary be considered a "public document" merely because it was on the Web, or did her diary also deserve some privacy protection because of the limited scope of its intended audience? Answers to these and related questions affecting blogs and the "blogosphere" are examined in Chapters 5, 9, and 11.

The Meier, Twitter, and Washingtonienne scenarios provide us with particular contexts in which we can begin to think about a cluster of ethical issues affecting the use of computers and cybertechnology. A number of alternative examples could also have been used to illustrate many of the moral and legal concerns that arise in connection with this technology. In fact, examples abound. One has only to read a daily newspaper or view regular television news programs to be informed about controversial issues involving computers and the Internet, including questions that pertain to property, privacy, security, anonymity, crime, and jurisdiction. Ethical aspects of these issues are examined in the chapters comprising this textbook. In the remainder of Chapter 1, we identify and examine some key foundational concepts and frameworks in cyberethics.

▶ 1.1 DEFINING KEY TERMS: CYBERETHICS AND CYBERTECHNOLOGY

Before we propose a definition of cyberethics, it is important to note that the field of cyberethics can be viewed as a branch of (applied) ethics. In Chapter 2, where we define ethics as "the study of morality," we provide a detailed account of what is meant by morality and a moral system, and we also focus on some important aspects of theoretical, as opposed to, applied ethics. For example, both ethical concepts and ethical theories are also examined in detail in that chapter. There, we also include a "Getting Started" section on how to engage in ethical reasoning in general, as well as reasoning in the case of some specific moral dilemmas. In Chapter 1, however, our main focus is on clarifying some key cyber and cyber-related terms that will be used throughout the remaining chapters of this textbook.

For our purpose, *cyberethics* can be defined as the study of moral, legal, and social issues involving cybertechnology. Cyberethics examines the impact of cybertechnology on our social, legal, and moral systems, and it evaluates the social policies and laws that have been framed in response to issues generated by its development and use. To grasp the significance of these reciprocal relationships, it is important to understand what is meant by the term *cybertechnology*.

1.1.1 What Is Cybertechnology?

Cybertechnology, as used throughout this textbook, refers to a wide range of computing and communication devices, from stand-alone computers to connected, or networked, computing and communication technologies. These technologies include, but need not be limited to, devices such as "smart" phones, iPods, (electronic) "tablets," personal computers (desktops and laptops), and large mainframe computers. Networked devices can be connected directly to the Internet, or they can be connected to other devices through one or more privately owned computer networks. Privately owned networks, in turn, include local area networks (LANs) and wide area networks (WANs). A LAN is a privately owned network of computers that span a limited geographical area, such as an office building or a small college campus. WANs, on the other hand, are privately owned networks of computers that are interconnected throughout a much broader geographic region.

How exactly are LANs and WANs different from the Internet? In one sense, the Internet can be understood as *the network of interconnected computer networks*. A synthesis of contemporary information and communications technologies, the Internet evolved from an earlier United States Defense Department initiative (in the 1960s) known as the ARPANET. Unlike WANs and LANs, which are privately owned computer networks, the Internet is generally considered to be a public network, in the sense that much of the information available on the Internet resides in "public space" and is thus available to anyone. The Internet, which should be differentiated from the World Wide Web, includes several applications. The Web, based on hypertext transfer protocol (HTTP), is one application; other applications include file transfer protocol (FTP), Telnet, and e-mail. Because many users navigate the Internet by way of the Web, and because the majority of users conduct their online activities almost exclusively on the Web portion of the Internet, it is very easy to confuse the Web with the Internet.

The Internet and privately owned computer networks, such as WANs and LANs, are perhaps the most common and well-known examples of cybertechnology. However, "cybertechnology" is used in this book to represent the entire range of computing systems, from stand-alone computers to privately owned networks to the Internet itself. "Cyberethics" refers to the study of moral, legal, and social issues involving those technologies.

1.1.2 Why the Term *Cyberethics*?

Many authors have used the term "computer ethics" to describe the field that examines moral issues pertaining to computing and information technology (see, for example, Barger 2008; Johnson 2010). Others use the expression "information ethics" (e.g., Capurro 2007) to refer to a cluster of ethical concerns regarding the flow of information that is either enhanced or restricted by computer technology.[4] Because of concerns about ethical issues involving the Internet in particular, some have also used the term "Internet ethics" (Langford 2000). Ethical issues examined in this textbook, however, are not limited to the Internet; they also include privately owned computer networks and interconnected communication technologies—i.e., technologies that we refer to collectively as cybertechnology. Hence, we use "cyberethics" to capture the wide range of moral issues involving cybertechnology.

For our purposes, "cyberethics" is more accurate than "computer ethics" for two reasons. First, the term "computer ethics" can connote ethical issues associated with computing *machines*, and thus could be construed as pertaining to stand-alone or "unconnected computers." Because computing technologies and communication technologies have converged in recent years, resulting in networked systems, a computer system may now be thought of more accurately as a new kind of *medium* than as a machine. Second, the term "computer ethics" might also suggest a field of study that is concerned exclusively with ethical issues affecting computer professionals. Although these issues are very important, and are examined in detail in Chapter 4 as well as in relevant sections of Chapters 6 and 12, we should note that the field of cyberethics is not limited to an analysis of moral issues that affect only professionals.

"Cyberethics" is also more accurate, for our purposes, than "information ethics." For one thing, "information ethics" is ambiguous because it can mean a specific methodological framework—i.e., *Information Ethics* (or *IE*)—for analyzing issues in cyberethics (Floridi 2007).[5] Or it can connote a cluster of ethical issues of particular interest to professionals in the fields of library science and information science (Buchanan and Henderson 2009). In the latter sense, "information ethics" refers to ethical concerns affecting the free flow of, and unfettered access to, information, which include issues such as library censorship and intellectual freedom. (These issues are examined in Chapter 9.) Our analysis of cyberethics issues in this text, however, is not limited to controversies often considered under the heading "information ethics."

Given the wide range of moral issues examined in this book, the term "cyberethics" is also more comprehensive, and more appropriate, than "Internet ethics." Although many of the issues considered under the heading cyberethics often pertain to the Internet, some issues examined in this textbook do not involve the Internet per se—for example, issues associated with computerized monitoring in the workplace, with professional responsibility for designing reliable computer hardware and software systems, and with the implications of cybertechnology for gender and race. We examine ethical issues that cut across the spectrum of devices and networked communication systems comprising cybertechnology, from stand-alone computers to networked systems.

Finally, we should note that some issues in the emerging fields of "agent ethics," "bot ethics," "robo-ethics," or what Wallach and Allen (2009) call "machine ethics," overlap with a cluster of concerns examined under the heading of cyberethics. Wallach and Allen define machine ethics as a field that expands upon traditional computer ethics because it shifts the main area of focus away from "what people do with computers to questions about what machines do by themselves." It also focuses on questions having to do with whether computers can be autonomous agents capable of making good moral decisions. Research in machine ethics overlaps with the work of interdisciplinary researchers in the field of artificial intelligence (AI).[6] We examine some aspects of this emerging field (or subfield of cyberethics) in Chapters 11 and 12.

▶ 1.2 THE CYBERETHICS EVOLUTION: FOUR DEVELOPMENTAL PHASES IN CYBERTECHNOLOGY

In describing the key evolutionary phases of cybertechnology and cyberethics, we begin by noting that the meaning of "computer" has evolved significantly since the 1940s. If you were to look up the meaning of that word in a dictionary written before World War II, you would most likely discover that a computer was defined as a person who calculated numbers. In the time period immediately following World War II, the term "computer" came to be identified with a (calculating) machine as opposed to a person (who calculated).[7] By the 1980s, however, computers had shrunk in size considerably and they were beginning to be understood more in terms of desktop machines (that manipulated symbols as well as numbers), or as a new kind of medium for communication, rather than simply as machines that crunch numbers. As computers became increasingly connected to one another, they came to be associated with metaphors such as the "information superhighway" and cyberspace; today, many ordinary users tend to think about computers in terms of various Internet- and Web-based applications made possible by cybertechnology.

In response to some social and ethical issues that were anticipated in connection with the use of electronic computers, the field that we now call cyberethics had its informal and humble beginnings in the late 1940s. It is interesting to note that during this period, when ENIAC (Electronic Numerical Integrator and Calculator)—the first electronic computer, developed at the University of Pennsylvania, became operational in 1946—some analysts confidently predicted that no more than five or six computers would ever need to be built. It is also interesting to point out that during this same period, a few insightful thinkers had already begun to describe some social and ethical concerns that would likely arise in connection with computing and cybertechnology.[8] Although still a relatively young academic field, cyberethics has now matured to a point where several articles about its historical development have appeared in books and scholarly journals. For our purposes, the evolution of cyberethics can be summarized in four distinct *technological phases*.[9]

Phase 1 (1950s and 1960s)
In *Phase 1*, computing technology consisted mainly of huge mainframe computers, such as ENIAC, that were "unconnected" and thus existed as stand-alone machines. One set of ethical and social questions raised during this phase had to do with the impact of computing machines as "giant brains." Today, we might associate these kinds of questions with the field of artificial intelligence (or AI). The following kinds of questions were introduced in Phase 1: Can machines think? If so, should we invent thinking

machines? If machines can be intelligent entities, what does this mean for our sense of self? What does it mean to be human?

Another set of ethical and social concerns that arose during Phase 1 could be catalogued under the heading of privacy threats and the fear of Big Brother. For example, some people in the United States feared that the federal government would set up a national database in which extensive amounts of personal information about its citizens would be stored as electronic records. A strong centralized government could then use that information to monitor and control the actions of ordinary citizens. Although networked computers had not yet come on to the scene, work on the ARPANET—the Internet's predecessor, which was funded by an agency in the United States Defense Department—began during this phase, in the 1960s.

Phase 2 (1970s and 1980s)

In *Phase 2*, computing machines and communication devices in the commercial sector began to converge. This convergence, in turn, introduced an era of computer/communications networks. Mainframe computers, minicomputers, microcomputers, and personal computers could now be linked together by way of one or more privately owned computer networks such as LANs and WANs (see Section 1.1.1), and information could readily be exchanged between and among databases accessible to networked computers.

Ethical issues associated with this phase of computing included concerns about personal privacy, intellectual property, and computer crime. Privacy concerns, which had emerged during Phase 1 because of worries about the amount of personal information that could be collected by government agencies and stored in a centralized government-owned database, were exacerbated because electronic records containing personal and confidential information could now also easily be exchanged between two or more commercial databases in the private sector. Concerns affecting intellectual property and proprietary information also emerged during this phase because personal (desktop) computers could be used to duplicate proprietary software programs. And concerns associated with computer crime appeared during this phase because individuals could now use computing devices, including remote computer terminals, to break into and disrupt the computer systems of large organizations.

Phase 3 (1990–Present)

During *Phase 3*, the Internet era, availability of Internet access to the general public has increased significantly. This was facilitated, in no small part, by the development and phenomenal growth of the World Wide Web in the 1990s. The proliferation of Internet- and Web-based technologies has contributed to some additional ethical concerns involving computing technology; for example, issues of free speech, anonymity, jurisdiction, and trust have been hotly disputed during this phase. Should Internet users be free to post any messages they wish on publicly accessible Web sites or even on their own personal Web pages—i.e., is that a "right" that is protected by free speech or freedom of expression? Should users be permitted to post anonymous messages on Web pages, or even be allowed to navigate the Web anonymously or under the cover of a pseudonym?

Issues of jurisdiction also arose because there are no clear national or geographical boundaries in cyberspace; if a crime occurs on the Internet, it is not always clear where—i.e., in which legal jurisdiction—it took place and thus it is unclear where it should be prosecuted. And as e-commerce emerged during this phase, potential consumers initially had concerns about trusting online businesses with their financial and personal information. Other ethical and social concerns that arose during Phase 3 include disputes about the public vs. private aspects of personal information that has become increasingly available on the Internet. Concerns of this type have been exacerbated by the amount of personal information included on social networking sites, such as Facebook and Twitter, and on other kinds of interactive Web-based forums (made possible by "Web 2.0" technology).

We should note that during Phase 3, both the interfaces used to interact with computer technology and the devices used to "house" it were still much the same as in Phases 1 and 2. A computer was still essentially a "box," i.e., a CPU, with one or more peripheral devices, such as a video screen, keyboard, and mouse, serving as interfaces to that box. And computers were still viewed as devices essentially external to humans, as things or objects "out there." As cybertechnology continues to evolve, however, it may no longer make sense to try to understand computers simply in terms of objects or devices that are necessarily external to us. Instead, computers will likely become more and more a part of who or what we are as human beings. For example, James Moor (2005) notes that computing devices will soon be a part of our clothing and even our bodies. This brings us to Phase 4.

Phase 4 (Present–Near Future)
Presently we are on the threshold of *Phase 4*, a point at which we have begun to experience an unprecedented level of convergence of technologies. We have already witnessed aspects of technological convergence beginning in Phase 2, where the integration of computing and communication devices resulted in privately owned networked systems, as we noted above. And in Phase 3, the Internet era, we briefly described the convergence of text, video, and sound technologies on the Web, and we noted how the computer began to be viewed much more as a new kind of medium than as a conventional type of machine. The convergence of information technology and biotechnology in recent years has resulted in the emerging fields of bioinformatics and computational genomics; this has also caused some analysts to question whether computers of the future will still be silicon-based or whether some may also possibly be made of biological materials. Additionally, biochip implant technology, which has been enhanced by developments in AI research (described in Chapter 11), has led some to predict that in the not-too-distant future it may become difficult for us to separate certain aspects of our biology from our technology.

Today, computers are also becoming ubiquitous or pervasive; i.e., they are "everywhere" and they permeate both our workplace and our recreational environments. Many of the objects that we encounter in these environments are also beginning to exhibit what Philip Brey (2005) and others call "ambient intelligence," which enables "smart objects" to be connected to one another via wireless technology. Some consider radio frequency identification (RFID) technology (described in detail in Chapter 5) to be the first step in what is now referred to as *pervasive* or *ubiquitous computing* (described in detail in Chapter 12).

What other kinds of technological changes should we anticipate as research and development continues in Phase 4? For one thing, computing devices will likely continue to become more and more indistinguishable from many kinds of noncomputing devices.

TABLE 1.1   Summary of Four Phases of Cyberethics

Phase	Time Period	Technological Features	Associated Issues
1	1950s–1960s	Stand-alone machines (large mainframe computers)	Artificial intelligence (AI), database privacy ("Big Brother")
2	1970s–1980s	Minicomputers and the ARPANET; desktop computers interconnected via privately owned networks	Issues from Phase 1 plus concerns involving intellectual property and software piracy, computer crime, and communications privacy
3	1990s–present	Internet, World Wide Web, and early "Web.2.0" applications, environments, and forums	Issues from Phases 1 and 2 plus concerns about free speech, anonymity, legal jurisdiction, behavioral norms in virtual communities
4	Present to near future	Convergence of information and communication technologies with nanotechnology and biotechnology; increasing use of autonomous systems	Issues from Phases 1–3 plus concerns about artificial electronic agents ("bots") with decision-making capabilities, and developments in nanocomputing, bioinformatics, and ambient intelligence

For another thing, a computer may no longer typically be conceived of as a distinct device or object with which users interact via an explicit interface such as a keyboard, mouse, and video display. We are now beginning to conceive of computers and cybertechnology in drastically different ways. Consider also that computers are becoming less visible—as computers and electronic devices continue to be miniaturized and integrated/embedded in objects, they are also beginning to "disappear" or to become "invisible" as distinct entities.

Many analysts predict that computers will become increasingly smaller in size, ultimately achieving the nano scale. (We examine some ethical implications of nano-technology and nanocomputing in Chapter 12.) Many also predict that aspects of nanotechnology, biotechnology, and information technology will continue to converge. However, we will not speculate any further in this chapter about either the future of cybertechnology or the future of cyberethics. The purpose of our brief description of the four phases of cybertechnology mentioned here is to provide a historical context for understanding the origin and evolution of at least some of the ethical concerns affecting cybertechnology that we will examine in this book.

Table 1.1 summarizes key aspects of each phase in the development of cyberethics as a field of applied ethics.

▶ 1.3 ARE CYBERETHICS ISSUES UNIQUE ETHICAL ISSUES?

Few would dispute the claim that the use of cybertechnology has had a significant impact on our moral, legal, and social systems. Some also believe, however, that cybertechnology has introduced new and unique moral problems. Are any of these problems genuinely unique moral issues? There are two schools of thought regarding this question.

Consider once again the three scenarios included in the chapter's opening section. Have any new ethical issues been introduced in these scenarios, or are the issues that arise in each merely examples of existing ethical issues that have been exacerbated in some sense by new technologies used to communicate and disseminate personal information (such as in blogs in the Washingtonienne and Twitter scenarios), or to harass and bully someone (as in the Meier scenario)? To see whether any new ethical issues arise because of cybertechnology in general, consider once again the cyberbullying scenario involving Megan Meier. Here, one could argue that there is nothing really new or unique in the bullying incident that led to Meier's death, because in the final analysis "bullying is bullying" and "crime is crime." According to this line of reasoning, whether someone happens to use cybertechnology to assist in carrying out a particular bullying incident is irrelevant. One might further argue that there is nothing special about cyberbullying incidents in general, regardless of whether or not they also result in a victim's death. Proponents of this position could point to the fact that bullying activities are hardly new, since these kinds of activities have been carried out in the off-line world for quite some time. So, cybertechnology might be seen simply as the latest in a series of tools or techniques that are now available to aid bullies in carrying out their activities.

Alternatively, some argue that forms of behavior made possible by cybertechnology have indeed raised either new or special ethical problems. Using the example of cyberbullying to support this view, one might point out the relative ease with which bullying activities can now be carried out. Simply by using a computing device with Internet access, one can bully others without having to leave the comfort of his or her home. A cyberbully can, as Lori Drew did, also easily deceive her victim under the cloak of an alias, or pseudoname. The fact that a user can bully a victim with relative anonymity makes it much more difficult for law enforcement agents to track down a bully, either before or after that bully has caused harm to the victim(s).

Also consider issues having to do with *scope* and *scale*: an Internet user can bully multiple victims simultaneously via the use of multiple "windows" on his or her computer screen or electronic device. The bully can also harass victims who happen to live in states and nations that are geographically distant from the bully. Bullying activities can now occur on a scale or order of magnitude that could not have been realized in the pre-Internet era. More individuals can now engage in bullying behavior because cybertechnology has made it easy, and, as a result, significantly more people can now become the victims of bullies.

But do these factors support the claim that cybertechnology has introduced any new and unique ethical issues? Walter Maner (2004) argues that computer use has generated a series of ethical issues that (a) did not exist before the advent of computing, and (b) could not have existed if computer technology had not been invented.[10] Is there any evidence to support Maner's claim? Next we consider two scenarios that, initially at least, might suggest that some new ethical issues have been generated by the use of cybertechnology.

▶ **SCENARIO 1–4:** Developing the Code for a Computerized Weapon System

Sally Bright, a recent graduate from Technical University, has accepted a position as a software engineer for a company called CyberDefense, Inc. This company has a contract with the U.S. Defense Department to develop and deliver applications for the U.S. military. When Sally reports to work on her first day, she is assigned to a controversial project that is developing the software for a computer system designed to deliver chemical weapons to and from remote locations. Sally is conflicted about whether she can, given her personal values, agree to work on this kind of weapon-delivery system, which would not have been possible without computer technology. ■

Is the conflict that Sally faces in this particular scenario one that is new or unique because of computers and cybertechnology? One might argue that the ethical concerns surrounding Sally's choices are unique because they never would have arisen had it not been for the invention of computer technology. In one sense, it is true that ethical concerns having to do with whether or not one should participate in developing a certain kind of computer system did not exist before the advent of computing technology. However, it is true only in a trivial sense. Consider that long before computing technologies were available, engineers were confronted with ethical choices involving whether or not to participate in the design and development of certain kinds of controversial technological systems. Prior to the computer era, for example, they had to make decisions involving the design of aircraft intended to deliver conventional as well as nuclear bombs. So, is the fact that certain technological systems happen to include the use of computer software or computer hardware components morally relevant in this scenario? Have any new or unique ethical issues, in a nontrivial sense of "unique," been generated here? Based on our brief analysis of this scenario, there does not seem to be sufficient evidence to substantiate the claim that one or more new ethical issues have been introduced.

▶ **SCENARIO 1–5:** Digital Piracy

Harry Flick is an undergraduate student at Pleasantville State College. In many ways, Harry's interests are similar to those of typical students who attend his college. But Harry is also very fond of classic movies, especially films that were made before 1950. DVD copies of these movies are difficult to find; those that are available tend to be expensive to purchase, and very few are available for loan at libraries. One day, Harry discovers a Web site that has several classic films (in digital form) freely available for downloading. Since the movies are still protected by copyright, however, Harry has some concerns about whether it would be permissible for him to download any of these films (even if only for private use). ■

Is Harry's ethical conflict one that is unique to computers and cybertechnology? Are the ethical issues surrounding Harry's situation new and thus unique to cybertechnology, because the practice of downloading digital media from the Internet—a practice that many in the movie and recording industries call "digital piracy"—would not have been possible if computer technology had not been invented in the first place? If so, this claim would, once again, seem to be true only in a trivial sense. The issue of piracy itself as a moral concern existed before the widespread use of computer technology. For example, people were able to "pirate" audio cassette tapes simply by using two or more analog tape recorders to make unauthorized copies of proprietary material. The important point to note here is that moral issues surrounding the pirating of audio cassette tapes are, at bottom, the same issues underlying the pirating of digital media. They arise in each case because, fundamentally, the behavior associated with unauthorized copying raises moral concerns about property, fairness, rights, and so forth. So, as in Scenario 1–4, there seems to be insufficient evidence to suggest that the ethical issues associated with digital piracy are either new or unique in some nontrivial sense.

1.3.1 Distinguishing between Unique Technological Features and Unique Ethical Issues

Based on our analysis of the two scenarios in the preceding section, we might conclude that there is nothing new or special about the kinds of moral issues associated with cybertechnology. In fact, some philosophers have argued that we have the same old ethical issues reappearing in a new guise. But is such a view accurate?

If we focus primarily on the moral issues themselves *as moral issues*, it would seem that perhaps there is nothing new. Cyber-related concerns involving privacy, property, free speech, etc., can be understood as specific expressions of core (traditional) moral notions, such as autonomy, fairness, justice, responsibility, and respect for persons. However, if instead we focus more closely on cybertechnology itself, we see that there are some interesting and possibly unique features that distinguish this technology from earlier technologies. Maner has argued that computing technology is "uniquely fast," "uniquely complex," and "uniquely coded." But even if cybertechnology has these unique features, does it necessarily follow that any of the moral questions associated with that technology must also be unique? One would commit a logical fallacy if he or she concluded that cyberethics issues must be unique simply because certain features or aspects of cybertechnology are unique. The fallacy can be expressed in the following way:

PREMISE 1. Cybertechnology has some unique technological features.

PREMISE 2. Cybertechnology has generated some ethical concerns.

CONCLUSION. At least some ethical concerns generated by cybertechnology must be unique ethical concerns.

As we will see in Chapter 3, this reasoning is fallacious because it assumes that characteristics that apply to a certain technology must also apply to ethical issues generated by that technology.[11]

1.3.2 An Alternative Strategy for Analyzing the Debate about the Uniqueness of Cyberethics Issues

Although it may be difficult to prove conclusively whether or not cybertechnology has generated any new or unique ethical issues, we must not rule out the possibility that many of the controversies associated with this technology warrant special consideration from an ethical perspective. But what, exactly, is so different about issues involving computers and cybertechnology that makes them deserving of special moral consideration? James Moor (2007) points out that computer technology, unlike most previous technologies, is "logically malleable"; it can be shaped and molded to perform a variety of functions. Because noncomputer technologies are typically designed to perform some particular function or task, they lack the universal or general-purpose characteristics that computing technologies possess. For example, microwave ovens and DVD players are technological devices that have been designed to perform specific tasks. Microwave ovens cannot be used to view DVDs, and DVD players cannot be used to defrost, cook, or reheat food. However, a computer, depending on the software used, can perform a range of diverse tasks: it can be instructed to behave as a video game, a word processor, a spreadsheet, a medium to send and receive e-mail messages, or an interface to Web sites. Hence, cybertechnology is extremely malleable.

Moor points out that because of its logical malleability, cybertechnology can generate "new possibilities for human action" that appear to be limitless. Some of these possibilities for action generate what Moor calls "policy vacuums," because we have no explicit policies or laws to guide new choices made possible by computer technology. These vacuums, in turn, need to be filled with either new or revised policies. But what, exactly, does Moor mean by "policy"? Moor (2004) defines policies as "rules of conduct, ranging from formal laws to informal, implicit guidelines for actions."[12] Viewing computer ethics issues in terms of policies is useful, Moor believes, because policies have the right level of generality to consider when we evaluate the morality of conduct. As noted, policies can range from formal laws to informal guidelines. Moor also notes that policies can have "justified exemptions" because they are not absolute; yet policies usually imply a certain "level of obligation" within their contexts.

What action is required to resolve a policy vacuum when it is discovered? Initially, a solution to this problem might seem quite simple and straightforward. We might assume that all we need to do is identify the vacuums that have been generated and then fill them with policies and laws. However, this will not always work, because sometimes the new possibilities for human action generated by cybertechnology also introduce "conceptual vacuums," or what Moor calls "conceptual muddles." In these cases, we must first eliminate the muddles by clearing up certain conceptual confusions before we can frame coherent policies and laws.

1.3.3 A Policy Vacuum in Duplicating Computer Software

A critical policy vacuum, which also involved a conceptual muddle, emerged with the advent of personal desktop computers (henceforth referred to generically as PCs). The particular vacuum arose because of the controversy surrounding the copying of software. When PCs became commercially available, many users discovered that they could easily duplicate software programs. They found that they could use their PCs to make copies of proprietary computer programs such as word processing programs, spreadsheets, and video games. Some users assumed that in making copies of these programs they were doing nothing wrong. At that time there were no explicit laws to regulate the subsequent use and distribution of software programs once they had been legally purchased by an individual or by an institution. Although it might be difficult to imagine today, at one time software was not clearly protected by either copyright law or the patent process.

Of course, there were clear laws and policies regarding the theft of physical property. Such laws and policies protected against the theft of personal computers as well as against the theft of a physical disk drive residing in a PC on which the proprietary software programs could easily be duplicated. However, this was not the case with laws and policies regarding the "theft," or unauthorized copying, of software programs that run on computers. Although there were intellectual property laws in place, it had not been determined that software was or should be protected by intellectual property (IP) law: It was unclear whether software should be understood as an idea (which is not protected by IP law), as a form of writing protected by copyright law, or as a set of machine instructions protected by patents. Consequently, many entrepreneurs who designed and manufactured software programs argued for explicit legal protection for their products. A policy vacuum arose with respect to duplicating software: Could a user make a backup copy of a program for herself? Could she share it with a friend? Could she give the original program to a friend? A clear policy was needed to fill this vacuum.

Before we can fill the vacuum regarding software duplication with a coherent policy or law, we first have to resolve a certain conceptual muddle by answering the question: what, exactly, is computer software? Until we can clarify the concept of software itself, we cannot frame a coherent policy as to whether or not we should allow the free duplication of software. Currently there is still much confusion, as well as considerable controversy, as to how laws concerning the exchange (and, in effect, duplication) of proprietary software over the Internet should be framed.

In Moor's scheme, how one resolves the conceptual muddle (or decides the conceptual issue) can have a significant effect on which kinds of policies are acceptable. Getting clear about the conceptual issues is an important first step, but it is not a sufficient condition for being able to formulate a policy. Finally, the justification of a policy requires much factual knowledge, as well as an understanding of normative and ethical principles.

Consider the controversies surrounding the original Napster Web site and the Recording Industry Association of America (RIAA), in the late 1990s, regarding the free exchange of music over the Internet. Proponents on both sides of this dispute experienced difficulties in making convincing arguments for their respective positions due, in no small part, to confusion regarding the nature and the status of information (digitized music in the form of MP3 files) being exchanged between Internet users and the technology (P2P systems) that facilitated this exchange. Although cybertechnology has made it possible to exchange MP3 files, there is still debate, and arguably a great deal of confusion as well, about whether doing so should necessarily be illegal. Until the conceptual confusions or muddles underlying arguments used in the Napster vs. RIAA case in particular, and about the nature of P2P file-sharing systems in general, are resolved, it is difficult to frame an adequate policy regarding the exchange of MP3 files in P2P transactions.

How does Moor's insight that cyberethics issues need to be analyzed in terms of potential policy vacuums and conceptual muddles contribute to our earlier question as to whether there is anything unique or special about cyberethics? First, we should note that Moor takes no explicit stance on the question as to whether any cyberethics issues are unique. However, he does argue that cyberethics issues deserve special consideration because of the nature of cybertechnology itself, which is significantly different from alternative technologies in terms of the vast number of policy vacuums it generates (Moor 2001). So, even though the ethical issues associated with cybertechnology—that is, issues involving privacy, intellectual property, and so forth—might not be new or unique, they nonetheless can put significant pressure on our conceptual frameworks and normative reasoning to a degree not found in other areas of applied ethics. Thus it would seem to follow, on Moor's line of reasoning, that an independent field of applied ethics that focuses on ethical aspects of cybertechnology is indeed justified.

▶ 1.4 CYBERETHICS AS A BRANCH OF APPLIED ETHICS: THREE DISTINCT PERSPECTIVES

Cyberethics, as a field of study, can be understood as a branch of *applied ethics*. Applied ethics, as opposed to theoretical ethics, examines practical ethical issues. It does so by analyzing those issues from the vantage point of one or more ethical theories. Whereas ethical theory is concerned with establishing logically coherent and consistent criteria in the form of standards and rules for evaluating moral problems, the principal aim of applied ethics is to analyze specific moral problems themselves through the application of ethical theory. As such, those working in fields of applied ethics, or practical ethics, are not inclined to debate some of the finer points of individual ethical theories. Instead, their interest in ethical theory is primarily with how one or more theories can be successfully applied to the analysis of specific moral problems that they happen to be investigating.

For an example of a practical ethics issue involving cybertechnology, consider again the original Napster controversy. Recall that at the heart of this dispute is the question: should proprietary information, in a digital format known as MP3 files, be allowed to be exchanged freely over the Internet? Those advocating the free exchange of MP3 files could appeal to one or more ethical theories to support their position. For example, they might appeal to utilitarianism, an ethical theory that is based on the principle that our policies and laws should be such that they produce the greatest good (happiness) for the greatest number of people. A utilitarian might argue that MP3 files should be distributed freely over the Internet because the consequences of allowing such a practice would make the majority of users happy and would thus contribute to the greatest good for the greatest number of persons affected.

Others might argue that allowing proprietary material to be exchanged freely over the Internet would violate the rights of those who created, and who legally own, the material. Proponents of this view could appeal to a nonutilitarian principle or theory that is grounded in the notion of respecting the rights of individuals. According to this view, an important consideration for an ethical policy is that it protects the rights of individuals—in this case, the rights of those who legally own the proprietary material in question—irrespective of the happiness that might or might not result for the majority of Internet users.

Notice that in our analysis of the dispute over the exchange of MP3 files on the Internet (in the Napster case), the application of two different ethical theories yielded two very different answers to the question of which policy or course of action ought to be adopted. Sometimes, however, the application of different ethical theories to a particular problem will yield similar solutions. We will examine in detail some standard ethical theories, including utilitarianism, in Chapter 2. Our main concern in this textbook is with applied, or practical, ethics issues, and not with ethical theory per se. Wherever appropriate, however, ethical theory will be used to inform our analysis of moral issues involving cybertechnology.

Understanding cyberethics as a field of applied ethics that examines moral issues pertaining to cybertechnology is an important first step. But much more needs to be said about the perspectives that interdisciplinary researchers bring to their analysis of the issues that make up this relatively new field. Most scholars and professionals conducting research in this field of applied ethics have proceeded from one of three different perspectives— professional ethics, philosophical ethics, or sociological/descriptive ethics.[13] Gaining a clearer understanding of what is meant by each perspective is useful at this point.

1.4.1 Perspective #1: Cyberethics as a Field of Professional Ethics

According to those who view cyberethics primarily as a branch of *professional ethics*, the field can best be understood as identifying and analyzing issues of ethical responsibility for computer and information-technology (IT) professionals. Among the cyberethics issues considered from this perspective are those having to do with the computer/IT professional's role in designing, developing, and maintaining computer hardware and software systems. For example, suppose a programmer discovers that a software product she has been working on is about to be released for sale to the public even though that product is unreliable because it contains "buggy" software. Should she blow the whistle?

Those who see cyberethics essentially as a branch of professional ethics would likely draw on analogies from other professional fields, such as medicine and law. They would point out that in medical ethics and legal ethics, the principal focus of analysis is on issues of moral responsibility that affect individuals as members of these *professions*. By analogy, they would go on to argue that the same rationale should apply to the field of cyberethics—i.e., the primary, and possibly even exclusive, focus of cyberethics should be on issues of moral responsibility that affect computer/IT professionals. Don Gotterbarn (1995) can be interpreted as defending a version of this position when he asserts

> The only way to make sense of 'Computer Ethics' is to narrow its focus to those actions that are within the control of the individual *moral* computer professional.[14] [Italics Gotterbarn]

So, in this passage, Gotterbarn suggests that the principal focus of computer ethics should be on issues of professional responsibility and not on the broader moral and social implications of that technology.

The analogies Gotterbarn uses to defend his argument are instructive. He notes, for example, that in the past, certain technologies have profoundly altered our lives, especially in the ways that many of us conduct our day-to-day affairs. Consider three such technologies: the printing press, the automobile, and the airplane. Despite the significant and perhaps revolutionary effects of each of these technologies, we do not have "printing press ethics," "automobile ethics," or "airplane ethics." So why, Gotterbarn asks, should we have a field of computer ethics apart from the study of those ethical issues that affect the professionals responsible for the design, development, and delivery of computer systems? In other words, Gotterbarn suggests that it is not the business of computer ethics to examine ethical issues other than those that affect computer professionals.

Professional Ethics and the Computer Science Practitioner

Gotterbarn's view about what the proper focus of computer ethics research and inquiry should be is shared by other practitioners in the discipline of computer science. However, some of those practitioners, as well as many philosophers and social scientists, believe that Gotterbarn's conception of computer ethics as simply a field of professional ethics is too narrow. In fact, some who identify themselves as computer professionals or as "information professionals," and who are otherwise sympathetic to Gotterbarn's overall attention to professional ethics issues, believe that a broader model is needed. For example, Elizabeth Buchanan (2004), in describing the importance of analyzing ethical issues in the "information professions," suggests that some nonprofessional ethics issues must also be examined because of the significant impact they have on noninformation professionals, including ordinary computer users. Consider that these issues can also affect people who have never used a computer.

Of course, Buchanan's category of "informational professional" is considerably broader in scope than Gotterbarn's notion of computer professional. But the central point of her argument still holds, especially in the era of the Internet and the World Wide Web. In the computing era preceding the Web, Gotterbarn's conception of computer ethics as a field limited to the study of ethical issues affecting computer professionals seemed plausible. Now, computers are virtually everywhere, and the ethical issues generated by certain uses of computers and cybertechnology affect virtually everyone, professional and nonprofessional alike.

Despite the critiques leveled against Gotterbarn's conception of the field, his position may turn out to be the most plausible of the three models we consider. Because of the social impact that computer and Internet technologies have had during the past three decades, we have tended to identify many of the ethical issues associated with these technologies, especially concerns affecting privacy and intellectual property, as computer ethics issues. But Deborah Johnson (2000) believes that in the future, computer-related ethical issues, such as privacy and property (that are currently associated with the field of computer ethics), may become part of what she calls "ordinary ethics." In fact, Johnson has suggested that computer ethics, as a separate field of applied ethics, may eventually "go away." However, even if Johnson's prediction turns out to be correct, computer ethics as a field that examines ethical issues affecting responsibility for computer professionals will, in all likelihood, still be needed. In this sense, then, Gotterbarn's original model of computer ethics might turn out to be the correct one in the long term.

Applying the Professional Ethics Model to Specific Scenarios

It is fairly easy to see how the professional ethics model can be used to analyze issues involving professional responsibility that directly impact computer/IT professionals. For example, issues concerned with the development and implementation of critical software would fit closely with the professional model. But can that model be extended to include cases that may only affect computer professionals indirectly?

We can ask how some of the issues in the scenarios described earlier in this chapter might be analyzed from the perspective of professional ethics. Consider the Washingtonienne scenario, which initially might seem to be outside the purview of computer ethics vis-à-vis professional ethics. However, some interesting and controversial questions arise that can have implications for computer/IT professionals as well as for professional bloggers. For example, should Internet service providers (ISPs) and SNSs hire programmers to design features that would support anonymity for individuals who post certain kinds of personal information (e.g., personal diaries such as Cutler's) to blogs aimed at sharing that information with a limited audience, as opposed to blogs whose content is intended to be available to the entire "online world"? Also, should providers of online services be encouraged to include applications that enable bloggers to delete, permanently, some embarrassing information they had entered in a blog in the past—e.g., information that could threaten their current employment (as in the case of Jessica Cutler) or harm their chances or future employment (e.g., if information they had previously posted to a blog were discovered by a prospective employer)? Consider the example of information about oneself that a person might have carelessly posted on Facebook when he or she was a first-year college student; the question of whether an individual's remarks entered in an online forum should remain there indefinitely (or should be stored in that forum's database in perpetuity) is one that is now hotly debated.

Another aspect of the professional ethics model as applied to blogs is whether bloggers themselves should be expected to comply with a professional "blogger code of ethics," as some have proposed. For example, there are ethical codes of conduct that professional journalists are expected to observe. (We examine professional codes of ethics in detail in Chapter 4.)

Also, consider the Megan Meier scenario. From the vantage point of professional ethics, one might argue that cyberbullying in general and the death of Meier in particular are not the kinds of concerns that are the proper business of computer ethics. We saw that someone such as Gotterbarn might ask why a crime that happened to involve the use of a computer should necessarily be construed as an issue for computer ethics. For example, he notes that a murder that happened to be committed with a surgeon's scalpel would not be considered an issue for medical ethics. While murders involving the use of a computer, like all murders, are serious moral and legal problems, Gotterbarn seems to imply that they are not examples of genuine computer ethics issues. However, Gotterbarn and the advocates for his position are acutely aware that software developed by engineers can have implications that extend far beyond the computing/IT profession itself.

Many of the ethical issues discussed in this book have implications for computer/IT professionals, either directly or indirectly. Issues that have a direct impact on computer professionals in general, and software engineers in particular, are examined in Chapter 4, which is dedicated to professional ethics. Computer science students and computer professionals will likely also want to assess some of the indirect implications that issues examined in Chapters 5 through 12 also have for the computing profession.

1.4.2 Perspective #2: Cyberethics as a Field of Philosophical Ethics

What, exactly, is *philosophical ethics* and how is it different from professional ethics? Since philosophical methods and tools are also used to analyze issues involving professional ethics, any attempt to distinguish between the two might seem arbitrary, perhaps even odd. For our purposes, however, a useful distinction can be drawn between the two fields because of the approach each takes in addressing ethical issues. Whereas professional ethics issues typically involve concerns of responsibility and obligation affecting individuals as members of a certain profession, philosophical ethics issues include broader concerns—social policies as well as individual behavior—that affect virtually everyone in society. Cybertechnology-related moral issues involving privacy, security, property, and free speech can affect everyone, including individuals who have never even used a computer.

To appreciate the perspective of cyberethics as a branch of philosophical ethics, consider James Moor's classic definition of the field. According to Moor (2007), cyberethics, or what he calls "computer ethics," is

> the analysis of the nature and social impact of computer technology and the corresponding formulation and justification of policies for the ethical use of such technology.[15]

Two points in Moor's definition are worth examining more closely. First, computer ethics (i.e., what we call "cyberethics") is concerned with the social impact of computers and cybertechnology in a broad sense, and not merely the impact of that technology for computer professionals. Secondly, this definition challenges us to reflect on the social impact of cybertechnology in a way that also requires a justification for our social policies.

Why is cyberethics, as a field of philosophical ethics dedicated to the study of ethical issues involving cybertechnology, warranted when there aren't similar fields of applied ethics for other technologies? Recall our earlier discussion of Gotterbarn's observation that we do not have fields of applied ethics called "automobile ethics" or "airplane ethics," even though automobile and airplane technologies have significantly affected our day-to-day lives. Moor could respond to Gotterbarn's point by noting that the introduction of automobile and airplane technologies did not affect our social policies and norms in the same kinds of fundamental ways that computer technology has. Of course, we have had to modify and significantly revise certain laws and policies to accommodate the implementation of new kinds of transportation technologies. In the case of automobile technology, we had to extend, and in some cases modify, certain policies and laws previously used to regulate the flow of horse-drawn modes of transportation. And clearly, automobile and airplane technologies have revolutionized transportation, resulting in our ability to travel faster and farther than was possible in previous eras.

What has made the impact of computer technology significantly different from that of other modern technologies? We have already seen that for Moor, three factors contribute to this impact: logical malleability, policy vacuums, and conceptual muddles. Because cybertechnology is logically malleable, its uses often generate policy vacuums and conceptual muddles. In Section 1.3.2 we saw how certain kinds of conceptual muddles contributed to some of the confusion surrounding software piracy issues in general, and the Napster controversy in particular. What implications do these factors have for the standard methodology used by philosophers in the analysis of applied ethics issues?

Methodology and Philosophical Ethics

Philip Brey (2004) notes that the standard methodology used by philosophers to conduct research in applied ethics has three distinct stages in that an ethicist must

1. identify a particular controversial practice as a moral problem,
2. describe and analyze the problem by clarifying concepts and examining the factual data associated with that problem,
3. apply moral theories and principles in the deliberative process in order to reach a position about the particular moral issue.[16]

We have already noted (in Section 1.3) how the first two stages in this methodology can be applied to an analysis of ethical issues associated with digital piracy. We saw that, first, a practice involving the use of cybertechnology to "pirate" or make unauthorized copies of proprietary information was *identified* as morally controversial. At the second stage, the problem was *analyzed* in descriptive and contextual terms to clarify the practice and to situate it in a particular context. In the case of digital piracy, we saw that the concept of piracy could be analyzed in terms of moral issues involving theft and intellectual property theory. When we describe and analyze problems at this stage, we will want to be aware of and address any policy vacuums and conceptual muddles that are relevant.

At the third and final stage, the problem must be *deliberated* over in terms of moral principles (or theories) and logical arguments. Brey describes this stage in the method as the "deliberative process." Here, various arguments are used to justify the application of particular moral principles to the issue under consideration. For example, issues involving digital piracy can be deliberated upon in terms of one or more standard ethical theories, such as utilitarianism (defined in Chapter 2).

Applying the Method of Philosophical Ethics to Specific Scenarios

To see how the philosophical ethics perspective of cyberethics can help us to analyze a cluster of moral issues affecting cybertechnology, we revisit the Washingtonienne, Twitter, and Meier scenarios introduced in the opening section of this chapter. In applying the philosophical ethics model to these scenarios, our first task is to identify one or more moral issues associated with each. We have already seen that these scenarios illustrate a wide range of ethical issues. For example, we saw that ethical issues associated with the Washingtonienne scenario include free speech, defamation, confidentiality, anonymity, and privacy with respect to blogs and blogging. But what kinds of policy vacuums and conceptual muddles, if any, arise in this case? For one thing, both the nature of a blog and the practices surrounding blogging are relatively new. Thus, not surprisingly, we have very few clear and explicit policies affecting the "blogosphere." To consider why this is so, we begin by asking: what, exactly, is a blog? For example, is it similar to a newspaper or a periodical (such as the *New York Times* or *TIME Magazine*), which is held to standards of accuracy and truth? Or is a blog more like a tabloid (such as the *National Inquirer*), in which case there is little expectation of accuracy? Our answers to these questions may determine whether bloggers should be permitted to post anything they wish, without concern for the accuracy of any of their remarks that may be false or defamatory, or both? At present, there are no clear answers to these and related questions surrounding blogs. So, it would seem that explicit policies are needed to regulate blogs and bloggers. But it would also seem that before we can frame explicit policies for blogging, we first need to resolve some important conceptual muddles.[17]

Next, consider the Twitter scenario. Among the ethical issues identified in that scenario were concerns affecting intellectual property. We can now ask whether any policy vacuums and conceptual muddles were generated in that scenario. The answer would clearly seem to be "yes." However, policy vacuums concerning intellectual property in the digital era are by no means new. For example, we noted earlier that the original Napster scenario introduced controversies with respect to sharing copyrighted information, in the form of proprietary MP3 files, online. The Twitter scenario, however, introduces issues that go beyond that kind of concern. Here, we have a dispute about who owns a list of names that can constitute both a company's customer list and a blogger's group of followers on a private SNS account. Should one party have exclusive ownership of this list of names? Can a list of names qualify as a "trade secret" for a corporation, as companies such as Phonedog Media claim? If a blogger generates a list of followers while blogging for an employer, should that employer have exclusive rights to the list of names?

Finally, consider the Meier scenario. Did MySpace have a clear policy in place regarding the creation of user accounts on its forum when Lori Drew set up the "Josh Evans" account? Do/Should SNS users have an expectation of anonymity or pseudonomity when they set up an account? Should SNSs, such as MySpace and Facebook, bear some moral responsibility, or at least some legal liability, for harm that is caused to users of its service, especially when users of that SNS have set up accounts with fictitious names and profiles? It would appear that the Meier scenario illustrates how a clear and significant policy vacuum arose in the case of the rules governing acceptable behavior on SNSs. Fortunately, many SNSs now, following the tragic incident involving Meier, have clear and explicit policies that require one to disclose his or her true identity to the SNS before setting up an account on its forum.

1.4.3 Perspective #3: Cyberethics as a Field of Sociological/Descriptive Ethics

The two perspectives on cyberethics that we have examined thus far—professional ethics and philosophical ethics—can both be understood as *normative* inquiries into applied ethics issues. Normative inquiries or studies, which focus on evaluating and prescribing moral systems, can be contrasted with *descriptive* inquiries or studies. Descriptive ethics is, or aims to be, nonevaluative in approach; typically, it describes particular moral systems and sometimes also reports how members of various groups and cultures view particular moral issues. This kind of analysis of ethical and social issues is often used by sociologists and social scientists; hence, our use of the expression "sociological/descriptive perspective" to analyze this methodological framework.

Descriptive vs. Normative Inquiries

Whereas descriptive investigations provide us with information about what *is* the case, normative inquiries evaluate situations from the vantage point of questions having to do with what *ought to be* the case. Those who approach cyberethics from the perspective of descriptive ethics often describe sociological aspects of a particular moral issue, such as the social impact of a specific technology on a particular community or social group. For example, one way of analyzing moral issues surrounding the "digital divide" (examined in Chapter 10) is first to describe the problem in terms of its impact on various socio-demographic groups involving social class, race, and gender. We can investigate whether, in fact, fewer poor people, non-whites, and women have access to cybertechnology than wealthy and middle-class persons, whites, and men. In this case, the investigation is one that is basically descriptive in character. If we were then to inquire whether the lack of access to technology for some groups relative to others was unfair, we would be engaging in a normative inquiry. For example, a normative investigation of this issue would question whether certain groups *should* have more access to cybertechnology than they currently have. The following scenario illustrates an approach to a particular cyberethics issue via the perspective of sociological/descriptive ethics.

▶ **SCENARIO 1–6:** The Impact of Technology X on the Pleasantville Community

AEC Corporation, a company that employs 8,000 workers in Pleasantville, has decided to purchase and implement a new kind of computer/information technology, Technology X. The implementation of Technology X will likely have a significant impact for AEC's employees in particular, as well as for Pleasantville in general. It is estimated that 3,000 jobs at AEC will be eliminated when the new technology is implemented during the next six months. ■

Does the decision to implement Technology X pose a normative ethical problem for the AEC Corporation, as well as for Pleasantville? If we analyze the impact that Technology X has with respect to the number of jobs that are gained or lost, our investigation is essentially descriptive in nature. In reporting this phenomenon, we are simply describing or stating what *is/is not* at issue in this case. If, however, we argue that AEC either should or should not implement this new technology, then we make a claim that is normative (i.e., a claim about what *ought/ought not* to be the case). For example, one might argue that the new technology should not be implemented because it would displace workers and thus possibly violate certain contractual obligations that may exist between AEC and its employees. Alternatively, one might argue that implementing Technology X would be acceptable provided that certain factors are taken into consideration in determining which workers would lose their jobs. For example, suppose that in the process of eliminating jobs, older workers and minority employees would stand to be disproportionately affected. In this case, critics might argue that a fairer system should be used.

Our initial account of the impact of Technology X's implementation for Pleasantville simply reported some descriptive information about the number of jobs that would likely be lost by employees at AEC Corporation, which has sociological implications. As our analysis of this scenario continued, however, we did much more than merely describe what the impact was; we also evaluated the impact for AEC's employees in terms of what we believed *ought* to have been done. In doing so, we shifted from an analysis based on claims that were merely descriptive to an analysis in which some claims were also normative.

Some Benefits of Using the Sociological/Descriptive Approach to Analyze Cyberethics Issues

Why is the examination of cyberethics issues from the sociological/descriptive ethics perspective useful? Huff and Finholt (1994) suggest that focusing on descriptive aspects of social issues can help us to better understand many of the normative features and implications. In other words, when we understand the descriptive features of the social effects of a particular technology, the normative ethical questions become clearer. So, Huff and Finholt believe that analyzing the social impact of cybertechnology from a sociological/descriptive perspective can better prepare us for our subsequent analysis of practical ethical issues affecting our system of policies and laws.

We have already noted that virtually all of our social institutions, from work to education to government to finance, have been affected by cybertechnology. This technology has also had significant impacts on different sociodemographic sectors and segments of our population. The descriptive information that we gather about these groups can provide important information that, in turn, can inform legislators and policy makers who are drafting and revising laws in response to the effects of cybertechnology.

From the perspective of sociological/descriptive ethics, we can also better examine the impact that cybertechnology has on our understanding of concepts such as community and individuality. We can ask, for instance, whether certain developments in social networking technologies used in Twitter and Facebook have affected the way that we conceive traditional notions such as "community" and "neighbor." Is a community essentially a group of individuals with similar interests, or perhaps a similar ideology, irrespective of geographical limitations? Is national identity something that is, or may soon become, anachronistic? While these kinds of questions and issues in and of themselves are more correctly conceived as descriptive rather than normative concerns, they can have significant normative implications for our moral and legal systems as well. Much more will be said about the relationship between descriptive and normative approaches to analyzing ethical issues in Chapters 10 and 11, where we examine the impact of cybertechnology on sociodemographic groups and on some of our social and political institutions.

Applying the Sociological/Descriptive Ethics Approach to Specific Scenarios

Consider how someone approaching cyberethics issues from the perspective of socio-logical/descriptive ethics might analyze the Washingtonienne and Meier scenarios, described above. In the Washingtonienne case, the focus might be on gathering socio-demographic and socioeconomic data pertaining to the kinds of individuals who are likely to view and interact in blogs. For example, some social scientists might consider the income and educational levels of bloggers, as compared to individuals who engage in alternative kinds of online activities or who do not use the Internet at all. Others might be interested in determining which kinds of users view their own blogs and online postings as simply an online outlet for the kind of personal information that traditionally was included only in one's (physical) diary. (Jessica Cutler's behavior seemed to fit this category.) Social and behavioral scientists might further inquire into why some individuals seem to display little-to-no concern about posting intimate details of their romantic and sexual encounters to online forums that could be read, potentially at least, by millions of people. They might also question why some bloggers (as well as ordinary users of SNSs such as Facebook and Twitter) are so eager to post personal information, including information about their location (at a given point in time) and about their recreational interests, to online forums, in an era when that kind of information is so easily tracked and recorded by individuals other than those for whom it is intended.

Next consider the Meier scenario with respect to how it might be analyzed by someone doing research from the point of view of sociological/descriptive ethics. For example, a researcher might inquire into whether there has been an increase in the number of bullying incidents. And if the answer to this question is "yes," the researcher might next question whether such an increase is linked to the widespread availability of cybertechnology. Also, the researcher might consider whether certain groups in the population are now more at risk than others with respect to being bullied in cyberspace. The researcher could inquire whether there are any statistical patterns to suggest that late-adolescent/early-teenage females are more likely to be bullied via cybertechnology than are individuals in other groups. The researcher could also ask if women in general are typically more vulnerable than men to the kinds of harassment associated with cyberbullying.

Also, a researcher approaching the Meier scenario from the sociological/descriptive ethics perspective might set out to determine whether an individual who never would have thought of physically bullying a victim in geographical space might now be inclined to engage in cyberbullying—perhaps because of the relative ease of doing so with cybertechnology? Or is it the case that some of those same individuals might now be tempted to do so because they believe that they will not likely get caught? Also, has the fact that a potential cyberbully realizes that he or she can harass a victim on the Internet under the cloak of relative anonymity/pseudonymity contributed to the increase in bullying-related activities online? These are a few of the kinds of questions that could be examined from the sociological/descriptive perspective of cyberethics.

Table 1.2 summarizes some key characteristics that differentiate the three main perspectives for approaching cyberethics issues.

In Chapters 4–12, we examine specific cyberethics questions from the vantage points of our three perspectives. Issues considered from the perspective of professional ethics are examined in Chapters 4 and 12. Cyberethics issues considered from the perspective of philosophical ethics, such as those involving privacy, security, and intellectual property and free speech, are examined in Chapters 5–9. And several of the issues considered in Chapters 10 and 11 are examined from the perspective of sociological/descriptive ethics.

TABLE 1.2   Summary of Cyberethics Perspectives

Type of Perspective	Associated Disciplines	Issues Examined
Professional	Computer Science	Professional responsibility
	Engineering	System reliability/safety
	Library/Information Science	Codes of conduct
Philosophical	Philosophy	Privacy and anonymity
	Law	Intellectual property
		Free speech
Sociological/Descriptive	Sociology/Behavioral Sciences	Impact of cybertechnology on governmental/financial/educational institutions and sociodemographic groups

▶ 1.5 A COMPREHENSIVE CYBERETHICS METHODOLOGY

The three different perspectives of cyberethics described in the preceding section might suggest that three different kinds of methodologies are needed to analyze the range of issues examined in this textbook. The goal of this section, however, is to show that a single, comprehensive method can be constructed, and that this method will be adequate in guiding us in our analysis of cyberethics issues.

Recall the standard model used in applied ethics, which we briefly examined in Section 1.4.2. There we saw that the standard model includes three stages, i.e., where a researcher must (1) identify an ethical problem, (2) describe and analyze the problem in conceptual and factual terms, and (3) apply ethical theories and principles in the deliberative process. We also saw that Moor argued that the conventional model was not adequate for an analysis of at least some cyberethics issues. Moor believed that additional steps, which address concerns affecting "policy vacuums" and "conceptual muddles," are sometimes needed before we can move from the second to the third stage of the methodological scheme. We must now consider whether the standard model, with Moor's additional steps included, is complete. Brey (2004) suggests that it is not.

Brey believes that while the (revised) standard model might work well in many fields of applied ethics, such as medical ethics, business ethics, and bioethics, it does not always fare well in cyberethics. Brey argues that the standard method, when used to identify ethical aspects of cybertechnology, tends to focus almost exclusively on the *uses* of that technology. As such, the standard method fails to pay sufficient attention to certain features that may be embedded in the technology itself, such as design features that may also have moral implications.

We might be inclined to assume that technology itself is neutral and that only the uses to which a particular technology is put are morally controversial. However, Brey and others believe that it is a mistake to conceive of technology, independent of its uses, as something that is value-free, or unbiased. Instead, they argue, moral values are often embedded or implicit in features built into technologies at the design stage. For example, critics, including some feminists, have pointed out that in the past the ergonomic systems designed for drivers of automobiles were biased toward men and gave virtually no consideration to women. That is, considerations having to do with the average height and typical body dimensions of men were implicitly built into the design specification. These critics also note that decisions about how the ergonomic systems would be designed were all made by men, which likely accounts for the bias embedded in that particular technological system.

1.5.1 A "Disclosive" Method for Cyberethics

As noted earlier, Brey believes that the standard, or what he calls "mainstream," applied ethics methodology is not always adequate for identifying moral issues involving cybertechnology. Brey worries that using the standard model we might fail to notice certain features embedded in the design of cybertechnology. He also worries about the standard method of applied ethics because it tends to focus on known moral controversies, and because it fails to identify certain practices involving the use of cybertechnology that have moral import but that are not yet known. Brey refers to such practices as having "morally opaque" (or morally nontransparent) features, which he contrasts with "morally transparent" features.

According to Brey, morally controversial features that are transparent tend to be easily recognized as morally problematic. For example, many people are aware that the practice of placing closed circuit video surveillance cameras in undisclosed locations is controversial from a moral point of view. Brey notes that it is, however, generally much more difficult to discern morally opaque features in technology. These features can be morally opaque for one of two reasons: either they are unknown, or they are known but perceived to be morally neutral.[18]

Consider an example of each type of morally opaque (or morally nontransparent) feature. Computerized practices involving data mining (defined in Chapter 5) would be unknown to those who have never heard of the concept of data mining and who are unfamiliar with data mining technology. However, this technology should not be assumed to be morally neutral merely because data mining techniques are unknown to non-technical people, including some ethicists as well. Even if such techniques are opaque to many users, data mining practices raise certain moral issues pertaining to personal privacy.

Next consider an example of a morally opaque feature in which a technology is well known. Most Internet users are familiar with search engine technology. What users might fail to recognize, however, is that certain uses of search engines can be morally controversial with respect to personal privacy. Consequently, one of the features of search engine technology can be morally controversial in a sense that it is not obvious or transparent to many people, including those who are very familiar with and who use search engine technology. So, while a well-known technology, such as search engine programs, might appear to be morally neutral, a closer analysis of practices involving this technology will disclose that it has moral implications.

Figure 1.1 illustrates some differences between morally opaque and morally transparent features.

Brey argues that an adequate methodology for computer ethics must first identify, or "disclose," features that, without proper probing and analysis, would go unnoticed as having moral implications. Thus, an extremely important first step in Brey's "disclosive

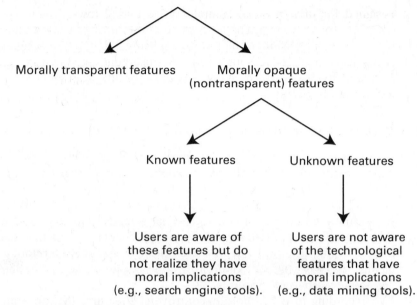

Figure 1.1 Embedded technological features having moral implications.

method" is to reveal moral values embedded in the various features and practices associated with cybertechnology itself.

1.5.2 An Interdisciplinary and Multilevel Method for Analyzing Cyberethics Issues

Brey's disclosive model is *interdisciplinary* because it requires that computer scientists, philosophers, and social scientists collaborate. It is also *multilevel* because conducting computer ethics research requires three levels of analysis:

- disclosure level
- theoretical level
- application level

First of all, the moral values embedded in the design of computer systems must be disclosed. To do this, we need computer scientists because they understand computer technology much better than philosophers and social scientists do. However, social scientists are also needed to evaluate system design and make it more user-friendly. Then philosophers can determine whether existing ethical theories are adequate to test the newly disclosed moral issues or whether more theory is needed. Finally, computer scientists, philosophers, and social scientists must cooperate by applying ethical theory in deliberations about moral issues.[19] In Chapter 2, we examine a range of ethical theories that can be used.

In the deliberations involved in applying ethical theory to a particular moral problem, one remaining methodological step also needs to be resolved. Jeroen van den Hoven (2000) has noted that methodological schemes must also address the "problem of justification of moral judgments." For our purposes, we use the strategies of logical analysis included in Chapter 3 to justify the moral theories we apply to particular issues.

TABLE 1.3 Brey's Disclosive Model

Level	Disciplines Involved	Task/Function
Disclosure	Computer Science Social Science (optional)	Disclose embedded features in computer technology that have moral import
Theoretical	Philosophy	Test newly disclosed features against standard ethical theories
Application	Computer Science Philosophy Social Science	Apply standard or newly revised/formulated ethical theories to the issues

Table 1.3 describes the academic disciplines and the corresponding tasks and functions involved in Brey's disclosive model.

It is in the interdisciplinary spirit of the disclosive methodology proposed by Brey that we will examine the range of cyberethics issues described in Chapters 4–12.

▶ 1.6 A COMPREHENSIVE STRATEGY FOR APPROACHING CYBERETHICS ISSUES

The following methodological scheme, which expands on the original three-step scheme introduced in Section 1.4.2, is intended as a strategy to assist you in identifying and analyzing the specific cyberethics issues examined in this book. Note, however, that this procedure is not intended as a precise algorithm for resolving those issues in some definitive manner. Rather, its purpose is to guide you in the identification, analysis, and deliberation processes by summarizing key points that we have examined in Chapter 1.

Step 1. *Identify* a practice involving cybertechnology, or a feature of that technology, that is controversial from a moral perspective.

    1a. Disclose any hidden or opaque features.

    1b. Assess any descriptive components of the ethical issue via the sociological implications it has for relevant social institutions and sociodemographic groups.

    1c. In analyzing the normative elements of that issue, determine whether there are any specific guidelines, i.e., social policies or ethical codes, that can help resolve the issue (for example, see the relevant professional codes of conduct described in Chapter 4 and Appendixes A–E).

    1d. If the normative ethical issue cannot be resolved through the application of existing policies, codes of conduct, etc., go to Step 2.

Step 2. *Analyze* the ethical issue by clarifying concepts and situating it in a context.

    2a. If a policy vacuums exists, go to Step 2b; otherwise, go to Step 3.

    2b. Clear up any conceptual muddles involving the policy vacuum and go to Step 3.

Step 3. *Deliberate* on the ethical issue. The deliberation process requires two stages.

3a. Apply one or more ethical theories (see Chapter 2) to the analysis of the moral issue, and then go to Step 3b.

3b. Justify the position you reached by evaluating it via the standards and criteria for successful logic argumentation (see Chapter 3).

Note that you are now in a position to carry out much of the work required in the first two steps of this methodological scheme. In order to satisfy the requirements in Step 1d, a step that is required in cases involving professional ethics issues, you will need to consult the relevant sections of Chapter 4. Upon completing Chapter 2, you will be able to execute Step 3a; and after completing Chapter 3, you will be able to satisfy the requirements for Step 3b.

▶ 1.7 CHAPTER SUMMARY

In this introductory chapter, we defined several key terms, including *cyberethics* and *cybertechnology*, used throughout this textbook. We also briefly described four evolutionary phases of cyberethics, from its origins as a loosely configured and informal field concerned with ethical and social issues involving stand-alone (mainframe) computers to a more fully developed field that is today concerned with ethical aspects of ubiquitous, networked computers. We then briefly considered whether any cyberethics issues are unique or special in a nontrivial sense. We next examined three different perspectives on cyberethics, showing how computer scientists, philosophers, and social scientists each tend to view the field and approach the issues that comprise it. Within that discussion, we also examined some ways in which embedded values and biases affecting cybertechnology can be disclosed and thus made explicit. Finally, we introduced a comprehensive methodological scheme that incorporates the expertise of computer scientists, philosophers, and social scientists who work in the field of cyberethics.

▶ REVIEW QUESTIONS

1. What, exactly, is *cyberethics*? How is it different from and similar to computer ethics, information ethics, and Internet ethics?
2. What is meant by the term *cybertechnology*? How is it similar to and different from computer technology?
3. Identify and briefly describe some key aspects of each of the "four phases" in the evolution of cyberethics as a field of applied ethics.
4. Why does Walter Maner believe that at least some cyberethics issues are unique? What arguments does he provide to support his view?
5. Why is it important to distinguish between unique technological features and unique ethical issues when evaluating the question, Are cyberethics issues unique?
6. What alternative strategy does James Moor use to analyze the question whether cyberethics issues are unique ethical issues?
7. Why does Moor believe that cybertechnology poses special problems for identifying and analyzing ethical issues?
8. Explain what Moor means by the expression "logical malleability," and why he believes that this technological feature of computers is significant.
9. What does Moor mean by the phrase "policy vacuum," and what role do these vacuums play in understanding cyberethics?

10. Explain what Moor means by a "conceptual muddle"? How can these muddles sometimes complicate matters when trying to resolve policy vacuums?

11. What is applied ethics, and how is it different from theoretical ethics?

12. Summarize the principal aspects of the perspective of cyberethics as a field of *professional* ethics.

13. Describe the principal aspects of the perspective of cyberethics as a field of *philosophical* ethics.

14. Summarize the key elements of the perspective of cyberethics as a field of *sociological/descriptive* ethics.

15. Describe the kinds of criteria used to distinguish normative ethical inquiries from those that are essentially descriptive.

16. What are the three elements of the standard, or "mainstream," method for conducting applied ethics research?

17. How is Philip Brey's "disclosive method" of computer ethics different from what Brey calls "mainstream computer ethics"?

18. What does Brey mean by "morally opaque" or "morally nontransparent" features embedded in computer technology?

19. In which ways is Brey's disclosive method "multilevel"? Briefly describe each level in his methodology.

20. In which ways is that method also "multidisciplinary" or interdisciplinary? Which disciplines does it take into consideration?

▶ DISCUSSION QUESTIONS

21. List and critically analyze some ethical concerns that arise in the Megan Meier cyberbullying incident on MySpace, which resulted in Meier's suicide. Should SNSs allow users to create accounts with fake identities?

22. Describe and critically evaluate some ethical/policy issues that arise in the scenario involving the dispute between Noah Kravitz and PhoneDog Media regarding the ownership of a Twitter account. Was PhoneDog simply protecting what it believed to be its intellectual property interests, or did the company go too far in this case? Explain.

23. Identify and critically analyze some ethical issues that arise in the "Washingtonienne" scenario. Should Jessica Cutler's anonymity have been protected, and should the contents of her online diary have been protected from their subsequent publication in *Wonkette*? Explain.

24. Assess Don Gotterbarn's arguments for the claim that computer ethics is, at bottom, a field whose primary concern should focus on moral-responsibility issues for computer professionals. Do you agree with his position?

▶ ESSAY/PRESENTATION QUESTIONS

25. Think of a controversial issue or practice involving cybertechnology that has not yet been identified as an ethical issue, but which might eventually be recognized as one that has moral implications. Apply Brey's "disclosive method" to see whether you can isolate any embedded values or biases affecting that practice. Next apply the "comprehensive strategy" for approaching cyberethics that we examined in Section 1.6.

26. We identified three main perspectives from which cyberethics issues can be examined. Can you think of any additional perspectives from which cyberethics issues might also be analyzed? In addition to the Washingtonienne, Twitter, and Meier scenarios that we examined, can you think of other recent cases involving cyberethics issues that would benefit from being analyzed from all three perspectives considered in Chapter 1?

Scenarios for Analysis

1. We briefly considered the question whether some cyberethics issues are new or unique ethical issues. In the following scenario,

   (a) identify the ethical issues that arise and
   (b) determine whether any of them are unique to cybertechnology. In which ways are the

ethical issues in this scenario both similar to, and different from those in the Megan Meier incident involving cyberbullying, which we analyzed earlier in this chapter (Scenario 1–1)?

In October 1999, twenty-year-old Amy Boyer was murdered by a young man who had stalked her via the Internet. The stalker, Liam Youens, was able to carry out most of the stalking activities that eventually led to Boyer's death by using a variety of tools and resources generally available to any Internet user. Via standard online search facilities, for example, Youens was able to gather personal information about Boyer. And after paying a small fee to Docusearch.com, an online information company, Youens was able to find out where Boyer lived, where she worked, and so forth. Youens was also able to use another kind of online tool, available to Internet users, to construct two Web sites, both dedicated to his intended victim. On one site, he posted personal information about Boyer as well as a photograph of her; on the other Web site, Youens described, in explicit detail, his plans to murder Boyer.[20]

2. Identify and evaluate the ethical issues that arise in the following scenario. In which ways are the

ethical issues in this scenario similar to, and different from, those in the incident involving Twitter and Phonedog Media (Scenario 1–2), which we analyzed earlier in this chapter?

In January 2003, a United States district court in the District of Columbia ruled that Verizon (an Internet service provider or ISP) must comply with a subpoena by the RIAA— an organization that represents the interests of the recording industry. The RIAA, in an effort to stop the unauthorized sharing of music online, requested from Verizon the names of two of its subscribers who allegedly made available more than 600 copyrighted music files on the Internet. Although many ISPs, such as Comcast, and many universities complied with similar subpoenas issued on behalf of the RIAA, Verizon refused to release the names of any of its subscribers. Verizon argued that doing so would violate the privacy rights of its subscribers and would violate specific articles of the U.S. Constitution. So, Verizon appealed the district court's decision. On December 19, 2003, the United States Court of Appeals for the District of Columbia overturned the lower court's decision, ruling in favor of Verizon.[21]

▶ ENDNOTES

1. See "Parents: Cyber Bullying Led to Teen's Suicide," *ABC News*, Nov. 17, 2007. Available at http://abcnews. go.com/GMA/Story?id=3882520.

2. See J. Biggs, "A Dispute Over Who Owns a Twitter Account Goes to Court." *New York Times*, Dec. 25, 2011. Available at http://www.nytimes.com/2011/12/26/ technology/lawsuit-may-determine-who-owns-a-twitter-account.html?_r=3.

3. See Richard Leiby, "The Hill's Sex Diarist Reveals All (Well Some)," *The Washington Post*, May 23, 2004, p. D03. Available at http://www.washingtonpost.com/ wp-dyn/articles/A48909-2004May22.html.

4. Some have used a combination of these two expressions. For example, Ess (2009) uses "information and computer ethics" (ICE) to refer to ethical issues affecting "digital media." And, Capurro (2007) uses the expression "Intercultural Information Ethics" (IIE).

5. Floridi (2007, p. 63) contrasts Information Ethics (IE) with computer ethics (CE), by noting that the former is the "philosophical foundational counterpart of CE."

6. Anderson and Anderson (2011) also use the term "machine ethics" to refer to this new field, which they

describe as one "concerned with giving machines ethical principles." They contrast the development of ethics for people who use machines with the development of ethics for machines. Others, however, such as Lin, Abney, and Bekey (2012), use the expression "robot ethics" to describe this emerging field.

7. See the interview conducted with Paul Ceruzzi in the BBC/PBS video series, *The Machine That Changed the World* (1990).

8. For example, Bynum (2008) notes that Norbert Weiner, in his writings on cybernetics in the late 1940s, anticipated some of these concerns.

9. My analysis of the four phases in this section is adapted from and expands on Tavani (2001). Note that what I am calling a "technological phase" is not to be confused with something as precise as the expression "computer generation," which is often used to describe specific stages in the evolution of computer hardware systems.

10. Maner (2004, p. 41) argues that computers have generated "entirely new ethical issues, unique to computing, that do not surface in other areas."

11. My analysis of the uniqueness debate here is adapted from Tavani (2002a).
12. Moor (2004), p. 107.
13. My scheme for analyzing computer-ethics issues from these perspectives is adapted from Tavani (2002b).
14. Gotterbarn (1995), p. 21.
15. Moor (2007), p. 31.
16. Brey (2004), pp. 55–56.
17. See, for example, Grodzinsky and Tavani (2010) for an analysis of this case in terms of these issues.
18. For more details on this distinction, see Brey (2004), pp. 56–57.
19. See Brey, pp. 64–65.
20. See A. J. Hitchcock, "Cyberstalking and Law Enforcement: Keeping Up With the Web," *Link-UP,* July/August 2000. Available at http://computeme.tripod.com/cyberstalk.html. Also see Grodzinsky and Tavani (2004).
21. See, for example, Grodzinsky and Tavani (2005).

▶ REFERENCES

Anderson, Michael, and Susan Leigh Anderson, eds. 2011. *Machine Ethics*. New York: Cambridge University Press.

Barger, Robert N. 2008. *Computer Ethics: A Case-Based Approach*. New York: Cambridge University Press.

Brey, Philip. 2004. "Disclosive Computer Ethics." In R. A. Spinello and H. T. Tavani, eds. *Readings in CyberEthics*. 2nd ed. Sudbury, MA: Jones and Bartlett Publishers, pp. 55–66. Reprinted from *Computers and Society* 30, no. 4 (2000): 10–16.

Brey, Philip. 2005. "Freedom and Privacy in Ambient Intelligence." *Ethics and Information Technology* 7, no. 4: 157–66.

Biggs, John. 2011. "A Dispute Over Who Owns a Twitter Account Goes to Court." *New York Times,* Dec. 25. Available at http://www.nytimes.com/2011/12/26/technology/lawsuit-may-determine-who-owns-a-twitter-account.html?_r=3.

Buchanan, Elizabeth A. 2004. "Ethical Considerations for the Information Professions." In R. A. Spinello and H. T. Tavani, eds. *Readings in CyberEthics*. 2nd ed. Sudbury, MA: Jones and Bartlett Publishers, pp. 613–24.

Buchanan, Elizabeth A., and Kathrine A. Henderson. 2009. *Case Studies in Library and Information Science Ethics*. Jefferson, NC: McFarland.

Bynum, Terrell Ward. 2008. "Milestones in the History of Information and Computer Ethics." In K. E. Himma and H. T. Tavani, eds. *The Handbook of Information and Computer Ethics*. Hoboken, NJ: John Wiley and Sons, pp. 25–48.

Capurro, Rafael. 2007. "Intercultural Information Ethics." In R. Capurro, J. Freübrauer, and T. Hausmanninger, eds. *Localizing the Internet*. Munich: Fink Verlag, pp. 21–38.

Ess, Charles. 2009. *Digital Media Ethics*. London, U.K.: Polity Press.

Floridi, Luciano. 2007. "Information Ethics: On the Philosophical Foundations of Computer Ethics." In J. Weckert, ed. *Computer Ethics*. Aldershot, U.K.: Ashgate, pp. 63–82. Reprinted from *Ethics and Information Technology* 1, no. 1 (1999): pp. 37–56.

Gotterbarn, Don. 1995. "Computer Ethics: Responsibility Regained." In D. G. Johnson and H. Nissenbaum, eds. *Computing, Ethics, and Social Values*. Upper Saddle River, NJ: Prentice Hall.

Grodzinsky, Francis S., and Herman T. Tavani. 2004. "Ethical Reflections on Cyberstalking." In R. A. Spinello and H. T. Tavani, eds. *Readings in CyberEthics*. 2nd ed. Sudbury, MA: Jones and Bartlett Publishers, pp. 561–70.

Grodzinsky, Frances S., and Herman T. Tavani. 2005. "P2P Networks and the *Verizon v. RIAA Case*." *Ethics and Information Technology* 7, no. 4: 243–50.

Grodzinsky, Frances S., and Herman T. Tavani. 2010. "Applying the 'Contextual Integrity' Model of Privacy to Personal Blogs in the Blogosphere." *International Journal of Internet Research Ethics* 3, no. 1: 38–47.

Huff, Chuck, and Thomas Finholt, eds. 1994. *Social Issues in Computing: Putting Computing in its Place*. New York: McGraw-Hill.

Johnson, Deborah G. 2000. "The Future of Computer Ethics." In G. Collste, ed. *Ethics in the Age of Information Technology*. Linköping, Sweden: Centre for Applied Ethics, pp. 17–31.

Johnson, Deborah G. 2010. *Computer Ethics*. 4th ed. Upper Saddle River, NJ: Prentice Hall.

Langford, Duncan. ed. 2000. *Internet Ethics*. New York: St. Martin's Press.

Lin, Patrick, Keith Abney, and George A. Bekey, eds. 2012. *Robot Ethics: The Ethical and Social Implications of Robotics*. Cambridge, MA: MIT Press.

Maner, Walter. 2004. "Unique Ethical Problems in Information Technology." In T. W. Bynum and S. Rogerson, eds. *Computer Ethics and Professional Responsibility*. Malden, MA: Blackwell, pp. 39–59. Reprinted from *Science and Engineering Ethics* 2, no. 2 (1996): 137–54.

Moor, James H. 2001. "The Future of Computer Ethics: You Ain't Seen Nothing Yet." *Ethics and Information Technology* 3, no. 2: 89–91.

Moor, James H. 2004. "Just Consequentialism and Computing." In R. A. Spinello and H. T. Tavani, eds. *Readings in CyberEthics*. 2nd ed. Sudbury, MA: Jones and Bartlett Publishers, pp. 407–17. Reprinted from *Ethics and Information Technology* 1, no. 1 (1999): 65–69.

Moor, James H. 2005. "Should We Let Computers Get Under Our Skin?" In R. Cavalier ed. *The Impact of the Internet on Our Moral Lives*. Albany, NY: State University of New York Press, pp. 121–38.

Moor, James H. 2007. "What Is Computer Ethics?" In J. Weckert, ed. *Computer Ethics*. Aldershot, UK: Ashgate, pp. 31–40. Reprinted from *Metaphilosophy* 16, no. 4 (1985): 266–75.

Tavani, Herman T. 2001. "The State of Computer Ethics as a Philosophical Field of Inquiry." *Ethics and Information Technology* 3, no. 2: 97–108.

Tavani, Herman T. 2002a. "The Uniqueness Debate in Computer Ethics: What Exactly Is at Issue, and Why Does it Matter?" *Ethics and Information Technology* 4, no 1: 37–54.

Tavani, Herman T. 2002b. "Applying an Interdisciplinary Approach to Teaching Computer Ethics." *IEEE Technology and Society Magazine* 21, no. 3: 32–38.

van den Hoven, Jeroen. 2000. "Computer Ethics and Moral Methodology." In R. Baird, R. Ramsower, and S. Rosenbaum, eds. *Cyberethics: Social and Moral Issues in the Computer Age*. Amherst, NY: Prometheus Books, pp. 80–94. Reprinted from *Metaphilosophy* 28, no. 3 (1997): 234–48.

Wallach, Wendell, and Colin Allen. 2009. *Moral Machines: Teaching Robots Right from Wrong*. New York: Oxford University Press.

▶ FURTHER READINGS

Abelson, Hal, Ken Ledeen, and Harry Lewis. *Blown to Bits: Your Life, Liberty and Happiness after the Digital Explosion*. Upper Saddle River, NJ: Addison-Wesley, 2008.

Capurro, Rafael, and Michael Nagenborg, eds. *Ethics and Robotics*. Heidelberg, Germany: IOS Press, 2009.

De Palma, Paul, ed. *Computers in Society 11/12*. 14th ed. New York: McGraw-Hill, 2011.

Floridi, Luciano. ed. *The Cambridge Handbook of Information and Computer Ethics*. Cambridge, MA: MIT Press, 2010.

Mitcham, Carl. ed. *Encyclopedia of Science, Technology, and Ethics*. 4 Vols. New York: Macmillan, 2005.

Moor, James H. "Why We Need Better Ethics for Emerging Technologies." In J.van den Hoven and J. Weckert, eds. *Information Technology and Moral Philosophy*. New York: Cambridge University Press, 2008, pp. 26–39.

van den Hoven, Jeroen. "Moral Methodology and Information Technology." In K. E. Himma and H. T. Tavani, eds. *The Handbook of Information and Computer Ethics*. Hoboken, NJ: John Wiley and Sons, 2008, pp. 49–67.

▶ ONLINE RESOURCES

Association for Computing—Special Interest Group on Computers and Society. http://www.sigcas.org/.

Bibliography on Computing, Ethics, and Social Responsibility. http://cyberethics.cbi.msstate.edu/biblio/index.htm.

Computer Professionals for Social Responsibility (CPSR). http://cpsr.org/.

Heuristic Methods for Computer Ethics. http://csweb.cs.bgsu.edu/maner/heuristics/maner.pdf.

International Center for Information Ethics (ICIE). http://icie.zkm.de/.

International Society for Ethics and Information Technology. http://www4.uwm.edu/cipr/collaborations/inseit/.

Research Center for Computing and Society. http://www.southernct.edu/organizations/rccs/.

Stanford Encyclopedia of Philosophy. http://plato.stanford.edu/.

CHAPTER

▼

2

Ethical Concepts and Ethical Theories: Establishing and Justifying a Moral System

In Chapter 1, we defined cyberethics as the study of moral issues involving cybertechnology. However, we have not yet defined what is meant by *ethics*, *morality*, and *the study of moral issues*. In Chapter 2, we define these terms as well as other foundational concepts, and we examine a set of ethical theories that will guide us in our deliberation on the specific cyberethics issues we confront in Chapters 4–12. To accomplish the objectives of Chapter 2, we provide answers to the following questions:

- What is ethics, and how is it different from morality or a moral system?
- What are the elements that make up a moral system?
- Where do the rules in a moral system come from, and how are they justified?
- How is a philosophical study of morality different from studying morality from the perspectives of religion and law?
- Is morality essentially a personal, or private, matter, or is it a public phenomenon?
- Is morality simply relative to particular cultures and thus culturally determined?
- How is meaningful dialogue about cyberethics issues that are global in scope possible in a world with diverse cultures and belief systems?
- What roles do classic and contemporary ethical theories play in the analysis of moral issues involving cybertechnology?
- Are traditional ethical theories adequate to handle the wide range of moral controversies affecting cybertechnology?

▶ 2.1 ETHICS AND MORALITY

Ethics is derived from the Greek *ethos*, and the term *morality* has its roots in the Latin *mores*. Both the Greek and the Latin terms refer to notions of custom, habit, behavior, and character. Although "ethics" and "morality" are often used interchangeably in everyday discourse, we draw some important distinctions between the two terms as we will use them in this textbook. First, we define ethics as the study of morality.[1] This definition, of course, raises two further questions:

a. What is *morality*?

b. What is *the study of morality*?

We had begun to answer question (b) in Chapter 1, where we described three approaches to cyberethics issues. You may want to review Section 1.4, which describes how moral issues can be studied from the perspectives of professional ethics, philosophical ethics, and sociological/descriptive ethics. We will say more about the study of morality from a philosophical perspective in Section 2.1.2. Before we examine the concepts and theories that comprise morality or a moral system, however, we briefly consider a classic example of a moral dilemma.

First, we should note that the phrase "moral dilemma" is often misused to describe a "moral issue." We will see that not every moral issue is a moral dilemma, and not every dilemma is necessarily moral in nature. A dilemma describes a situation where one is confronted with two choices, neither of which is desirable. Sometimes it may mean choosing between (what one may perceive to be) the lesser of two evils. But our primary interest in this chapter is not so much with the specific choices one makes; instead it is with (i) the principle that one uses in making his or her choice, and (ii) whether that principle can be applied systematically and consistently in making moral decisions in similar kinds of cases. We next consider a dilemma that has become a classic in the ethics literature.

▶ **SCENARIO 2–1:** The Runaway Trolley: A Classic Moral Dilemma

Imagine that you are driving a trolley and that all of a sudden you realize that the trolley's brake system has failed. Further imagine that approximately 80 meters ahead of you on the trolley track (a short distance from the trolley's station) five crew men are working on a section of the track on which your trolley is traveling. You realize that you cannot stop the trolley and that you will probably not be able to prevent the deaths of the five workers. But then you suddenly realize that you could "throw a switch" that would cause the trolley to go on to a different track. You also happen to notice that one person is working on that track. You then realize that if you do nothing, five people will likely die, whereas if you engage the switch to change tracks, only one person would likely die.[2] ■

What would you do in this situation—let the trolley take its "natural" course, expecting that five people will likely die, or intentionally change the direction of the trolley, likely causing the death of one person who otherwise would have lived? If you use what some call a "cost-benefits" approach in this particular situation, you might reason in the following way: throwing the switch will have a better outcome, overall, because more human lives would be saved than lost. So, in this case you conclude that throwing the switch is the right thing to do because the net result is that four more people will live. If the reasoning process that you used in this particular case is extended to a general principle, you have embraced a type of consequentialist or utilitarian ethical theory (described later in this chapter). But can this principle/theory be consistently extended to cover similar cases?

Next consider a variation of this dilemma, which also involves a runaway trolley, but this time you are a spectator. Imagine that you are standing on a bridge overlooking the track on which a runaway trolley is traveling. You observe that the trolley is heading for the station where there are many people gathered outside. Standing next to you on the bridge is a very large and obese person (weighing approximately 500 pounds), who is leaning forward over the rail of the bridge to view the runaway trolley. You realize that if you gently pushed the obese person forward as the trolley approaches, he would fall off the bridge and land in front of the trolley; the impact would be sufficient to stop the trolley. Thus you could save the lives of many people who otherwise would die.

Would you be willing to push the obese person off the bridge? If not, why not? What has changed in the two scenarios? After all, if you are reasoning from the standpoint of a utilitarian/consequentialist theory, the same outcome would be realized—one person dies, while many others live. But studies have shown that most people find it far more difficult to push (intentionally) one person to his death, even though doing so would mean that several persons will live as a result. However, in this case, you might reason that intentionally causing someone's death (especially by having a "direct hand" in it) is morally wrong. You may also reason that actively and deliberately causing one person's death (as opposed to another's) is unjust and unfair, and that it would be a dangerous moral principle to generalize. In this case, your reasoning would be nonutilitarian or nonconsequentialist.

Perhaps you see the inconsistency in the means used to make decisions in the two similar scenarios. However, you might react initially by saying that it is permissible to flip-flop on moral principles, depending on the particular circumstances you face. But we will see that it is difficult to have a coherent moral system where the ethical theories used to frame policies are inherently inconsistent. Fortunately, there is no need for us to resolve these questions at this point in the chapter. Rather, the purpose of posing this dilemma now is to get us to begin thinking about how we can respond to dilemmas that we will invariably face in our professional as well as personal lives. Later in this chapter, we revisit this dilemma and we complicate it somewhat by replacing the trolley's human driver with an autonomous computer system. We then examine in detail some specific ethical theories that can be applied in our analyses of this and other moral dilemmas. First, however, we examine some basic concepts that comprise morality and a moral system.

2.1.1 What Is Morality?

As noted above, we defined ethics as the study of morality. However, there is no universally agreed upon definition of "morality" among ethicists and philosophers. For our purposes, however, *morality* can be defined as a system of rules for guiding human conduct, and principles for evaluating those rules. Note that (i) morality is a *system*, and (ii) it is a system comprised of moral *rules* and *principles*. Moral rules can be understood as rules of conduct, which are very similar to the notion of policies, described in Chapter 1. There, "policies" were defined as rules of conduct that have a wide range of application. According to James Moor (2004), policies range from formal laws to informal, implicit guidelines for actions.

There are two kinds of rules of conduct:

1. *Directives* that guide our conduct as individuals (at the microlevel)
2. *Social policies* framed at the macrolevel

Directives are rules that guide our individual actions and direct us in our moral choices at the "microethical" level (i.e., the level of individual behavior). "Do not steal" and "Do not harm others" are examples of directives. Other kinds of rules guide our conduct at the "macrolevel" (i.e., at the level of social policies and social norms).

Rules of conduct that operate at the macroethical level guide us in both framing and adhering to social policies. For example, rules such as "Proprietary software should not be duplicated without proper authorization," or "Software that can be used to invade the privacy of users should not be developed," are instances of social policies. Notice the correlation between the directive "Do not steal" (a rule of conduct at the microlevel), and the social policy "Unauthorized duplication of software should not be allowed" (a rule of conduct at the macrolevel). In Section 2.1.2 we will see that both types of rules of conduct are derived from a set of "core values" in a moral system.

The rules of conduct in a moral system are evaluated against standards called *principles*. For example, the principle of social utility, which is concerned with promoting the greatest good for the greatest number, can be used as a "litmus test" for determining whether the policy "Proprietary software should not be copied without permission" can be justified on moral grounds. In this case, the policy in question could be justified by showing that not allowing the unauthorized copying of software will produce more overall social good than will a policy that permits software to be duplicated freely.

Similarly, the policy "Users should not have their privacy violated" might be justified by appealing to the same principle of social utility. Or a different principle such as "respect for persons," or possibly a principle based on the notion of fairness, might be used to justify the social policy in question. Figure 2.1 illustrates the different kinds of rules and principles that comprise a moral system.

What Kind of a System Is a Moral System?

According to Bernard Gert (2005, 2007), morality is a "system whose purpose is to prevent harm and evils." In addition to preventing harm, a moral system aims at promoting human flourishing. Although there is some disagreement regarding the extent to which the promotion of human flourishing is required of a moral system, virtually all ethicists believe that, at a minimum, the fundamental purpose of a moral system is to prevent or alleviate harm and suffering. We have already seen that at the heart of a moral system are rules of conduct and principles of evaluation. We next consider some other characteristics that define a moral system.

Gert describes a moral system as one that is both public and informal. The system is *public*, he argues, because everyone must know what the rules are that define it. Gert uses the analogy of a game, which has a goal and a corresponding set of rules. The rules are understood by all of the players, and the players use the rules to guide their behavior in legitimately achieving the goal of the game. The players can also use the rules to evaluate or judge the behavior of other players in the game. However, there is one important difference between a moral system and a game: Not everyone is required to participate in a game, but we are all obligated to participate in a moral system.

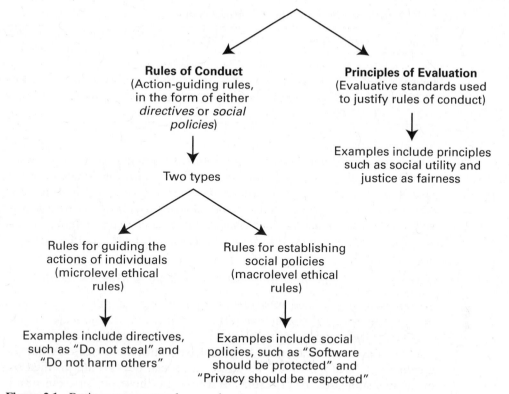

Figure 2.1 Basic components of a moral system.

Morality is also *informal* because, Gert notes, a moral system has no formal authoritative judges presiding over it. Unlike games in professional sports that have rules enforced by referees in a manner that approaches a legal system, morality is less formal. A moral system is more like a game of cards or a "pickup game" in baseball or basketball. Here the players are aware of the rules, but even in the absence of a formal official or referee to enforce the game's rules, players generally adhere to them.

Gert's model of a moral system includes two additional features: *rationality* and *impartiality*. A moral system is rational in that it is based on principles of logical reason accessible to ordinary persons. Morality cannot involve special knowledge that can be understood only by privileged individuals or groups. The rules in a moral system must be available to all rational persons who, in turn, are (what ethicists call) *moral agents*, bound by the system of moral rules. We do not hold nonmoral agents (such as young children, mentally challenged persons, and pets) morally responsible for their own actions, but moral agents often have responsibilities to nonmoral agents. (We examine the concepts of "agency" and "moral agency" in detail in Chapter 12.)

A moral system is *impartial* in the sense that the moral rules are ideally designed to apply equitably to all participants in the system. In an ideal moral system, all rational persons are willing to accept the rules of the system, even if they do not know in advance what their particular place in that system will be. To ensure that impartiality will be built into a moral system, and that its members will be treated as fairly as possible,

TABLE 2.1   Four Features of Gert's Moral System

Public	Informal	Rational	Impartial
The rules are known to all of the members.	The rules are informal, not like formal laws in a legal system.	The system is based on principles of logical reason accessible to all its members.	The system is not partial to any one group or individual.

Gert invokes his "blindfold of justice" principle. Imagine that you are blindfolded while deciding what the rules of a moral system will be. Since you do not know in advance what position you will occupy in that system, it is in your own best interest to design a system in which everyone will be treated fairly. As an impartial observer who is also rational, you will want to ensure against the prospect of ending up in a group that is treated unfairly.[3]

Table 2.1 summarizes four key features in Gert's model of a moral system.

2.1.2   Deriving and Justifying the Rules and Principles of a Moral System

So far, we have defined morality as a system that is public, informal, rational, and impartial. We have also seen that at the heart of a moral system are rules for guiding the conduct of the members of the system. But where, exactly, do these rules come from? And what criteria can be used to ground or justify these rules? Arguably, the rules of conduct involving individual directives and social policies are justified by the system's evaluative standards, or principles. But how are those principles in turn justified?

On the one hand, rules of conduct for guiding action in the moral system, whether individual directives or social policies, are ultimately derived from certain core *values*. Principles for evaluating rules of conduct, on the other hand, are typically grounded in one of three systems or sources: religion, law, or (philosophical) ethics.

We next describe the core values in a society from which the rules of conduct are derived.

Core Values and Their Role in a Moral System
The term *value* comes from the Latin *valere*, which means having worth or being of worth. Values are objects of our desires or interests; examples include happiness, love, and freedom. Some philosophers suggest that the moral rules and principles comprising a society's moral system are ultimately derived from that society's framework of values.[4]

Philosophers often distinguish between two types of values, *intrinsic* and *instrumental*. Any value that serves some further end or good is called an instrumental value because it is tied to some external standard. Automobiles, computers, and money are examples of goods that have instrumental value. Values such as life and happiness, on the other hand, are *intrinsic* because they are valued for their own sake. Later in this chapter, we will see that utilitarians argue that happiness is an intrinsic value. And in Chapter 5, we will see that some ethicists believe personal privacy is a value that has both intrinsic and instrumental attributes.

Another approach to cataloguing values is to distinguish *core values*, some of which may or may not also be intrinsic values, from other kinds of values. James Moor (2004), for example, believes that life, happiness, and autonomy are core values because they are

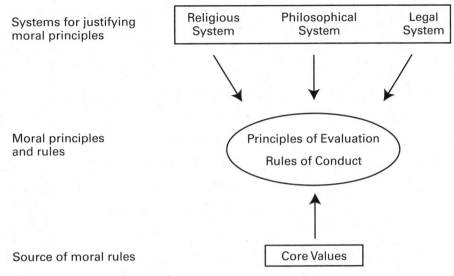

Systems for justifying moral principles

Moral principles and rules

Source of moral rules

Figure 2.2 Components of a moral system.

basic to a society's thriving and perhaps even to its survival. Autonomy, Moor argues, is essentially a cluster of values that includes ability, security, knowledge, freedom, opportunity, and resources. Although core values might be basic to a society's flourishing, and possibly to that society's survival, it does not follow that each core value is also a moral value.

Sometimes descriptions of morals and values suggest that morals are identical to values. Values, however, can be either moral or nonmoral, and moral values need to be distinguished from the broader set of nonmoral values. Consider again the roles that rationality and impartiality play in a moral system. Rationality informs us that it is in our interest to promote values consistent with our own survival, happiness, and flourishing as individuals. When used to further only our own self-interests, these values are not necessarily moral values. Once we bring in the notion of impartiality, however, we begin to take the moral point of view. When we frame the rules of conduct in a moral system, we articulate one or more core moral values, such as autonomy, fairness, and justice. For example, the rule of conduct "Treat people fairly" is derived from the moral value of impartiality. Figure 2.2 illustrates how the rules and principles that comprise a moral system are both derived from core values and justified on grounds that that tend to be either religious, legal, or philosophical in nature.

Three Approaches for Grounding the Principles in a Moral System
We have seen how the rules of conduct in a moral system can be derived from a society's core values. Now we will consider how the principles that are used to justify the rules of conduct are grounded. As we suggested in Section 2.1.2, the principles are grounded in one of three sources: religion, law, and philosophical ethics. We now consider how a particular moral principle can be justified from the vantage point of each scheme. As an illustration, we can use the rule of conduct "Do not steal," since it underpins many cyberethics controversies involving software piracy and intellectual property. Virtually every moral system includes at least one rule that explicitly condemns stealing. But why,

exactly, is stealing morally wrong? This particular rule of conduct is evaluated against one or more principles such as "We should respect persons" or "We should not cause harm to others"; but how are these principles, in turn, justified? The answer depends on whether we take the religious, the legal, or the philosophical/ethical point of view.

Approach #1: Grounding Moral Principles in a Religious System Consider the following rationale for why stealing is morally wrong:

> Stealing is wrong because it offends God or because it violates one of God's Ten Commandments.

Here the "moral wrongness" in the act of stealing is grounded in religion; stealing, in the Judeo-Christian tradition, is explicitly forbidden by one of the Ten Commandments. From the point of view of these particular institutionalized religions, then, stealing is wrong because it offends God or because it violates the commands of a divine authority. Furthermore, Christians generally believe that those who steal will be punished in the next life even if they are not caught and punished for their sins in the present life.

One difficulty in applying this rationale in the United States is that American society is pluralistic. While the United States was once a relatively homogeneous culture with roots in the Judeo-Christian tradition, American culture has in recent years become increasingly heterogeneous. So people with different religious beliefs, or with no religious beliefs at all, can disagree with those whose moral beliefs are grounded solely on religious convictions that are Judeo-Christian based. Because of these differences, many argue that we need to ground the rules and principles of a moral system on criteria other than those provided by any particular organized religion. Some suggest that civil law can provide the foundation needed for a moral system to work.

Approach #2: Grounding Moral Principles in a Legal System An alternative rationale to the one proposed in the preceding section is as follows:

> Stealing is wrong because it violates the law.

One advantage of using law instead of religion as the ground for determining why stealing is wrong is that it eliminates certain kinds of disputes between religious and nonreligious persons and groups. If stealing violates the law of a particular jurisdiction, then the act of stealing can be declared wrong independent of any religious beliefs or disbeliefs — Christian, Muslim, or even agnostic or atheist. And since legal enforcement of rules can be carried out independent of religious beliefs, there is a pragmatic advantage to grounding moral principles (and their corresponding rules) in law rather than in religion: those breaking a civil law can be punished, for example, by either a fine or imprisonment, or both.

But laws are not uniform across political boundaries: Laws vary from nation to nation and state to state within a given nation. In the United States, the unauthorized copying and distribution of proprietary software is explicitly illegal. However, in certain Asian countries, the practice of copying proprietary software is not considered criminal (or even if it is technically viewed as a crime, actual cases of piracy may not be criminally prosecuted). So there can be a diversity of legal systems just as there is a diversity of religious systems.

Perhaps a more serious flaw in using a legal approach is that history has shown that certain laws, although widely accepted, institutionalized, and practiced within a society, have nonetheless been morally wrong. For example, slavery was legally valid in the United States until 1865. And in South Africa, apartheid was legally valid until 1991. So if we attempt to ground moral principles in law, we are still faced with serious challenges. Also, we can ask whether it is possible, or even desirable, to institutionalize morality such that we require specific laws for every possible moral issue?

Approach #3: Grounding Moral Principles in a Philosophical System of Ethics   A third way to approach the problem of how to ground moral systems is to say:

> Stealing is wrong because it is wrong.

Notice what this statement implies. The moral rightness or wrongness of stealing is not grounded in any external authority, theological or legal. So regardless of whether God condemns stealing or whether stealing violates existing civil laws, stealing is held to be wrong in itself. On what grounds can such a claim be made? Many philosophers and ethicists argue that reason alone is sufficient to show that stealing is wrong—reason informs us that there is something either in the very act of stealing or in the consequences of the act that makes stealing morally wrong.

In the case of both religion and law, sanctions in the form of punishments can be applied to deter individuals from stealing. In the first case, punishment for immoral behavior is relegated to the afterlife. And in the second case, punishment can be meted out here and now. In the case of philosophical ethics, sanctions take the form of social disapprobation (disapproval) and, possibly, social ostracism, but there is no punishment in a formal sense.

According to the system of philosophical ethics, stealing is morally wrong by criteria that reason alone is sufficient to determine. Of course, we need to specify what these criteria are; we will do this in Sections 2.4–2.7, where we discuss four kinds of ethical theories.

The Method of Philosophical Ethics: Logical Argumentation and Ethical Theory

In Chapter 1, we briefly described the philosophical method and saw how it could be used to analyze cyberethics issues. We also saw that the method philosophers use to analyze moral issues is normative, in contrast to the descriptive method that is used by many social scientists. We saw that sociological and anthropological studies are descriptive because they describe or report how people in various cultures and groups behave with respect to the rules of a moral system. For example, a sociologist might report that people who live in nations along the Pacific Rim believe that it is morally permissible to make copies of proprietary software for personal use. However, it is one thing simply to report or describe what the members of a particular culture believe about a practice such as duplicating proprietary software, and it is something altogether different to say that people ought to be permitted to make copies of that proprietary material. When we inquire into moral issues from the latter perspective, we engage in a normative investigation.

We have seen that normative analyses of morality can involve religion and law as well as philosophy. We have also seen, however, that what separates philosophy from the other two perspectives of normative analysis is the methodology used to study the moral issues. To approach these issues from the perspective of philosophical ethics is, in effect, to engage in a philosophical study of morality.

If you are taking a course in ethics for the first time, you might wonder what is meant by the phrase "philosophical study." We have already described what is meant by a descriptive study, which is essentially a type of scientific study. Philosophical studies and scientific studies are similar in that they both require that a consistent methodological scheme be used to verify hypotheses and theories; and these verification schemes must satisfy the criteria of rationality and impartiality. But philosophical studies differ from scientific studies in one important respect: Whereas scientists typically conduct experiments in a laboratory to confirm or refute one or more hypotheses, philosophers do not have a physical laboratory to test ethical theories and claims. Instead, philosophers confirm or reject the plausibility of the evidence for a certain claim or thesis via the rules of logical argumentation (which we will examine in Chapter 3); these rules are both rational and impartial. Another important feature that distinguishes a philosophical study of morality from other kinds of normative investigation into morality is the use of ethical theory in the analysis and deliberation of the issues.

Ethicists vs. Moralists

We note that ethicists who study morality from the perspective of philosophical methodology, and who thus appeal to logical arguments to justify claims and positions involving morality, are very different from moralists. Moralists often claim to have all of the answers regarding moral questions and issues. Many moralists have been described as "preachy" and "judgmental." And some moralists may have a particular moral agenda to advance. Ethicists, on the other hand, use the philosophical method in analyzing and attempting to resolve moral issues; they must remain open to different sides of a dispute, and their primary focus is on the study of morality and the application of moral theories. As such, they approach moral issues and controversies by way of standards that are both rational (based on logic) and impartial (open to others to verify). We also examine some of these important distinctions in our analysis of key differences between moral absolutism and moral objectivism, later in this chapter.

▶ 2.2 DISCUSSION STOPPERS AS ROADBLOCKS TO MORAL DISCOURSE

We have suggested that impartial and objective standards, such as those provided by ethical theory and the rules of logical argumentation, can be used in our analysis of moral issues. However, many people might be surprised that tests and standards of any kind can be applied to disputes about morality and moral issues. So before beginning our examination of the ethical theory, perhaps we should first acknowledge and try to address some concerns that many people frequently encounter when either they willingly engage in, or find themselves involuntarily drawn into, discussions involving moral issues. We will see why these concerns are often based on some conceptual confusions about the nature of morality itself.

Have you ever been engaged in a serious conversation about a moral issue when, all of a sudden, one party in the discussion interjects with a remark to the effect, "But who's to say what is right or wrong anyway?" Or perhaps someone might interject, "Who are we to impose our values and ideas on others?" Such clichès are just two examples of the kinds of simplistic or nonreflective questions that we are likely to hear in discussions involving moral issues. I call remarks of this type "discussion stoppers" because often they close down prematurely what otherwise might be a useful discussion. These stoppers can take many different forms, and some are more common than others, but we can analyze them in terms of four distinct questions:

1. People disagree about morality, so how can we reach an agreement on moral issues?
2. Who am I/who are we to judge others and to impose my/our values on them?
3. Isn't morality simply a private matter?
4. Isn't morality simply a matter that different cultures and groups should determine for themselves?

2.2.1 Discussion Stopper #1: People Disagree on Solutions to Moral Issues

Because different people often have different beliefs as to the correct answer to many moral questions, some infer that there is no hope of reaching any kind of agreement on answers to *any* moral question. And from this inference, some conclude that any meaningful discourse about morality is impossible. Three crucial points that people who draw these and similar inferences about morality fail to recognize, however, are as follows:

I. Experts in other fields of study, such as science and mathematics, also disagree as to the correct answers to certain questions.
II. There is common agreement as to answers to some moral questions.
III. People do not always distinguish between disagreements about general principles and disagreements about factual matters in disputes involving morality.

We briefly examine each of these points.

Experts in Many Fields Disagree on Fundamental Issues

First, we should note that morality is not the only area in which intelligent people have disagreements. Scientists and mathematicians disagree among themselves about core issues in their disciplines, yet we do not dismiss the possibility of meaningful discourse in science and mathematics merely because there is some disagreement among experts in those fields. Consider also that computer scientists disagree among themselves whether open source code is better than proprietary code, whether Linux is a better operating system than Windows 7, or whether C++ is a better programming language than Java.

One example of how natural scientists can disagree among themselves is apparent in the classic and contemporary debate in physics regarding the nature of light. Some physicists argue that light is ultimately composed of particles, whereas others claim that light is essentially composed of waves. Because physicists can disagree with each other, should we conclude that physics itself must be a totally arbitrary enterprise? Or, alternatively, is it not possible that certain kinds of disagreements among scientists might indeed be healthy for science? The debate about the nature of light has actually contributed to moving the field of physics forward in ways that it otherwise might not progress. In this sense, then, a certain level of disagreement and dispute among scientists is a positive and constructive function in the overall enterprise of scientific discovery. Similarly, why not assume that certain kinds of disagreements in ethics—that is, those that are based on points aimed at achieving constructive resolutions—actually contribute to progress in the field of ethics?

Also note that disagreement exists among contemporary mathematicians as to whether or not numbers are constructed (as opposed to having an independent existence). Because mathematicians disagree about the truth of certain claims pertaining to foundational issues in mathematics, does it follow that the field of mathematics itself is arbitrary? Does it also follow that we should give up any hope of eventually reaching an agreement about basic truths in mathematics? And should we dismiss as arbitrary the theories of mathematics as well as the theories of physics, simply because there is some level of disagreement among scholars in both academic fields? Would it be reasonable to do so? If not, then why should one dismiss ethics merely because there is some disagreement among ethicists and among ordinary persons as to the correct answers to some moral issues?

Note that certain conditions (parameters, rules, etc.) must be satisfied in order for a particular claim or a particular theory to qualify as acceptable in debates among scientists and among mathematicians. We will see that certain rules and parameters must also be satisfied in order for a particular claim or theory to qualify as acceptable in debates among ethicists. Just as there are claims and theories in physics and in mathematics that are not considered plausible by the scientific and mathematical communities, similarly, not every claim or theory involving morality is considered reasonable by ethicists. Like mathematicians and scientists, ethicists continue to disagree with one another; for example, they will likely continue to debate about which ethical theories should be applied in the case of cloning and genomic research. But like scientists and mathematicians, ethicists will continue to work within the constraints of certain acceptable rules and parameters in advancing their various theories.

Common Agreement on Some Moral Issues

We can now turn to our second point: People have demonstrated considerable agreement on answers to some moral questions, at least with respect to moral principles. We might be inclined to overlook the significant level of agreement regarding ethical principles, however, because, as Gert (2005, 2007) notes, we tend to associate moral issues with highly controversial concerns such as the death penalty, euthanasia, abortion, and cloning, all involving life and death decisions. We tend to forget that there are also many basic moral principles on which we do agree; for instance, nearly everyone believes that people should tell the truth, keep promises, respect their parents, and refrain from activities involving stealing and cheating. And most people agree that "Murder is wrong." It would be prudent for us to pay closer attention to our beliefs regarding these core moral principles in order to find out why there is such agreement.

So if we agree on many basic moral principles, such as our commonly held beliefs that murder is wrong and stealing is wrong, then why do many people also believe that disputes about moral issues are impossible to resolve? Beliefs and assumptions regarding morality may be based on certain conceptual confusions, and one source of confusion may be our failure to distinguish between the alleged factual matters and the general principles that constitute moral issues. This brings us to our third point.

judgment that such practices, as well as the system that permits those practices, are immoral?

So it would seem that some serious confusions exist with respect to two distinct situations: (1) someone making a judgment about X, and (2) someone being a judgmental person. With that distinction in mind, we can avoid being judgmental and yet still make moral judgments when appropriate, and especially when we are obligated to do so.

2.2.3 Discussion Stopper #3: Morality Is Simply a Private Matter

Many people assume that morality is essentially personal in nature and must, therefore, be simply a private matter. Initially, such a view might seem reasonable, but it is actually both confused and problematic. In fact, "private morality" is essentially an oxymoron, or contradictory notion. For one thing, morality is a *public* phenomenon—recall our discussion of Gert's account of morality as a "public system" in Section 2.1.1, where we saw that a moral system includes a set of public rules that apply to all of the members of that system. Thus morality cannot be reduced to something that is simply private or personal.

We have already seen that morality is a system of normative rules and standards whose content is studied by ethicists in the same way that mathematicians study the content of the field of mathematics. Would it make sense to speak of personal mathematics, personal chemistry, or personal biology? Such notions sound absurd because each discipline has a content area and a set of standards and criteria, all of which are open and available to all to examine. Since public rules make up the content of a moral system, which itself can be studied, we can reasonably ask how it would make sense to speak of private morality.

If morality were simply a private matter, then it would follow that a study of morality could be reduced to a series of descriptive reports about the personal preferences or personal tastes of individuals and groups. But is such an account of morality adequate? Are the moral choices that we make nothing more than mere personal choices? If you happen to prefer chocolate ice cream and I prefer vanilla, or if you prefer to own a laptop computer and I prefer to own a desktop computer, we will probably not choose to debate these preferences. You may have strong personal beliefs as to why chocolate ice cream is better than vanilla and why laptop computers are superior to desktop computers; however, you will most likely respect my preferences for vanilla ice cream and desktop computers, and, in turn, I will respect your preferences.

Do moral choices fit this same kind of model? Suppose you happen to believe that stealing is morally wrong, but I believe that stealing is okay (i.e., morally permissible). One day, I decide to steal your laptop computer. Do you have a right to complain? You would not, if morality is simply a private matter that reflects an individual's personal choices. Your personal preference may be not to steal, whereas my personal preference is for stealing. If morality is grounded simply in terms of the preferences that individuals happen to have, then it would follow that stealing *is* morally permissible for me but *is not* for you. But why stop with stealing? What if I happen to believe that killing human beings is okay? So, you can probably see the dangerous implications for a system in which moral rules and standards are reducible to personal preferences and personal beliefs.

The view that morality is private and personal can quickly lead to a position that some ethicists describe as *moral subjectivism*. According to this position, what is morally right or wrong can be determined by individuals themselves, so that morality would seem to be in the "eye of the beholder." Moral subjectivism makes pointless any attempt to engage in meaningful ethical dialogue.

2.2.4 Discussion Stopper #4: Morality Is Simply a Matter for Individual Cultures to Decide

Some might assume that morality can best be understood not so much as a private or a personal matter but as something for individual cultures or specific groups to determine. According to this view, a moral system is dependent on, or relative to, a particular culture or group. Again, this view might initially seem quite reasonable; it is a position that many social scientists have found attractive. To understand some of the serious problems inherent in this position, it is useful to distinguish between *cultural relativism* and *moral relativism*.

Cultural Relativism

Cultures play a crucial role in the transmission of the values and principles that constitute a moral system. It is through culture that initial beliefs involving morality are transmitted to an individual. In this sense cultures provide their members with what ethicists often refer to as "customary morality," or conventional morality, where one's moral beliefs are typically nonreflective (or perhaps prereflective). For example, if asked whether you believe that acts such as pirating software or invading someone's privacy are wrong, you might simply reply that both kinds of behavior are wrong because your society taught you that they are wrong. However, is it sufficient for one to believe that these actions are morally wrong merely *because* his or her culture says they are wrong? Imagine, for example, a culture in which the principle "Murder is wrong" is not transmitted to its members. Does it follow that murdering people would be morally permissible for the members of that culture?

The belief that morality is simply a matter for individual cultures to decide is widespread in our contemporary popular culture. This view is often referred to as *cultural relativism*, and at its base is the following assumption:

A. Different cultures have different beliefs about what constitutes morally right and wrong behavior.

Note that this assumption is essentially descriptive in nature, because it makes no normative judgment about either the belief systems of cultures or the behavior of people in those cultures. Although it is generally accepted that different cultures have different conceptions about what is morally right and morally wrong behavior, this position has been challenged by some social scientists who argue that some of the reported differences between cultures have been greatly exaggerated. Other social scientists suggest that all cultures may possess some universal core moral values.[5]

However, let us assume that claim (A) is true and ask whether it logically implies (B).

B. We should not morally evaluate the behavior of people in cultures other than our own (because different cultures have different belief systems about what constitutes morally right and wrong behavior).

Note that (B) is a different kind of claim than (A). Also note that to move from (A) to (B) is to move from cultural relativism to *moral relativism*.

Moral Relativism

What are the differences between the two forms of relativism? We saw that cultural relativism is essentially a descriptive thesis, merely reporting that people's moral beliefs vary from culture to culture. Moral relativism, on the contrary, is a normative thesis because it asserts that one *should not* make moral judgments about the behavior of people who live in cultures other than one's own. However, critics point out that if moral relativists are correct, then any kind of behavior can be morally acceptable—provided that such behavior is approved by the majority of people in a particular culture.

Critics also note that the moral relativist's reasoning is flawed. For example, they point out that sometimes it is appropriate for people to question certain kinds of behavioral practices, regardless of where those practices are carried out. Consider a specific case involving a practice in some cultures and tribes in West Africa, where a ritual of female circumcision is performed. Is it wrong for those living outside these cultures to question this practice from the perspective of morality or human rights? Although this practice has been a tradition for generations, some females living in tribes that still perform it on teenage girls have objected. Let us assume, however, that the majority of members of cultures that practice female circumcision approve it. Would it be inappropriate for those who lived outside of West Africa to question whether it is morally wrong to force some women to experience this ritual against their wishes? And if so, is it inappropriate (perhaps even morally wrong) to question the practice simply because the persons raising such questions are not members of the particular culture?

If we embrace that line of reasoning used by the moral relativist, does it follow that a culture can devise any moral scheme it wishes as long as the majority of its members approve it? If so, is moral relativism a plausible thesis? Perhaps the following scenario can help us to understand further the flawed reasoning in moral relativism.

▶ **SCENARIO 2–2:** The Perils of Moral Relativism

Two cultures, Culture A and Culture B, adjoin each other geographically. The members of Culture A are fairly peaceful people, tolerant of the diverse beliefs found in all other cultures. And they believe that all cultures should essentially mind their own business when it comes to matters involving morality. Those in Culture B, on the contrary, dislike and are hostile to those outside their culture. Culture B has recently developed a new computer system for delivering chemical weapons that it plans to use in military attacks on other cultures, including Culture A. Since Culture A subscribes to the view of moral relativism, and thus must respect the views of all cultures with regard to their systems of moral beliefs, can it condemn, in a logically consistent manner, Culture B's actions as immoral?   ■

rBecause Culture A embraces moral relativism, it must be tolerant of all of Culture B's practices and actions, as it would in the case of all cultures. Furthermore, Culture A cannot condemn the actions of Culture B, since, in the relativist's view, moral judgments about Culture B can be made only by those who reside in that culture. So, Culture A cannot say that Culture B's actions are morally wrong.

Moral relativists can only say that Cultures A and B are different. They cannot say that one is better than another, or that the behavior in one is morally permissible while the other is morally impermissible. Consider that while the systems for treating Jews used by the Nazis and by the British in the 1940s were clearly different, moral relativists could not say, with any sense of logical consistency, that one system was morally superior to the other. In the same way, Culture B cannot be judged by Culture A to be engaging in morally wrong conduct even though Culture B wishes to destroy A and to kill all of its members. Perhaps you can see that there is a price to pay for being a moral relativist. Is that price worth paying?

Although moral relativism might initially seem attractive as an ethical position, we can now see why it is conceptually flawed. To debate moral issues, we need a conceptual and methodological framework that can provide us with impartial and objective criteria to guide us in our deliberations. Otherwise, ethical debate might quickly reduce to a shouting match in which those with the loudest voices or, perhaps worse yet, those with the "biggest sticks" win the day.

Moral Absolutism and Moral Objectivism

Why is moral relativism so attractive to so many people, despite its logical flaws? Pojman (2006) notes that many people tend to assume that if they reject moral relativism, they must automatically endorse some form of *moral absolutism*. But do they necessarily need to make an either/or choice here? Pojman and others believe that it is possible to hold a view called *ethical objectivism*, which is between the two extremes.[6] Recall our earlier distinction between ethicists and moralists at the end of Section 2.2; the group that we identified there as moralists are similar to moral absolutists in that both believe they have all of the correct answers for every moral question. Whereas absolutists argue that there is only one uniquely correct answer to every moral question, moral relativists assume that there are no universally correct answers to any moral questions. Moral objectivists disagree with both positions; they disagree with absolutists by pointing out that there can be more than one acceptable answer to some moral questions, despite the fact that most cultures agree on the answers to many moral issues. For example, we saw that there is considerable agreement across cultures on principles such as "murder is morally wrong" and that "stealing is morally wrong." However, objectivists also acknowledge that reasonable people can nonetheless disagree on what the correct answers are to some moral questions.

Objectivists also differ from relativists in at least one important respect. Relativists suggest that *any* answer to a moral question can be appropriate, as long the majority in a culture hold that view. Objectivists such as Gert (2005, 2007) counter by arguing that even if there is no uniquely correct answer to every moral question, there are nonetheless many incorrect answers to some of these questions.[7] To illustrate this point, consider an analogy involving a normative dispute that happens to be nonmoral in nature—viz., a debate about who was the greatest baseball player of all time. Reasonable people could disagree on the correct answer to this normative question. For example, some might argue that it was Babe Ruth or Hank Aaron; others could reasonably claim that it was Ty Cobb or Joe DiMaggio. All four answers are objectively plausible. But someone could not reasonably defend the claim that the best baseball player was Danny Ainge or Stan Papi, since those answers are clearly unacceptable (even if we, as individuals, happen to like these former baseball players). So, there are definitely some wrong answers to this normative question, and thus we cannot endorse the "anything goes" view of relativists in defending a rational answer to the question concerning the greatest baseball player of all time. The rationale used in this scenario can be extended to the analysis of normative questions that are moral in nature.

We can now see how moral objectivism offers an alternative to the extreme views of moral relativism and moral absolutism. Unlike moral absolutism, objectivism allows for a plurality of plausible answers to some controversial moral questions, provided that certain rational criteria are satisfied. But unlike relativists, objectivists would not find every answer acceptable, because some answers would fall outside the criteria of (rationally defensible) moral behavior, in the same way that some answers fell outside the criteria for rationally acceptable answers to the normative question about the greatest baseball player. Because moral objectivism allows for the possibility that there may be more than one (rationally) acceptable answer to at least some moral questions, it is compatible with a view that some call "ethical pluralism" (Ess 2006). Although objectivism and pluralism do not entail moral relativism, they allow for multiple ethical theories—provided, of course, that those theories satisfy objective criteria. Because relativism fails to satisfy such criteria, however, it cannot be included in the list of "objective" ethical theories we will examine (such as utilitarianism, deontology, etc.) in the remaining sections of this chapter.

Fortunately, ethical theory can provide us with criteria for objectively analyzing moral issues so that we can avoid the problems of moral relativism without having to endorse moral absolutism. Before proceeding directly to our discussion of ethical theories, however, it would be useful to summarize some of the key points in our analysis of the four discussion stoppers. Table 2.2 summarizes these points.

TABLE 2.2 Summary of Logical Flaws in the Discussion Stoppers

Stopper #1	Stopper #2	Stopper #3	Stopper #4
People disagree on solutions to moral issues.	*Who am I to judge others?*	*Ethics is simply a private matter.*	*Morality is simply a matter for individual cultures to decide.*
1. Fails to recognize that experts in many areas disagree on key issues in their fields.	1. Fails to distinguish between the act of judging and being a judgmental person.	1. Fails to recognize that morality is essentially a public system.	1. Fails to distinguish between descriptive and normative claims about morality.
2. Fails to recognize that there are many moral issues on which people agree.	2. Fails to distinguish between judging as condemning and judging as evaluating.	2. Fails to note that personally based morality can cause major harm to others.	2. Assumes that people can never reach common agreement on some moral principles.
3. Fails to distinguish between disagreements about principles and disagreements about facts.	3. Fails to recognize that sometimes we are required to make judgments.	3. Confuses moral choices with individual or personal preferences.	3. Assumes that a system is moral because a majority in a culture decides it is moral.

▶ 2.3 WHY DO WE NEED ETHICAL THEORIES?

In our analysis of the four discussion stoppers, we saw some of the obstacles that we encounter when we debate moral issues. Fortunately, there are ethical theories that can guide us in our analysis of moral issues involving cybertechnology. But why do we need something as formal as ethical theory? An essential feature of theories in general is that they guide us in our investigations and analyses. Science uses theory to provide us with general principles and structures with which we can analyze our data. Ethical theory, like scientific theory, provides us with a framework for analyzing moral issues via a scheme that is internally coherent and consistent as well as comprehensive and systematic. To be coherent, a theory's individual elements must fit together to form a unified whole. To be consistent, a theory's component parts cannot contradict each other. To be comprehensive, a theory must be able to be applied broadly to a wide range of actions. And to be systematic, a theory cannot simply address individual symptoms peculiar to specific cases while ignoring general principles that would apply in similar cases.

Recall our brief analysis of the moral dilemma involving the runaway trolley (Scenario 2–1) in the opening section of this chapter. There we saw how easy it might be for a person to use two different, and seemingly inconsistent, forms of reasoning in resolving the dilemma, depending on whether that person was driving the trolley or merely observing it as a bystander on a bridge. Of course, we might be inclined to think that it is fine to flip-flop on moral decisions, since many people seem to do this much of the time. But philosophers and logicians in general, and ethicists in particular, point out many of the problems that can arise with inconsistent reasoning about moral issues.

Some critics, however, might be inclined to respond that philosophers and ethicists often dream up preposterous moral dilemmas, such as the trolley case, to complicate our decision-making process. Yet, the trolley scenario may not be as far-fetched as some critics might assume. Consider that classic dilemmas involving humans in general, and human drivers of vehicles in particular, will likely take on even more significance in the near future when human drivers of commercial vehicles are replaced by computer systems, which are typically referred to as "autonomous systems." In fact, the transport systems connecting terminal buildings in some large airports are now operated by ("driverless") autonomous systems. (In Chapter 12, we examine some specific challenges we will need to face as autonomous systems replace more and more humans who currently drive commercial vehicles.)

Next consider a slight variation or twist in Scenario 2–1. Imagine that a "driverless" trolley—i.e., a trolley being "driven" by an autonomous computer system—is in the same predicament as the one facing the human driver described in that scenario.[8] If you were a software engineer or a member of the team developing the computer system designed to "drive" this trolley, what kind of "ethical-decision-making" instructions would you recommend be built into the autonomous system? Should the autonomous computer system be instructed (i.e., programmed) to reason in a way that it would likely reach a decision to "throw the switch" to save five humans who otherwise would die (as a result of the failed braking system), thus steering the trolley instead in a direction that will intentionally kill one human? In other words, should the "computerized driver" be embedded mainly (or perhaps even exclusively) with a programming code that would influence (what we earlier called) consequentialist- or utilitarian-like moral-decision making? Alternatively, should programming code that would support non-consequentialist decision-making considerations also be built into this autonomous system. We postpone our analysis of these kinds of questions (involving "machine ethics") until Chapter 12; for now, we focus on challenges that ordinary humans have in determining how to apply ethical theories in their deliberations.

Next imagine that as a result of an accident (involving a runaway trolley), five people are rushed to the hospital. Each patient, whose condition is "critical," is in need of a vital human organ to live, and there is not sufficient time to get these organs from a transplant-donor bank located outside the hospital. Also, the hospital happens to be understaffed with surgeons at the time the accident victims are admitted to the emergency ward. So a medical physician (Dr. Smith) on duty at the hospital, who is administering a post-surgery physical exam to a patient in one room, is suddenly called into the emergency room. Dr. Smith determines that one patient needs a heart, and another a kidney; a third patient needs a liver; a fourth, a pancreas; and a fifth, a pair of lungs. Smith also determines that unless the victims receive the organ transplants immediately, each will die. Then it suddenly occurs to Dr. Smith that the hospital patient on whom he had been conducting the physical exam is in excellent health. If the healthy patient's organs were removed and immediately given to each accident victim, all five would live. Of course, the healthy patient would die as a result. But the net effect would be that four more humans would live. What should Smith do in this case? What would you do if you were in the doctor's shoes?

As you have probably determined at this point, it is helpful to have in place a systematic, comprehensive, coherent, and consistent set of principle or rules to guide us in our moral decisions. To that end, various kinds of ethical theories have been developed. We next examine four standard types of ethical theories: consequence-based, duty-based, contract-based, and character-based.

▶ 2.4 CONSEQUENCE-BASED ETHICAL THEORIES

Some have argued that the primary goal of a moral system is to produce desirable consequences or outcomes for its members. For these ethicists, the consequences (i.e., the ends achieved) of actions and policies provide the ultimate standard against which moral decisions must be evaluated. So if one must choose between two courses of action—that is, either "Act A" or "Act B"—the morally correct action will be the one that produces the most desirable outcome. Of course, we can further ask the question, "Whose outcome" (i.e., "the most desirable outcome for whom")? Utilitarians argue that the outcome or consequences for the greatest number of individuals, or the majority, in a given society is paramount in moral deliberation. According to the utilitarian theory,

> An individual act (X) or a social policy (Y) is morally permissible if the consequences that result from (X) or (Y) produce the greatest amount of good for the greatest number of persons affected by the act or policy.

Utilitarians stress the "social utility" or social usefulness of particular actions and policies by focusing on the consequences that result from those actions and policies. Jeremy Bentham (1748–1832), who was among the first philosophers to formulate utilitarian ethical theory in a systematic manner, defended this theory via two claims:

I. Social utility is superior to alternative criteria for evaluating moral systems.

II. Social utility can be measured by the amount of happiness produced.

According to (I), the moral value of actions and policies ought to be measured in terms of their social usefulness (rather than via abstract criteria such as individual rights or social justice). The more utility that specific actions and policies have, the more they can be defended as morally permissible actions and policies. In other words, if Policy Y encourages the development of a certain kind of computer software, which in turn would produce more jobs and higher incomes for those living in Community X, then Policy Y would be considered more socially useful and thus the morally correct policy. But how do we measure overall social utility? That is, which criterion can we use to determine the social usefulness of an act or a policy? The answer to this question can be found in (II), which has to do with happiness.

Bentham argued that nature has placed us under two masters, or sovereigns: pleasure and pain. We naturally desire to avoid pain and to seek pleasure or happiness. However, Bentham believed that it is not the maximization of individual pleasure or happiness that is important, but rather generating the greatest amount of happiness for society in general. Since it is assumed that all humans, as individuals, desire happiness, it would follow on utilitarian grounds that those actions and policies that generate the most happiness for the most people are most desirable. Of course, this reasoning assumes:

a. All people desire happiness.

b. Happiness is an intrinsic good that is desired for its own sake.

We can ask utilitarians what proof they have for either (a) or (b). John Stuart Mill (1806–1873) offered the following argument for (a):

> The only possible proof showing that something is audible is that people actually hear it; the only possible proof that something is visible is that people actually see it; and the only possible proof that something is desirable is that people actually desire it.

From the fact that people desire happiness, Mill inferred that promoting happiness ought to be the criterion for justifying a moral system. Unlike other goods that humans desire as means to one or more ends, Mill argued that people desire happiness for its own sake. Thus, he concluded that happiness is an intrinsic good. (Recall our earlier discussion of intrinsic values in Section 2.1.2.)

You might consider applying Mill's line of reasoning to some of your own goals and desires. For example, if someone asked why you are taking a particular college course (such as a course in cyberethics), you might respond that you need to satisfy three credit hours of course work in your major field of study or in your general education requirements. If you were then asked why you need to satisfy those credit hours, you might respond that you would like to earn a college degree. If next someone asks you why you wish to graduate from college, you might reply that you wish to get a good-paying job. If you are then asked why you want a good-paying job, your response might be that you wish to purchase a home and that you would like to be able to save some money. If asked why again, you might reply that saving money would contribute to your long-term financial and emotional security. And if further asked why you want to be financially and emotionally secure, you might respond that ultimately you want to be happy. So, following this line of reasoning, utilitarians conclude that happiness is an intrinsic good—that is, something that is good in and of itself, for its own sake, and not merely a means to some further end or ends.

2.4.1 Act Utilitarianism

We noted above that utilitarians look at the expected outcomes or consequences of an act to determine whether or not that act is morally permissible. However, some critics point out that because utilitarianism tends to focus simply on the roles that individual acts and policies play in producing the overall social good (the greatest good for the greatest number), it is conceptually flawed. Consider a hypothetical scenario in which a new controversial policy is being debated.

► **SCENARIO 2–3:** A Controversial Policy in Newmerica

A policy is under consideration in a legislative body in the nation of Newmerica, where 1% of the population would be forced to work as slaves in a manufacturing facility to produce computer chips. Proponents of this policy argue that, if enacted into law, it would result in lower prices for electronic devices for consumers in Newmerica. They argue that it would also likely result in more overall happiness for the nation's citizens because the remaining 99% of the population, who are not enslaved, would be able to purchase electronic devices and other computer-based products at a much lower price. Hence, 99% of Newmerica's population benefit at the expense of the remaining 1%. This policy clearly seems consistent with the principle of producing the greatest good for the greatest number of Newmerica's population, but should it be enacted into law? ■

The above scenario illustrates a major flaw in at least one version of utilitarianism, viz., *act utilitarianism*. According to act utilitarians,

> An act, X, is morally permissible if the consequences produced by doing X result in the greatest good for the greatest number of persons affected by Act X.

All things being equal, actions that produce the greatest good (happiness) for the greatest number of people seem desirable. However, policies and practices based solely on this principle can also have significant negative implications for those who are not in the majority (i.e., the greatest number). Consider the plight of the unfortunate few who are enslaved in the computer chip-processing plant in the above scenario. Because of the possibility that such bizarre cases could occur, some critics who embrace the goals of utilitarianism in general reject act utilitarianism.

Critics who reject the emphasis on the consequences of individual acts point out that in our day-to-day activities we tend not to deliberate on each individual action as if that action were unique. Rather, we are inclined to deliberate on the basis of certain principles or general rules that guide our behavior. For example, consider some principles that may guide your behavior as a consumer. Each time that you enter a computer store, do you ask yourself, "Shall I steal this particular software game in this particular store at this particular time?" Or have you already formulated certain general principles that guide your individual actions, such as: it is never morally permissible to steal? In the latter case, you are operating at the level of a rule or principle rather than deliberating at the level of individual actions.

2.4.2 Rule Utilitarianism

Some utilitarians argue that the consequences that result from following *rules* or principles, not the consequences of individual acts, ultimately matter in determining whether or not a certain practice is morally permissible. This version of utilitarian theory, called *rule utilitarianism*, can be formulated in the following way:

> An act, X, is morally permissible if the consequences of following the general *rule*, Y, of which act X is an instance, would bring about the greatest good for the greatest number.

Note that here we are looking at the consequences that result from following certain kinds of rules as opposed to consequences resulting from performing individual acts. Rule utilitarianism eliminates as morally permissible those cases in which 1% of the population is enslaved so that the majority (the remaining 99%) can prosper. Rule utilitarians believe that policies that permit the unjust exploitation of the minority by the majority will also likely have overall negative social consequences and thus will not be consistent with the principal criterion of utilitarian ethical theory.

How would a rule utilitarian reason in the case of the trolley accident involving five victims (described in the preceding section) each of whom needs an organ transplant to survive? For an (extreme) act utilitarian, the decision might be quite simple: remove the five organs from the one healthy patient (even though he will die) so that five humans who otherwise would die could now live. But would a rule utilitarian see this particular action as justifiable on rule-utilitarian grounds—i.e., could it form the basis for an acceptable policy (in general) for hospitals and medical facilities?

Imagine a society in which it is possible for a person to report to a medical center for a routine physical exam only to discover that his or her vital organs could be removed in order to save a greater number of people. Would anyone be willing to submit to a routine physical exam in such a society? Of course, a rule utilitarian could easily reject such a practice on the following grounds: Policies that can intentionally cause the death of an innocent individual ought not to be allowed, even if the net result of following such policies meant that more human lives would be saved. For one thing, such a policy would seem unfair to all who are adversely affected. But perhaps more importantly from a rule utilitarian's perspective, adopting such a policy would not result in the greatest good for society.

Rule utilitarianism would seem to be a more plausible ethical theory than act utilitarianism. However, some critics reject all versions of utilitarianism because they believe that no matter how this theory is expressed, utilitarianism is fundamentally flawed. These critics tend to attack one or both of the following aspects of utilitarian theory:

I. Morality is basically tied to the production of happiness or pleasure.

II. Morality can ultimately be decided by consequences (of either acts or policies).

Critics of utilitarianism argue that morality can be grounded neither in consequences nor in happiness. Hence, they argue that some alternative criterion or standard is needed.

▶ 2.5 DUTY-BASED ETHICAL THEORIES

Immanuel Kant (1724–1804) argued that morality must ultimately be grounded in the concept of duty, or obligations that humans have to one another, and never in the consequences of human actions. As such, morality has nothing to do with the promotion of happiness or the achievement of desirable consequences. Thus Kant rejects utilitarianism in particular, and all consequentialist ethical theories in general. He points out that, in some instances, performing our duties may result in our being unhappy and may not necessarily lead to consequences that are considered desirable. Theories in which the notion of duty, or obligation, serves as the foundation for morality are called *deontological* theories because they derive their meaning from the Greek root *deon*, which means duty. How can a deontological theory avoid the problems that plague consequentialist theories such as utilitarianism? Kant provides two answers to this question, one based on our nature as rational creatures, and the other based on the notion that human beings are ends-in-themselves. We briefly consider each of Kant's arguments.

What does Kant mean when he says that humans have a rational nature? Kant argues that what separates us from other kinds of creatures, and what binds us morally, is our rational capacity. Unlike animals who may be motivated only by sensory pleasure, humans have the ability to reason and deliberate. So Kant reasons that if our primary nature were such that we merely seek happiness or pleasure, as utilitarians suggest, then we would not be distinguishable from other creatures in morally relevant ways. But because we have a rational capacity, we are able to reflect upon situations and make moral choices in a way that other kinds of (nonrational) creatures cannot. Kant argues that our rational nature reveals to us that we have certain duties or obligations to each other as "rational beings" in a moral community.

We can next examine Kant's second argument, which concerns the roles of human beings as ends-in-themselves. We have seen that in focusing on criteria involving the happiness of the majority, utilitarians allow, even if unintentionally, that the interests and well-being of some humans can be sacrificed for the ends of the greatest number. Kant argues that a genuinely moral system would never permit some humans to be treated simply as means to the ends of others. He also believes that if we are willing to use a standard based on consequences (such as social utility) to ground our moral system, then that system will ultimately fail to be a moral system. Kant argues that each individual, regardless of his or her wealth, intelligence, privilege, or circumstance, has the same moral worth. From this, Kant infers that each individual is an end in him- or herself and, therefore, should never be treated merely as a means to some end. Thus we have a duty to treat fellow humans as ends.

2.5.1 Rule Deontology

Is there a rule or principle that can be used in an objective and impartial way to determine the basis for our moral obligations? For Kant, there is such a standard or objective test, which can be formulated in a principle that he calls the *categorical imperative*. Kant's imperative has a number of variations, and we will briefly examine two of them. One variation of his imperative directs us to

Act always on that maxim or principle (or rule) that ensures that all individuals will be treated as ends-in-themselves and never merely as a means to an end.

Another variation of the categorical imperative can be expressed in the following way:

Act always on that maxim or principle (or rule) that can be universally binding, without exception, for all human beings.[9]

Kant believed that if everyone followed the categorical imperative, we would have a genuinely moral system. It would be a system based on two essential principles: universality and impartiality. In such a system, every individual would be treated fairly since the same rules would apply universally to all persons. And because Kant's imperative observes the principle of impartiality, it does not allow for one individual or group to be privileged or favored over another. In other words, if it is morally wrong for you to engage in a certain action, then it is also morally wrong for all persons like you—that is, all rational creatures (or moral agents)—to engage in that action. And if you are obligated to perform a certain action, then every moral agent is likewise obligated to perform that action. To illustrate Kant's points about the role that universal principles play in a moral system, consider the following scenario.

► **SCENARIO 2–4:** Making an Exception for Oneself

Bill, a student at Technical University, approaches his philosophy instructor, Professor Kanting, after class one day to turn in a paper that is past due. Professor Kanting informs Bill that since the paper is late, he is not sure that he will accept it. But Bill replies to Professor Kanting in a way that suggests that he is actually doing his professor a favor by turning in the paper late. Bill reasons that if he had turned in the paper when it was due, Professor Kanting would have been swamped with papers. Now, however, Kanting will be able to read Bill's paper in a much more leisurely manner, without having the stress of so many papers to grade at once. Professor Kanting then tells Bill that he appreciates his concern about his professor's well being, but he asks Bill to reflect a bit on his rationale in this incident. Specifically, Kanting asks Bill to imagine a case in which all of the students in his class, fearing that their professor would be overwhelmed with papers arriving at the same time, decided to turn their papers in one week late. ■

On deontological grounds, Bill can only make an exception for himself if everyone else (in this case, every other student in Bill's class) had the right to make exceptions for him- or herself as well. But if everyone did that, then what would happen to the very notion of following rules in a society? Kant believed that if everyone decided that he or she could make an exception for him- or herself whenever it was convenient to do so, we couldn't even have practices such as promise keeping and truth telling. For those practices to work, they must be universalizable (i.e., apply to all persons equally) and impartial. When we make exceptions for ourselves, we violate the principle of impartiality, and we treat others as means to our ends.

In Kant's deontological scheme, we do not consider the potential consequences of a certain action or of a certain rule to determine whether that act is morally permissible. Rather, the objective rule to be followed—that is, the litmus test for determining when an action will have moral worth—is whether the act complies with the categorical imperative.

For a deontologist such as Kant, enslaving humans would always be immoral, regardless of whether the practice of having slaves might result in greater social utility for the majority (e.g., being able to purchase consumer products at a lower price) than the practice of not allowing slavery. The practice of slavery is immoral, not because it might have negative social consequences in the long term, but because

a. it allows some humans to be used only as a means to an end; and

b. a practice such as slavery could not be consistently applied in an objective, impartial, and universally binding way.

Kant would ask, for example, whether we could consistently impose a universal maxim that would allow slavery. He believed that we could not consistently (in a logically coherent sense) formulate such a principle that would apply to all humans, unless we also were willing to be subject to slavery. If we allow for the practice that some individuals can be enslaved but not others, then we would be allowing for exceptions to the moral rule. We would also allow some individuals to be used merely as a means to the ends of others rather than having a system in which all humans are treated as ends-in-themselves.

Although Kant's version of deontological ethics avoids many of the difficulties of utilitarianism, it, too, has been criticized as an inadequate ethical theory. Critics point out, for example, that even if Kant's categorical imperative provides us with the ultimate test for determining when some particular course of action is our duty, it will not help us in cases where we have two or more conflicting duties. Consider that, in Kant's system, we have duties both to keep promises and tell the truth. Thus, acts such as telling a lie or breaking a promise can never be morally permissible. However, Kant's critics point out that sometimes we encounter situations in which we are required *either* to tell the truth and break a promise *or* to keep a promise and tell a lie. In these cases, we encounter genuine moral dilemmas. Kant's deontological theory does not provide us with a mechanism for resolving such conflicts.

2.5.2 Act Deontology

Although Kant's version of deontology has at least one significant flaw, some philosophers believe that a deontological account of morality is nonetheless the correct kind of ethical theory. They also believe that a deontological ethical theory can be formulated in a way that avoids the charges of Kant's critics. One attempt at reformulating this theory was made by David Ross (1930). Ross rejects utilitarianism for many of the same reasons that Kant does. However, Ross also believes that Kant's version of deontology is not fully adequate.

Ross argues that when two or more moral duties clash, we have to look at individual situations in order to determine which duty will override another. Like act utilitarians, then, Ross stresses the importance of analyzing individual situations to determine the morally appropriate course of action to take. Unlike utilitarians, however, Ross believes that we must not consider the consequences of those actions in deliberating over which course of action morally trumps, or outweighs, another. Like Kant, Ross believes that the notion of duty is the ultimate criterion for determining morality. But unlike Kant, Ross does not believe that blind adherence to certain maxims or rules can work in every case for determining which duties we must ultimately carry out.

Ross believes that we have certain *prima facie* (or self-evident) *duties*, which, all things being equal, we must follow. He provides a list of prima facie duties such as honesty, benevolence, justice, and so forth. For example, each of us has a prima facie duty not to lie and a prima facie duty to keep a promise. And if there are no conflicts in a given situation, then each prima facie duty is also what he calls an *actual duty*. But how are we to determine what our actual duty is in situations where two or more prima facie duties conflict with one another? Ross believes that our ability to determine what our actual duty will be in a particular situation is made possible through a process of "rational intuitionism" (similar to the one used in mathematics).[10]

We saw that for Kant, every *prima facie* duty is, in effect, an absolute duty because it applies to every human being without exception. We also saw that Kant's scheme does not provide a procedure for deciding what we should do when two or more duties conflict. However, Ross believes that we can determine what our overriding duty is in such situations by using a deliberative process that requires two steps:

a. Reflect on the competing *prima facie* duties.

b. Weigh the evidence at hand to determine which course of action would be required in a particular circumstance.

The following scenario illustrates how Ross's procedure can be carried out.

▶ **SCENARIO 2–5:** A Dilemma Involving Conflicting Duties

You promise to meet a classmate one evening at 7:00 in the college library to study together for a midterm exam for a computer science course you are taking. While driving in your car to the library, you receive a call on your cell phone informing you that your grandmother has been taken to the hospital and that you should go immediately to the hospital. You consider calling your classmate from your car, but you realize that you don't have his phone number. You also realize that you don't have time to try to reach your classmate by e-mail. What should you do in this case? ▪

All things being equal, you have a moral obligation to keep your promise to your friend. You also have a moral obligation to visit your grandmother in the hospital. On both counts, Kant and Ross are in agreement. But what should we do when the two obligations conflict? For a rule deontologist like Kant, the answer is unclear as to what you should do in this scenario, since you have two absolute duties. For Ross, however, the following procedure for deliberation is used. You would have to weigh between the two prima facie duties in question to determine which will be your actual duty in this particular circumstance. In weighing between the two conflicting duties, your actual duty in this situation would be to visit your grandmother, which means, of course, that you would have to break your promise to your friend. However, in a different kind of situation involving a conflict of the same two duties, your actual duty might be to keep the promise made to your friend and not visit your grandmother in the hospital.

Notice that in cases of weighing between conflicting duties, Ross places the emphasis of deliberation on certain aspects of the particular situation or context, rather than on mere deliberation about the general rules themselves. Unlike utilitarians, however, Ross does not appeal to the consequences of either actions or rules in determining whether a particular course of action is morally acceptable. For one thing, Ross argues that he would have to be omniscient to know what consequences would result from his actions. So, like all deontologists, Ross rejects the criteria of consequences as a viable one for resolving ethical dilemmas.

One difficulty for Ross's position is that, as noted above, it uses a process called "rational intuitionism." Appealing to the intuitive process used in mathematics to justify certain basic mathematical concepts and axioms, Ross believes that the same process can be used in morality. However, his position on moral intuitionism is controversial and has not been widely accepted by contemporary ethicists. And since intuitionism is an important component in Ross's theory of act deontology, many ethicists who otherwise

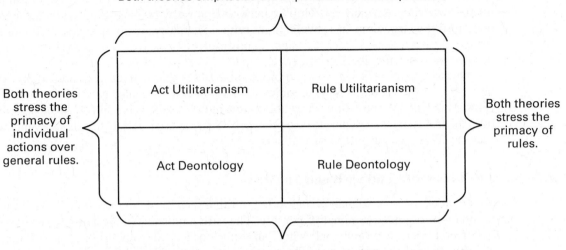

Both theories emphasize the importance of consequences.

Both theories stress the primacy of individual actions over general rules.

Act Utilitarianism | Rule Utilitarianism

Act Deontology | Rule Deontology

Both theories stress the primacy of rules.

Both theories emphasize the importance of duty or obligation.

Figure 2.3 Acts vs. rules and consequences vs. duties.

might be inclined to adopt Ross's theory have been skeptical of it. Nevertheless, variations of that theory have been adopted by contemporary deontologists.

Figure 2.3 summarizes key features that differentiate act and rule utilitarianism and act and rule deontology.

▶ 2.6 CONTRACT-BASED ETHICAL THEORIES

During the past two centuries, consequence-based and duty-based ethical theories have tended to receive the most attention from philosophers and ethicists. However, other kinds of ethical theories, such as those that emphasize criteria involving social contracts and individual rights, have recently begun to receive some serious attention as well.

From the perspective of some social contract theories, a moral system comes into being by virtue of certain contractual agreements between individuals. One of the earliest formal versions of a contract-based ethical theory can be found in the writings of Thomas Hobbes (1588–1679). In his classic work *Leviathan*, Hobbes describes an original "premoral" state that he calls the "state of nature." It is premoral because there are no moral (or legal) rules yet in existence. In this state, each individual is free to act in ways that satisfy his or her own natural desires. According to Hobbes, our natural (or physical) constitution is such that in the state of nature we act in ways that will enable us to satisfy our desires (or appetites) and to avoid what Hobbes calls our "aversions." While there is a sense of freedom in this natural state, the condition of our day-to-day existence is hardly ideal. In this state, each person must continually fend for herself, and, as a result, each must also avoid the constant threats of others, who are inclined to pursue their own interests and desires.

Hobbes describes this state of nature as one in which life is "solitary, poor, nasty, brutish, and short." Because we are rational creatures, and because we see that it would be in our best interests to band together, Hobbes notes that we eventually establish a formal legal code. In doing this, Hobbes believes that we are willing to surrender some of our "absolute" freedoms to a sovereign. In return, we receive many benefits, including a system of rules and laws that are designed and enforced to protect individuals from being harmed by other members of the system.

One virtue of the social contract model of ethics is that it gives us a motivation for being moral. We see that it is in our individual self-interest to develop a moral system with rules. This type of motivation for establishing a moral system is conspicuously absent in both the utilitarian and deontological theories.[11] So a contract-based ethical theory might seem to have one advantage over them.

2.6.1 Some Criticisms of Contract-Based Theories

Some critics, such as Pojman (2006), point out that contract-based theories provide the foundation for only a minimalist morality. They are minimalist in the sense that we are obligated to behave morally only where an explicit or formal contract exists. So if I have no express contract with you, or if a country such as the United States has no explicit contract with a developing nation, there is no moral obligation for me to help you or for the United States to come to the aid of that developing nation. Of course, we can think of many situations involving morality where there are no express contracts or explicit laws describing our obligations to each other. Yet we also tend to believe that in at least some of these cases we are morally obligated to help others when it is in our power to do so.

Consider the case of Kitty Genovese who was murdered outside her apartment building in Queens, New York in 1964, as thirty-eight neighbors in her apartment building watched. During the incident, none of Genovese's neighbors came to her rescue or called the police. When interviewed after the fact, some of her neighbors responded that they did nothing wrong.[12] In one sense, they were correct, since there was no explicit law requiring that they do anything at all. So technically, these neighbors were correct, at least from a legal perspective. But we can certainly ask whether her neighbors had a moral obligation to do something rather than simply be indifferent. It is in this sense, then, that social contract theory can be seen as being minimalist and legalistic, and not a robust theory of morality.

Another way to think about minimalist morality is to think of the difference between two principles: (a) doing no harm, and (b) doing good. A minimalist morality would insist merely that we do not harm others. As such, it does not require that we come to the aid of others. But is that an adequate view of morality? Should we accept such a moral system as complete? If you happen to see a child drowning in water that is four feet deep, and it is in your power to rescue the child, are you not morally obligated to do so? Are you under no moral obligation to assist simply because you may have no explicit legal contract requiring you to rescue that particular child?

According to a minimalist account of morality, you are not *required* to make any effort to save the child. All that is required is that you not actively harm the child (or anyone else). But some argue that a moral system demands much more of us than simply doing no harm. That is, it may also obligate us to do good when it is in our power to do so. According to the latter view of morality, then, if we could rescue the child without any significant inconvenience to ourselves, we would be morally obligated to do so (even if we have no explicit contract).

2.6.2 Rights-Based Contract Theories

Closely associated with social contract ethical theories are rights-based theories of morality. Some philosophers have argued that independent of whether individuals happen to have any legal rights, all humans have certain moral rights or natural rights. Philosophers such as Thomas Aquinas (1225–1274), as well as several of the Founders of the United States, believed that humans possess some natural rights. In the Declaration of Independence, for example, Thomas Jefferson asserted that all humans are entitled to life, liberty, and the pursuit of happiness because these rights are "inalienable" and "self-evident."

Of course, it is one thing for philosophers and legal scholars to assert that humans are endowed with natural or moral rights; and it is something altogether different to ensure that such rights are guaranteed and protected by the state. Hence, the need for explicit legal rights identified in a governing charter or constitution. Legal rights are grounded in "positive law," or civil law, whereas moral rights or natural rights are not. However, some argue that moral rights are derived from natural law; and because of this, they further argue that these rights exist independently of any legal rights that might happen to be granted to citizens of a certain nation via that nation's system of positive laws.[13]

Philosophers and legal scholars often differentiate between two kinds of legal rights: *positive rights* and *negative rights*. Having a negative right to something simply means that one has the right not to be interfered with in carrying out the privileges associated with that right. For example, your right to vote and your right to own a computer are both negative rights. They are negative rights in the sense that as a holder of those rights, you have the right (and the expectation) not to be interfered with in exercising your right to go to polls to cast your vote in a particular election or your right to purchase a computer. However, as the holder of a negative right, you cannot demand (or even expect) that others must either physically transport you to the voting polls if you are unable to travel there on your own, or provide you with a computer if you cannot afford to purchase one.

Positive rights, it turns out, are very rare. And since those rights tend to be far more controversial than negative rights, philosophers and legal scholars have had a much more difficult time justifying them. In the United States, one's right to receive an education (through the twelfth grade of high school) is a positive right. All American citizens are entitled to such an education; thus they must be provided with a free public education through the twelfth grade. An interesting question, for our purposes, is, what would happen in the event that our formal education process requires that each student own a computer and that he or she has access at home to the Internet? In that case, would students also have to be provided with a home computer and free Internet access? (We take up the question of universal access issues and the "digital divide" in Chapter 10.)

Some would argue that access to adequate health care should also be a positive right as well, because they believe health care is something that citizens have a right to be provided (even if they cannot afford to pay for it). In Canada as well as in many European countries, universal health care is viewed as a positive right. In the United States, however, this view is still being debated (as of July 2012). Although the Patient Protection and Affordable Care Act, also informally known as "Obamacare," was enacted into law in March 2010, it has since come under severe criticism and serious challenges from opponents. Depending on the outcome of the fall 2012 presidential elections, this law could be repealed, in which case health care in the United States would not be a positive right.

Discussion about the nature of rights can be both confusing and controversial. In the United States, many conservative political and religious leaders believe that in recent years far too much emphasis has been placed on individual rights. As a result, they believe that we have not paid enough attention to corresponding responsibilities that individuals also have by virtue of possessing those rights. However, we will not pursue that line of controversy here.

► 2.7 CHARACTER-BASED ETHICAL THEORIES

A fourth type of ethical theory that must be considered, especially in light of the recent attention it has received, is *virtue ethics* (also sometimes described as "character ethics"). This ethical theory ignores the special roles that consequences, duties, and social contracts play in moral systems, especially with respect to determining the appropriate standard for evaluating moral behavior. Rather, it focuses on criteria having to do with the character development of individuals and their acquisition of good character traits from the kinds of habits they develop. The fundamental principles of virtue ethics were introduced in the writings of Plato and Aristotle nearly 2,500 years ago. In more recent times, virtue ethics has gained respect among ethicists as a viable contemporary ethical theory, in part, through the influential work of Philippa Foot, Alasdair MacIntyre, and others.[14]

2.7.1 Being a Moral Person vs. Following Moral Rules

Aristotle believed that ethics was something not merely to be studied, but rather to be lived or practiced. In fact, Aristotle thought of ethics as a "practical science," like politics. To become an ethical person, in Aristotle's view, one is required to do more than simply memorize and deliberate on certain kinds of rules. What is also needed, Aristotle argued, is that people develop certain *virtues*. The Greek word for virtue is *arete*, which means excellence. Aristotle believed that to be a moral person, one had to acquire the right virtues (strengths or excellences). Through the proper training and acquisition of good habits and character traits, Aristotle believed that one could achieve moral virtues such as temperance and courage that are needed to "live well."

Because virtue ethics focuses primarily on character development and moral education, it does not need to rely on a system of formal rules. Consider that both utilitarians and deontologists depend on having a system of rules when they ask a question such as, What should we do in such and such a case or situation? For utilitarians, the answer could be found by measuring the anticipated outcomes of following a general rule or principle. And for deontologists the answer can be determined by using a formal rule such as the categorical imperative as a principle for determining which duties you have. For contract theorists, questions involving moral obligation ultimately rest on the principle or rule, What is the nature of my contract, if any, in this particular situation? Virtue ethicists take a very different tack. Instead of asking, "What should I *do* in such and such a situation?" a virtue ethicist asks, *What kind of person should I be*? Hence, the emphasis on *being a moral person*, and not simply on understanding what moral rules are and how they apply in certain situations. Whereas deontological and utilitarian theories are action-oriented and rule-oriented, virtue ethics is "agent-oriented" because it is centered on the moral development and character of the agent herself.

Virtue ethicists believe that a moral person is one who is necessarily disposed to do the right thing. They correctly point out that when we engage in routine acts in our daily lives, including many of our nonnormative actions, we do not deliberate by asking ourselves, What ought I to do in such and such a case? In our earlier criticism of act utilitarianism, we considered a situation in which an individual would be required to deliberate over whether or not to steal an item each time he or she entered a store. A virtue ethicist would point out that if that person had developed the right kind of moral character (through the acquisition of the "correct" moral habits), he or she would not be in a position that required such deliberation. That is, the moral person is already disposed not to steal items from stores (or from fellow human beings) because of the kinds of character traits that he or she has previously developed. And in the example involving the drowning child, considered in our criticism of contract-based ethical theory, a virtue ethicist would also likely point out that a moral person would not have to deliberate. Regardless of whether someone had an explicit legal contract to help rescue the child, the virtue ethicist would point out that a moral person is predisposed to attempt to rescue the child if it were in his or her power to do so.

2.7.2 Acquiring the "Correct" Habits

Consider the following illustration of a disposition to behave in a certain way. When you woke up this morning and began to prepare for your day's events, did you ask yourself the question, Should I brush my teeth today? Most likely, this question never crossed your mind. Why not? The answer, of course, is that you have already developed certain habits such that you are disposed to brush your teeth in the morning without having to question it or even think about it. Of course, the act of brushing one's teeth is not an act that has any moral significance. But it is the process of character formation, especially the development of moral habits, that is crucial to becoming a fully moral person, from the perspective of virtue ethics.

As noted above, Aristotle believed that ethics was something to be lived and practiced, not simply studied. Thus some philosophers and ethicists believe that to teach ethics, one must first be an ethical person. The teacher who instructs students on the virtues but who himself lacks them would be a poor model for aspiring students. James Moor (2002) suggests that virtue ethics instruction is the "first level" in teaching (computer) ethics. He believes that building habits of character such as kindness, truthfulness, honesty, trustworthiness, helpfulness, generosity, and justice are important prerequisites in preparing for the second level of instruction. Once students have mastered the virtues, they can then move to the second level where they learn the established rules of a moral system.

Some instructors have argued that their students are better able to relate to classroom examples that involve virtue ethics than to those illustrating other traditional theories. For this reason, Frances Grodzinsky (1999) has suggested that aspects of virtue ethics should be incorporated into the ethics training for computing professionals. Grodzinsky believes that aspiring computer professionals who wish to develop an appropriate level of sensitivity to ethical aspects of their profession often find the principles of virtue ethics far more useful than the kinds of rigid rules required in ethical theories such as utilitarianism and deontology. She notes that action-guiding rules associated with utilitarian and deontological theories often tend to be perceived by students as too abstract and formal. On the contrary, however, many of those students are able to grasp what it means to develop certain character traits and thus become (or be) a certain kind of person.

It would seem that the re-emergence of virtue ethics, despite the fact that its origins can be traced back to classical Greece, has provided ethicists with some fresh insights. However, we should also note that virtue ethics is not without its critics. One of the chief drawbacks of taking virtue ethics as a complete theory of ethics is that it neither helps resolve conflicts that can arise among the competing virtues nor encourages examination of consequences. Some critics point out that a virtue- or character-based ethics would seem to have a better chance of taking hold in a society that is homogeneous rather than in one that is heterogeneous or pluralistic. The ancient Greek society could be considered fairly homogeneous in the sense that the world that Plato and Aristotle inhabited included a consensus as to what the ideal values, including the moral education of the young, were. In contemporary America, which is much more heterogeneous than classical Greek society, we have a diversity of views about which ideals and values are most important.

It is also worth pointing out that character-based ethical systems would most likely flourish in cultures where the emphasis placed on community life is stronger than that accorded to the role of individuals themselves. Beginning with the Enlightenment period in the West in the seventeenth and eighteenth centuries, considerable emphasis has been placed on the importance of individual autonomy and individual rights. As you might already have suspected, aspects of utilitarianism, deontological ethics, and contractualist ethics are strongly tied to the notions of individual rights and responsibilities. In the ancient Greek world of Aristotle's time, the notion of community was paramount. Thus virtue ethics faces certain challenges in contemporary Western society that it would not have had to endure in the classical Greek *polis*, or city-state.

▶ 2.8 INTEGRATING ASPECTS OF CLASSICAL ETHICAL THEORIES INTO A SINGLE COMPREHENSIVE THEORY

We have completed our examination of the four main types of ethical theories, and we have noted some of the strengths and weaknesses of each theory. Consequentialist theories such as utilitarianism are useful because they aim at promoting happiness and the social good. Yet, we also saw that utilitarians tend to ignore the importance of justice and fairness in their preoccupation with promoting social utility for the majority. Deontologists, on the contrary, stress the importance of obligation and respect for all persons, and thus emphasize the principles of fairness and justice. However, we saw that deontologists fail to pay sufficient attention to the promotion of happiness and the social good.

Contract theory seems useful in that it provides a motivation for being moral and it enables us to articulate which explicit moral obligations we have and do not have, both as individuals and as a society. However, the weakness of the social contract view is that it

TABLE 2.3 Four Types of Ethical Theory

Type of Theory	Advantages	Disadvantages
Consequence-based (utilitarian)	Stresses promotion of happiness and utility	Ignores concerns of justice for the minority population
Duty-based (deontology)	Stresses the role of duty and respect for persons	Underestimates the importance of happiness and social utility
Contract-based (rights)	Provides a motivation for morality	Offers only a minimal morality
Character-based (virtue)	Stresses character development and moral education	Depends on homogeneous community standards for morality

provides us with only a minimalist theory of morality. Virtue ethics stresses character development and the acquisition of good habits on the part of individuals, but its disadvantage is that it depends on homogeneous community standards for determining the correct virtues. Thus each theory has its weakness, despite its strengths. Table 2.3 summarizes the advantages and disadvantages of each of the four ethical theories we examined.

Because of problems with the four types of traditional ethical theories that we considered, some have advocated for alternative ethical theories including feminist ethics. Alison Adam (2008) has drawn from some of the insights of Carol Gilligan,[15] as well as from other authors who have contributed to the literature on feminist ethics, in making her case for why at least some computer ethics issues would be better understood if they were analyzed from the perspective of feminist ethical theory. We examine Adam's arguments for a "gender-informed" computer ethics in Chapter 10, where we consider gender issues affecting cybertechnology.

Others have proposed ways in which elements of two or more traditional theories can be integrated into a single, more comprehensive framework. For example, Bernard Gert (2005, 2007) has integrated aspects of two theories by incorporating Kant's insights on the importance of impartiality with the claims of utilitarians about consequences, but he thinks that each theory, in itself, is inadequate. Gert has also shown how his moral system, which he calls "common morality," can be directly applied to issues involving computer ethics such as copying proprietary software.[16] Recall our discussion of Gert's notion of the moral system and its corresponding "moral rules" in Section 2.1.1.

Influenced by the work of Gert and others, Moor (2004) has proposed a scheme that integrates aspects of utilitarian and deontological theories into a framework he calls "just consequentialism." We next examine some key aspects of this theory.

2.8.1 Moor's Just-Consequentialist Theory and Its Application to Cybertechnology

Moor believes that only an ethical approach that combines considerations of consequences of action with more traditional deontological considerations of duties, rights, and justice can provide us with a defensible ethical theory—viz., just consequentialism—that yields a useful framework for applied ethics. Moor begins by considering what kind of conduct we want ethics to regulate. He believes first and foremost everyone wants to be protected against suffering unnecessary harms. We don't want to be killed or suffer great pain or have our freedom taken away. Human nature is such that people value the same kind of basic goods (life, happiness, abilities, security, knowledge, freedom, opportunities, and resources). The specifics of these may manifest somewhat differently in different cultures (some kinds of freedom may be more important in some cultures than others, for example), but the general set of goods, which Moor calls "core values" (see Section 2.1.2), is shared by all. Losing any of these goods counts as harm, and all of us want ethics to protect us from others causing us harm. This point is captured by the familiar ethical maxim "Do no harm," described earlier. Stealing someone's computer causes a loss of resources to that person, and lying about software bugs undermines the purchaser's knowledge. Thus, it is not surprising that we regard stealing and lying as unethical activities in light of their harmful consequences.

Another desirable objective of ethics, according to Moor, is to support justice, rights, and duties. We want others to keep their promises and agreements, to obey the law, and to fulfill their duties in whatever roles they play. These specific obligations are generated within societies, and to the extent that they spring from just agreements, laws, and social situations, we justifiably expect others to fulfill their duties toward us. For example, we want a software engineer to produce reliable software. We believe it is her duty as a professional to develop effective and safe software and that we have a right to expect good quality when we buy it. Another familiar maxim of ethics is "Do your duty," where "duty" here designates specific duties people acquire by their roles in society such as a signer of contract, a citizen, a parent, an employer, or an employee. Violating one's just duty, such as knowingly designing defective software for later production and sales, in the absence of contravening considerations, is clearly unethical.

Moor believes that if all we had to do to be ethical were to do no harm and perform our duties, ethics would be challenging but at least easy to understand. But, as Moor argues, the ethical life is not nearly so simple. Often actions involve a mixture of goods and evils as well as conflicts among duties. Sometimes we need to make exceptions to our general policies for action. How do we decide what to do? His answer involves two steps: the deliberation stage and the selection stage. First, at the *deliberation stage*, we should consider the various possible policies for action from an impartial point of view. Impartial does not mean that everyone is treated the same but that the policy is regarded as a rule governing the situation without consideration of the particular individuals who happen to be involved. This is what Gert has in mind by his "blindfold of justice" (see Section 2.1.1) or what Rawls suggests with his "veil of ignorance." This is a technique to establish the justice of a policy—it will not be just if one will not accept the policy as a general rule of conduct, not knowing who plays which roles in the situation.

For example, consider the cyberbullying scenario discussed in Chapter 1, in which Lori Drew (under the alias of Josh Evans) bullied Megan Meier to the point that eventually led to Meier's suicide. Let us assume that Drew was obsessed with her victim and got significant gratification out of her deeds. If we consider a policy for justifying such an action impartially, we will clearly reject it. We will not endorse a policy of allowing someone to bully and harass us even if such bullies get significant pleasure from it. It is easy to reject such a policy as unjust and unethical when considered from an impartial point of view.

However, many policies will pass the impartiality test, and we will still need to consider whether we should adopt them. We need to move to the second step in the decision-making process, the *selection stage*, and carefully weigh the good consequences and the bad consequences of the remaining policies. In this second step, it may be less of a choice between ethical vs. unethical policies than between better vs. worse policies. Although we may be able to at least partially rank policies, legitimate disagreements about the rankings often exist.

For instance, consider the controversial issues as to whether we should adjust or even have a policy of intellectual property protection. For many years in many places there were no laws protecting intellectual property. It is far from clear that this situation was unjust or even bad. A culture might maintain that sharing information and invention is more valuable to the society's members' welfare and the society's cohesiveness than trying to protect intellectual property. Witness the rationale given for the "open source movement" in software development. Critics of this movement, however, might maintain that having intellectual-property protection laws is important to protect creators and to produce innovative products for everyone's benefit.

According to Moor, it is important to keep in mind that although we may disagree about the merits of various policies and how to rank them, rational discussion of the relevant policies is very possible and highly desirable. People may overlook values embedded in a situation and may change their rankings once informed. People may not be fully aware of the consequences of various policies. Moor does not believe that complete agreement on controversial policies can or necessarily should be reached, as people may ultimately rank benefits and harms differently. Nevertheless, considerable consensus about some policies being better than others can often be generated. Moor points out that frequently much of the disagreement hinges on differences about the facts of the case than on value differences. (Recall our early analysis of differences involving "disagreements about principles" and "disagreements about facts" in Section 2.2.1, in our discussion of discussion stoppers in ethics.) It would radically change much of the debate about the need for protecting MP3 files, for example, if it could be demonstrated that, *as a matter of fact*, downloading MP3 files to preview them dramatically increases sales or if it could be demonstrated that, *as a matter of fact*, downloading MP3 files to preview them dramatically decreased the quality of music that was produced.

2.8.2 Key Elements in Moor's Just-Consequentialist Framework

Moor's ethical framework of just consequentialism can be summarized in terms of a strategy that includes the following steps:

1. *Deliberate* over various policies from an impartial point of view to determine whether they meet the criteria for being ethical policies. A policy is ethical, if it
   a. does not cause any unnecessary harms to individuals and groups, and
   b. supports individual rights, the fulfilling of duties, etc.
2. *Select* the best policy from the set of just policies arrived at in the deliberation stage by ranking ethical policies in terms of benefits and (justifiable) harms. In doing this, be sure to
   a. weigh carefully between the good consequences and bad consequences in the ethical policies, and

    b. distinguish between disagreements about facts and disagreements about principles and values, when deciding which particular ethical policy should be adopted. (Knowledge about the facts surrounding a particular case should inform the decision-making process.)

As we noted in our discussion of virtue ethics in Section 2.7.2, Moor points out that developing the appropriate habits of character such as kindness, truthfulness, honesty, trustworthiness, helpfulness, generosity, and justice is an important prerequisite in moral behavior. So if one has not already developed the "correct" habits required for moral behavior, it may be difficult for an individual to successfully carry out the steps in Moor's just-consequentialist model. In this sense, elements of virtue ethics or character-based ethics are also presupposed in Moor's framework.

We apply the just-consequentialist framework, wherever appropriate, in suggesting policies in response to moral issues that arise from specific cyberethics issues examined in Chapters 4–12 of this textbook.

▶ 2.9 CHAPTER SUMMARY

In this chapter, we defined ethics as the study of morality. In elaborating on that definition, we drew some useful distinctions between morality (as a system of rules and principles) and ethics (as the study of that system). Acknowledging the distinction between normative and descriptive studies of morality, we saw that normative investigations into morality can be conducted from the perspectives of religion and law as well as from philosophy. We also noted that only philosophical ethics offers a method to analyze moral issues based exclusively on the application of ethical theory and logical argumentation. We briefly identified and analyzed some common "discussion stoppers" that are frequently invoked in ways that prematurely close down, even if unintentionally, the possibility of constructive ethical dialogue.

We also examined the roles that ethical theories ideally play in guiding us in our moral deliberations about cyberethics issues. We saw that consequence-based, duty-based, contract-based, and character-based theories each had certain strengths and weaknesses. Finally, we examined James Moor's proposal for a framework that incorporates aspects of consequence-based and duty-based theories (and to some extent character-based theories) into one unified, comprehensive theory, called "just consequentialism." We summarized Moor's framework into a two-step process that we will use, wherever possible, in our analysis of the cyberethics issues examined in this textbook.

▶ REVIEW QUESTIONS

1. What is *ethics*, and how can it be distinguished from *morality*?

2. What is meant by a *moral system*?

3. What are some of the key differences between the "rules of conduct" and the "principles of evaluation"

that comprise a moral system? Give an example of each.

4. Describe the key differences between rules of conduct that are individual "directives" and those that are "social policies." Provide an example of each.

5. What does Bernard Gert mean when he describes morality in terms of a system that is both "public" and "informal"?

6. Describe how the ideals of "rationality" and "impartiality" function in Gert's moral system.

7. What are *values*, and what are some of the key differences between moral values and nonmoral values? Provide some examples of "basic moral values" and "core nonmoral values."

8. How do religion, law, and philosophy each provide different grounds for justifying a moral principle? How can each perspective be applied to the analysis of the moral principle "Stealing is wrong?"

9. What are the basic differences separating ethicists from moralists?

10. Identify and briefly summarize four different kinds of "discussion stoppers" in ethical discourse.

11. Why are these "discussion stoppers" problematic for the advancement of dialogue and debate about ethical issues?

12. What is moral relativism? How is it different from cultural relativism?

13. What is moral objectivism, and how is it different from moral absolutism?

14. What is ethical theory, and what important functions do ethical theories play in the analysis of moral issues?

15. What are the distinguishing features of consequence-based ethical theories?

16. Describe some of the key differences between act utilitarianism and rule utilitarianism.

17. Which features distinguish duty-based ethical theories from alternative types of theories?

18. Describe some of the main differences between act deontology and rule deontology.

19. What is meant by the expression "contract-based" ethical theories?

20. What features distinguish "character-based" (or "virtue-based") ethical theories from alternative schemes of morality?

► DISCUSSION QUESTIONS

21. Why does Gert believe that the notion of "personal morality" is an oxymoron? For Gert, how is a moral system both similar to, and different from, a game? Apply Gert's notion of a moral system to the analysis of a contemporary ethical issue affecting cybertechnology. Analyze that issue in terms of the four features that comprise a moral system for Gert.

22. How does James Moor's "just-consequentialist" theory incorporate aspects of utilitarian and deontological theories into one comprehensive ethical framework? Describe the strategies used in the two different stages of Moor's theory: the deliberation and the selection stage. Identify a contemporary moral issue affecting cybertechnology, and apply Moor's just-consequentialist theory to it.

► ESSAY/PRESENTATION QUESTIONS

23. Recall the four types of "discussion stoppers" that we examined in this chapter. Is that collection of "stoppers" complete? Can you think of any additional discussion stoppers that might also block or shut down moral discourse? Why is it so easy to fall victim to one or more of those stoppers when discussing moral issues in general, as well as moral issues involving the use of cybertechnology in particular?

24. Are any of the four traditional ethical theories we examined—i.e., consequence-based, duty based,

contract-based, and character-based—adequate to handle moral issues that arise as a result of cybertechnology? If not, is an alternative kind of ethical theory needed, as some have argued (e.g., Adam 2008)? Or can a comprehensive, integrated theory, such as the one proposed by James Moor (i.e., his theory of "just consequentialism") be used successfully to resolve moral issues involving cybertechnology?

Scenarios for Analysis

1. In analyzing the following scenario, describe how an *act utilitarian*, a *rule utilitarian*, a *rule deontologist*, and an *act deontologist* would each reach a solution to this dilemma. Which solution seems most plausible? Finally, apply Moor's Just-Consequentialism framework in your analysis of this scenario.

You have just been appointed to the board of directors of XYZ.com. Unfortunately, the dot-com company has been experiencing some difficult financial times, resulting in revenue losses in three of the last four quarters. As you assume your new position, you discover that two proposals are on the table. Each proposal has been put forth as a means for dealing with XYZ's immediate financial problems. Proposal #1 recommends that all employees be retained, but that an immediate freeze on salary increases (raises) for all employees be imposed for the next six months. (Employees may even be asked to take a 5% cut in pay if things do not improve by the end of that period.) Proposal #2 recommends that wages not be frozen, but that 5% of the XYZ's work force be laid off. (One piece of reasoning behind this proposal is that taking more drastic measures will "protect" 95% of XYZ's workers and will send a message to Wall Street and local investors that XYZ is serious about improving its financial position and that it will soon be a stable company once again.) The board is evenly split, seven members favoring proposal# 1 and seven favoring proposal #2. Yours will be the tie-breaking vote.

2. Analyze the dilemma in the following scenario from the vantage point of both utilitarian and deontological ethical theories. In particular, how might Ross's theory of act-deontology apply?

The United States government, with the approval of the majority of Americans, has decided to round up all Arab-Americans and relocate them into internment camps. You have a friend who is an American citizen of Arab descent. She asks you to protect her from the authorities. You have known this person all of your life, and you are convinced that she is a loyal American. So you agree to hide her in the third floor of your house. Next, imagine that a United States federal agent knocks on your door and asks if you know the whereabouts of the person you are hiding. How would you respond to that agent?

You realize that you cannot both keep your promise to your friend and tell the truth to the federal agent. Initially, your gut reaction might suggest that the solution to your dilemma is really quite simple: a far greater good will be served by lying to the federal agent than by breaking your promise to your friend. However, to embrace the moral principle underlying that line of reasoning is to embrace a form of utilitarianism. And we have already seen some of the difficulties that can result from trying to be a consistent and thoroughgoing utilitarian. Furthermore, could you consistently universalize a moral principle that states: Whenever you must choose between telling the truth to authorities and breaking a promise to a friend, you should always keep your promise? Will that principle always work?

► ENDNOTES

1. This classic definition of ethics has been defended by many philosophers. See, for example, Paul W. Taylor's *Principles of Ethics: An Introduction* (Belmont CA: Wadsworth, 1980).

2. Analyses of moral dilemmas based on examples using the (now classic) "trolley problem" have proliferated since this "thought experiment" was introduced by philosopher Philippa Foot in 1967. For an interesting variation of this dilemma, see Wallach and Allen (2009).

3. Gert's "blindfold of justice" is similar in some ways to John Rawls' well-known "veil of ignorance," articulated in Rawls' class work *A Theory of Justice* (rev. ed. 1999). However, the two notions also differ in key respects.

4. See, for example, Pojman (2006).

5. For example, some critics point out that while there appear to be differences affecting moral beliefs at the surface level, a closer analysis will suggest ("deep") universal or core moral beliefs that lie under the surface.

6. Bernard Gert suggests that his ten "moral rules" are objective in nature. However, Gert does not use the label "objectivism" to describe his moral system.

7. Although Gert does not call himself a moral objectivist, I interpret his position to be compatible with the view I describe as moral objectivism.

8. Wallach and Allen (2009) also consider a variation of the "trolley case" in which the trolley's driver has been replaced by a computerized system.

9. The variations of Kant's categorical imperative expressed here closely follow the original.

10. For more detail on this strategy, see Ross (1930).

11. Pojman (2006) explains in more detail how this theory provides a motivation for being moral.

12. For the original account of this incident, see "Queens Woman is Stabbed to Death in Front of Home," *New York Times*, March 14, 1964.

13. This is a basic distinction in Natural Law, a theory of ethics that we are not able to examine in detail in this chapter.

14. See, for example, see Foot's *Theories of Ethics* (Oxford University Press, 1967) and MacIntyre's *After Virtue* (Notre Dame IN: University of Notre Dame Press, 1981).

15. Gilligan's classic book *In a Different Voice* (Cambridge MA: Harvard University Press, 1982) has influenced feminist ethics.

16. See Gert (2004).

▶ REFERENCES

Adam, Alison. 2008. "The Gender Agenda in Computer Ethics." In K. E. Himma and H. T. Tavani, eds. *The Handbook of Information and Computer Ethics.* Hoboken, NJ: John Wiley and Sons, pp. 589–619.

Aristotle. 1962. *Nicomachean Ethics.* Trans. M. Oswald. New York: Bobbs-Merrill.

Bentham, Jeremy. 1948. *Introduction to the Principles of Morals and Legislation.* W. Harrison, ed. London: Oxford University Press.

De George, Richard T. 1999. *Business Ethics.* 5th ed. Upper Saddle River NJ: Prentice Hall.

Ess, Charles. 2006. "Ethical Pluralism and Global Information Ethics." *Ethics and Information Technology* 8, no. 4: 215–66. p. 63–82.

Gert, Bernard. 2004. "Common Morality and Computing." In R. A. Spinello and H. T. Tavani, eds. *Readings in CyberEthics.* 2nd ed. Sudbury, MA: Jones and Bartlett, pp. 96–106. Reprinted from *Ethics and Information Technology* 1, no. 1 (1999): 37–56.

Gert, Bernard. 2005. *Morality: Its Nature and Justification.* Rev. ed. New York: Oxford University Press.

Gert, Bernard. 2007. *Common Morality: Deciding What to Do.* New York: Oxford University Press.

Grodzinsky, Frances S. 1999. "The Practitioner from Within: Revisiting the Virtues." *Computers and Society* 29, no. 1: 9–15.

Hobbes, Thomas. 1962. *Leviathan.* New York: Collier Books.

Kant, Immanuel. 1965. *Fundamental Principles of the Metaphysics of Morals.* Trans. T. K. Abbott. London: Longman's.

Mill, John Stuart. 1965. *Utilitarianism.* New York: Bobbs-Merrill.

Moor, James H. 2002. "The Importance of Virtue in Teaching Computer Ethics." In M. Ochi, et al., eds. *Proceedings of the Foundations of Information Ethics.* Hiroshima, Japan: Hiroshima University Press, pp. 29–38.

Moor, James H. 2004. "Just Consequentialism and Computing." In R. A. Spinello and H. T. Tavani, eds. *Readings in CyberEthics.* 2nd ed. Sudbury, MA: Jones and Bartlett, pp. 107–13.

Pojman, Louis P. 2006. *Ethics: Discovering Right and Wrong.* 5th ed. Belmont, CA: Wadsworth.

Rawls, John. 1999. *A Theory of Justice.* Rev. ed. New York: Oxford University Press.

Ross, W. D. 1930. *The Right and the Good.* London: Oxford University Press.

Wallach, Wendell, and Colin Allen. 2009. *Moral Machines: Teaching Robots Right from Wrong.* New York: Oxford University Press.

▶ FURTHER READINGS

Arthur, John, ed. *Morality and Moral Controversies.* 8th ed. Upper Saddle River, NJ: Prentice Hall, 2009.

Cahn, Steven, and Peter Markie, eds. *Ethics: History, Theory, and Contemporary Issues.* 5th ed. New York: Oxford University Press, 2012.

Hinman, Lawrence M. *Ethics—A Pluralistic Approach to Moral Theory.* 5th ed. Belmont, CA: Wadsworth Publishing, 2013.

Rachels, James, and Stuart Rachels. *The Elements of Moral Philosophy.* 7th ed. New York: McGraw-Hill, 2012.

Sterba, James, and Peter Bornschein. *Morality in Practice.* 8th ed. New York: Cengage, 2013.

Triplett, Timm. "Bernard Gert's *Morality* and Its Application to Computer Ethics." *Ethics and Information Technology* 4, no. 1 (2002): 79–92.

CHAPTER

3

Critical Reasoning Skills for Evaluating Disputes in Cyberethics

You may wonder why a chapter dedicated to *critical reasoning* skills is included in a book on cyberethics.[1] To appreciate the important role that these skills play in our examination of cyberethics issues, recall the methodological framework that we developed in Chapter 1. There we saw that the final step of that methodology requires that we defend or justify our position by evaluating it against the rules of logical argumentation.[2] In Chapter 3 we examine some basic critical reasoning concepts needed to do this. To accomplish these objectives, we

- examine the structure of a *logical argument* and show how arguments are used in resolving disputes affecting ethical aspects of cybertechnology;
- evaluate the strength of arguments by distinguishing between arguments that are valid and invalid, sound and unsound, inductive and fallacious;
- identify some common logical fallacies that occur in everyday reasoning and show how they apply to arguments affecting cyberethics issues.

Additional material on critical reasoning skills is included in Appendix G, available at www.wiley.com/college/tavani.

▶ 3.1 GETTING STARTED

In Chapter 2, we learned how to apply ethical theories to cyberethics issues and we saw how those theories provided a consistent and systematic approach to analyzing ethical issues. For example, we saw how a typical cyberethics issue could be systematically approached from the vantage point of a standard ethical theory, such as utilitarianism, deontology, etc. At some point, however, we may also need to defend—give a reason for why—we selected one particular ethical theory over another. Additionally, we may sometimes need to convince others about which ethical theory is best for analyzing cyberethics issues in general.

It is also possible that others may try to convince you with regard to why a particular theory or framework is best for analyzing some ethical issue. Or, they may try to persuade you either to accept or violate policies and laws that have ethical implications—e.g., they may wish to convince you to endorse a specific Internet user policy. They may also try to persuade you as to how one ought to behave online, based on their perceptions or beliefs about the legitimacy or nonlegitimacy of certain policies and laws. Consider, for instance, disputed policies involving digital intellectual property and the appropriateness of downloading copyrighted material from the Internet. It is possible that you may be unclear about some of those laws and policies, or unclear about how to behave appropriately in light of those laws and policies—especially ones that might not initially seem to be unethical (even if they are illegal).

In the following scenario, where you are conflicted about whether or not to download a software application from the Internet, a friend tries to convince you why you should take one course of action rather than another.

▶ **SCENARIO 3–1:** Reasoning About Whether to Download a File from "Sharester"

You are contemplating downloading a software application that is available on a Web site called Sharester, a peer-to-peer (P2P) site set up for file sharing. Sharester is not officially designated as a "pirate site" because it provides users mainly with access to (freely available) open-source software applications. However, the site also enables users to download a few proprietary (or copyrighted) software programs. It turns out that the particular software application you are interested in downloading is proprietary, and there is no reason to believe that the copyright holder of that application has authorized its being freely downloaded by users on this P2P site. You want to download this application for personal use (only) but you are conflicted about what to do, and you discuss your concerns with a good friend.

Your friend tries to convince you not to download the proprietary software program, using the following rationale: Downloading proprietary software (without permission from the copyright holder) is identical to stealing physical property. Stealing physical property is morally wrong. Therefore, downloading proprietary software (without permission) is morally wrong. ■

Is the reasoning process used by your friend a good one? How do we determine that? If we rely solely on our intuitions, we might be inclined to think that the reasoning process used here is very solid (and in this case, the conclusion reached in the reasoning process would indeed seem to be true). But what about the reasoning process itself, i.e., the "reasoning form," used in this case. Is the evidence provided by your friend sufficient to guarantee the truth of the conclusion reached? Also, can we always trust our intuitions (solely) when reasoning about what to do in situations similar to this one? Fortunately, there are some objective criteria that we can use to distinguish good and bad reasoning (what we will call valid vs. invalid/fallacious reasoning).

Later in this chapter (at the end of Section 3.8), we apply a seven-step strategy to evaluate the reasoning process used in the above scenario. First, however, we need to understand some basic terms and concepts used by logicians to analyze the strength of reasoning forms called arguments.

3.1.1 Defining Two Key Terms in Critical Reasoning: Claims and Arguments

Critical reasoning is a branch of informal logic. It aims at assisting us in evaluating the strength of *arguments* and in analyzing (the truth or falsity of) *claims*. Claims, also called statements or assertions, comprise a form of reasoning called a logical argument or argument.

For our purposes, an argument, which contains at least two claims, can be defined as a reasoning form, or structure, that attempts to establish the truth of one claim (called a *conclusion*) based on the assumed truth of the evidence in other claims (called *premises*) provided to support the conclusion. Thus, an argument is a *form of reasoning* that has two important characteristics or features in that it

    i. includes at least two claims (but can include an indefinite number of claims);

    ii. aims at establishing a conclusion (i.e., the truth of one claim) based on evidence provided by one or more other claims, called premises.

We will see that whereas arguments are either *valid* or *invalid*, the claims that comprise them are either *true* or *false*. First, however, we examine an important role that arguments can play when someone is trying to support or defend a position that may be in some dispute.

3.1.2 The Role of Arguments in Defending Claims

Consider a hypothetical scenario involving a claim about the development of a controversial and powerful new computer chip—code-named Chip X—in Japan. This new chip is purported to be so powerful in speed and performance that it will eclipse any computer chips that manufacturers in the United States, such as Intel or AMD, will be capable of producing during the next several years. Chip X will also enable the manufacturer to monitor certain activities of those users whose computers contain the chip in ways that pose serious threats to personal privacy.

Suppose I claim that Chip X is currently under development by Mishito Corporation. Let us further suppose that you are skeptical about my claim. There are a number of ways I could attempt to convince you: I could persuade you to accompany me on a trip to Japan to see first-hand whether or not Chip X is being developed there. In this case, we could obtain direct evidence about my claim. But if you are unable or unwilling to accompany me to Japan, I will have to use some other, less direct mode of verification to convince you. For example, I could show you a copy of the design specifications for Chip X, extracted from a confidential Mishito Corporation document that I happened to acquire. Or perhaps I could ask a mutual colleague of ours who recently studied as an exchange student at the University of Hiroshima, where the field testing for this new chip is being carried out, to corroborate my claim regarding Chip X. That is, I can put together various pieces of evidence to construct a logical argument that supports my claim.

Now we are in a position to debate the merits of my argument regarding Chip X without having to go to Japan to verify the truth of my claim. Before we debate the strength of my argument, however, we must first understand some essential features of an argument's *structure*.

3.1.3 The Basic Structure of an Argument

We noted in Section 3.1 that an argument consists of two or more claims, one of which is called the conclusion; the others are called the premises. The standard form for representing an argument is to list the premises first and then state the conclusion. The following structure represents an argument's standard form:

PREMISE 1
PREMISE 2 (optional)
PREMISE 3 (optional)
.
.
.
PREMISE *n* (optional)

CONCLUSION

To support my claim that Chip X is currently being developed in Japan, in the conclusion of my argument, I would need to list the evidence in the form of one or more premises. For example, I could use the following argument form:

PREMISE 1. When I recently visited the Computer Science Department at the University of Hiroshima in Japan, I noticed that graduate students and professors there were field-testing a new computer chip, whose code name is Chip X.

PREMISE 2. I have a copy of the design specifications for Chip X, which shows that it will be several times faster than any chip currently available in the United States.

PREMISE 3. Lee Smith, a mutual colleague of ours who was recently an exchange student in the computer science program at the University of Hiroshima and who participated in the field-testing of Chip X, will corroborate my claim.

CONCLUSION. Chip X is currently being developed in Japan.

This particular argument includes three premises and a conclusion; additional premises could be added. However, an argument requires at least one premise along with a conclusion. In this section, we are concerned only with an argument's structure and not with how strong the argument might be. An argument, however weak it may ultimately be, still qualifies as an argument if its structure (or reasoning form) includes one or more premises and a conclusion.

You might have observed that the claim expressed in the conclusion to our argument about Chip X could also be verified (i.e., determined to be either true or false) independent of the evidence provided in the argument's premises. Since the conclusion contains a statement that is descriptive, or empirical (i.e., capable of being observed through sensory experience), the truth or falsity of the conclusion could be resolved in this case simply by going to Japan to see whether such a chip was actually being developed there.

However, not all arguments have empirical or descriptive statements as their conclusions. Suppose that a friend wants to convince you that Internet users should be allowed to write a blog on how to build a bomb. (Note that this is a normative claim because it includes the word "should"; you may want to consult the distinction we drew in Chapter 1 between normative and descriptive claims.) Further, suppose that his reason for holding this view is based on the principle that people are allowed to write books on how to build bombs, and authors of blogs should have the same rights and freedoms as authors of books. And suppose your friend bases his reasoning for this claim on the right of authors to express themselves as guaranteed in the First Amendment of the United States Constitution. His argument could be constructed as follows:

> **PREMISE 1.** A person's right to author a book on how to build a bomb is protected by the First Amendment (of the U.S. Constitution).
>
> **PREMISE 2.** Authoring a book is similar to authoring a blog on the Internet.
>
> **CONCLUSION.** A person's right to author a blog on how to build a bomb ought to be protected by the First Amendment.

Notice how this argument differs from the preceding one. For one thing, we can't simply go to Japan to determine whether this conclusion is true or false. For another, the conclusion contains a normative statement (one that includes "ought"). Unlike the previous argument, which contained a descriptive statement in its conclusion that could be verified independent of the argument, we now depend on the *form of reasoning* alone to help us determine whether the conclusion is true. In doing this, we will *assume* that the premises in this argument are true and then ask whether the conclusion would logically follow from them.

Initially, the reasoning in this argument might seem plausible: the person constructing the argument cleverly uses an analogy based on a legal right that applies in physical space. So, we might assume that any legal rights that citizens enjoy in physical space should automatically be extended to cyberspace.

In this argument, we are also asked to consider certain features or characteristics that are common to both (printed) books and blogs. Clearly, we can draw a number of analogies here. For example, both books and blogs can communicate and disseminate information to readers; each is authored by one or more persons; and so forth. However, there is a danger in pushing some of these analogies too far: Whereas traditional books are tangible items existing in physical space, blogs are not. And the scope of a blog allows it to be accessed by members of the international community, some of whom may have no access to physical books or may lack sufficient funds to purchase such books. We now begin to see dissimilarities between books and blogs, so we must be cautious about drawing conclusions when reasoning by analogy. Later in this chapter, we will see why arguments of this kind are not valid. First, however, we consider some strategies for constructing arguments.

▶ 3.2 CONSTRUCTING AN ARGUMENT

Think of some situations in which arguments are used by those in powerful positions, as well as by ordinary persons. Lawyers, for example, use arguments to try to persuade juries; and politicians often use arguments to convey their positions to their constituencies. All of us use arguments when we try to convince a friend, a spouse, or a boss about some point or other. If you try to convince your parents that they should buy you a new iPod, for example, you will most likely be making an argument of some sort. Ultimately, arguments will succeed or not succeed depending on (a) how well they are constructed and (b) how strong their reasoning forms are. We refer to (b) as *argument strength*, and we examine that concept in Section 3.3 in our discussion of valid vs. invalid arguments. In this section, we focus on how arguments are constructed.

Arguments often appear as editorials in newspapers and periodicals where they are sometimes expressed in prose forms that can obscure the argument, making it difficult to isolate and analyze. When this happens we must locate the arguments concealed in the text before we can analyze them. Consider the political debate over the need for a new national missile defense (NMD) system, which has been controversial from both a domestic and an international perspective. A fairly straightforward argument in favor of NMD in the editorial section of a newspaper might look something like the following:

> We must build a national missile defense system because without such a system we are vulnerable to nuclear attacks from rogue nations that might arise in the future. Engineers and computer scientists have testified that they can design a computer-guided missile defense system that is effective, safe, and reliable. It is our obligation as Americans to take whatever measures we can to protect the safety of our citizens.

Before we analyze this argument, however, it is perhaps worth making a few parenthetical remarks about certain events leading up to NMD. The debate in the U.S. Congress over NMD that occurred during the George W. Bush administration can be viewed as an updated version of the earlier "Star Wars" debate, officially known as the Strategic Defense Initiative (or SDI). That debate, which took place during the Reagan administration in the 1980s, was significant for cyberethics because it was one of the first ethical controversies to catch the attention of a group of computer ethics pioneers.[3] We will examine some specific ethical issues pertaining to Star Wars and NMD of interest to computer professionals in Chapter 4. Our primary purpose in this chapter, however, is to consider the NMD controversy only insofar as it illustrates how logical arguments can be constructed and analyzed.

There has been strong support for NMD among many conservative politicians in the United States. As suggested above, a proponent of the NMD system could construct an argument for his or her case by first asserting that without such a new missile system, the United States is vulnerable to future attacks from potential "rogue" nations that might acquire nuclear weapons. The proponent might next want to assure us that there is sufficient and compelling evidence that such a missile defense system would be safe and reliable. Finally, the NMD supporter might assume the following principle: "We must do whatever is necessary to preserve the safety of America and its people." The structure of the proponent's argument can be represented as follows:

PREMISE 1. Without the NMD, the United States is vulnerable to nuclear attacks in the future from rogue nations.

PREMISE 2. Computer scientists and engineers have testified before Congress that they can design a computer-guided missile defense system that is both safe and reliable.

PREMISE 3. The United States must do whatever is necessary to preserve the military defense of the nation and the safety of its citizens.

CONCLUSION. The United States should build the NMD.

So far, we have considered only the structure of this argument. That is, we have described its two basic components—its premises and conclusion—and we have represented it in standard logical form. Now we ask: Is the reasoning used in the argument strong? Are there rules that will enable us to determine this? To answer these questions, we first need to understand the difference between valid and invalid arguments.

▶ 3.3 VALID ARGUMENTS

The first question we could ask about the sample argument described in the preceding section is whether its reasoning is strong or weak—that is, is the argument's reasoning *valid* or is it *invalid*? "Valid" and "invalid" are technical terms in logic. Whereas claims (the individual statements that make up an argument) are either true or false, arguments will be either valid or invalid; it is incorrect to refer to an argument as either true or false, and it is incorrect to refer to a claim as either valid or invalid.

How can we determine whether a particular argument is valid or invalid? In formal systems of logic, elaborate schemes that consist of symbols, rules, and tables have been constructed for determining when arguments are valid or invalid. Alternatively, however, some "informal" systems of logic, such as the system developed by John Nolt (2002), also enable us to accomplish this task. Nolt's system does not require that we know anything about the *actual* truth or falsity of the claims in an argument's premise(s) in order to determine whether an argument is valid or invalid. Instead, we need only to determine whether the argument's conclusion would necessarily follow from its premises, when those premises are all *assumed* to be true.[4] In other words, we ask,

> Is the relationship between the premises and the conclusion such that if all of the premises in the argument are assumed true, it would be impossible for the conclusion to be false?

The concern here is with the relationship of truth conditions *vis-à-vis* the premises and the conclusion. The premises and the conclusion could be true or false (in the actual world) independent of each other, but that is not relevant for testing the argument's validity. We ask only whether the assumed truth of the premises is sufficient to guarantee the truth of the conclusion. If the answer is yes, then the argument is valid. If, however, it is logically possible for the argument's conclusion to be false at the same time that its premises are (assumed) true, then the argument is invalid.

You can apply this test for validity to the argument for the new national missile defense system that we considered above. Imagine that all of the argument's premises are true statements. Is it possible—that is, could you conceive of a possible instance such that—when those premises are true, the conclusion could still be false? Of course, the premises could be imagined to be false, and the conclusion could be imagined to be false as well. But the relevant questions here are: What happens when all of the premises are imagined to be true? Could the claim in the argument's conclusion (i.e., "The United States should build the new NMD.") be false, even when Premises 1–3 are assumed true? The answer is yes. Hence, the argument is invalid.

The Counterexample Strategy

To show that an argument is invalid, all we need to do is to produce one *counterexample* to the argument. A counterexample is

> a logically possible case in which the argument's conclusion could be imagined to be false while (at the same time) the argument's premises are assumed true.[5]

In the NMD argument, we can coherently imagine a logically possible situation (i.e., a situation that does not involve a logical contradiction) where the conclusion "The United States should build the new NMD" is false when the claims stated in Premises 1–3 are assumed true. For example, we can imagine a situation or case in which all three premises are true but some alternative strategy not involving the development of a new missile defense system could provide for the safety of America. So a counterexample is possible; thus the argument is invalid.

Note, however, although this particular argument has been shown to be invalid, it does not follow that the argument's conclusion is, in fact, false. All that has been shown is that the argument is invalid because the form of reasoning it uses does not succeed in guaranteeing that the conclusion must be true. It is still possible, of course, that the conclusion could be true. But a different argument would need to be constructed to show that the inference is valid.

Suppose we added a fourth premise, "The new NMD system is necessary to preserve the defense and safety of the United States and its citizens," to the argument. The amended argument would be as follows:

PREMISE 1. Without the NMD, the United States is vulnerable to nuclear attacks in the future from rogue nations.

PREMISE 2. Computer scientists and engineers have testified before Congress that they can design a computer-guided missile defense system that is both safe and reliable.

PREMISE 3. The United States must do whatever is necessary to preserve the military defense of the nation and the safety of its citizens.

PREMISE 4. The new NMD system is necessary to preserve the defense and safety of the United States and its citizens.

CONCLUSION. The United States should build the NMD.

This argument would now be valid. If all of its premises are assumed true, then the conclusion cannot be false. Of course, we could next ask whether all of the premises in this argument are in fact true. Premises 1 and 2 are fairly uncontroversial claims, though Premise 2 might be challenged by programmers who believe that building a completely

Arguments

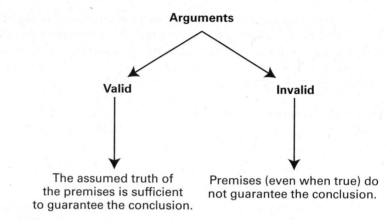

Valid

The assumed truth of
the premises is sufficient
to guarantee the conclusion.

Invalid

Premises (even when true) do
not guarantee the conclusion.

Figure 3.1 Valid and invalid arguments.

reliable computer system is not possible. However, both Premises 3 and 4 are controversial: Premise 4 can be shown to be false if it can be demonstrated that the United States could be adequately protected without the newly proposed missile defense system; Premise 3, which is a normative statement, can also be shown to be false if, for instance, we can provide an exception to the principle included in it. For one thing, we could ask both whether indeed the United States *must* do whatever is necessary to make the United States safe and what exactly we mean by the phrase "whatever is necessary"? For example, what if making the United States safe entailed closing down all systems of transportation, all government offices, and all schools for an indefinite period of time that could go on for years? It might protect U.S. citizens but would it be an acceptable alternative? And U.S. citizens might be willing to make trade-offs rather than shut down major institutions essential to their day-to-day lives. So Premise 3, as stated, is also false. However, even if all of the premises are eventually shown to be false, the argument itself is still valid because its conclusion follows from the premises if they are assumed true.

Figure 3.1 illustrates the basic distinction between valid and invalid arguments.

Next consider the following argument:

PREMISE 1. People who own iMac's are smarter than those who own PCs.

PREMISE 2. My roommate owns an iMac.

PREMISE 3. I own a PC.

CONCLUSION. My roommate is smarter than me.

This argument meets all of the criteria for validity: *if* all three of the premises in this argument are assumed true, then the conclusion ("My roommate is smarter than me.") must be true. In other words, no counterexample to this argument's reasoning form is possible. However, the argument's validity alone is not sufficient to establish that the argument succeeds in the final analysis (as we will see in the following sections). It only shows that when all of the premises are assumed true, the conclusion would also be true.

This argument, like all valid arguments, is valid by virtue of its *logical form*; an argument's logical form, not its content, determines its validity and invalidity. An example of a valid logical form is as follows:

PREMISE 1. Every A is a B.

PREMISE 2. C is an A.

CONCLUSION. C is a B.

Any argument that has this form is valid, regardless of the content represented by A, B, or C. As long as the premises "Every A is a B" and "C is an A" are both assumed true, there is no way that the conclusion "C is a B" could be coherently conceived to be false. Even if the two premises in this particular argument turn out to be false in the actual world, the argument continues to be valid by virtue of its logical form.

We can now see that it is important to separate two distinct questions:

a. What is the *strength of reasoning* of the argument (i.e., is it valid or invalid)?

b. Are the argument's premises true in the actual world?

To say that an argument is valid does not necessarily mean that its premises are true in the actual world. An argument can be valid in terms of its logical form and yet still be unsound. One more step is required for an argument to qualify as a *sound argument*. To be sound, all of the premises (included in the valid argument) must be true in the real world, and not merely assumed true as in the case of the test for validity. For information on how to determine whether a statement is true or false, see Appendix G, available at www.wiley.com/college/tavani.

▶ 3.4 SOUND ARGUMENTS

To assume that the premises of an argument are true is an important first step in the process of evaluating arguments, because doing so enables us to determine the logical relationship between the argument's premise(s) and conclusion and thus determine the argument's strength of reasoning. The reasoning strength will be one of either validity or invalidity. If we can produce one counterexample by showing a possible case where the argument's conclusion can be false even when all of its premises are assumed true, we have shown the argument to be invalid. If the argument is shown to be invalid, we can stop here for the time being. To show that the argument was valid, all that we had to do was to show that no counterexample was possible. And to do that, we considered the hypothetical or assumed truth of the argument's premises vis-à-vis the argument's conclusion. If the argument is valid, then we must determine if it is sound by going on to the next step, where we test the premises to see whether they are true or false in the actual world.

Consider again the two arguments in the preceding section: one involving an NMD system, and the other involving the intelligence of iMac users. Both arguments were shown to be valid. (The argument defending the need for an NMD system had to be modified, but once we modified it, it met the criteria for validity.) We can now further examine each argument to see if it is also sound. An argument will be sound if (a) the argument is valid and (b) all of the premises are actually true (and not merely assumed to be true).

First consider the NMD system. If one or more of Premises 1–4 are false, then the argument will be unsound. Premise 3, "The United States must do whatever is necessary to preserve the military defense of the nation and the safety of its citizens," is clearly questionable. Surely, the goal of national defense is one of the highest priorities of a political administration. But we have already seen that the phrase "whatever is necessary" is problematic. For example, would such a principle give the United States government the right to use *any* means that it happened to deem necessary to bring about some desired end?

Suppose some government officials believed that it was necessary to put all non-United States citizens under house arrest? Or suppose that some of those officials believed that all United States citizens should be subject to constant search and seizure, both within and outside their homes? Would these measures be acceptable? Perhaps under the most severe and dire circumstances some proposals of this type might seem plausible. But it is still not exactly clear that such drastic measures would be necessary. So Premise 3 in the missile defense argument cannot be confirmed to be true, even if Premises 1, 2, and 4 can. Thus, this argument is not sound even though it is valid. Because it is unsound, the argument does not succeed. However, once again we should be careful to note that even when an argument is unsound, or even when it is invalid, it does not necessarily follow that the argument's conclusion is false. Rather, we can only infer that the evidence given, that is, the particular premises used to support the argument's conclusion, is not adequate because (when used alone) the premises fail to meet certain logical requirements.

Returning to the argument involving claims about the intelligence of iMac users, we saw that when we assume the truth of all three premises of that argument, the conclusion cannot be imagined to be false; hence the argument is valid. But is it also sound? We need to examine each premise in more detail. Premises 2 and 3—"My roommate owns an iMac computer" and "I own a PC," respectively—are relatively easy to verify because both are descriptive claims. To see if they are true or false, we simply go to the dormitory room or to the apartment where my roommate and I live and observe whether my roommate indeed owns an iMac computer and whether I own a PC.

Premise 1—"People who own iMac computers are smarter than those who own PCs"—however, is more controversial and hence more difficult to verify than the other premises. Clearly, more evidence would be needed to show that Premise 1 is true; in fact, it certainly seems suspect. So despite the fact that the argument is valid by virtue of its logical form, we cannot yet say that it is sound. Thus the argument would appear, at best, to be not sound, but inconclusive.

As you might suspect, sound arguments are not very common, and often they are about matters that are either trivial or uncontroversial. Consider the following argument:

PREMISE 1. CEOs of major computer corporations are high-school graduates.

PREMISE 2. Bill Gates was the CEO of a major computer corporation.

CONCLUSION. Bill Gates is a high-school graduate.

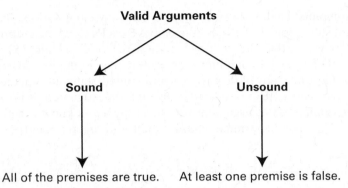

Figure 3.2 Sound and unsound (valid) arguments.

This argument is clearly valid because no counterexample can be constructed; that is, there is no possible case where Premises 1 and 2 could both be (assumed) true and the conclusion could be false at the same time. As it turns out, the premises are also true in the actual world, so this argument is sound; however, it is also not terribly informative. Perhaps you can now see why there are so few sound arguments that are also informative: relatively few valid arguments are sound, and relatively few sound arguments are informative or nontrivial.

Figure 3.2 illustrates the basic differences between valid arguments that are sound and those that are unsound.

At this point, you might ask, what good is a valid argument if it contains false premises? You might also wonder whether certain types of invalid arguments whose premises are true in the actual world are stronger than valid arguments that contain one or more false premises.

► 3.5 INVALID ARGUMENTS

Consider the following argument:

> **PREMISE 1.** All CEOs of major United States computer corporations have been United States citizens.
>
> **PREMISE 2.** Steve Jobs was a United States citizen.
>
> **CONCLUSION.** Steve Jobs was a CEO of a major computer corporation in the United States.

Even though all three of the claims included in this argument (i.e., the two premises and the conclusion) are true in the actual world, we can show that this argument is invalid by producing at least one counterexample. We can imagine a possible case where the premises in this argument are both true, but the conclusion—(the late) Steve Jobs was the CEO of a major computer corporation—is false. For example, we can imagine that he had been a consultant or a programmer, or he could have been employed outside the computer field. However, there is an even more serious flaw in this argument: If we substitute for "Steve Jobs" the names Sara Palin, Michael Jordan, Julia Roberts, or Brad Pitt, we see that although each of these persons is a United States citizen, none has been a CEO of a major computer corporation. Yet by the logic used in the argument, it would follow that if any of these people is a United States citizen, then he or she must also be or have been a CEO. We have shown that this argument is invalid. If you noticed that the reasoning in this argument was weak, now you know exactly why.

We next determine whether the following argument is valid or invalid:

PREMISE 1. Most CEOs of major computer corporations are college graduates.

PREMISE 2. Steve Ballmer is the CEO of a major computer corporation.

CONCLUSION. Steve Ballmer is a college graduate.

Notice that all of the statements included in this argument happen to be true in the real world. But is the reasoning valid? Clearly not! All we need is one counterexample to show why. If we substitute the name "Bill Gates" for "Steve Ballmer," the present CEO of Microsoft, the premises of the argument remain true but the conclusion is false. The argument is invalid, but because the premises are true, this particular invalid argument is stronger overall than either of the two arguments we considered that were valid but unsound. Overall argument strength, as opposed to an argument's strength of reasoning, takes into account the actual truth condition of the argument's premises. We saw that an argument's strength of reasoning is concerned only with the hypothetical or assumed truth of those premises.

▶ 3.6 INDUCTIVE ARGUMENTS

Not all invalid arguments are necessarily weak arguments; in fact, some are quite strong. Hence, we should not automatically discard every invalid argument simply because it is not valid. Some invalid arguments are *inductive*. Although inductive arguments do not necessarily guarantee the truth of their conclusions in the way that valid arguments do, inductive arguments nonetheless provide a high degree of probability for their conclusions. Those invalid arguments that are not inductive are fallacious arguments; we will discuss them in the next section. In this section, we describe the criteria that must be satisfied for an argument to be inductive.

Let's determine the strength of reasoning of the following argument:

PREMISE 1. Seventy-five percent of people who own iPods also own iMacs.

PREMISE 2. My roommate owns an iPod.

CONCLUSION. My roommate owns an iMac.

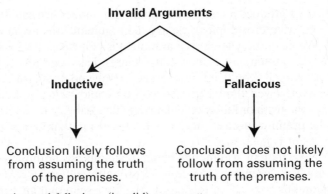

Figure 3.3 Inductive and fallacious (invalid) arguments.

Based on the technique discussed earlier in this chapter, we can see that this argument is not valid: a counterexample to the argument is possible. For instance, we can assume that both premises are true while the conclusion ("My roommate owns an iMac computer") is false. There is no contradiction in doing this since my roommate could be among the 25% of people who currently own iPods but who never owned iMacs. So the argument is clearly invalid.

This argument and the argument in the preceding section designed to show that Bill Gates is the CEO of a major computer corporation are both invalid, but they are different in their strength of reasoning. The argument that tried to show that Gates must be or have been a CEO because "Gates is a United States citizen" and "all CEOs of major computer corporations have been United States citizens" has weak reasoning. On the other hand, the form of reasoning used in the argument to show that my roommate owns an iMac computer is much stronger. In fact, the conclusion ("My roommate owns an iMac computer") is *very likely* to be true when we assume the truth of both premises. Hence this (invalid) argument is inductive.

As suggested above, some inductive arguments, although invalid, can be stronger-overall than some valid arguments. But how is that possible? We have seen examples of valid arguments that contained premises that were false in the actual world. Inductive arguments consisting of premises that are all true in the actual world are generally stronger than arguments that are valid but unsound. As you consider the various arguments involving privacy, free speech, security, etc., in Chapters 4–9, determine which ones meet the criteria of being inductive with all true premises. Such arguments will be much more successful in establishing their positions (i.e., they will be much stronger) than will deductive arguments that contain one or more false premises.

Figure 3.3 illustrates the basic differences between invalid arguments that are inductive and invalid arguments that are fallacious.

▶ 3.7 FALLACIOUS ARGUMENTS

Recall the argument that we examined in Section 3.5 to show that Bill Gates was the CEO of a major corporation. All of the statements or claims in that particular argument were true in the actual world, so the argument might have seemed fairly strong. Yet, because we could produce a counterexample (and, in fact, we saw that we could easily produce several counterexamples), clearly the argument was invalid.

We next ask whether the argument is inductive or fallacious. That is, how likely is it that the argument's conclusion, "Gates has been the CEO of a major computer corporation," would be true based simply on the assumed truth of the argument's premises? Even though the conclusion could be true—and even though it is, in fact, true—the truth or falsity would have to be established on grounds other than those given in the premises used to support the conclusion that Gates has been a CEO. Hence this argument is *fallacious*.

Note that an argument's being fallacious has nothing to do with the actual truth or falsity of its premises, so you have probably noticed a certain irony with respect to an argument's strength of reasoning. We have seen that an argument can be valid and yet contain one or more false premises and a false conclusion; and, conversely, an argument can be fallacious despite the fact that all of its premises as well as its conclusion could be true.

Next, consider an argument in which someone tries to convince you that Internet users should not expect to retain their privacy when they engage in online activities, because the Internet is essentially a public forum or public space. Expressed in standard form, the argument reads:

PREMISE. The Internet is in public space.

CONCLUSION. Those who use the Internet should not expect to retain any personal privacy.

When we evaluate this argument's strength of reasoning, that is, whether it is valid or invalid, we first ask if a counterexample can be produced. Let us assume that the premise—The Internet is in public space—is true. We next ask: Is it possible for that statement to be true, and for the conclusion (Internet users cannot expect to retain their privacy) to be false, at the same time? The answer is "yes." For example, a person's backpack can be in public space, yet its owner enjoys some expectation of privacy regarding the contents enclosed in the backpack. So a counterexample can be produced, and the argument is invalid. We can next ask whether the argument is inductive or fallacious. In the argument's current form, the conclusion does not likely follow from the premise, even when that premise is assumed true. So the argument is fallacious.

Also recall an argument that we examined in Chapter 1 for the view that at least some ethical issues involving cybertechnology must be unique. The argument had the following form:

PREMISE 1. Cybertechnology has some unique technological features.
PREMISE 2. Cybertechnology has generated some ethical concerns.

CONCLUSION. Some ethical concerns generated by cybertechnology must be unique ethical concerns.

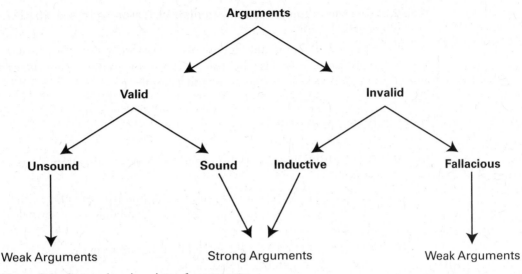

Figure 3.4 Comprehensive view of arguments.

You can no doubt see why this argument is fallacious. First, we construct a counter-example to show the argument is invalid; that is, we can imagine a case where both premises are true, but the conclusion is false. For example, we can imagine some ethical concern generated by the use of cybertechnology to be simply a variation of a traditional ethical problem that is neither not new or unique. Furthermore, we can construct a range of possible cases where both premises are assumed true, but the conclusion could be false. (In fact, in the majority of such cases, the conclusion would not likely be true merely because of what is assumed to be true in the premises). As we noted in Chapter 1, this argument wrongly assumes that a characteristic that applies to the technology—viz., uniqueness—must also apply to the ethical issues generated by this technology. Of course, it is possible that some cyberethics issues may turn out to be unique ethical issues. But if that happens, it is not because of the evidence supplied in the premises of the above argument.

In Section 3.9, we will examine some "informal logical fallacies" that tend to recur in everyday reasoning. There, we will also examine techniques for spotting some of the more common fallacies, or "fallacy types," that occur in ordinary discourse. These techniques do not require the counterexample strategy that we used to distinguish invalid from valid arguments. First, however, we include a scheme that summarizes the techniques we have used so far to differentiate among valid and invalid, sound and unsound, and inductive and fallacious arguments.

Figure 3.4 presents an overview of the different kinds of argument forms that we have examined in this chapter.

▶ 3.8 A SEVEN-STEP STRATEGY FOR EVALUATING ARGUMENTS

The following strategy, which consists of seven steps, summarizes the techniques we used in Sections 3.3–3.7 to evaluate an argument's overall strength of reasoning:

Step 1. Convert the argument into standard form. (List the premises, followed by the conclusion.)

Step 2. Test the argument for its strength of reasoning to see whether it is valid or invalid.

Strategy: Assume the premises to be true, and ask yourself whether the conclusion must also be true when those premises are assumed true. Is a counterexample to the argument possible?

Step 3. Is the argument valid?

If yes, go to Step 4.

If no, go to Step 5.

Step 4. Is the (valid) argument also sound? That is, are the premises true in the actual world?

Strategy: To determine whether a claim is true or false in the actual world, see the guidelines in Appendix G (available at www.wiley.com/college/tavani).

a. If the argument is valid and if all of the premises are true in the actual world, then the argument is also sound.

b. If the argument is valid, but one or more premises can be shown to be false, then the argument is unsound. (Note that if one or more premises are unable to be verified, i.e., determined to be either true or false, then the overall argument is inconclusive.)

Step 5. Is the (invalid) argument inductive or fallacious?

Strategy: To determine this, ask how likely the conclusion would be true when the premises are assumed true.

a. If the conclusion would likely be true because the premises are assumed true (i.e., the evidence for the conclusion is strong), the argument is inductive.

b. If the conclusion would not likely be true even when the premises are assumed true, the argument is fallacious.

Note: Keep in mind that a fallacious argument can be made up of individual claims or statements that are themselves true in the actual world.

Step 6. Determine whether the premises in your argument are either true or false in the actual world.

Strategy: Consult the guidelines for determining the truth or falsity of statements in Appendix G, available at www.wiley.com/college/tavani.

Step 7. Make an overall assessment of the argument by determining both (a) the argument's strength of reasoning (valid, inductive, or fallacious) *and* (b) the truth conditions of each of the argument's premises.

Strategy: Determine, for example, whether the argument's overall strength is

- sound
- valid but unsound
- inductive with all true premises,
- inductive with some false premises,

- fallacious with a mixture of true and false premises,
- some other combination.

Remember that an inductive argument with premises that are all true can be stronger overall than a valid argument with one or more false premises, which will be (valid but) unsound.

We next apply the seven-step strategy to the argument included in Scenario 3–1, at the beginning of this chapter. Applying Step 1, we convert the argument into standard form (which, in this case, it already happens to be presented):

> **PREMISE 1.** Downloading proprietary software (without permission from the copyright holder) is identical to stealing physical property.
>
> **PREMISE 2.** Stealing physical property is morally wrong.
>
> **CONCLUSION.** Downloading proprietary software (without permission) is morally wrong.

At Step 2, we examine the argument's strength of reasoning and determine that the argument is valid because if we assume the truth of both its premises (Premises 1 and 2), the conclusion cannot be false (i.e., the combination of true premises and false conclusion in this example would be a logical contradiction). Having determined that the argument is valid (Step 3), we next go to Step 4 and ask whether it is sound or unsound. Whereas Premise 2 is a true statement (and is easily verifiable), the truth or falsity of Premise 1 is less clear cut. Although there would certainly seem to be a strong analogy between stealing physical property and downloading unauthorized software, there are also some disanalogies. Thus, the two behaviors are not, strictly speaking at least, "identical." (We examine this and some other disanalogies in Chapter 8 in our discussion of intellectual property.) So, Premise 1 may be either false or indeterminate (i.e., it is not literally true, as stated), and we now see that this argument is *unsound*.

However, the argument is still valid; so we can skip Step 5, which applies only to invalid arguments. At Step 6, we note that both Premise 2 and the conclusion are true, while Premise 1 may be either false or indeterminate (since it is not literally true). So our overall evaluation of this argument, at Step 7, is: *valid but unsound*. Here, we note that the conclusion happens to be true, even though its truth is not logically supported by the argument's premises.

The seven-step strategy is a useful tool for evaluating a wide range of arguments. However, we should note that some less formal techniques are also available for spotting fallacious arguments that commonly occur in ordinary, everyday reasoning. In the next section we will see that there is an informal, and arguably simpler, way of identifying and cataloging many logical fallacies that frequently appear in everyday discourse.

▶ 3.9 IDENTIFYING SOME COMMON FALLACIES

Contrary to what many people assume, "fallacy" does not mean false statement; rather, it means *faulty reasoning*. As we saw in Section 3.6, it is possible for an argument to contain all true statements and still be fallacious. (We also saw that an argument can contain all false statements and still be valid, solely by virtue of its logical form.)

At this point, you might be unsure about your ability to recognize a fallacious argument without using the counterexample strategy described in this chapter or without applying some of the more sophisticated rules that comprise formal systems of logic. Because so many fallacies appear in everyday reasoning, logicians have categorized them in ways that are convenient for us to recognize. We refer to these kinds of fallacious arguments as *informal logical fallacies*.

The following ten informal fallacies, or "fallacy types," each illustrated with one or more examples involving computers and cybertechnology, are typical of fallacious arguments that surface time and again in ordinary everyday discourse.

3.9.1 *Ad Hominem* Argument

In the *ad hominem* argument, an attack is directed at the person rather than the substance of the person's argument. For example, imagine that the late Senator Ted Kennedy had opposed a bill before Congress that supported the construction of a controversial national missile defense system (we saw an argument for this view in Section 3.2). Further suppose that Kennedy opposed the bill even though its passage would have meant thousands of new jobs for computer professionals in Massachusetts. Next imagine that a proponent of this legislation, Senator Smith, offered the following objection to Kennedy's position:

> How can we take seriously a position regarding the future of our national defense that has been proposed by a senator who has been arrested for drunken driving and who has been involved in extramarital affairs?

What is wrong with Senator Smith's attack, and why does the reasoning used in it commit a logical fallacy? Note that Senator Smith did not attack the merits or weaknesses of Kennedy's position on the national missile defense system; rather he attacked the personal character of the senator. Even if Kennedy's personal character was questionable, that point was irrelevant to whether the bill he opposed should be passed or defeated, or whether it was a well-conceived piece of legislation or one that was ill-founded. Unfortunately, the debate over the merits or deficiencies of the bill could be cut short, or at least temporarily derailed, because of the *ad hominem* attack.

One might object that if Kennedy's character had been attacked in this scenario because of allegations that were made against him on different grounds—e.g., a charge that he had sold secrets to foreign governments—then the personal attack against Kennedy might have been justified. Although national security-related allegations might have greater relevance in the argument as to why Kennedy's position on the missile defense system debate should not have been taken seriously, the argument would still be fallacious because the attack fails to focus on the merits of the issues being debated; instead it focuses on a person's character.

3.9.2 Slippery Slope Argument

The slippery slope argument has the form, "X could possibly be abused; therefore, we should not allow X." For example, one might argue:

We should not continue to allow computer manufacturers to build computer systems that include CD burners. If we allow them to do so, young users will burn copies of copyrighted music illegally. If the rate of unauthorized copying of music continues, recording artists will lose more money. If they lose more money, the entire music industry could be in jeopardy. If the music industry in America declines, the entire U.S. economy will suffer. So, we must prohibit computer manufacturers from providing CD burners as part of the computer systems they build.

It should be fairly easy to spot the fallacy here: The author assumes that allowing computer manufacturers to continue to include CD burners as part of their computer systems will inevitably lead to an abusive slippery slope that logically implies a downturn in the overall U.S. economy. It is certainly possible that in the future, the U.S. economy does experience a downturn while computer manufacturers continue to produce computers with CD burners. And it may well be that some users abuse CD burners to make unauthorized copies of music. However, any claim that the bad economy was an inevitable result of the use of CD burners in computers cannot be substantiated merely in terms of the evidence provided in the above argument.

3.9.3 Fallacy of Appeal to Authority

Arguments that conform to the fallacy of authority (*argumentum ad vericundiam*) have the following form:

PREMISE 1. X is an authority in field Y.
PREMISE 2. X said Z.

CONCLUSION. Z.

As an example, imagine that Tim Berners-Lee, who designed the HTTP protocol that became the standard for the World Wide Web, has agreed to do an advertisement for Twitter, a social networking service (SNS). Further imagine that someone draws the following inference from the ad:

Tim Berners-Lee believes that Twitter is superior to SNSs such as Facebook and MySpace. And Berners-Lee is clearly an expert on matters involving the Web and the Internet. So, Twitter must be superior to alternative SNSs such as Facebook and MySpace.

Can you spot the fallacy here? It is true that Berners-Lee is an expert on Web design; it may also be true that Twitter is superior to alternative SNSs (e.g., in certain respects). However, is the argument's conclusion that Twitter is superior to Facebook and other SNSs, even if true, warranted by the premises? Simply because Berners-Lee wrote the code that became the standard protocol for the World Wide Web, and thus is an expert on some matters involving the Web, does that make him an authority on SNSs?

3.9.4 False Cause Fallacy

The false cause argument (*post hoc ergo propter hoc*—after this, therefore because of this) reasons from the fact that event X preceded event Y to the conclusion that event X is necessarily the cause of event Y. Consider the following argument about the Microsoft's Windows 7 operating system:

> Shortly after the release of the Microsoft Windows 7 operating system in 2009, Microsoft's stock plummeted severely. Hence, there is no doubt that the release of Windows 7 is responsible for the decline in Microsoft's loss in the stock market.

Can you identify the fallacy in the above argument? Even though it might be tempting to attribute Microsoft's decline in the price of its stock to the release of the Windows 7 operating system, the person making this argument has overlooked the possibility of other factors that might have caused this decline. For example, maybe there were factors in the economy in 2009 that affected all high tech stock prices, or maybe there were overall declines in the market during that year.

3.9.5 Begging the Question

An argument commits the fallacy of begging the question when its premise(s) presuppose the truth of the conclusion it is trying to establish. In such a case, the reasoning is circular. Consider the following argument:

> Object-oriented programming (OOP) languages are superior to nonstructured programming languages because OOP languages are structured.

Why is this reasoning fallacious? Here the author of the argument has reasoned in a circle—instead of establishing that OOP languages are superior, the author assumes that to be the case; that is, the truth of the premise presupposes the truth of the conclusion, rather than supplying evidence for the conclusion.

3.9.6 Fallacy of Composition/Fallacy of Division

The fallacy of composition confuses the characteristics that apply to the parts of a whole, or to the individual members of a group, with the characteristics of the whole itself. For example, consider the following form of reasoning:

> The new XYZ desktop computer is the best system on the market. XYZ has the fastest processor currently available on any PC, it comes with twice the amount of RAM than any of its competitors, and it comes equipped with a suite of office applications that are superior to those on any currently available system. Also, its monitor has the best resolution and graphic display currently available on any commercial desktop computer.

Here the fallacy should be obvious. Each of the components of this desktop computer is the best that is currently available. However, it clearly does not follow that the system will necessarily be the best one available. The connections between the various parts of this system might not be well designed; we are not told how reliable the computer system is vis-à-vis its competitors. These kinds of flaws are apparent in all argument forms that commit the fallacy of composition. A film that has the best cast (Tom Hanks, Julia Roberts), one of the best directors (Steven Spielberg), and one of the best soundtrack composers (John Williams) might still be a flop. The quality of the individual parts does not necessarily guarantee the same quality in the overall product.

Next consider the flip side of this fallacy: the fallacy of division. The fallacy of division mistakenly infers that the same attributes or characteristics that apply to the whole or to the group must also apply to every part of the whole or to every member of the group. See if you can spot the fallacy in the following argument:

> Harvard University is the highest-ranked university in the U.S. Thus, Harvard must have the nation's best computer science department.

Does the conclusion to the above argument follow from its premise? Clearly not! Harvard might be ranked first overall among universities in the United States, but the possibility remains that MIT, Stanford University, or some other institution has the nation's highest-ranked computer science department.

3.9.7 Fallacy of Ambiguity/Equivocation

Fallacious reasoning can occur whenever one or more terms are used either ambiguously or equivocally; ambiguous terms have more than one interpretation, and it is not always clear which interpretation the author intends. A term is used equivocally, on the contrary, when it has two (or more) different senses or meanings. Consider the following argument:

> Humans can think, and highly-sophisticated AI (artificial intelligence) computer systems can think; therefore, highly-sophisticated AI computer systems are human.

In this case, it is possible that both premises are true in the actual world. However, the sense in which AI computer systems are said to think is not necessarily the same sense in which humans, in fact, think. Here, the term "think" is used equivocally. So even if it is true that computers can think in one sense of that term, it doesn't necessarily follow that computers can think in the same sense that humans do. Even if computers and humans could both think in the same sense, it doesn't follow that computers must be human. Consider that some animals, such as orangutans, do many things in ways that are similar to humans, yet we do not infer that orangutans are humans. (One might object to the above argument being called a fallacy by noting that if thinking is defined as something that only humans could do, then, by definition, computers (that "think") would have to be human. While this kind of move might avoid the fallacy of ambiguity/equivocation, it introduces other problems since the premise "computers can think" would now be more controversial and require further analysis.)

Another example of the fallacy of ambiguity/equivocation can be found in the following argument:

> Computers have memory. Humans have memory. Having memory enables humans to recall some of their childhood experiences. Therefore, computers can recall their childhood experiences.

Notice that "memory" is used in two different senses in the above argument.

Although both examples of the fallacy of ambiguity/equivocation illustrate exaggerated cases, which might seem implausible, we should note that many arguments used in everyday discourse commit variations of this fallacy.

3.9.8 Appeal to the People (Argumentum ad Populum)

Sometimes people appeal to the notion that there is strength in numbers. I remember once seeing a jacket to a record album that contained the following expression: "Fifty million Elvis fans can't be wrong." Does it follow that because Elvis Presley had fifty million fans, that those numbers alone were sufficient to prove that Elvis was a great recording artist? Are sheer numbers sufficient to establish this claim? Suppose that 150 million Americans believed that slavery was okay. Would that mean that slavery must be okay? The fallacy of the appeal to the people assumes that because X is popular, or because the majority of people agree with X, then X must be an acceptable standard. The following argument commits the fallacy of popular appeal.

> The majority of Americans believe that it is perfectly acceptable to share copyrighted music over the Internet. So, despite the objections of greedy entrepreneurs in the recording industry, peer-to-peer (P2P) networks such as LimeWire and Pirate Bay should be allowed to serve the wishes of the American people.

You should be able to spot the fallacy in this argument quite easily. Perhaps there are good reasons for why LimeWire should be allowed to operate as a site for downloading music. However, those reasons have not been well articulated in this argument. What if the majority of Americans believed that all software should be distributed free of charge, does it follow that it should? The appeal to popular opinion has been an effective strategy, and in a democracy there are cases where such an appeal is clearly warranted and appropriate. The fallacy, of course, is to assume that every kind of issue—especially those concerning moral questions—can be decided in terms of a popular referendum.

3.9.9 The Many/Any Fallacy

This fallacy assumes that because many things of a certain kind have a feature, anything of that kind has that feature. It has the following form:

PREMISE. Many items of a certain kind, A, have property B.

CONCLUSION. Any item of the kind A has B.

Clearly, many items of a certain kind can have a property B without all of them having B. Note that many intellectual-property-protection policies could be justifiable, but does it follow that any intellectual-property-protection policy is justifiable? Similarly, we can ask whether it follows from the fact that many sorting algorithms are efficient that *any* sorting algorithm is efficient. In his description of this fallacy, James Moor (2004) made the point that there are many acceptable ways to travel from Boston to Madrid. For example, one could travel to Madrid from Boston via flights connecting in London, Paris, Zurich, and so forth. However, it doesn't follow that any way of traveling between the two cities is acceptable. Consider that traveling from Boston to Madrid via the South Pole or even by way of Bangkok, Thailand would not be acceptable, at least not for most travelers.

Next, consider how a variation on this fallacy could arise in a discussion involving the use of programming languages to write a particular kind of software application. Theoretically, there are many programming languages—Basic, Algol60, Ada, Cobol-Script, Java, C++, and so forth—that *could* be used to write the code for a particular kind of software application, but it doesn't follow that any programming language can be used to write the code *efficiently*. While there might be legitimate disputes as to whether C++ or Java is better for writing a particular Internet application, most programmers would agree that for Internet applications either of these two languages is superior to Fortran or Cobol.

3.9.10 The Virtuality Fallacy

The *virtuality fallacy*, coined by James Moor, has the following form:

> **PREMISE 1.** X exists in cyberspace.
> **PREMISE 2.** Cyberspace is virtual.
>
> _____
>
> **CONCLUSION.** X (or the effect of X) is not real.[6]

Those who defend questionable forms of online behavior, such as launching viruses and engaging in unauthorized entries into computer systems, sometimes suggest that these activities cause no real harm to people. Some reason that because these activities are carried out in the virtual world, their effects are only virtual and thus not real. You should be able to spot the fallacy in this line of reasoning. Imagine that someone has posted an insulting remark about you on Facebook or some other online forum. Arguably, the locus of offense is in cyberspace, or virtual space, as opposed to real (physical) space. Does it follow that the particular harm caused to you is any less real than it would have been had it occurred in a physical setting? In Chapter 11, we examine some arguments used by members of virtual communities who reason that no real harm can result in these forums because they are only in virtual space. There, we will see how the virtuality fallacy applies.

We have considered some techniques for identifying fallacy types in ordinary language. The common fallacy types identified in this section represent only a small sample of those identified and labeled by logicians and philosophers. Yet all have one feature in common: their reasoning is so weak that even when the premises are assumed true, the conclusion would not likely be true because of the weak or insufficient evidence supporting it.

You can devise your own labels for some of the fallacious arguments we have encountered that have not yet been given names. For example, consider the fallacious argument we examined in Section 3.7 that tried to show that computer ethics issues must be unique because (a) computers have some unique technological features and (b) computers raise ethical issues. We could call this the "Computer Ethics is Unique Fallacy." Also consider the fallacy we examined earlier in this chapter, which reasoned that Internet users should have no expectation of personal privacy while they are online because the Internet is in public space. We could label this the "Privacy in Public Fallacy." You can no doubt come up with additional labels for fallacious arguments that you encounter in your analysis of cyberethics issues. (For the names of some standard logical fallacies not covered in this chapter, see http://yourlogicalfallacyis.com/.)

These techniques for spotting logical fallacies in ordinary, everyday discourse are useful in helping us to evaluate some of the arguments we will examine in the remaining chapters in this textbook. We should also note that some authors, including John Artz (2000), have suggested that "narrative reasoning" in the form of stories, as opposed to strict logical reasoning (even in the informal sense described in this chapter), can be very useful in helping us to understand and evaluate some cyberethics issues. However, we will not pursue this claim here, because the aim of Chapter 3 has been to show how conventional critical reasoning skills for analyzing informal logical arguments can be applied in the context of cyberethics.

▶ 3.10 CHAPTER SUMMARY

In this chapter, we considered some basic critical reasoning skills and we examined both the structure and the strength of logical arguments. We considered key criteria for differentiating among arguments that were valid and invalid, sound and unsound, and inductive and fallacious. We then considered a seven-step strategy for determining an argument's overall strength of reasoning. We also identified ten common fallacies, or "fallacy types," that illustrated flaws in reasoning in the context of cybertechnology and cyberethics; and we considered some techniques that will help us to spot additional informal logical fallacies that occur in everyday reasoning. In the remaining chapters of this textbook, we will see how the critical reasoning skills introduced in Chapter 3 can be used to evaluate arguments affecting many cyberethics disputes.

▶ REVIEW QUESTIONS

1. What is critical reasoning, and how can it be applied to ethical issues involving cybertechnology?
2. What is a logical argument, and how is it different from a claim or a statement?
3. Identify and briefly describe the two important characteristics or features of an argument?
4. What role or purpose do arguments play in helping us to resolve issues in cyberethics?
5. Describe the basic structure of an argument.
6. What is meant by "argument strength" (as opposed to argument structure)?
7. What is the essential difference between an argument that is valid and one that is invalid? Construct an example of each.
8. What is a counterexample, and how can it be used to show that an argument is invalid?
9. How is it possible for an argument to be valid but not successful?
10. What is required for an argument to be sound? Construct an example of a sound argument.
11. What is the main difference between invalid arguments that are inductive and invalid arguments that are fallacious? Construct an example of each.
12. What is an "informal logical fallacy"?

13. What is the *Ad Hominem Fallacy*? Provide an example of this fallacy in the context of cyberethics.
14. What is the *Slippery Slope Fallacy*? Provide an example of this fallacy in the context of cyberethics.
15. What is the *Fallacy of Appeal to Authority (Ad Vericundiam)*? Provide an example of this fallacy in the context of cyberethics.
16. What is the *False Cause Fallacy*? Provide an example of this fallacy in the context of cyberethics.
17. What is the difference between the *Fallacy of Composition* and the *Fallacy of Division*? Provide an example of each fallacy in the context of cyberethics.
18. What is the *Fallacy of Ambiguity/Equivocation*? Provide an example of this fallacy involving either an issue in cyberethics or an aspect of cybertechnology.
19. What is the *Fallacy of Appeal to the People (Ad Populum)*? Provide an example of this fallacy in the context of cyberethics.
20. What is the *Virtuality Fallacy*? Provide an example of this fallacy in the context of cyberethics.

▶ DISCUSSION QUESTIONS

21. Construct an argument for the view that your university should/should not have the right to monitor student e-mail. Next, analyze your argument to see if it is either valid or invalid. If it is valid, determine

whether it is also sound. If it is invalid, determine whether it is inductive or fallacious.

22. Identify some of the arguments that have been made on both sides in the debate about sharing copyrighted MP3 files on the Internet. Evaluate the arguments in terms of their strength of reasoning. Can you find any valid arguments? Can you find any inductive arguments?

▶ ESSAY/PRESENTATION QUESTIONS

23. Based on what you have learned in this chapter, construct an argument to support or to refute the view that all undergraduate students should be required to take a course in cyberethics. Next, apply the seven-step strategy (in Section 3.8) to your argument.

24. Construct an argument for the view that privacy protection should be improved for ordinary users who conduct searches on Google. Next evaluate your argument via the rules for validity vs. invalidity. If your argument is invalid, check to see if it also includes any of the informal fallacies we examined in Section 3.9.

Scenarios for Analysis

1. Apply the seven-step strategy (in Section 3.8) to your evaluation of the argument in the following scenario.

   A major association representing the music industry in the U.S. has determined that 4,000 copies of a new album featuring a popular rock group, called DUO, had been illegally downloaded last month. The cost of this album for those who download it legally from online music stores is $10 per copy. So the association concludes that the music company that holds the copyright to this album lost $40,000 dollars in revenue last month (on that album alone).

2. Determine whether the strength of reasoning used in the argument in the following scenario is valid or invalid. If it is invalid, does it commit any of the fallacies we examined in Section 3.9?

   You are engaged in an intense discussion with your friend, Bill, who works in the IT department at your university. Bill complains that many students are using P2P file-sharing applications on the university's network to download excessive amounts of unauthorized copyrighted material. He also claims that the most effective solution to this problem would be to disable student access to all (existing) P2P sites and to prevent students at your institution from setting up their own P2P sites for any reason whatsoever (even to include noncopyrighted material). You convey to Bill your belief that this measure is too drastic. However, Bill argues that the only way to eliminate unauthorized file sharing among students at your institution is to disable access to all P2P software on the university's network.

▶ ENDNOTES

1. Following Thomson (2009), Cederblom and Paulsen (2012), and others, I use the expression "critical reasoning" instead of "critical thinking" to describe the reasoning skills examined in this chapter. In my view, "critical thinking" has become far too broad a term, and it can now be interpreted to mean very different things in different academic disciplines. For our purposes, "critical reasoning" better captures the kind of precision and rigor required in the strategies and techniques used in this textbook to evaluate informal logical arguments.

2. Many ethics instructors now recognize the importance of rigorous critical reasoning skills for analyzing issues examined in ethics courses, and an increasing number of introductory ethics and applied ethics textbooks include a separate chapter on logical arguments and

critical reasoning. See, for example, Bowyer (2001), Vaughn (2008), and Waller (2008). See also Ruggiero (2007) who devotes an entire text to critical thinking in the context of ethics.

3. An analysis of issues and arguments surrounding the classic SDI controversy, as well as NMD, are included in Bowyer (2001, 2002) and Yurcik and Doss (2002).

4. Both the methodology and the terminology that I use for argument evaluation in Sections 3.3–37 closely follow a model of informal logic used by Nolt (2002). In those sections, I also include several examples from my (Wiley custom) textbook on reasoning (Tavani 2010).

5. This description of a counterexample closely follows the definition in Nolt.

6. Moor described this fallacy in a talk entitled "Just Consequentialism and Computing," at the *2000–2001 Humanities Lecture Series*, Rivier University, Nashua NH, February 2001.

► REFERENCES

Artz, John M. 2000. "Narrative vs. Logical Reasoning in Computer Ethics." In R. Baird, R. Ramsower, and S. Rosenbaum, eds. *Cyberethics: Social and Moral Issues in the Computer Age.* Amherst, NY: Prometheus, pp. 73–79.

Bowyer, Kevin W. 2001. *Ethics and Computing: Living in a Computerized World.* 2nd ed. New York: IEEE Press.

Bowyer, Kevin W. 2002. "Star Wars Revisited: Ethics and Safety Critical Software." *IEEE Technology and Society* 21, no. 1: 13–26.

Cederblom, Jerry, and David W. Paulsen. 2012. *Critical Reasoning: Understanding and Criticizing Arguments and Theories.* 7th ed. Boston, MA: Wadsworth.

Moor, James H. 2004. "Reason, Relativity, and Responsibility in Computer Ethics." In R. A. Spinello and H. T. Tavani, eds. *Readings in CyberEthics.* 2nd ed. Sudbury, MA: Jones and Bartlett, pp. 40–54.

Nolt, John E. 2002. *Informal Logic: Possible Worlds and Imagination.* New York: McGraw-Hill.

Ruggiero, Vincent R. 2007. *Thinking Critically About Ethical Issues.* 7th ed. New York: McGraw-Hill.

Tavani, Herman T. 2010. *The Elements of Reasoning: A Short Introduction to Informal Logic.* Hoboken, NJ: John Wiley and Sons (Custom Learning Solutions).

Thomson, Anne. 2009. *Critical Reasoning: A Practical Introduction.* 3rd ed. New York: Routledge.

Vaughn, Lewis. 2008. *Doing Ethics: Moral Reasoning and Contemporary Issues.* New York: W. W. Norton.

Waller, Bruce N. 2008. *Consider Ethics.* 2nd ed. New York: Pearson.

Yurcik, William, and David Doss. 2002. "Software Technology Issues for a U.S. National Missile Defense System." *IEEE Technology and Society Magazine* 21, no. 2: 36–46.

► FURTHER READINGS

Bergmann, Marie, James H. Moor, and Jack Nelson. *The Logic Book.* 5th ed. New York: McGraw-Hill, 2009.

Copi, Irving M., and Carl Cohen. *Introduction to Logic.* 14th ed. Upper Saddle River, NJ: Prentice Hall, 2011.

Hurley, Patrick. *A Concise Introduction to Logic.* 11th ed. Belmont, CA: Wadsworth Publishing, 2012.

Kahane, Howard, and Nancy Cavender. *Logic and Contemporary Rhetoric: The Use of Reason in Everyday Life.* 11th ed. Belmont, CA: Wadsworth Publishing, 2010.

Moore, Brooke Noel, and Richard Parker. *Critical Thinking.* 10th ed. New York: McGraw-Hill, 2011.

Munson, Ronald, and Andrew Black. *The Elements of Reasoning.* 6th ed. Boston, MA: Wadsworth. 2012.

Ruggiero, Vincent R. *Beyond Feelings: A Guide to Critical Thinking.* 9th ed. New York: McGraw-Hill, 2012.

CHAPTER

4

Professional Ethics, Codes of Conduct, and Moral Responsibility

In this chapter, we examine a range of issues often categorized under the general heading "professional ethics." More specifically, we analyze the following questions:

- What do we mean by "professional ethics" in a computing or information-technology (IT) context?

- What are professional codes of ethics, and what important functions do they serve in the computing/IT profession?

- What is "whistle-blowing," and when is it permissible or perhaps even required for computer/IT professionals?

- Which standards of moral responsibility, legal liability, and accountability should apply in cases of computer malfunctions, especially in safety-critical computer systems?

- Is an adequate model of risk analysis for developing software, especially for safety-critical and life-critical systems, possible?

Issues involving software reliability and risk are also examined from the perspective of cybersecurity, in Chapter 6, where concerns about the vulnerability and reliability of computer systems are considered from the vantage point of attacks on computer systems from external sources, such as malicious hackers. In this chapter, our concern with unreliable computer systems centers primarily on issues that arise as a result of malfunctions and errors generated from "internal" sources; that is, we are concerned with reliability and safety issues that can be traced to the coding and testing of software and to the manufacturing of hardware components used in computer systems.

A principal objective of this chapter is to determine the extent to which computer/IT professionals should be held accountable for malfunctions involving computer systems. Why is this important? For one thing, advanced and sophisticated technologies, developed by computer/IT professionals, are increasingly used in military defense systems and warfare. In 2007, the South African army deployed a semi-autonomous robotic canon that malfunctioned, killing nine "friendly" soldiers and wounding fourteen others (Wallach and Allen, 2009). And in 2010, the U.S. military lost control of a helicopter drone for more than 30 minutes during a test flight; the drone veered toward Washington, D.C., violating air space intended to protect the White House and other official government buildings (Lin, 2012).

We should note, however, that computer malfunctions involving life-critical applications are by no means new. Consider two incidents, now viewed as classic cases, which occurred in the 1980s. In 1988, the USS *Vincennes*, a U.S. Navy ship equipped with the Aegis Radar System, accidentally shot down an Iranian passenger airliner, killing 290 people. A poorly designed user interface to the computerized radar system contributed significantly to this accident.[1] Between 1985 and 1987, a series of malfunctions involving the Therac-25, a computerized radiation-therapy machine, resulted in six serious accidents and three deaths. The problem was eventually traced to a bug in a software program that, in certain instances, caused massive overdoses of radiation to be administered to patients.[2]

Both the Therac-25 and the Aegis incidents are examined in detail in this chapter, in Sections 4.5.2 and 4.6, respectively. Accidents of this type are sometimes categorized as "computer error" or "computer malfunction." But who, exactly, is responsible for these computer errors and malfunctions? It would seem reasonable to hold the manufacturers of unreliable computer systems legally liable for harms caused by faulty design interfaces or "buggy" software. But we must also ask to what extent the computer/IT professionals, especially the software engineers who design and develop "safety-critical" and "life-critical" applications, bear responsibility for the harmful consequences that result from unreliable computer systems.

While the Aegis and Therac incidents each raise concerns about professional responsibility for safety-critical and life-critical systems, our analysis of responsibility and reliability issues in Chapter 4 is also concerned with failures and malfunctions of computer systems, which might not be "safety-critical," but which can cause businesses and ordinary users to lose work, time, and money. For example, problems in the computerized baggage system at the Denver International Airport caused both damage to luggage and routing problems, which, in turn, cost the airport millions of dollars and significantly delayed its opening. Before examining specific cases involving unreliable computer systems, however, we first briefly consider some foundational issues in professional ethics.

▶ 4.1 PROFESSIONAL ETHICS

Recall that in Chapter 1 we described professional ethics as one of the three main perspectives through which cyberethics issues can be identified and analyzed. We saw that, when applied to computing, professional ethics is a field of applied ethics concerned with moral issues that affect computer professionals. You may also recall from our discussion of professional ethics in Chapter 1 that Don Gotterbarn suggested that professional ethics is the principal, perhaps even exclusive, perspective through which ethical issues involving the computing field should be examined.[3] Although this claim is controversial and will not be further considered here, we have devoted this chapter to an analysis of computer ethics issues from the vantage point of professional ethics.

Why have a category called "professional ethics"? After all, one could reasonably argue that independent of whether a particular moral issue happens to arise in either a professional or a nonprofessional context, ethics is ethics; the same basic ethical rules apply to professionals as to ordinary individuals. In response, many ethicists argue that some moral issues affecting professionals are sufficiently distinct and specialized to warrant a separate field of study. Some ethicists also argue that, at least in certain cases, professionals have special moral obligations, which exceed those of ordinary individuals. To grasp the essential points in the arguments advanced by these ethicists, it is useful first to understand what is meant by "profession" and "professional."

4.1.1 What Is a Profession?

The meaning of "profession" has evolved significantly over time. Harris, Pritchard, and Rabins (2004) note that the term was once associated with people "professing a religious or monastic life," before taking on a more secular meaning in the late seventeenth century, when it was first used to refer to one who "professed to be duly qualified."[4] In more recent times, a profession has come to be associated with a certain kind of vocation or an occupation in which a person has a specific set of skills or a mastery of knowledge in a particular field.

A profession can be distinguished from many ordinary occupations in terms of certain kinds of characteristics, such as having a code of ethics. Consider that the field of computing/IT has a number of professional societies with ethical codes (see Section 4.3), as do professions such as medicine and law. However, the computing/IT profession also differs from traditional professions such as medicine and law in at least one key respect. While many doctors and lawyers work in private practice, most computer/IT professionals are not self-employed; even though some work as independent consultants, most are employed by corporations. So, some may question whether the computer/IT field is a "true profession." But Robert Barger (2008) argues that it qualifies as a genuine profession because the field satisfies two criteria that have traditionally characterized a profession: (1) expert knowledge, which he describes as a "special technical knowledge that is certified by some authority and is not possessed by the layperson"; and (2) autonomy with respect to "independence in conducting one's professional practice."[5]

4.1.2 Who Is a Professional?

As in the case of "profession," the term "professional" has also evolved over time. Traditional professionals included lawyers, medical doctors, and professors. In our current and expanded use of that term, we refer to a broader range of professional categories, such as real-estate professionals, marketing professionals, and so forth. A defining attribute of traditional professions, such as medicine and law, is that members often find themselves in situations in which their decisions and actions can have significant social effects; for example, medical doctors can prescribe the use of certain drugs for their patients, who otherwise would have no legal access to them, and lawyers are bound by special obligations such as client confidentiality that would not apply if they were acting as ordinary citizens. In these cases, a professional's roles and responsibilities can exceed those of ordinary individuals. Sometimes these roles and responsibilities are said to *differentiate* professionals from nonprofessionals.

Elizabeth Buchanan (2004) believes that the roles and responsibilities of professionals are differentiated from ordinary individuals because:

> . . . professionals are experts in a field, which provides them an advantage over the lay person and that professional's work has the potential to impact—either positively or negatively—the general public at large.[6]

Buchanan goes on to note that "information professionals" have the potential to adversely affect an "increasingly large and diverse clientele by failing to act responsibly, fairly, timely, and appropriately." So it would seem that these roles and responsibilities differentiate professionals working in the fields of computing and information technology from ordinary individuals. The extent to which a computer/IT professional's roles and responsibilities are "highly differentiated," however, is a matter of some dispute. To understand why this is so, it would first help to understand what, exactly, is meant by the expression "computer/IT professional."

4.1.3 Who Is a Computer/IT Professional?

Broadly speaking, a *computer/IT professional* is anyone employed in the computing and IT fields—from software and hardware engineers, to specialists such as support personnel, network administrators, and computer repair technicians. Computer professionals can also include faculty and instructors who teach in computer science and information management departments at universities, as well as in industry settings. We could possibly even extend "computer/IT professional" to include professionals who are responsible for providing unfettered access to electronic information in libraries, although they may prefer to describe themselves as "information professionals" or "information science professionals."[7]

A computer/IT professional might also be thought of in more narrow terms, in which case only software engineers would be included. Of course, there are various gradients in between the two ends of this spectrum. A computer/IT professional could be defined in a way that would exclude professionals in the fields of communications and library science, yet still include professionals whose computer-specific job descriptions extend beyond software engineering per se, such as software technical writers, software quality analysts, and managers and supervisors who play key roles in the software development process and make up a *software engineering team*.[8]

For purposes of this chapter, we will consider "computer/IT professionals" to include software/hardware engineers and software/hardware engineering teams, as well as computer science instructors in colleges, universities, and industry settings who are responsible for educating and training the members of software engineering teams. We will also include IT professionals in end-user support roles (e.g., network administrators and computer support personnel) in our definition of computer professionals. However, we will not include lawyers, accountants, nurses, or other professionals who are employed by computer companies or who work closely with computers as part of their regular employment.

▶ 4.2 DO COMPUTER/IT PROFESSIONALS HAVE ANY SPECIAL MORAL RESPONSIBILITIES?

Some ethicists believe that all professionals, regardless of their practice, have special moral obligations *as professionals*. But are there also specific moral obligations that apply to computer/IT professionals in the more narrow sense in which we have defined the term? As noted above, many computer/IT professionals are software engineers or members of software engineering teams. An important question for us to ask is: Does this group of professionals have any special moral obligations that differentiate them from other professionals who work in the computing/IT fields? Gotterbarn (2001) believes that because software engineers and their teams are responsible for developing safety-critical systems, they have significant opportunities to

i. do good or cause harm,

ii. enable others to do good or cause harm,

iii. influence others to do good or cause harm.

Thus Gotterbarn suggests that the roles and responsibilities involved in the development of safety-critical systems constitute a differentiating factor.

4.2.1 Safety-Critical Software

What, exactly, is safety-critical software? Kevin Bowyer (2001) points out that the phrase "safety-critical system" is often used to refer to computer systems that can have a "direct life-threatening impact." He notes that, under this definition, examples of safety-critical software applications typically include

- aircraft and air traffic control systems,
- mass transportation systems,
- nuclear reactors,
- missile systems,
- medical treatment systems.

However, Bowyer believes that an understanding of safety-critical systems that includes only these examples is too narrow. He suggests that a broader definition be adopted in which safety-critical systems are also understood as software applications used in the design of physical systems and structures whose failures can also have an impact that is life threatening. Here, the range of safety-critical applications can be expanded to include software used in the

- design of bridges and buildings,
- selection of water disposal sites,
- development of analytical models for medical treatment.[9]

We use the expanded sense of "safety-critical software" in this chapter. And we examine two important cases of computer malfunctions involving safety-critical software in our discussions of moral-accountability and risk-assessment issues in Sections 4.5 and 4.6, respectively.

A related question is whether the computer profession itself (as opposed to the individuals comprising that profession) has any special moral obligations. In other words, are there any macro-ethical, as opposed to micro-ethical (see Chapter 2 for this distinction), obligations that are special or unique to the computer profession? And do some computer corporations, because of the significant scope of their influence, have special moral obligations. In Section 4.7, we briefly consider whether major search engine companies such as Google have special moral obligations because of the social role they play as "gatekeepers of information." We also question whether computer companies that are now developing autonomous systems, i.e., "machines" capable of making life-critical decisions independent of human oversight, may have some special moral obligations.

▶ 4.3 PROFESSIONAL CODES OF ETHICS AND CODES OF CONDUCT

We have already seen that many professions have established professional societies, which in turn have adopted codes of conduct. For example, the medical profession established the American Medical Association (AMA), and the legal profession established the American Bar Association (ABA). Both associations have formal codes of ethics/conduct for their members. The computing profession has also established a number of professional societies, the largest of which are the Association for Computing Machinery (ACM) and the Institute for Electrical and Electronics Engineers-Computer Society (IEEE-CS). Both organizations have adopted professional codes of ethics, and the full texts of these two codes are included in Appendixes A and E (www.wiley.com/college/tavani), as well as at the ACM and IEEE sites.

Both the ACM and the IEEE codes contain general statements about what is expected, and in some cases what is required, to be a member in good standing. The IEEE Code of Ethics contains ten general directives; the first four instruct members to

1. accept responsibility in making engineering decisions consistent with the safety, health, and welfare of the public . . . ;
2. avoid real or perceived conflicts of interest wherever possible . . . ;
3. be honest . . . ;
4. reject bribery in all its forms; . . . [10]

The ACM Code of Ethics and Professional Conduct, on the other hand, is more complex. It contains twenty-four imperatives, formulated as statements of personal responsibility. Like the IEEE Code, the ACM Code also lists general moral imperatives:

1.1 contribute to society and human well being,

1.2 avoid harm to others,

1.3 be honest and trustworthy,

1.4 be fair and take action not to discriminate,

1.5 honor property copyrights and patents,

1.6 give proper credit for intellectual property,

1.7 respect the privacy of others,

1.8 honor confidentiality.

From these general imperatives, a list of more specific professional responsibilities follows. These include the directives:

2.1 Strive to achieve the highest quality . . . in . . . work.

2.2 Acquire and maintain professional competence.

These directives are then followed by six "organizational leadership imperatives," which include:

3.1 Articulate social responsibilities of members . . .

3.2 Manage personnel and resources to design and build information that enhance the quality of working life.

The fourth component of the ACM Code stresses "compliance with the code," and consists of two imperatives:

4.1 Uphold and promote the principles of this code.

4.2 Treat violations of this code as inconsistent with membership of the ACM.[11]

4.3.1 The Purpose of Professional Codes

Professional codes of ethics serve a variety of functions. For example, Gotterbarn and Miller (2009) note that these codes are often perceived as a way to "regulate members of a profession." Bynum and Rogerson (2004) believe that for computer/IT professionals, codes of ethics have five important functions: inspiration, education, guidance, accountability, and enforcement. For example, they point out that codes *inspire* members of the profession by "identifying values and ideals" to which members can aspire. Bynum and Rogerson believe that codes *educate* by informing members about the profession's values and standards, and that they *guide* members by specifying "standards of good practice." Additionally, codes describe the level of *accountability* and responsibility that is expected and demanded by a professional society. Finally, codes have an *enforcement* function with regard to behavior deemed to be "ethically unacceptable" in a society.[12] Martin and Schinzinger (2004) describe this feature as a "disciplinary or penal function" that codes can serve when members violate one or more policies stipulated by the professional code.

To be effective, a professional code must be broad, yet specific. Perlman and Varma (2002) point out that a code must be broad enough to cover the ethical conflicts and concerns likely to arise in its professional field (such as computing), but, at the same time, a code cannot be so broad that it covers extraneous incidents. It must also be sufficiently specific to serve as a guide to making sound decisions for practical action in actual circumstances that are likely to arise in the computing field. To accomplish the first objective, Perlman and Varma believe that a code needs to encompass the principles that guide professions, in general, and ethics, in particular. And to satisfy the second objective, a code is measured by the degree to which its rules serve as "effective guides" for computer/IT professionals and practitioners. Perlman and Varma also note that in engineering contexts, professional codes face a special challenge because the practice of engineering often dictates secrecy, whereas the ethics of engineering requires transparency, or openness.

4.3.2 Some Criticisms of Professional Codes

Initially, it might seem surprising that anyone would be critical of professional codes in general or of specific codes developed for computer/IT professionals. However, critics have pointed out that the ethical codes adopted by professional computer societies have no "teeth." For example, violations of the ACM or the IEEE codes, unlike violations of professional codes in the fields of medicine and law, do not necessarily threaten the employment of those who violate them. Also, computer professionals are not usually required to be members of the ACM, IEEE, or any other professional society to be employed in the computing field or to practice as computer/IT professionals.

Michael Davis (1995) has pointed out some ways in which professional codes are often dismissed. For example, he notes that they are often perceived as "self-serving, unrealistic, inconsistent, mere guides for novices, too vague, or unnecessary."[13] To Davis's list, we could add one more characteristic—professional codes also tend to be incomplete. Ben Fairweather (2004) believes that codes of conduct for computing professionals have been influenced by a conception of computer and information ethics that is limited to four traditional areas of concern: privacy, accuracy, property, and accessibility. He argues that a professional code built on a foundation that includes such a narrow range of ethical concerns can provide certain loopholes for unethical behavior in an organization.

John Ladd (1995) has criticized ethical codes on slightly different grounds, arguing that these codes rest on a series of confusions that are both "intellectual and moral." His complex arguments can, for our purposes, be summarized in three main points. First, Ladd notes that ethics is basically an "open ended, reflective, and critical intellectual activity." Because ethics is a field of study that consists of issues to be examined, explored, discussed, deliberated, and argued, it requires a process of deliberation and argumentation. (Recall our definition of ethics in Chapter 2.) Directives listed in a professional code may give an employee the mistaken notion that all he or she needs to do is to locate a directive and then blindly follow it. More importantly, however, Ladd notes that individuals are not told what to do in a situation where two or more principles or directives (in a code) conflict with one another. Here the individual needs to deliberate; yet professional codes do not typically provide any hierarchy of principles or any mechanism for choosing one directive over another.

Second, Ladd is critical of codes because of the confusions they introduce with respect to responsibilities involving microethics vs. macroethics issues (i.e., confusions about which responsibilities apply to individual professionals and which responsibilities apply to the profession itself). Recall that we briefly discussed the microethical/macroethical distinction in Chapter 2. In the context of professional ethics, microethical issues apply to personal relationships between individual professionals and other individuals, such as clients. Macroethical issues, on the contrary, apply to social problems that confront members of a profession collectively, or as a group. As such, most microethical issues involve the application of ordinary moral notions (such as honesty and civility) that would also hold when dealing with other individuals in nonprofessional contexts. Macroethical issues, however, are more complex, since they involve the formulation of policies at the level of social organizations. Ladd believes that we need to distinguish between questions such as "Which responsibilities do I, as a computer professional, have in such and such a situation?" and "Which responsibilities does the computing profession, as a profession, have in such and such a situation?" He concludes that professional codes of ethics cannot help us to make this important distinction.

Third, Ladd believes that attaching disciplinary procedures and sanctions to codes effectively turns them into legal rules or "authoritative rules of conduct" rather than ethical rules. The role of ethics in general, he argues, is to appraise, criticize, and even defend the principles, rules, and regulations, but it is not to dictate or to punish. Also, when individuals are compelled to obey directives, they are deprived of their autonomy, that is, their ability to choose, which is crucial in moral deliberation. So Ladd argues that professional codes rest on some mistaken notions about both the nature and the purpose of morality, which ultimately result in a series of intellectual and moral confusions.

4.3.3 Defending Professional Codes

It is very important to point out at this stage of our discussion of professional codes that not everyone has been critical of them. In fact, even some critics who have identified specific limitations or weaknesses in professional codes have also defended and praised them. For example, Robert Barger (2003), who concedes that the hope of finding a single professional code that everyone would accept might seem "dim," also notes that we should not infer that an effort to do so is futile. And Davis, whose criticisms of professional codes were described in the previous section, has argued that codes are extremely important for engineering professionals because they are central to guiding individual engineers in how to behave morally as professionals. Since an engineer cannot always rely on his or her own private conscience when making moral decisions, Davis believes that codes play an essential role in "advising individual engineers in how to conduct themselves."[14] He also believes that codes of conduct can help individual engineers to better understand "engineering as a profession." Bynum and Rogerson (2004), who also describe some positive functions that codes serve, point out that we should acknowledge the "limitations of codes." For example, they note that professional codes should not be viewed simply as laws or algorithms, or as "exhaustive checklists."

Gotterbarn (2000) has suggested that some of the criticism leveled against professional codes might be eliminated if we think of them as serving three important, but distinct, functions; that is,

- Codes of ethics
- Codes of conduct
- Codes of practice

Gotterbarn describes *codes of ethics* as "aspirational," because they often serve as mission statements for the profession and can thus provide vision and objectives. *Codes of conduct*, on the other hand, address the professional and the professional's attitude and behavior. Finally, *codes of practice* relate to operational activities within a profession. Gotterbarn points out that the degree of enforcement possible with respect to specific violations of a professional code is dependent on the type of code violated. For example, he notes that violations involving codes of ethics, which are primarily aspirational, are often considered no more than "light concerns." Consequently, violations of these codes may not have any serious consequences for individuals. Violations involving codes of conduct, on the other hand, can range from warnings

TABLE 4.1   Some Strengths and Weaknesses of Professional Codes

Strengths	Weaknesses
Codes inspire the members of a profession to behave ethically.	Codes include directives that tend to be too general and too vague.
Codes guide the members of a profession in ethical choices.	Codes are not always helpful when two or more directives conflict.
Codes educate the members about their professional obligations.	Codes comprise directives that are neither complete nor exhaustive.
Codes discipline members when they violate one or more directives.	Codes are ineffective (have no "teeth") in disciplinary matters.
Codes inform the public about the nature and roles of the profession.	Codes sometimes include directives that are inconsistent with one another.
Codes "sensitize" members of a profession to ethical issues and alert them to ethical aspects they otherwise might overlook.	Codes do not always distinguish between microethics issues and macroethics issues.
Codes enhance the profession in the eyes of the public.	Codes can be self-serving for the profession.

given to an individual to the possibility of exclusion from practicing in a profession. Violations of codes of practice go one step further, however, in that they may also lead to legal action.

Gotterbarn notes that the hierarchy in the three types of codes parallels the three levels of obligation owed by professionals. The first level includes a set of ethical values, such as integrity and justice, which professionals share with other humans by virtue of a shared humanity. The second level of responsibility is shared by all professionals, regardless of their fields of specialization. The third (and deeper) level comprises several obligations that derive directly from elements unique to a particular professional practice, such as software engineering. This threefold distinction is incorporated in a professional code developed by a joint task force of the IEEE-CS/ACM, which we examine in the next section.

Table 4.1 lists some of the strengths and weaknesses of professional codes.

4.3.4   The IEEE-CS/ACM Software Engineering Code of Ethics and Professional Practice

In the 1990s, the ACM and IEEE approved a joint code of ethics for software engineers: the IEEE-CS/ACM Software Engineering Code of Ethics and Professional Practice (SECEPP). Gotterbarn (2001) believes that SECEPP, as a professional code for software engineers, is unique for two reasons: First, it is intended as *the* code for the software engineering profession, unlike the individual codes (such as those of the ACM and IEEE) designed for particular professional societies within the computing profession. Second, Gotterbarn believes that SECEPP is distinctive in that it has been adopted by two international computing societies: ACM and IEEE-CS.

SECEPP is organized into two main parts: a short version and a longer, or full, version. Each version has its own preamble, and the full text for each version is included in Appendix E (www.wiley.com/college/tavani). SECEPP comprises eight core principles:

1. **PUBLIC** Software engineers shall act consistently with the public interest.
2. **CLIENT AND EMPLOYER** Software engineers shall act in a manner that is in the best interests of their client and employer, consistent with the public interest.
3. **PRODUCT** Software engineers shall ensure that their products and related modifications meet the highest professional standards possible.
4. **JUDGMENT** Software engineers shall maintain integrity and independence in their professional judgment.
5. **MANAGEMENT** Software engineering managers and leaders shall subscribe to and promote an ethical approach to the management of software development and maintenance.
6. **PROFESSION** Software engineers shall advance the integrity and reputation of the profession consistent with the public interest.
7. **COLLEAGUES** Software engineers shall be fair to and supportive of their colleagues.
8. **SELF** Software engineers shall participate in lifelong learning regarding the practice of their profession and shall promote an ethical approach to the practice of the profession.[15]

Does SECEPP Provide an Appropriate Balance between Generality and Specificity?

We noted above that professional codes are often criticized for being too vague and too general to be useful, yet there is also a danger in being too specific. If a professional code is too specific, it might fail to instruct members about general principles regarding ethical behavior and ethical decision making. SECEPP does include some very specific language, but it also has general prescriptions found in most professional codes. And, at the general level, SECEPP emphasizes the profession's obligation to the public at large, including concern for the public's health, safety, and welfare. For example, in the preamble to the full version of the code, software engineers are encouraged to

- consider broadly who is affected by their work;
- examine if they and their colleagues are treating other human beings with due respect;
- consider how the public, if reasonably well informed, would view their decisions;
- analyze how the least empowered will be affected by their decisions.

The preamble to the short version of SECEPP summarizes aspirations at a high level of abstraction. The specific clauses included in the full version, on the other hand, give examples of how these aspirations change the way that software engineering professionals act *as* professionals. The code's principal authors note that "without the aspirations, the details can become legalistic and tedious; without the details, the aspirations can become high sounding but empty; together, the aspirations and the details form a cohesive code."[16] SECEPP's supporters believe that this code achieves an ideal balance between the general and the specific.

Does SECEPP Avoid Criticisms of Earlier Professional Codes?

One criticism often directed at professional codes is that they are incomplete; recall Ben Fairweather's argument in Section 4.3.2. Another criticism notes that most codes provide no mechanism for choosing between principles when two or more of them conflict; recall John Ladd's critique, included in Section 4.3.2. Gotterbarn (2000) believes that SECEPP has overcome both difficulties.

Regarding the charge of incompleteness, Gotterbarn is willing to concede that the principles included in SECEPP are not intended to be exhaustive. He also acknowledges that no code could reasonably anticipate every possible moral controversy that can arise. However, he believes that SECEPP addresses the problem of completeness by providing "general guidance for ethical decision making." Gotterbarn argues that ethical tensions that arise can best be addressed by "thoughtful consideration of fundamental principles, rather than blind reliance on detailed regulations." He also points out that SECEPP should not be viewed as a simple algorithm that generates ethical decisions. And Gotterbarn notes that the individual principles that comprise SECEPP are not intended to be used in isolation from one another.

With respect to the second major criticism of professional codes, Gotterbarn points out that SECEPP has a "hierarchy of principles." This hierarchy enables engineers to prioritize their roles and responsibilities and to determine which ones are overriding when two or more conflict. Recall the list of eight principles that make up SECEPP: the ordering of these principles is intended to offer some guidance in cases where two or more rules conflict. SECEPP's hierarchy of principles states that concern for the health, safety, and welfare of the public is primary in all ethical judgments.

In concluding Section 4.3, we acknowledge that professional codes clearly have some limitations. However, we should be careful not to underestimate the important contributions that well-developed professional codes, such as SECEPP, have made to the computing profession so far. Critics may be correct in pointing out that following the directives of a professional code can never be a substitute for the kind of careful moral deliberation that is needed in certain controversial cases. Nevertheless, well-developed codes of conduct provide professionals with an important first step in the overall ethical deliberation process.

▶ 4.4 CONFLICTS OF PROFESSIONAL RESPONSIBILITY: EMPLOYEE LOYALTY AND WHISTLE-BLOWING

What, exactly, is employee loyalty? Do employees and employers have a special obligation of loyalty to each other? Should loyalty to one's employer ever preclude an employee's "blowing the whistle" in critical situations? In which cases can whistle-blowing be justified? Each of these questions is examined in this section.

4.4.1 Do Employees Have an Obligation of Loyalty to Employers?

Many ethicists believe that while loyalty may not be an obligation that is absolute, we nonetheless have a *prima facie* obligation of loyalty in employment contexts. In other words, all things being equal, an employee should be loyal to his or her employer and vice versa. What is the origin of the concept of employee loyalty in an engineering context?

Carl Mitcham (1997) points out that, historically, engineers believed that they had a basic obligation to be loyal to institutional authority. Originally, an engineer was a "soldier who designed military fortifications or operated engines of war, such as catapults."[17] Mitcham notes that early civil engineering could be viewed as peacetime military engineering in which engineers were "duty bound to obey their employer," which was often some branch of the government. So it may well be the case that this historical precedent has contributed to the sense of loyalty many engineers currently have for their institutions and employers.

Does employee loyalty still make sense in the context of a large computer corporation in the twenty-first century? Skeptics might argue that loyalty makes sense only in employment contexts where there is a mutual commitment on the part of both parties involved—employer and employee. In good economic times, employees may have the sense that their employers are very loyal to them. And in the past, it was not uncommon for employees in many professional fields to expect to be able to spend their entire career working for one employer, provided he or she was a loyal employee. But downturns in the U.S. economy, especially during the past three decades, have caused many employers to reassess their obligations to employees. As a result of significant downsizing in many corporations in the 1980s and 1990s, and continuing into this century, employees can reasonably question the degree of loyalty that their employers offer them. In fairness to corporations, however, CEOs also have an obligation of loyalty to stockholders to ensure that the company remains viable and profitable. This obligation can sometimes conflict with a corporation's obligations to its employees.

In one sense, the skeptic's arguments seem plausible. Consider, for instance, how many corporations have gone through downsizing and restructuring phases in which loyal employees who have served a company faithfully for several years have been laid off or dismissed as part of restructuring plans. Also consider that many computer programming jobs in the United States are now being "outsourced" by major corporations to countries where programmers are willing to write the software code for much lower wages.

On the contrary, however, some employers have shown what would certainly appear to be a strong sense of loyalty to employees. For example, there have been instances where an employer will keep an employee on the payroll even though that employee has a chronic illness that causes her to miss several months of work. There have also been cases in which several employees have been kept on by a company despite the fact that their medical conditions have caused the corporation's health insurance costs to increase significantly, thereby reducing the company's overall profits. You may also have heard of a case involving the owner of Malden Mills, whose physical plant in Massachusetts was destroyed by fire. The mill's proprietor, Aaron Feuerstein, could have been excused from any future obligations to his employees, and he could have chosen to rebuild his facility in a different state or country where employees would work for lower wages. Instead, Feuerstein continued to pay and provide benefits for his employees while a new facility was being built in Massachusetts. So there have been instances where employers have been very loyal to their employees.

How should the notion of employee loyalty apply in computing/IT contexts? Do computer/IT professionals necessarily have an obligation to be loyal to their employers? Let us assume for the sake of argument that, all things being equal, computer/IT professionals should be loyal to their employers. However, sometimes an employee's obligation of loyalty can conflict with other obligations, such as those to society in general, especially where health and safety considerations are at stake.

How are computer/IT professionals supposed to balance their obligation of loyalty to an employer against their obligations of loyalty that lie elsewhere? Even if a computer/IT professional has a *prima facie* obligation (i.e., all things being equal) of loyalty to his or her employer, it does not follow that he or she has an absolute obligation of loyalty! Consider that computer/IT professionals, because of the nature of the critical-safety projects they work on, can also have an obligation to society as a whole, especially since safety and health issues can arise. Divided loyalties of this type, of course, can result in serious conflicts for employees, and in certain cases the moral dilemmas they generate are so profound that an employee must determine whether to blow the whistle.

4.4.2 Whistle-Blowing Issues

What, exactly, is whistle-blowing? Sisela Bok (2003) defines a whistle-blower as an individual who makes "revelations meant to call attention to negligence, abuses, or dangers that threaten the public interest." She goes on to note that whistle-blowers often "sound an alarm" from within the organizations in which they work. Bok also notes that whistle-blowing can be viewed as a form of *dissent*, because those who blow the whistle make public their disagreement with their employers or with some authority. Although Bok defends whistle-blowing in certain cases, where other alternatives have been "considered and rejected," she also believes that it should remain as a "last alternative" due to its "destructive side effects."[18]

Determining When to Blow the Whistle
When should an employee blow the whistle? Consider a whistle-blowing incident in which Colleen Rowley, an FBI employee, came forth to describe how critical messages had failed to be sent up the Federal Bureau's chain of command in the days immediately preceding the tragic events of September 11, 2001. Was it appropriate for her to blow the whistle on her supervisor? Was she disloyal to her supervisor and her fellow employees in doing so?

Should individuals in positions of authority in corporations such as Enron and WorldCom have blown the corporate whistle about their illegal accounting practices, which were discovered in early 2002? One could argue that failing to blow the whistle in the Enron case resulted in thousands of people losing their retirement savings and, in some cases, their entire life savings. On similar grounds, one could argue that if someone had blown the whistle on Bernie Madoff (and other notorious investment advisors who used "Ponzi" schemes that deceived investors) prior to the 2008/2009 financial crisis in the U.S., the financial losses suffered by many investors, as well as the damage to the U.S. economy in general, might not have been as severe as it was.

There are, no doubt, cases where a decision to blow the whistle might have saved human lives. Consider, for example, the Space Shuttle *Challenger* disaster in January 1986, which resulted in the deaths of the seven crew members. Engineers who designed the space shuttle were aware of the safety risks in launching the shuttle in cooler temperatures. In fact, some engineers, when learning the *Challenger* was scheduled for launch on a cool January morning, went to their supervisors to express their concerns. However, a decision was made to stick with the original launch date. Having received no support from their supervisors, should those engineers have gone directly to the press? Would whistle-blowing at that level have saved the lives of the Challenger's crew?

In the Challenger case, many believe that the engineers involved had a responsibility to blow the whistle on their management team. We next briefly examine a classic case of whistle-blowing in a computing context involving national defense.[19]

▶ **SCENARIO 4–1:** Whistle-Blowing and the "Star Wars" Controversy

In the early 1980s, a U.S. military proposal called the Strategic Defense Initiative (SDI) was introduced and debated. SDI, also referred to as "Star Wars" in the media, was a national missile defense (NMD) system that would provide a "defense shield" against incoming ballistic missiles. The SDI proposal, which was vigorously supported by the Reagan administration, soon became very controversial. While SDI's supporters argued that the missile system was essential for America's national defense, critics argued that the system's software was unreliable. One critic, David Parnas, decided to go public with his concerns about SDI.[20]   ■

David Parnas, a consultant on the Star Wars project, was paid $1,000 per day (in the 1980s) for his expertise. However, shortly after he joined the SDI project team, Parnas became convinced that it was not possible to construct SDI software that could confidently be expected to work when needed. His conclusion that SDI was inadequate was based on concerns he had about the design specifications and the testing of the software involved. Parnas (1990) argued that the specifications were not known with sufficient confidence and that the SDI software would not be able to undergo adequate testing. Additionally, Parnas determined that there would not be sufficient time during an attack to repair and reinstall software that failed.

When Parnas went public with his position, some of SDI's supporters accused him of disloyalty and of acting out of his own self-interest. Many of Parnas's defenders, however, pointed out that Parnas walked away from a lucrative consulting contract. Did Parnas do the right thing? It is interesting to note that William Yurcik and David Doss (2002) believe that the arguments used by Parnas in the case of SDI also apply in the controversy involving the National Missile Defense (NMD) proposal put forth by the Bush administration in 2001. In Chapter 3, we briefly examined some arguments advanced for and against NMD.

Can Professional Codes Guide Engineers in Whistle-Blowing Decisions?

As noted above, legislation has been enacted at both the federal and the state levels in the United States to protect employees who go public with certain kinds of information. We also noted that individual state laws vary considerably with the amount and kind of protection offered to whistle-blowers. It would seem appropriate to ask what measures the engineering and computing professions themselves have taken to protect whistle-blowers. Perhaps a more fundamental question is: What kind of guidance do the ethical codes adopted by engineering and computing professions provide members when they are confronted with specific dilemmas that could lead to a whistle-blowing decision? Sections 6.12 and 6.13 of SECEPP state that an engineer is obligated to

- express concerns to the people involved when significant violations of this Code are detected unless this is impossible, counterproductive, or dangerous;

- report significant violations of this Code to appropriate authorities when it is clear that consultation with people involved in these significant violations is impossible, counterproductive, or dangerous.

Although guidelines such as these are useful, many believe that they are still too vague. It would be helpful if engineers had more straightforward criteria for determining when they are permitted, or perhaps even required, to blow the whistle.

Being Morally Permitted vs. Being Morally Required to Blow the Whistle

Richard De George (1999) has offered some specific conditions for when an engineer is (a) *morally permitted* to blow the whistle, and (b) *morally obligated* to do so. De George believes that engineers and other workers are morally permitted to go public with information about the safety of a product if three conditions are satisfied. For our purposes, we can summarize De George's three conditions as follows:

1. The product will do "serious and considerable harm" to the public.
2. The engineer(s) have reported the "serious threat" to their immediate supervisor.
3. The engineer(s) have "exhausted the internal procedures and possibilities" within the company, including going to the board of directors, having received no support from their immediate supervisor.[21]

Although De George argues that one is morally permitted to blow the whistle when conditions 1–3 are satisfied, he does not believe that a person is yet morally required to do so. To have a strict moral obligation to blow the whistle, De George believes that two additional conditions must be satisfied:

4. The engineer(s) have "accessible, documented evidence that would convince a reasonable, impartial, observer that one's view of the situation is correct."
5. The engineer(s) have "good reasons to believe that by going public the necessary changes will be brought about."[22]

Applying De George's Criteria

De George provides us with a carefully developed and articulate model in which to assess whistle-blowing in an engineering context. Next, we apply De George's model to the SDI case, described above. Because Parnas's actions seem to comply with De George's first three conditions, we can assume that his whistle-blowing in the SDI case was morally permissible. But was Parnas also morally obligated to blow the whistle in this case? While his actions would seem to comply with Condition 4, we should note that Parnas was challenged by an expert who offered a different analysis of the risks involved. Also, regarding Condition 5, it is not obvious from what we have seen so far that Parnas had "good reasons" for believing that going public would necessarily bring about the intended changes. Additionally, we should note that De George includes a caveat with Condition 5, pointing out that the engineer's chance of "being successful must be worth the risk one takes and the danger to which one is exposed."[23] So, using De George's criteria, it is by no means clear that Parnas was morally obligated to blow the whistle on SDI, even though he was morally permitted to do so.

Of course, we can question whether De George's criteria are too stringent, as some have suggested, or too lenient as others have argued.[24] However, we will not pursue that debate here. Nor will we question the merits of De George's whistle-blowing model outside the context of an engineering environment. We conclude our discussion by noting that one virtue of De George's model is that it provides clear and straightforward guidelines for engineers to consider in a morally complex case without also requiring engineers to be (what De George calls) "moral heroes" or "moral saints."

4.4.3 An Alternative Strategy for Understanding Professional Responsibility

Michael McFarland offers an alternative model with regard to whistle-blowing, arguing that engineers must see themselves in a "wider social context." He claims that unless individual engineers

 a. see their work in relation to society, an adequate account of their ethical responsibilities cannot be given.

 b. learn to act in collaboration with others, both inside and outside their profession, they will not be able to meet their responsibilities.[25]

McFarland suggests that, collectively, engineers might be held to a higher standard of social responsibility than ordinary individuals, but that the onus of responsibility should not fall directly on engineers as individual engineers. Rather, it should be shouldered by engineers as members of the engineering profession.

McFarland's model is based on the assumption that, as moral agents, we have a *prima facie* obligation to come to the aid of others. In describing the nature of this obligation, he uses a nonengineering analogy involving the Kitty Genovese case. (We briefly examined this incident in Chapter 2.) Recall that Genovese was murdered in Queens, New York in 1964 as 38 people in and around her apartment building watched or listened. It has since been argued that if some of Genovese's neighbors had banded together to come to her aid, she would have survived. The analogy for engineers that McFarland wishes to draw is that when no other sources of help are available, engineers should take responsibility by banding together.

McFarland recognizes that if engineers act as individuals, they might not always have the ability to help. If they act collectively, however, they might be able to accomplish goals that would otherwise not be possible. Consider that if Genovese's neighbors had acted individually to intervene in her behalf, they might have put themselves at great risk. However, if they had acted collectively as a group, the neighbors could have overcome Genovese's assailant. Thus McFarland's model encourages engineers to shift their thinking about responsibility issues from the level of individual responsibility (the microethical level) to responsibility at the broader level of the profession itself (the macroethical level).

▶ 4.5 MORAL RESPONSIBILITY, LEGAL LIABILITY, AND ACCOUNTABILITY

So far, our examination of issues involving the moral responsibility of computing/IT professionals has focused mainly on questions concerning employee loyalty and whistle-blowing. We have seen that some of these questions have centered on the responsibilities of computing/IT professionals as individuals, whereas others have dealt with responsibilities facing the computing/IT profession itself. We have also noted that these questions illustrate essential differences between issues of responsibility involving microethics and macroethics. However, we have not yet fully considered the concept of moral responsibility itself.

Philosophers often describe the concept of moral responsibility in terms of two conditions that must be satisfied: *causality* and *intent*. In other words, some agent, X, is held morally responsible for an act, Y, if X caused Y. Here, a person could be held responsible even if he or she did not intend the outcome. Consider a scenario in which a camper, whose careless behavior in failing to put out a camp fire properly resulted in a major forest fire that caused millions of dollars in damage, claims that he did not intend the damage that resulted. Nonetheless, the camper can be held responsible as a moral "agent" for the outcome *caused* by his careless behavior. Agents can also be held morally responsible when they *intend* for something to happen, even if they ultimately fail to cause (or to bring about) the intended outcome. For example, consider a scenario in which a disgruntled student intends to blow up a college's computer lab, but at the last minute is discovered and prevented from doing so. Even though the student failed to carry out his objective—cause the bomb to detonate in the computer lab—we hold the student morally culpable because of his intentions.

4.5.1 Distinguishing Responsibility from Liability and Accountability

It would be helpful at this point to distinguish responsibility from the related notions of liability and accountability. Responsibility differs from liability in that the latter is a legal concept, sometimes used in the narrow sense of "strict liability." To be strictly liable for harm is to be liable to compensate for it even though one did not necessarily bring it about through faulty action. Here, the moral notion of blame may be left out. A property owner may be legally liable for an injury to a guest who falls in the property owner's house, but it does not necessarily follow that the property owner was also morally responsible for any resulting injury. (We elaborate on the notion of liability in Section 4.5.4, where we examine some legal-liability issues affecting producers of defective computer software.)

Helen Nissenbaum (2007) distinguishes between responsibility and accountability by suggesting that responsibility is only part of what is covered by the "robust and intuitive notion of accountability." In Nissenbaum's scheme, *accountability* is a broader concept than responsibility, and means that someone, or some group of individuals, or perhaps even an entire organization, is *answerable*. In a computing context, she notes that accountability means

> there will be someone, or several people to *answer* not only for malfunctions in life-critical systems that cause or risk grave injuries and cause infrastructure and large monetary losses, but even for the malfunctions that cause individual losses of time, convenience, and contentment.[26]

Table 4.2 summarizes the elements we have used to differentiate moral responsibility, legal liability, and accountability.

Nissenbaum believes that the notion of accountability has been "systematically undermined" in the computer era, despite the fact that we are increasingly dependent on safety-critical and life-critical systems controlled by computers. In Section 4.2, we saw that safety-critical applications included software used in aircraft and air traffic control systems, in nuclear reactors, in missile systems, and in medical treatment systems, as well

TABLE 4.2   Responsibility, Legal Liability, and Accountability

Moral Responsibility	Legal Liability	Accountability
Attributes blame (or praise) to individuals.	Does not attribute blame or fault to those held liable.	Does not necessarily attribute blame (in a moral sense).
Usually attributed to individuals rather than collectivities or groups.	Typically applies to corporations and property owners.	Can apply to individuals, groups of individuals, and corporations.
Notions of guilt and shame apply, but no legal punishment or compensation need result.	Compensation can be required even when responsibility in a formal sense is not admitted.	Someone or some group is answerable (i.e., it goes beyond mere liability).

as in the selection of water-disposal sites and in the design of bridges and buildings. Nissenbaum argues that a major barrier to attributing accountability to the developers of safety-critical software is the problem of "many hands."

4.5.2   Accountability and the Problem of "Many Hands"

Computer systems are typically developed in large organizational settings. Because these systems are the products of engineering teams or of corporations, as opposed to the products of a single programmer working in isolation, Nissenbaum notes that "many hands" are involved in their development. Thus it is very likely that no single individual grasps all of the code used in developing a particular safety-critical system.[27] As a result, it is difficult to determine who exactly is accountable whenever one of these safety-critical systems results in personal injury or harm to individuals; it is not always clear whether the manufacturer of the system hardware (the machine) or the engineering teams that developed the system's software, or both, should be held accountable.

When thinking about the problem of many hands from the perspective of strict moral responsibility, as opposed to accountability, two difficulties arise: first, we tend to attribute moral responsibility for an accident to an individual, but not to groups or "collectivities." Thus we sometimes encounter difficulties when we try to attribute blame to an organization. Nissenbaum suggests that by using "accountability" we can avoid the tendency to think only at the level of individuals in matters typically associated with assigning moral responsibility.

The second difficulty arises because the concept of moral responsibility is often thought of as exclusionary, as Ladd (1995) points out. In other words, if we can show that A is responsible for C, then we might infer that B cannot be held responsible for C. Ladd believes that moral responsibility should be viewed as nonexclusionary because both A and B (and possibly others) can be responsible for C. Nissenbaum suggests that we can avoid this confusion if we use "accountability" instead of "responsibility"; in her scheme, holding Sally accountable for making unauthorized copies of proprietary software does not necessarily preclude holding Harry accountable as well (for example, if Harry pays Sally for making copies of the pirated software).

So Nissenbaum believes that holding one individual accountable for some harm need not necessarily let others off the hook, because several individuals may be accountable.

Nor does it mean letting organizations off the hook, because they too may be account-able. As Nissenbaum puts the matter, "We should hold each fully accountable because many hands ought not necessarily lighten the burden of accountability." The following scenario (involving the Therac-25 machine, which we described briefly in the opening section of this chapter) illustrates how the involvement of "many hands" can obscure the process in determining accountability for accidents affecting some safety-critical systems.

▶ **SCENARIO 4–2:** The Therac-25 Machine

The Therac-25 was a computer-controlled radiation treatment machine built by Atomic Energy of Canada Limited (AECL). Between 1985–1987, there were six reported incidents in which patients were severely overdosed by the Therac-25. As a result of the severe burns caused by the excessive radiation dosages, three individuals died and three others had irreversible injuries.[28] ■

Eventually the Therac-25 malfunction was traced not to a single source but to numerous faults, including two significant software coding errors ("bugs") and a faulty microswitch. One bug involved radiation dosage errors: if a subsequent request to change a previously entered radiation dosage was entered in a certain sequence through the user interface, a software bug caused the new entry to be ignored, and the entry instructing the original dosage was used. Instead of receiving 200 RADs, one radiation patient received 20,000 RADs; this patient died shortly afterwards from excessive radiation (Leveson and Turner 2001).

Several interesting questions regarding the locus of responsibility were raised in the wake of the Therac-25 accidents. Who, exactly, should be held accountable for the deaths and injuries that resulted from the computer malfunction? Is the hospital, which may be found legally liable, also accountable in a larger sense? Should the company that manufactured and sold the Therac system to the hospital be held accountable? Were the engineers and programmers who worked on the design and development of this system ultimately responsible for the injuries and deaths caused to the radiation patients? Should they be held legally liable?

Nissenbaum argues that guidelines for producing safer and more reliable computers should include a standard of care that incorporates (a) a formal analysis of system modules (as well as of the entire system), (b) meaningful quality assurance and independent auditing, and (c) built-in redundancy.[29] She believes that a standard comprising these criteria would provide a nonarbitrary means for determining accountability; it would offer a tool for distinguishing between malfunctions due to inadequate practices and those that occur in spite of a programmer or designer's best efforts. Nissenbaum also suggests that if such standard had existed at the time Therac-25 was produced, the software developers of the system could have been held accountable for the deaths and injuries that resulted.

4.5.3 Legal Liability and Moral Accountability

In Section 4.5.1, we saw that legal liability can be distinguished from both moral responsibility and accountability. Nissenbaum believes that in computer/IT contexts, it is important to keep "accountability" distinct from "liability to compensate." She concedes that liability offers a partial solution to problems resulting from computer malfunctions, because at least it addresses the needs of the victims; however, she also notes that accepting liability as a substitute for accountability can further obscure the process of determining who is accountable for computer malfunctions.

Is it reasonable to hold computer corporations legally liable for products they sell that are either unreliable or defective? Supporters of liability law believe that holding owners legally liable makes sense because owners are typically in the best position to directly control their property. Nissenbaum believes that because ownership implies a "bundle of rights," it should also imply responsibilities such as being liable. Software owners (who are also usually the software's producers) are in the best position to directly affect the quality of the software they release to the public. Yet, ironically, the trend in the software industry, Nissenbaum points out, is to "demand maximal property protection while denying, to the extent possible, accountability." Software manufacturers frequently include disclaimers of liability on their products such as "This software is sold as is."

Nissenbaum also suggests that strict liability would shift the accountability to the producers of defective software, thereby addressing an anomaly (perhaps even a paradox) with respect to our current understanding of overall accountability: While liability laws protect the public against potential harm, most producers of software deny accountability for software errors. Producers sometimes base their argument on the notion that software is prone to error in ways that other technologies are not. Nissenbaum concludes that strict liability laws can send a message cautioning software producers to take extraordinary care to produce safe and reliable systems. Strict liability laws may also cause manufacturers to reassess the level of risk tolerated in the process of developing software.

▶ 4.6 RISK ASSESSMENT IN THE SOFTWARE DEVELOPMENT PROCESS

Some analysts have suggested that in order to reduce software failures, we must first address issues involving the level of risk currently associated with the development of computer systems. Gotterbarn (2004) argues that ethical risks associated with the entire "software development life cycle" must also be taken into consideration. For Gotterbarn, the life cycle of software includes the maintenance phase as well as the design and development stages.

Bruce Schneir (2004) notes that in the context of computer/IT security, risk assessment models can be used to make informed decisions about the most cost-effective controls in order to limit risks to one's assets. Gotterbarn worries that while much attention has been paid to cost-effectiveness, very little thought has been given to ethical considerations in the models of risk used in the software development process. In these models, risk has typically been understood in terms of scheduling, budgeting, or specification requirements. Gotterbarn argues that software can satisfy all three conditions and still fail to meet an acceptable standard of risk assessment. To see how this is possible, we examine a case involving the Aegis Radar System, which was briefly described in the opening section of this chapter.

▶ SCENARIO 4–3: The Aegis Radar System

The Aegis Radar System was developed by the United States Navy. Its purpose was to enable U.S. ships to monitor space around them. A serious incident involving the Aegis system occurred in July 1988 on board the USS *Vincennes*. The ship accidentally shot down an Iranian passenger aircraft, killing 290 people. Many believe that a contributing element to—and arguably the key reason for—the accident was the poor design of the Aegis system's user interface.[30] ■

In response to the *Vincennes* incident, some critics have argued that system designers need to realize the importance of building features that affect human abilities and limitations into the interfaces of safety-critical systems. Some analysts believe that accidents such as the one involving the Aegis system on the *Vincennes* are inevitable because they result from the mathematical errors in calculation. Critics of this interpretation, however, believe that the Aegis accident was an error of engineering judgment, that is, an error not reducible to engineering science or to mathematics. They also believe that similar errors could be better understood if an adequate model of risk assessment were used.

The Aegis Radar System met all of the requirements that the developer and customer had set for it; in fact, it satisfied the three conditions specified above: it was on schedule, it was within budget, and it satisfied design specification requirements. Yet the use of the Aegis system resulted in the deaths of 290 airline passengers and crew members. Are risks involving accidents of this magnitude acceptable in schemes for the development of software?

Gotterbarn suggests that software failures like the one involving the Aegis system are the result of two defects in current models of risk assessment for software development:

1. an overly narrow conception of risk, and
2. a limited notion of system stakeholders.

With respect to (1), Gotterbarn argues that a model of risk assessment based solely on cost effectiveness and using only criteria such as budget and schedule is overly narrow. He suggests that the assessment model be enlarged to include social, political, and ethical issues. Regarding (2), Gotterbarn notes that the only stakeholders typically given consideration in risk assessment models for software development are the software developers and the customers, and he argues that this limited notion of "system stakeholders" leads to the development of systems that have unanticipated negative effects. Gotterbarn concludes that unless an adequate risk model for software development is framed, we may be doomed to experiencing future computer malfunctions similar to that of the Aegis system on the USS *Vincennes*.[31]

We will discuss software risk, reliability, and vulnerability in detail in Chapter 6, which examines computer security issues. In Chapter 6, we focus on risks affecting intrusions into computer systems from external sources such as malicious hackers. A model for analyzing risk, especially as it applies to securing our computer network-dependent infrastructure, is also included in that chapter.

▶ 4.7 DO SOME COMPUTER CORPORATIONS HAVE SPECIAL MORAL OBLIGATIONS?

Before concluding our chapter on professional responsibility, we return to a question raised earlier (in Section 4.2) concerning whether computer/IT professionals, in particular, or the computing profession in general, have any special moral responsibilities. There we noted the importance of professional-responsibility-related issues in developing life-critical and safety-critical applications. However, we postponed our consideration of whether some computer corporations, by virtue of the scope and impact of their products and services, might also have some special moral obligations to society. Next, we briefly consider two very different kinds of computer corporations in terms of specific moral responsibilities they may have, given their profound societal impact: (i) search engine companies, and (ii) companies that develop autonomous systems and robots.

4.7.1 Special Responsibilities for Search Engine Companies

Do search engine companies have any special moral or social obligations because of their privileged place in our society as "gatekeepers of the Web"? Lawrence Hinman (2005) identifies four reasons why major search engine companies should shoulder significant social responsibility, when he points out that contemporary search engines:

1. "play an absolutely crucial role in the access to information" and that without them, the Web would "simply be inaccessible to us" and thus "almost useless,"

2. provide "access to information that is crucial for responsible citizenship" (and "citizens in a democracy cannot make informed decisions without access to accurate information"),

3. are now "central to education" (and students now search on Google and other major search engines more frequently than they visit libraries),

4. are owned by private corporations—i.e., by businesses that are mostly interested in making a profit.[32]

Regarding (1)–(3), some critics worry about the degree of commercial control that major search engine companies now have over the distribution of information in digital format. For example, Carr (2011) suggests that this control could ultimately lead to "restrictions on the flow of knowledge." And Hinman (2008) believes that the control of knowledge that these companies have, which is fundamentally a "public trust," is now "firmly ensconced in private hands and behind a veil of corporate secrecy."

With regard to (4), we see how conflicts can easily arise between corporate profits (on the part of search engine companies) and the interests of the general public good. For example, Nicas (2011) notes that many search engine companies, which in the past were "content to simply produce search results," now offer "everything from online music to local coupons to mobile phones." Initially, this might not seem problematic. But Nicas points out that when Google recently entered into the online travel business, it "began placing its new flight-search service atop general search results" (e.g., above those of Expedia, Oribitz, and other major players in the online travel business). So it would seem that there are good reasons to be concerned about conflicts of interest involving some search engine companies and their role as gatekeepers of the Web.

We already noted Hinman's concern about the veil of corporate secrecy that shields search engine companies from exposure to the public. Much of this secrecy is closely tied to the proprietary search algorithms that major search engines use. But why is this problematic? For one thing, critics argue that the ranking and ordering of Web sites returned to users' search queries often reflects "bias," where some sites are systematically favored over others (see, for example, Introna and Nissenbaum, 2000). This concern, in turn, raises the question of whether the search algorithms used by these companies should be more transparent to the general public. Many critics believe that they should. However, Elgesem (2008) argues that while search engine companies should be required to make their policies more transparent (and to follow those policies), they should not be required to disclose information about their proprietary search algorithms. Unfortunately, we are unable to examine Elgesem's argument in the detail that it deserves.[33]

While a thorough examination of controversies affecting social and moral responsibility issues for search engine companies is beyond the scope of this chapter, it would seem that Hinman and others are correct in claiming that these companies should shoulder a fair degree of social responsibility. We further examine ethical aspects of search engines in Chapters 5 and 10, where we consider some implications that current search technologies have for privacy and democracy, respectively.

4.7.2 Special Responsibilities for Companies that Develop Autonomous Systems

An influential report published in the UK by The Royal Academy of Engineering (2009) notes that *autonomous systems*—from "unmanned vehicles and robots on the battlefield, to autonomous robotic surgery devices, applications for technologies that can operate without human control, learn as they function and ostensibly make decisions"—will soon be available and that these systems raise a number of ethical, legal, and social issues. To this list, we could also add *professional-responsibility issues* for the companies that develop them.

Wendell Wallach and Colin Allen (2009) describe an actual case that closely mirrors one kind of concern anticipated in the Royal Academy's report—i.e., an incident in which a prototype of an autonomous system (designed to make decisions "independent of human oversight") has already malfunctioned and resulted in human casualties. The incident, as noted in the opening section of this chapter, involved a "semiautonomous robotic cannon" (used by the South African army in 2007) that accidentally killed 9 soldiers and wounded 14 others. Wallach and Allen also describe a hypothetical scenario set in the not-too-distant future in which autonomous software agents have been designed to make financial recommendations for their human clients about when to buy and sell stock. A cluster of financial transactions initiated by these autonomous agents then triggers a series of cascading events in which other agents make decisions that ultimately result in an international catastrophe where (a) hundreds of people lose their lives, and (b) billions of dollars are lost in the financial sector. Wallach and Allen ask whether disasters of this kind could be avoided if autonomous systems are embedded with the appropriate kinds of ethical decision-making procedures (software code) that will enable them to make "good moral decisions."

Should the companies that develop these machines be held responsible for "moral-decision-making software code" that they build into them? Wallach, Allen, and others suggest that they should.[34] But to whom, exactly, should these companies be responsible, in the event that the autonomous machines they develop result in accidental human deaths or in severe economic loss? The lack of a clear answer to this question would seem to suggest that explicit policies and laws are needed to anticipate, rather than have to react to, these and related concerns in light of the profound societal impact that autonomous systems will likely have.[35]

In Chapter 12, we examine some broader ethical issues involving the development and use of autonomous machines. There, for example, we consider some implications that the future development of these machines will likely have for our notions of autonomy and trust. In this chapter, however, we simply pose the question of whether the companies that develop autonomous machines may have some special moral responsibilities to society. It would seem that a plausible case can be made for the view that they do.

We conclude this section and chapter by noting that there may indeed be other kinds of computer corporations that also have special responsibilities to society in light of the significant social impacts of their products and services. In some ways, concerns of this type are more appropriately analyzed under the category "business ethics." To the extent that these concerns particularly affect computer/IT professionals, however, they also warrant discussion within the context of cyberethics and professional responsibility as well.

► 4.8 CHAPTER SUMMARY

In this chapter, we examined some ethical problems that confront computer/IT professionals, and we focused on the kinds of issues and challenges that software engineers and their team members sometimes face in the development of safety-critical software. We saw that professional codes of ethics/conduct are useful insofar as they inspire and educate professionals entering and working in the field of computing and information technology. We also saw, however, that many professional codes have serious limitations. We noted that the IEEE-CS/ACM SECEPP was designed to avoid many of the shortcomings of earlier professional codes of ethics.

We also considered questions having to do with employee loyalty, especially in cases where computer/IT professionals have conflicting obligations involving their employers and the public good. We examined circumstances where engineers may be "permitted" to blow the whistle vs. situations in which they might also be "required" to blow the whistle. We also saw that because the notion of accountability in the context of computing has become diffused by the "problem of many hands," it is not always easy to determine where accountability and responsibility for computer malfunctions and errors in safety-critical software systems ultimately lie. Next, we examined some models of risk assessment used in developing software for safety-critical systems. Finally, we asked whether some computer corporations may have special moral responsibilities due to the significant societal impact of the technologies they develop.

Among the relevant professional ethics concerns not considered in this chapter are issues surrounding "open" vs. "closed" software development methodologies. Some ethical aspects of methodologies used in software development are examined in Chapter 8 in our discussion of open source software (OSS) and free software foundation (FSF) development. An ethical issue that also has implications for computer professionals but not examined in this chapter involves the global outsourcing of programming jobs. This controversy is briefly examined in Chapter 10 in connection with our discussion of globalization and the transformation of work. Another professional ethics question not considered in Chapter 4 is whether computer professionals should participate in nano-computing research and development, given certain kinds of controversies surrounding nanotechnology. This question is examined in Chapter 12.

▶ REVIEW QUESTIONS

1. What is professional ethics?
2. What is a profession, and who is a professional?
3. Who is a computer/IT professional?
4. Do computer/IT professionals have special moral responsibilities that ordinary computer users do not have?
5. How do Don Gotterbarn, Keith Miller, and Simon Rogerson propose that we define the profession of software engineering?
6. According to Gotterbarn, what responsibilities do software engineers and their teams have that differentiate them from other professionals working in the computer field?
7. How is "safety-critical software" defined by Kevin Bowyer?
8. What are professional codes of ethics, and what functions do they serve?
9. Briefly describe John Ladd's criticisms of professional codes.
10. Explain Gotterbarn's threefold distinction: codes of ethics, codes of conduct, and codes of practice.
11. Do Gotterbarn's distinctions help to eliminate any of the criticisms that have been raised against professional codes?
12. How does the IEEE-CS/ACM SECEPP improve on earlier professional codes affecting software engineers?
13. What, exactly, is whistle-blowing?
14. Can professional codes guide engineers in determining when it would be appropriate to blow the whistle?
15. What does Helen Nissenbaum mean by *accountability* in a computing context?
16. How is Nissenbaum's notion of accountability different from both liability and responsibility?
17. What does Nissenbaum mean by "the problem of many hands" in a computing/IT context?
18. Describe the conventional criteria used in assessing risk in the software-development process.
19. According to Gotterbarn, what is required for an adequate model of risk analysis for the development of safety-critical systems?
20. Do some computer corporations, including search engine companies and companies that develop autonomous systems, have any special societal obligations?

▶ DISCUSSION QUESTIONS

21. Evaluate Richard De George's criteria for when it is morally permissible, as opposed to when it is morally required for an engineer to blow the whistle (described in Section 4.4.2). Apply these criteria to a recent controversy where you believe that blowing the whistle would have been morally permissible or perhaps even morally required.
22. Revisit Michael McFarland's argument for the position that we described as an "alternative strategy" for understanding the concept of professional responsibility for engineers (in Section 4.4.3). Does McFarland present a practical alternative? How could this model help individual engineers who, as members of the broader engineering profession, find themselves in a situation where they believe it would be appropriate to blow the whistle?

▶ ESSAY/PRESENTATION QUESTIONS

23. Describe some virtues of the ethical codes of conduct adopted by professional societies such as the ACM and IEEE-CS, and list some shortcomings of these professional codes as well. In the final analysis, do the advantages of having a code outweigh the prospects of not having one? Use either an actual or a hypothetical case to establish the main points in your answer. Do you believe that a coherent and comprehensive code of conduct for the computing/IT profession is possible? Does SECEEP satisfy those conditions?
24. Recall the various arguments that we examined as to when it is appropriate, and sometimes mandatory, for software engineers and IT professionals to blow the whistle. The criteria for when whistle-blowing is permissible, at least for those working in

some federal government agencies, changed following the September 11, 2001 terrorist attacks. In November 2002, the Homeland Security Act was passed in both houses of Congress and was signed into law by former President George W. Bush. On one interpretation of the revised law, whistle-blowing acts similar to that of Colleen Rowley—who blew the whistle on her FBI superiors who failed to act on information they received in the days preceding September 11—would be illegal and thus a punishable offense. What implications could this have for software engineers and other computer professionals whose employment comes under the auspices of the Homeland Security Department? In this case, what set of rules should computer/IT professionals follow?

Scenarios for Analysis

1. Describe the process of ethical deliberation that you would use in trying to resolve the following dilemma.

    You have been working for the XYZ Computer Corporation as an entry-level software engineer since you graduated from college last May. You have done very well so far; you are respected by the management team, are well liked by your fellow engineers, and have been assigned to a team of engineers that has consistently worked on the most critical and valued projects and contracts that XYZ Corp. has secured. XYZ's most recent contract is for a United States defense project involving the missile defense system, and again you have been assigned to the engineering team that will develop the software for this project. However, you are staunchly opposed to the project's objectives, so you ask to be reassigned. Your supervisor and coworkers, as well as upper management, are disappointed to learn of your strong feelings about this project. You are asked to reconsider your views, and you are promised a bonus and a substantial pay increase if you agree to work on this project during the next year. You also discover from a colleague that refusing to work on this project would greatly diminish your career advancement at XYZ and may even make you vulnerable in the event of future layoffs. To compound matters, you and your spouse are expecting your first child in about three months and you recently purchased a home. What would you do?

2. In analyzing the following scenario, what course of action would you take? Would you be willing to blow the whistle? Explain your position.

    For the past six months you have worked on a project to develop a transportation-related software program for the city of Agropolis, a project designed to make some much needed improvements to Agropolis's system of public transportation. You and your team of programmers have worked very hard on this project, but you have encountered difficulties that could not possibly have been anticipated in the original design plan; these difficulties have put your project significantly behind schedule. The city transportation planners are nervous, because they depend on the software from your company to get the new transportation system up and running. And the management at your company is very uncomfortable because it signed a contract to deliver the required software on time. Although the software is not yet foolproof, testing so far reveals that it works about 99% of the time. The few glitches that remain apply only to the transportation system's backup code, which arguably would be needed in only the most severe emergencies. Residents of the city are also eager to have the new transportation system in place.

    A decision is made by the management of your company and by the managers of the city transportation system to go ahead and implement the software as it is. They base their decision on the probability that a backup system would not be needed for several months (at which time the remaining bugs should be fixed). A decision was also made by the management groups on both sides not to announce publicly that the software still has a few bugs. You and a few of your coworkers believe that the bugs are more dangerous than the managemers are willing to admit. What would you do in this case?

▶ ENDNOTES

1. See George C. Wilson. "Navy Missile Downs Iranian Jetliner on 4th of July," *Washington Post* (July 4, 1998), p. A01.
2. See Leveson and Turner (2001).
3. See, for example, Gotterbarn (1995).
4. Harris, Pritchard, and Rabins (2004), p. 9.
5. Barger (2008), p. 85.
6. Buchanan (2004), p. 620.
7. Buchanan suggests that an "information professional" can be conceived of along these lines.
8. Gotterbarn, Miller, and Rogerson (1999) suggest that a software engineering team can be thought of as those who contribute by direct participation to "the analysis, specification, design, development, certification, maintenance and testing of software systems."
9. See Bowyer (2001), p. 165.
10. The full text of IEEE Code of Ethics is available at http://www.ieee.org/web/membership/ethics/code_ethics.html.
11. The full text of the ACM Code of ethics is available at http://web.mit.edu/afs/athena.mit.edu/course/2/2.95j/Codes-of-Ethics/ACM-Code-of-Ethics.html.
12. For a full description of these five features, see Bynum and Rogerson (2004), pp. 135–36.
13. Davis (1995), p. 586.
14. *Ibid*, p. 586.
15. The text of both versions of this code (short and full) is available at http://seeri.etsu.edu/Codes/TheSECode.htm.
16. See Gotterbarn, Miller, and Rogerson (1999).
17. Mitcham (1997), p. 262.
18. Bok (2003), p. 53.
19. Another classic whistle-blowing case in a computer/engineering context involved the Bay Area Rapid Transit (BART) in California in the late 1960s/early 1970s. For a description of this case, see Bok, pp. 51–52.
20. For more information on this case, see Bowyer (2002).
21. The full text for these three conditions is included in De George (1999), pp. 251–53.
22. See De George, pp. 250–56, for the full text of his five conditions for whistle-blowing.
23. De George, pp. 255–56. De George's fourth and fifth conditions are also presented in summarized form here.
24. See Johnson (1991) for some classic articles that critique De George's model for whistle-blowing.
25. McFarland (1991), pp. 159–60.
26. Nissenbaum (2007), p. 274. [Italics Added]
27. See Nissenbaum, p. 275.
28. For more detail, see Leveson and Turner (2001).
29. See Nissenbaum, p. 279. She also includes some additional guidelines, such as "independent auditing" and "excellent documentation."
30. For more information on this case, see Gotterbarn (2004).
31. See Gotterbarn (2004), p. 675. An expanded version of his model is included in Gotterbarn, Clear, and Kwan (2008).
32. See Hinman (2005), p. 21.
33. My analysis of professional-ethics-related issues affecting search engines in this section draws from Tavani (2012).
34. See, for example, the views expressed on this topic by various authors included in M. Anderson and S. Anderson (2011).
35. My analysis of professional-ethics-related issues affecting autonomous machines in this section draws from Tavani (2011).

▶ REFERENCES

Anderson, Michael, and Susan Leigh Anderson, eds. 2011. *Machine Ethics*. Cambridge: Cambridge University Press.

Barger, Robert N. 2003. "Can We Find a Single Ethical Code?" In M. David Ermann and Michele S. Shauf, eds. *Computers, Ethics, and Society*. New York: Oxford University Press, pp. 42–47.

Barger, Robert N. 2008. *Computer Ethics: A Case-Based Approach*. New York: Cambridge University Press.

Bok, Sisela. 2003. "The Morality of Whistle Blowing." In M. David Ermann and Michele S. Shauf, eds. *Computers, Ethics, and Society*. 3rd ed. New York: Oxford University Press, pp. 47–54.

Bowyer, Kevin, ed. 2001. *Ethics and Computing: Living Responsibly in a Computerized World*. 2nd ed. New York: IEEE Press.

Bowyer, Kevin. 2002. "Star Wars Revisited: Ethics and Safety-Critical Software." *IEEE Technology and Society* 21, no. 1: 13–26.

Buchanan, Elizabeth A. 2004. "Ethical Considerations for the Information Professions." In R. A. Spinello and H. T. Tavani, eds. *Readings in CyberEthics*. 2nd ed. Sudbury, MA: Jones and Bartlett Publishers, pp. 613–24.

Bynum, Terrell Ward, and Simon Rogerson, eds. 2004. *Computer Ethics and Professional Responsibility*. Malden, MA: Blackwell.

Carr, Nicholas. 2011. *The Shallows: What the Internet is Doing to Our Brain*. New York: Norton.

Davis, Michael. 1995. "Thinking Like an Engineer." In D. G. Johnson and H. Nissenbaum, eds. *Computing Ethics and*

Social Values. Englewood Cliffs, NJ: Prentice Hall, pp. 586–97.

De George, Richard T. 1999. *Business Ethics.* 3rd ed. Upper Saddle River, NJ: Prentice Hall.

Elgesem, Dag. 2008. "Search Engines and the Public Use of Reason." *Ethics and Information Technology* 10, no. 4: 233–42.

Fairweather, N. Ben. 2004. "No PAPA: Why Incomplete Codes of Ethics are Worse Than None at All." In T. W. Bynum and S. Rogerson, eds. *Computer Ethics and Professional Responsibility.* Malden, MA: Blackwell, pp. 142–56.

Gotterbarn, Don. 1995. "Computer Ethics: Responsibility Regained." In D. G. Johnson and H. Nissenbaum, eds. *Computers, Ethics and Social Values.* Englewood Cliffs, NJ: Prentice Hall, pp. 18–24.

Gotterbarn, Don. 2000. "Computer Professionals and YOUR Responsibilities." In D. Langford, ed. *Internet Ethics.* New York: St. Martin's Press, pp. 200–19.

Gotterbarn, Don. 2001. "The Ethical Software Engineer." In K. W. Bowyer, ed. *Ethics and Computing: Living Responsibly in a Computerized World.* 2nd ed. New York: IEEE Press, p. 67.

Gotterbarn, Don. 2004. "Reducing Software Failures: Address Ethical Risks With Software Development Impact Statements." In R. A. Spinello and H. T. Tavani, eds. *Readings in CyberEthics.* 2nd ed. Sudbury, MA: Jones and Bartlett Publishers, pp. 674–89.

Gotterbarn, Don, Tony Clear, and Choon-Tuck Kwan. 2008. "A Practical Mechanism for Ethical Risk Assessment—A SoDIS Inspection." In K. E. Himma and H. T. Tavani, eds. *The Handbook of Information and Computer Ethics.* Hoboken, NJ: John Wiley and Sons, pp. 429–71.

Gotterbarn, Don, and Keith Miller. 2009. "The Public is Priority: Making Decisions Using the Software Code of Ethics," *IEEE Computer* 42, no. 6: 66–73.

Gotterbarn, Don, Keith Miller, and Simon Rogerson. 1999. "Software Engineering Code of Ethics Approved." *Communications of the ACM* 42, no. 10: 102–07.

Harris, Charles E., Michael S. Pritchard, and Michael J. Rabins. 2004. *Engineering Ethics: Concepts and Cases.* 3rd ed. Belmont, CA: Wadsworth.

Hinman, Lawrence M. 2005. "Esse Est Indicato in Google: Ethical and Political Issues in Search Engines." *International Review of Information Ethics* 3: 19–25.

Hinman, Lawrence M. 2008. "Searching Ethics: The Role of Search Engines in the Construction and Distribution of Knowledge." In A. Spink and M. Zimmer, eds. *Web Search: Multidisciplinary Perspectives.* Berlin: Springer–Verlag, pp. 67–76.

Introna, Lucas, and Helen Nissenbaum. 2000. "Shaping the Web: Why the Politics of Search Engines Matters." *The Information Society.* 16, no. 3: 169–185.

Johnson, Deborah G., ed. 1991. *Ethical Issues in Engineering.* Englewood Cliffs, NJ: Prentice Hall.

Ladd, John. 1995. "The Quest for a Code of Professional Ethics: An Intellectual and Moral Confusion." In D. G. Johnson and H. Nissenbaum, eds. *Computers, Ethics and Social Values.* Englewood Cliffs, NJ: Prentice Hall, pp. 580–85.

Leveson, Nancy G., and Clark S. Turner. 2001. "An Investigation of the Therac-25 Accidents." In K. W. Bowyer, ed. *Ethics and Computing: Living Responsibly in a Computerized World.* 2nd ed. New York: IEEE Press, pp. 200–24.

Lin, Patrick. 2012. "Introduction to Robot Ethics." In P. Lin, K. Abney, and G. Bekey, eds. *Robot Ethics: The Ethical and Social Implications of Robotics.* Cambridge, MA: MIT Press, pp. 3–16.

Martin, Michael W., and Roland Schinzinger. 2004. *Ethics in Engineering.* 4th ed. New York: McGraw-Hill.

McFarland, Michael C. 1991. "The Public Health, Safety, and Welfare: An Analysis of the Social Responsibility of Engineers." In D. G. Johnson, ed. *Ethical Issues in Engineering.* Englewood Cliffs, NJ: Prentice Hall, pp. 159–74.

Mitcham, Carl. 1997. "Engineering Design Research and Social Responsibility." In K. Schrader-Frechette and L. Westra, eds. *Technology and Values.* Lanham, MD: Rowman and Littlefield, pp. 261–78.

Nicas, Jack. 2011. "Google Roils Travel." *Wall Street Journal,* 12/27. Available at http://online.wsj.com/article/SB10001424052970203686204577116700668483194.html.

Nissenbaum, Helen. 2007. "Computing and Accountability." In J. Weckert, ed. *Computer Ethics.* Aldershot, UK: Ashgate, pp. 273–80. Reprinted from *Communications of the ACM* 37 (1994): 37–40.

Parnas, David Lorge. 1990. "Professional Responsibility to Blow the Whistle on SDI." In M. D. Ermann, M. B. Williams, and C. Guiterrez, eds. *Computers, Ethics, and Society.* New York: Oxford University Press, pp. 359–72.

Perlman, Bruce, and Roli Varma. 2002. "Improving Engineering Practice," *IEEE Technology and Society* 21, no. 1: 40–47.

Schneir, Bruce. 2004. *Secrets and Lies: Digital Security in a Networked World.* Rev. ed. New York: John Wiley & Sons.

Tavani, Herman T. 2011. "Can We Develop Artificial Agents Capable of Making Good Moral Decisions?" *Minds and Machines* 21: 465–74.

Tavani, Herman T. 2012. "Search Engines and Ethics." In E. Zalta, ed. *Stanford Encyclopedia of Philosophy.* Available at http://plato.stanford.edu/entries/ethics-search.

The Royal Academy of Engineering. 2009. *Autonomous Systems: Social, Legal and Ethical Issues.* London, UK. Available at www.raeng.org.uk/autonomoussystems.

Wallach, Wendell, and Colin Allen. 2009. *Moral Machines: Teaching Robots Right from Wrong.* New York: Oxford University Press.

Yurcik, William, and David Doss. 2002. "Software Technology Issues for a U.S. National Missile Defense System." *IEEE Technology and Society* 21, no. 2: 36–46.

▶ FURTHER READINGS

Allen, Colin, and Wendell Wallach. "Moral Machines: Contradiction in Terms or Abdication of Human Responsibility." In P. Lin, K. Abney, and G. Bekey, eds. *Robot Ethics: The Ethical and Social Implications of Robotics*. Cambridge, MA: MIT Press, 2012, pp. 55–68.

Birsch, Douglas. "Moral Responsibility for Harm Caused by Computer System Failures." *Ethics and Information Technology* 6, no. 4 (2004): 233–45.

Buchanan, Elizabeth A., and Kathrine A. Henderson. *Case Studies in Library and Information Science Ethics*. Jefferson, NC: McFarland, 2009.

Friedman, Batya, Peter H. Kahn, Jr., and Alan Borning. "Value Sensitive Design and Information Systems." In K. E. Himma and H. T. Tavani, eds. *The Handbook of Information and Computer Ethics*. Hoboken, NJ: John Wiley and Sons, 2008, pp. 69–101.

Moor, James H. "If Aristotle Were a Computing Professional." In R. Baird, R. Ramsower, and S. E. Rosenbaum, eds. *Cyberethics: Social and Moral Issues in the Computer Age*. Amherst, NY: Prometheus, 2000, pp. 34–40.

Rashid, Awais, John Weckert, and Richard Lucas. "Software Engineering Ethics in a Digital World." *IEEE Computer* 42, no. 6 (2009): 34–41.

CHAPTER

▼

5

Privacy and Cyberspace

Of all the ethical issues associated with the use of cybertechnology, perhaps none has received more media attention than concern about the loss of personal privacy. In this chapter, we examine issues involving privacy and cybertechnology by asking the following questions:

- How are privacy concerns generated by the use of cybertechnology different from privacy issues raised by earlier technologies?
- What, exactly, is personal privacy, and why is it valued?
- How do computerized techniques used to gather and collect information, such as Internet "cookies" and radio frequency identification (RFID) technology, raise concerns for personal privacy?
- How do the transfer and exchange of personal information across and between databases, carried out in computerized merging and matching operations, threaten personal privacy?
- How do tools used to "mine" personal data exacerbate existing privacy concerns involving cybertechnology?
- Can personal information we disclose to friends in social networking services (SNS), such as Facebook and Twitter, be used in ways that threaten our privacy?
- How do the use of Internet search engines and the availability of online public records contribute to the problem of protecting "privacy in public"?
- Do privacy-enhancing tools provide Internet users with adequate protection for their online personal information?
- Are current privacy laws and data protection schemes adequate?

Concerns about privacy can affect many aspects of an individual's life—from commerce to healthcare to work to recreation. For example, we speak of consumer privacy, medical and healthcare privacy, employee and workplace privacy, and so forth. Unfortunately, we cannot examine all of these categories of privacy in a single chapter. So we will have to postpone our analysis of certain kinds of privacy issues until later chapters in the book. For example, we will examine some ways that medical/genetic privacy issues are aggravated by cybertechnology in our discussion of bioinformatics in Chapter 12, and we will examine some particular employee/workplace privacy issues affected by the use of cybertechnology in our discussion of workplace surveillance and employee monitoring in Chapter 10. Some cyber-related privacy concerns that conflict with cybersecurity issues and national security interests will be examined in Chapter 6, where privacy-related concerns affecting "cloud computing" are also considered. In our discussion of emerging and converging technologies in Chapter 12, we examine some issues that affect a relatively new category of privacy called "location privacy," which arise because of the use of embedded chips, RFID technology, and global positioning systems (GPS).

Although some cyber-related privacy concerns are specific to one or more spheres or sectors—i.e., employment, healthcare, and so forth—others cut across multiple dimensions of our lives, affecting virtually all persons regardless of their employment or health status. The privacy issues involving cybertechnology examined in this chapter affect each of us, whether or not we have ever owned or even used a networked computer. Consider that in carrying out many of our day-to-day activities, we supply information to organizations that use computers to record, store, and exchange those data. These activities can include information we provide in filling out various forms, or they can include information acquired from our commercial transactions in a bank or a store. Also consider that many people now engage in online commerce activities, and this raises some additional consumer-related privacy worries. But users who navigate the Web solely for recreational purposes are also at risk with respect to their privacy. For example, personal data about one's interests and preferences can be acquired by organizations and by individuals whose need for this information is not always obvious. Furthermore, personal data about us collected via our online activities and transactions can then be sold to third parties.

Also consider that applications such as Google Street View (a feature of Google Earth and Google Maps) make use of satellite cameras and GPS software that enable Internet users to zoom in on your house or place of employment and potentially record information about you. Additionally, closed circuit television cameras (CCTVs) located in public places and in shopping malls record many of your daily movements as you casually stroll through those environments. So even if you have never used a computer, cell phone, (Internet-enabled) electronic device, etc., your privacy is threatened in ways that were not possible in the past.

In this chapter, we examine a wide range of privacy concerns affecting the day-to-day activities of ordinary individuals carried out in both online and offline contexts. We also note, however, that cybertechnology is not the first technology to threaten personal privacy. We begin by looking at some ways to distinguish current issues associated with cybertechnology from privacy concerns involving earlier technologies.

▶ 5.1 ARE PRIVACY CONCERNS ASSOCIATED WITH CYBERTECHNOLOGY UNIQUE OR SPECIAL?

Concerns about personal privacy existed long before the advent of computers and cybertechnology. Prior to the information era, for example, technologies such as the camera and the telephone presented challenges for privacy. So we can ask: what, if anything, is special about the privacy concerns that are associated with cybertechnology?

Consider the impact that changes involving this technology have had on privacy with respect to the

- *amount* of personal information that can be collect,
- *speed* at which personal information can be transmitted,
- *duration* of time that the information can be retained,
- *kind* of information that can be acquired and exchanged.

Cybertechnology makes it possible to collect and store much more information about individuals than was possible in the precomputer era. The *amount* of personal information that could be collected in the precomputer era was determined by practical considerations, such as the physical space required to store the data and the time and difficulty involved in collecting the data. Today, of course, digitized information that can be stored electronically in computer databases takes up very little storage space and can be collected with relative ease.

Consider the *speed* at which information is exchanged and transferred between databases. At one time, records had to be physically transported between filing destinations; the time it took to move them depended upon the transportation systems—e.g., motor vehicles, trains, airplanes, and so forth—that carried the records. Now, of course, records can be transferred between electronic databases in milliseconds through wireless technologies, high-speed cable lines, or even ordinary telephone lines.

With so much information being collected and transferred so rapidly, many have expressed concerns about its accuracy as well as the difficulties in tracking down and correcting any inaccuracies that might have been transferred. In an interview conducted for the BBC TV series *The Machine that Changed the World*, Harvard law professor Arthur Miller points out that trying to correct such information is like "chasing a greased pig"—you may get your hands on the pig, but it is very difficult to keep the pig firmly in your grip.[1] Although issues concerning the accuracy of personal information are clearly distinguishable from those concerning privacy *per se*, accuracy issues are frequently associated with privacy issues, and both are impacted by cybertechnology.

Also, consider the *duration* of information—that is, how long information can be kept. Before the information era, information was manually recorded and stored in file cabinets and then in large physical repositories; it is unlikely that report cards my parents received as high school students still exist somewhere as physical records in file cabinets, for at that time, report cards were not computerized but instead existed, literally, as ink marks on paper. But the report cards my daughter received when she was a high school student were both generated and stored using computer technology. As an electronic record, her report card can be kept indefinitely, and the grades she received as a high school student (as well as the grades she received in elementary school and in college) can follow her throughout her life.

In the past, practices involving the retention of personal data were perhaps more "forgiving." Because of practical limitations, such as physical storage space, that affected how long personal data could be kept on file, much of the personal information collected and stored had to be destroyed after a certain number of years. Since information could not be archived indefinitely, people with blemished records sometimes had the opportunity to start over again by physically relocating. Today, however, one's electronic dossier would likely follow, making it very difficult, if not impossible, for that person to start over with a clean slate. We can argue whether the current means of data retention is a good thing, but it is difficult to dispute the claim that now, because of cybertechnology, most of us have what Arthur Miller calls a "womb-to-tomb dossier."

Cybertechnology has also generated privacy concerns because of the *kind* of personal information that can now be collected. For example, every time you engage in an electronic transaction, such as making a purchase with a credit card or withdrawing money from an ATM, transactional information is collected and stored in several computer databases; this information can then be transferred electronically across commercial networks to agencies that request it. Personal information, retrieved from transactional information that is stored in computer databases, has been used to construct electronic dossiers containing detailed information about an individual's commercial transactions, including purchases made and places traveled—information that can reveal patterns in a person's preferences and habits.

Additionally, we should note that cybertechnology raises privacy concerns because of the myriad ways in which it enables our personal information to be *manipulated* (e.g., merged, matched, and "mined") once it has been collected. For example, unrelated pieces of information about us that reside in separate databases can be *merged* together to construct electronic personal dossiers or profiles. Also, information about us included in one database can be *matched* against records in other databases that contain information about us. Furthermore, our personal information can be *mined* (from databases, as well as from our activities on the Web) to reveal patterns in our behavior that would have been very difficult to discern in the precomputer era. (We examine controversies associated with data merging, matching, and mining practices in Sections 5.5 and 5.6.) Of course, our personal data could have been, and in some instances was, manipulated in the precomputer era as well. But there were practical limitations to the amount of information merging, matching, and mining that could be done manually by humans.

Although the privacy concerns that we now associate with cybertechnology may not be totally new, or even altogether different in kind, from those we associate with earlier technologies, few would dispute the claim that cybertechnology has exacerbated them. In Sections 5.4–5.7, we examine specific uses of cybertechnology that raise concerns for personal privacy. First, however, we examine the concept of personal privacy to better understand what privacy is and why we value it.

▶ 5.2 WHAT IS PERSONAL PRIVACY?

Although many definitions of privacy have been put forth, there is no universally agreed upon definition of this concept. To illustrate this point, consider some of the metaphors that are typically associated with privacy. Sometimes we speak of privacy as something that can be *lost* or *diminished*, suggesting that privacy can be understood in terms of a repository of personal information that can be either diminished altogether or gradually eroded. Contrast this view with descriptions of privacy as something that can be *intruded upon* or *invaded*, where privacy can be understood in terms of a spatial metaphor, such as a zone, that deserves protection. Alternatively, privacy is sometimes described as something that can be violated or breached, when we think of it in terms of either a right or an interest that deserves legal protection. Because of these different conceptions of privacy, we will see that it is useful to distinguish between the notions of one's having privacy (in a descriptive sense) and one's having a (normative) right to privacy. We will say more about this distinction in Section 5.2.4.

Privacy analysts have pointed out that in the United States, the meaning of privacy has evolved since the eighteenth century. Initially, privacy was understood in terms of freedom from (physical) intrusion. Later it became associated with freedom from interference into one's personal affairs, including one's ability to make decisions freely. Most recently, privacy has come to be closely identified with concerns affecting access to and control of personal information—a view that is also referred to as "informational privacy." Although the main emphasis in this chapter is on informational privacy, we also briefly examine the other two views.

5.2.1 Accessibility Privacy: Freedom from Unwarranted Intrusion

In a seminal paper on privacy, Samuel Warren and Louis Brandeis suggested that privacy could be understood as "being let alone" or "being free from intrusion." Appearing in the *Harvard Law Review* in 1890, the Warren and Brandeis article made the first explicit reference to privacy as a legal right in the United States. Many Americans are astonished to find out that there is no explicit mention of privacy in either the Constitution or its first ten amendments, the Bill of Rights. However, some legal scholars believe that a right to privacy can be inferred from the Fourth Amendment, which protects citizens against unreasonable searches and seizures of personal affects (i.e., papers, artifacts, etc.) by the government. Many legal scholars believe that the Fourth Amendment also provides legal grounds for a right to privacy protection from nongovernmental intrusion as well.

Warren and Brandeis also suggested that our legal right to privacy is grounded in our "right to inviolate personality." In part, they were responding to a certain use of a new technology—not the computer, of course, but rather the camera—which had begun to threaten individual privacy in new ways.[2] Photographs of people began to appear in newspapers, for example, in gossip columns, along with stories that were defamatory and sometimes even false. Warren and Brandeis believed that individuals have a (legal) right not be intruded upon in this manner. Because this definition of privacy as freedom from unwarranted intrusion focuses on the harm that can be caused through physical access to a person or to a person's possessions, Judith DeCew (1997) and others have described this view as *accessibility privacy*.

5.2.2 Decisional Privacy: Freedom from Interference in One's Personal Affairs

Privacy is also sometimes conceived of as freedom from interference in one's personal choices, plans, and decisions; some refer to this view as *decisional privacy*. This kind of privacy has also been associated with reproductive technologies having to do with contraception. In *Griswold v. Connecticut* (1965), the court ruled that a person's right to get counseling about contraceptive techniques could not be denied by state laws. The view of privacy as freedom from external interference into one's personal affairs has since been appealed to in legal arguments in a series of controversial court cases, such as those involving abortion and euthanasia. For example, this view of privacy was appealed to in the landmark Supreme Court decision on abortion (*Roe v. Wade* 1973), as well as in a state court's decision involving Karen Ann Quinlan's right to be removed from life-support systems and thus her "right to die."[3] Because it focuses on one's right not to be interfered with, decisional privacy can be distinguished from both accessibility privacy and informational privacy.

5.2.3 Informational Privacy: Control over the Flow of Personal Information

Because of the increasing use of technology to gather and exchange personal information, many contemporary analysts view privacy in connection with one's ability to restrict access to and control the flow of one's personal information. Privacy concerns are now often framed in terms of questions such as: Who should have access to one's personal information? To what extent can individuals control the ways in which information about them can be gathered, stored, mined, combined, recombined, exchanged, and sold? These are our primary concerns in this chapter, where we focus on *informational privacy*.

Table 5.1 summarizes the three views of privacy.

5.2.4 A Comprehensive Account of Privacy

James Moor (2000) has introduced an account of privacy that incorporates important elements of the nonintrusion, noninterference, and informational views of privacy. According to Moor,

> An individual [has] privacy *in a situation* with regard to others if and only if in that situation the individual [is] *protected from intrusion, interference,* and *information access* by others.[4]

An important element in this definition is Moor's notion of "situation," which he deliberately leaves broad so that it can apply to a range of contexts, or zones, that can be "declared private." For example, a situation can be an "activity" or a "relationship," or it can be the "storage and access of information" in a computer.

Central to Moor's theory is a distinction between *naturally private* and *normatively private* situations, enabling us to differentiate between the conditions required for (a) having privacy and (b) having a right to privacy. This distinction, in turn, enables us to differentiate between a loss of privacy and a violation of privacy. In a naturally private situation, individuals are protected from access and interference from others by natural means, for example, physical boundaries such as those one enjoys while hiking alone in the woods. In this case, privacy can be *lost* but not *violated*, because there are no norms—conventional, legal, or ethical—according to which one has a *right*, or even an expectation, to be protected. In a normatively private situation, on the other hand, individuals are protected by conventional norms (e.g., formal laws and informal policies) because they involve certain kinds of zones or contexts that we have determined to need

TABLE 5.1 Three Views of Privacy

Accessibility privacy	Privacy is defined as one's physically being let alone, or being free from intrusion into one's physical space.
Decisional privacy	Privacy is defined as freedom from interference in one's choices and decisions.
Informational privacy	Privacy is defined as control over the flow of one's personal information, including the transfer and exchange of that information.

normative protection. The following two scenarios will help us to differentiate between normative and natural (or descriptive) privacy.

▶ **SCENARIO 5–1:** Descriptive Privacy

Mary arrives in the computer lab at her university at 11:00 PM to work on a paper that is due the next day. No one else is in lab at the time that Mary arrives there, and no one enters the lab until 11:45 PM, when Tom—the computer lab coordinator—returns to close the lab for the evening. As Tom enters, he sees Mary typing on one of the desktop computers in the lab. Mary seems startled as she looks up from her computer and discovers that Tom is gazing at her. ◾

Did Mary lose her privacy when Tom entered the lab and saw her? Was her privacy violated? Before Tom noticed her in the lab, we could say that Mary had privacy in the descriptive, or natural, sense of the term because no one was physically observing her while she was in the lab. When Tom entered and noticed that Mary was typing on a computer, Mary lost her natural (or descriptive) privacy in that situation. However, we should not infer that her privacy was violated in this incident, because a university's computer lab is not the kind of situation or zone that is declared normatively private and thus protected.

▶ **SCENARIO 5–2:** Normative Privacy

Tom decides to follow Mary, from a distance, as she leaves the computer lab to return to her (off-campus) apartment. He carefully follows her to the apartment building, and then stealthily follows Mary up the stairway to the corridor leading to her apartment. Once Mary is safely inside her apartment, Tom peeps through a keyhole in the door. He observes Mary as she interacts with her laptop computer in her apartment. ◾

Has Mary's privacy been violated in this scenario? In both scenarios, Tom observes Mary interacting with a computer. In the first scenario, the observation occurred in a public place. There, Mary may have lost some privacy in a descriptive or natural sense, but she had no expectation of preserving her privacy in that particular situation. In the second scenario, Mary not only lost her privacy but her privacy was violated as well, because apartments are examples of zones or "situations" that we, as a society, have declared normatively private.

We have explicit rules governing these situations with respect to privacy protection. Note that it was not merely the fact that Tom had observed Mary's interactions with a computer that resulted in her privacy being violated in the second scenario. Rather, it was because Tom had observed her doing this in a normatively protected situation. So, there was nothing in the information *per se* that Tom acquired about Mary that threatened her privacy; it was the situation or context in which information about Mary was acquired that caused her privacy to be violated in the second scenario.

5.2.5 Privacy as "Contextual Integrity"

We have seen the important role that a situation, or context, plays in Moor's privacy theory. But some critics argue that the meaning of a situation or context is either too broad or too vague. Helen Nissenbaum (2004a, 2010) elaborates on the notion of a context in her model of privacy as "contextual integrity," where she links adequate privacy protection to "norms of specific contexts." She notes that the things we do, including the transactions and events that occur in our daily lives, all take place in some context or other. In her scheme, contexts include "spheres of life" such as education, politics, the marketplace, and so forth.

Nissenbaum's privacy framework requires that the processes used in gathering and disseminating information (a) are "appropriate to a particular context" and (b) comply with norms that govern the flow of personal information in a given context.[5] She refers to these two types of informational norms as follows:

1. Norms of appropriateness.
2. Norms of distribution.

Whereas norms of appropriateness determine whether a given type of personal information is either appropriate or inappropriate to divulge within a particular context, norms of distribution restrict or limit the flow of information within and across contexts. When either norm has been "breached," a violation of privacy occurs; conversely, the contextual integrity of the flow of personal information is maintained when both kinds of norms are "respected."[6]

As in the case of Moor's privacy model, Nissenbaum's theory demonstrates why we must always attend to the context in which information flows, and not to the nature of the information itself, in determining whether normative protection is needed. To illustrate some of the nuances in her framework of privacy as contextual integrity, consider the following scenario in which a professor collects information about students in his seminar.

▶ **SCENARIO 5–3:** Preserving Contextual Integrity in a University Seminar

Professor Roberts teaches a seminar on social issues in computing to upper division undergraduate students at his university. Approximately half of the students who enroll in his seminar each semester are computer science (CS) students, whereas the other half are students majoring in humanities, business, etc. At the first class meeting for each seminar, Professor Roberts asks students to fill out an index card on which they include information about their major, their year of study (junior, senior, etc.), the names of any previous CS courses they may have taken (if they are non-CS majors), their preferred e-mail address, and what they hope to acquire from the seminar. Professor Roberts then records this information in his electronic grade book. ■

Has Professor Roberts done anything wrong in requesting and collecting this information? For the most part, it is information that he could have gathered from the registrar's office at his university—e.g., information about which CS courses the students took, and so forth. But Roberts finds it much more convenient to collect information in the classroom, and he informs the students that he uses that information in determining which kinds of assignments he will decide to give to the class in general, and which kinds of criteria he will use to assign students to various group projects.

Because Professor Roberts has informed the students about how the information they provided to him will be used in the context of the classroom, and because the students have consented to give him the information, no privacy violation seems to have occurred. In fact, the process used by Professor Roberts satisfies the conditions for Nissenbaum's norm of appropriateness with respect to contextual integrity.

Next, suppose that Professor Roberts has lunch a few weeks later with a former student of his, Phil, who recently graduated and now has a job as a software engineer for a publishing company. Phil's company plans to release its first issue of a new magazine aimed at recent CS graduates, and it has launched an advertising campaign designed to attract undergraduate CS majors who will soon graduate. Phil asks Professor Roberts for the names of the CS majors in the seminar he is teaching. Professor Roberts is initially inclined to identify some students that Phil would likely know from classes that he had taken the previous year at the university. But should Professor Roberts reveal those names to Phil?

If he did, Professor Roberts would violate the privacy norm of distribution within the context of the seminar he is teaching. Consider that the students gave information about themselves to Professor Roberts for use in the context of that seminar. While his use of that information for purposes of the seminar is context-appropriate, passing on (i.e., distributing) any of that information to Phil is not, because it would violate the integrity of that context. Even though the information about the students that Professor Roberts has collected is not highly sensitive or confidential information, it was given to him for use only in the context of the seminar he is teaching. Insofar as Professor Roberts uses the information in that context, he preserves its integrity. But if he elects to distribute the information outside that context, he violates its integrity and breaches the privacy of his students.

► 5.3 WHY IS PRIVACY IMPORTANT?

Of what value is privacy? Why does privacy matter, and why should we care about it? In 1999, Scott McNealy, then CEO of Sun Microsystems, uttered his now famous remark to a group of reporters: "You have zero privacy anyway. Get over it." Is the idea of personal privacy merely a relic of the past? Michael Froomkin (2000) and Simson Garfinkel (2000) both speak of the "death of privacy." But not everyone has conceded defeat in the battle over privacy. Some privacy advocates staunchly believe that we should be vigilant about retaining what little privacy we may still have. Others note that we do not appreciate the value of privacy until we lose it, and by then it is usually too late. They point out that once privacy has been lost, it is difficult, if not impossible, to get back. So perhaps we should heed their warnings and try to protect privacy to the degree that we can.

We might also question whether the current privacy debate needs to be better understood in terms of differences that reflect generational attitudes. For many so-called Millennials, who are now college-aged, privacy does not always seem to be of paramount importance. Most Millennials, as well as many members of Generations X and Y, seem all too eager to share their personal information widely on social networking services such as Facebook, and many also seem willing to post "away messages" on AIM or Skype that disclose their whereabouts at a given moment to a wide range of people. But for many older Americans, including Baby Boomers, privacy is something that is generally still valued. So the relative importance of privacy may vary considerably among the generations; however, we will proceed on the assumption that privacy has value and thus is important.

Is privacy universally valued? Or is it valued mainly in Western, industrialized societies where greater importance is placed on the individual? It has been argued that some non-Western nations and cultures do not value individual privacy as much as we do in the West. Alan Westin believes that countries with strong democratic political institutions consider privacy more important than do less democratic ones.[7] Nations such as Singapore and the People's Republic of China seem to place less importance on individual privacy and greater significance on broader social values, which are perceived to benefit the state's community objectives. Even in countries such as Israel, with strong democratic systems but an even stronger priority for national security, individual privacy may not be as important a value as it is in most democratic nations. So, even though privacy has at least some universal appeal, it is not valued to the same degree in all nations and cultures. As a result, it may be difficult to get universal agreement on privacy laws and policies in cyberspace.

5.3.1 Is Privacy an Intrinsic Value?

Is privacy something that is valued for its own sake—that is, does it have intrinsic value? Or is it valued as a means to an end, in which case it has only instrumental worth? Recall our discussion of intrinsic and instrumental values in Chapter 2. There we saw that happiness has intrinsic value because it is desired for its own sake. Money, on the other hand, has instrumental value since it is desired as a means to some further end or ends.

While few would argue that privacy is an intrinsic value, desired for its own sake, others, including Charles Fried (1990), argue that privacy is not merely an instrumental value or instrumental good. Fried suggests that unlike most instrumental values that are simply one means among others for achieving a desired end, privacy is also essential, that is, necessary to achieve some important human ends, such as trust and friendship. We tend to associate intrinsic values with necessary conditions and instrumental values with contingent, or nonnecessary conditions; so while privacy is instrumental in that it is a means to certain human ends, Fried argues that it is also a necessary condition for achieving those ends.

Although agreeing with Fried's claim that privacy is more than merely an instrumental value, James Moor (2004) takes a different approach to illustrate this point. Like Fried, Moor argues that privacy itself is not an intrinsic value. Moor believes that privacy is an articulation, or "expression" of the "core value" *security*, which in turn is essential across cultures, for human flourishing. (We examine the concept of security as it relates to privacy in Chapter 6.) And like Fried, Moor shows why privacy is necessary to achieve certain ends. Moor further suggests that as information technology insinuates itself more and more into our everyday lives, privacy becomes increasingly important for expressing (the core value) security.

Does privacy play a key role in "promoting human well-being," as Richard Spinello (2010) claims? Perhaps one way it does is by serving as a "shield" that protects us from interference. Judith DeCew (2006), who believes that the value of privacy lies in the "freedom and independence" it provides for us, argues that privacy shields us from "pressures that preclude self-expression and the development of relationships."[8] She claims that privacy also acts as a shield by protecting us from coercion and the "pressure to conform." In her view, the loss of privacy leaves us vulnerable and threatened because we are likely to become more conformist and less individualistic.

5.3.2 Privacy as a Social Value

Based on the insights of DeCew and others, one might infer that privacy is a value that simply benefits individuals. However, some authors have pointed out the social value that privacy also provides, noting that privacy is essential for democracy. Priscilla Regan (1995) points out that we often frame debates over privacy simply in terms of how to balance privacy interests as individual goods against interests involving the larger social good; in such debates, Regan believes, interests benefiting the social good will generally override concerns regarding individual privacy. If, however, privacy is understood as not solely concerned with individual good but as contributing to the broader social good, then in debates involving the balancing of competing values, individual privacy might have a greater chance of receiving equal consideration.

Since privacy can be of value for greater social goods, such as democracy, as well as for individual autonomy and choice, it would seem that it is important and worth protecting. But privacy is increasingly threatened by new cyber and cyber-related technologies. In Sections 5.4–5.6, we examine how privacy is threatened by three different kinds of practices that use cybertechnology:

a. *Data gathering* techniques used to collect and record personal information, often without the knowledge and consent of users.

b. *Data exchange* techniques used to transfer and exchange personal data across and between computer databases, typically without the knowledge and consent of users.

c. *Data mining* techniques used to search large databases in order to generate consumer profiles based on the behavioral patterns of certain groups.

▶ 5.4 GATHERING PERSONAL DATA: MONITORING, RECORDING, AND TRACKING TECHNIQUES

Collecting and recording data about people is hardly new. Since the Roman era, and possibly before then, governments have collected and recorded census information. Not all data gathering and data recording practices have caused controversy about privacy. However, cybertechnology makes it possible to collect data about individuals without their knowledge and consent. In this section, we examine some controversial ways in which cybertechnology is used to gather and record personal data, as well as to monitor and track the activities and locations of individuals.

5.4.1 "Dataveillance" Techniques

Some believe that the greatest threat posed to personal privacy by cybertechnology lies in its capacity for surveillance and monitoring. Others worry less about the monitoring *per se* and more about the vast amounts of transactional data recorded using cybertechnology. Roger Clarke uses the term *dataveillance* to capture both the surveillance (data monitoring) and data recording techniques made possible by computer technology.[9] There are, then, two distinct controversies about dataveillance: one having to do with surveillance as a form of data monitoring, and one having to do with the recording and processing of data once the data are collected. We examine both controversies, beginning with a look at data monitoring aspects of surveillance.

First, we should note the obvious, but relevant, point that privacy threats associated with surveillance are by no means peculiar to cybertechnology. Long before the advent of cybertechnology, individuals (e.g., private investigators and stalkers) as well as organizations, including governmental agencies all over the world, have used both electronic and nonelectronic devices to monitor individuals and groups.

Telephone conversations have been subject to government surveillance by wiretapping, but phone conversations have also been monitored in the private sector as well; for example, telephone conversations between consumers and businesses are frequently monitored, sometimes without the knowledge and consent of the consumers who are party to them. So surveillance is neither a recent concern nor one that should be associated exclusively with the use of cybertechnology to monitor and record an individual's online activities. However, surveillance has clearly been exacerbated by cybertechnology. Consider that video cameras now monitor consumers' movements while they shop at retail stores, and scanning devices used by "intelligent highway vehicle systems," such as E-ZPass, subject motorists to a type of surveillance while they drive through tollbooths. And Sue Halpern (2011) notes that approximately 500 companies are now able to monitor and track all of our movements online.

In the past, it was not uncommon for companies to hire individuals to monitor the performance of employees in the workplace. Now, however, there are "invisible supervisors," that is, computers, that can continuously monitor the activities of employees around the clock without failing to record a single activity of the employee. We will examine workplace monitoring in detail, including some arguments that have been used to defend and to denounce computerized monitoring, in Chapter 10, where we consider some impacts that cybertechnology has for the contemporary workplace. In the remainder of this section, we consider surveillance techniques that involve non-workplace-related monitoring and recording of personal data in both off- and online activities.

Although users may not always realize that they are under surveillance, their online activities are tracked by Web site owners and operators to determine how frequently users visit their sites and to draw conclusions about the preferences users show while accessing their sites. We next consider some controversies associated with a type of online surveillance technology known as *cookies*.

5.4.2 Internet Cookies

Cookies are files that Web sites send to and retrieve from the computer systems of Web users, enabling Web site owners to collect information about an individual's online browsing preferences whenever a person visits a Web site. The use of cookies by Web site owners and operators has generated considerable controversy, in large part because of the novel way that information about Web users is collected and stored. Data recorded about the user are stored on a file placed on the hard drive of the user's computer system; this information can then be retrieved from the user's system and resubmitted to a Web site the next time the user accesses that site.

Those who defend the use of cookies tend to be owners and operators of Web sites. Proprietors of these sites maintain that they are performing a service for repeat users of a Web site by customizing the user's means of information retrieval. They also point out that, because of cookies, they are able to provide a user with a list of preferences for future visits to that Web site. Privacy advocates, on the other hand, see the matter quite differently. They argue that activities involving the monitoring and recording of an individual's activities while visiting a Web site and the subsequent downloading of that information onto a user's computer (without informing the user) clearly cross the privacy line. Some privacy advocates also point out that information gathered about a user via cookies can eventually be acquired by online advertising agencies, which can then target that user for online ads.

Initially, you might feel a sense of relief in discovering that, generally, owners and operators of one Web site cannot access cookies-related information pertaining to a user's activities on another Web site. However, information about a user's activities on different Web sites can, under certain circumstances, be compiled and aggregated by online advertising agencies such as DoubleClick that pay to place advertisements on Web sites. DoubleClick can also acquire information about you from data that it retrieves from other Web sites you have visited and where DoubleClick advertises. The information can then be combined and cross-referenced in ways that enable a marketing profile of that user's online activities to be constructed and used in more direct advertisements.

Several privacy advocates have argued that because cookies technology involves monitoring and recording a user's activities while visiting Web sites (without the user's knowledge and consent) as well as the subsequent downloading of that information onto a user's computer system, it violates the user's privacy. To assist Internet users in their concerns about cookies, a number of privacy-enhancing tools, which are discussed in detail in Section 5.8, are available. In most Web browsers, users now also have an option to disable cookies, so that they can either opt-in or opt-out of cookies, assuming that they (i) are aware of cookies technology and (ii) know how to enable/disable that technology on their Web browsers. However, some Web sites will not grant users access unless they accept cookies.

Many privacy advocates object to the fact that the default status for most Web browsers is such that cookies will automatically be accepted unless explicitly overridden by the user. As we noted above, cookies technology involves downloading the information it gathers about users onto the user's computer system. So, cookies technology also raises concerns involving encroachment or intrusion into a user's physical space as well as privacy concerns regarding the clandestine method used to gather data about users who visit Web sites.

5.4.3 RFID Technology

Another mode of surveillance made possible by cybertechnology involves the use of RFID technology. In its simplest form, RFID technology consists of a tag (microchip) and a reader. The tag has an electronic circuit, which stores data, and an antenna that broadcasts data by radio waves in response to a signal from a reader. The reader also contains an antenna that receives the radio signal, and it has a demodulator that transforms the analog radio information into suitable data for any computer processing that will be done (Lockton and Rosenberg 2005).

Although the commercial use of RFIDs was intended mainly for the unique identification of real-world objects (e.g., items sold in supermarkets), the tags can also be used to monitor those objects after they are sold. For example, Helen Nissenbaum notes that prior to the use of RFID tags

> . . . customers could assume that sales assistants, store managers, or company leaders recorded point-of-sale information. RFID tags extend the duration of the relationships, making available to . . . others a range of information about customers that was not previously available.[10]

In one sense, the use of these tags in inventory control would seem uncontroversial. For example, Simson Garfinkel (2002) notes that a company such as Playtex could place an RFID tag in each bra to make sure that shipments of bras headed for Asia are not diverted to New York. He also points out, however, that a man with a handheld (RFID) reader in his pocket who is standing next to a woman wearing such a bra can learn the make and size of her bra. Additionally, and perhaps more controversially, RFID technology can be used for tracking the owners of the items that have these tags. So, on the one hand, RFID transponders in the form of "smart labels" make it much easier to track inventory and protect goods from theft or imitation. On the other hand, these tags pose a significant threat to individual privacy. Critics of this technology, which include organizations such as the Electronic Privacy Information Center (EPIC) and the American Civil Liberties Union (ACLU), worry about the accumulation of RFID transaction data by RFID owners and how those data will be used in the future.

RFID technology is already widely used—as Garfinkel notes, it has been incorporated into everything from automobile keys to inventory control systems to passports. If you have an E-ZPass (or some other intelligent highway system) transponder in your car, for example, you are already carrying a wireless tag; E-ZPass uses the serial number to debit your account when your car passes through a tollbooth. Garfinkel notes that these tags now also appear in clothing.

Ranchers in the United States track cattle by implanting RFID tags in the animals' ears. In the future, major cities and municipalities might require RFID tags for pets; in Taiwan, owners of domesticated dogs are now required to have a microchip containing an RFID tag, which identifies the animal's owner and residence, inserted in their pet dog's ear. Policies requiring RFID tags for humans, especially for children and the elderly, may also be established in the near future. In the United States, some nursing homes now provide their patients with RFID bracelets. And chips (containing RFID technology) can be implanted in children so that they can be tracked if abducted; however, Alison Adam (2005) fears that we may come to rely too heavily on these technologies to care for children. Because RFID technology is now included in chips being embedded in humans, which enables them to be tracked, it has raised concerns for many privacy advocates.

In light of these and related privacy concerns, Garfinkel has proposed an "RFID Bill of Rights" to protect individuals and guide businesses that use RFID tags. In this scheme, individuals would have the right to (a) know whether products contain RFID tags, (b) have the tags removed or deactivated when they purchase products, (c) access the tag's stored data, and (d) know when, where, and why the tags are being read.

Like Internet cookies and other online data gathering and surveillance techniques, RFID clearly threatens individual privacy. But unlike surveillance concerns associated with cookies, which track a user's habits while visiting Web sites, RFID technology can be used to track an individual's location in the offline world. We examine some specific privacy and surveillance concerns affecting RFID in connection with "location privacy" and "pervasive surveillance" issues in Chapter 12 in our discussion of ambient intelligence.

5.4.4 Cybertechnology and Government Surveillance

So far, we have examined some surveillance techniques involving cybertechnology that are used mainly in the business and commercial sectors to monitor the activities of consumers and to record data about them. Another mode of surveillance that is also associated with cybertechnology involves governments and government agencies that monitor the activities of citizens, a practice that is sometimes referred to as "domestic spying." As already noted, this practice is not exactly new, but as the technologies used by governments to monitor their citizens' activities become more sophisticated, intrusive, and pervasive, the threats posed to privacy and civil liberties become exacerbated.

Some cybertechnologies, despite their initial objectives and intent, can facilitate government surveillance. Consider, for example, that cell phone companies in the United States are required by the Federal Communications Commission (FCC) to install a GPS locator chip, in compliance with an "enhanced 911 mandate," in all of the cell phones manufactured after December 2005. This technology, which assists 911 operators in emergencies, also enables any cell phone user to be tracked within 100 meters of his or her location. However, privacy advocates worry that this information can also be used by the government to spy on individuals.

Government agencies currently use a variety of technologies that enable them to intercept and read private e-mail messages. In Chapter 6, we will see that this practice, initiated by the George W. Bush administration to monitor e-mail between U.S. residents and people living outside the United States, has been controversial. And in Section 5.7.1, we will see why the U.S. government's decision to subpoena the records of online search requests made by users of search engines such as Google, which are recorded and archived in computer databases, has also been controversial. In Chapter 7, we describe in detail some of the specific technologies (such as Internet pen registers, keystroke monitoring, and biometric technologies) that have been used by government agencies in the United States to conduct surveillance on individuals. There, we will also see why these technologies, which have been used to combat terrorism and crime in cyberspace, have been controversial from the point of view of privacy and civil liberties.

While few would object to the desirable ends that increased security provides, we will see that many oppose the means—i.e., the specific technologies and programs supporting surveillance operations, as well as legislation such as the USA Patriot Act—that the U.S. government has used to achieve its objectives. In Chapter 7, we will see why the Patriot Act, enacted into law in October 2001 and renewed in March 2006, has been controversial from the point of view of civil liberties. Our purpose in this section has been to briefly describe how government surveillance of citizens illustrates one more way that cyber-technology both contributes to and enhances the ability of organizations to gather and record data about individuals.

In concluding this section, we note that plans are well underway for the construction of a government data center in Bluffdale, Utah, under the egis of the National Security Agency (NSA). It is estimated that this $2 billion center should be operational by September 2013. James Bamford (2012) notes that with the sophisticated tools and databases planned for this center, NSA will be able to "intercept, decipher, analyze, and store" vast amounts of the world's communications. He also points out that these communications and data may include "the complete contents of private emails, cell phone calls, and Google searches, as well as all sorts of personal data trails—parking receipts, travel itineraries, bookstore purchases, and other digital 'pocket litter.'" NSA's original charter was to conduct foreign surveillance; now, however, the agency's mission appears to have been broadened, as surveillance on U.S. citizens is also now conducted by NSA.

▶ 5.5 EXCHANGING PERSONAL DATA: MERGING AND MATCHING ELECTRONIC RECORDS

In the previous section, we examined ways in which personal data could be gathered using surveillance techniques and then recorded electronically in computer databases. Other tools have been devised to transfer and exchange those records across and between computer databases. Simply collecting and recording personal data, *per se*, might not seem terribly controversial if, for example, the data were never used, transferred, exchanged, combined, or recombined. Some would argue, however, that the mere collection of personal data is problematic from a privacy perspective, assuming that if data are being collected, there must be some motive or purpose for their collection. Of course, the reason, as many now realize, is that transactions involving the sale and exchange of personal data are a growing business.

Much of the personal data gathered electronically by one organization is later exchanged with other organizations; indeed, the very existence of certain institutions depends on the exchange and sale of personal information. Some privacy advocates believe that professional information gathering organizations, such as Equifax, Experion (formerly TRW), and Trans Union (credit reporting bureaus), as well as the Medical Information Bureau (MIB), violate the privacy of individuals because of the techniques they use to facilitate the exchange of personal information across and between databases. These techniques include computer merging and computer matching.

5.5.1 Merging Computerized Records

Few would dispute the claim that organizations, in both the public and the private sectors, have a legitimate need for information about individuals in order to make intelligent decisions concerning those individuals. For example, if you are applying for a credit card, it would be reasonable for the credit company to request information about you. However, few would also disagree with the claim that individuals should have a right to keep some personal information private. A crucial question, then, is: What kind of control can an individual expect to retain over the personal information that he or she has given to an organization? Can, for example, an individual expect that personal information provided to an organization for legitimate use in a specific context will remain within that organization? Or will it instead be exchanged with other organizations who can then combine or merge it with existing information?

Computer merging is the technique of extracting information from two or more unrelated databases that contain information about some individual or group of individuals, and then integrating that information into a composite file. It occurs whenever two or more disparate pieces of information contained in separate databases are combined. Consider the following sequence of events in which you voluntarily give information about yourself to three different organizations. First, you give information about your income and credit history to a lending institution in order to secure a loan.

You next give information about your age and medical history to an insurance company to purchase life insurance. You then give information about your views on certain social issues to a political organization you wish to join. Each of these organizations can be said to have a legitimate need for information to make certain decisions about you—insurance companies have a legitimate need to know about your age and medical history before agreeing to sell you life insurance, and lending institutions have a legitimate need to know about your income and credit history before agreeing to lend you money to purchase a house or a car. And insofar as you voluntarily give these organizations the information requested, no breach of your privacy has occurred.

Now suppose that without your knowledge and consent, information about you that resides in the insurance company's database is transferred and merged with information about you that resides in the lending institution's database or in the political organization's database. Even though you voluntarily gave certain information about yourself to three different organizations, and even though you voluntarily authorized each organization to have the information, it does not follow that you authorized any one organization to have some combination of that information.[11] When organizations merge information about you in a way that you did not specifically authorize, the "contextual integrity" of your information has been violated. (Recall Nissenbaum's criteria for preserving the contextual integrity of personal information, described in Section 5.2.5.)

Next, consider a case of computer merging involving DoubleClick, an online advertising company. In our discussion of cookies technology in the previous section, we described how DoubleClick was able to compile data from multiple Web sites on which it placed DoubleClick ads. If, for example, DoubleClick advertised on 1,000 Web sites, it could retrieve cookie files from any user who visited any of those sites and clicked on its ads. Thus, DoubleClick can compile and cross-reference cookies-related information in ways that individual Web site proprietors cannot. This, in turn, has caused concern among DoubleClick's critics, including privacy advocates.

▶ **SCENARIO 5–4:** Merging Personal Information in Unrelated Computer Databases

DoubleClick planned to purchase Abacus Direct Corporation, a database company, in late 1999. Abacus's databases contained not only records of consumer's catalogue purchases but also actual names and telephone numbers that had been collected by Abacus primarily from offline transactions. With this acquisition, DoubleClick could merge records in the Abacus database with its own database, which consisted of information gained primarily from Internet cookies files. And with its newly merged data, DoubleClick would have an information mosaic about individuals that included not merely anonymous and indirect information (such as IP addresses and ISP-related information) but also direct personal information. The Web profiles in DoubleClick's original database, gathered via cookies, included data about which Web sites that users (who are identified and tracked via an IP address) visit, how long they visit a particular site, and so on. That information would be able to be compared to and combined with explicit personal information (gathered offline and stored in Abacus's databases), including names, addresses, and phone numbers.[12] ■

The planned merger involving the two companies, which generated considerable controversy at the time, was canceled in January 2000, when DoubleClick was sued by a woman who complained that her right to privacy had been violated. The woman claimed that DoubleClick's business practices were deceptive, because the company had quietly reversed an earlier policy by which it provided businesses with only anonymous data about Internet users (acquired from cookies files). Because of public pressure, Double-Click backed off from its proposal to purchase Abacus, but many users were able to see for the first time the privacy threats that can result from merging electronic data. However, DoubleClick continued to function as an online advertising company, and in March 2008, it was acquired by Google. This acquisition has caused concerned for many privacy advocates, because Google integrates information gathered from cookies with its wide array of applications and services, which include Gmail, Google+, Google Chrome, and others. As Michael Zimmer (2008) notes, Google's ability to integrate this information provides the search engine company with a "powerful infrastructure of dataveillance" in which it can monitor and record users' online activities.

5.5.2 Matching Computerized Records

Computer matching is a variation of the technology used to merge computerized records. It involves cross-checking information in two or more unrelated databases to produce matching records, or "hits." In federal and state government applications, this technique has been used by various agencies and departments for the express purpose of creating a new file containing a list of potential law violators, as well as individuals who have actually broken the law or who are suspected of having broken the law.[13]

Consider a scenario in which you complete a series of forms for various federal and state government agencies, such as the Internal Revenue Service (IRS), your state government's motor vehicle registration department, or your local government's property tax assessment department. You supply the specific information requested and, in addition, you include general information requested on each form, such as your social security number and driver's license number, which can be used as identifiers in matching records about you that reside in multiple databases. The information is then electronically stored in the agencies' respective databases, and routine checks (matches) can be made against information (records) contained in those databases. For example, your property tax records can be matched against your federal tax records to see whether you own an expensive house but declared only a small income. Records in an IRS database of divorced or single fathers can be matched against a database containing records of mothers receiving welfare payments to generate a list of potential "deadbeat parents."

In filling out the various governmental forms, you agreed to give some information to each government agency. It is by no means clear, however, that you authorized information given to any one agency to be exchanged with other agencies. You had no say in the way information that you authorized for use in one context was subsequently used in another. Because of this contextual violation of personal information, some have argued that practices involving computerized matching of records containing personal data raise serious threats for personal privacy. The debate over computerized record matching has been hotly contested, and it has been denounced because of its implications for stereotyping and profiling certain classes or groups of individuals. Computerized record matching has also been criticized by civil liberties groups who fear that such a practice might lead to a new form of social control.

Defenders of this practice justify the matching of computer records because it enables us to track down deadbeat parents, welfare cheats, and the like. Although few would object to the ends that could be achieved, we can question whether the practice of computerized matching is compatible with individual privacy. Even if computerized record matching does help to root out governmental waste and fraud, would that fact alone justify such a practice? Consider this counterexample: Suppose that 24-hour video surveillance and daily drug testing of all government employees also help to root out government waste and fraud—would such means also be justifiable in order to reach the desired end?

Proponents of computer matching might argue that 24-hour video surveillance and daily drug testing of government workers would violate the privacy of workers in ways that matching computerized records does not. However, critics have pointed out that computer matches have been made even when there was no suspicion that a particular individual or group of individuals had violated the law. For example, computer records of entire categories of individuals, such as government employees, have been matched against databases containing records of welfare recipients on the chance that a "hit" will identify one or more welfare cheats. One line of argumentation sometimes used to defend a practice such as computer matching against the charge of violating privacy rights is as follows:

PREMISE 1. Privacy is a legal right.

PREMISE 2. Legal rights are conditional, not absolute.

PREMISE 3. When one violates the law (i.e., commits a crime), one forfeits one's legal rights.

CONCLUSION. Criminals have forfeited their legal right to privacy.

Initially, this line of reasoning seems quite plausible, but does it apply in the case of computerized record matching? First of all, this argument assumes that we have an explicit legal right to privacy. Let us assume, for the sake of argument, that we have such a right and that all legal rights are (or ought to be) conditional only. Even with the addition of these two assumptions, problems remain: for example, those who maintain that a deadbeat parent has, in violating the law, given up his right to privacy seem to either disregard or ignore any right to privacy accorded to individuals who have not broken the law. For it was only by matching the records of mostly innocent individuals whose names were included in multiple government databases that a "hit," identifying one or more alleged criminals, was generated. So even if criminals do forfeit their right to privacy, the process of identifying these criminals via computerized record matching entails that several noncriminals will be required to forfeit that right as well.

Next, consider a computerized matching technique involving biometric identifiers that also has been used by some government agencies.

▶ **SCENARIO 5–5:** Using Biometric Technology at Super Bowl XXXV

At Super Bowl XXXV in January 2001, a facial recognition technology scanned the faces of individuals entering the stadium. The digitized facial images were then instantly matched against images in a centralized database of suspected criminals and terrorists. Those who attended the sporting advent were not told that their faces had been scanned. The day after the super bowl, many learned what had happened via a newspaper story, which caused considerable controversy at the time. Many privacy advocates and civil liberties proponents criticized the tactics used by the government at this major sports event.[14] ∎

Although this incident generated some controversy in early 2001, the attitudes of many Americans who were initially critical of the government's use of biometrics at Super Bowl XXXV changed later that year, following the tragic events of September 11. We will examine this biometric technique in greater detail in Chapter 7, where we discuss cybercrime. However, it is useful at this point to show how this biometric-based matching technique differs from the computerized record-matching practice involving government workers, which we considered earlier in this section.

Initially, one might argue that the biometric-based matching technique used to scan and match faces of individuals at stadiums and airports, as well as other public places, is essentially no different from the computerized record-matching operations previously used to catch welfare cheats and deadbeat parents. But in traditional computerized record matching, all of the databases involved contain records of individuals who were (or should have been) assumed to be innocent. As we saw, records of government workers (presumed to be innocent) were matched against records of welfare recipients (also presumed to be innocent) to ferret out any persons who just happen to be in both groups. In the case of the face recognition program used at Super Bowl XXXV, however, images of persons entering the football stadium were matched against a database of persons already known (or at least suspected) to be criminals and terrorists. So the objectives of the targeted matches at Super Bowl XXXV were much more specific than those involving the "fishing expeditions" used in some earlier computerized record-matching practices. Perhaps this is one reason why the biometric-based matching operations aimed at catching terrorists and dangerous criminals have been less controversial than traditional record-matching practices used by federal and state governments.

▶ 5.6 MINING PERSONAL DATA

A form of data analysis that uses techniques gained from research and development in artificial intelligence (AI), described in Chapter 11, has been used to "mine" personal data. Formally referred to as Knowledge Discovery in Databases, or KDD, the process is now more commonly known as *data mining*. Essentially, data mining involves the indirect gathering of personal information through an analysis of implicit patterns discoverable in data. Data mining activities can generate new and sometimes non-obvious classifications or categories; as a result, individuals whose data are mined can become identified with or linked to certain newly created groups that they might never have imagined to exist. This is further complicated by the fact that current privacy laws offer individuals virtually no protection with respect to how information about them acquired through data mining activities is subsequently used, even though important decisions can be made about those individuals based on the patterns found in the mined personal data. So, data mining technology can be used in ways that raise special concerns for personal privacy.

5.6.1   How Does Data Mining Threaten Personal Privacy?

What is so special about the privacy concerns raised by data mining? For example, how do they differ from privacy issues introduced by more traditional data retrieval techniques, such as computerized merging and matching operations that we examined in

Section 5.5? For one thing, privacy laws as well as informal data protection guidelines have been established for protecting personal data that are

- *explicit* in databases (in the form of specific electronic records),
- *confidential* in nature (e.g., data involving medical, financial, or academic records),
- exchanged between or across databases.

However, virtually no legal or normative protections apply to personal data manipulated in the data mining process, where personal information is typically

- *implicit* in the data,
- *nonconfidential* in nature,
- *not exchanged* between databases.

Unlike personal data that reside in explicit records in databases, information acquired about persons via data mining is often derived from implicit patterns in the data. The patterns can suggest "new" facts, relationships, or associations about a person, placing that person in a "newly discovered" category or group. Also, because most personal data collected and used in data mining applications is considered neither confidential nor intimate in nature, there is a tendency to presume that such data must, by default, be *public* data. And unlike the personal data that are often exchanged between or across two or more databases in traditional database retrieval processes, in the data mining process personal data are often manipulated within a single database, and typically within a large *data warehouse*.

Next consider a scenario involving data mining practices at a bank in determining whether or not to grant loans to its customers. As you consider the privacy issues raised in the following scenario, keep in mind Nissenbaum's distinction between "norms of appropriateness" and "norms of distribution" for determining contextual integrity (described in Section 5.2.5).

▶ **SCENARIO 5–6:** Data Mining at the XYZ Bank

Lee, a junior executive at ABE Marketing Inc., has recently applied for an automobile loan at the XYZ Bank. To secure the loan, Lee agrees to complete the usual forms required by the bank for loan transactions. He indicates that he has been employed at the ABE Marketing Company for more than 3 years and that his current annual salary is $240,000. He also indicates that he has $30,000 in a separate savings account, a portion of which he intends to use as a down payment for a new BMW. On the loan form, Lee also indicates that he is currently repaying a $15,000 personal loan used to finance a family vacation to Europe the previous year.

Next, the bank's computing center runs a data mining program on information in its customer databases and discovers a number of patterns. One reveals that executives earning more than $200,000 but less than $300,000 annually, who purchase luxury cars (such as BMWs), and who take their families on international vacations, are also likely start their own businesses within their first 5 years of employment. A second data mining algorithm reveals that the majority of marketing entrepreneurs declare bankruptcy within 1 year of starting their own businesses. The data mining algorithms can be interpreted to suggest that Lee is a member of a group that neither he nor possibly even the loan officers at the bank had ever known to exist—viz., the group of marketing executives likely to start a business and then declare bankruptcy within a year. With this new category and new information about Lee, the bank determines that Lee, and people that fit into Lee's group, are long-term credit risks.[15]

Does the mining of data about Lee by the XYZ Bank raise concerns for privacy? At one level, the transaction between Lee and the bank seems appropriate. To borrow money from XYZ Bank, Lee has authorized the bank to have the information about him, that is, his current employment, salary, savings, outstanding loans, and so forth, that it needs to make an informed decision as to whether or not to grant him the loan. So, if we appeal to Nissenbaum's framework of privacy as contextual integrity, it would seem that there is no breach of privacy in terms of norms of appropriateness. However, Lee gave the bank information about himself for use in one context, viz., to make a decision about whether or not he should be granted a loan to purchase a new automobile. He was assured that the information given to the bank would not be exchanged with a third party without first getting Lee's explicit consent. So, unlike cases involving the computerized merging and matching of records that we considered in Section 5.5, no information about Lee was either exchanged or cross-referenced between databases—i.e., there is no breach of the norms of distribution (in Nissenbaum's model). However, it is unclear whether the bank has agreed not to use the information it now has in its databases about Lee for certain in-house analyses.

Although Lee voluntarily gave the bank information about his annual salary, about previous personal loans, and about the type of automobile he intended to purchase, he gave each piece of information for a specific purpose and use, in order that the bank could make a meaningful determination about Lee's request for an automobile loan. It is, however, by no means clear that Lee authorized the bank to use disparate pieces of that information for more general data mining analyses that would reveal patterns involving Lee that neither he nor the bank could have anticipated at the outset. Using Lee's information for this purpose would now raise questions about "appropriateness" in the *context* involving Lee and the XYZ Bank.

The mining of data in Lee's case is controversial from a privacy perspective for several reasons. For one thing, the information that Lee is someone likely to start his own business, which would probably lead to his declaring personal bankruptcy, was not explicit in any of the data (records) about Lee; rather it was implicit in patterns of data about people similar to Lee in certain respects but vastly different from him in other respects. For another thing, Lee's case illustrates how data mining can generate new categories and groups such that the people whom the data mining analysis identifies with those groups would very likely have no idea that they would be included as members. And we have seen that, in the case of Lee, certain decisions can be made about members of these newly generated groups simply by virtue of those individuals being identified as members. For example, it is doubtful that Lee would have known that he was a member of a group of professional individuals likely to start a business, and that he was a member of a group whose businesses were likely to end in bankruptcy. The "discovery" of such groups is, of course, a result of the use of data mining tools.

Even though no information about Lee was exchanged with databases outside XYZ, the bank did use information about Lee internally in a way that he had not explicitly authorized. And it is in this sense—unauthorized internal use by data users—that data mining raises serious concerns for personal privacy. Note also that even if Lee had been granted the loan for the automobile, the bank's data mining practices would still have raised serious privacy concerns with respect to the contextual integrity of his personal information. Lee was merely one of many bank customers who had voluntarily given certain personal information about themselves to the bank for use in one context—in this example, a loan request—and subsequently had that information used in ways that they did not specifically authorize.

Consumer Profiling

Of course, the scenario involving Lee is merely hypothetical. But some relatively recent evidence now suggests that banks and consumer credit organizations are using data mining techniques to determine an individual's "credit worthiness" in ways that are not so different from the example involving Lee. In these cases, a consumer's credit rating could actually be determined via profiling schemes that can suggest "guilt by association." For example, a consumer could have the spending limit on her credit card reduced, or have that card revoked altogether, because of where she shops or where she lives. Following the economic turndown in the United States that began in 2008, many private homes have been lost to foreclosure. So people living in neighborhoods where there was a high rate of foreclosures, or people holding mortgages with certain banks or lending institutions that have experienced high rates of home foreclosures, may now be considered credit risks by virtue of their association with either a certain neighborhood or bank, even though they have been responsible in paying their mortgages and other loans on time. Similarly, if individuals shop at a certain kind of retail store, say Wal-Mart, information about their purchases at such a store can associate them with other individuals who shop there, and who may have a higher-than-average default rate on their credit cards.

Mike Stuckey (2008) describes an incident where a 37-year-old computer consultant had two of his American Express cards canceled and the limit on a third card reduced. The consumer was told that the credit card company's decision was based in part on criteria having to do with *where* he shopped and with *whom* held his mortgage. American Express informed this customer that included in the criteria it uses to decide to reduce the spending limit on someone's credit card are the company's

> "credit experience with customers who have made purchases at establishments where you have recently used your card."

> "analysis of the credit risk associated with customers who have residential loans from the creditor(s) indicated in your credit report."

While there had been suspicion for some time that credit card companies engage in the kind of profiling scheme used by American Express, consumer advocates and credit analysts believe that this may be the first time that a major credit company admitted to using such criteria. In its defense, however, American Express claimed that it needs to analyze its exposure to risk as it reviews its cardholder's credit profiles in light of the economic turndown in the United States that severely affected the credit industry (Stuckey 2008).

We have seen how data mining can be used to threaten consumer privacy. But can it also be used to protect consumers against fraudulent activities? Perhaps not surprisingly, data mining, like other technologies, can be viewed as a "double-edged sword" with respect to consumers' interests, as the following story suggests. One day, to my surprise, I received a telephone call from my credit card company informing me that a purchase, which the company apparently viewed as suspicious, had been charged earlier that day to my credit card account. When asked about the purchase, I informed the company's representative that it had not been made by me, and I also thanked the person for notifying me so promptly about this transaction. The company representative then immediately canceled my existing credit card and issued me a new card with a new account number.

Why did the company suspect that the purchase made that day with my credit card was questionable? It would seem that the data mining algorithms used by the credit card company to determine the patterns of my purchases—which kinds of purchases and credit card transactions I typically make, with whom and where I make them, and when—revealed the anomaly of the questionable purchase made that day with my credit card. So in this instance, data mining appeared to have been used in a way that protected the interests of a consumer.

5.6.2 Web Mining

Initially, the mining of personal data depended on large (offline) commercial databases called data warehouses, which stored the data, consisting primarily of transactional information. Data mining techniques are now also used by commercial Web sites to analyze data about Internet users, which can then be sold to third parties. This process is sometimes referred to as "Web mining," which has been defined as the application of data mining techniques to discover patterns from the Web.[16] The kinds of patterns discovered from Web mining can be useful to marketers in promotional campaigns. The following scenario, involving Facebook, illustrates one way in which mining can be done on the Web.

▶ **SCENARIO 5–7:** The Facebook Beacon Controversy

Facebook (originally called "The Facebook") is a popular social networking service founded by Mark Zuckerberg in 2004, when he was a student at Harvard University. As in the case of other SNSs (examined in detail in Chapter 11), Facebook enables its members to share information about themselves with "friends" and to make additional friends through its range of services. In November 2007, Facebook announced a marketing initiative called Facebook Beacon, which would let Facebook friends share information about what they do online, including the purchases they make. Although this feature, made possible by external Web sites that sent data about individuals to Facebook, enabled users to share their online activities with their friends, it also allowed targeted advertisements by the Web sites sending the data. Essentially, Beacon allowed affiliate Web sites (including Blockbuster, Fandago, and many others) to send stories about a user's online activities to Facebook, which were then displayed to that user's "friends" in the form of news feeds and Social Ads.

However, the Beacon initiative proved to be very controversial; for one reason, it disclosed what purchases users made at certain Web sites. Also, when Facebook introduced Beacon, it stated that it would not share any personally identifiable information in the Social Ads, and it claimed that users would only see those ads to the extent that they were willing to share that information with others. But Facebook was soon criticized for collecting more user information for advertisers than it had originally admitted. In December 2007, Zuckerberg publicly apologized for the way that the Beacon project had been set up, admitting that it was established as an "opt-out" system instead of an "opt-in" system. So, by default, if a Facebook user did not explicitly decline to share something, Beacon would share the advertising information with that person's friends via the user's profile.[17] ■

Many Facebook users complained when they discovered what was happening with the information about their online purchases and activities. But were the practices used in the Beacon program incompatible with Facebook's privacy policy at that time? Facebook's original privacy agreement stated

> We may use information about you that we collect from other sources, including but not limited to newspapers and Internet sources such as blogs, instant messaging services, Facebook Platform developers, and other users of Facebook, to supplement your profile.

A controversial clause in its privacy policy was Facebook's right to sell a user's data to private companies, which stated

> We may share your information with third parties, including responsible companies with which we have a relationship.

However, Facebook officials claimed that they had never provided, nor had they intended to provide, users' information to third-party companies. But Facebook nonetheless decided to change its privacy policy in response to the controversy generated by Beacon.[18]

The Beacon controversy also generated other privacy concerns for Facebook users, independent of Web mining. One concern had to do with Facebook's policy for users wishing to delete their accounts. Some users worried about what would happen to the personal information that Facebook had collected about them while their accounts were active. Did Facebook own that information? Could it be used in future Web mining or sold to third parties, or both? Facebook's initial policy stated that users could only "deactivate" their accounts. Once deactivated, the user's profile would no longer be visible on Facebook. However, that information would remain on Facebook's servers. Again, many users were not satisfied, because they wished to delete their accounts permanently. For example, some users wished to permanently remove information that may have been embarrassing or highly sensitive, including photos of them drinking at parties or in their dormitory rooms. In response to pressure from users, Facebook has since changed its policy for deleting accounts. The new policy enables users to contact Facebook to request that their accounts be permanently deleted.

In Table 5.2, we summarize some of the differences in mining, matching, and merging techniques used to process personal information.

The Facebook Beacon controversy illustrates how easily personal data can be mined on the Web. Because the amount of data on the Internet is so vast, one might assume that it is impossible to mine those data in ways that could be useful. However, current data mining tools employ sophisticated and advanced AI technology that enable the users of

TABLE 5.2 Mining, Matching, and Merging Techniques for Manipulating Personal Data

*Data **Merging***	A data exchange process in which personal data from two or more sources is combined to create a "mosaic" of individuals that would not be discernable from the individual pieces of data alone.
*Data **Matching***	A technique in which two or more unrelated pieces of personal information are cross-referenced and compared to generate a match, or "hit, " that suggests a person's connection with two or more groups.
*Data **Mining***	A technique for "unearthing" implicit patterns in large single databases, or "data warehouses," revealing statistical data that associates individuals with nonobvious groups; user profiles can be constructed from these patterns.

those tools to "comb" through massive amounts of data that would not have been possible to analyze with traditional information retrieval techniques. Also, sophisticated search engines have programs (called "spiders") that "crawl" through the Web in order to uncover general patterns in information across multiple Web sites. Sue Halpern (2011) points out that approximately 500 companies now mine the "raw material of the Web" and then sell it to data mining companies. And Eli Pariser (2011) notes that one of these companies, Acxiom, has managed to accumulate 1500 pieces of data, on average, for each person in its database; this personal data ranges from people's credit scores to the kinds of medications they use.

Pariser also notes that Google and other major search engine companies use "prediction engines" to construct and refine theories about us and the kinds of results we desire from our search queries. (We examine Google's 2012 Privacy Policy, which has been criticized by privacy advocates, in Section 5.9.1.) In Section 5.7.1, we examine some specific ways in which the use of Internet search engines raise privacy concerns, even though the kind of personal information about us that is acquired by search engine companies might not initially seem to warrant explicit privacy protection. To see why such protection might indeed be needed in these cases, however, we first examine some questions underlying a concern that Helen Nissenbaum (2004b) calls the "problem of privacy in public."

▶ 5.7 PROTECTING PERSONAL PRIVACY IN PUBLIC SPACE

So far, we have examined how cybertechnology can be used to gather, exchange, and mine personal information. With the exception of data mining, which manipulates personal, but nonconfidential information, the kind of personal information gathered and exchanged was often confidential and intimate in nature. For example, we saw how financial and medical records could be exchanged between two or more databases using computerized merging and matching. This confidential and very personal information is referred to as nonpublic personal information (NPI). Privacy analysts are now concerned about a different kind of personal information—public personal information (PPI), which is neither confidential nor intimate and which is also being gathered, exchanged, and mined using cybertechnology.

PPI includes information about you, such as where you work or attend school or what kind of car you drive. Even though it is information about you as a particular person, PPI has not enjoyed the privacy protection that has been granted to NPI.

Until recently, most concerns about personal information that was gathered and exchanged electronically were limited to NPI, and because of the attention it has received, privacy laws and policies were established to protect NPI. But now privacy advocates are extending their concern to PPI; they are arguing that PPI deserves greater legal and normative protection than it currently has. As noted above, Nissenbaum refers to this challenge as the problem of protecting privacy in public.

Why should the collection and exchange of PPI raise privacy concerns? Suppose that I discover some information about you: you are a junior at Technical University, you frequently attend your university's football games, and you are actively involved in your university's computer science club. In one sense, the information that I have discovered about you is personal, because it is about *you* (as a person), but it is also public, because it pertains to things that you do in the public sphere. Should you be worried that this information about you is so easily available?

In the past, the public availability of such seemingly harmless and uncontroversial information about you was no cause for concern. Imagine that 80 years ago a citizen petitioned his or her congressperson to draft legislation protecting the privacy of each citizen's movements in public places. It would have been difficult then to make a strong case for such legislation; no one would have seen any need to protect that kind of personal information. But now some are arguing that we need to protect privacy in public, that our earlier assumptions are no longer tenable. Nissenbaum (2004b) believes that many in the commercial sector proceed from an assumption that she believes is "erroneous"—viz., "There is a realm of public information about persons to which no privacy norms apply."[19] Keep this assumption in mind as you consider the following scenario.

▶ **SCENARIO 5–8:** Shopping at SuperMart

One day, you decide to shop for groceries at SuperMart. If I happen to see you enter or leave SuperMart, or if we are both shopping in this store at the same time, I now have information that you shop (or, at least, have once shopped) at SuperMart. (This information could be considered "public" because it was acquired in a public forum and because it is neither intimate nor confidential in nature.) If I also happen to pass by you in one of the aisles at SuperMart, I can observe the contents of your shopping basket; I may notice that you are purchasing several bottles of wine but relatively little food. Again, I have acquired this information about you by observing your activity in a public forum. ■

Because the information I have acquired about you in the above scenario can be considered public information, it would not warrant any legal privacy protection. And even though this information is about *you as a person*, it is not the kind of personal information to which we, as a society, would typically grant normative privacy protection. What, exactly, is the privacy problem regarding the kind of personal information about your public activities in shopping at SuperMart? Why should you be concerned about information that is gathered about what you do at SuperMart or, for that matter, in any public place? Let us continue the shopping metaphor, but this time we consider shopping that takes place in an online forum.

▶ **SCENARIO 5–9:** Shopping at Nile.com

Imagine that you visit an online bookstore called *Nile.com* to locate a particular book that you are considering purchasing. Because you are visiting this bookstore via a computer or electronic device located in your own home, you cannot be observed by people in physical space nor can you be seen by other customers on the *Nile.com* Web site. However, from the moment you log on to *Nile.com*, information about you is being intentionally gathered and carefully recorded—i.e., information about the exact time that you entered Nile, as well as the exact time that you leave. As you make contact with the Nile Web site, Nile requests a cookie file from your computer to determine whether you have previously visited this site. If you have visited this site before and have clicked on items that interested you, Nile can find a record of these items. The information stored in that cookie file can also be used by Nile to alert you to newly released books that it believes might interest you, based on an analysis of the data Nile collected from your previous visits to its site. ■

The information that Nile now has about you does not seem categorically different from the information that SuperMart might also have about you (assuming that you used that store's "courtesy card" or discount card in making your purchases). However, there are significant differences in the ways that information about you can be gathered, recorded, and then used as a result of your shopping at each store.

When you shopped in physical space at SuperMart, only your actual purchases could be recorded and stored in SuperMart's databases. Items that might have only caught your attention and items that you might also have picked up or even placed in your cart at one point while shopping but did not eventually purchase at the checkout register are not recorded by SuperMart's data collection system. However, as you shop, or even browse, at Nile, there is a record of virtually every move you make—every book that you search, review, etc., as well as the one(s) you purchase. Yet, just like the information gathered about your shopping habits in physical space at SuperMart, this personal information that Nile has gathered about your browsing and shopping habits online is considered and treated as public information.

Now we can see why some people worry about having their movements online tracked and recorded. The information Nile gathered about you is, in effect, *Nile's* information, even though it pertains to *you* as a person; Nile now owns that information about you, as well as the information it has about its other customers, and is, in principle at least, free to do with that information whatever it chooses. On the one hand, the information seems fairly innocuous—after all, who really cares which books you happen to browse or purchase? On the other hand, however, this information can be combined with other information about your online transactions at additional Web sites to create a consumer profile of you, which can then be sold to a third party.

One argument that online entrepreneurs might advance to defend these business practices is that if a user puts information about him- or herself into the public domain of the Internet, then that information is no longer private. Of course, one response to this line of reasoning could be to question whether users clearly understand the ways that data they submit might subsequently be used.

In the Nile.com scenario, Nile used information about you in ways that you neither authorized nor intended—an example of the kind of practice that Nissenbaum (2004a, 2010) describes as violating "contextual integrity" (see Section 5.2.5). Also, we can question whether businesses, such as Nile, should be able to "own" the information about us that they collect and then do with that information whatever they please for as long as they want? Joseph Fulda (2004) questions whether the old legal rule that states, "Anything put by a person in the public domain can be viewed as public information," should still apply. He admits that such a rule may have served us well, but only before data were "mined" to produce profiles and other kinds of patterns about individuals.[20]

5.7.1 Search Engines and the Disclosure of Personal Information

Internet search engines are valuable for directing us to available online resources for academic research, commerce, recreation, and so forth; so it might be surprising to find that search engine technology, too, can be controversial from the perspective of personal privacy. How can search engine technology conflict with personal privacy? At least two different kinds of concerns affecting privacy arise because of practices involving search engines: (1) search engine companies such as Google record and archive each search request made by users and (2) search engines enable users to acquire a wealth of personal information about individuals, with relative ease. We begin with a brief examination of (1).

Google and the Controversy Surrounding Records of Users' Searches

Google creates a record of every search made on its site, which it then archives. The topic searched for, as well as the date and time the specific search request is made by a user, are included in the record. These data can be linked to the IP address and the ISP of the user requesting the search. So individual searches made by a particular user could theoretically be analyzed in ways that suggest patterns of that individual's online behavior, and, perhaps more controversially, these records could later be subpoenaed in court cases. Yet, until relatively recently, many (if not most) Google users were unaware of the company's policy regarding the recording and archiving of users' search requests.

On the one hand, this information might seem relatively innocuous—after all, who would be interested in knowing about the kinds of searches we conduct on the Internet, and who would want to use this information against us? On the other hand, however, consider the case of a student, Mary, who is writing a research paper on Internet pornography. Records of Mary's search requests could reveal several queries that she made about pornographic Web sites, which in turn might suggest that Mary was interested in viewing pornography. In early 2006, Google users discovered that any worries they may have had about the lack of privacy protection concerning their Internet searches were justified, in light of the events described in the following scenario.

▶ **SCENARIO 5–10:** Tracking Your Search Requests on Google

In 2005, the George W. Bush administration informed Google that it must turn over a list of all users' queries entered into its search engine during a 1-week period (the exact dates were not specified by Google). But Google refused to comply with the subpoena on the grounds that the privacy rights of its users would be violated. Both Yahoo Inc. and Microsoft Corp. MSN, companies that operated the second- and third-most-used search engines, respectively, also had their search records subpoenaed by the Bush administration. Yahoo, unlike Google, complied with the subpoena. It was not clear whether Microsoft also turned over its records to the government, since it declined to say one way or another.[21]   ■

The Bush administration's decision to seek information about the search requests of ordinary users has since drawn significant criticism from many privacy advocates. Critics argued that although the Bush administration claimed that it had the authority to seek electronic information in order to fight the "war on terror" and to prevent another September 11-like attack, the records at issue in this particular case had to do with the number of users requesting information about, or inadvertently being sent to, pornographic Web sites. Some critics further argued that the Bush administration was interested in gathering data to support its stance on the Child Internet Pornography Act (CIPA), which had been challenged in a U.S. District Court (see Chapter 9). So, many critics were quick to point out that the Bush administration's rationale for obtaining records of search requests made by ordinary citizens seemed politically and ideologically motivated, and may have had nothing to do with protecting national security.

Using Search Engines to Acquire Information about People

It is not only the fact that an individual's search requests are recorded and archived by major companies such as Google that make Internet search engines controversial from the perspective of personal privacy. Search engine-related privacy issues also arise because that technology can be used for questionable purposes such as stalking. In fact, one search facility—Gawker-Stalker (www.gawker.com/stalker)—has been designed specifically for the purpose of stalking famous people, including celebrities. For example, suppose that Matt Damon is spotted ordering a drink at an up-scale café in Boston. The individual who spots Damon can send a "tip" via e-mail to Gawker-Stalker, informing the site's users of Damon's whereabouts. The Gawker site then provides its users, via precise GPS software, with information about exactly where, and at what time, Damon was sighted. Users interested in stalking Damon can then follow his movements electronically, via the Gawker site, or they can locate and follow him in physical space, if they are in the same geographical vicinity as Damon.

But it is not just celebrities who are vulnerable to information about them being acquired by others via search engines. Consider the amount and kind of personal information about ordinary individuals that is now available to search engines. In some cases, that information may have been placed on the Internet inadvertently, without the knowledge and consent of those affected. Yet information about those persons can be located by an Internet user who simply enters their names in a search engine program's entry box. The fact that one can search the Internet for information about someone might not seem terribly controversial. After all, people regularly place information about themselves on Web sites (or perhaps they authorize someone else to do it for them) and on social networking services such as Facebook and LinkedIn. And it might seem reasonable to assume that any online personal information that is currently available to the public should be viewed simply as public information. But should such information about persons be unprotected by privacy norms merely because it is now more easily accessible for viewing by the public?

We have seen how the use of search engines can threaten the privacy of individuals in two distinct ways: (1) by recording and archiving records of a user's search queries that reveal the topic of the search and the time the request was made by the user and (2) by providing users of search engines with personal information about individuals who may have no idea of the wealth of personal information about them that is available online (and have no control over how it is accessed and by whom it is accessed). The latter concern is further complicated by the fact that individuals who are the subject of online searches enjoy no legal protection because of the presumed "public" nature of the personal information about them that is available via online searches.

So far, we have seen how our personal information can be collected and then manipulated by search engines in ways that are controversial. We next consider some controversies that involve access to personal information that resides in public records available online.

5.7.2 Accessing Online Public Records

Another kind of personal information that can also be considered public in nature is information about us stored in records located in municipal buildings, which are accessible to the general public. Public records have generally been available to anyone willing to go to those municipal buildings and request hardcopy versions of them. Some municipalities charge a small fee to retrieve and copy the requested records. Many of these public records can now also be accessed online. Has this changed anything?

Consider that information merchants were always able to physically or manually collect all of the public records they could acquire. But traditional "information entrepreneurs" without computer technology would have had to hire legions of clerks to collect the (publicly available) data, sort the data according to some scheme, and then compile and print the data for sale. The process would have been physically impractical and hardly profitable, given the labor it involved; it would probably never have occurred to anyone even to attempt it prior to the advent of sophisticated information technology.

We could ask why public records were made public in the first place. Were they made public so that information merchants could profit from them, or were they instituted to serve broader societal and governmental ends? In order for governmental agencies at all levels to operate efficiently, records containing personal information are needed. For example, municipal governments need real estate information for tax assessment purposes, state governments need information about motor vehicle owners and operators, and federal governments need social security and income tax information. Records have to be easily accessible to and transferable and exchangeable between governmental agencies at various levels. Since they contain information that is neither confidential nor intimate, they are, with good reason, public records. It has been assumed that the availability of public records causes no harm to individuals, and that communities are better served because of the access and flow of those records for what seems to be legitimate purposes. But information gathering companies now access those public records, manipulate them to discover patterns useful to businesses, and then sell that information to third parties.

Many information merchants seem to assume that offices responsible for maintaining public records now have a legal obligation to make *all* public records available online. Their presumption is that the government has no right to restrict or limit, in any way, information that has been deemed appropriate for inclusion in public records. Is this a reasonable presumption? Consider two incidents, one involving public records at the city level and the other at the state level, which have caused controversy.

► **SCENARIO 5–11:** Accessing Online Public Records in Pleasantville

The city of Pleasantville has recently made all of its public records, including real estate records, available online; with a networked computer or electronic device, one can simply enter the address of any house in Pleasantville and retrieve the current tax assessment for the house, the price paid by the most recent owner, and a description of the physical layout of the house, including the location of doors and windows. Many of Pleasantville's citizens were outraged when they learned that this information was available online, even though the same information had previously been available as public records, stored in physical file cabinets at City Hall.[22]   ■

Why should the residents of Pleasantville be so concerned? For one thing, some might worry that prospective burglars could plan break-ins by accessing the detailed physical layouts of their homes, which were readily available online. Consider that public records in the form of motor vehicle information have also been made available online, and, as in the Pleasantville scenario involving access to records about one's home, this practice has also outraged many citizens.

► **SCENARIO 5–12:** Accessing a State's Motor Vehicle Records Online

In the late 1990s, information from the state of Oregon's Department of Motor Vehicle became accessible online. An independent computer consultant used the means available to any private citizen to purchase data from that state's department, which was already available offline to anyone willing to pay a small fee. Once he purchased the information and converted it to electronic format, the consultant set up a Web site where any Internet user could, for a small fee, enter an Oregon license plate number and obtain the name and address of the owner of the registered vehicle. Many of Oregon's residents were outraged when they heard about this practice; eventually, the state's governor intervened and persuaded the consultant to close down the Web site.[23] ■

We ask again, What was the purpose of making such records public in the first place? There is no reason to believe that it was to facilitate commerce in the private sector. Of course, selling information, as the State of Oregon did, is now an important source of revenue for many state governments. But we also need to consider the privacy (and other ethical) implications of states selling information about their residents to online merchants, especially in an era where technology makes it so easy to erode personal privacy. Can technology also provide us with tools to protect our privacy?

► 5.8 PRIVACY-ENHANCING TECHNOLOGIES

We have seen how cybertechnology has exacerbated privacy concerns. Ironically, perhaps, cybertechnology also provides tools that can help users to protect their privacy. For example, *privacy-enhancing technologies* or *PETs* have been developed to help users protect (a) their personal identity while navigating the Internet and (b) the privacy of their online communications (such as e-mail). An example of (b) is encryption tools that encode and decode e-mail messages. Our main focus in this section is on whether PETs actually accomplish (a).

Some PETs enable users to navigate the Internet either anonymously or pseudonymously; one of the best-known anonymity tools is available from *Anonymizer.com*. It is important to note that although Anonymizer users enjoy anonymity while visiting Web sites, they are not anonymous to *Anonymizer.com* or to their own ISPs. A user's activities on a Web site can be recorded in server log files and can thus be traced back to a specific ISP and IP address. To enjoy complete anonymity on the Internet, online users need tools that do not require them to place their trust in a single "third party" (such as Anonymizer).

Another useful tool is TrackMeNot (http://cs.nyu.edu/trackmenot/), which was designed to work with the Firefox Web browser to protect users against surveillance and data profiling by search engine companies. Rather than using encryption or concealment tools to accomplish its objectives, TrackMeNot instead uses "noise and obfuscation." In this way, a user's Web searches become "lost in a cloud of false leads." By issuing randomized search queries to popular search engines such as Google and Bing, TrackMeNot "hides users' actual search trails in a cloud of 'ghost' queries." This technique makes it difficult for search engine companies to aggregate the data it collects into accurate user profiles.

Although PETs such as Anonymizer and TrackMeNot assist users in navigating the Web with relative anonymity, they are not useful for e-commerce transactions in which users must reveal their actual identities. Many e-commerce sites now provide users with a stated privacy policy that is backed by certified "trustmarks" or trust seals (discussed in more detail in Section 5.9.1). These trust agreements between users and e-commerce sites can also be viewed as PETs in that they are intended to protect a user's privacy during a consumer transaction. But are they adequate to the task? To answer this question, we next analyze PETs in relation to two specific challenges: consumer education and informed consent.[24]

5.8.1 Educating Users about PETs

How are users supposed to find out about PETs? Consider that Web sites are not required to inform users about the existence of PETs or to make those tools available to them. Furthermore, online consumers must not only discover that PETs are available, but they must also learn how to use these tools. So at present, responsibility for learning about PETs and how to use them is incumbent upon consumers. Is it reasonable and is it fair to expect users to be responsible for these tasks?

Recall our earlier discussion of cookies. Although many Web browsers allow users to reject cookies, the default is that cookies will be accepted unless the user explicitly rejects them. But why shouldn't the default setting be changed such that Web sites would have to get a user's permission to send a cookie file to that user's computer system? The Web site could also inform, and possibly educate, the user about the existence of cookies, and then ask whether he or she is willing to accept them. Why not presume that users do not want cookie information recorded and stored on their computer systems, and then set the default conditions on Web browsers accordingly? And why not further presume that users do not want their personal data used in ways they did not explicitly authorize when they initially disclosed it in a commercial transaction? Following Judith DeCew (2006), we could "presume in favor of privacy" and then develop ways that would allow individuals to determine for themselves how and when that presumption should be overridden. (This is part of a process that DeCew refers to as "dynamic negotiation.") Independent of questions about where the presumption should reside, however, the widespread application and use of PETs will require a massive educational effort.

5.8.2 PETs and the Principle of Informed Consent

Even if the consumer-education-related issues involving PETs can be resolved, other questions need to be asked. For example, do PETs adequately support users in making *informed* decisions about the disclosure of their personal data in commercial transactions? Traditionally, the principle of informed consent has been the model, or standard, in contexts involving the disclosure of one's personal data. However, users who willingly consent to provide information about themselves for one purpose (e.g., in one transaction) may have no idea how that information can also be used in secondary applications.

Some in the commercial sector argue that because no one is forcing users to reveal personal data, the disclosure of such data is done on a completely voluntary basis. Assume that a user has willingly consented to disclose personal data in an e-commerce transaction. Has the user also consented to having that information used for additional, "secondary" purposes? Recall our discussion in Section 5.6 about data mining, where we saw that specific information given by a consumer for use in one context could be subsequently "mined."

We can also ask whether businesses that collect personal data could possibly know in advance exactly how those data will be used in secondary and future applications? When data mining technology is involved, for example, it would seem that businesses could *not* adequately inform users about exactly how their personal data might be used in secondary applications. What kind of *informed* choice, then, could users make in these cases? (In Chapter 12, we examine how the principle of informed consent has become nontransparent or "opaque" in genomic research that employs data mining technology.)

Some in the e-commerce sector have responded to critics by pointing out that in most cases, users are provided with the means to either "opt-in" or "opt-out" of having their personal data collected, as well as having those data made available for secondary use. But the default is such that if no option is specified by the user when he or she discloses personal data for use in one context, then those disclosed personal data are also available for secondary use. Hence, the policy is "presumed consent," not informed consent. Is that presumption fair to online consumers?

Because PETs provide users with some ways of protecting their identity and also provide them some choice in controlling the flow of their personal information, they would seem to be an empowering rather than a disabling technology. But PETs alone are insufficient for resolving many privacy concerns affecting e-commerce.

▶ 5.9 PRIVACY LEGISLATION AND INDUSTRY SELF-REGULATION

We saw in the previous section that even though PETs offer users a means to protect their identity in certain kinds of activities, they are not the "magic bullet" many of their staunchest supporters have suggested. Recognizing the limitations of PETs, some privacy advocates believe that stronger privacy laws will protect consumers, whereas others in the commercial sector, for example, believe that additional privacy legislation is neither necessary nor desirable. Instead, they suggest strong industry controls regulated by standards.

Generally, privacy advocates have been skeptical of voluntary controls, including industry standards for "self-regulation initiatives." Instead, they argue for stricter privacy legislation and data protection principles to protect the interests of users. We begin this section with a look at certain self-regulatory schemes for privacy protection that is provided to consumers by industry standards.

5.9.1 Industry Self-Regulation Initiatives Regarding Privacy

Some industry representatives who advocate for the use of "voluntary controls" might concede that tools such as PETs, in themselves, are not adequate to protect the privacy of consumers in e-commerce transactions. However, they also believe that alternatives to additional privacy legislation are possible. These advocates point to the establishment of industry standards that have already been accepted and implemented. Some of these standards are similar to PETs in the sense that they are intended to protect a user's privacy, but unlike PETs in that they are not themselves tools.

An industry-backed (self-regulatory) initiative called TRUSTe was designed to help ensure that Web sites adhere to the privacy policies they advertise. TRUSTe uses a branded system of "trustmarks" (graphic symbols), which represent a Web site's privacy policy regarding personal information. Trustmarks provide consumers with the assurance that a Web site's privacy practices accurately reflect its stated policies. Through this PET-like feature, users can file a complaint to TRUSTe if the Web site bearing its trust seal does not abide by the stated policies. Any Web site that bears the TRUSTe mark and wishes to retain that seal must satisfy several conditions: The Web site must clearly explain in advance its general information-collecting practices, including which personally identifiable data will be collected, what the information will be used for, and with whom the information will be shared. Web sites that bear a trust seal but do not conform to these conditions can have their seal revoked. And Web sites displaying trust seals, such as TRUSTe, are subject to periodic and unannounced audits of their sites.

Critics have pointed out some of the difficulties in implementing TRUSTe. For example, the amount of information users are required to provide can easily discourage them from carefully reading and understanding the agreement. Also, the various warnings displayed may appear unfriendly and thus might discourage users; "friendlier" trustmarks, on the contrary, might result in users being supplied with less direct information that is important for protecting their privacy. But advocates of tools such as TRUSTe argue that, with these tools, users will be better able to make informed choices regarding electronic purchasing and other types of online transactions.

Critics worry that such programs do not go far enough. Consider, for example, the case of *Toysmart.com*, an e-commerce site that operated in Massachusetts. Consumers who purchased items from Toysmart were assured, via an online trust seal, that their personal data would be protected. The vendor's policy stated that personal information disclosed to Toysmart would be used internally but would not be sold to or exchanged with external vendors. So, users who dealt with Toysmart expected that their personal data would remain in that company's databases and not be further disclosed or sold to a third party. In the spring of 2000, however, Toysmart was forced to file for bankruptcy.[25]

In the bankruptcy process, Toysmart solicited bids for its assets, which included its databases containing the names of customers. Were the parties interested in purchasing that information under any obligation to adhere to the privacy policy that Toysmart had established with its clients? If not, whoever either took over Toysmart or purchased its databases, would, in principle, be free to do whatever they wished with the personal information in them, despite the fact that such information was given to Toysmart by clients under the belief that information about them would be protected indefinitely.

The Toysmart incident illustrates a situation in which users had exercised control over their personal information in one context—that is, in electing whether to disclose information about themselves to Toysmart in online transactions—based on specific conditions stated in Toysmart's privacy policy. However, it also turned out that these individuals were not guaranteed that the personal information they disclosed to Toysmart would be protected in the future. Thus, it would seem that controls beyond those provided by trustmarks and e-commerce vendors are needed.

Another concern has to do with various privacy policies established by search engine companies. Unlike e-commerce sites, which users can easily avoid if they wish, virtually every Internet user depends on search engines to navigate the Web. In Section 5.7.1, we saw how major search engine companies such as Google record and keep a log of users' searches. This practice, as we also saw, has generated privacy concerns. In early 2012, Google announced a new comprehensive privacy policy, as described in the following scenario.

▶ **SCENARIO 5–13:** Controversies Involving Google's Privacy Policy

Google Inc., perhaps the most well-known search engine company in the world, also owns and/or operates several subsidiary services and Web-based applications. These include, Gmail, Google Maps, Google+, Google Calendar, Google Chrome, Picasa, Adsense/Adwords, and so forth. In the past, each had its own privacy policy. In 2012, however, Google replaced the individual policies with one comprehensive privacy policy across all of its services. When it implemented this change, Google also announced that the company would share user account data across all its services. Critics note that a user's search engine history could be shared with YouTube, or vice versa, and that a user's Google+ account data might be shared with Adwords to generate more targeted advertising.[26] ∎

Google's new privacy policy, while explicit and transparent, has nonetheless been controversial for several reasons. For one thing, it is not clear how Google will use all of the personal information that it can now access so easily. For another, no one outside Google fully understands how the search engine company uses that information to manipulate (i.e., tailor or personalize) the search results a user receives for his or her search queries. Additionally, it is not clear whether one's personal information collected from the various Google services will be used only internally, or will also be available to advertisers and information merchants outside the company (e.g., those Web sites that include embedded Google ads to generate revenue).

Others worry whether users can trust Google—a company that officially embraces the motto: "do not be evil"—to abide by its new privacy policy. Some note, for example, that many people who used Apple's Safari Web browser on their computers and iPhones were under the impression that Google was not able to track their browsing activities. In early 2012, however, it was discovered Google had used software code that tricked the Safari browser, thus enabling Google to track the activities of those using that browser. Google disabled the controversial software code shortly after the incident was reported in *The Wall Street Journal*, and Safari users were informed by Google that they could rely on Safari's privacy settings to prevent tracking by Google in the future (Anguin and Valentino-DeVries 2012). But some critics remain skeptical.

Because of concerns involving distrust of Google and other commercial Web sites to regulate themselves, privacy advocates believe that explicit privacy laws are needed to protect users. We next briefly examine some existing privacy legislation.

5.9.2 Privacy Laws and Data Protection Principles

Many nations have enacted strong privacy legislation. The United States, however, has not taken the lead on legislation initiatives; some would argue that the United States is woefully behind the European nations in this regard. In fact, in the United States there is currently very little privacy protection in legal statutes. In 1974, Congress passed the Privacy Act, which has been criticized both for containing far too many loopholes and for lacking adequate provisions for enforcement. It applies only to records in federal agencies and thus is not applicable in the private sector. Subsequent privacy legislation in the United States has resulted mostly in a "patchwork" of individual state and federal laws that are neither systematic nor coherent. In 2003, the Health Insurance Portability and Accountability Act (HIPAA), which provides protection for "individually identifiable" medical records from "inappropriate use and disclosure," was enacted into law. (HIPAA is examined in Chapter 12 in connection with our discussion of bio-informatics.) But the kind of privacy protection provided by HIPAA does not apply to an individual's nonmedical/health records such as consumer data.

Generally, U.S. lawmakers have resisted requests from privacy advocates for stronger consumer privacy laws, siding instead with business interests in the private sector who believe that such legislation would undermine economic efficiency and thus adversely impact the overall economy. Critics point out, however, that many of those businesses who have subsidiary companies or separate business operations in countries with strong privacy laws and regulations, such as nations in Western Europe, have found little difficulty in complying with the privacy laws of the host countries; profits for those American-owned companies have not suffered because of their compliance. In any event, there has been increased pressure on the U.S. government, especially from Canada and the European Union (EU), to enact stricter privacy laws, and pressure on American businesses to adopt stricter privacy polices and practices because of global e-commerce pressures.

EU nations have, through the implementation of strict data protection principles, been far more aggressive than the United States in addressing privacy concerns of individuals. In the early 1990s, the European community began to consider synthesizing the data protection laws of the individual European nations.[27] The European Community has since instituted a series of directives, including the EU Directive 95/46/EC of the European Parliament and of the Council of Europe of 24 October 1995, which is referred to as the EU Directive on Data Protection, designed to protect the personal data of its citizens by prohibiting the "transborder flow" of such data to countries that lack adequate protection of personal data.[28]

Dag Elgesem (2004) has pointed out that a central focus of the EU Directive, unlike earlier privacy legislation in Europe that focused simply on the recording and the storage of personal information, is on the *processing* and *flow* of personal data. Several principles make up the European Directive; among them are the principles of Data Quality, Legitimate Purposes, Sensitive Data, and The Right to Be Informed. Whereas the Data Quality Principle is concerned with protecting the data subject's reasonable expectations concerning the processing of data about that subject, the Legitimate Purposes Principle lists the purposes for which the processing of personal data about the data subject are considered legitimate. What helps to ensure that each of these principles is enforced on behalf of individuals, or "data subjects," is the presence of privacy protection commissions and boards in the various European nations. As in the case of Canada, which has also set up privacy oversight agencies with a Privacy Commissioner in each of its provinces, many European countries have their own data protection agencies.

So far, we have considered various kinds of proposals aimed at addressing privacy concerns. Some have called for stricter privacy laws on the part of governments and for the formation of privacy oversight commissions to enforce those laws. Others call for more serious self-regulatory measures by those in the commercial sector. And some proposals have suggested the need for technological solutions that empower online users by providing them with privacy-enhancing tools. Can these various proposals, or at least relevant aspects of them, be successfully combined or integrated into one comprehensive proposal?

While there has been no uniform consensus on a comprehensive privacy policy, especially one that could be implemented across international borders, there does seem to be considerable agreement on at least one point: any comprehensive privacy policy should be as transparent as possible. In examining James Moor's theory of privacy in Section 5.2.4, we saw that personal privacy could be protected in "situations" or zones that were declared "normatively private." We also saw that Moor requires that the rules for setting up normatively private situations be "public" and open to debate. This point is made explicit in his *Publicity Principle*, which states that the rules and conditions governing private situations should be "clear and known to persons affected by them" (Moor 2000). Thus, a critical element in Moor's model for an adequate privacy policy is openness, or transparency, so that all parties in the "situation," or context, are kept abreast of what the rules are at any given point in time. In this sense, Moor's publicity principle would seem to provide a key foundational element in any comprehensive privacy policy that incorporates legislation, self-regulation, and privacy-enhancing tools.

▶ 5.10 CHAPTER SUMMARY

We began by examining some ways that cybertechnology has exacerbated privacy concerns introduced by earlier technologies. We then briefly examined the concept of privacy and some theories that have attempted to explain and justify privacy. We saw that "informational privacy" could be distinguished from "accessibility privacy" and "decisional privacy," and that Moor's privacy theory was able to integrate key components of three traditional theories into one comprehensive theory of privacy. We also saw that privacy is an important value, essential for human ends such as friendship and autonomy.

We saw how NPI is threatened by data gathering and data exchanging techniques, including computerized matching and merging of records. And we also saw how PPI is threatened by data mining technology. We examined some privacy threats posed by the use of RFID technology, Internet cookies, and search engine technology. We also considered whether technology itself, in the form of privacy-enhancing technologies or PETs, could be used to preserve personal privacy or whether stronger privacy legislation and better industry self-regulation are needed.

We also noted at the outset that not all computer-related privacy concerns could be examined in Chapter 5. For example, specific kinds of privacy concerns pertaining to computerized monitoring in the workplace are discussed in Chapter 10, and privacy issues affecting computerized medical and healthcare information are examined in Chapter 12. Also examined in Chapter 12 are surveillance concerns affecting "location privacy" made possible by pervasive computing and GPS technologies. Although some privacy concerns affecting personal information about individuals collected by governmental organizations were also briefly considered in this chapter, additional privacy issues in this area are examined in Chapter 6 in the context of our discussion of computer security. Our main focus in Chapter 5 has been with privacy and cybertechnology concerns affecting the collection, exchange, and mining of personal data acquired from a typical individual's day-to-day activities, both on- and offline.

▶ REVIEW QUESTIONS

1. Identify and briefly describe four ways in which the privacy threats posed by cybertechnology differ from those posed by earlier technologies.
2. What is personal privacy, and why is privacy difficult to define?
3. Describe some important characteristics that differentiate "accessibility privacy," "decisional privacy," and "informational privacy."
4. How does James Moor's theory of privacy combine key elements of these three views of privacy? What does Moor mean by a "situation," and how does he distinguish between "natural privacy" and "normative privacy"?
5. Why is privacy valued? Is privacy an intrinsic value or is it an instrumental value? Explain.
6. Is privacy a social value, or is it simply an individual good?
7. What does Roger Clarke mean by "dataveillance"? Why do dataveillance techniques threaten personal privacy?
8. What are Internet cookies, and why are they considered controversial from the perspective of personal privacy?
9. What is RFID technology, and why is it a threat to privacy?
10. Explain computerized merging. Why is it controversial from the perspective of personal privacy?
11. Describe the technique known as computerized matching? What problems does it raise for personal privacy?
12. What is data mining, and why is it considered controversial?
13. What is the difference between PPI and NPI?
14. What is meant by "privacy in public"? Describe the problem of protecting personal privacy in public space.
15. Why are certain aspects and uses of Internet search engines controversial from a privacy perspective?
16. Why does online access to public records pose problems for personal privacy?
17. What are privacy-enhancing technologies (PETs)? How is their effectiveness challenged by concerns related to (user) education and informed consent?
18. Describe some of the voluntary controls and self-regulation initiatives that have been proposed by representatives from industry and e-commerce. Are they adequate solutions?
19. What are some of the criticisms of U.S. privacy laws such as HIPAA and the Privacy Act of 1974?
20. Describe some principles included in the EU Directive on Data Protection. What do you believe to be some of the strengths and weaknesses of those principles when compared to privacy laws in America?

▶ DISCUSSION QUESTIONS

21. Review Helen Nissenbaum's framework of privacy in terms of "contextual integrity." What are the differences between what she calls "norms of appropriateness" and "norms of distribution"? Give an example of how either or both norms can be breached in a specific context.
22. Through the use of currently available online tools and search facilities, ordinary users can easily acquire personal information about others. In fact, anyone who has Internet access can, via a search engine such as Google, find information about us that we ourselves might have had no idea is publicly available there. Does this use of search engines threaten the privacy of ordinary people? Explain.
23. In debates regarding access and control of personal information, it is sometimes argued that an appropriate balance needs to be struck between individuals and organizations: individuals claim that they should be able to control who has access to their information, and organizations, including government and business groups, claim to need that information in order to make appropriate decisions. How can a reasonable resolution be reached that would satisfy both parties?
24. Reexamine the arguments made by the U.S. government and by Google regarding the government's requests for information about users' search requests made during the summer of 2005. Are the government's reasons for why it should have access to that information reasonable? Does Google have an obligation to protect the personal information of its users, with respect to disclosing information about their searches? Could this obligation be overridden by certain kinds of national defense interests? If, for example, the government claimed to need the information to

prevent a potential terrorist attack, would that have changed your analysis of the situation? Or does the government have the right, and possibly an obligation to the majority of its citizens, to monitor the searches if doing so could positively affect the outcome of child pornography legislation?

▶ ESSAY/PRESENTATION QUESTIONS

25. Initially, privacy concerns involving computer technology arose because citizens feared that a strong centralized government could easily collect and store data about them. In the 1960s, for example, there was talk of constructing a national computerized database in the United States, and many were concerned that George Orwell's prediction of Big Brother in his classic book *1984* had finally arrived. The centralized database, however, never materialized. Prior to September 11, 2001, some privacy advocates suggested that we have fewer reasons to be concerned about the federal government's role in privacy intrusions (Big Brother) than we do about privacy threats from the commercial sector (Big Bucks and Big Browser). Is that assessment still accurate? Defend your answer.

26. Apply Helen Nissenbaum's framework of "privacy as contextual integrity" (examined in Section 5.2.5) to personal blogs that contain online personal diaries, such as the "Washingtonienne" (involving Jessica Cutler) scenario that we briefly described in Chapter 1. (At this point, you may want to revisit Scenario 1–3 in Chapter 1.) An important question that we were unable to analyze in our earlier analysis of that case was whether Cutler's privacy had been violated. Using Nissenbaum's framework, however, we can further refine our initial question by asking whether the incident violated the integrity of the norms of appropriateness or the norms of distribution, or both, in that context. Consider that, when Cutler set up her blog, she did not bother to protect it with a password. Is that point relevant in your assessment? Because the information included in her blog could, in principle, be read by anyone on the Internet, could Cutler plausibly claim that her privacy had been violated when her online diary was discovered and then posted in *Wonkette*, the Washington DC online gossip column? Also consider the six men implicated in her blog? Was it appropriate for her to include that information in her online diary? Did the distribution of information about them via Cutler's diary violate their privacy? Explain.

Scenarios for Analysis

1. In the days and weeks immediately following the tragic events of September 11, 2001, some political leaders in the United States argued that extraordinary times call for extraordinary measures; in times of war, basic civil liberties and freedoms, such as privacy, need to be severely restricted for the sake of national security and safety. Initially, the majority of American citizens strongly supported the Patriot Act, which passed by an overwhelming margin in both houses of Congress and was enacted into law on October 21, 2001. However, between 2001 and 2005 support for this act diminished considerably. Many privacy advocates believe that it goes too far and thus erodes basic civil liberties. Some critics also fear that certain provisions included in the act could easily be abused. Examine some of the details of the Patriot Act (which can be viewed on the Web at www.govtrack.us/congress/bills/107/hr3162/text), and determine whether its measures are as extreme as its critics suggest. Are those measures also consistent with the value of privacy, which many Americans claim to embrace? Do privacy interests need to be reassessed, and possibly recalibrated, in light of ongoing threats from terrorists? To what extent does the following expression, attributed to Benjamin Franklin, affect your answer to this question: "They who can give up essential liberty to obtain a little temporary safety, deserve neither liberty nor safety."

2. At the beginning of Chapter 5, we suggested that concerns about the loss of privacy may have a generational dimension or element— i.e., younger people may be less concerned about privacy loss involving cybertechnology than older people. To further explore this possibility, conduct a series of informal interviews with individuals that represent three generations: Millennials, Gen X/Y, and Baby Boomers. Ask members of each group how much they value their privacy and how much of it they are willing to trade off for the convenience of cybertechnology. Compare the results of the answers you get from the three groups. Are their respective views about the importance of privacy as far apart as some might expect? Explain.

▶ ENDNOTES

1. See the interview with Arthur Miller in the video "The World at Your Fingertips" in the BBC/PBS Series, *The Machine That Changed the World*, 1990.
2. See Warren and Brandeis (1890) for more detail.
3. For a discussion of the right to privacy in the Quinlan case, see "Court at the End of Life—The Right to Privacy: Karen Ann Quinlan" at http://www.libraryindex.com/pages/582/Court-End-Life-RIGHT-PRIVACY-KAREN-ANN-QUINLAN.html.
4. Moor (2000), p. 207. [Italics added]
5. Nissenbaum (2004a), p. 137.
6. *Ibid*, p. 135. For analyses of how Nissenbaum's contextual-integrity model of privacy can be applied to the blogosphere and to "the Cloud," see Grodzinsky and Tavani (2010, 2011), respectively.
7. See Westin (1967) for more detail on this point.
8. DeCew (2006), p. 121. Moor (2006, p. 114) also describes privacy as a kind of "shield" that protects us.
9. See Clarke's account of dataveillance, available at http://www.rogerclarke.com/DV/.
10. Nissenbaum (2004a), p. 135.
11. Mason (2007, p. 42) makes a similar point when he notes that "I may authorize one institution to collect 'A' about me, and another institution to collect 'B' about me: but I might not want anyone to possess 'A and B' about me at the same time."
12. See, for example, Scott Chapman and Gurpreet S. Dhillon (2002). "Privacy and the Internet: The Case of DoubleClick, Inc." In G. Dhillon, ed. *Social Information in the Information Age: issues and Controversies.* Hershey PA: Idea Group, pp. 75–88.
13. My discussion of computerized matching here draws from Tavani (1996).
14. For more information about this incident, see Brey (2004).
15. This scenario is adapted from Tavani (1999).
16. See "Web Mining." *Wikipedia*. Available at http://en.wikipedia.org/wiki/Web_mining.
17. See http://en.wikipedia.org/wiki/Facebook.
18. *Ibid*.
19. Nissenbaum (2004b), p. 455.
20. Fulda (2004), p. 472.
21. See, for example, Nissenbaum (2010).
22. This scenario is based in part on an actual controversy involving online public records in Merrimack, NH.
23. See Scanlan (2001) for a more detailed account of the issues involved in this scenario.
24. My analysis of PETs in this section draws from Tavani (2000) and Tavani and Moor (2001).
25. For more information about this scenario, see Nicholas Morehead (2000). "Toysmart: Bankruptcy Litmus Test." *Wired* 7, no. 12. Available at http://www.wired.com/techbiz/media/news/2000/07/37517.
26. See Werner (2012) for a more detailed analysis of this controversy.
27. See http://www.oecd.org/document/18/0, 3343, en_2649_34255_1815186_1_1_1_1, 00.html.
28. See http://www.cdt.org/privacy/eudirective/EU_Directive_.html.

▶ REFERENCES

Adam, Alison. 2005. "Chips in Our Children: Can We Inscribe Privacy in a Machine?" *Ethics and Information Technology* 7, no. 4: 233–42.

Anguin, Julia, and Jennifer Valentino-DeVries. 2012. "Google's iPhone Tracking: Web Giant, Others Bypassed Apple Browser Settings for Guarding Privacy." *Wall Street Journal*, February 17. Available at http://online.wsj.com/article_email/SB10001424052970204880404577225380456599176-lMyQjAxMTAyMDEwNjExNDYyWj.html.

Bamford, James. 2012. "The NSA Is Building the Country's Biggest Spy Center (Watch What You Say)." *Wired*, March 15. Available at http://m.wired.com/threatlevel/2012/03/ff_nsadatacenter/all/1.

Brey, Philip. 2004. "Ethical Aspects of Facial Recognition Systems in Public Places." In R. A. Spinello and H. T. Tavani, eds. *Readings in Cyberethics*. 2nd ed. Sudbury MA: Jones and Bartlett, pp. 585–600.

DeCew, Judith W. 1997. *In Pursuit of Privacy: Law, Ethics, and the Rise of Technology*. Ithaca NY: Cornell University Press.

DeCew, Judith W. 2006. "Privacy and Policy for Genetic Research." In H. T. Tavani, ed. *Ethics, Computing, and Genomics*. Sudbury MA: Jones and Bartlett, pp. 121–35.

Elgesem, Dag. 2004. "The Structure of Rights in Directive 95/46/EC on the Protection of Individuals with Regard to the Processing of Personal Data and the Free Movement of Such Data." In ªR. A. Spinello and H. T. Tavani, eds. *Readings in CyberEthics*. 2nd ed. Sudbury MA: Jones and Bartlett, pp. 418–35.

Fried, Charles. 1990. "Privacy: A Rational Context." In M. D. Ermann, M. B. Williams, and C. Gutierrez, eds. *Computers, Ethics, and Society*. New York: Oxford University Press, pp. 51–67.

Froomkin, Michael. 2000. "The Death of Privacy?" *Stanford Law Review* 52. Available at www.law.miami.edu/~froomkin/articles/privacy-deathof.pdf.

Fulda, Joseph S. 2004. "Data Mining and Privacy." In R. A. Spinello and H. Tavani, eds. *Readings in CyberEthics*. 2nd ed. Sudbury MA: Jones and Bartlett, pp. 471–75.

Garfinkel, Simson. 2000. *Database Nation: The Death of Privacy in the 21st Century*. Cambridge MA: O'Reilly and Associates.

Garfinkel, Simson. 2002. "RFID Bill of Rights." *Technology Review*, October. Available at http://www.technologyreview.com/article/401660/an-rfid-bill-of-rights/.

Grodzinsky, Frances S., and Herman T. Tavani. 2010. "Applying the 'Contextual Integrity' Model of Privacy to Personal Blogs in the Blogosphere," *International Journal of Internet Research Ethics* 3, no. 1: 38–47.

Grodzinsky, Francis, S., and Herman T. Tavani. 2011. "Privacy in 'the Cloud': Applying Nissenbaum's Theory of Contextual Integrity." *Computers and Society* 41, no. 1: 38–47.

Halpern, Sue. 2011. "Mind Control and the Internet." *New York Review of Books*, June 23. Available at http://www.nybooks.com/articles/archives/2011/jun/23/mind-control-and-internet/.

Lockton Vance, and Richard S. Rosenberg. 2005. "RFID: The Next Serious Threat to Privacy." *Ethics and Information Technology* 7, no. 4: 221–31.

Mason, Richard O. 2007. "Four Ethical Issues of the Information Age." In J. Weckert, ed. *Computer Ethics*. Aldershot UK: Ashgate, pp. 31–40. Reprinted from *MIS Quarterly* 10: 5–12.

Moor, James H. 2000. "Towards a Theory of Privacy for the Information Age." In R. M. Baird, R. Ramsower, and S. E. Rosenbaum, eds. *Cyberethics: Moral, Social, and Legal Issues in the Computer Age*. Amherst NY: Prometheus Books, pp. 200–12.

Moor, James H. 2004. "Reason, Relativity, and Responsibility in Computer Ethics." In R. A. Spinello and H. T. Tavani, eds. *Readings in CyberEthics*. 2nd ed. Sudbury MA: Jones and Bartlett, pp. 40–54.

Moor, James H. 2006. "Using Genetic Information While Protecting the Privacy of the Soul." In H. T. Tavani, ed. *Ethics, Computing, and Genomics*. Sudbury MA: Jones and Bartlett, pp. 109–19.

Nissenbaum, Helen. 2004a. "Privacy as Contextual Integrity." *Washington Law Review* 79, no. 1: 119–57.

Nissenbaum, Helen. 2004b. "Toward an Approach to Privacy in Public: Challenges of Information Technology." In R. A. Spinello and H. T. Tavani, eds. *Readings in Cyber-Ethics*. 2nd ed. Sudbury MA: Jones and Bartlett, pp. 450–61. Reprinted from *Ethics and Behavior* 7, no. 3 (1997): 207–19.

Nissenbaum, Helen. 2010. *Privacy in Context: Technology, Policy, and the Integrity of Social Life*. Palo Alto, CA: Stanford University Press.

Pariser, Eli. 2011. *The Filter Bubble: What the Internet Is Hiding from You*. New York: Penguin.

Regan, Priscilla M. 1995. *Legislating Privacy: Technology, Social Values, and Public Policy*. Chapel Hill NC: The University of North Carolina Press.

Scanlan, Michael. 2001. "Informational Privacy and Moral Values." *Ethics and Information Technology* 3, no. 1: 3–12.

Spinello, Richard A. 2010. "Informational Privacy." In G. Brenkert and T. Beauchamp, eds. *Oxford Handbook of Business Ethics*. Oxford, UK: Oxford University Press, pp. 366–87.

Stuckey, Mike. 2008. "Amex Rates Credit Risk by Where You Live, Shop." *MSNBC.Com*. Available at http://www.msnbc.msn.com/id/27055285/ (accessed May 18, 2009).

Tavani, Herman T. 1996. "Computer Matching and Personal Privacy: Can They Be Compatible?" In C. Huff, ed. *Proceedings of the Symposium on Computers and the Quality of Life*. New York: ACM Press, pp. 97–101.

Tavani, Herman T. 1999. "Informational Privacy, Data Mining and the Internet." *Ethics and Information Technology* 1, no. 2: 137–45.

Tavani, Herman T. 2000. "Privacy-Enhancing Technologies as a Panacea for Online Privacy Concerns: Some Ethical Considerations." *Journal of Information Ethics* 9, no. 2: 26–36.

Tavani Herman T., and James H. Moor. 2001. "Privacy Protection, Control over Information, and Privacy-Enhancing Technologies." *Computers and Society* 31, no. 1: 6–11.

Warren, Samuel, and Louis Brandeis. 1890. "The Right to Privacy." *Harvard Law Review* 4, no. 5: 193–220.

Werner, Jeff. 2012. "Should You Be Worried about Google's New Privacy Policy?" *NWFDailyNews.com*, March 25. Available at http://www.nwfdailynews.com/articles/google-48355-new-policy.html.

Westin, Alan. 1967. *Privacy and Freedom*. New York: Atheneum Press.

Zimmer, Michael. 2008. "The Gaze of the Perfect Search Engine: Google as an Institution of Dataveillance." In A. Spink and M. Zimmer, eds. *Web Search: Multidisciplinary Perspectives*. Berlin: Springer-Verlag, pp. 77–99.

▶ FURTHER READINGS

Alfino, Mark. "Misplacing Privacy." *Journal of Information Ethics* 10, no. 1 (2001): 5–8.

Cavoukian, Ann."Privacy in the Clouds: A White Paper on Privacy and Digital Identity: Implications for the Internet." Available at http://www.ipc.on.ca/images/resources/privacyintheclouds.pdf, 2008.

Shoemaker, David W. "Self Exposure and Exposure of the Self: Informational Privacy and the Presentation of Identity." *Ethics and Information Technology* 12, no. 1 (2010): 3–15.

Solove, Daniel J. *Understanding Privacy*. Cambridge, MA: Harvard University Press, 2008.

Spinello, Richard A. "Privacy and Social Networking." *International Review of Information Ethics* 16 (2011): 42–46.

Zimmer, Michael. "Surveillance, Privacy, and the Ethics of Vehicle Safety Communication Technologies." *Ethics and Information Technology* 7, no. 4 (2005): 201–10.

CHAPTER

6

Security in Cyberspace

Can cyber intrusions (including cyberattacks and computer break-ins) ever be justified on ethical grounds? This is one of many cybersecurity issues that we will examine in Chapter 6. Other questions include the following:

- What is cybersecurity, and how are security issues involving computers and cybertechnology different from privacy issues in cyberspace?
- How are violations involving cybersecurity similar to and different from issues of cybercrime?
- Which key features differentiate data security, system security, and network security?
- What is "cloud computing," and which kinds of challenges does it pose for cybersecurity?
- What is meant by "hacking" and the "hacker ethic"?
- Can a clear distinction be drawn between "hacktivism" and cyberterrorism?
- What is the difference between cyberterrorism and information warfare (IW)?

We begin our analysis of security issues in cyberspace with a brief discussion of some basic concepts and definitions.

▶ 6.1 SECURITY IN THE CONTEXT OF CYBERTECHNOLOGY

What, exactly, do we mean by "computer security" and "cybersecurity"? Like privacy, *security*—especially, in the context of computing and cybertechnology—has no universally agreed-upon definition. The expressions *computer security* and *cybersecurity* are often associated with issues having to do with the reliability, availability, and safety, of computers systems, as well as with the integrity, confidentiality, and protection of data. Richard Epstein (2007) suggests that security concerns affecting computers and cybertechnology can be viewed in terms of three key elements:

- confidentiality,
- integrity,
- accessibility.

Whereas confidentiality is "about preventing unauthorized persons from gaining access to unauthorized information," integrity, in computer security contexts, is about "preventing an attacker from modifying data." In Epstein's scheme, accessibility has to do with "making sure that resources are available for authorized users."[1]

Are any additional elements or criteria useful for understanding cybersecurity? Peter Neumann (2004) notes that, in addition to providing desired confidentiality, integrity, and accessibility, cybersecurity aims at preventing "misuse, accidents, and malfunctions" with respect to computer systems. Neumann also notes, however, that cybersecurity can be a "double-edged sword"; for example, it can be used to protect privacy, but it can also be used to undermine "freedom of access" to information for users.[2]

In defining cybersecurity, it is important to point out that sometimes issues involving security in cyberspace overlap with concerns pertaining to cybercrime; other times they intersect with issues involving privacy. We briefly examine some ways in which security issues intersect and overlap with both kinds of concerns, also noting how security concerns can be distinguished from those of privacy and crime.

6.1.1 Cybersecurity as Related to Cybercrime

How are cybersecurity violations both similar to and different from cybercrime? First, we should note that some cyberethics textbooks link together issues involving cybersecurity and cybercrime by covering them in the same chapter. Consequently, these issues could easily be viewed as subcategories of a single cyberethics category. But while most intentional cybersecurity violations are illegal and often criminal, not every crime in cyberspace involves a breach, or violation, of cybersecurity.

Consider three cyber-related crimes that have no direct implications for cybersecurity: a pedophile can use a computer to solicit sex with young children, a drug dealer can use the Internet to traffic in drugs, and a student can use an electronic device to pirate copyrighted music. Although each of these activities is clearly illegal, it is not clear that any of them necessarily result from insecure computers. Perhaps greater security mechanisms on computer networks could deter crimes and detect criminals in cyberspace, but cyber-assisted crimes involving pedophilia, drug trafficking, and pirating music do not typically result from security flaws in computer system design. There are, then, important distinctions between issues of security and crime involving cybertechnology. We will discuss cybercrime in Chapter 7, and focus our attention in this chapter on actual and potential threats to security in cyberspace.

Just as cybersecurity issues are sometimes lumped together with cybercrime, security concerns involving cybertechnology can also overlap with worries about personal privacy. We briefly considered some of these privacy-related security concerns in our discussion of PETs in Chapter 5. Now we ask: How are issues pertaining to security in cyberspace different from those involving privacy?

6.1.2 Security and Privacy: Some Similarities and Some Differences

The concepts of privacy and security are not always easy to separate, especially when civil liberties and basic human rights are discussed. In the United States, arguments for a right to privacy that appeal to the Fourth Amendment have often been made on the basis of *securing* the person (and the person's papers, and so forth) from the physical intrusion of searches and seizures. Paul Thompson (2001) believes that many of our claims involving a right to privacy are grounded in the notion of security and can be better understood as arguments concerning a "right to being secure."

Although cyber-related issues involving privacy and security can overlap, some important distinctions are nonetheless worth drawing. Privacy concerns affecting cyber-technology often arise because people fear losing control over personal information that can be accessed by organizations (especially businesses and government agencies), many of whom claim to have some *legitimate* need for that information in order to make important decisions. Security concerns, on the contrary, can arise because people worry that personal data or proprietary information, or both, could be retrieved and possibly altered, by unauthorized individuals and organizations.

Privacy and security concerns can be thought of as two sides of a single coin: People need personal privacy and they wish to control those who have information about them as well as how that information is accessed by others. Making sure that personal information stored in computer databases is secure is important in helping them achieve and maintain their privacy. In this sense, then, the objectives would seem compatible with, and even complementary to, security. In another sense, however, there is a certain tension between privacy and security. From the perspective of security, the protection of system resources and proprietary data is generally considered more critical, whereas from the vantage point of privacy, the protection of personal information and personal autonomy will receive a higher priority.

In analyzing the tension involving privacy vs. security interests, Kenneth Himma (2007a) has argued that threats to security outweigh comparable threats to the right to privacy. On the contrary, Helen Nissenbaum (2010) offers a more sympathetic appeal to the value of privacy in her analysis of the trade-offs between the two competing interests. The following quotation, attributed to Ben Franklin (1706–1790), is sometimes cited by privacy advocates to express their interpretation of what is at stake in the dispute involving security vs. privacy interests: "They who can give up essential liberty to obtain a little temporary safety, deserve neither liberty nor safety." However, in an era where concerns about cyberterrorism now influence our public policy debate, many people may be more willing to give up aspects of their liberty and privacy for greater security. (We examine some impacts that cyberterrorism has for this debate in Section 6.5.)

In the context of cybersecurity, privacy-related concerns include protecting personal data from unauthorized access, abuse, and alteration, and thus reflect values that preserve individual autonomy and individual respect for persons. And while anonymity tools (briefly described in Chapter 5) help to protect the privacy of individuals navigating in cyberspace, those tools can also cause serious concerns for security because anonymous behavior makes it difficult to identify security violators. So, in some cases, there is a natural tension between security and privacy, as we have seen; at other times, however, the objectives and goals of privacy and security—for example, with respect to confidentiality and data integrity—are the same.[3]

▶ 6.2 THREE CATEGORIES OF CYBERSECURITY

Security issues involving cybertechnology span a range of concerns having to do with three distinct kinds of vulnerabilities:

I. Unauthorized access to *data*, which are either resident in or exchanged between computer systems.

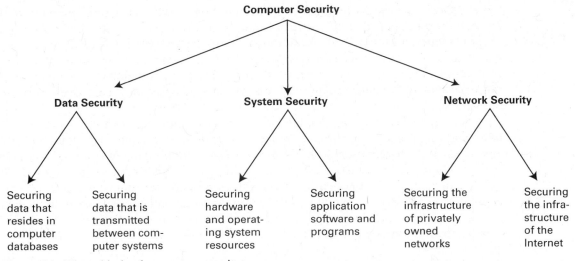

Figure 6.1 Three kinds of computer security.

II. Attacks on *system resources* (such as computer hardware, operating system software, and application software) by malicious computer programs.

III. Attacks on *computer networks*, including the infrastructure of privately owned networks and the Internet itself.[4]

We refer to the first of these three categories of security concerns as "data security." The second category of concerns can be described under the heading "system security," and the third can be understood as "network security."

We briefly describe some key aspects of each category of security, as summarized in Figure 6.1.

6.2.1 Data Security: Confidentiality, Integrity, and Availability of Information

Data security is concerned with vulnerabilities pertaining to unauthorized access to data. Those data can either (a) reside in one or more computer storage devices or (b) be exchanged between two or more computer systems, or both. In particular, data security issues affect the confidentiality, integrity, and availability of information. Richard Spinello (2000) aptly describes what is required for data security when he points out that

> . . . proprietary or sensitive information under one's custodial care is kept confidential and secure, that information being transmitted is not altered in form or content and cannot be read by unauthorized parties, and that *all* information being disseminated or otherwise made accessible through Web sites and online data repositories is as accurate and reliable as possible.[5]

Three points in this description are worth highlighting. First, the information to be protected can be either *proprietary* or *sensitive*, or both. (Proprietary information, as we will see in Chapter 8, is legally protected by schemes such as copyrights and patents and thus can be "owned" by corporations or by individuals, while sensitive information is generally considered to be intimate or confidential because it includes personal, medical, and financial records.)

Second, the information must be secured not only from tampering and alteration by unauthorized parties but also from merely being accessed (and read) by those parties. Third, and finally, the stored information must be accurate, readily available, and accessible to authorized parties. So, not only must the information residing in a computer database or in a password-protected Web site be available at optimal times, it must be able to be accessed by authorized users at any time—i.e., accessible "on demand."

Data security is now also threatened by "cloud-computing" services, as more and more corporations and ordinary users elect to store their data in "the Cloud." Cloud storage devices provide users with one means to secure their data by ensuring that their data could survive (a) "crashes" on the hard drives of their personal computers, and (b) physical damages involving their electronic "tablets" and electronic devices. However, cloud storage also poses a threat to data security because unauthorized users could gain access to, and potentially manipulate, personal data that is stored there. We examine cloud computing in detail in Section 6.3.

6.2.2 System Security: Viruses, Worms, and Malware

System security is concerned with vulnerabilities to system resources such as computer hardware, operating system software, and application software. As such, it is concerned with various kinds of viruses, worms, and related "malicious programs" that can disrupt and sometimes destroy computer systems. What are the differences between computer viruses and worms? According to Ed Skoudis (2004), a virus is a self-replicating piece of software code that "attaches itself to other programs and usually requires human action to propagate." He defines a worm in contrast as a self-replicating piece of code that "spreads via networks and usually doesn't require human interaction to propagate." Michael Simpson (2006) points out that worms replicate and propagate without needing a host or program.

Some security analysts differentiate further between the two types of disruptive programs by pointing out that a worm is less virulent than a virus. However, worms can spread more quickly than viruses, because worms, unlike viruses, do not need any human action to trigger them. We already noted that viruses cannot run on their own and are often activated when an unsuspecting user opens an e-mail attachment. Worms, on the contrary, can move from machine to machine across networks and can have parts of themselves running on different machines. The following scenario describes some effects of one notorious worm.

▶ **SCENARIO 6–1:** The Conficker Worm

In 2009, the Conficker Worm—also referred to as Kido, Downup, and Downadup—gained international attention. The worm spread quickly via a vulnerability described as a "buffer overflow" in the Microsoft Windows operating system. Later versions of Conficker also spread through both network file systems and USB drives. George Lawton (2009) notes that the worm turned the computers it infected into "a botnet capable of launching mass attacks" and that in a 4-day period in January 2009, the number of "individual infections grew from 2.4 to 8.9 million." Among the international organizations affected by Conficker were the German armed forces and the U.K. Ministry of Defense.[6] ∎

Other worms and viruses have also become well known—not only in the computer community but in the popular media as well. For example, you may have heard of the ILOVEYOU virus (also known as the "Love Bug") that wreaked havoc for computer users around the world in 2000. Other classic viruses and worms have had names such as "Blaster," "Slammer," and "Code Red."[7] (In our analysis of information warfare in Section 6.6, we examine some controversies involving the Stuxnet worm and the Flame virus, which generated controversy when they were exposed in June 2012 in connection with cyber-attacks on Iran.) If the distinction between viruses and worms were not confusing enough, some analysts suggest that we further differentiate disruptive programs to include Trojan horses and logic bombs. A *Trojan horse* often appears to be a benign program, but it can do significant system damage behind the scenes. *Logic bombs*, on the contrary, check for certain conditions or states in a computer system and then execute when one of those conditions arises. Some now refer collectively to these various kinds of "malicious programs," including viruses and worms, under the single heading "malware."

Simpson (2006) notes that malware can take many forms and can also include "spyware." The effects of malware can range from minor annoyances with individual computer systems, to preventing an entire organization from operating, to shutting down computer networks, to disrupting major segments of the Internet.

6.2.3 Network Security: Protecting our Infrastructure

A third category of computer security, which we call *network security*, is concerned with securing computer networks—i.e., from privately owned computer networks (such as LANs and WANs) to the Internet itself—against various kinds of attacks. The Internet's infrastructure has been the victim of several attacks. These attacks have ranged from programs launched by individuals with malicious intentions to individuals who claimed their intentions were benign. In many cases, these attacks have severely disrupted activities on segments of the Internet. In a few cases, they have also rendered the Internet virtually inoperable.

We should note that it is not always easy to determine whether a major computer network disruption is the result of the work of malicious individuals who launch various kinds of malware or is due to the failure of some aspect of the network infrastructure itself. For example, a significant power outage experienced by the AT&T long distance telephone service in 1990 was attributed to a software glitch in the system's programming code that caused the network to crash. However, some have questioned the official explanation given by AT&T, suggesting instead that the crash may have resulted from an attack involving malware.

Because many nations now depend on a secure cyberspace for their physical infrastructures, including power grids, there has been increased concern over threats from international hacking groups, including governments and state-sponsored organizations. The following scenario illustrates how vulnerable our national infrastructure may be to attacks by foreign governments.

▶ **SCENARIO 6–2:** The GhostNet Controversy

In 2009, The Information Warfare Monitor (IWM), a Canadian organization that monitors cyberespionage, discovered a network of at least 1,295 compromised computers in 103 countries. Approximately 30% of these were considered "high-value" targets, which (according to the IWM

TABLE 6.1 Data, System, and Network Security

Cybersecurity Category	Corresponding Area(s) of Concern
Data security	Concerned with vulnerabilities pertaining to unauthorized access to *data*, as well as with threats to the confidentiality, integrity, and availability of data that resides in computer storage devices or is exchanged between computer systems.
System security	Concerned with attacks on *system* resources (such as computer hardware, operating system software, and application software) by malicious programs.
Network security	Concerned with attacks on computer *networks*, including the infrastructure of privately owned networks as well as the Internet itself.

Report) included ministries of foreign affairs, embassies, international organizations, news media, and nongovernmental organizations (NGOs). The computer systems were compromised in ways that suggested China was responsible, but the IWM report refused to identify any one nation. The circumstantial evidence implicating China was tied to the fact that IWM's investigation was launched in response to a request by the Dali Lama, the exiled leader of Tibet (and long-time enemy of the Chinese government), who reported that his computer network had been hacked. (The IWM report referred to the cyberespionage system as "GhostNet" because it resembled the ghOst RAT Trojan horse malware that was traced back to Hainan, China.) The IWM report concluded that regardless of which country or countries were responsible for the cyberespionage, the discovery of these activities should serve as a warning to policy makers that network security requires serious attention.[8] ◼

In one sense, this scenario might initially seem to be more concerned with information warfare, which we discuss in Section 6.6, than with network security. However, the GhostNet controversy has also raised concerns about the vulnerability of a nation's network-based infrastructure, including its power grids. We will return to the GhostNet controversy later in this chapter in our discussion of information warfare, where we also discuss the impact of the Stuxnet worm and Flame virus in 2012.

In this section, we have differentiated three categories of cybersecurity, and we have briefly described some typical kinds of threats associated with each category. Table 6.1 summarizes key concerns identified with each cybersecurity category.

For the most part, the specific cybersecurity issues we identified in this chapter tend to fall into one (or at most two) of these categories. However, in the next section we will see why some relatively recent security issues associated with "cloud computing" can potentially span all three of the categories comprising our security framework.

▶ 6.3 "CLOUD COMPUTING" AND SECURITY

What is meant by *cloud computing*? Eric Knorr and Galen Gruman (2008) note that in the past, "the cloud" has often been used as a "metaphor for the Internet." In fact, the graphical interfaces on the screens of older desktop computers typically included an icon or visual of a cloud, which a user could click on to connect to the Internet. But in the current context of "cloud computing," Knorr and Gruman point out that "the cloud" (in its broad sense) can now refer to any computer resources that are used "outside the firewall."

According to the National Institute of Standards and Technology (NIST), cloud computing is officially defined as

> a model for enabling ubiquitous, convenient, on-demand network access to a shared pool of configurable computing resources (e.g., networks, servers, storage, applications and services).

Among the "essential characteristics" included in the NIST definition of cloud computing are three key elements: "on-demand self-service," "broad network access," and "resource pooling" (Mell and Grance 2011).

Ke Zeng and Ann Cavoukian (2010) note that while cloud computing is still at an early stage of development, it currently provides a wide range of services—i.e., from "full-blown applications to storage services to spam filtering." The authors also believe that cloud computing is changing the way we now think about computing by "decoupling data" and "in effect, divorcing components from location." Consider, for example, that this technology affects not only where users can store their data but also where many of the applications they use can ultimately reside. Four popular examples of cloud-computing applications include photo storing services, such as Google's Picassa; Web-based email services, such as Yahoo; file transfer services, such as YouSendit; and online computer backup services, such as Mozy (Privacy Rights Clearinghouse 2008).

6.3.1 Deployment and Service/Delivery Models for the Cloud

The NIST definition of cloud computing identifies four distinct "deployment models" and three kinds of "service models," which are also sometimes also referred to as "delivery models" (Zeng and Cavoukian). Deployment models include the following:

1. Private Cloud.
2. Community Cloud.
3. Public Cloud.
4. Hybrid Cloud.

Whereas (1) is "provisioned for exclusive use by a single organization comprising multiple consumers (e.g., business units)," and while (2) is "provisioned for use by a specific community of consumers from organizations that have shared concerns," (3) is "provisioned for open use by the general public." The infrastructure of (4) is a "composition of two or more distinct cloud infrastructures (private, community, or public) that remain unique entities" but also "bound together by standardized or proprietary technology that enables data and application portability" (NIST 2011; Mell and Grance 2011).

As mentioned above, cloud computing also provides three important *service* (or *delivery*) models:

- Software as a Service (or SaaS).
- Platform as a Service (PaaS).
- Infrastructure as a Service (IaaS).

TABLE 6.2   Possible Configurations of Cloud Computing

SaaS—Private Cloud	PaaS—Private Cloud	IaaS—Private Cloud
SaaS—Community Cloud	PaaS—Community Cloud	IaaS—Community Cloud
SaaS—Public Cloud	PaaS—Public Cloud	IaaS—Public Cloud
SaaS—Hybrid Cloud	SaaS—Hybrid Cloud	SaaS—Hybrid Cloud

Zeng and Cavoukian note that while a SaaS model "delivers applications to consumers (either individuals or enterprises) using a multitenant architecture," a PaaS model "delivers development environments to consumers." An IaaS model, on the contrary, "delivers resources such as servers, connections, and related tools necessary to build an application from scratch" (Zeng and Cavoukian). So if we consider the possible configurations of the cloud-computing services generated by the combination of deployment and service/delivery models, 12 distinct permutations of cloud computing are possible (i.e., based on private/community/public/hybrid modes of deployment and SaaS/PaaS/IaaS modes. of service/delivery). Table 6.2 illustrates the permutations.[9]

So it would appear that there is no monolithic scheme for describing and understanding cloud computing in general, given the multifaceted nature of the cloud services currently available. And perhaps more importantly for our purposes, there is no single "context" from which security concerns involving *the* cloud can be analyzed (Grodzinsky and Tavani 2011). Thus, it would seem that any attempt to frame a comprehensive cloud-security policy, would need to take into account all 12 elements in Table 6.2. Additionally, it is worth noting that the kinds of challenges involved in securing these elements can impact all three categories of cybersecurity (described in Section 6.2): data security, system security, and network security. In the following section, we focus our discussion of cloud-security concerns that pertain to data-information security, in particular.

6.3.2   Securing User Data Residing in the Cloud

Cavoukian (2008) argues that for cloud computing to be fully realized, users will have to be confident that their personal information is protected and that their data (in general) is both secure and accessible. At present, however, users have at least four kinds of worries along these lines. One concern has to do with how users can control their data stored in the cloud—currently, users have very little "control over or direct knowledge about how their information is transmitted, processed, or stored" (Privacy Rights Clearinghouse). Another concern involves the integrity of the data—for example, if the host company goes out of business, what happens to the users' data? A third concern affects access to the data; i.e., can the host deny a user access to his/her own data? And a fourth concern has to do with who actually "owns" the data that is stored in the cloud (Privacy Rights Clearinghouse).

Despite these concerns, Cavoukian notes that the Cloud offers flexibility and security to users, because they no longer have to worry about how to protect their data. She also notes that the Cloud enables users to work on local, less expensive platforms, which could appeal to business owners who would be relieved of the burden of having to secure their data. However, Cavoukian argues that cloud computing can only be effective if users and businesses trust their cloud service providers. But do users have good reasons to place their trust in the businesses that currently provide cloud-computing services? Consider that in March 2009, Google reported that a bug in Google Docs (a cloud storage system) had allowed unintended access to some private documents, and it was estimated that "0.05% of documents stored via the service were affected by the bug"; however, Google claimed that the bug had been fixed within a few days (Breitbart 2010).

According to David Talbot (2011), many businesses—especially those in the health-care and finance sectors—remain leery about turning over their data to third parties. In particular, Talbot identifies three main kinds of concerns that these businesses have (i) accidental loss of data, (ii) fear of hacking attacks, and (iii) theft by "rogue employees of cloud providers." So it would seem that until these kinds of concerns are resolved, users have good reasons to be skeptical about placing their trust in cloud-computing services to protect their data.

In addition to questions concerning confidence and trust on the part of businesses and ordinary users who subscribe, or are considering subscribing, to cloud-computing services, some related concerns affecting risk analysis also arise. We briefly examine a few cloud-computing-related controversies from the perspective of risk in Section 6.7. So far in Chapter 6, we have examined some key elements in cybersecurity, but we have not yet elaborated on their ethical implications. Next, we examine ethical aspects of cybersecurity that pertain to hacking-related activities.

▶ 6.4 HACKING AND "THE HACKER ETHIC"

Individuals who have launched malicious programs of various kinds, which we collectively refer to as malware, have commonly been described in the media as computer *hackers*. Who are hackers, and what is hacking in the context of computers and cybertechnology? According to Simpson (2006), a hacker is anyone who "accesses a computer system or network without authorization from the owner." (He defines "crackers," on the contrary, as hackers who break into a computer system with "the intention of doing harm or destroying data.") Note that we also examine the concept of hacking in our discussion of cybercrime in Chapter 7, where we discuss hacking as it relates to crime and criminal behavior. In this chapter, we examine hacking and the notion of a "hacker ethic" as it relates to cybersecurity.

Many in the computer science community are unhappy with how the word "hacker," which now has a negative connotation, is used in the conventional media. Kaufman, Perlman, and Speciner (2002) describe "true computer hackers" in a very different way—i.e., as individuals who play with computers for the "pure intellectual challenge" and as "master programmers, incorruptibly honest, unmotivated by money, and careful not to harm anyone." They go on to note that people identified in the media as hackers tend to be malicious individuals who are neither brilliant nor accomplished. The authors also note that "early hackers" have been described as individuals who aimed at accessing computer systems to see how they worked, not to cause any harm to those systems.

In this chapter, we use "hacker" in the sense of the term often attributed to early computer enthusiasts. In documenting early computer hackers, many of whom were associated with the "MIT culture," some authors have used the expressions "hacker ethic" and "hacker code of ethics."

6.4.1 What Is "The Hacker Ethic"?

Steven Levy (2001) suggests that a strong and distinctive code of ethics could be found in the original hacker community. He describes the hacker code as "a philosophy, an ethic, and a dream," based on the following principles:

I. Access to computers should be unlimited and total.

II. All information should be free.

III. Mistrust authority–promote decentralization.

IV. Hackers should be judged by their hacking (not by bogus criteria such as degrees, age, race, or position).

V. You can create art and beauty on a computer.

VI. Computers can change your life for the better.[10]

Perhaps what Levy really describes is not so much a code of ethics but rather a code for the way that hackers approach their craft, that is, in terms of a certain *ethic*, as in "work ethic." Pekka Himanen (2001) has described the hacker ethic as a "new work ethic," which he contrasts with the classic "Protestant work ethic" (coined originally by Max Weber in his classic work *The Protestant Ethic and the Spirit of Capitalism*). In addition to an ethic, hackers also seem to have a distinct "ethos"—that is, they have a distinct way of looking at the world, especially the world of computers.

Many of the early hackers believed that computer systems were inherently flawed and thus needed to be improved. As a result, some hackers believed that they needed total access to all computer systems in order to take them apart, see how they work, and make the needed improvements. Not surprisingly, then, these hackers wanted to remove any barriers to free access to computers. Many hackers have embraced and some continue to embrace, either explicitly or implicitly, the following three principles:

1. Information should be free.

2. Hackers provide society with a useful and important service.

3. Activities in cyberspace are virtual in nature and thus do not harm real people in the real (physical) world.

We briefly examine each principle.

Information Should Be Free

Should information be totally free? If so, on what grounds can this claim be justified? The expression "Information wants to be free" has become a mantra for many hackers who see proprietary software and systems as obstacles to realizing the freedom of the Internet, where users would otherwise have total access to information. The debate over whether information should be free, or even to what extent information should be freely accessible to Internet users, is a complicated one. As we shall see in Chapter 8, this debate is rooted in complex property laws and policies that have been disputed in the courts, resulting in Supreme Court decisions. So we will postpone our fuller discussion of this particular point raised by hackers until our analysis of intellectual property in cyberspace. However, a few brief comments need to be made at this point.

Some critics regard the view that information should be free as idealistic or romantic. According to Eugene Spafford (2007), it is also a very naïve view. He points out that if information were free, privacy would not be possible because individuals could not control how information about them was collected and used. Also, it would not be possible to ensure integrity and accuracy of that information, since information that was freely available could always be modified and changed by anyone who happened to access it. So from the points of view of privacy and confidentiality, a world in which all information was literally and completely free would not be desirable. Thus, there would seem to be good reasons for not embracing the principle that information should be free.

Hackers might object, however, by pointing out that they do not claim that all information should be free because they recognize that some information should be kept private. Hence they would argue for a position along the following lines: keep private any information that should be private, and keep free any information that should be free. They recognize that there is much information that should be kept private but is not, and there is much information that should be publicly available but is not.[11]

Hackers Provide Society with an Important Service

Does the second hacker principle fare any better? Many are suspicious of claims that hackers perform a useful service for society by searching for and exposing security holes in cyberspace. According to this rationale, hackers are doing us a favor, because pointing out these security holes will force those responsible for the holes to fix them.

Spafford has produced a series of counterexamples to this version of the hacker argument, and he uses an analogy to counter the hacker's position that exposing security vulnerabilities is doing the computer user community a favor. Spafford asks whether we would permit someone to start a fire in a crowded shopping mall in order to expose the fact that the mall's sprinkler system was not adequate. Similarly, we could also ask whether you would be willing to thank a burglar, who in the process of burglarizing your house, was able to show that your home security system was inadequate. If you would not, then why, Spafford would ask, should we thank hackers for showing us that our computers are insecure? We return to Spafford's argument in Section 6.4.2.

However, we will see how some nonmalicious hackers have discovered holes in security systems that have also revealed questionable, and possibly illegal, behavior on the part of content providers in cyberspace. For example, a type of hacking activity led to a discovery of a security flaw in a Digital Rights Management (DRM) system (described in Chapter 9) used by Sony BGM. This discovery also revealed that Sony was able to control the computers of customers running its music CDs and to spy on these customers. So, one might make a utilitarian argument that computer users are better served if such abuses are discovered by nonmalicious hackers.

Hacking Causes Only Virtual Harm, Not Real Harm

According to third principle we identified, unauthorized access in cyberspace causes no real harm because those activities occur only in the *virtual* world. This argument commits a logical fallacy in that it confuses the relationship between the notions of "harm" and "space" by reasoning that

the virtual world is not the real (physical) world; so any harms that occur in the virtual world are not real harms.

Consider how this reasoning is flawed. If someone sends you an e-mail message in which they unfairly accuse you of being a malicious person, they have communicated with you in cyberspace, which is "virtual," as opposed to physical, space. But does it follow that the content of the e-mail is any less real than if it had been printed in a hardcopy letter that had been sent to you in the physical mail? Would any harm you experience because of the e-mail's content be any less real than the harm you would experience from identical information in a letter written on physical paper? James Moor[12] has described a variation of this type of reasoning involving incidents in virtual contexts as the "virtuality fallacy," which we briefly examined in Chapter 3. In Chapters 9 and 11, respectively, we will see how harms involving virtual child pornography and a "virtual rape" in cyberspace can arguably cause real harms to real people, even if they involve only virtual (or computer-generated) images or virtual characters.

Of course, nonmalicious hackers could argue that they are not causing any harm, virtual or real. In fact, some might argue that they are helping to reduce the amount of harm that can occur because of abuses of power by content providers on the Internet (as we will see in our analysis of the Sony BMG controversy in Chapter 9).

We have now considered some counterexamples for each of the three principles that we identified as key elements in the "hacker code of ethics." And we have considered some ways in which nonmalicious hackers can respond to those counterexamples. In the following section, we consider the question of whether unauthorized access to a computer in the form of an explicit break-in could ever be ethically justified.

6.4.2 Are Computer Break-ins Ever Ethically Justifiable?

Spafford believes that in certain extreme cases, breaking into a computer could be the "right thing to do."[13] He also argues, however, that computer break-ins always cause harm, which suggests that they are not ethically justified. How can Spafford defend what some might interpret as a contradictory claim: sometimes it could be right to do something that is ethically unjustifiable? Spafford asks us to consider a scenario in which vital medical data that resided in a computer are needed in an emergency to save someone's life. Further imagine that the authorized users of the computer system cannot be located. In this case, Spafford believes that breaking into that computer system would be the right thing to do. We might assume that Spafford's rationale in this situation is based on utilitarian grounds because, arguably, a greater good (or at least a lesser harm) would result—and conversely, a greater wrong would be committed if the break-in did not occur.

However, Spafford does not appeal to utilitarian or consequentialist principles to defend his position. Instead, he bases his argument on deontological grounds (see the discussion of deontological and nonconsequentialist ethical theories in Chapter 2) because he believes that morality is determined by actions, not results. He correctly notes that we cannot evaluate morality based on consequences or results because we would not "know the full scope of those results," which are based on the "sum total of all future effect." Thus, Spafford believes that we must base our moral decisions primarily on the actions themselves and not on possible results. In this sense, his view is compatible with the ethical theory of Act Deontology, which we analyzed in Chapter 2.

Critics might point out that Spafford has not provided us with a general principle for determining which kinds of break-ins are ethically justifiable. But using the act deontologist criteria, Spafford could respond by noting that each extreme situation would have to be analyzed on a case-by-case basis, in order to weigh the seriousness of the particular situation. In deliberating and weighing the specific circumstances involving each of those situations, however, Spafford claims that we cannot simply base our decision on absolute duties (as in Kant's version of rule deontology) or on consequentialist considerations based on the anticipated outcomes of rules and actions. (You may want to review David Ross's account of act deontology in Chapter 2 to see how it applies to Spafford's position on justifying a computer break-in affecting extreme cases.)

Independent of whether some computer break-ins can be justified on moral grounds is the question whether certain forms of hacking, especially for nonmalicious purposes, ought to be legally permissible (a question we examine in detail in Chapter 7). Another interesting question is whether the expression "ethical hacker" is an oxymoron. We should note that at least one organization believes that there can be "ethical hackers," and they offer a program that certifies individuals to engage in authorized hacking activities for companies who employ them. According to the Certified Ethical Hacker (CEH) Web site, an ethical hacker is

> an individual who is usually employed with the organization and who can be trusted to undertake an attempt to penetrate networks and/or computer systems using the same methods as a Hacker [but] has authorization to probe the target . . . A Certified Ethical Hacker is a skilled professional who understands and knows how to look for the weaknesses and vulnerabilities in target systems and uses the same knowledge and tools as a malicious hacker.[14]

Of course, few would disapprove of training people—whether or not we choose to call them "ethical hackers"—to thwart the malicious actions carried by individuals that, for better or worse, we have traditionally called hackers. And the official process of certifying such individuals would seem to give them a sense of legitimacy. But these are not the kind of hackers—if we still wish to use that term to describe these individuals—whose activities would seem to raise moral concerns. However, insofar as these certified hackers' activities also allow "preemptive" hacking attacks, we can question the moral and legal status of some of their actions. We take up this particular question in Chapter 7.

Additional questions regarding hacking could include whether we should distinguish between "white hat" and "black hat" hackers, and whether we need to distinguish between hacking and "cracking," as some computer security analysts do. We also address these and similar questions in Chapter 7, where we examine legal issues involving hacking in connection with our discussion of cybercrime.

We have not yet considered the various implications that break-ins involving malicious hacker attacks have had for our financial infrastructure, which increasingly depends on available networked computers. Nor have we yet considered some of the threats that certain forms of malicious hacking pose to our national security. In the next two sections we examine both security-related concerns.

► 6.5 CYBERTERRORISM

Concerns about the threats posed by cyberterrorism have been on the rise in the United States and around the world. In 2002, the U.S. Congress passed legislation that specifically addressed this new kind of terrorism. In 2009, President Barack Obama established a "cybersecurity czar" to address concerns about cyberterrorism. He also described his plans to create a top-level post called "Cyber Security Coordinator" to oversee "a new comprehensive approach to securing America's digital infrastructure" and to respond to the threat of cyberattacks from Al Qaeda and other terrorist groups.[15]

What, exactly, is cyberterrorism? Dorothy Denning (2004) defines it as the "convergence of terrorism and cyberspace."[16] As such, cyberterrorism covers politically motivated hacking operations intended to cause grave harm—that is, resulting in either loss of life or severe economic loss, or both. Denning (2007) also notes that acts of cyberterrorism are typically performed by "non-state actors" in their goal of intimidating or coercing governments and societies. In some cases, however, it is difficult to separate acts of malicious hacking (e.g., computer break-ins and cybervandalism) from cyberterrorism. As noted in our discussion of network security in Section 6.2.3, it is sometimes even difficult to determine whether a major computer network disruption is due to a system failure (in either the hardware or the software of a networked computer system) or is the result of the work of either malicious hackers or cyberterrorists.[16] Additionally, it is possible that some of these disruptions are caused a third group: hacktivists.

6.5.1 Cyberterrorism vs. Hacktivism

In early 2000, several coordinated cyberattacks directed at major e-commerce Web sites, such a Yahoo and eBay, prevented tens of thousands of people from accessing them. These cyber intrusions, called distributed denial-of-service (DDoS) attacks, resulted in severe economic loss for major corporations. Should these DDoS attacks be classified as cyberterrorism? Or are they better understood as a form of hacking by individuals with some particular political agenda or ideology—a kind of behavior that Mark Manion and Abby Goodrum (2004) describe as *hacktivism* or "electronic political activism"?

Noting that some hackers and political activists have expressed their outrage over the ways in which the Internet has become "commodified," Manion and Goodrum question whether the actions taken by these individuals can be viewed as a new form of "civil disobedience" that integrates the talent of traditional computer hackers with the interests and social consciousness of political activists. They also point out that while many hackers continue to be portrayed in the media as vandals, terrorists, and saboteurs, only a few have considered the possibility that at least some of these individuals might be hacktivists. But they also point out that a key factor in making this distinction is to show that political activists are engaging in acts of electronic civil disobedience (ECD).

Is the distinction drawn by Manion and Goodrum plausible? Can acts of hacktivism be justified on grounds of civil disobedience? Kenneth Himma (2007b) describes the line of reasoning that hacktivists and their supporters use to justify their acts of civil disobedience via the following argument:

PREMISE 1. Because civil disobedience is justifiable as a protest against injustice, it is permissible to commit digital intrusions as a means of protesting injustice.

PREMISE 2. Insofar as it is permissible to stage a sit-in in a commercial or governmental building to protest, say, laws that violate human rights, it is permissible to intrude on commercial or government networks to protest such laws.

CONCLUSION. Digital intrusions that would otherwise be morally objectionable are morally permissible if they are politically motivated acts of electronic civil disobedience, or hacktivism.[17]

Based on our analysis of arguments in Chapter 3, we see that the form of this argument is valid. But in order to be a sound argument, the premises must also be true; otherwise the argument will be valid and unsound. Both of the argument's premises are controversial, and they assume that an appropriate analogy can be drawn between civilly disobedient acts in the physical and the electronic realms. But how are we to understand the notion of "electronic civil disobedience"? Manion and Goodrum claim that for an act to qualify as "civilly disobedient," it must satisfy the following conditions:

- No damage done to persons or property.
- Nonviolent.
- Not for personal profit.
- Ethical motivation—the strong conviction that a law is unjust, or unfair, to the extreme detriment of the common good.
- Willingness to accept personal responsibility for the outcome of actions.[18]

Based on these criteria, Manion and Goodrum believe that a number of nonviolent, politically motivated cyberattacks qualify as ECD. They cite, as an example, a person who had protested against the policy for assigning Internet domain names (described in Chapter 9) as a hacktivist that met the condition required for ECD; this person carried out his act nonanonymously and he was willing to go to jail.

Denning (2008), however, argues that Manion and Goodrum's analysis of hacktivism suggests that some acts of Web defacement may also be morally justified as ECD insofar as they are "ethically motivated." But she points out that defacing a Web site seems to be incompatible with Manion and Goodrum's first condition for ECD—i.e., "no damage." As Denning notes, defacements can "cause information property damage that is analogous to physical property damage" and both forms of damage can "require resources to repair."[19] So she suggests that at least some of the cases that Manion and Goodman count as hacktivism are questionable, given their own criteria.

Based on Denning's analysis of criteria involving ECD and hacktivism, we ask whether the incident described in the following scenario can be justified on hacktivist grounds.

▶ **SCENARIO 6–3:** *Anonymous* and the "Operation Payback" Attack

In January 2012, a self-described hacktivist group called *Anonymous* launched a series of DDoS attacks against commercial and government Web sites, in response to two different incidents. For one thing, the group stated that its attack, called "Operation Payback," was in retaliation against the (U.S.) Department of Justice for taking down Megaupload, a massive file-sharing site. For another, Anonymous stated that it was supporting the coordinated January 18 online protest against two controversial legislative proposals in the U.S. Congress: PIPA (Protect Intellectual Property Act) and SOPA (Stop Online Piracy Act).

While most of the participants in this online protest, including Wikipedia and Google, used tactics that were nondisruptive, Anonymous launched DDoS attacks against the Web sites of organizations that supported the two congressional bills. The sites attacked included not only at the RIAA (Recording Industry Association of America) and MPAA (Motion Picture Association of America) sites but also at the sites for the U.S. Copyright Office and Broadcast Music, Inc. (BMI), which collects fees from business that use music. (The online protest involving SOPA and PIPA, as well as the controversial aspects of these two legislative proposals that sparked this protest, are described in detail in Chapter 8.) ■

Can these attacks by Anonymous qualify as hacktivism? One could argue that attacks of this scale border on cyberterrorism, which raises the question of whether a meaningful distinction can be drawn between acts of hacktivism and cyberterrorism? Denning (2001) has drawn some distinctions between them. She notes that hacktivism, the convergence of activism and computer hacking, uses hacking techniques against a target Internet site in a way that (a) intends to disrupt normal operations, but (b) does not intend to cause serious damage. Denning also notes that these disruptions could be caused by "e-mail bombs" and by "low-grade viruses" that can cause minimal disruption but would not result in severe economic damage or loss of life.

Cyberterrorism, as we saw earlier, consists of activities intended to cause great harm, such as loss of life or severe economic damage, or both. For example, a cyberterrorist might attempt to bring down the U.S. stock market or take control of a transportation unit in order to cause trains to crash. Denning believes while these conceptual distinctions can be used to differentiate hacktivism and cyberterrorism, the boundaries can become fuzzy as we progress from the former to the latter. For example, should an e-mail bomb sent by a hacker who is also a political activist be classified as a form of hacktivism or as an act of cyberterrorism? Many in law enforcement would no doubt argue that rather than trying to understand the ideological beliefs, goals, and objectives of those who engage in malicious forms of hacking, much more effort should be devoted to finding ways to deter and catch these individuals. However, the category distinctions that Denning has drawn can help determine the degree of punishment that these individuals should receive.

6.5.2 Cybertechnology and Terrorist Organizations

A major security concern, especially since September 11, 2001, has been how and when terrorist organizations, such as Al Qaeda, might use cybertechnology to carry out their objectives. We discovered that the terrorists who carried out the highly coordinated attacks on the Twin Towers of the World Trade Center communicated by e-mail in the days preceding the attack. We also have discovered that many members of Al Qaeda, despite the fact that some operated out of caves in Afghanistan and Pakistan, had fairly sophisticated computer devices. Yet it does not seem that these terrorists have taken full advantage of currently available forms of cybertechnology in executing their campaigns.

Why not? One possible explanation is that they have not yet gained the needed expertise with cybertechnology. This, of course, may change as the next generation of terrorists, who will likely be more skilled in the use of computers and cybertechnology, replace current leadership. Two terrorists gave up their lives in targeting the Navy ship USS *Cole* in Yemen in 2000. Similar activities might be done remotely in the future via cybertechnology, in which case no terrorists would be required to give up their lives in carrying out their missions. A scenario is also possible in which terrorists gain control of an airplane's onboard computer systems and even block the ability of a pilot to override those controls.

Denning (2007) notes that there is evidence that terrorist groups and "jihadists" are interested in conducting cyberattacks. She also notes that there is evidence to suggest they have at least some capability to carry out such attacks, and that they are undergoing online training on how to develop the necessary skills. However, Denning also points out that there is no evidence to suggest either that the threat of cyberattacks from these terrorist groups is imminent or that they have acquired the knowledge or the skills to conduct "highly damaging attacks against critical infrastructure."[20] Nevertheless, Denning suggests that there are "indicators" showing that these terrorist groups have an interest in acquiring the relevant knowledge and skills. This kind of threat would certainly seem to warrant close attention by government actors. As noted earlier, U.S. President Barack Obama created a new post for a Cyber Security Coordinator in 2009 in response to threats of cyberattacks from terrorist groups.

▶ 6.6 INFORMATION WARFARE (IW)

In the preceding section, we saw that it is not always easy to differentiate acts of cyberterrorism from those of hacktivism. It can also be difficult to distinguish between acts of cyberterrorism and acts of IW. Denning (1999) defines IW as "operations that target or exploit information media in order to win some objective over an adversary." But certain aspects of cyberterrorism also conform to Denning's definition of IW, so what distinguishes the latter from the former? For our purposes, information warfare is distinguishable from cyberterrorism in three ways. First, IW can include cyberattacks that send misleading information to an enemy. Second, while IW is disruptive and sometimes destructive, it need not involve loss of life or severe economic loss, even though such results can occur. Third, IW typically involves cyberattacks launched by sovereign nations, or nation states, as opposed to "rogue" political organizations and terrorist groups.

6.6.1 Information Warfare vs. Conventional Warfare

James Moor (2004) notes that while information has always played a vital role in warfare, now its importance is overwhelming, because the battlefield is becoming increasingly computerized. In the past, warfare was conducted by physical means: human beings engaged in combat, using weapons such as guns, tanks, and aircraft. Moor notes that during the first Gulf War, in the early 1990s, we saw for the first time the importance of information technology in contemporary warfare strategies. Arguably, the war was won quickly by the multinational coalition because it had advantages in cybertechnology. Destroying the Iraqi communications technologies at the outset put the Iraqi army at a severe disadvantage. Moor points out that in the future, warfare may have more to do with information and cybertechnology than with human beings going into combat.

Some analysts point out that IW, unlike conventional or physical warfare, often tends to be more disruptive than destructive. The "weapons" of IW, consisting of logic bombs, viruses, worms, and DDoS attacks deployable from cyberspace, typically strike at a nation's infrastructure. Although these are not the traditional weapons of warfare, the disruption can be more damaging than physical damage from conventional weapons.

Consider once again the GhostNet controversy (described in Scenario 6–2) and its implications for IW. Recall that a report issued by the *Information Warfare Monitor* (2009) included circumstantial evidence that linked various cyberattacks (associated with GhostNet) to China, but also suggested that other countries might be involved as well. For example, in 2009, the government of South Korea accused North Korea of running a cyberwarfare unit that attempted to hack into both U.S. and South Korean military networks to gather confidential information and to disrupt service. North Korea was also suspected of launching the DDoS attacks that disrupted the Web sites of 27 American and South Korean government agencies as well as commercial Web sites such as the New York Stock Exchange, Nasdaq, and Yahoo's finance section (Sang-Hun and Markoff 2009). Next, we consider an IW incident that allegedly involves two Western nations: the United States and Israel.

▶ **SCENARIO 6–4:** The Stuxnet Worm and the "Olympic Games" Operation

In June 2012, *The New York Times* reported that the U.S. and Israeli governments had been cooperating on an initiative code-named *Olympic Games*. First developed during the George W. Bush administration, this initiative aimed at disrupting Iran's uranium enrichment program and thus damaging that nation's nuclear capability (Charette 2012). At the core of this joint operation was a computer worm known as Stuxnet, a "cyberweapon" that targeted "electronic program controllers" developed by Siemens Corporation (in Germany) for industrial control computers (ICCs) that were installed in Iran. This worm was allegedly responsible for (a) sending misleading data to computer monitors in Iran, and (b) causing several of that nation's centrifuges—i.e., fast-spinning machines that enrich uranium—to spin out of control. The Stuxnet attack is estimated to have destroyed approximately 1,000 of Iran's 6,000 centrifuges (Nakashima and Warrick 2012). ∎

Does Operation Olympic Games qualify as an example of IW (or "cyberwarfare")? In so far as the Stuxnet worm sent misleading information to the Iranian government and its scientists, it complies with one aspect of IW. And because this worm was disruptive (regarding Iran's nuclear program), as well as destructive (i.e., with respect to its effect on Iran's centrifuges), it complies with another aspect of IW. Third, the Stuxnet attacks were launched (allegedly, at least) by two nation states. So, Stuxnet complies with all three elements of IW (described above). It is perhaps also worth noting that in the Olympic Games incident, there had been no formal declaration of war among the three nation states allegedly involved.

6.6.2 Potential Consequences for Nations that Engage in IW

Why has the Stuxnet/Operation Olympic Games incident caused so much controversy at the international level? Recall some of the concerns that arose in the international community in response to the 2009 IW incidents allegedly involving China (in GhostNet) and South Korea. One question that arises in the aftermath of the Stuxnet attacks is whether the U.S. and Israeli governments are now guilty of the same kind of questionable behavior attributed to China and North Korea 3 years earlier. If so, should the U.S. government worry about the possible repercussions that its involvement in "Olympic Games" could have for its standing in the international community, as well as for its credibility involving any future complaints that it might make against other nations, especially China? David Sanger (2012) suggests that the United States has not thought through the international implications of its use of cyberwarfare in the Olympic Games operations (just as he believes that it also had not thought through some of the major political and legal consequences of its policy regarding use of armed drones).

Another question is whether the U.S. government, and the nation's infrastructure and commerce, will also become focal points of retaliation for its IW activities involving

Olympic Games. Jaikumar Vijayan (2012) notes that the United States, as a result of the Stuxnet attacks, may have "painted a huge target on [its] back." And the Obama administration seemed to recognize this vulnerability when it warned American businesses—immediately following the media's announcement of the effects that Stuxnet had in Iran—to prepare for similar attacks by bolstering the security apparatus on their computers.

We should note that the Stuxnet worm, discovered in 2010, is sometimes confused with the Flame virus (also known as "Flamer" and "Skywiper"). Like Stuxnet, this virus also has significant implications for IW. Richard Ladner (2012) points out that the Flame virus, discovered in May 2012, is "an espionage tool" that can "eavesdrop on data traffic, take screenshots and record audio and keystrokes." Vitaly Kamlyuk (2012), a security (malware) expert at the Kepersky Lab in Russia, describes Flame as the "most powerful computer virus in history." Pointing to some differences between Stuxnet and Flame, Kamlyuk notes that while the former was a "small application developed for a particular target with the specific objective to interact with industrial control systems," the latter is a "universal attacking tool kit used mostly for cyberespionage."

Some security experts, including Kamlyuk, also point to a few things that Flame and Stuxnet have in common, in addition to the widely held view that both pieces of malware were developed by nation states. David Lee (2012) points out that there is growing evidence to suggest that the development teams responsible for Stuxnet and Flame worked together, in the early stages, on the code for both malware applications. One way in which the two applications are similar is that both take advantage of a "zero day" type of "vulnerability" in the systems they attack. In most cases, software developers are the first to become aware of vulnerabilities (such as bugs or "holes") in their systems that need to be fixed. But in some cases, these vulnerabilities are initially discovered and exploited by malicious hackers. In this sense, the vulnerability is discovered on the "zeroth day," or a(ny) day preceding the discovery of that software's vulnerability by its developer(s).

We should note that IW-related concerns affecting both the Flame virus and Stuxnet worm are further complicated by the recent development of a new kind of search engine, called *Shodan*. Not only can Shodan locate and return the URLs for relevant Web sites (as traditional search engines do) but it is also able "to map and capture the specifications of everything from desktop computers to network printers to Web servers" that are connected to the internet (Charette 2012). Robert O'Harrow (2012) points out that between 2010 and 2012, Shodan gathered data on approximately 100 million devices, "recording their exact locations and the software systems that run them." He also notes that during that period, Shodan users had discovered numerous ("uncounted") industrial control computers—i.e., the systems that automate power grids and water plants—and that these computers were "linked in, and in some cases they were wide open to exploitation by even moderately talented hackers." As Charette observes, it is not difficult to imagine what "a government intent on doing harm to U.S. infrastructural and business systems could do with that information." So, it would seem that the United States (and other countries as well) may indeed have something to worry about in the aftermath of the IW activities involving Stuxnet and the Olympic Games operation.

In concluding our discussion of IW, we acknowledge that some controversial issues surrounding this topic were not able to be examined. One interesting question concerns

TABLE 6.3   Hacktivism, Cyberterrorism, and Information Warfare

Hacktivism	The convergence of political activism and computer hacking techniques to engage in a new form of civil disobedience.
Cyberterrorism	The convergence of cybertechnology and terrorism for carrying out acts of terror in (or via) cyberspace.
Information warfare	Using malware in cyberattacks designed to mislead the enemy and disrupt/damage an opponent's military defense system and its critical infrastructure.

whether IW could, in principle, satisfy the conditions traditionally required for a "just war." For example, one requirement is that a distinction between combatants and noncombatants be drawn and respected. Another condition is that attacks typically cannot be pre-emptive. However, it may not be possible for these and other conventional just-war requirements to be satisfied in the context of IW. So, some conclude that IW can never be justified solely on moral grounds. Unfortunately, however, an examination of the necessary conditions articulated for just-war theory in the context of IW is beyond the scope of this chapter.[21]

In this and the preceding section, we have discussed various security threats, from malicious hacking to hacktivism, and from cyberterrorism to information warfare. Table 6.3 summarizes these distinctions. In the next section, we examine cybersecurity concerns from the perspective of risk analysis.

▶ 6.7 CYBERSECURITY AND RISK ANALYSIS

You may recall that we briefly discussed the concept of risk in Section 4.6, where we examined a model for analyzing risk in the development of safety-critical software systems. We now examine risk in the context of cybersecurity. Bruce Schneier (2004), who argues that security is an ongoing process, believes that a key element in that process involves an understanding of *risk*.

6.7.1 The Risk Analysis Methodology

Risk analysis is used in a wide range of sectors, including commerce. Consider, for example, that banks and credit card companies can tolerate a considerable amount of credit risk because they know how to anticipate losses and how to price their services accordingly. But what, exactly, is the level of risk that can be acceptable in securing computer systems? For example, can a mere cost-benefits analysis be applied to computer security issues that impact the safety and lives of individuals? Financial considerations alone might be adequate for determining the "bottom line" for some corporations and organizations deciding how to increase their computer security. But can/should all decisions involving risk and cybersecurity simply be market driven?

Schneier claims that risk can be understood and analyzed in terms of the net result of the impacts of five elements: assets, threats, vulnerabilities, impact, and safeguards. Schneier's model is fairly sophisticated, but can it help us to frame an adequate security policy that also addresses ethical challenges? Recall our discussion in Chapter 4 where Don Gotterbarn (2004) claimed that an expanded sense of both "ethical risks" and "system stakeholder" should be taken into account in models of risk analysis for software development.

The ethical implications affecting risk analysis in the context of securing our national infrastructure are significant; as we saw in the preceding section, they affect the public safety and can result in the deaths of millions of people. But if businesses in the private sector are not willing to pay for enhanced security for their computer systems, which could ultimately impact the larger national infrastructure, who should? For example, does the government have an obligation to do so?

Unfortunately, it is not altogether clear where, exactly, the moral responsibility for ensuring greater cybersecurity lies, even in contexts that do not necessarily involve risks to our national infrastructure. One reason why it is difficult to determine *who* is responsible for securing cyberspace may have to do with a factor that Wolter Pieters and Andre van Cleeff (2009) call the "de-perimeterization" of the security landscape.

6.7.2 The Problem of "De-Perimeterization" of Information Security for Analyzing Risk

In arguing that the information security landscape has become increasingly "de-perimeterized," Pieters and van Cleeff point out that IT systems now "span the boundaries of multiple parties" and they "cross the security perimeters" that these parties have put in place for themselves. The authors note that we can no longer achieve adequate cyber-security by simply building a "digital fence" around a single organization. In their view, IT security has become de-perimeterized because of the following trends:

- Many organizations now outsource their information technology processes.
- Many employees expect to be able to work from home.
- Mobile devices make it possible to access data from anywhere.
- 'Smart buildings' are being equipped with small microchips that allow for constant communication between buildings and their headquarters.[22]

To illustrate some of the security concerns that arise because of de-perimeterization, especially with respect to the interdependencies that now exist between two or more organizations or parties, Pieters and van Cleeff cite an example involving Skype, a popular voice over Internet protocol (VOIP) system, and Microsoft. They note that in 2007 Skype had to go offline for a period of time, following an automatic software update from Microsoft. As a result, Skype users had to log back in once the service was available again online. Because many users decided to log back on at the same time, they experienced a denial-of-service (DoS) condition (described in Section 6.5.1). Pieters and van Cleeff point out that before the incident, neither Microsoft nor Skype realized the extent of the dependency that existed between their two applications.

Pieters and van Cleeff also believe that de-perimeterization-related concerns lead to "uncertain risk" for IT security, because of the lack of clear boundaries defining the security landscape. In Section 6.3, in our discussion of cloud computing, we saw some of the security challenges posed by the increasingly common practice of having third parties store users' data remotely (in the Cloud). There, we also saw that for cloud computing to be fully realized, users would have to be able to trust businesses that store their data (and that also, increasingly, provide many of their applications-based services).[23] But to the extent that there is no secure "fence" or perimeter safeguarding the users' data, it would seem that ordinary users and businesses alike will be required to assume the kind of "uncertain risk" described by Pieters and van Cleeff.

We conclude this section by noting that if Pieters and van Cleeff are correct, the de-perimeterization of IT security indeed poses a significant challenge for measuring security-related risk and for achieving adequate security in cyberspace. But in responding to this challenge with an alternative framework for analyzing risk, Pieters and van Cleeff also make an important contribution to achieving a security-related objective that Rashid, Weckert, and Lucas (2009) call *ethics-aware software engineering*—i.e., a model where "ethical considerations are explicitly taken into account across the software development cycle and are an integral part of the risk assessment and acceptance criteria."[24]

▶ 6.8 CHAPTER SUMMARY

In this chapter, we examined the ethical implications of a wide range of cybersecurity issues, including the question whether unauthorized computer break-ins can ever be ethically justified. We argued that it is useful to draw distinctions involving data, system, and network security, and distinctions between concepts such as hacking and hacktivism, and information warfare and cyberterrorism. Finally, we described some ethical challenges involved in trying to understand cybersecurity issues in terms of models for risk analysis, especially in light of challenges posed by current cloud-computing services and the "de-perimeterization" of information security.

We also drew some distinctions between the traditional and current meanings of "hacker," in our discussion of the "hacker ethic." In Chapter 7, we will examine some criminal aspects of (malicious) hacking from a legal perspective.

▶ REVIEW QUESTIONS

1. What do we mean by "computer security" or "cybersecurity"?
2. How can cybersecurity concerns be differentiated from issues in cybercrime?
3. How are cybersecurity issues similar to and different from privacy issues affecting cyber-technology?
4. Identify and briefly describe the key distinguishing features separating data security, system security, and network security.
5. What is cloud computing, and what challenges does it pose for securing one's personal information in cyberspace?
6. How do security issues in cyberspace raise ethical concerns?
7. Who are computer hackers, and how has the term "hacker" evolved?
8. What is meant by the expression "hacker code of ethics"?
9. According to Steve Levy, what are the six "principles" of this code?
10. Describe and briefly evaluate the argument used by some hackers, who assert that "information wants to be free."
11. Assess the argument that (nonmalicious) hackers can provide society with a valuable service. Is it a plausible argument?
12. Describe the argument that some hackers use to show that hacking causes only virtual harm, not real harm.

13. What, exactly, is cyberterrorism?
14. What is meant by "hacktivism"? How is it distinguished from traditional computer hacking?
15. Can "hacktivist activities" be justified on the grounds of civil disobedience toward unjust laws?
16. What is meant by "information warfare"?
17. How can information warfare be distinguished from cyberterrorism?

18. How might our understanding of cybersecurity be enhanced by using models of risk analysis?
19. Identify the five elements that Bruce Schneir recommends for assessing risk in the context of cybersecurity.
20. How has the information security landscape become increasingly "de-perimeterized," and what additional challenges does this factor pose for risk analysis models?

▶ DISCUSSION QUESTIONS

21. Is the expression "ethical hacker" an oxymoron? Do you agree that some individuals should be allowed to be "certified" as hackers to work on behalf of industry or for the interests of other organizations? Do the kinds of activities permitted by certified hackers in the CEH Program raise any moral issues? Explain.
22. Revisit the GhostNet controversy described in Scenario 6–2, and the "Olympic Games" incident

discussed in Scenario 6–4. What kinds of actions should sovereign nations take against countries that engage in cyberespionage and that launch cyberattacks in the form of various worms, viruses, and DDoS requests? Would such attacks be acceptable between nations that have formally declared war with one another?

▶ ESSAY/PRESENTATION QUESTIONS

23. In Section 6.4.1, we examined some issues surrounding a "hacker code of ethics." We also saw why this code, containing the six principles described by Steven Levy, has been controversial. Is it possible to establish an *appropriate* set of guidelines for a hacker code of ethics, i.e., for nonmalicious hackers, without becoming a moral relativist? You may want to revisit our discussion of moral relativism in Chapter 2 in deciding your answer to this question.

24. Assess the claims made by Wolter Pieters and Andre van Cleeff regarding the "de-perimeterization" of information security. Are their claims plausible? Can you think of any other factors that can contribute to the de-perimeterization process? What implications does this process have for our ability to assess the risks involved in adequately securing our national infrastructure? Explain.

Scenarios for Analysis

1. In our discussion of hacking-related security concerns, we saw how some forms of anonymous behavior in cyberspace can cause harm to others. What course of action would you recommend be taken in the following scenario?

   A very close political race is underway in your state, where two candidates who are running for a seat in the U.S. Senate. The weekend before citizens will cast their votes, one

   candidate decides to defame his opponent by using an anonymous remailer service (which strips away the original address of the sender of the e-mail) to send a message of questionable truth to an electronic distribution list of his opponent's supporters. The information included in this email is so defamatory that it may threaten the outcome of the election by influencing many undecided voters, as well as the libeled candidate's regular supporters, to vote against her. Does the "injured" candidate in this instance have the right to demand that the identity of the person using the anonymous remailer (whom she suspects is her opponent in this election) be revealed?[25]

2. Recall Eugene Spafford's argument as to why computer break-ins can be justified under extraordinary circumstances. Apply his rationale in the following scenario.

You determine that you will need to break into a neighbor's car in order to drive a friend, who will otherwise die, to the hospital. You realize that you are morally obligated to save a person's life when it is in your power to do so. But you are also obligated to obey the law, which forbids breaking into someone's motor vehicle. How is the reasoning process that you use to evaluate this scenario similar to, or different from, the one Spafford used in determining whether it is morally permissible to break into a computer database containing the medical information needed to save someone's life?

▶ ENDNOTES

1. Epstein (2007), p. 176. Kizza (2007), who has a similar threefold distinction regarding the key elements of cybersecurity, describes the third element as *availability* rather than *accessibility*.
2. See Neumann (2004, pp. 208–09), for more examples of how security can be viewed as a double-edged sword that "cuts both ways."
3. Some of the distinctions I draw between privacy and security are adapted from Tavani (2000).
4. My analysis of cybersecurity in terms of these categories is adapted from Spinello and Tavani (2004) and Tavani (2007).
5. Spinello (2000), p. 158. [Italics Spinello]
6. This scenario is based on the account of the Conficker Worm in Lawton (2009).
7. Bottis (2007) points out that Code Red infected approximately 395,000 servers during a 14-hour period in 2000.
8. See Maidment (2009) and the Information Warfare Monitor Report (2009). See also "Tracking GhostNet: Investigating a Cyber Espionage Network (2009)." Available at http://www.scribd.com/doc/13731776/Tracking-GhostNet-Investigating-a-Cyber-Espionage-Network.
9. My analysis of cloud computing in this section draws from material in Grodzinsky and Tavani (2011).
10. See Levy (2001) for a full explanation of these principles.
11. I am grateful to Mason Cash for pointing out this distinction to me.
12. Moor described this fallacy in a talk titled "Just Consequentialism and Computing," presented at the Humanities Lecture Series, Rivier University, Nashua, NH, February 2001.
13. Spafford (2007), p. 57.
14. See www.eccouncil.org/ceh.htm. I am grateful to Hien Nguyen for pointing out this Web site to me.
15. See http://edition.cnn.com/2009/POLITICS/05/29/cyber.czar.obama/index.html.
16. Denning (2004), p. 536.
17. Himma (2007b), pp. 73–74. Note that Himma's original text has been transposed into the form of a logical argument (with the author's permission). See also Himma (2008).
18. Manion and Goodrum (2004), p. 528.
19. Denning (2008), p. 421.
20. Denning (2007), p. 136.
21. See, for example, Arquilla (2002), De George (2003), Denning (2008), and Lin, Allhoff, and Rowe (2012) for some excellent discussions of just warfare in the cyber era.
22. Pieters and van Cleeff (2009), p. 50.
23. For an empirical study of risk in the context of cloud computing, see Pauley (2012).
24. Rashid, Weckert, and Lucas (2009), p. 36.
25. I am grateful to an anonymous reviewer who suggested this hypothetical scenario, illustrating an ethical dilemma involving Internet anonymity.

▶ REFERENCES

Arquilla, John. 2002. "Can Information Warfare Ever Be Just?" In J. Rudinow and A. Graybosch, eds. *Ethics and Values in the Information Age.* Belmont CA: Wadsworth, pp. 403–14.

Bottis, Maria Canellopoulu. 2007. "Disclosing Software Vulnerabilities." In K. E. Himma, ed. *Internet Security: Hacking, Counterhacking, and Society.* Sudbury MA: Jones and Bartlett, pp. 255–68.

Breitbart, Andrew. 2010. "Google software bug shared private online documents." Available at http://www.breitbart.com/article.php?id=CNG.54c3200980573ae4c.

Cavoukian, Ann. 2008. "Privacy in the Clouds: A White Paper on Privacy and Digital Identity: Implications for the Internet." Available at http://www.ipc.on.ca/images/resources/privacyintheclouds.pdf.

Charette, Robert N. 2012. "Gone Missing: The Public Policy Debate on Unleashing the Dogs of Cyberwar." *IEEE Spectrum*, June 4. Available at http://spectrum.ieee.org/riskfactor/telecom/security/gone-missing-the-public-policy-debate-on-unleashing-the-dogs-of-cyberwar/?utm_source=techalert&utm_medium=email&utm_campaign=060712.

De George, Richard T. 2003. "Post-September 11: Computers, Ethics, and War." *Ethics and Information Technology* 5, no. 4: 183–90.

Denning, Dorothy E. 1999. *Information Warfare and Security*. New York: ACM Press, and Reading MA: Addison Wesley.

Denning, Dorothy E. 2001. "Activism, Hacktivism, and Cyberterrorism: The Internet as a Tool for Influencing Foreign Policy." In J. Arquilla and D. Ronfelt, eds. *Networks and Netwars*. Santa Monica CA: Rand Corp., pp. 229–88.

Denning, Dorothy E. 2004. "Cyberterrorism." In R. A. Spinello and H. T. Tavani, eds. *Readings in CyberEthics*. 2nd ed. Sudbury MA: Jones and Bartlett, pp. 536–41.

Denning, Dorothy E. 2007. "A View of Cyberterrorism Five Years Later." In K. E. Himma, ed. *Internet Security: Hacking, Counter-Hacking, and Society*. Sudbury MA: Jones and Bartlett, pp. 123–29.

Denning, Dorothy E. 2008. "The Ethics of Cyber Conflict." In K. E. Himma and H. T. Tavani, eds. *The Handbook of Information and Computer Ethics*. Hoboken NJ: John Wiley & Sons, pp. 407–28.

Epstein, Richard G. 2007. "The Impact of Computer Security Concerns on Software Development." In K. Himma, ed. *Internet Security: Hacking, Counter-Hacking, and Society*. Sudbury MA: Jones and Bartlett, pp. 171–202.

Gotterbarn, Don. 2004. "Reducing Software Failures: Address Ethical Risks with Software Development Impact Statements." In R. A. Spinello and H. T. Tavani, eds. *Readings in CyberEthics*. 2nd ed. Sudbury MA: Jones and Bartlett Publishers, pp. 674–89.

Grodzinsky, Francis S., and Herman T. Tavani. 2011. "Privacy in 'the Cloud': Applying Nissenbaum's Theory of Contextual Integrity." *Computers and Society* 41, no. 1: 38–47.

Himanen, Pekka. 2001. *The Hacker Ethic: A Radical Approach to the Philosophy of Business*. New York: Random House.

Himma, Kenneth Einar. 2007a. "Privacy vs. Security: Why Privacy is Not an Absolute Value or Right," *University of San Diego Law Review* 45, 857–921.

Himma, Kenneth Einar. 2007b. "Hacking as Politically Motivated Digital Civil Disobedience: Is Hacktivism Morally Justified?" In K. E. Himma, ed. *Internet Security: Hacking, Counter-Hacking, and Society*. Sudbury MA: Jones and Bartlett, pp. 61–71.

Himma, Kenneth Einar. 2008. "Ethical Issues Involving Computer Security: Hacking, Hacktivism, and Counterhacking." In K. E. Himma and H. T. Tavani, eds. *The Handbook of Information and Computer Ethics*. Hoboken NJ: John Wiley and Sons, pp. 191–217.

Kamlyuk, Vitaly. 2012. "'Flame' Virus Explained: How it Works and Who's Behind it." Interview in *RT*, May 29. Available at http://www.rt.com/news/flame-virus-cyberwar-536/.

Kaufman, Charlie, Radia Perlman, and Mike Speciner. 2002. *Network Security: Private Communication in a Public World*. 2nd ed. Upper Saddle River NJ: Prentice Hall.

Kizza, Joseph M. 2008. *Ethical and Social Issues in the Information Age*. 3rd ed. New York: Springer-Verlag.

Knorr, Eric, and Galen Gruman. 2008. "What Cloud Computing Really Means." *InfoWorld*. Available at http://www.infoworld.com/d/cloud-computing/what-cloud-computing-really-means-031?page=0,0.

Ladner, Richard. 2012. "Sophisticated Cyber-battles Raise Fears of Cyber-blowback." *MSNBC News*, June 2. Available at http://www.msnbc.msn.com/id/47658329/ns/technology_and_science-security/.

Lawton, George. 2009. "On the Trail of the Conficker Worm." *IEEE Computer* 42, no. 6: 19–22.

Lee, David. 2012. "Flame and Stuxnet Makers 'Co-operated' on Code." *BBC News*, June 11. Available at http://www.bbc.co.uk/news/technology-18393985.

Levy, Steve. 2001. *Hackers: Heroes of the Computer Revolution*. Rev. ed. New York: Penguin.

Lin, Patrick, Fritz Allhoff, and Neill Rowe. 2012. "Is It Possible to Wage a Just Cyberwar?" *The Atlantic*, June 5. Available at http://www.theatlantic.com/technology/archive/2012/06/is-it-possible-to-wage-a-just-cyberwar/258106/.

Maidment, Paul. 2009. "GhostNet in the Machine." *Forbes.com*. Available at http://www.forbes.com/2009/03/29/ghostnet-computer-security-internet-technology-ghostnet.html.

Manion, Mark, and Abby Goodrum. 2004. "Terrorism or Civil Disobedience: Toward a Hacktivist Ethic." In R. A. Spinello and H. T. Tavani, eds. *Readings in CyberEthics*. 2nd ed. Sudbury MA: Jones and Bartlett, pp. 525–35. Reprinted from *Computers and Society* 30, no. 2 (2000): 14–19.

Mell, Peter, and Timothy Grance. 2011. *The NIST Definition of Cloud Computing*. National Institute of Standards and Technology. U.S. Department of Commerce. Available at http://csrc.nist.gov/publications/nistpubs/800-145/SP800-145.pdf.

Moor, James H. 2004. "Reason, Relativity, and Responsibility in Computer Ethics." In R. A. Spinello and H. T. Tavani, eds. *Readings in CyberEthics*. 2nd ed. Sudbury MA: Jones and Bartlett, pp. 40–54.

Nakashima, Ellen, and Joby Warrick. 2012. "Stuxnet Was Work of U.S. and Israeli Experts." *The Washington Post*, June 1. Available at http://www.washingtonpost.com/world/national-security/stuxnet-was-work-of-us-and-israeli-experts-officials-say/2012/06/01/gJQAlnEy6U_story.html.

National Institute of Standards and Technology. 2011. *The NIST Definition of Cloud Computing*. U.S. Department of Commerce. Special Publication 800-145. Available at http://csrc.nist.gov/publications/nistpubs/800-145/SP800-145.pdf.

Neumann, Peter G. 2004. "Computer Security and Human Values." In T. W. Bynum and S. Rogerson, eds. *Computer Ethics and Professional Responsibility*. Malden MA: Blackwell, pp. 208–26.

Nissenbaum, Helen. 2010. *Privacy in Context: Technology, Policy, and the Integrity of Social Life*. Palo Alto, CA: Stanford University Press.

O'Harrow, Robert. 2012. "Cyber Search Engine Shodan Exposes Industrial Control Systems to New Risks." *The Washington Post*, June 3. Available at http://www.washingtonpost.com/investigations/cyber-search-engine-exposes-vulnerabilities/2012/06/03/gJQAIK9KCV_story.html.

Pauley, Wayne. 2012. *An Empirical Study of Privacy Risk Methodologies in Cloud Computing Environments*. Dissertation. Nova Southeastern University.

Pieters, Wolter, and Andre van Cleeff. 2009. "The Precautionary Principle in a World of Digital Dependencies." *IEEE Computer Society* 42, no. 8: 50–56.

Privacy Rights Clearinghouse. 2008. "The Privacy Implications of Cloud Computing." Available at http://www.privacy rights.org/ar/cloud-computing.htm.

Rashid, Awais, John Weckert, and Richard Lucas. 2009. "Software Engineering Ethics in a Digital World." *IEEE Computer* 42, no. 8: 34–41.

Sanger, David. 2012. "Mutually Assured Cyberdestruction." *New York Times*, June 2. Available at http://www.nytimes.com/2012/06/03/sunday-review/mutually-assured-cyberdestruction.html?

Sang-Hun, Choe, and John Markoff. 2009. "Cyberattacks Jam Government and Commercial Web Sites in U.S. and South Korea." *New York Times*, July 9. Available at http://www.nytimes.com/2009/07/09/technology/09cyber.html.

Schneier, Bruce. 2004. *Secrets and Lies: Digital Security in a Networked World*. Rev. ed. New York: John Wiley and Sons.

Simpson, Michael T. 2006. *Hands-On Ethical Hacking and Network Defense*. Boston MA: Thomson.

Skoudis, Ed. 2004. *Malware: Fighting Malicious Code*. Upper Saddle River NJ: Prentice Hall.

Spafford, Eugene H. 2007. "Are Computer Hacker Break-Ins Ethical?" In K. Himma, ed. *Internet Security: Hacking, Counter-Hacking, and Society*. Sudbury MA: Jones and Bartlett, pp. 49–59. Reprinted from *Journal of Systems Software*, 17: 41–47.

Spinello, Richard A. 2000. "Information Integrity." In D. Langford, ed. *Internet Ethics*. London UK: Macmillan, pp. 158–80.

Spinello, Richard A., and Herman T. Tavani. 2004. "Introduction: Security and Crime in Cyberspace." In R. A. Spinello and H. T. Tavani, eds. *Readings in Cyberethics*. 2nd ed. Sudbury MA: Jones and Bartlett, pp. 501–12.

Talbot, David. 2011. "Improving the Security of Cloud Computing," *Technology Review*, June 15. Available at http://www.technologyreview.com/business/37683/.

Tavani, Herman T. 2000. "Privacy and Security." In D. Langford, ed. *Internet Ethics*. London UK: Macmillan, and New York: St. Martin's Press, pp. 65–95.

Tavani, Herman T. 2007. "The Conceptual and Moral Landscape of Computer Security." In K. E. Himma, ed. *Internet Security: Hacking, Counter-Hacking, and Society*. Sudbury MA: Jones and Bartlett, pp. 29–45.

Thompson, Paul B. 2001. "Privacy, Secrecy, and Security." *Ethics and Information Technology* 3, no. 1: 13–19.

Vijayan, Jaikumar. 2012. "Government Role in Stuxnet Could Increase Attacks Against U.S. Firms." *Computer World*, June 2. Available at http://www.computerworld.com/s/article/9227696/Government_role_in_Stuxnet_could_increase_attacks_against_U.S._firms.

Zeng, Ke, and Ann Cavoukian. 2010. "Modeling Cloud Computing Architecture without Compromising Privacy: A Privacy by Design Approach." Available at www.privacybydesign.ca.

► FURTHER READINGS

Bidgoli, Hossein, ed. *The Handbook of Information Security*. Hoboken NJ: John Wiley and Sons, 2005.

Jordan, Tim. *Hacking*. Cambridge, UK: Polity Press, 2008.

Schneir, Bruce. *Liars and Outliers: Enabling the Trust that Society Needs to Thrive*. Hoboken, NJ: John Wiley and Sons, 2012.

Tetmeyer, Annette, and Hossein Saiedian. "Security Threats and Mitigating Risk for USB Devices." *IEEE Technology and Society Magazine* 29, no. 4 (2010): 44–49.

Wallace, Kathleen A. "Online Anonymity." In K. E. Himma and H. T. Tavani, eds. *The Handbook of Information and Computer Ethics*. Hoboken NJ: John Wiley and Sons, 2008, pp. 165–89.

Wright, Marie, and John Kakalik. *Information Security: Contemporary Cases*. Sudbury MA: Jones and Bartlett, 2007.

7

Cybercrime and Cyber-Related Crimes

In Chapter 6, we examined cybersecurity issues independent of their implications for crime, even though issues involving crime and security in cyberspace sometimes overlap. In Chapter 7, we focus specifically on criminal activities involving cybertechnology. Among the questions examined in this chapter are:

- What is cybercrime, and how can it be distinguished from cyber-related crimes?
- Is there a typical cybercriminal?
- Can a meaningful distinction be drawn between hacking and "cracking" in the context of cybertechnology?
- What is "active defense hacking" or counter hacking, and is it morally permissible?
- Can biometric technologies be used to assist law enforcement groups in identifying criminals and terrorists in ways that are ethically permissible?
- Why are jurisdictional issues problematic for prosecuting some cybercrimes?
- Are the "journalistic" practices used by the WikiLeaks organization defensible under a free press, or are they criminal?

We begin our examination with a brief look at some classic cybercrimes that have received worldwide media attention.

▶ 7.1 CYBERCRIMES AND CYBERCRIMINALS

Reports of criminal activities involving cybertechnology have appeared as cover stories in periodicals, as headlines in major newspapers, and as lead stories on television news programs in the United States and around the globe. In the 1970s and 1980s, we heard about numerous crimes that involved the use of computers to launch viruses and to break into financial and government institutions. In the 1990s, as the Internet insinuated itself into mainstream society, we heard stories about crimes involving digital piracy, cyberstalking, cyberpornography, and Internet pedophilia. In the first decade of this century, high-profile cyber-related crimes have expanded to include cyberbullying, sexting, phishing, and so forth. In light of the evolutionary aspects of crimes involving cybertechnology, David Wall (2007) differentiates "three generations" of computer crimes.

In the past few years, there have been reports of "hacks" into people's pacemakers, and even into a person's genome.[1] It seems as if novel cyber-related crimes continue to arise as new cyber-related technologies are developed and implemented. But we will see that despite the increase in the number and kinds of cyber-related crimes in recent years, the use of computers and cybertechnology to carry out criminal activities is not exactly new.

7.1.1 Background Events: A Brief Sketch

In our analysis of cybercrime, it is useful to trace the developments of some key criminal activities involving computers and cyberspace. As noted above, some of the earliest incidents occurred in the 1970s. During that period, stories about disgruntled employees who altered files in computer databases or who sabotaged computer systems to seek revenge against employers surfaced. Other highly publicized news stories described computer-savvy teenagers, sometimes described in the media as "hackers," breaking into computer systems, either as a prank or for malicious purposes. There were also reports, frequently sensationalized and occasionally glamorized by some members of the press, involving "hackers" who used computers to transfer money from wealthy individuals and corporations to poorer individuals and organizations.

In Chapter 6, we saw that malicious hackers have engaged in a wide range of illicit, or at least questionable, activities. As a society, our attitude toward activities associated with hacking, as that concept has been used in the media, has changed. In the past, young computer enthusiasts who figured out ways of gaining unauthorized access to computer systems were sometimes portrayed as countercultural heroes who single-handedly took on the establishment, like David taking down Goliath (i.e., big government or big business) or Robin Hood robbing the rich to give to the poor. By the turn of the twenty-first century, however, there was a growing concern in both the private and the public sectors that no types of activities leading to unauthorized access should be tolerated. The media, which itself had become a victim of cyberattacks (e.g., distributed denial-of-service (DDoS) attacks on the *New York Times* and the CNN Web sites), as well as ordinary computer users shifted their attitude considerably. Perhaps this change in sentiment is due to our society's increased dependence on networked computers and the Internet, as we noted in Chapter 6.

Of course, unauthorized break-ins are only one of the many kinds of crimes made possible by computers and cybertechnology. Richard Power (2000), who believes that most computer crimes involve either fraud or abuse, or both, distinguishes between the two notions in the following way: He identifies *computer fraud* as computer-related crimes involving "deliberate misrepresentation or alteration of data in order to get something of value"; he defines *computer abuse,* on the contrary, as "willful or negligent unauthorized activity that affects the availability, confidentiality, or integrity of computer resources." Power notes that these abuses can include "embezzlement, theft, malicious damage, unauthorized use, denial of service, and misappropriation."[2]

Analysts believe that many cybercrimes go unreported. Wall (2007) notes that in at least some cases, organizations are reluctant to report cybercrimes because of the embarrassment it might cause them. Other analysts believe that many of these crimes go unreported because the victims fear the negative repercussions: reporting the crimes would be tantamount to admitting that their computer security practices are inadequate. Consider, for example, what might happen if a customer discovered that the bank where she deposits and saves money had been broken into—she might decide to transfer her funds to a bank that she perceives to be more secure. And if cyber-related crimes committed by employees working inside a financial institution were reported and publicized, the institution could also suffer a loss of customer confidence.

7.1.2 A Typical Cybercriminal

Can we construct a profile for a typical cybercriminal? Some people associate cybercriminals with "hackers," or what we described in Chapter 6 as "malicious hackers." Many people think of the typical computer hacker as the very bright, technically sophisticated, young white male in the popular 1983 movie *War Games*. Is such a portrayal accurate? Donn Parker, one of the first authors to write on the topic of computer crime, points out that a traditional hacker tended to perceive himself "as a problem solver rather than as a criminal."[3] Parker's classic study also suggested that we should carefully distinguish between hackers who commit crimes, i.e., as people who are primarily nonprofessional or amateur criminals, and "professional criminals." He believes that stereotypical computer hackers, unlike most professional criminals, are not generally motivated by greed; some seem to thrive on a kind of "joyriding" (the thrill experienced in figuring out how to break into unauthorized systems). Along somewhat similar lines, Sagiroglu and Canbek (2009) point out that in the early days of computing, "idealistic hackers" were inclined to attack computers merely to prove that they could or to "show off" to one another. Characteristics such as these would seem to differentiate many traditional hackers from professional criminals.

Although many malicious hackers are considered amateur criminals, some possess an expertise with computers comparable to that of the best technical experts in computer science. However, it is also worth noting that many malicious hackers do not possess outstanding technical skills but are savvy enough to locate sophisticated "hacking tools" that can be downloaded from the Internet for free, and many of these individuals are sufficiently astute to take advantage of "holes" in computer systems and programs. Michael Simpson (2006) notes that these individuals, who tend to be young and inexperienced, are sometimes referred to by sophisticated computer programmers as "script kiddies" or "packet monkeys," because they copy code from knowledgeable programmers as opposed to creating the code themselves.

▶ 7.2 HACKING, CRACKING, AND COUNTERHACKING

We have already noted that computer criminals are often referred to in the media as hackers, and that, as a result, "hacker" now has a negative connotation. In Chapter 6, we saw why this definition of "hacker" is controversial and why many believe it to be both an inaccurate and unfortunate use of the term. Pekka Himanen (2001) notes that "hacker" originally meant anyone who "programmed enthusiastically" and who believed that "information sharing is a powerful positive good." The hacker Jargon File (maintained on the Web by Eric Raymond at www.tuxedo.org/esr/jargon) defines a hacker as "an expert or enthusiast of any kind." Note that, according to this definition, a hacker need not be a computer enthusiast; for example, someone could be an astronomy hacker. In fact, a hacker, in the generic sense of the term, might have no interest in computers or cybertechnology at all.

7.2.1 Hacking vs. Cracking

Himanen points out that the meaning of "hacker" began to change in the 1980s when the media started applying the term to criminals using computers. In order to avoid confusion with virus writers and intruders into information systems, traditional hackers began calling these destructive computer users *crackers*. According to the hacker Jargon File, a cracker is one "who breaks security on a system." Crackers often engage in theft and vandalism once they have gained access to computer systems.

Some authors, including Wall (2007), also use the expressions *white hat* and *black hat* to distinguish between the two types of hacking behavior. The phrase "white hat hackers" is used to refer to those "innocent," or nonmalicious, forms of hacking, while "black hat hackers" refers roughly to what we described above as "cracking." However, distinctions between hacking and cracking, and between white-hat and black-hat hackers, are generally not recognized and observed in the world beyond the computer community. So the media often refers to crackers, or "black hat hackers," simply as hackers. This, in turn, has perpetuated the negative image of hackers and hacking in society at large.

In this chapter, our uses of "hacker" sometimes reflect the broader societal (i.e., negative) meaning of the term. Because of the way "hacker" has been used in the media, it is difficult, if not impossible, to refer to some classic cases of cybercrime without invoking it. So it is important to keep in mind that many activities and crimes described in this chapter in terms of hacking would be better understood as instances of cracking.

7.2.2 Active Defense Hacking: Can Acts of "Hacking Back" or Counter Hacking Ever Be Morally Justified?

A more recent controversy associated with hacking activities has to do with *active defense hacking*, sometimes also referred to as "counter hacking" or "hacking back against hackers." Counter hacking activities have been carried out both by individuals and corporations; they are directed against those who are suspected of originating the hacker attacks. In some cases, counter hacking has been pre-emptive; in other cases, it has been reactive. Both forms are controversial, but pre-emptive counter hacking is arguably more difficult to defend. Is counter hacking an act of "self-defense," as some argue? Or is it simply another case of "two wrongs making a right"? Should counter hacking be legalized? Can it ever be ethically justified?

In Chapter 6, we saw that at least one organization offers a certification program to train "ethical hackers." Individuals who successfully complete this program—i.e., Certified Ethical Hackers—are trained and certified not only in the use of defensive measures to ensure the security of their employers, but also appear to be authorized to engage in security-related activities that involve pre-emptive strikes as well. According to the Certified Ethical Hacker (CEH) Web site (www.eccouncil.org/ceh.htm):

> The goal of the ethical hacker is to help the organization take *preemptive measures* against malicious attacks by attacking the system himself; all the while staying within legal limits . . . an Ethical Hacker is very similar to a Penetration Tester . . . When it is done by request and under a contract between an Ethical Hacker and an organization, it is legal. [Italics added]

But is it, or should it be, legal to engage in pre-emptive hacking attacks? Some who defend pre-emptive acts of counter hacking believe that they can be justified on utilitarian, or consequentialist, grounds. For example, they argue that less overall harm will likely result if pre-emptive strikes are allowed. However, it would seem that many of the same difficulties that arose in applying a utilitarian justification for computer break-ins in extraordinary cases (examined in Chapter 6) also arise in the case of extending a utilitarian argument to defend counter hacking in its pre-emptive form.

Because counter hacking can cause harm to innocent individuals, we can question whether this practice can be defended on moral grounds. Kenneth Himma (2004, 2008) points out that in the case of hacking back against those who launch DDoS attacks, many innocent persons are adversely affected because the attacks are routed through their computer systems. As we noted in Chapter 6, perpetrators of DDoS attacks use "host computers," which often include the computers of innocent persons, to initiate their attacks (a technique sometimes referred to as "IP spoofing"). This would suggest to the victims of these attacks that they originated from the host computer, as opposed to the computer of the initiator of the attack. So when victims hack back, they can unintentionally cause the intermediate computer to be assaulted.

So, even if utilitarian arguments showed that counter hacking resulted in more desirable outcomes for the majority of society, deontologists (and other nonconsequentialists) would argue that such practices are morally unacceptable if they do not respect the rights of innocent individuals. In this case, those individuals would be unfairly used as a means to an end, which, as we saw in Chapter 2, is not permissible in deontological ethical theories.

It is difficult to provide a moral justification for counter hacking; and from a legal perspective, it is not clear whether "hacking back" can be viewed in a way that is not criminal. For example, if hacking is illegal, then it would seem that hacking back would be no less illegal. However, until a case of counter hacking—especially one that involves a pre-emptive attack in the form of a DDoS—is officially tried in court, it is difficult to say how our legal system will respond.

In Chapter 6, we considered whether at least some computer break-ins, under extraordinary conditions, might be ethically justifiable. In this chapter, we analyze computer break-ins and hacking-related issues mainly from a legal perspective. For example, we ask, Should all forms of computer hacking be declared illegal? Should every hacker be prosecuted as a criminal?[4] Before answering these questions, however, we examine some reasons why it is important to define what we mean by "cybercrime."

▶ 7.3 DEFINING CYBERCRIME

We have seen that crimes affecting cybertechnology, especially those associated with hacking, have received considerable attention in the popular press. The criteria used for determining which kinds of crimes should be labeled "computer crimes" or "cybercrimes" have been neither clear nor consistent. Initially, some news reporters and journalists seemed to suggest that any crime involving the use, or even the presence, of a computer is a computer crime; others, however, have argued that there was nothing special about crimes that happen to involve computers. Don Gotterbarn has criticized much of the media hype surrounding computer-related crimes as "a new species of yellow journalism."[5] As we saw in Chapter 1, Gotterbarn argues that a crime in which an individual uses a surgeon's scalpel to commit a murder would not be considered an issue in medical ethics, even though a medical instrument was used in the criminal act; so, by analogy, Gotterbarn concludes that crimes involving computers are not necessarily issues in computer ethics.

Gotterbarn's position can be interpreted in a way to suggest that no distinct category of computer crime or cybercrime is needed. Stephane Leman-Langlois (2008) makes a similar suggestion in stating that cybercrime, or what she calls "technocrime," "does not exist." In Leman-Langlois' view, cybercrime "is simply a convenient way to refer to a set of concepts . . . shaping the ways we understand matters having to do with the impact of technology on crime, criminals and our reactions to crime—and vice versa."[6]

If Gotterbarn and Leman-Langlois are correct, we can reasonably ask whether a separate category, cybercrime, is necessary or even useful. Consider the crimes that have involved technologies other than computers. Do we have separate categories for them? People steal televisions, but we don't have a category, television crime. People also steal automobiles, and some people have used automobiles to assist criminals in "getaway" operations, but we don't have a category, automobile crime. So why do we need a separate category, cybercrime, for criminal acts involving cybertechnology? Yet lawmakers have determined it necessary, or at least useful, to enact specific laws for crimes involving computers and cybertechnology.

In this chapter, we use "computer crime" and "cybercrime" interchangeably, even though some authors draw a distinction between the two. For example, Robert Moore (2011) notes that a computer crime can be viewed as a "subdivision" of cybercrime and thus warrants its own definition. Moore prefers the expression "high technology crime," which he uses to refer to any crime "involving the use of a high-technology device in its commission." However, in following the conventional nomenclature in the cyberethics ethics literature, we use "cybercrime" and "computer crime" to refer to the full range of crimes covered in Moore's category of high technology crime.

We next take up the question of criteria for distinguishing computer/cyber crimes from other kinds of crimes. In particular, we ask whether the criteria used by lawmakers to frame various categories of computer crime or cybercrime been coherent.[7]

7.3.1 Determining the Criteria

Do any of the following three incidents, each of which illustrates criminal activity involving a computer lab, convincingly demonstrate the need for a distinct category of computer crime?

a. Sandra steals a computer device (e.g., a laser printer) from a computer lab.

b. Bill breaks into a computer lab and then snoops around.

c. Ed enters a computer lab that he is authorized to use and then places an explosive device, set to detonate a short time later, on a computer system in the lab.

Clearly, (a)–(c) are criminal acts, but should any of these acts necessarily be viewed as a computer crime or cybercrime? One could point out that it would not have been possible to commit any of them if computer technology had never existed, and this might initially influence some to believe that the three criminal acts are somehow unique to computer technology. Even though each act involves the presence of computer technology, each of them can easily be understood and prosecuted as a specific example of ordinary crime involving theft, breaking and entering, and vandalism, respectively. So we might infer that there are no legitimate grounds for having a separate category of computer crime. Can we justify such an inference?

7.3.2 A Preliminary Definition of Cybercrime

Moore (2011) suggests that a computer crime can include any criminal activity involving a computer, while a cybercrime would include any criminal activity involving a computer and a network. He also claims that a computer "may or may not have played an instrumental part in the commission of the crime." But some authors would find these definitions far too broad. Perhaps a computer crime could, as Forester and Morrison suggest, be defined as "a criminal act in which a computer is used as the *principal tool*" [italics added].[8] According to this definition, the theft of a computer hardware device (or, for that matter, the theft of an automobile or a television which also happened to contain a computer component) would not qualify as a computer crime. If we apply the definition to incidents (b) and (c) above—i.e., breaking and entering into the computer lab and vandalizing a computer system in the lab, respectively—Forester and Morrison's definition eliminates these criminal acts as well. So their definition of computer crime might seem plausible. But is it adequate? Consider the following scenario.

▶ **SCENARIO 7–1:** Using a Computer to File a Fraudulent Tax Return

Sheila uses a computer to enter the data for her annual income tax forms, which she will submit electronically. In the process of completing her income tax forms, she decides to enter false information and thus files a fraudulent tax return. Since income tax fraud is a crime and Sheila uses a computer in committing this crime, is this criminal act a computer crime? ■

Arguably, Sheila has used a computer as the "principal tool" to commit fraud in this scenario. So according to Forester and Morrison's definition, it would seem that Sheila has committed a computer crime. But has she? Sheila could commit the same crime by manually filling out a hard-copy version of the income tax forms using a pencil or pen. Sheila's using a computer is coincident with, but by no means essential to, this particular criminal act, so Forester and Morrison's definition of computer crime, which fails to rule out Sheila's criminal act of income tax fraud as a computer crime, is not adequate.

Roy Girasa (2002) defines cybercrime as a crime that involves a "computer as a central component." Is this definition any more helpful than Forester and Morrison's? What does it mean for a crime to have a computer as its "central component"? Was a computer a central component in our example of Sheila's filing a fraudulent income tax return? It is difficult to distinguish which crimes have and which do not have a computer as their central component, so Girasa's definition of computer crime is not much of an improvement over the one advanced by Forester and Morrison.

7.3.3 Framing a Coherent and Comprehensive Definition of Cybercrime

Recall our discussion in Chapter 1 of James Moor's insight that computer technology is "logically malleable" and thus creates "new possibilities for human action." We saw that these new possibilities, in turn, sometimes generate both "policy vacuums" and "conceptual muddles" (Moor 2007). By extension, these new possibilities for human action include new possibilities for crime. Many of these possibilities have resulted in criminal actions that have forced us to stretch traditional concepts and laws dealing with crime. Applying Moor's insight, we can further ask whether any new forms of crime have been made possible by cybertechnology. If we answer "yes," then some crimes may be unique to computers and cybertechnology.

By thinking about cybercrimes in terms of their unique or special features—i.e., conditions that separate them from ordinary crimes—we could distinguish authentic or "genuine" cybercrimes from other crimes that merely involve the use or the presence of cybertechnology. We propose a definition of a genuine cybercrime as a crime in which

the criminal act can be carried out only through the use of cybertechnology and can take place only in the cyberrealm.

Note that this definition would rule out the scenario where Sheila used a computer to file a fraudulent income tax return as an example of a genuine cybercrime. Of course, it also rules out the three examples of crimes involving a computer lab that we considered.

▶ 7.4 THREE CATEGORIES OF CYBERCRIME: PIRACY, TRESPASS, AND VANDALISM IN CYBERSPACE

Using our definition of cybercrime, we can further categorize genuine cybercrimes as follows:

1. **Cyberpiracy**—using cybertechnology in unauthorized ways to
   a. reproduce copies of proprietary information, or
   b. distribute proprietary information (in digital form) across a computer network.
2. **Cybertrespass**—using cybertechnology to gain unauthorized access to
   a. an individual's or an organization's computer system, or
   b. a password-protected Web site.
3. **Cybervandalism**—using cybertechnology to unleash one or more programs that
   a. disrupt the transmission of electronic information across one or more computer networks, including the Internet, or
   b. destroy data resident in a computer or damage a computer system's resources, or both.

Consider three incidents that can each illustrate one of the three categories: (a) the unleashing of the Conficker computer virus in 2009 (described in Chapter 6), which infected computers around the world; (b) the launching of cyberattacks on major (commercial and government) Web sites in January 2012, in response to PIPA and SOPA legislation (described in Chapter 8), that resulted in "denial-of-service" to thousands of users wishing to access those sites; andthe unauthorized exchanging of copyrighted music files over the Internet (beginning with the original Napster site). Using our model of cybercrime, activities involving the unauthorized exchange of copyrighted music on the Internet via Napster and subsequent P2P-related file-sharing sites are examples of cyberpiracy (Category 1); the launching of the Conficker virus is an instance of cybervandalism (Category 3); and the DDoS attacks on government and commercial Web sites illustrate an example of cybertrespass (Category 2), because they involved the breaking into, as well as the unauthorized use of, third-party computer systems to send spurious requests to commercial Web sites (as opposed to the kind of "genuine" requests sent by users who wish to access those sites for legitimate purposes). Since DDoS attacks also cause serious disruption of services for the targeted Web sites, they can also be classified as cybervandalism (Category 3); some cybercrimes will span more than one category.

If our model is correct, then many crimes that use cybertechnology are not genuine cybercrimes. For example, crimes involving pedophilia, stalking, and pornography can each be carried out with or without computers and cybertechnology; there is nothing about them that is unique to cybertechnology, so crimes such as Internet pedophilia, cyberstalking, and Internet pornography would not qualify as genuine cybercrimes. (We will see below that they are examples of *cyber-related* crimes.)

In Chapter 6, we saw that it was difficult to draw a coherent distinction between cyberterrorism and hacktivism. We now see that both can be understood as instances of cybertrespass, regardless of whether they were perpetrated by "electronic political activists" (called hacktivists) or by cyberterrorists. If, however, hacktivists and cyber-terrorists also break into computer systems in order to disrupt or vandalize computer systems and networks, then they have committed cybervandalism as well. Using our definition of cybercrime, there is no need to consider motive, political cause, ideology, etc., when determining how the criminal acts best fit into one of our three categories. (However, motive or intention could influence the ways that cybercrimes are prosecuted and that convicted cybercriminals are sentenced.)

▶ 7.5 CYBER-RELATED CRIMES

So far we have differentiated genuine cybercrimes, i.e., crimes that are specific to cybertechnology, from crimes that are cyber-related. We next see that *cyber-related* crimes can, in turn, be divided into two subcategories: *cyberexacerbated* crimes and *cyberassisted* crimes. This distinction enables us to differentiate between a crime in which someone merely uses cybertechnology (e.g., a personal computer to file a fraudulent income tax return) from crimes such as Internet pedophilia and cyberstalking, which are significantly affected by computers and cybertechnology. The role that cybertechnology plays in the first example seems at best trivial and possibly altogether irrelevant, but in the latter two examples, cybertechnology does much more than merely *assist* someone in carrying out a crime—cybertechnology *exacerbates* the crimes.

7.5.1 Some Examples of Cyber-Exacerbated vs. Cyber-Assisted Crimes

Certain kinds of crimes aided by cybertechnology can increase significantly because of that technology. For example, in the case of cyberexacerbated crimes, the scale on which crimes of a certain type can be carried out is significantly affected. Consider the potential increase in the number of stalking-, pornography-, and pedophilia-related crimes that can now occur because of cybertechnology, vs. the likely increase in the number of income tax crimes, which are also assisted by computer technology.

Along lines that are somewhat similar to the distinctions we have drawn in separating three categories of cybercrime—cyberassisted, cyberexacerbated, and cyberspecific (or genuine cyber) crimes—Wall (2007) proposes the following scheme based on three "generations" of cybercrime. What we call cyberassisted crimes, he describes as "first generation" cybercrimes that are, in effect, "traditional" or "ordinary" crimes that happen to involve the use of a computer. Corresponding to our category of cyber-exacerbated crimes is Wall's notion of second generation or "hybrid crimes." For this set of cyber-related crimes, Wall points out that network technology has "created entirely new global opportunities." His third generation of cybercrimes comprises a category that Wall calls "true cybercrimes," which corresponds to our category of genuine cybercrimes in that they are "solely the product of the Internet" (or, in our case, the product of cybertechnology).

Wall notes that in the case of cybercrimes involving the first two generations, individuals and organizations could still find ways of carrying out the criminal activities in the event that either the computer or the Internet was eliminated. In the case of true cybercrimes, however, Wall points out that if you eliminate the Internet, those crimes "vanish." He uses the examples of spamming and phishing to illustrate this point. These examples complement the set of crimes we identified above as genuine cybercrimes.

Figure 7.1 illustrates some ways in which crimes involving the use of cybertechnology can be catalogued according to this threefold scheme.

We should not underestimate the significance of many cyber-related crimes, even if they fail to qualify as genuine or true cybercrimes. Consider that many professional or career criminals, including those involved in organized crime, are using cybertechnology

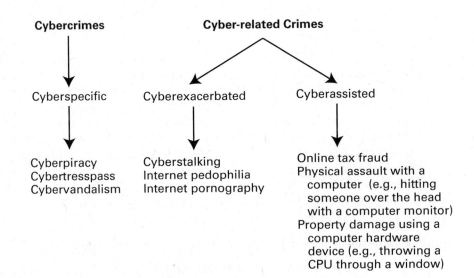

Figure 7.1 Cybercrimes and cyber-related crimes.

to conduct illicit gambling, drug trafficking, and racketeering scams. When cybertechnology is used, these crimes can be viewed as cyber-related crimes. Yet these kinds of crimes, which some describe as "old-style" crimes, receive far less attention in the popular media than those perpetrated by malicious hackers, many of whom are young and could be viewed as "amateur criminals." Because stories about these amateur criminals tend to grab the headlines, our attention is diverted from crimes committed in cyberspace by professionals. Power (2000) believes that youthful hacker stereotypes provide a "convenient foil" for both professional criminals and foreign intelligence agents. In Section 7.1.2 we saw that unlike many individuals who are described in the media as "hackers," and who are amateurs, professionals do not seek technological adventure; rather they hope to gain a financial advantage. But Power points out that since professional criminals have superior skills, they are less likely than amateurs to get caught in carrying out their criminal acts.

Also consider that some cyber-related crimes, including cyberstalking and cyberbullying, have resulted in deaths.[9] Paul Bocij (2004) describes the wide range of criminal activities made possible by cyberstalking in a book dedicated to that topic.[10] And Kowalski, Limber, and Agatston (2008), in their book on cyberbullying, identify many of the ways by which cybertechnology has provided new opportunities for traditional bullying.[11] Although the authors of both books suggest that there may be some aspects of cyberstalking (vs. offline stalking) crimes and cyberbullying (vs. traditional bullying) crimes, respectively, that challenge our conventional laws, neither succeeds in making a convincing case for why those criminal acts should qualify as examples of what we call genuine cybercrimes. But, in describing the many ways that stalking and bullying crimes have increased significantly because of cybertechnology, the authors make a very strong case for why those cyber-related crimes would qualify as cyberexacerbated crimes rather than merely cyberassisted crimes.[12]

Next we examine, in more detail, a cyber-related crime that also has been significantly exacerbated by cybertechnology: identity theft.

7.5.2 Identity Theft

What is identity theft, and how is it exacerbated by cybertechnology? Lininger and Vines (2005) define identity theft as

> a crime in which an imposter obtains key pieces of personal information, such as social security or driver's license numbers, in order to impersonate someone else. The information can be used to obtain credit, merchandise, and services in the name of the victim, or to provide the thief with false credentials.[13]

Identity-theft crimes can also include the taking of another person's identity through the fraudulent acquisition of personal information in credit card numbers. However, Wall (2007) notes that identity theft is often mistakenly used to describe crimes involving credit card theft. So, not all instances of the latter kind of theft qualify as identity theft.

Of course, identity theft, like other cyber-related crimes, does not require cybertechnology. In the past, identity thieves have combed through dumpsters (and some still do) looking for copies of bank statements and for papers containing account information on credit card bills that people dispose of in their trash. (This behavior is sometimes referred to as "dumpster diving.") But identity thieves have been very successful in scams involving cybertechnology in general (e.g., in recording credit card "swipes"), independent of the Internet per se.

Factors such as lax security and carelessness involving customer information contained in computer databases and in company-owned laptop computers has made it easy for some identity thieves to acquire personal information about their victims. Ellen Simon describes two examples that occurred in 2005: (a) the Bank of America lost computer tapes containing data on 1.2 million federal employees; and (b) ChoicePoint Inc. and Lexis-Nexis disclosed that the dossiers of more than 170,000 Americans on the companies' databases had been illegally accessed by criminals, and that at least 750 of them had their identities stolen. The information in these databases contained the addresses and social security numbers of individuals—all of the information that identity thieves needed to open up a credit card account. Simon points out that another incident linked to lax security and carelessness involved an MCI laptop computer containing the names of 165,000 MCI employees. (MCI was acquired by Verizon Communications in 2005.) The computer was stolen from the car of an MCI employee, which was parked in front of his home garage.[14]

As we saw in Chapter 5, information merchants purchase and sell personal information, including social security numbers and credit card information. And many are willing to pay for this information. So information brokering has become a lucrative business, and this has not gone unnoticed by professional criminals as well as by some employees in organizations that have access to sensitive information about people's financial records. Simon describes an incident where a former bank employee of Wachovia Corporation allegedly sold information about account numbers and account balances to a person who then sold them to data collection agencies. Some data brokers, such as ChoicePoint, have tried to screen customers, to avoid selling information to criminals. But critics, especially privacy advocates, remain skeptical; many believe that for information brokers, concerns about privacy and security are more of an "afterthought" than a priority.[15]

Many kinds of identity-theft scams have also been carried out on the Internet. One common example is a scheme involving e-mail that appears to have been sent by a reputable business. For example, you may receive e-mail that looks as if it were sent by eBay, Amazon, or PayPal. Often these e-mail messages include the official logos of the companies they purport to represent; the message informs you that your account is about to expire and that you need to update it by verifying your credit card number. Although the e-mail might look legitimate, it could have been sent to you by identity thieves or other individuals whose objective is to get your credit card number as well as other kinds of personal information. How can a potential victim differentiate legitimate e-mail sent from businesses such as eBay or PayPal from that sent by identity thieves? Typically, e-mail from identity thieves will not address the potential victim by name; so this can be an indication that the e-mail is not from a legitimate source. Users wishing to verify the authenticity of the e-mail can contact the company by phone, or through the company's legitimate e-mail address, if they are in doubt.

Many e-mail messages sent from identity thieves are generated through spam (examined in Chapter 9). Using spam to gather personal information is sometimes referred to as *phishing*, which Lininger and Vines (2005) describe as "automated identity theft." They point out that phishing "combines the power of the Internet with human nature to defraud millions of people out of billions of dollars."[16] They also believe that phishing may soon overtake spam as "the main Internet headache." Lininger and Vines cite a study by the Anti-Phishing Working Group (APWG), which reports that the number of phishing incidents is increasing at a rate of about 56% per month.[17]

An automated version of phishing, sometimes called "pharming," automatically "redirects the victim to the offending site" (Wall 2007). Activities involving pharming and phishing, along with conventional e-mail spam, increase the amount of identity theft that can be accomplished over the Internet. And we have seen how other, non-networked uses of cybertechnology also exacerbate identity-theft crimes.

In our analysis of cybercrime and cyber-related crimes so far, we have examined some ways in which individuals and organizations have used cybertechnology to carry out criminal activities. Some of these crimes were "genuine" cybercrimes because they could not have been committed without the use of cybertechnology; others, however, were crimes that were either assisted or exacerbated by the use of cybertechnology. Not only has this technology enabled criminals to carry out their crimes, it has also provided law enforcement agencies with new tools to track down criminals, including cybercriminals. We have already examined some ethical issues that arise because of the ways individuals can use cybertechnology to carry out criminal acts. Next, we consider some ways by which the use of cybertechnology by law enforcement agencies to combat crime can also raise ethical concerns.

▶ 7.6 TECHNOLOGIES AND TOOLS FOR COMBATING CYBERCRIME

In our discussion of privacy in Chapter 5, we saw some examples of how the U.S. government has used cybertechnology to track down criminals via a technique called computerized record matching. We also saw why this technique was considered controversial when it was used to match records in databases containing the names of federal government employees against the records in databases with the names of welfare recipients in order to identify welfare cheats. There, our analysis of computerized matching focused mainly on implications for personal privacy. But we also noted some of the concerns that practices involving record matching can raise when used to combat crime. One popular line of reasoning frequently used to defend computerized techniques (including record matching) in tracking down individuals suspected of committing crimes is: If you have done nothing wrong, you have nothing to worry about.[18] Critics, however, argue that this line of reasoning misses an important point— one that is illustrated in the following scenario.

▶ **SCENARIO 7–2:** Intercepting Mail that Enters and Leaves Your Neighborhood

You live in a peaceful community in Sunnyside Valley, USA. The local law enforcement authorities there have heard rumors that members of an organized crime syndicate have been communicating via the United States Postal Service with someone living in your neighborhood. The authorities decide to intercept the mail sent to and from homes in Sunnyside Valley and then compare the information included in the return and destination addresses on the envelopes against a list of names and addressees of suspected mobsters. When you discover what the authorities are doing and you object to it, you are told, "If you have nothing to hide, you have nothing to worry about." Of course, you could respond that even though you have nothing to hide, you believe that you still have quite a bit to worry about; that is, you have to worry about how to retain your basic freedoms and civil liberties as a United States citizen under such conditions.[19] ■

Computerized record matching is like the cross-checking procedures in the above scenario. Although many citizens might be inclined to view the kind of electronic surveillance implicit in computer matching as less intrusive, or at least less objectionable, than the physical surveillance techniques used in intercepting and cross-checking the mail sent to and from a particular neighborhood, both practices raise serious concerns for civil liberties. From a utilitarian perspective, it could be argued that the end (e.g., catching welfare cheats or "deadbeat" parents) justifies the means used (matching the records of many innocent citizens in the process). But we can also see why techniques involving the computerized record matching of ordinary citizens (who are presumed to be innocent) can raise concerns about basic civil liberties.[20]

Civil liberties issues often lie at the heart of the controversies surrounding the use of cybertechnology by law enforcement agencies in tracking down criminals. Not surprisingly, law enforcement organizations desire to use the latest available technologies in pursuing criminals, including cybercriminals. We next consider some controversies surrounding the use of biometric technologies to fight crime.

7.6.1 Biometric Technologies

Biometric technologies have also been used by law enforcement agencies to combat crime and terrorism. Power defines biometrics as "the biological identification of a person, which includes eyes, voice, hand prints, finger prints, retina patterns, and hand-written signatures."[21] Irma van der Ploeg (1999, 2004) points out that through biometric technologies, one's iris can be read in the same way that one's voice can be printed. She also notes that one's fingerprints can be read by a computer that, in turn, has become touch sensitive and endowed with hearing and seeing capacities. The digital representation of these biometric data is usually transformed via some algorithm to produce a template, which is stored in a central computer database.

In 2002 a biometric identification scheme was tested at London's Heathrow Airport; the iris-scanning device captures a digital image of one's iris, which is then stored in a database and can then be matched against images of the irises of other individuals entering and leaving public places such as airports.[22] As biometric technologies improve, security officials at airports such as Heathrow and elsewhere may consider adopting them for authenticating an individual's identity, in combination with (or possibly even in place of) passports.

Possibly you have heard the expression, "Eyes are the window to the soul." In an age of biometrics, however, one's eyes may become the window to one's identity in a much more tangible sense than the classic metaphor ever intended. While biometric devices are a highly accurate means for validating an individual's identity, they are also controversial. Recall our analysis of a scenario in Chapter 5 involving Super Bowl XXXV (in January 2001), where a biometric identification tool using face-recognition technology scanned the faces of people entering the football stadium. The scanned images were then instantly matched against the facial templates of suspected criminals and terrorists, which were contained in a central computer database.[23]

Initially, the use of this technology at Super Bowl XXXV drew scathing criticism from civil liberties groups and privacy advocates. In the post-September 11 world, however, practices that employ biometric technologies such as face-recognition devices have received overwhelming support from the American public; a poll conducted in

October 2001, for example, indicated that more than 86% of Americans approved of using biometric technologies in public places, including sports stadiums and airports.[24]

Does the use of biometric technologies violate human rights? Do arguments against the government's traditional uses of computerized record matching apply equally in the case of biometric techniques? In nonbiometric-based computerized matching, including earlier record-matching techniques used by the U.S. government in the 1970s, the databases that were used contained records of individuals all of whom were presumed to be innocent; for example, records of government workers were matched against records of welfare recipients to generate one or more hits. In matching practices involving biometric technology, such as the one used at Super Bowl XXXV, images of people who are presumed innocent are recorded and matched against a database of known or suspected criminals and terrorists. So, there is at least one noticeable difference involving these two examples of computerized matching.

But critics still raise questions regarding the use of biometric technologies by law enforcement agencies. Philip Brey (2004) notes that critics of face-recognition technologies in particular, and biometrics in general, point to at least three problems: error, abuse, and privacy. He notes that errors occur in matches resulting from biometrics technology, and the rate of error increases when the criteria used to determine what qualifies as an acceptable match is expanded. Second, the uses for which biometric technologies are originally authorized can expand significantly and can lead to possible abuses. And finally, some privacy advocates argue that the net security gained in the use of biometrics is not commensurate with the loss of privacy and civil liberties for individuals. But those who favor using biometric technology argue that it provides increased security, even if using this technology undercuts some civil liberties for ordinary citizens.

7.6.2 Keystroke-Monitoring Software and Packet-Sniffing Programs

In addition to biometric technologies, law enforcement agencies have used other forms of cybertechnology to track the activities of criminals who themselves use cybertechnology. One such technique is *keystroke monitoring*, which Power describes as "a specialized form of audit-trail software . . . that records every key struck by a user and every character of the response that the system returns to the user."[25] This software can trace the text included in electronic messages back to the original sequence of keys and characters entered at a user's computer keyboard. So it is especially useful in tracking the activities of criminals who use encryption tools to encode their messages. Wall (2007) notes that "keystroke loggers" were originally designed to "identify errors in systems." The later use of this technology by law enforcement groups, however, has been controversial.

Government agencies such as the Federal Bureau of Investigation (FBI) have also tracked criminals and their activities via *Carnivore*, a "packet sniffing" program that monitors the data traveling between networked computers; a packet sniffer or "sniffer" is a program that captures data across a computer network. However, these kinds of software programs have also been used by malicious hackers to capture user IDs and passwords. So Carnivore became somewhat controversial, and because of the negative publicity it received in the media, the FBI officially changed the name from Carnivore to DCS1000. However, DCS (Digital Collection System) has functioned in much the same way as Carnivore.[26]

▶ 7.7 PROGRAMS AND TECHNIQUES DESIGNED TO COMBAT CYBERCRIME IN THE UNITED STATES

In the preceding section we saw that the government and law enforcement groups, in their efforts to track suspected criminals, have used a variety of technologies and tools—including biometrics, keystroke-monitoring software, and packet-sniffing programs—all of which are controversial from the perspective of civil liberties groups. Next, we examine some programs and practices, as well as some interpretations of controversial laws, that government and law enforcement agencies have also used to apprehend and catch individuals, including professional criminals who use cybertechnology to carry out their criminal activities. We begin with a look at the practice of entrapment on the Internet.

7.7.1 Entrapment and "Sting" Operations to Catch Internet Pedophiles

Police and federal agents have used "sting" operations and entrapment techniques to catch members of organized crime involved in drug dealing, gambling, pornography, and so forth. Consider a controversial case of entrapment involving cybertechnology that was intended to lure and catch a pedophile who used the Internet to solicit sex with an under-aged person.

▶ **SCENARIO 7–3:** Entrapment on the Internet

Using an alias or pseudonamé, detective James McLaughlin of Keene, New Hampshire posed as a young boy in "boy-love chat rooms" on the Internet. There he searched for adults attempting to solicit sex with underage boys, and gathered evidence from conversations recorded in the chat rooms. Philip Rankin, a British marine-insurance expert living in Norway, communicated with McLaughlin under the assumption that the police officer was a young boy. Rankin then agreed to travel to Keene to meet his online contact in person at a Dunkin' Donuts restaurant. Upon his arrival at the restaurant, Rankin was arrested by McLaughlin on the charge of using the Internet to solicit sex with an under-aged person.[27] ∎

Critics of Internet entrapment have questioned whether such practices for catching child molesters are ethically justifiable, even if they are legal. In the United States, numerous cases of child molestation have been investigated by the FBI where pedophiles have crossed over a state line to meet and molest children they met via an Internet forum such as a chat room. Sometimes police officers have entered chat rooms, posing as young girls to lure unsuspecting pedophiles. In 2003, a three-week sting operation was conducted in Spokane, Washington, where a policeman posing as a 13-year-old girl in an Internet chat room arrested a twenty-two-year-old man on charges of attempted (second-degree) rape of a child.[28]

Supporters of online entrapment operations argue that they can save many innocent lives and can significantly lessen the harm that might otherwise occur to some individuals. For example, one could speculate about the outcome of the Amy Boyer stalking incident (described in a scenario in Chapter 1) if an entrapment scheme, similar to the one used in Scenario 7-3, had been in place to catch cyberstalkers such as Liam Youens. Of course, a critical question from the point of view of many civil libertarians is whether the ends achieved by entrapment operations justify the means. Are such means morally acceptable? At the root of this question are some of the same issues involving civil liberties that we examined in Scenario 7-2 (involving the interception of physical mail entering and leaving a certain neighborhood), where we saw that the end achieved, catching criminals, was desirable, but the means used to accomplish this end were questionable.

7.7.2 Enhanced Government Surveillance Techniques and the Patriot Act

Another controversial practice involving government surveillance of criminal activities is supported by provisions in the USA (United and Strengthening America) PATRIOT (Provide Appropriate Tools Required to Intercept and Obstruct Terrorism) Act. This act, which was passed by the U.S. Congress in October 2001 and renewed (in a slightly modified form) in March 2006, provides law enforcement agencies with increased powers to track down suspected terrorists and criminals by allowing those agencies to closely monitor e-mail communications and cell phone conversations.

The Patriot Act works in conjunction with, and in some cases expands on, two related acts: the Foreign Intelligence Surveillance Act (FISA) of 1978, and the Electronic Communications Privacy Act (ECPA) of 1986. The original FISA, which was amended in 2008, established legal guidelines for federal investigations of foreign intelligence targets.[29] The Patriot Act amended FISA: whereas the original FISA applied only to "snooping" in foreign intelligence investigations, the Patriot Act permits "domestic surveillance" as well.

ECPA, which includes provisions for "access, use, disclosure, interception and privacy protections of electronic communications," allows the government to attach two kinds of devices to a criminal suspect's phone: "pen registers" and "trap-and-trace devices." When a suspect makes a phone call, a pen register displays the number being dialed, and when the suspect receives a phone call, the trap-and-trace device displays the caller's phone number.[30] A pen register used on the Internet can reveal the URLs of Web sites visited by a suspect. The Patriot Act allows police to install Internet pen registers without having to demonstrate a probable cause and without having to demonstrate that the suspect is engaged in criminal activity.

In late 2005, reports began to surface that the George W. Bush administration had been monitoring the e-mails and phone calls of U.S. citizens who were communicating with individuals outside the United States. Opponents of this practice, including many members of the U.S. Congress, argued that the administration's practices violated the law because no court order was requested in conducting the surveillance on U.S. citizens. Others, however, supported the Bush administration's decision because of the positive effect it could have on national security. Some supporters also noted that it is legal for the National Security Agency (NSA) to conduct wiretaps on non-U.S. citizens, because of the authority given to it by FISA. However, critics objected that NSA is not authorized to intercept the communications of American citizens without first getting a court order. But, in its defense, the Bush administration argued that it was acting within the law because its primary obligation was to protect the American public against terrorist attacks.

While many conservative organizations have supported the enhanced domestic surveillance provisions made possible by the Patriot Act, critics argue that this increased surveillance has eroded basic civil liberties. Some critics also worry that certain provisions in this act could be abused by those in power, under the convenient excuse of crime prevention and national defense, to achieve certain political ends. So, controversial aspects of the Patriot Act once again illustrate the classic tension between interests involving civil liberties and national security (as it affects terrorism and crime).[31]

► 7.8 NATIONAL AND INTERNATIONAL LAWS TO COMBAT CYBERCRIME

Laws are typically limited in jurisdiction to nations where they are enacted. For example, the Economic Espionage Act is enforceable only in the United States. Some laws involving cybercrime are intended to have international reach, but issues involving legal jurisdiction have often impeded their prosecution in many instances.

7.8.1   The Problem of Jurisdiction in Cyberspace

Traditionally, crimes are prosecuted in the legal jurisdictions in which they were committed. In certain cases, suspected criminals have been extradited from one legal jurisdiction to another (and sometimes from one country to another) to stand trial for an accused crime. Girasa (2002) points out that jurisdiction is based on the concept of boundaries, and laws are based on "territorial sovereignty." Because cyberspace has no physical boundaries, it can be difficult to prosecute cybercrimes involving multiple nations, as well as multiple states within nations. So, some have questioned whether the concept of legal jurisdiction makes any sense in cyberspace.

Enforcing Cybercrime Laws across States/Provinces within Nations
States and provinces within nations have often been challenged in determining how to enforce local laws when crimes are committed within their jurisdictional boundaries by criminals residing outside those boundaries. In the United States, for example, different states have different laws regarding gambling. How can those laws be prosecuted in the case of online gambling, which can span multiple states? Individual state laws affecting online gambling are evolving and thus seem to be in flux. In the following (hypothetical) scenario, we will assume that online gambling is legal in the state of Nevada but not in Texas.

► SCENARIO 7–4: A Virtual Casino

Sarah and Phil are U.S. citizens who live in different states. Phil, a resident of Nevada, has decided to set up an online gambling site called "Virtual Casino." His casino, which complies with all of Nevada's gambling regulations, is fully licensed by the state. Sarah, a resident of Texas, decides to visit Phil's Virtual Casino, which is physically located on a server in Nevada. She then places a bet at one of the virtual tables in Phil's casino.[32]   ■

When Sarah engages in gambling activities on Phil's site (located on a server in Nevada) from her home computer, she has technically broken the law in Texas; but where, exactly, has the violation of the law taken place—in Texas, where the illegal gambling activities are carried out from Sarah's home, or in Nevada where the server for the Virtual Casino resides? And where should this "crime" be prosecuted? Can the state of Texas demand the extradition of the Nevada resident who owns and operates the online gambling site, on grounds that the Web site owner has assisted (or has made possible) the "crime" that was committed by the resident of Texas?

Note that in this scenario, no interstate transmission of illegal material, in the strict legal sense of that definition, has occurred. Interstate statutes have been established to prosecute that type of crime.

Although our scenario is merely hypothetical, there have been some actual jurisdictional quagmires involving cybertechnology. A now classic incident involved an online forum, whose California-based server contained pornographic material that was legal in that state. But this content was illegal in Tennessee, where it had been viewed online by a resident of that state. We examine this incident in detail in our discussion of pornography laws in Chapter 9.

Enforcing Cybercrime Laws Involving Multiple Nations

Not only have there been problems in prosecuting Internet crimes that span state borders within nations, but criminal enforcement has been hampered as well by a lack of international legal agreements and treaties. Consider the case of the ILOVEYOU virus that wreaked havoc worldwide in 2001 and which was allegedly launched by Onel de Guzman from the Philippines.

Where, exactly, did the crime take place? In the Philippines? In the United States? In Europe? Or in all of the above? Even though it originated in the Philippines, its effect was global. And if in the Philippines there is no explicit crime against launching computer viruses, did an actual crime even occur? Furthermore, if no crime was committed by Guzman in the Philippines, should he have been extradited to nations that do have cyber-related crime laws, and should he be required to stand trial in those nations?

On the one hand, it might be argued that Guzman should stand trial in any country that was affected by the virus he launched; after all, individuals and institutions in those countries were harmed by Guzman's act. On the other hand, we might also wish to consider the flip side of that argument: Would we want all cases of crimes or of controversial Internet practices that have a global reach prosecuted by multiple nations? Consider the following scenario.

▶ **SCENARIO 7–5:** Prosecuting a Computer Corporation in Multiple Countries

XYZ Corporation, a major computer company in the United States, has developed and released a new software product that has been distributed globally. However, this product has a serious defect that causes computer systems using it to crash under certain conditions. These system crashes, in turn, result in both severe disruption and damage to system resources. QTRON, a company headquartered in eastern Asia that purchased this product from XYZ, has experienced multiple system crashes since installing it, which has also resulted in a severe loss of revenue for that company. What legal recourse does/should QTRON have in its complaint against XYZ Corp., given that its complaint involves companies in two sovereign nations? ∎

In the United States, there are strict liability laws, but there are also disclaimers and caveats issued by manufacturers to protect themselves against litigation. Suppose that several countries where XYZ Corporation has sold its new software product also have strict liability laws but do not recognize disclaimers. Should XYZ Corporation be held legally liable in each of these countries? Would the fact that some of those countries did not recognize XYZ's disclaimer clause for computer products it sells in those countries have any bearing on deciding this question. It would seem that we need to think through some of the ramifications that broadening the sphere of legal jurisdiction at the international level could have for corporations that produce software products, which are susceptible to system failures in ways that other kinds of products are not.

For information about specific cybercrime laws in the United States, see http://www.cybercrime.gov. We next examine some international laws and treaties.

7.8.2 Some International Laws and Conventions Affecting Cybercrime

The Council of Europe (COE) has considered ways to implement an international legal code that would apply to members of the European Union. Because cybercrimes can involve multiple law enforcement agencies and multiple ISPs in diverse countries under diverse rules of law, the G8 countries met in May 2000 to discuss an international treaty involving cybercrime. (The G8 was, at that time, an informal group of eight countries: Canada, France, Germany, Italy, Japan, Russia, the United Kingdom, and the United States of America.) In conjunction with the G8 conference, the COE released its first draft of the COE Convention on Cybercrime on April 27, 2000 (http://conventions.coe.in/treaty/en/projects/cybercrime.htm).[33] It addresses four types of criminal activity in cyberspace:

- offenses against the confidentiality, availability, and integrity of data and computer systems
- computer-related offenses (such as fraud)
- content-related offenses (such as child pornography)
- copyright-related offenses.

Crimes involving economic espionage are not considered in the COE draft. However, international crimes involving copyright offenses are included, and this may prove to be important because of the sheer volume of unauthorized file sharing at the global level.

Many crimes affecting digital intellectual property are international in scope. Beginning in the late 1990s, Internet users around the world downloaded proprietary music from the original Napster Web site, whose central servers resided in the United States. In subsequent years, many illicit file-sharing sites that built upon the Napster system have operated outside the United States. For example, the servers for KaZaA, a well-known P2P file-sharing site, resided in the Netherlands before it ceased operations in 2005. But other sites, including Limewire, have taken the place of earlier sites such as Napster and KaZaA and have enabled the illicit sharing of proprietary music internationally. Perhaps one of the most "successful" sites dedicated to the unauthorized sharing of proprietary music, videos, games, and other copyrighted materials was The Pirate Bay, which operated out of Sweden. In 2009, an international trial took place, which determined the fate of that site.

▶ **SCENARIO 7–6:** The Pirate Bay Web Site

Established in 2003 by a Swedish anti-copyright organization, Pirate Bay is a well-known Web site that tracks and indexes files known as BitTorrent or "torrent" files. (Torrents are small files that contain "metadata," which are required to download the data files from other users.) In 2008, Pirate Bay announced that it had more than 25 million "unique peers" (unregistered users) and about 3,600,000 registered users. (Only users who wanted to download pornography from that site were required to register.) In 2006, Pirate Bay's servers were raided by Swedish police. Since then, Pirate Bay has faced a series of legal battles. In 2009, the four cofounders of Pirate Bay were found guilty by a Swedish court of "assisting the distribution of illegal content online." The verdict has since been appealed.[34] ◼

The prosecution of Pirate Bay received international attention, and the verdict in this case no doubt pleased those who favor the strict international enforcement of intellectual property laws. In this case, there was no need to dispute jurisdictional boundaries and no need to extradite individuals across nationally sovereign borders to prosecute a cyber-crime that was international in scope.

▶ 7.9 CYBERCRIME AND THE FREE PRESS: THE WIKILEAKS CONTROVERSY

In the previous section, we examined some challenges for law-enforcement groups in their efforts to prosecute cybercrimes in the international arena. A relatively recent challenge for law enforcement in cyberspace, especially at the international level, has emerged in response to controversial "journalistic" practices involving some new online media outlets and organizations. Do these practices explicitly violate existing laws, in which case they would clearly qualify as criminal? Or, should they be viewed as journalistic activities that are protected by a free press? This question lies at the heart of the WikiLeaks controversy.

WikiLeaks was founded in 2006 by the Sunshine Press organization (allegedly under the direction of Julian Assange, who has since become the "face of WikiLeaks"). Describing itself as a "not-for-profit media organization," WikiLeaks claims that its main objective is "to bring important news and information to the public" by publishing original source material so that readers "can see evidence of the truth" (http:wikileaks .org). Comparing itself to other "media outlets" that conduct "investigative journalism," WikiLeaks states that it accepts (but does not solicit) sources of information that are anonymous. However, Wikileaks also states that unlike the other outlets, it provides a "high security anonymous drop box" and that when it receives new information, the organization's journalists analyze and verify the material, before writing a "news piece about it describing its significance to society." The organization then publishes "both the news story and the original material" so that readers can analyze the story "in the context of the original source material themselves" (http:wikileaks.org/About.html).

By 2010, WikiLeaks had released thousands of controversial documents, in redacted form, to five traditional media organizations: *The Guardian*, *Le Monde*, *Der Spiegel*, *El Pais*, and the *New York Times* (Benkler 2011). The released documents included:

- a video of a U.S. helicopter attack in which the crew members allegedly fired on and killed innocent civilians, in addition to enemy soldiers;

- two large-scale documents involving the Iraq and Afghanistan Wars;
- several U.S. State Department diplomatic cables.

We analyze the WikiLeaks controversy in terms of three key questions: (1) Can WikiLeaks' practices be justified on ethical grounds (even if they may be criminal)?; (2) Do WikiLeaks' practices clearly violate existing laws (and thus rise to the level of a crime)?; and (3) Should WikiLeaks' practices be interpreted as a new form of journalism (and thus be protected under the provisions of a free press)?

7.9.1   Are WikiLeaks' Practices Ethical?

WikiLeaks claims that it "combines high-end security technologies with journalism and *ethical principles*" (http:wikileaks.org/About.html Italics Added). However, many critics have challenged WikiLeaks' claim regarding its adherence to ethical principles. For example, David Weineke (2010), who describes the organization's objectives and practices as naïve, reckless, and dangerous, believes that WikiLeaks' activities are unethical for at least two reasons: (a) the leaks involved have been "vast and indiscriminate," and (b) the leaks were intended more to "embarrass" rather than to "fix." So, Weineke exposes two kinds of concerns that would make it difficult for WikiLeaks to defend its claim regarding the organization's compliance with ethical principles.

Luciano Floridi (2010) also examines some ethics-related aspects of WikiLeaks' activities, which he analyzes from the vantage point of whistleblowing. He identifies two key problems with trying to support the organization's (whistleblowing) activities on ethical grounds: (i) WikiLeaks' motivation was based on resentment (and the intent to cause harm to its target), and (ii) WikiLeaks' activities put some innocent people at risk. Floridi also points out that some of WikiLeaks' supporters have tried to justify the organization's practices by appealing either to consequentialist (e.g., utilitarian) or deontological theories (see Chapter 2), or both. But Floridi believes that neither kind of ethical theory can be used successfully to justify WikiLeaks' practices.

Floridi also questions WikiLeaks' so-called "information liberation" argument, which holds that its practice of publishing leaked documents "improves transparency, and this transparency creates a better society for all people" (http://www.wikileaks.ch/about.html). He believes that this argument is "naïve," at best. Additionally, Floridi is concerned that the kind of threat/retaliation tactics used by Wikileaks constitute a form of "whitemail"—i.e., because it blackmails organizations by threatening to disclose even more damaging information about them via the organization's "insurance file," in the event anything should happen to WikiLeaks or to Julian Assange. Following Floridi, we question whether an organization that threatens its adversaries with these kinds of retaliatory measures can be viewed as acting ethically? We conclude this section by noting that both Floridi and Weineke provide some compelling examples to show why it is difficult to justify WikiLeaks' practices on ethical grounds.

7.9.2   Are WikiLeaks' Practices Criminal?

Many see WikiLeak's activities as not only unethical but also crossing the threshold of criminal behavior. But do these activities rise to the level of a cybercrime? And if they do, what specific criminal statutes do they violate? U.S. Attorney General Eric Holder and U.S. Senator Diane Feinstein (D-CA) believe that Julian Assange, as the spokesman for (and generally recognized leader of) WikiLeaks, should be prosecuted under the U.S. Espionage Act. But others, including U.S. Congressman Peter King (R-NY), have taken a different tack by arguing that WikiLeaks should be placed on the list of terrorist organizations that includes Al Qaeda. And some analysts have interpreted former U.S. Vice Presidential candidate Sara Palin's remarks as (effectively) calling for the assassination of Assange, when Palin suggested that Assange be treated the same as a high ranking member of Al Qaeda.

Should Assange be assassinated, as Palin and a few other conservative politicians in the United States seem to imply? Would that be ethically justifiable? And is Assange really a "high-tech terrorist," as U.S. Vice President Joseph Biden asserts? It would certainly be helpful if we could separate the rhetoric used by some political leaders from the "facts" (or descriptive accounts) of the WikiLeaks criminal case. What we do know so far is that Pfc. Bradley Manning (U.S. Army), who was accused of leaking the sensitive military information to WikiLeaks, is facing a court martial at the time of this writing (March 2012) on 22 counts. Specific charges against him include downloading and sending a vast amount of diplomatic cables and sensitive documents to WikiLeaks. He is also being charged with indirectly aiding Al Qaeda. The U.S. military's prosecutors claim that the documents sent by Manning to WikiLeaks included "nearly half a million sensitive battlefield reports from Iraq and Afghanistan" as well as "hundreds of thousands of diplomatic cables" that WikiLeaks, in effect, shared with the world.[35]

Of course, the criminal charges that have been brought against Manning (for leaking sensitive military/national security information to WikiLeaks) are very different from the kinds of criminal charges being levied against the WikiLeaks organization itself for disseminating that information. In the remainder of this section, we limit our discussion to assessing the grounds (or lack thereof) for the criminal charges directed against WikiLeaks and Julian Assange.

Despite what would appear to be widespread international support for prosecuting Assange, some countries see the matter differently. For example, law enforcement authorities in Australia, where Assange is a citizen (but not currently residing), are not convinced that he has violated any Australian laws. Also, some U.S. legal scholars and analysts do not believe that WikiLeaks' activities qualify as criminal under American Law. Yochai Benkler, an eminent Harvard Law Professor, argues that "there is no sound Constitutional basis for a criminal prosecution of Assange" and that neither WikiLeaks nor Assange should be treated any differently than the *New York Times* (and its reporters). Benkler also believes that the reports issued by both the American news media and the U.S. government have dramatically overstated the extent of the "actual threat of WikiLeaks." He further argues that the vast overreaction by both groups has helped to frame and reinforce an image of Wikileaks as some kind of terrorist organization, as opposed to presenting an accurate picture of what the organization, in his view, is: a "journalistic enterprise."[36]

7.9.3 WikiLeaks and the Free Press

We next briefly consider the interests of the "free press" tradition in the dispute about whether it was legal to shut down WikiLeaks and to prosecute Assange. Benkler believes that WikiLeaks' activities were "fundamentally a moment of journalistic exposure," despite the fact that public and political response was, in his view, over-stated, overheated, and irresponsible. If Benkler is correct, then it would seem plausible to argue that the journalistic protections consonant with a free press should also apply to WikiLeaks. But some disagree that this organization's activities can be defended under the guise of "journalistic exposure," at least not in the traditional sense of that phrase. For example, Weineke (2010) argues that if WikiLeaks' motivation had been simply "to disseminate factual information," there would have been little distinction between an attempt to prosecute Assange or other WikiLeaks organizers and "more established media outlets" such as the *New York Times* and its journalists. Of course, a critic might point out that it was precisely the status of so-called "factual information" previously reported in the media that was being challenged in some of the leaked documents and reports. That critic might further point out that exposing (and correcting) false information previously reported in the press is an important part of "responsible journalism."

Can the WikiLeaks organization qualify as a traditional journalistic organization, in which case it would also qualify for the legal protections that apply to traditional journalists and their organizations? Benkler argues that WikiLeaks can best be under-stood as participating in a "joint venture" with "other traditional news organizations." In this role, Benkler believes that WikiLeaks has (whether intentionally or not) helped to form a new mode of journalism —i.e., one that cannot be adequately understood simply as a "traditional media organization." But we can still ask whether this "new" kind of media organization deserves the same legal protections that have been accorded to traditional media outlets and their journalists.

Benkler believes that there is a "difficult but important relationship" between the traditional media and the "new, networked media" that have now come together to characterize what he calls the "new media environment." This environment, Benkler points out, is much more global and diverse, and it also includes a wider "range of actors." And in response to the kinds of journalistic practices made possible by this new media environment, Benkler believes that we need a "reformed legal regime." He also believes that these laws are needed to protect forms of "unpopular speech" that otherwise would not be able to be expressed in this new environment.

We conclude this section by noting that the WikiLeaks controversy seems far from settled. We also note that there are aspects of this controversy that could not be examined in this chapter. For example, we did not consider WikiLeaks vis-à-vis concerns affecting national security, as issues affecting that topic were examined in Chapter 6. While it may be difficult to defend the view that Wikileaks should be rewarded for "exposing corruption around the world," as some proponents seem to suggest, it also not clear that "vigilante groups" that support the U.S. government's concerns—e.g., some private commercial organizations—should be encouraged to continue their efforts to shut down WiKiLeaks by launching DDoS attacks on that organization's Web site. And even if international law enforcement agencies succeed in permanently shutting down WikiLeaks, other like-minded Web sites will probably emerge sooner or later. In the meantime, however, it would seem prudent to follow Benkler's advice as far as gaining a better understanding of what constitutes the new media environment for journalism, so that we can enact the appropriate legislation that may be needed.

▶ 7.10 CHAPTER SUMMARY

In this chapter, we examined crimes involving cybertechnology. We considered arguments as to whether a profile for a typical cybercriminal could be constructed and whether a reasonable distinction could be drawn between hacking and cracking. We also questioned whether "hacking back" or counter hacking is ever morally permissible. We then drew a distinction between "genuine" cybercrimes and cyber-related crimes and considered some examples of each type. We also considered some roles that biometric technologies can play in assisting law enforcement to combat crime in cyberspace. Next, we identified and briefly described some international laws that have been enacted in response to criminal activities involving cybertechnology. Finally, we described problems that the WikiLeaks controversy poses for both understanding and prosecuting international cybercrimes where journalistic interests involving a free press are at stake.

It is important to note that many cyber-related crimes were either not examined, or not discussed in the detail they would seem to deserve, in this chapter. Our intent here was to clear up some conceptual confusion about the way that many of the crimes involving cybertechnology are analyzed, rather than to provide an exhaustive analysis of cyber-related crimes. As a result, very little was said about crimes affecting software piracy, spam, sexting, online child pornography, etc.—all of which use cybertechnology at some level. These topics are discussed in detail in appropriate sections of later chapters. For example, criminal aspects of software piracy are examined in our discussion of intellectual property in Chapter 8. Issues affecting spam, child pornography, and sexting are discussed in our examination of regulatory challenges affecting cyberspace in Chapter 9.

▶ REVIEW QUESTIONS

1. How did the popular media's portrayal of computer-related crimes carried out in the 1970s and 1980s romanticize the behavior of some individuals who engaged in these activities?
2. Can we construct a profile of a "typical cybercriminal"?
3. Why do many in the computer community oppose the use of "hacker" to describe cybercriminals?
4. Can a meaningful distinction be drawn between hacking and "cracking"?
5. What is meant by "active defense hacking" or "counter hacking"?
6. Can this kind of hacking be justified on either legal or ethical grounds?
7. What are the objectives of the Certified Ethical Organization (CEH)?
8. Can CEH's practices be justified on ethical grounds, even if they happen to be legal?
9. What, exactly, is cybercrime?
10. How can a coherent definition of cybercrime be framed?
11. Identify and briefly describe the three categories of "genuine cybercrime" that we examined.
12. How can we distinguish between genuine cybercrimes and "cyber-related" crimes?
13. How might we distinguish between cyber-related crimes that are "cyberexacerbated" and those that are "cyberassisted"?
14. What is identity theft, and how has it been exacerbated by cybertechnology?
15. What are biometric technologies, and how are they used in fighting cybercrime?
16. How have packet-sniffing programs and keystroke-monitoring technologies assisted law enforcement authorities in fighting cybercrime?
17. What is "entrapment on the Internet," and why has is it been controversial?
18. What is the Patriot Act, and why is it controversial?
19. What problems do issues of jurisdiction pose for understanding and prosecuting crimes committed in cyberspace?
20. What is WikiLeaks, and why is it controversial?

▶ DISCUSSION QUESTIONS

21. Recall the case of Internet entrapment involving pedophiles that we described in Section 7.7.1. Which arguments can be made in favor of entrapment and "sting operations" on the Internet? From a utilitarian perspective, entrapment might seem like a good thing because it may achieve desirable consequences. Should sting operations be used to lure pedophiles? Justify your position by appealing to one or more of the ethical theories described in Chapter 2.

22. Recall the distinctions that we drew between cyberspecific and cyber-related crimes. Why would cyberstalking be classified as a cyber-related crime, according to this distinction? Among cyber-related crimes, is it useful to distinguish further between cyberexacerbated and cyberassisted crimes? Why would cyberstalking also be categorized as a "cyberexacerbated," rather than a cyberassisted, crime? Why not simply call every crime in which cybertechnology is either used or present a cybercrime? Would doing so pose any problems for drafting coherent cybercrime legislation involving cybertechnology?

▶ ESSAY/PRESENTATION QUESTIONS

23. Assess arguments for and against the use of biometric technologies for security, especially in airports and large stadiums. Should biometric technologies such as face-recognition programs and iris scanners be used in public places to catch criminals? In the post-September 11 world, there is much more support for these technologies than there was when biometrics were used at Super Bowl XXXV in January 2001. Granted that such technologies can help the government to catch criminals and suspected terrorists, what kinds of issues do they raise from a civil liberties perspective? Compare the arguments for and against the use of biometric technologies in tracking down criminals to arguments we examined for and against computerized record matching in our discussion of privacy in Chapter 5. Do you support the use of biometrics in large, public gathering places? Defend your answer.

24. What implications does the conviction of the four cofounders of the Pirate Bay Web site (in 2009) have for international attempts to prosecute intellectual property crimes globally? Should the four men also have been required to stand trial in all of the countries in which copyrighted material had been downloaded from their Web site? Will the outcome of the Pirate Bay trial likely deter individuals and organizations, worldwide, from setting up future P2P sites that allow the illicit file sharing of copyrighted material?

Scenarios for Analysis

1. Your brother, Phil, is a sergeant in the U.S. Army. He has just returned home (on military leave) from his second tour of duty in Iraq, where he was part of a multi-nation security coalition (peace keeping force) during the transition period for a new government regime in that country. Phil's first tour in Iraq went relatively smoothly, but during his second tour he witnessed a tragic event involving "friendly fire" in his unit, which has since troubled him deeply. He tells you that three members of his platoon were killed by coalition forces as a result of mistaken identity, although the official report issued by the U.S. Army was that the three soldiers were killed by enemy combatants. Phil also tells you that he was advised by his close friends in the military not to report the truth about this incident to the press, for fear of possible retaliation by some of Phil's (Army) superiors. It turns out that you are aware of controversial journalistic/media outlet (similar to WikiLeaks) that accepts anonymous tips about incidents falsely reported by governments and military organizations around the world.

Phil has made it clear to you that he will not report the incident to the media outlet in question. However, you believe that the truth about the cover-up should be reported (while you also believe that your anonymity, as well as Phil's, should be protected). So, you seriously consider giving the information to this media outlet; but you also have some concerns about how the release of this information might adversely affect the families of the three victims, once the truth about their deaths is revealed. After much deliberation, you decide to send the information to the media organization through an "anonymous drop box." Later, you learn that this organization has been under criminal investigation for leaks of sensitive diplomatic and military information in the past. Even after learning this, you still believe that providing the information about the cover-up of the "friendly fire" incident to this organization was the right thing to do. Next, assume that that media organization releases the information about this incident and that it is subsequently charged with criminal behavior for doing so. Would it be appropriate for you to be considered an accessory to that crime? Explain.

2. In France and Germany, it is illegal to sell Nazi memorabilia (from the World War II era), as well as neo-Nazi items, on Web auction sites. In fact, France had a dispute with Yahoo, Inc. about this point in 2000, and Yahoo agreed to install filtering technology that would block access to information about these items on the Yahoo site in France (even though advertising and selling the same kinds of items on U.S. Web auction sites is legal). Your sister, Jane, has recently founded a new Web auction site in the United States, which, of course, will have to compete with well known sites such as eBay to succeed. Jane's newly launched auction site is eager to attract as much business as it can, as long as the items being traded on it are in compliance with U.S. law. Two potential clients, both of whom are U.S. citizens living in America, wish to auction some Nazi memorabilia and neo-Nazi items on this new site.

Initially, Jane is conflicted about what to do, but she is then informed by a few of her business associates that auctioning these items on Web sites in the United States is perfectly legal. Jane also realizes that if she turns down the prospective clients, they will only go elsewhere to a site that will list the items in question. What would you advise Jane to do in this case? Suppose her Web auction company decides to accept these items, and further suppose that they eventually end up for sale in Germany or France where they would have been acquired illegally? Would Jane and her online auction site bear any responsibility in aiding and abetting a crime in a country outside the United States?

▶ ENDNOTES

1. See, for example Ragan (2009), Feder (2009), and Aldhous and Reilly (2009).
2. Power (2000), p. 329.
3. Parker (1988), p. 142.
4. Some critics suggest that many of today's "computer heroes," including some successful entrepreneurs in the computer industry could also be accused of having been hackers in the past (see, for example, Jordan 2008).
5. Gotterbarn (1995), p. 19.
6. Leman-Langlois (2008), p. 1
7. My analysis of cybercrime in Sections 7.3 and 7.4 is adapted from Tavani (2004).
8. Forester and Morrison (1994), p. 29.
9. For example, Amy Boyer was murdered in 1999 by a cyberstalker, and Meghan Meier committed suicide in 2006 as a result of a cyberbullying incident.
10. Bocij (2004, p. 14) defines cyberstalking as a "group of behaviors in which an individual, group of individuals, or an organization uses information and communications technology to harass another individual, group of individuals, or organization."
11. Kowalski, Limber, and Agatston (2008, p. 1) define cyberbullying as "bullying through e-mail, instant messaging (IM), in a Chat Room, on a Web site, or through digital messages or images sent to a cellular phone."
12. See the argument by Grodzinsky and Tavani (2001) for why cyberstalking crimes do not qualify as "genuine cybercrimes."
13. Lininger and Vines (2005), p. 268.
14. For more detail, see the account of these incidents in Simon (2005).
15. Ibid.
16. Lininger and Vines (2005), p. 5.
17. Ibid, p. xxi.
18. For an interesting critique of this view, see Solove (2011).

19. This scenario is adapted from Tavani (1996).
20. For a critical analysis of computerized-matching techniques from the perspective of personal privacy, see Chapter 5.
21. Power (2000), p. 328.
22. See http://goliath.ecnext.com/coms2/gi_0199-657504/Protecting-the-zone-London-City.html.
23. See the account in Brey (2004).
24. See the Harris Interactive Poll taken in late September 2001.
25. Power (2000), p. 332.
26. See http://en.wikipedia.org/wiki/Carnivore_(FBI).
27. This scenario is based on an analysis of Internet entrapment issues in Sinnott-Armstrong (1999).
28. See the account of this in Michael Martinez, "To Catch a Predator: An Ethical Analysis of Sting Journalism." Available at http://www.michaelmartinez.org/document.pdf.
29. See http://www.fas.org/irp/agency/doj/fisa/.
30. See http://personalinfomediary.com/ECPAof1986_info.htm.
31. Critics note that many, possibly even most, crimes involving cybertechnology have involved neither terrorists nor members of organized crime syndicates. So, they ask whether the government should be permitted to use the same aggressive tactics that it claims are needed to counter terrorism and organized crime in catching lesser criminals who commit crimes that do not impact our security and safety as a nation.
32. For more information about online gambling, see Wikipedia. Available at http://en.wikipedia.org/wiki/Online_gambling.
33. The former G8 countries have since expanded to include Australia, Belgium, Spain, Switzerland, and others, and are now referred to as the G20.
34. See Jemima Kiss. "The Pirate Bay Trial: Guilty Verdict." *The Guardian*, April 17, 2009. Available at http://www.guardian.co.uk/technology/2009/apr/17/the-pirate-bay-trial-guilty-verdict.
35. See "Bradley Manning Hearing: Attorney Asks For Dismissal In WikiLeaks Case." *Huffington Post*, March 16, 2012. Available at http://www.huffingtonpost.com/2012/03/15/bradley-manning-trial-attorney-dismiss-case_n_1349309.html.
36. References to Benkler's views in the remaining sections of this chapter are from the transcript of his interview with June Wu, in *Harvard Law Today* (Wu 2011).

▶ REFERENCES

Aldhous, Peter, and Michael Reilly. 2009. "Special Investigation: How my Genome was Hacked."*New Scientist.* Available at http://www.newscientist.com/article/mg20127013.800-special-investigation-how-my-genome-was-hacked.html.

Benkler, Yochai. 2011. "A Free Irresponsible Press: Wikileaks and the Battle over the Soul of the Networked Fourth Estate." *Harvard Civil Rights—Civil Liberties Journal,* 46, 311.

Bocij, Paul. 2004. *Cyberstalking: Harassment in the Internet Age and How to Protect Your Family.* Westport, CT: Praeger.

Brey, Philip. 2004. "Ethical Aspects of Facial Recognition Systems in Public Places." In R. A. Spinello and H. T. Tavani, eds. *Readings in CyberEthics.* 2nd ed. Sudbury, MA: Jones and Bartlett, pp. 585–600.

Feder, Barnaby J. 2008. "A Heart Device Is Found Vulnerable to Hacker Attacks." *New York Times,* March 12. Available at http://www.nytimes.com/2008/03/12/business/12heart-web.html?_r=1.

Floridi, Luciano. 2010. "The Ethics of WikiLeaks." *Philosophy of Information.* Dec. 8. Available at http://thephilosophyofinformation.blogspot.com/2010/12/ethics-of-wikileaks.html.

Forester, Tom, and Perry Morrison. 1994. *Computer Ethics: Cautionary Tales and Ethical Dilemmas in Computing.* 2nd ed. Cambridge, MA: MIT Press.

Girasa, Roy J. 2002. *Cyberlaw: National and International Perspectives.* Upper Saddle River, NJ: Prentice Hall.

Gotterbarn, Don. 1995. "Computer Ethics: Responsibility Regained." In D. G. Johnson and H. Nissenbaum, eds. *Computers, Ethics, and Social Values.* Englewood Cliffs, NJ: Prentice Hall, pp. 18–24.

Grodzinsky, Frances S., and Herman T. Tavani. 2001. "Is Cyberstalking a Special Type of Computer Crime?" In T. W. Bynum, et al., eds. *Proceedings of the Fifth International Conference on the Social and Ethical Impacts of Information and Communications Technologies: Ethicomp 2001.* Vol. 2 Gdansk, Poland: Mikom Publishers, pp. 73–85.

Himanen, Pekka. 2001. *The Hacker Ethic: A Radical Approach to the Philosophy of Business.* New York: Random House.

Himma, Kenneth. 2004. "Targeting the Innocent: Active Defense and the Moral Immunity of Innocent Persons from Aggression." *Journal of Information, Communication, and Ethics in Society* 2, no. 1: 31–40.

Himma, Kenneth Einar. 2008. "Ethical Issues Involving Computer Security: Hacking, Hacktivism, and Counterhacking." In K. E. Himma and H. T. Tavani, eds. *The Handbook of Information and Computer Ethics.* Hoboken, NJ: John Wiley & Sons, pp. 191–217.

Jordan, Tim. 2008. *Hacking. Digital Media and Technological Determinism.* Malden, MA: Polity.

Kowalski Robin, M., Susan P. Limber, and Patricia W. Agaston. 2008. *Cyber Bullying*. Malden, MA: Blackwell.

Leman-Langlois, Stephane, ed. 2008. *Technocrime: Technology, Crime, and Social Control*. Portland, OR: Willan Publishing.

Lininger, Rachael, and Russell Dean Vines. 2005. *Phishing: Cutting the Identity Theft Line*. Indianapolis, IN: John Wiley and Sons.

Moor, James H. 2007. "What Is Computer Ethics?" In J. Weckert, ed. *Computer Ethics*. Aldershot, UK: Ashgate, pp. 31–40. Reprinted from *Metaphilosophy* 16, no. 4 (1985): 266–75.

Moore, Robert. 2011. *Cybercrime: Investigating High-Technology Cybercrime*. 2nd ed. Burlington, MA: Anderson Publishing.

Parker, Donn B. 1998. *Fighting Computer Crime: A Framework for Protecting Information*. New York: John Wiley and Sons.

Power, Richard. 2000. *Tangled Web: Tales of Digital Crime from the Shadows of Cyberspace*. Indianapolis, IN: Que Corp.

Ragan, Steve. 2009. "Facebook Accounts Hacked for $100." *The Tech Herald*. Sep. 18. Available at http://www.thetechherald.com/article.php/200938/4468/Facebook-accounts-hacked-for-100.

Sagiroglu, Seref, and Gurol Canbek. 2009. "Keyloggers: Increasing Threats to Computer Security and Privacy." *IEEE Technology and Society Magazine* 28, no. 3: 11–17.

Simon, Ellen. 2005. "Identities Get Harder to Keep." *The Nashua Telegraph*, 24, 14–15.

Simpson, Michael. 2006. *Hands-On Ethical Hacking and Network Defense*. Boston, MA: Thompson.

Sinnott-Armstrong, Walter. 1999. "Entrapment in the Net?" *Ethics and Information Technology* 1, no. 2: 95–104.

Solove, Daniel J. 2011. *Nothing to Hide: The False Tradeoff Between Privacy and Security*. New Haven, CT: Yale University Press.

Tavani, Herman T. 1996. "Computer Matching and Personal Privacy: Can They Be Compatible?" In C. Huff, ed. *Proceedings of the Symposium on Computers and the Quality of Life*. New York: ACM Press, pp. 97–101.

Tavani, Herman T. 2004. "Defining the Boundaries of Computer Crime: Piracy, Trespass, and Vandalism in Cyberspace." In R. A. Spinello and H. T. Tavani, eds. *Readings in CyberEthics*. 2nd ed. Sudbury, MA: Jones and Bartlett, pp. 513–24.

van der Ploeg, Irma. 1999. "The Illegal Body: Eurodac and the Politics of Biometric Identification." *Ethics and Information Technology* 1, no. 2, 295–302.

van der Ploeg, Irma. 2004. "Written on the Body: Biometrics and Identity." In R. A. Spinello and H. T. Tavani, eds. *Readings in CyberEthics*. 2nd ed. Sudbury, MA: Jones and Bartlett, pp. 571–84.

Wall, David S. 2007. *Cybercrime: The Transformation of Crime in the Information Age*. Malden, MA: Polity.

Weineke, David. 2010. "Is WikiLeaks Ethical, Criminal, or an Immune Nuisance?" *Useful Arts*. Dec 3. Available at http://usefularts.us/2010/12/03/is-wikileaks-ethical-criminal-or-an-immune-nuisance/.

Wu, June. 2011. Interview (with Yochai Benkler): "Benchler Argues Against the Prosecution of WikiLeaks." *Harvard Law Today*. Available at http://www.law.harvard.edu/news/2011/03/14_benkler-argues-against-prosecution-of-wikileaks.html.

▶ FURTHER READINGS

Brin, David. "Crime and Lawfulness in an Age of All-Seeing Techno-Humanity." In S. Leman-Langlois, ed. *Technocrime: Technology, Crime, and Social Control*. Portland, OR: Willan Publishing, 2008, pp. 14–26.

Easttom, Chuck, and Jeffrey Taylor, eds. *Computer Crime, Investigation, and the Law*. Boston, MA: Course Technology/Cengage. 2011.

Fairweather, N. Ben, and S. Rogerson. "Biometric Identification." *Journal of Information, Communication and Ethics in Society* 2, no. 1 (2004): 3–8.

Gagnon, Benoit. "Cyberwars and Cybercrimes." In S. Leman-Langlois, ed. *Technocrime: Technology, Crime, and Social Control*. Portland, OR: Willan Publishing, 2008, pp. 46–65.

Singel, Ryan. "National ID: Biometrics Pinned to Social Security Cards." In P. De Palma, ed. *Computers in Society 08/09*. New York: McGraw-Hill, 2008, pp. 48–49.

Schneir, Bruce. *Liars and Outliers: Enabling the Trust that Society Needs to Thrive*. Hoboken, NJ: John Wiley and Sons, 2012.

Willard, Nancy. *Cyber Bullying and Cyberthreats: Responding to the Challenge of Online Social Threats*. Eugene, OR: Center for Safe and Responsible Internet Use, 2006.

CHAPTER

8

Intellectual Property Disputes in Cyberspace

What, exactly, is intellectual property? And how should it be protected in cyberspace? These are two of the questions examined in Chapter 8. Other questions include the following:

- Should computer software be protected by copyright law as well as by patent law?
- How does the principle of fair use apply to proprietary information in digital format?
- What are the similarities and differences between the Free Software Movement and the Open Source Initiative (OSI)?
- What kinds of philosophical and legal arguments are used to justify protecting intellectual property?
- Do current intellectual property laws sufficiently balance the interests of the public good against those of individuals and corporations who own copyrights and hold patents?

The debate over intellectual property rights in cyberspace has become one of the defining ethical issues of the digital era. Deciding who should have ownership rights to, and thus control over, digitized information will ultimately determine who can and cannot access that form of information. Disputes about intellectual property rights in cyberspace range from claims pertaining to ownership of software programs to arguments about who has the right to distribute (or even make available for use) proprietary information on the Internet. Perhaps no property issue has been more contentious in the past decade than the question as to whether computer users should be able to freely download and exchange copyrighted music in the form of MP3 files.

▶ 8.1 WHAT IS INTELLECTUAL PROPERTY?

An adequate analysis of *intellectual property* issues requires that we first have an understanding of the concept of property in general. Like privacy, property is a complex notion that is not easy to define. Yet, as legal scholars and philosophers have pointed out, property laws and norms play a fundamental role in shaping a society and in preserving its legal order; that is, laws and norms involving property rights establish relationships between individuals, different sorts of objects, and the state. When discussing issues involving property, we tend to think of tangible items. Originally, property referred to land; however, it now also includes objects that an individual can own, such as an automobile, articles of clothing, or a stamp collection.[1]

However, many legal theorists and philosophers suggest that property should not be understood simply in terms of objects or things, but rather as a *relationship between individuals in reference to things*. Hence, there are three elements to consider:

1. an individual, X
2. an object, Y
3. X's relation to other individuals (A, B, C, etc.) in reference to Y.

In this sense, X (as the owner of property Y) can control Y relative to persons A, B, C, and so forth. So if Tom owns a Dell laptop computer, then he can control who has access to his computer and how it is used; for example, Tom has the right to exclude Mary from using the laptop computer, or, as its owner, he can grant her unlimited access to it. Ownership claims involving "intellectual objects" are similar in certain respects but are also less straightforward, in other respects, than claims involving the ownership of tangible objects.

8.1.1 Intellectual Objects

Some philosophers use the expression *intellectual objects* when referring to forms of intellectual property.[2] Unlike physical property, intellectual property consists of objects that are not tangible. These nontangible, or intellectual, objects represent literary/ creative works and inventions, which are the manifestations or expressions of ideas. Unlike tangible objects, which are exclusionary in nature, intellectual objects (e.g., software programs) are *nonexclusionary*: Consider once again Tom's laptop computer, which is a physical object. If Tom owns it, then Mary cannot own it, and vice versa. Tom's laptop is an exclusionary object. Next consider a word processing program that resides in Tom's computer. If Tom makes a copy of that program, then both Mary and Tom have copies of it. The word processing program is nonexclusionary.

Note that scarcity (which often causes competition and rivalry when applied to physical objects) need not exist in the case of intellectual objects, which can be easily reproduced. Note also that there are practical limitations to the number of physical objects one can own and that there are natural as well as political limitations to the amount of land that can be owned; however, countless digital copies of a software program can be produced and each at a relatively low cost.

Another feature that distinguishes intellectual objects from physical objects has to do with exactly what it is that one can lay legal claim to. One cannot own an idea in the same sense that one can own a physical object; ideas themselves are not the kinds of things for which governments are willing to grant ownership rights to individuals. As Adam Moore (2008) points out, ownership rights do not apply to an intellectual object as an "abstract physical entity" but rather to the control of "physical manifestations or expressions" of that object. In other words, legal protection is given only to the tangible *expression* of an idea that is creative or original.

For a literary or artistic idea to be protected it must be expressed (or "fixed") in some tangible medium such as a physical book or a sheet of paper containing a musical score. If the idea is functional in nature, such as an invention, it must be expressed as a machine or a process. Whereas authors are granted copyright protections for expressions of their literary ideas, inventors are given an incentive, in the form of a patent protection, for expressions of their functional ideas. Both copyright law and patent law, along with other legal schemes for protecting intellectual property, are discussed in detail in Sections 8.2 and 8.3.

8.1.2 Why Protect Intellectual Objects?

What is our basis for saying that intellectual property, or for that matter any kind of property, ought to be protected? One answer lies in our current system of laws. Of course, we could then further ask, On what philosophical grounds are our laws themselves based? In Section 8.5, we will see that in Anglo-American law the philosophical justification for granting property rights is generally grounded in two different theories about property. One theory is based on the rationale that a property right is a type of "natural right" that should be granted to individuals for the products that result from the labor expended in producing a creative work or a practical invention. The other theory is based on the notion that property rights themselves are not natural rights but rather social constructs designed to encourage creators and inventors to better serve society in general by bringing forth their creative works and practical inventions into the market-place. To encourage authors and inventors, utilitarians believe that it is necessary to grant them property rights in the form of limited monopolies that can result in financial advantages for them.

In many continental European countries, neither individual labor nor social utility are used as a justification for granting intellectual property rights and corresponding protections. Instead, creative works and inventions represent the expressions and personalities of their creators and inventors, who should, it is argued, have the right to determine how their works are displayed and distributed. This view is sometimes referred to as the personality theory of intellectual property. In Section 8.5, where we consider examples of each kind of property theory, we will see that some critics reject the notion that intellectual property rights should be extended to computer software.

Philosophers and legal theorists point out that the introduction of computer software has created questions regarding intellectual property laws for which there are no easy answers. Innovations in computer hardware, on the contrary, have clearly qualified for patent protection, and in this sense, computer hardware inventions are no different than other kinds of inventions involving physical objects. But questions about whether and how software, as a kind of intellectual object, should be protected have been vehemently debated in the courts.

8.1.3 Software as Intellectual Property

Is computer software a special kind of intellectual object that deserves both copyright and patent protection? Software, which consists of lines of programming code (or codified thought), is not exactly expressed, or "fixed," in a tangible medium as literary works are. To complicate matters, a program's code takes many forms: source code, object code, and the final executable code. Because of conceptual muddles and confusions surrounding the nature of programming code, computer programs were not, initially, eligible for either copyright or patent protection. Eventually, however, they were granted both forms of legal protection. Although software programs seem to be like inventions that could be patented, they also resemble algorithms, which, like mathematical ideas or "mental steps," are not typically eligible for patent protection.

Initially, software was not conceived of as a distinct commodity, since computer corporations tended to bundle together their software and hardware offerings as part of a single package. But Grodzinsky, Miller, and Wolf (2004) note that in the late 1960s, IBM adopted a new marketing policy that separated software (and services) from hardware, which also suggested the need for "closed source software" so that its programming division could be profitable. Grodzinsky et al. also note that the practice of separating these components became further entrenched when IBM contracted with Intel and Microsoft to develop the personal computer in 1981. However, in the early 1970s, AT&T Bell Laboratories in New Jersey decided to make the source code for one of its software products "open" or freely accessible. AT&T gave away the source code and licenses for its Unix operating system to universities.[3] So two very different strategies emerged in the 1970s with respect to whether software code should be protected as proprietary information.

As late as the 1970s and early 1980s, software programs and software code were often freely exchanged among computer enthusiasts without concern for copyright law. I worked in the software industry in the early 1980s, and I recall incidents where software developers freely exchanged with each other copies of programs on which they were working: A software developer might lend a fellow developer a copy of a database program in return for a copy of a word processing program. (As we will see in our discussion of the Free Software Movement and the Open Source Initiative in Section 8.6, some programmers believe that these kinds of exchanges actually improved the quality of the software products that eventually went to market.) By the mid-1980s, the cavalier attitude that once surrounded the exchange of software programs had changed considerably, and by the 1990s, software companies carefully guarded their proprietary software, sometimes to the point of encouraging law enforcement officials to raid private homes where they suspected that unauthorized software was being used.

Some people believe that a distinction should be drawn between an individual's unauthorized copying of a friend's software program for personal use and the pirating of software in a systematic way for profit by corporations and criminals. The economic impact of systematic software piracy by organizations is far more significant than the impact of a few individuals copying their friends' programs. From a moral point of view, however, if unauthorized copying of proprietary software is wrong, then it is just as wrong for individuals as it is for organizations interested in profiting from it.

8.1.4 Evaluating an Argument for Why It is Wrong to Copy Proprietary Software

Why, exactly, is the unauthorized copying of proprietary software morally wrong? The software industry has made the following kind of argument:

PREMISE 1. Stealing a tangible object is morally wrong.

PREMISE 2. Making an unauthorized copy of a proprietary software program is identical to stealing a tangible object.

CONCLUSION. Making an unauthorized copy of a proprietary software program is morally wrong.

If we apply the rules for logical validity that we examined in Chapter 3, we see that this argument is valid because of its logical form—in other words, if Premises 1 and 2 are both assumed to be true, the conclusion cannot be false. Even though the argument's form is valid, however, we could still show the argument to be unsound if either or both of the premises are false. (You may want to review the rules for valid and sound arguments in Chapter 3.)

Premise 1 is fairly straightforward, and few would question its truth. But Premise 2 is more controversial and thus we can question whether it is empirically true. For example, is duplicating a software program *identical* to stealing a physical item? We noted that intellectual objects, such as software programs, are nonexclusionary, which means that my having a copy of Program X does not exclude you from also having a copy of that program, and vice versa. The computer hardware on which that software program runs—e.g., my laptop computer—is exclusionary in the sense that if I own it, you do not, and vice versa. So, the act of your making an unauthorized copy of the proprietary software program that resides on my laptop computer is *not* identical to your stealing my (physical) computer, in at least one important sense. Because the truth of Premise 2 is questionable, we cannot infer that the above argument (in its present form) is sound.

Even if the original argument turns out to be unsound, however, it does not follow that its conclusion is false. Note that the conclusion—"Making unauthorized copies of a proprietary software program is morally wrong"—could be true for reasons other than those stated in the original argument's premises. In fact, there could be several reasons why the conclusion can be true, despite the fact that the second premise may be false. For example, even if duplicating software is not identical to stealing physical property, we can show that it may cause harm. Consider that copying the proprietary software program, like the theft of someone's physical property, deprives the property owner of the legitimate use of his or her property. If someone steals my laptop, he deprives me of my right to use a device that I own; similarly, when someone makes an unauthorized copy of a proprietary program that I own (as the copyright holder), he deprives me of income to which I am entitled. Richard Spinello (2008) argues that unauthorized copying is harmful because it is a misuse, misappropriation, or "unfair taking" of another person's property against the property owner's will.

But some still might object by claiming that while an individual programmer, who is self-employed, may be harmed by the unauthorized copying of his program, most proprietary software programs are owned by wealthy corporations; for instance, they might argue that Microsoft is so well-off that it will not suffer if it loses the revenue from a few sales of its Word program. However, you can probably see the danger that might result if everyone used this line of reasoning. (Recall our discussion of the Slippery Slope

Fallacy in Chapter 3.) Thus, the unauthorized copying of software can be shown to be morally wrong, independent of whether it has a negative financial impact for the company that has ownership rights to the program.

Many nations have enacted specific laws and statutes to protect the rights and interests of "owners" of computer software programs and applications (as forms of intellectual property). We examine four different types of schemes for protecting intellectual property rights: copyright law, patents, trademarks, and trade secrets.

▶ 8.2 COPYRIGHT LAW AND DIGITAL MEDIA

Legal scholars trace the development of Anglo-American copyright law to a response to the widespread publishing of pamphlets made possible by the printing press. On the one hand, the British monarchy wanted to control the spread of "subversive" and "heretical" works that were being printed. On the other hand, authors had a vested interest in protecting their works from unauthorized reproduction. The English Statute of Anne, enacted in 1710, was the first law to give protection to authors for works attributed to them. The American colonies followed English law regarding copyright; the Framers later included these ideas in Article 1, Section 8, of the U.S. Constitution:

> The congress shall have the power . . . to promote the Progress of Science and the useful Arts, by securing for limited Times to authors and inventors the exclusive Rights to their respective Writings and Discoveries.

8.2.1 The Evolution of Copyright Law in the United States

The first copyright law in the United States, enacted in 1790, applied primarily to books, maps, and charts. As newer forms of media were developed, it was extended to include photography, movies, and audio recordings. In 1909, the copyright law was amended to include any form that could be seen and read visually by humans; this modification was motivated by a new technology (namely, the player piano) in which a song could be copied onto a perforated roll. Since the musical copy could not be read from the piano roll visually (by humans), the copy was not considered a violation of the song's copyright. The "machine readable" vs. "human readable" distinction has implications for decisions as to whether software programs qualify for copyright protection: Although a program's source code can be read by humans, its executable code, which runs on a computer, cannot. Beginning in the 1960s, arguments were made that computer programs, or at least parts of computer programs, should be eligible for copyright protection.

The Copyright Act was amended in 1980 to address the status of software programs, and the concept of a literary work was extended to include programs, computers, and "databases that exhibit authorship." The amendment defined a computer program as "a set of statements or instructions to be used directly in a computer in order to bring about certain results." To obtain a copyright for a computer program, however, its author had to show that the program contained an original expression (or arrangement) of ideas and not simply the ideas themselves.[4]

In 1998, two important amendments were made to the Copyright Act: the Sonny Bono Copyright Term Extension Act (SBCTEA) and the Digital Millennium Copyright Act (DMCA). The SBCTEA extended the length of copyright protection from the life of the author plus 50 years to the life of the author plus 70 years. Protection for works of hire produced before 1978 were extended from 75 to 95 years. (When an author receives payment from a corporation or organization to produce a creative or artistic work, it can be considered a work of hire.) Critics of the SBCTEA noted that the law was passed just in time to keep Mickey Mouse from entering the public domain, and they also pointed out that the Disney Corporation lobbied very hard for the passage of this act.

The DMCA has also been severely criticized—not because it extends the amount of time that a copyrighted work is protected, but because of the manner in which copyrights are extended. For example, Henderson, Spinello, and Lipinski (2007) point out that DMCA's critics identify three areas of controversy that need to be addressed: its "chilling effect" on *fair use*, its suppression of *innovation*, and its *overreach*. (We examine each of these points in later sections of this chapter.) Many critics also believe that these controversies are, in turn, closely linked to DMCA's highly controversial anticircumvention clause, which prohibits the development of any software or hardware technology that *circumvents* (or devises a technological workaround) to copyrighted digital media.

DMCA laws have also been passed at the state level. These laws, sometimes called "Super-DMCA" or "S-DMCA," have been very controversial because some are interpreted as exceeding the conditions specified in the federal DMCA. Critics, including the Electronic Frontier Foundation (EFF), argue that the Motion Picture Association of America (MPAA) has been pressing states to pass S-DMCA-type legislation that is aimed at criminalizing the possession of what the MPAA calls "unlawful communication and access devices." EFF also believes that this legislation would constitute "an unprecedented attack on the rights of technologists, hobbyists, tinkerers and the public at large."[5]

8.2.2 The Fair-Use and First-Sale Provisions of Copyright Law

To balance the exclusive controls given to copyright holders against the broader interests of society, two provisions have been developed: *fair use* and *first sale*. According to the fair-use principle, every author or publisher may make limited use of another person's copyrighted work for purposes such as criticism, comment, news, reporting, teaching, scholarship, and research. This principle is important to the computer industry in particular, and to engineering in general, because it supports the practice of "reverse engineering," which allows someone to buy a product for the purpose of taking it apart to see how it works.[6]

Another balancing scheme in copyright law is the first-sale provision, which applies once the original work has been sold for the first time. At this point, the original owner loses rights over the previously protected work. For example, once you purchase a copy of a (physical) book, you are free to give away, resell, or even destroy your copy. It is not clear, however, that one can give away media in digital format that is licensed for use but not, strictly speaking, owned by a user.

Critics believe that the fair-use provision of copyright law is threatened by both SBCTEA and DMCA. Some believe that SBCTEA threatens fair use because it has delayed many proprietary works from entering the public domain and being freely available for general use. Critics argue that the DMCA also has serious implications for the fair-use principle, mainly because its anticircumvention clause makes it illegal to reverse engineer a competitor's product to see how it works. Innovators and competitors have depended on the use of reverse engineering, which has been protected by the

Copyright Act's fair-use principle. The DMCA also has implications for the first-sale provision because works formatted in digital media are typically licensed by a user rather than purchased and owned by a consumer.

We next consider two scenarios that illustrate some concerns affecting the fair-use and first-sale provisions of the current copyright law. The first scenario demonstrates one way in which the SBCTEA threatens access to older books about to enter the public domain. The second scenario illustrates how the DMCA threatens our ability to use e-books in the same way that we have been able to use physical books.

▶ **SCENARIO 8–1:** Making Classic Books Available Online

Eric Eldred operated a personal, nonprofit Web site on which he included electronic versions of classic books that are in the public domain. While helping his daughters locate some older and out-of-print books for a high school literature project, Eldred discovered that it was difficult to find electronic versions of books such as *The Scarlet Letter*, so he decided to set up a Web site (www.eldritchpress.org) dedicated to online versions of older books. He included on his site, for example, the complete works of Nathaniel Hawthorne. Legally, Eldred was allowed to include electronic versions of these books on his site because their copyright protection had expired. But with the passage of SBCTEA in 1998, some of the books that were about to enter the public domain (and would thus be eligible for inclusion on Eldred's site) would instead remain under copyright protection. Eldred decided to challenge the legality of the amended Copyright Act, which he argued is incompatible with the fair-use provision and in violation of Article 1, Section 8, Clause 8, of the U.S. Constitution (see the opening of Section 8.4). His court challenge (*Eldred v. Attorney General John Ashcroft*) was turned down by a U.S. circuit court.[7] ■

Eldred appealed his case to the Supreme Court, and some of his advocates believed that the circuit court's decision might be overturned. In 2003, however, the high court upheld the lower court's decision in a 7–2 ruling.

▶ **SCENARIO 8–2:** Decrypting Security on an e-Book Reader

Dimitri Sklyarov, a Russian citizen, was arrested by U.S. federal agents in 2001 while attending a computer security conference in Las Vegas. Sklyarov had in his possession a copy of a program he had written to decrypt the code for the book-reading software developed by Adobe. (At that time, Adobe's Acrobat e-Book Reader software enabled computer users to read digital books, available online for a fee.) Adobe was concerned that with Sklyarov's program, users would be able to read e-books for free. However, the U.S. government seemed more interested in arresting Sklyarov in order to test the controversial anticircumvention clause of the DMCA, which had been enacted in 1998 but was not enforceable until 2000.[8] ■

Sklyarov's arrest caused considerable controversy and protest, especially in the software engineering community, where there was concern that the principle of fair use was being threatened by Adobe's e-book-reading technology. This technology could also be seen as threatening the principle of first sale. Consider that in the case of a physical (i.e., "paper and glue") book, one can do whatever one wishes after purchasing it. For example, one can give the book to a friend. Also, one can resell that book, in compliance with the first-sale provision of copyright law. The same is not true, however, of e-books, because the digitized information contained in those books cannot be subsequently exchanged without permission of the copyright holder. Note, for example, that if you own a Kindle (or some competitor to this e-book reader) and you purchase an e-book, you have the right to read that book but not to legally exchange the book with a friend in the same way that you could a physical book.

8.2.3 Software Piracy as Copyright Infringement

With the proliferation of personal computers in the 1980s, many users discovered how easy it was to duplicate software; but as we saw in Chapter 1, there was some legitimate confusion during that period as to whether it was legal to make a copy of someone else's software program. So, a policy vacuum existed with respect to copying proprietary software for personal use. This "vacuum" arose, in large part, because of certain confusions or conceptual muddles in our understanding of software. Earlier in this chapter, we noted that in the 1970s and early 1980s, software developers sometimes shared and exchanged programs with one another, and that by the late 1980s, many software companies had become extremely zealous when it came to protecting their proprietary software.

Software manufacturers, who claim to have lost millions of dollars of potential revenue because of software piracy, seem justified in their concerns regarding the pirating of proprietary software by individuals and organizations, both nationally and globally. However, some critics have argued that claims made by American software manufacturers about their loss of revenue due to the use of pirated software in developing countries are either greatly exaggerated or altogether bogus. They point out that many people and organizations in those countries could not afford to pay the prices set by American software companies for their products, so the companies have not lost any (real) revenues, because their (expensive, by American standards) software would not sell on the open market in most developing countries.

Software companies also worry about revenues lost in developed nations, including the United States, due to the illegal copying of software. Corporations such as Microsoft have been far more concerned with piracy as a form of organized crime, both domestically and internationally, than they have been about individuals making occasional unauthorized copies of their proprietary software. From a financial point of view, it would seem to make perfectly good sense for Microsoft to allow some illicit copying of its software by individuals rather than spend money to pursue their arrest and prosecution. However, many corporations have been quite willing to pursue those who engage in software piracy for commercial gain. And corporations have been especially concerned about the ways that their proprietary information can be pirated over a computer network. As we saw in Chapter 7, cyberpiracy applies to more than the mere unauthorized copying of software; it also covers the unauthorized distribution (or facilitation of the distribution) of digital information on a computer network. The software industry confronted this phenomenon for the first time in 1994 in an incident involving Robert LaMacchia, then a student at MIT.

LaMacchia operated an online forum at MIT called Cynosure. He invited Cynosure's users to upload and download (for free) copyrighted software to and from an anonymous server that resided in Finland. LaMacchia was arrested on charges that he had pirated software, but since he did not make unauthorized copies of the proprietary software, and since he did not receive a fee for his services, law enforcement authorities had a difficult time bringing piracy charges against him. In fact, they had a difficult time finding any clear criminal grounds for prosecuting LaMacchia at that time—there were no explicit provisions in the 1986 Computer Fraud and Abuse Act (see Chapter 7) under which he could be prosecuted. Eventually, federal authorities decided to bring charges against him by appealing to the Wire Fraud Act, a federal statute. Charges against LaMacchia were eventually dropped, however, and the indictment was officially struck down by a district judge who ruled that any criminal copyright charge must be brought under copyright laws and not under general federal criminal laws.[9]

The software industry followed the case closely, and, not surprisingly, was disappointed with the outcome. It had hoped that a conviction in the LaMacchia case would set a clear precedent. In the aftermath of this incident, however, the 1986 Computer Fraud and Abuse Act was amended to broaden the scope of criminal behavior that could be prosecuted under it, and the No Electronic Theft (NET) Act was passed in 1997, criminalizing the "dissemination" of copyrighted information by electronic means. While many agree with the spirit of the NET Act, some also believe that it went too far. Prior to the NET Act, a person had to "infringe a copyright willfully" and for "purposes of commercial or financial gain" in order to be punished under the criminal provisions of the Copyright Act. The NET Act, however, has made criminal the reproduction or distribution, including by electronic means, of one or more copyrighted works, which have a total retail value of more than $1,000.[10]

Andrew Grosso (2000) has argued that the meaning of copyright infringement was "expanded" under the Net Act. He points out that a copyright infringement can now occur either in fixation (in print or paper) or in virtual space, that is, by means of a mere electronic distribution, regardless of whether the copyrighted work is ever printed on paper or downloaded on to a disk, etc. According to the NET Act, merely viewing a copyrighted work posted on the Internet can be interpreted as a criminal violation of copyright. One possible interpretation is that "fixation" occurs in online viewing, because a temporary copy is "fixed" in the memory (i.e., in RAM) of the host computer, no matter how briefly the information is stored there.

8.2.4 Napster and the Ongoing Battles over Sharing Digital Music

In some ways, the LaMacchia incident foreshadowed many issues in the highly publicized Napster case. Although Napster provided a distribution center for proprietary digital information, it did not facilitate the distribution of software. Napster's users exchanged copyrighted music files, in MP3 format, with one another. In December 1999, the Recording Industry Association of America (RIAA) sued the Napster Web site for illegally distributing copyrighted music on the Internet. Napster responded by arguing that its activities were perfectly legal under the fair-use doctrine. However, the courts ultimately ruled against Napster.[11] Although the original Napster site ceased operations, it later reopened as a pay-per-song Web site, similar to iTunes, in cooperation with the RIAA.

The Napster controversy was just the beginning of an ongoing battle involving the recording industry and file-sharing sites over the unauthorized exchange of proprietary music online. Internet music providers such as Morpheus, KaZaA, and LimeWire have also supported the online exchange of MP3 files containing copyrighted music. Initially, they were able to avoid the plight of Napster, which used a centralized distribution point consisting of a centralized server, index, and registry of names in the file-exchange process. The later file-sharing services used either decentralized or "supernode" systems, based on peer-to-peer (P2P) technologies developed by Gnutella. As P2P file-sharing sites have evolved, they have become increasingly decentralized.

Spinello (2008) notes that the methods for indexing the files that are exchanged in P2P systems comprise three categories: (a) a centralized indexing system (such as in the original Napster site), (b) a decentralized indexing system, and (c) a supernode system (where a group of computers can act as indexing servers). Another P2P protocol is Bit Torrent, which enables large files, such entire music CDs, to be exchanged more efficiently through a system of networked computers designated as "peers" and "seeds." Whereas KaZaA used the supernode system, the Pirate Bay service used the Bit Torrent protocol. (We briefly examined the outcome of the trial involving the Pirate Bay site in Chapter 7.)

The recording industry, in its effort to crack down on illicit file sharing, has not been deterred by the fact that later P2P systems were able to avoid the legal pitfalls surrounding the centralized indexing method used by Napster. Alternatively, the recording industry employed some new strategies and techniques in the ongoing battle with file-sharing sites. For example, it began to track down individuals that it suspected of exchanging proprietary music online. In 2003, the recording industry issued court subpoenas to Internet service providers (ISPs) such as Comcast and Verizon, as well as to major universities, for the names of users who it suspected of downloading and exchanging large volumes of copyrighted music via those online services. While many ISPs and universities complied with the recording industry's request, Verizon challenged the RIAA in court on the grounds that complying with such requests violated specific articles of the U.S. Constitution (*Verizon v. RIAA*, 2003). Since that time, most universities have developed strict policies that prohibit the use of their networks to exchange copyrighted music; some have even disabled their P2P file-sharing systems altogether.[12]

The recording industry has also taken other tacks in its efforts to deter the unauthorized sharing of copyrighted music files online. For example, one way it fought back was by uploading "corrupted" music files onto the popular P2P sites, so that users downloading these files would be discouraged from using those sites again. And in what could be viewed as an even more aggressive attempt to prevent students from freely downloading copyrighted music on university campuses, the RIAA tried to tie the unauthorized downloading of files by college students to a loss of financial aid. Legislation introduced in 2007 to amend and extend the Higher Education Bill of 1965 included the controversial Section 494, entitled Campus-based digital theft prevention. Kalara (2007) points out that under this controversial section of the bill, eligible institutions that participate in the federal aid program would be required to provide "annual disclosure/ warnings to the students applying for or receiving financial aid," which inform them that "P2P file sharing may subject them to civil and criminal liability." The bill also would require that the universities offer subscription services to their student bodies, giving them an alternative to illegal file sharing. This legislation was opposed by the American Association of Universities, who worried that many innocent students could be deprived of financial aid, if universities did not comply.[13]

The debate over sharing copyrighted material in P2P systems has not been limited to copyrighted music files. The motion picture industry has also been concerned about the ease with which copyrighted movies can be freely exchanged in file-sharing systems. In 2003, Metro-Goldwyn-Mayer (MGM) Studies Inc. sued two P2P file-sharing services.

▶ **SCENARIO 8–3:** The Case of *MGM v. Grokster*

MGM and several music and motion picture studios sued Grokster (and Morpheus, who was owned by Streamcast) for "contributory copyright infringement" through its file-sharing service. MGM claimed that over 90% of the material exchanged on Grokster was copyrighted material and that the P2P service was legally liable. A district court disagreed with MGM, ruling that Grokster could not be held liable for the distribution of copyrighted material for two reasons: (a) it lacked sufficient knowledge of the infringement and (b) it did not "materially contribute" to it. MGM then appealed the decision to the Ninth Circuit Court of Appeals, which upheld the lower court's decision. Next, MGM appealed to the U.S. Supreme Court. In their deliberations, the justices considered two key principles that seemed to be in conflict: (i) the need to "protect new technologies" (such as P2P networks) and (ii) the need to provide "remedies against copyright infringement." Although the Court was unable to reach consensus on whether Grokster should be protected from liability for copyright infringement, it unanimously confirmed that using Grokster's service for exchanging copyrighted material is illegal.[14] ∎

A central argument made by Grokster in the MGM case involved a precedent from *Sony Corp of America v. Universal City Studios Inc.* (1984), which had to resolve whether it is legal to prohibit the use of technology merely because it *could* result in copyright infringement. In that case, Universal sued to ban the sale of video recorder (VCR) technology, claiming that Sony, who manufactured the Betamax home video recorder (a rival of later VHS-based recording devices), was liable for copyright infringement, either directly or indirectly, because the new technology could be used to make illegal copies of movies. Sony argued, however, that people who used VCR machines could record movies already being televised at a certain time and then view those movies at their own convenience.

By a very narrow decision—one decided by a 5–4 vote—the Supreme Court ruled in favor of Sony. (It is very difficult to imagine the consequences for both the entertainment industry and consumers if the decision had gone the other way.) The Court ruled that simply because VCR technology could be used to do something illegal is not sufficient grounds for banning that technology. In essence, it concluded that as long as the technology was capable of "substantial noninfringing uses" (SNIU), it could not be barred from sale and distribution. So, in effect, the Court also determined that VCRs did not violate copyright law merely because they were capable of substantial copyright infringement. (This interpretation has since come to be known as the "Sony Safe Harbor" precedent.) The courts have since been reluctant to ban or limit the use of technological advances because of this precedent. And since P2P networks are considered a "technological advance" that is capable of SNIU, they would seem to fall under the Sony precedent (Samuelson 2004).

As previously noted, MGM argued that 90% of the material exchanged on Grokster's P2P system was copyrighted material; they also argued that this clearly met the threshold of substantial copyright infringement. In this sense, MGM seemed to be challenging the legitimacy of the Sony safe harbor precedent itself. But the Supreme Court justices were careful not to appeal to the Sony precedent in their ruling, which disagreed with the lower courts. Instead they found Grokster liable for "inducing" copyright infringement through their practices such as advertising; but the Court did not rule that P2P technology itself violated copyright law. So some legal analysts such as Pamela Samuelson (2005) believe that MGM did not get the victory in court that it sought, even though Grokster was forced to pay $50 million to the music and recording industries.

▶ 8.3 PATENTS, TRADEMARKS, AND TRADE SECRETS

We noted earlier that in addition to copyright law, three alternative legal frameworks have been devised to protect intellectual property: patents, trademarks, and trade secrets. We examine examples of each form of protection with respect to how each can be applied to cybertechnology.

8.3.1 Patent Protections

A patent is a form of legal protection given to individuals who create an invention or process. Unlike copyright protection, patents offer a 20-year exclusive monopoly over an expression or implementation of a protected work. Patent protection can be applied to inventions and discoveries that include "utilitarian or functional" devices such as machines and "articles of manufacture." Patent law requires that inventions satisfy three conditions: (i) usefulness, (ii) novelty, and (iii) nonobviousness.

First, an invention must have a certain *usefulness*, or utility, in order to be awarded a patent; inventing a machine or process that does nothing "useful" would not merit its inventor a patent. Also, the invention must be *novel*, or new, in order to qualify for a patent. One cannot simply modify an existing invention and expect to be granted a patent for it; the modification would have to be significant enough to make a qualified difference. Finally, the invention or process must be *nonobvious*.[15] For example, it is possible that no one has yet recorded directions for how to travel from Buffalo, New York, to Cleveland, Ohio, through Pittsburgh, Pennsylvania, but describing the route would not satisfy the condition of nonobviousness.

Although computer hardware inventions clearly satisfied the requirements of patent law, this was not initially the case with computer software. John Snapper (1995) points out that in the 1960s, most of the discussion involving the protection of software focused on patents. He also notes that in a series of decisions beginning with *Gotshalk v. Benson* (1972), the U.S. Patent Office and the courts established a strong opposition to patenting software. Benson applied for a patent for an algorithm that translated the representation of numbers from base 10 to base 2; such an algorithm is an important feature of all programs. So, critics worried that if Benson had been granted a patent for his algorithm, he would have controlled almost every computer in use for a number of years.

However, Benson was denied the patent because his algorithm was viewed as an abstract process or mathematical formula that could be performed by a series of mental steps with the aid of pencil and paper (Snapper 1995). But the goal of obtaining patents for computer programs did not end with Benson. And in 1981, the U.S. Supreme Court ruled in what many now consider a landmark case for patents affecting computer software: *Diamond v. Deihr*.

In that pivotal case, the Supreme Court decided 5–4 that a patent could be awarded for a computer program under certain conditions; in this instance, the program assisted in converting rubber into tires. On the one hand, Deihr had developed a new process that physically transformed raw rubber into rubber tires; on the other hand, Deihr had only a new computer program, since every other part of the machinery used in the conversion process consisted of traditional technology. Initially, Deihr's request for a patent was denied by Diamond, the director of the Patent Office. But Deihr appealed, and his case was eventually heard by the Supreme Court, which ruled in Deihr's favor. However, in their ruling, the justices also continued to affirm the view that computer algorithms themselves are not patentable. They pointed out that the patent awarded to Deihr was not for the computer program but for the rubber tire transformation process as a whole.[16]

Since the Deihr case, numerous patents have been granted to computer programs and software applications. Some fear that now patent protection has gone too far. Gregory Aharonian (2001) points out that between 1990 and 1999, the number of patents increased from 1,300 to 22,500; and between 1993 and 1999, the number of patents issued increased tenfold. He also points out that between 1979 and 1999, more than 700,000 patents were issued for electronics inventions, including software products.

8.3.2 Trademarks

A trademark is a word, name, phrase, or symbol that identifies a product or service. In 1946, the Lanham Act, also referred to as the Trademark Act, was passed to provide protection for registered trademarks.[17] To qualify for a trademark, the "mark" is supposed to be distinctive. Consider, for example, the apple that has come to symbolize Apple and Macintosh computers and products. As Debora Halbert (1999) notes, however, the trademark "uh-huh," which is not very "distinctive," was granted to Pepsi-Cola. Because of decisions such as this, critics have argued that trademark protections are being expanded in ways that are inappropriate.

Consider the following example, which may support the view that some entrepreneurs have tried to expand the scope of trademark protection inappropriately. America Online (AOL) applied for trademarks for its expressions "You've Got Mail," "Buddy List," and "IM" (Instant Messenger). If AOL had been allowed to own these trademarks, other ISPs that used these or very similar expressions could have been sued for infringing on AOL's registered trademarks. So, AT&T decided to challenge AOL. In this case, the court ruled that the expressions were not unique to AOL.[18]

We briefly examine some additional issues affecting trademarks in cyberspace in Chapter 9, where we consider the process used to register Internet domain names.

8.3.3 Trade Secrets

A *trade secret* consists of information that is highly valuable and considered crucial in the operation of a business or other enterprise. The "secret" is accessible to only a few select individuals within the organization. Trade secrets can be used to protect formulas (such as the one used by Coca-Cola) and blueprints for future projects. They can also protect chemical compounds and processes used in manufacturing. Owners of a trade secret have exclusive rights to make use of it, but they have this right only as long as the secret is maintained.[19]

One problem with protecting trade secrets is that trade secret law is difficult to enforce at the international level. Not only have corporate spies in the United States tried to steal secrets from their corporate rivals, but there is evidence to suggest that international industrial espionage has become a growing industry. The TRIPS

(Trade Relationship Aspects of Intellectual Property Standards) agreement, which was part of the WIPO (World Intellectual Property Organization) agreements, includes a provision for protecting trade secrets at the international level; specifically, Article 39 of the TRIPS agreement protects trade secrets by stating explicitly that disclosure of trade secrets comes within the meaning of unfair competition in the global community.[20] (Both WIPO and TRIPS are described in detail in Section 8.4.)

Of course, protecting trade secrets is not something that is peculiar to the high-tech industry. However, because of the considerable amount of research and development conducted in that industry, and the fortunes that can be made from computer-based products, it is highly vulnerable to trade secret violations.

▶ 8.4 JURISDICTIONAL ISSUES INVOLVING INTELLECTUAL PROPERTY LAWS

The specific intellectual property laws described in this chapter apply mostly to the United States even though their implications are global. Some international treaties pertaining to intellectual property have also been signed; for example, the TRIPS agreement has implemented requirements from the Berne Convention for the Protection of Literary and Artistic Works.[21] This agreement is recognized by signatories to WIPO.[22]

International intellectual property laws have been very difficult to enforce globally, in large part because of jurisdictional issues. In recent years, however, there has been considerable international cooperation in prosecuting digital piracy cases across jurisdictional lines. For example, in 2009, the owners and operators of the internationally controversial (Sweden-based) Pirate Bay site, who were found guilty of "unlawful transfer" of copyrighted material, received both fines and jail sentences.[23]

In countries such as the United States, some laws affecting intellectual property also apply at the state level. These laws apply to the sale of goods, as well as to contracts involved in those sales, and they often vary from state to state. With regard to sales and contracts involving computers and electronic devices, two pieces of legislation have aimed at establishing uniformity across states: the Uniform Computer and Information Transactions Act (UCITA) and the Uniform Electronic Transactions Act (UETA).[24] Whereas UETA applies to electronic contracts in general, UCITA is designed to govern transactions, including contracts, involving the development, sale, licensing, maintenance, and support of computer software. It would also extend to all shrink-wrap licenses and "click-wrap" agreements. Roy Girasa (2002) points out that click-wrap agreements give the user an on-screen choice to agree or not agree with the product requirements, also noting that a program might not open until a user consents by clicking on the words "I agree." So far, UCITA has been enacted into law in the states of Virginia and Maryland.

Even though UCITA is not law in most states, critics point out that its effects can be felt in all states because contracts involving electronic goods and services can span multiple states and thus potentially involve Virginia and Maryland law in the process. Although there is general agreement that a uniform law across states pertaining to electronic contracts would be desirable, critics worry about the effects that universal passage of UCITA would have for American consumers. While UCITA has been supported by major companies in the software industry, it has been criticized by the Software Engineering Ethics Research Institute and the American Library Association,

TABLE 8.1 Acronyms Corresponding to Intellectual Property Laws and Agreements

DMCA	Digital Millennium Copyright Act
NET Act	No Electronic Theft Act
PLT	Patent Law Treaty
SBCTEA	Sonny Bono Copyright Term Extension Act
S-DMCA	Super-DMCA (DMCA legislation passed at the state level in the United States)
TRIPS	Trade Relationship Aspects of Intellectual Property Standards
UCC	Uniform Commerce Code
UCITA	Uniform Computer and Information Transactions Act
UETA	Uniform Electronic Transactions Act
UTSA	Uniform Trade Secrets Act
WIPO	World Intellectual Property Organization

as well as by many consumer advocacy groups. Some critics worry that UCITA would undermine existing consumer protection laws and threaten current copyright exceptions for fair use and first sale.

In our discussion of various schemes for protecting intellectual property, we used several acronyms and abbreviations to describe and refer to national and international policies, treaties, and statutes. Table 8.1 contains a list of those acronyms.

▶ 8.5 PHILOSOPHICAL FOUNDATIONS FOR INTELLECTUAL PROPERTY RIGHTS

Even though some philosophers and political theorists have opposed the notion of private property rights, we will assume that property ownership is justifiable. We should note that some believe that property ownership rights make sense in the physical realm but are skeptical that property rights can be extended to intellectual objects in cyberspace. We will examine arguments for this position in Section 8.6.

In Section 8.1.2, we alluded to three philosophical theories—labor, utilitarian, and personality theories—that have been used to justify property rights. We next examine each of those theories in greater detail.

8.5.1 The Labor Theory of Property

The labor theory of property traces its origins to seventeenth-century philosopher John Locke. In his *Second Treatise on Civil Government*, Locke argues that when a person "mixes" his or her labor with the land, that person is entitled to the fruit of his or her labor. So if a person tills and plants crops on a section of land that is not already owned by another—an act which, Locke notes, requires considerable toil—that person has a right to claim ownership of the crops. Analogously, if a person cuts down a tree in the woods and saws it into several pieces, then the person is entitled to the pieces of wood that result from his or her labor. Hence, for Locke, a person's right to property is closely tied to that person's labor.

Locke also includes an important qualification with respect to the appropriation of property, which has come to be known as the "Lockean proviso." The proviso states that when someone either encloses a section of land from the commons or appropriates objects from it, "enough and as good" must be left for others. So, in Locke's account of property, a person has neither the right to cut down all of the trees in a "commons" nor the right to take the last tree. Even with this qualification, however, some argue that Locke's theory fails to provide an adequate account of property rights.

Locke's property theory has been attacked on several fronts. For example, some critics argue that even if Locke's labor theory makes sense for physical property, it does not follow that it can be extended to intellectual property. Noting that Locke associates labor with arduous physical work, these critics point out that the production of intellectual objects does not necessarily require the same kind of onerous toil (or "sweat of the brow") that goes into producing tangible goods. But we can see how an author might claim a right to the ownership of intellectual objects generated by his or her labor, because writing a book, a poem, or a software program can often require a fair amount of mental toil.

Other critics of Locke's property theory point out that intellectual objects are nonexclusionary in nature (as we saw in Section 8.1.2) and thus are not scarce. From this, they go on to infer that there is no need to grant property rights for those objects in a way that would be strictly analogous to rights involving physical property.

Others dispute Locke's claim that a property right is a *natural right*. They ask, What evidence is there for Locke's assertion that an individual's right to own property is a natural right, as opposed to an artificial (or man-made) right? Also, Locke's theory of property presupposes that persons making property claims "own their own bodies." If the right to own property is indeed a natural right, then it should apply to all persons, but consider the example of slavery, a relevant issue in Locke's time. Slaves do not legally own their bodies and it would seem to follow, on Locke's reasoning, that they have no claim to the fruits of their labor—that is, they do not have property rights. So property rights, according to Locke's labor theory, do not apply equally to all people; if they did, Native Americans who mixed their labor with the soil should have been granted property rights to their land in North and South America. It is not clear how Locke can claim that property ownership is a natural right, and yet at the same time imply that such a right could possibly be denied to some individuals who happen to be slaves or Native Americans.

Despite these objections, however, some believe that Locke's property theory can be used to justify the protection of intellectual objects. We next consider a scenario in which an appeal for copyright protection is made on the basis of the labor theory of property.

▶ **SCENARIO 8–4:** DEF Corporation vs. XYZ Inc.

DEF Corporation, a software company with 80 employees, has spent the last year developing a sophisticated database program that it is about to release. Thirty software developers have been employed full time on this project, and each software developer worked an average of 60 hours per week. The company expects that it will take more than 1 year to recoup the investment of labor and time put into this project. DEF applies for a copyright for its product.

XYZ Inc., which also produces database software, files a suit against DEF Corporation for allegedly infringing on its copyright: XYZ claims that DEF has copied a feature used in the interface in one of XYZ's software products. DEF objects by arguing that the feature is, in fact, not original and thus XYZ Inc. should not be eligible for copyright protection. More importantly, DEF further argues that it has invested considerable labor and "sweat" in its database program, so it should be rewarded for its hard work. ∎

Does DEF's claim make sense in light of the labor theory of property? Is the labor expended on a particular project, in itself, sufficient to make the case for copyright protection? According to Locke's labor theory, DEF would seem to have a reasonable case, but XYZ sees the matter very differently. Do you agree with DEF's position or with the case made by XYZ?

8.5.2 The Utilitarian Theory of Property

Critics of the labor theory argue that a rationale for granting property rights should not be confused with an individual's labor or with a natural right; rather, property rights are better understood as artificial rights or conventions devised by the state to achieve certain practical ends. According to utilitarian theory, granting property rights will maximize the good for the greatest number of people in a given society. (Recall our Chapter 2 discussion of utilitarianism, and Jeremy Bentham's and John Stuart Mill's arguments for it.) Arguably, utilitarian theory was used by the framers of the U.S. Constitution to justify the granting of property rights for intellectual objects (creative works and inventions) to individuals. The Founders seemed to assume that incentives in the form of copyrights and patents would motivate individuals to bring out their creative products and that, as a result, American society in general would benefit.

An advantage of the utilitarian theory is that it does not need to appeal to the abstract principle of a natural right to justify the granting of property rights to creators and inventors of intellectual objects. However, utilitarians have their critics as well. In Chapter 2, we saw some shortcomings of utilitarian theory with respect to protecting the interests of individuals who fall outside the scope of the greatest number (or majority) in a given society. Also, utilitarians tend to appeal to an economic/financial incentive as a necessary motivation for bringing creative works into the marketplace. For these reasons, many critics find the utilitarian rationale for granting property rights to be inadequate. The following scenario considers some incentives one might have for bringing forth a creative work based on the utilitarian argument for property rights.

▶ **SCENARIO 8–5:** Sam's e-Book Reader Add-on Device

Sam is a very talented and creative person, but he is not terribly industrious when it comes to following through with his ideas. He has an idea for an add-on device that would enable a popular e-book reader to store and play music (MP3 files) on the e-reader. Many of Sam's friends are interested in his idea, and some have strongly encouraged him to develop this device so that they can use it on their e-book readers. But Sam remains unconvinced and unmotivated. Then Sam's friend, Pat, tells him that an acquaintance of hers patented an analogous invention and has since earned several thousand dollars. Pat tries to persuade Sam that not only would his invention benefit his friends but also that he would stand to gain financially if he patents the product and it is successful. After considering Pat's advice, Sam decides to work on his invention and apply for a patent for it. ■

Was a utilitarian incentive (i.e., in the form of a financial benefit) necessary to get Sam to follow through on his invention? Would he have brought his invention into the marketplace if there were not a financial enticement? Do people only produce creative works because of financial rewards they might receive? On the one hand, it would seem that financial incentives could motivate some individuals, such as Sam, to produce a creative work that benefits society in general. However, it is not clear that all great musical composers have written works of music solely because of the prospects of becoming wealthy. It is possible, for example, that some gifted composer wrote music for the sheer enjoyment it brought him or her as a creator of artistic works. So there may be factors other than financial incentives that influence creators to bring forth their works.

8.5.3 The Personality Theory of Property

Critics of the labor and utilitarian theories believe that a theory that links the granting of property rights to either (a) an individual's onerous labor or (b) the notion of social utility misses an important point about the nature of the creative work involved in the production of intellectual objects. Both the labor and utilitarian theories appeal to criteria external to the individual himself as the rationale for granting a property right. Note that in each case, the criterion is a reward that is directly monetary in the case of utilitarian theory, and indirectly monetary in the case of labor theory. Both theories assume an extrinsic criterion—i.e., either one's labor or some economic incentive—for justifying property rights; neither considers the possibility that an internal criterion could justify these rights. In this sense, both theories underestimate the role of the persona or *personality* of the creator of the intellectual work. According to the personality theory of property, the intellectual object is an extension of the creator's personality (i.e., the person's being, or soul). And it is because of this relationship between the intellectual object and the creator's personality that advocates of the personality theory believe that creative works deserve legal protection.

The personality theory traces its origins to the writings of G. W. F. Hegel, a nineteenth century philosopher, and it has served as a foundational element in intellectual property laws enacted by nations in continental Europe. In France, the personality account of property is sometimes referred to as the "moral rights" (*droits morals*) theory of property. The personality theory provides an interesting interpretation of *why* an author should have control over the ways in which his or her work can be displayed and distributed. To ensure this control, personality theorists suggest that authors should be given protection for their artistic work even if they have no legal claim to any monetary reward associated with it.

Consider a case in which the personality theory of property might apply—viz., the use of a Beatles' song in commercial advertisement. In mid-1987, the Nike Corporation aired a television commercial for its sneakers that featured the song "Revolution," composed by John Lennon in the late 1960s (when he was a member of the Beatles). Lennon was murdered in 1980, so when the Nike ad aired on commercial television, he could neither approve nor disapprove of how his song was being used. Many of Lennon's fans, however, were outraged that a song penned by Lennon to address the serious political and social concerns of the turbulent 1960s could be used so frivolously in a TV commercial. Critics argued that Lennon would not have approved of his song being used in this manner. However, even if Lennon had been alive, he may not have had any legal recourse when the TV commercial aired, because the entire Lennon-McCartney corpus of songs was purchased by Michael Jackson prior to 1987; Michael Jackson owned the copyright to "Revolution."[25]

By appealing to the personality theory, however, the case could be made that Lennon—or in this instance, his widow—should have some say in how his song was represented in a commercial forum. Next consider a hypothetical scenario in which we can also apply the personality theory of property.

▶ **SCENARIO 8–6:** Angela's B++ Programming Tool

Angela, a graduate student who has been struggling to make ends meet, has developed a new programming tool, called B++. This software application, which employs the notion of a "reduced instruction set" technique, can be used in conjunction with the standard C++ programming language to execute certain tasks more quickly than the C++ instruction set. Angela has recently published an article that describes, in detail, the reduced set of instructions, how they work, and why she was motivated to develop B++. She was delighted to have her article published in the prestigious journal *CyberTechnology*. As part of the conditions for publication, however, Angela had to agree to sign over the copyright for her article to CyberPress (the publisher of *CyberTechnology*).

Angela is then informed that a textbook publisher, CyberTextbooks Inc., wishes to include a portion of her article in a textbook. As the copyright holder for Angela's article, CyberPress is legally authorized to allow CyberTextbooks to reprint all or selected portions of her article. Suppose, however, that Angela protests that mere excerpts from her article neither truly convey the important features of her programming tool nor explain how it works. She further argues that the article is an extension of her persona and that only in total does the article reveal her creative talents as a programmer. ■

Does Angela have a legitimate objection in this case? Should she, the original author of the article and the creator of the new programming tool, have the right to prevent her article from being published in abridged form? Can her argument, based on the notion of intellectual property as an expression of one's personality, be defended on moral grounds? Because she signed over the copyright for her article to CyberPress, she has no legal grounds for objecting to how that article is subsequently used. However, on moral grounds, she could claim that the publication of her abridged article does not fairly present her creative work.

Table 8.2 summarizes the three philosophical theories of property.

TABLE 8.2 Three Philosophical Theories of Property

Labor theory	Argues that a property right is a natural right and that property rights can be justified by the labor, or toil, that one invests in cultivating land or in creating a work of art.
Utilitarian theory	Argues that property rights are not natural rights but rather artificial rights created by the state. Property rights are granted to individuals and to corporations because they result in greater overall social utility.
Personality theory	Argues that a property right is a moral right and that property rights are justified not because of labor or social utility but because creative works express the personalities of the authors who create them.

▶ 8.6 THE FREE SOFTWARE AND THE OPEN SOURCE MOVEMENTS

We have examined three traditional theories that have been used to justify the protection of intellectual property from a philosophical perspective. In the introduction to Section 8.5, however, we also noted that some have argued for the view that no formal legal protection should be given to intellectual property even if we do grant such protection to physical property. One of the best known, and perhaps most controversial, arguments for why conventional intellectual property rights should not be granted to computer software has been made by Richard Stallman (2004), who views software ownership as a form of "hoarding" that disregards the general welfare of society. As an alternative to this trend, Stallman proposes that programmers work together to make software freely available for humankind rather than supporting efforts to restrict its use.

Although Stallman has been a staunch advocate for the view that software should be free, we should note that he intends "free" to refer to liberty, not to price (or "free" as in free speech vs. free beer). Grodzinsky, Miller, and Wolf (2004) suggest that Stallman's position on why software should be free may have been influenced by the culture of the 1970s at the Massachusetts Institute of Technology, where source code could be freely exchanged. As we saw in Section 8.3, however, that practice began to change in the late 1970s and early 1980s. Also during that period, the burgeoning computer industry hired many of the best software developers and programmers from academic computing labs, and some of those individuals took the software they developed with them. As a result, some of that software eventually became proprietary. In response to these trends, Stallman began his GNU (Gnu's Not Unix) project in 1984. GNU's goal was to develop an entire Unix-like operating system, complete with system utilities, that was "open" and freely accessible.

8.6.1 GNU and the Free Software Foundation

As stronger intellectual property rights began to be granted to software "owners" in the early 1980s, and as more and more software became proprietary, some programmers were concerned about whether they would be able to exchange software programs with each other in the future. They also worried that someone other than themselves would "own" their creative works. In 1985, the Free Software Foundation (FSF) was formed in response to these concerns, as well as to support Stallman's GNU project.

According to FSF, four "freedoms" are essential for free software. These include *freedom to*

1. run the program, for any purpose;
2. study how the program works, and adapt it for your needs;
3. redistribute copies so you can help your neighbor;
4. improve the program, and release your improvements to the public so that the whole community benefits.[26]

The software that is produced by programmers adhering to "free software" requirements (freely downloadable from www.fsf.org/) is typically accompanied by a licensing agreement that is designed to keep it freely available to other users "downstream," who can continue to modify the source code. The best known of these is the GNU Public License (GPL). The kind of protection granted by this license is also known as *copyleft*.

("Copyleft" refers to a group of licenses that currently apply to documents, music, and art, as well as software.) Whereas copyright law is seen by FSF's proponents as a way to restrict the right to make and redistribute copies of a particular work, a copyleft license included in GPL uses an alternative scheme that "subverts" the traditional copyright mechanism in order to ensure that every person who receives a copy, or derived version of a work, can use, modify, and also redistribute both the work and the derived version of the work. All derivative works of GPL software must also be licensed under GPL. In this way, the four freedoms of FSF are propagated in future software developed under this agreement.[27]

By the early 1990s, the GNU project had produced many important software development tools in compliance with FSF guidelines and the specifications for Unix-like source code. Throughout the 1980s, however, there was some confusion as to just what "Unix" meant, since several versions of that operating system existed—some at universities such as Berkeley, and others in the private sector such as AT&T Bell Laboratories where Unix was originally developed. This resulted in lawsuits and counter lawsuits regarding which sections of Unix software source code could be freely distributed and which sections were proprietary. The legal problems created some difficulties for Stallman and the GNU project because GNU still lacked the core of its (Unix-like) operating system—that is, the kernel. However, this issue was finally resolved in the early 1990s, when Linus Torvalds developed the kernel for a Unix-like operating system that he called Linux. At this point, GNU realized its goal of having a complete, functional operating system with all of the source code freely available for inspection, modification, and improvement.[28] The GNU project and FSF significantly influenced another, related software development initiative known as the Open Source Software (OSS) movement.

8.6.2 The "Open Source Software" Movement: OSF vs. FSF

OSS, which began in 1988, shares many of the same goals as FSF—most notably, the ability of a software user to look at, understand, modify, and redistribute the source code for that software. Like FSF, OSS requires that its source code be freely available. So, both movements are similar with respect to their requirements for the free use of their source code in the software development process. And some authors, including Chopra and Dexter (2009), use the expression "FOSS" to describe "free and open source software." However, as Eric Raymond (2004) notes, there are significant differences in the "attitudes" or philosophies of these two groups. Whereas FSF continues to focus on promoting its philosophical position that software should be free, OSS has concentrated its efforts more on promoting the open source model as an alternative methodology to "closed-source" development for software. OSS and FSF also differ with respect to requirements for how the software is used downstream. For example, FSF requires that all derivative pieces of software be subject to the original requirements and thus remain "open" and nonproprietary. OSS, on the contrary, is more flexible with respect to its derivative software. Unlike FSF, which requires that users strictly adhere to its GPL license in all derivative uses of its software, OSS supports less restrictive licenses such as Berkeley's Software Distribution (BSD) and Netscape's Mozilla Public License (MPL). These licenses are considered more "lenient" than GPL because they permit programmers to alter the open source software and to release it as a proprietary product.[29]

Another difference between OSS and FSF can be found in their attitudes toward the business community. The former is less anticommercial than the latter. In fact, many in the open source community interact comfortably with members of the business community. Because of its success in the software world, OSS now poses a significant threat to companies that produce proprietary software, such as Microsoft Corp. In addition to the Linux operating system, other well-known open source products include the Apache Web server and the Perl programming language. Whereas Torvalds believes that OSS and commercial software can coexist, Stallman does not believe that this is possible in the long run because of the profit incentives that drive investors in the commercial sector. Stallman also condemns the business community's practice of producing proprietary or "closed" code as unethical, and he claims that signing a typical software licensing agreement is like "betraying your neighbor." Richard Spinello (2003) notes that some of Stallman's followers have gone so far as to suggest that FSF is "morally superior" to proprietary software. However, we will not pursue that debate here. Instead, a more important question for our purposes is how the OSS and FSF movements can help us to think about at an issue at the heart of the contemporary intellectual property debate: Is the free flow of information still possible in a digital world?

As we saw in Chapter 6, some of Stallman's followers subscribe to the mantra *information wants to be free.* We should not assume that Stallman himself holds this view with respect to all information, however, because he focuses his arguments specifically on why computer software should be free. One point that Stallman makes in his discussion of software is particularly useful in helping us think about issues involving the concept of information (in general) vis-à-vis intellectual property from a radically different perspective—namely, information is something that humans desire to *share* with one another. Although this insight undergirds Stallman's view that software should be free, we do not need to embrace his position on software to appreciate the force of Stallman's insight with respect to the broader notion of information. In order to be shared, information must be communicated; so elaborate intellectual property structures and mechanisms that prohibit, or even discourage, the communication of information would seem to undermine its very purpose as something to be shared.

► 8.7 THE "COMMON-GOOD" APPROACH: AN ALTERNATIVE FRAMEWORK FOR ANALYZING THE INTELLECTUAL PROPERTY DEBATE

In the preceding section we focused our discussion on the question of whether software should be unrestricted and thus freely available to distribute and modify in conformance with certain "open" or "free" licensing agreements, as opposed to being legally protected by strict copyright and patent laws. Although our discussion centered on computer software, in particular, we saw that a more general question that arises is whether the free flow of information itself, in digital form, should be restricted. While not everyone may agree with the claim that software should be free, we noted that some have found Stallman's insight about the nature and purpose of *information* (i.e., as something that humans naturally want to share and communicate) to be compelling.

Some authors writing on the topic of intellectual property have noted that Stallman's insights are compatible with key elements in virtue ethics, which we discussed in

Chapter 2. Michael McFarland (2004, 2005), who suggests that we can draw from principles in virtue ethics in understanding and analyzing issues involving intellectual property, appeals to Stallman's insight that the essential purpose of information is to be shared. McFarland also notes how this insight supports the "common-good" view of intellectual property.

McFarland's notion of a "common-good" view of computer ethics incorporates aspects of Aristotle's *Nicomachean Ethics*. In Chapter 2, we saw that key elements of Aristotle's theory serve as the cornerstone for virtue ethics, but how can this view provide a framework for discussing intellectual property issues? McFarland suggests the following strategy. First, it is important to note that Aristotle believed that every object had a nature, end, or purpose, which he called its *good*. Following his method of inquiry, we begin any philosophical investigation by asking what the good, or purpose, of an object *is*. To investigate information as an intellectual object, we should aim at understanding its ultimate purpose.

Although information can certainly be understood as a form of self-expression (as the personality theory rightly suggests), and as a product that performs some useful functions (as utilitarians correctly suggest), it also has an even more fundamental purpose than personal expression and utility. Information, McFarland argues, is ultimately about communication; hence the nature and purpose of intellectual property in the form of information is communication, and thus an adequate account of the purpose of information (as something to be communicated) must take that into consideration.

McFarland believes that traditional concepts of property often overlook the ethically significant relationships that some kinds of property have with the rest of society. The three traditional theories of property that we examined in Section 8.6 focus on criteria such as an individual's (or a corporation's) labor, social utility (cost benefits), or the author's personality. But they fail to consider that the purpose of information is something whose essential nature is to be shared and communicated. Hence, McFarland believes that a common-good analysis of property, which examines the nature of information in terms of a broader social context, can provide us with an attractive alternative to the traditional property theories.

How is a common-good approach to intellectual property issues, which takes into account the overall good of society, different from a utilitarian theory? We noted earlier that a utilitarian system's primary concern is with maximizing the good for the majority, but utilitarianism does not always take individual rights into consideration in producing the greatest good for the greatest number. McFarland points out that a utilitarian analysis based solely on cost-benefits criteria might determine that it is desirable to publish a person's private diary because many people would enjoy reading it. Although the benefit to the overall majority would outweigh any embarrassment to the individual writer of the diary, such a practice is not morally correct, because it violates the basic right of humans to be respected.

McFarland also points out that if we begin our analysis of intellectual property issues simply by analyzing the notion of property itself, then the central point of debate tends to be about ownership and control; this is indeed how property issues are typically conceived and debated. McFarland believes that if we are willing to step outside that conventional framework, we can get a more complete view of the important societal role that information plays in intellectual property debate. In doing this, we gain the insight that an adequate theory of information must take into account its *social nature*, an important feature that we tend to overlook when we think of information only in terms of rights and property.

Before proceeding any further, it is important to ask, What do we mean by "information" in the context of our common-good approach to intellectual property disputes? We should note that there are both technical and colloquial (or everyday) senses of "information." While many highly technical definitions of "information" have been proposed by scholars in the field of information science (especially since the 1950s), our concern in this chapter is with the term's colloquial use and meaning. Rafael Capurro and Birger Hjørland (2003) point out that "the concept of information as we use it in everyday English, in the sense *knowledge communicated*, plays a central role in contemporary society" (Italics Capurro and Hjørland). We limit our analysis to this sense of "information" (i.e., in the broad context of "knowledge communicated"), which includes academic, literary, scientific, health, (and general) information that either already is or eventually should be in the "public domain." It is this sense of "information" that Capurro, Hjørland, McFarland, and others believe plays a very important social role.

8.7.1 Information Wants to be Shared vs. Information Wants to be Free

Arguably, a new (guiding) principle can be derived from the insights of Stallman and McFarland: Information wants to be shared.[30] Note, however, that this principle is very different from the claim "information wants to be free." We do not need to embrace the latter in order to defend the former. As we saw in Chapter 6, the view that all information should be free is not only naïve, it is conceptually flawed. For example, Eugene Spafford (2007) has described some of the undesirable consequences that such a principle would have for protecting individual privacy if all personal information were freely accessible. Also, Kenneth Himma (2005) has shown why the view that information should be free is problematic as a "normative principle" since it is not clear who, exactly, should be responsible for making it free. For example, is the government or the state obligated to make this information freely available to its citizens? So it is important to distinguish the principle we defend in this chapter from the more controversial view that all information should be free. Perhaps it is also important to reiterate that our sense of "information" in this context has to do with "knowledge communicated" (and thus does not necessarily apply to all forms of information).

Not only is the principle *information wants to be shared* clearly compatible with McFarland's "common-good" approach to intellectual property, it is also compatible with positions that others have expressed with regard to the social benefits of being able to share knowledge and information freely. For example, Richard De George (2003) points out that because cyber technology enables us to share information in ways that were not previously possible, it has also provided us with the opportunity of greater information access at the level of community. Yet he also notes that, paradoxically, by focusing on information as a commodity, the software industry has highlighted its commercial value, and, as a result, policies and schemes have been constructed to control information for commercial purposes rather than to share it freely.

To see the force of De George's claim, consider that copyright laws, originally intended to cover print media, were designed to encourage the distribution of information. We have seen that these laws have since been extended to cover digital media, inhibiting the distribution of electronic information. The distribution of digitized information is now being discouraged in some sectors. To illustrate this point, consider the traditional practice of borrowing books from public libraries. Physical books had always been available for an indefinite number of loans for library patrons; that is, there was no limit on how many times a book could circulate. However, the same practice does not hold in the case of all e-books. Consider that in 2011, HarperCollins had a policy that any e-book it published could be checked out of a library a maximum of 26 times before the e-book's license expired. (HarperColins has since changed its policy in response to protests by librarians and library patrons.) But consider that some publishers do not even allow their e-books to circulate at all in public libraries. Such practices clearly tend to discourage the sharing of copyrighted information in digital format.

Copyright laws were originally designed to encourage the flow of information in print media, via their fair-use provisions. Yet, for digital media they have been revised in a way that discourages the flow, and thus the sharing, of electronic information. What implications could this trend have for the future? Consider that the ability to share, not to hoard, information contributed to the development of the World Wide Web. Also consider what might have happened if the inventors of the Internet and the Web had been more entrepreneurial-minded and less concerned with sharing information. Tim Berners-Lee, who invented HTTP (the protocol used on the Web), never bothered to apply for a patent for his invention or for a copyright for his programming code. As a physicist working at CERN (a physics laboratory on the Franco-Swiss border), he desired to develop a common protocol for Internet communication so that scientists could share information more easily with each other. Note that Berners-Lee's goal in developing the Web was to provide a forum where information could be *shared*. A person whose interests were more entrepreneurial could have sought intellectual property protection for his or her contributions, thereby reducing the amount of information that could be shared. Also consider that Doug Englebart, who invented the mouse, received no patent for his contribution, but virtually every major computer manufacturer, as well as every computer user who has used a graphical interface, has benefited from his seminal contribution to what came to be called the "windows interface" in computing.

Consider also how the sharing of information has benefited many of those entrepreneurs who now seek to control the flow of information in cyberspace. It has been argued that Microsoft benefited significantly from the work done by Apple Corporation on its graphical user interface (the system of icons that users can point to and click on to accomplish a task). And it is well known that when Steve Jobs was at Apple, he visited Xerox PARC (Palo Alto Research Center), where he discovered that a graphical interface had already been invented by researchers there. So it is reasonably accurate to say that current user interfaces have benefited from the sharing of information along the way. Would it be fair to credit any one company or person with exclusive rights to a graphical user interface? Would doing so not also eliminate, or certainly impede, the possibility of incremental development and innovation? And more importantly, would it not also prevent us from sharing that important information?

Shelly Warwick (2004) argues that the original copyright framework, which valued the interests of the people as a whole over the interests of creators of intellectual property, is being "slowly dismantled" to give more weight to the interests of the latter group. And Dan Burk (2003) notes that "overreaching" in copyright licensing is now beginning to be recognized by some courts to "constitute a new form of misuse." In fact, many critics worry that digital information is now becoming less available and that we, as a society, are worse off because of it. Some also fear that if the public domain of ideas continues to shrink, our "information commons" may eventually disappear.

8.7.2 Preserving the Information Commons

What do we mean by *information commons*? One way of understanding this concept is by comparing it to a "physical commons," a common area that has been set aside and is open to the general public or to residents of a community. Garret Hardin, in his classic account of the "tragedy of the commons," describes the disappearance of the public space, or commons, that farmers living in a certain community had once enjoyed. In Hardin's tale, a public plot of land is shared by many farmers but owned by none of them; by sharing the land in a reasonable and mutually agreed manner, the commons benefits all of the farmers. Suppose that they agree collectively that each is allowed to have no more than ten cows graze on the commons on a given day. Further suppose, however, one day a farmer decides to cheat a little by having 11 or 12 of his cattle graze on the commons, reasoning that having 1 or 2 additional cows graze will not deplete the land's resources and will also enable him to profit slightly.[31] If other farmers also use the same rationale, you can see that before long the entire commons would be depleted.

It is very easy to underestimate the importance of the commons, or the public domain. We often take for granted the public parks, public beaches, and public gathering places that have been set aside for general use. Imagine the quality of our lives without them, and consider that without proper foresight, planning, and management, our parks could easily have been turned over to entrepreneurs for private development. Imagine, for example, if early city planners in New York City had not had the wisdom to set aside the area of Manhattan called Central Park; yet there was nothing inevitable about this. An entrepreneurial-minded city council might have sold the land to developers and businesses on the grounds that doing so would bring revenue to the city. In the short term, the city might have realized significant financial gain, but they would have been very shortsighted, and it would likely have been economically disadvantageous in the long term as well. Although Central Park is a tourist attraction that draws many people to New York City, it is not valued simply as a tourist attraction—it is a gathering place for city residents as well as visitors—a place to hear a concert on a summer evening, have a picnic in the fall, or ice skate in the winter. Imagine if Central Park were to disappear from the New York City landscape.

We have briefly considered some ways in which the physical commons has been threatened, but how is this analogous to the current threat posed to the information commons? Elizabeth Buchanan and James Campbell (2005) describe the information commons as

> a body of knowledge and information that is available to anyone to use without the need to ask for or receive permission from another, providing any conditions placed on its use are respected.[32]

Just as the physical commons in England began to vanish in the seventeenth and eighteenth centuries when property laws were passed by Parliament that prohibited peasants from fishing and hunting in newly enclosed territories that had previously been accessible to everyone, some now worry that the information commons is now undergoing a similar fate.[33] James Boyle (2006), who describes this trend as the "second enclosure movement," draws some useful comparisons to the original enclosure movement that resulted in the "fencing off" of much of the "grassy commons of old England." In the current enclosure movement, of course, it is ideas and information that are being fenced off or enclosed. So, just as there is reason to be concerned about the tragedy of the physical commons, as described by Hardin, there would also seem to be good reasons to worry about what Harlan Onsrud (1998) calls "the tragedy of the information commons." Buchanan and Campbell note that what is especially tragic is that the information commons is now

> . . . being enclosed or even destroyed by a combination of law and technology that is privatizing what had been public and may become public, and locking up and restricting access to ideas and information that have heretofore been shared resources.[34]

A different way of expressing the concern about what is being lost in this second enclosure movement is offered by Michael Heller (1998) in his description of the "tragedy of the anti-commons"—a phenomenon that occurs whenever resources are *underconsumed* or *underutilized*. As more and more of the information commons is fenced off because of strong intellectual property laws, critics such as Heller fear that fewer and fewer intellectual resources will be available to ordinary individuals and that, as a result, our information resources will be underutilized.

8.7.3 The Fate of the Information Commons: Could the Public Domain of Ideas Eventually Disappear?

Now imagine what it would be like if the public domain of ideas, which we have all enjoyed and benefited from, disappeared. In a book subtitled *The Fate of the Commons in a Connected World*, Lawrence Lessig (2002) raises some serious concerns about the future of ideas in a medium that is overly regulated and controlled by economic interests. Recall Section 8.2.2, where we discussed Eric Eldred's Web site, which included classic books from the public domain that he made available in electronic form. We saw that the SBCTEA, which extended copyright protection by 20 years, thwarted Eldred's plans to include on his site books that were about to enter the public domain. Legislative changes such as SBCTEA seem to run counter to the notion in which the public domain of ideas has traditionally become populated—i.e., intellectual objects are supposed to enter the public domain after a reasonable period of time. As Wolfgang Coy (2007) notes, this factor distinguishes intellectual objects from physical objects, since the latter can always remain proprietary.

Of course, governments could continue to pass laws extending the term limits of copyright law (as in the case of SBCTEA in the United States) to the point where precious little, if anything, will enter the public domain in the future. We have already seen how the Digital Millennium Copyright Act, with its controversial anticircumvention clause, contributes to the erosion, and possible future elimination, of the information commons. We may wish to consider the short-term vs. long-term gains and losses that can result from current trends in information policy. In the near term, corporations and some individuals will profit handsomely from privatization of information policy. In the long term, however, our society may be worse off intellectually, spiritually, and even economically if the short-term goals of privatization are not balanced against the interests of the greater public good.

Imagine if more of the information that we have traditionally shared freely were to disappear from the public domain and enter the world of copyright protection. Suppose, for example, that beginning tomorrow every recipe will be copyrighted and thus not be able to be disseminated without the permission of the new rights holder (i.e., the legal owner of that recipe). We would not even be permitted to use, let alone improve on, a particular recipe without first getting permission from the copyright holder. In the past, chefs could use recipes freely and improve upon them. Would it be fair if those chefs who had previously benefited from the sharing of recipes were all of a sudden awarded exclusive rights to them? And would it be fair if they were awarded the exclusive rights simply because they just happened to be experimenting with food at a time when the legal system favored the privatizing of information for commercial interests? Does it matter that society would be deprived of communicating freely the kind of information it has always had the luxury to share? What would this mean for the public domain of ideas and for ordinary discourse and information exchange?

Writing in response to worries about the disappearance of the public domain of ideas, Boyle (2004) advocated for the formation of a political movement similar to the environmental movement that arose in the 1970s. Just as a political movement was essential to save the environment from further erosion, so is a similar kind of movement needed to preserve the intellectual commons. Boyle points out that the environment could have disappeared because of simplistic claims based on (highly individualistic) property rights, and in a similar way the public domain of information is disappearing under an intellectual property system built around the interests of the current stakeholders. As the environmental movement invented the concept of "the environment" so that farmers, consumers, hunters, and bird watchers could all "discover themselves as environmentalists," Boyle suggests that we need to frame the concept of the public domain to call into being the coalition of interested parties to protect it. Boyle is optimistic that we might still be able to reclaim the public domain of ideas if we act responsibly.

In defending the view that the ultimate purpose of information is something to be shared and communicated, we have made the case that the public domain of ideas should be preserved. Of course, the rights and interests of both software manufacturers and individual creators of literary and artistic works also deserve serious consideration in any debate about intellectual property rights in cyberspace. And we do not need to advocate for the controversial view that all information should be absolutely free to move the debate forward. Indeed, companies and individuals need fair compensation for both their costs and the risks they undertake in developing their creative products and bringing them to market. The key phrase here, of course, is "fair compensation"; a fair intellectual property system is one that would enable us to achieve a proper balance. In reaching that state of equilibrium, however, we must not lose sight of the fact that information is more than merely a commodity that has commercial value.

If we defend the principle that information wants to be shared (but not totally free), then perhaps it will be possible to frame reasonable intellectual property policies that would both encourage the flow of information in digital form *and* reward fairly the creators of intellectual objects, including software manufacturers. One promising scheme for accomplishing these objectives can be found in the kind of licensing agreements currently issued in the Creative Commons (CC) initiative.

8.7.4 The Creative Commons

The Creative Commons, a nonprofit organization launched in 2001, was founded by Lawrence Lessig and others. The principal aim of this organization is to provide creative solutions to problems that current copyright laws pose for sharing information. One of CC's goals is to expand the range of creative work available to others legally to build upon and share. To accomplish this objective, CC provides a set of licensing options that help artists and authors give others the freedom and creativity to build upon their creativity. Lessig (2004) points out that such a "creative" scheme for licensing is needed because many people now realize that the current intellectual property rights regime does not make sense in the digital world.

We should note that CC does not aim to undermine the principle of copyright. Lessig concedes that copyrights protect important values and are essential to creativity, even in a digital age. He also believes that if the essence of copyright law is to allow creators to have control, then there should be a way to maintain ownership of copyrighted works and still make it possible for the average person to license the use of those works. Lessig notes that, unfortunately, the current version of copyright, which was not written for a world of digital creativity, "restricts more than it inspires." Traditional copyright regimes tend to promote an "all or nothing" kind of protection scheme with their "exclusive rights" clauses. According to Thomas Goetz (2004), CC provides a "middle ground" with respect to copyright protection because it makes possible a "some rights reserved" approach vs. an "all rights reserved" policy.

Lessig believes that the Internet allows for an "innovation commons" and that the CC licensing schemes help to promote this vision. CC provides a menu of options in its licensing and contract schemes, available on its Web site (http://creativecommons.org) free of charge, that enable copyright holders to grant some of their rights to the public while retaining others. The following options are provided:

- **Attribution**—permit others to copy, distribute, display, and perform the work and derivative works based upon it only if they give you credit.

- **Noncommercial**—permit others to copy, distribute, display, and perform the work and derivative works based upon it only for noncommercial purposes.

- **Derivative**—permit others to copy, distribute, display, and perform only verbatim copies of the work, not derivative works based upon it.

- **Share alike**—permit others to distribute derivative works only under a license identical to the license that governs your work.

By specifying one or more of these options, you can retain the copyright for your creative work while also allowing for uses of it under some circumstances.

Suppose you have composed a musical score. If you wish to protect that musical composition under a CC license, you choose the combination of options from the above menu. You may want to allow your musical composition to be used at certain kinds of noncommercial functions—for example, concerts or political rallies supporting some social or environmental cause—but not used for commercial purposes. You may also allow that, in certain cases, derivative works from your composition can be made, provided that you are given credit. Perhaps an accomplished musical group, which is also commercially successful, would like to include a variation of your work in a forthcoming album. That group could consult the terms of your CC license to see whether they are permitted to do so.

Assuming that you have granted such permission, you could receive increased exposure as a musical composer, and at the same time still retain control over your composition.

Lessig believes that artists, authors, and other creators who use the CC license are, in effect, saying,

> We have built upon the work of others. Let others build upon ours.

Building on the notion that every author "stands on the shoulders of giants," CC's proponents believe that musicians and artists who use the CC license are, in effect, "standing on the shoulders of peers" and allowing peers to "stand on their shoulders."

Goetz points out that because CC grants musicians, authors, and other creators a flexible "opt-in" licensing system that lets them determine what secondary uses are allowed and under what conditions, a musician or artist will not have to call a lawyer before building on or sharing a CC-licensed work. A work released under that license grants (or denies) "before-the-fact" permission, which explicitly specifies under what circumstances and under which conditions that work may be used by others. Pointing out that John Coltrane did not need a lawyer to create his immortal version of *The Sound of Music*'s "My Favorite Things," Lessig asks: Why should today's young musicians need one?

We can see how CC, via its creative and flexible licensing schemes, both encourages the flow of information in digital form and protects the legal rights and interests of artists and authors. Artists and authors can be recognized and rewarded, financially and otherwise, for their creative contributions, yet still share their works (or portions of their works) with others. This, in turn, enables us to realize Lessig's notion of an "innovation commons" because it allows authors and artists to build upon the works of others. It also contributes to the future of the commons, and it promotes the kind of spirit of cooperation and sharing among creators that Stallman and the FSF movement advocate for software development (although FSF does not endorse CC's licensing scheme). In promoting these and related goals, CC provides an implementation scheme for the presumptive principle defended in this chapter—viz., "information wants to be shared." Implementing our presumptive principle through a mechanism such as CC enables us to frame intellectual property policies that avoid the kinds of problems inherent in both (a) the claim that information should be absolutely free and (b) overly strong copyright laws that discourage sharing and innovation and also diminish the information commons.

▶ 8.8 PIPA, SOPA, AND RWA LEGISLATION: CURRENT BATTLEGROUNDS IN THE INTELLECTUAL PROPERTY WAR

In the previous sections, we argued in favor of a principle that presumes in favor of sharing information, which would help to prevent the information commons from further erosion; however, we did not argue that copyright protection should be eliminated. In Section 8.2, we saw that the intent of the original U.S. Copyright Act (1790) was to promote the progress of the sciences and useful arts, thereby encouraging creative production for society's benefits, by giving authors exclusive rights over literary and artistic works (for a limited time). Alina Ng (2011) argues that while this was clearly a "desirable goal" on the part of the Founders, granting exclusive rights to authors can, unfortunately, also "unnecessarily limit society's ability to access works in the public domain" (as we saw in Section 8.7).

(on topical themes) for many of these journals. Yet, contributing scholars typically receive no payment for either their (authored) publications or their reviewing and guest-editing services. While this is generally not a problem for many professors seeking promotion or tenure at their universities—as their professional service can enhance their academic careers—many scientists argue that their published research (which was both freely submitted by them and funded by taxpayer money) should be more generally available to the public.

However, most scholars have virtually no control over how their published work is either disseminated or restricted, because they are typically required to transfer copyright of their work to publishers such as Elsevier. This means that the publisher and not the author(s), or the taxpayers who helped fund the research, have total control over the publications. As a result, access to these published works can be limited only to large or well-off universities that can pay the high prices charged by Elsevier and other major publishers.

RWA's critics also worry about the profit incentives that drive major publishers. Whereas scholars enjoy having their published work widely accessible, publishing companies are motivated by the corporate profit model. So, restricting access to scholarly papers can work in the publisher's favor by driving up the cost to ensure greater revenue and profit margins. In 2011, Elsevier's revenues were in excess of 3.2 billion dollars (US) and its profit rate was 36%, which is well above the average of many industries.[38] Elsevier has defended its profits by pointing to its efficient business model. But critics have responded by noting that those profits were significantly subsidized by both "free labor" from scholars and taxpayer-funded research. In light of the Elsevier Boycott and other protests, RWA's cosponsors—Darrell Issa (R-CA) and Carolyn Maloney (D-NY)—announced that they would not proceed with pushing the bill through the formal legislative process.

As of this writing, it is difficult to say how long the Elsevier boycott will last or if it will spread to other major academic publishers. One thing is fairly clear, however, the dispute about whether academic information should be greatly restricted or freely accessible remains hotly contested. One factor that may also influence the future direction of academic publishing is the recent proliferation of "open access" journals. Just as open source software is freely available to the computer community (as we saw in Section 8.6), open access journals are freely available to the academic community, as well as to ordinary users. These journals are still relatively new and have not yet earned the reputation of many of the prestigious journals published by Elsevier and other leading academic publishers. So, some skeptics of open access publishing fear that the quality of the articles published in these journals may not be as high as those in journals using the traditional model. However, the current trend seems to be favoring a movement toward open access, especially as many of these journals are gaining respect in the academic community. And if this trend continues, it may help to preserve the information commons.

8.8.3 Intellectual Property Battles in the Near Future

We conclude this section and chapter by noting that current intellectual property disputes over digital information seem to be as contentious as ever. Both sides stand prepared to muster their resources for the future battles that inevitably lie ahead. Copyright owners and corporations will no doubt continue to lobby the U.S. Congress for stronger copyright protections. On the other side, academic and library organizations will likely continue to press hard with their objective of keeping online scientific and academic information freely accessible to students and ordinary users.

One thing that is clearly at stake in the ongoing dispute is the future status of the information commons, which as we saw in Section 8.7 appears to be shrinking. We have seen how difficult it can be to strike a balance that is acceptable to both sides in the dispute. However, we have argued that if we employ the presumptive principle defended in this chapter—information wants to be shared—in our future policy debates about intellectual property rights vs. the free flow of information, it may be possible to prevent the information commons from further erosion.

► 8.9 CHAPTER SUMMARY

In this chapter, we have examined disputes involving intellectual-property-right claims affecting digital information. In particular, we considered how current intellectual property laws, especially those involving copyright and patents, can be applied to software and other forms of digital media. We saw that three distinct philosophical theories of property have been used to defend our current schemes of legal protection, and we examined some arguments used in the Free Software and Open Source Software movements. We also saw that an alternative framework for analyzing property disputes affecting digital media, based on the "common-good" approach, suggests that we need to take into account the fact that information's essential purpose or nature is to be shared and communicated. Ironically, however, we noted that recent copyright laws, such as the DMCA, restrict the distribution, and thus the sharing, of information. We defended the view that *information wants to be shared* as a guiding principle that can inform the contemporary debate about intellectual property rights affecting digitized information. We saw how the Creative Commons initiative provides a scheme that enables us to implement our principle in the digital world. Finally, we examined three recent legislative proposals that threaten the future of the information commons.

► REVIEW QUESTIONS

1. What is intellectual property?
2. How is intellectual property different from tangible property?
3. What is meant by the expression "intellectual object"?
4. Describe the difficulties that arose in determining whether computer software (as a kind of intellectual object) should be eligible for the kinds of legal protection (i.e., copyrights and patents) that are typically granted to authors and inventors of creative works.
5. Describe some of the key differences in the four legal schemes designed to protect intellectual property: copyrights, patents, trademarks, and trade secrets.

6. What is the SBCTEA, and why is it controversial?
7. What is the DMCA, and why is it controversial?
8. What is the principle of fair use?
9. What is the principle of "first sale" with respect to copyright law?
10. How is the principle of fair use, as illustrated in Scenarios 8-1 and 8-2, threatened by recent changes to copyright law?
11. How were some controversies in the Napster dispute anticipated in the LaMacchia incident (involving Cynosure) at MIT in the mid-1990s?
12. What are the arguments for and against protecting software with patents?

13. Describe the rationale behind the labor theory of property. Is it a plausible philosophical theory when used to justify intellectual property rights?

14. What is the utilitarian theory of property? Can it justify the protection of software?

15. How does the personality theory of property differ from both the labor and the utilitarian property theories?

16. What is the Free Software Foundation, and what does it advocate?

17. What is GNU?

18. What is the Open Source Initiative, and how is it different from the Free Software Movement?

19. What is meant by the expression "information commons"?

20. What is the Creative Commons (CC) Initiative?

21. What are PIPA and SOPA, and why are they controversial?

22. What is RWA, and how did it influence "The Cost of Knowledge" Boycott?

▶ DISCUSSION QUESTIONS

23. Why does Richard Stallman believe that software should be free? How is Stallman's view about the ownership of computer programs both similar to and different from that advocated by the Open Source Initiative? What do we mean by the expression "Information wants to be shared"? How is it different from the position "Information wants to be free"?

24. Why does Lawrence Lessig believe that the information commons, or what he calls the "innovations commons," is disappearing? How can Lessig's position be compared to Boyle's analysis of the "fencing off" of digital information in what he calls the "second enclosure" movement? Why does Boyle believe that a political movement, similar to the environmental movement in the 1970s, may be needed to save the information commons? Can the CC initiative help to preserve the information commons? Explain.

▶ ESSAY/PRESENTATION QUESTIONS

25. Critics argue that more and more information in digital form is being "fenced off" because of recent copyright legislation. Yet owners of proprietary information fear that they could lose control of their property without those laws. How can we achieve an appropriate balance between those who hold legal rights to proprietary information and ordinary users who wish to access, share, and communicate that information?

26. In Chapter 5, we saw that privacy advocates argue for greater control of personal information by individuals, while many in the commercial sector argue for increased access to that information. In this chapter, we saw that those positions have become reversed—entrepreneurs argue for control of the flow of information on the Internet, while ordinary users argue for access to that information. Is there an irony, perhaps even an inconsistency, here? Can this inconsistency be resolved in a logically coherent manner? How? Explain.

Scenarios for Analysis

1. You are taking a course on the history of computing at your university. One of the requirements for the course is a 25-page research paper. Your professor for that course is concerned that some students may be purchasing research papers from Internet sites, while others may be submitting papers that are highly plagiarized. So, your professor decides to use an online plagiarism-detecting system to have all of the papers submitted in this class verified (by being matched against a large repository or database of student papers) for their originality and authenticity. The company that owns the plagiarism detecting system, however, has a controversial policy with regard to ownership of student papers.

Specifically, they claim to own—i.e., hold the copyright to—every paper your professor submits to them, so that those papers can be included in the company's proprietary database. Thus, all of the students in your class are required to sign a transfer of copyright form when they submit their research papers. You are very annoyed by this, however, because you want to maintain ownership of your paper. In fact, you plan to use some material in your paper in a senior thesis project. Next, you approach your professor about your concern. Although she is sympathetic to your position, she also points out that she is not able to make any exceptions because of the agreement the university has with the company contracted to verify the authenticity of student papers.

What would you do in this scenario? Based on the theories of property that we examined in Chapter 8, what kind of argument would you make to your professor (and to your university's administration, if necessary) that you, and you alone, should be able to retain ownership (i.e., hold the copyright) for your paper?

2. Professor Bill Smith, who teaches computer science courses at Technical University in the United States, recently received an email from a graduate student in India, named Raj, who is working on a master's degree in computer science. Raj notes in the email that he came across an abstract of a paper by Smith, which appears to be very important for a final project that is required for Raj to complete his master's degree. Unfortunately, the library at the university where Raj is studying does not subscribe to the journal in which Smith's paper is published. When Raj contacted the journal about purchasing the article, he was informed that the cost was $50 (US). Unfortunately, Raj does not have the money to pay for this article; so he asks Professor Smith if he would be willing to email him a copy for personal use (i.e., to read and reference in his project). Smith is eager to help Raj, but is also concerned about copyright issues in distributing the article electronically. Although Smith has a copy of the article (in PDF format) on his desktop computer, he is reluctant to send Raj an electronic copy because of his interpretation of the DMCA (described in Section 8.2). But Smith is conflicted because he is eager to help Raj. Smith also wishes to have his article available as widely as possible for scholars to use; furthermore, he believes that the publisher is charging Raj (and others) an excessive price for the article. What should Professor Smith do in this situation?

▶ ENDNOTES

1. My analysis of intellectual property issues in this chapter draws from material in Tavani (2002, 2007).
2. See, for example, Hettinger (1997) and Spinello and Tavani (2005).
3. See Grodzinsky, Miller, and Wolf (2004) for more detail.
4. See http://www.austlii.edu.au/au/legis/cth/num_act/caa1980213/.
5. See http://w2.eff.org/IP/DMCA/states/200304_sdmca_eff_analysis.php.
6. Http://w2.eff.org/IP/eff_fair_use_faq.php.
7. For more information about the Eldred case, see Lessig (2002).
8. For more detail, see Jennifer Lee (2001). "Technology; U.S. Arrests Russian Cryptographer as Copyright Violator." *New York Times*, July 18. Available at http://query.nytimes.com/gst/fullpage.html?res=9901EED91F3BF93BA25754C0A9679C8B63.
9. See *United States v. Lamachia*. (1994). 871 F Supp 535.
10. See http://www.gseis.ucla.edu/iclp/hr2265.html.
11. See *A&M Records Inc. v. Napster Inc.* (2001). 239 F 3d 1004.
12. See Grodzinsky and Tavani (2005).
13. See S. Kalara (2007). "Now the RIAA wants Universities to get campus-wide Napster subscription or 'lose all federal aid,'" http://www.bizorigin.com/2007/riaa_nuclear_option. Also see Grodzinsky and Tavani (2008).
14. *MGM Studios Inc. v. Grokster Ltd.* (2005). 545 US 913.
15. See http://www.uspto.gov/.
16. See *Diamond v. Diehr* (1981). 45 U.S. 175.
17. See http://www.uspto.gov/#.
18. See *America Online Inc. v. AT&T Corp.* 243 F. 3d 812.
19. See http://www.wipo.int/sme/en/ip_business/trade_secrets/trade_secrets.htm.
20. See http://www.wto.org/english/tratop_E/trips_e/trips_e.htm.
21. See http://www.wipo.int/treaties/en/ip/berne/trtdocs_wo001.html.
22. See http://www.wipo.int/portal/index.html.en.

23. See http://torrentfreak.com/the-pirate-bay-trial-the-verdict-090417/.
24. See http://www.law.cornell.edu/ucc/; http://www.law.upenn.edu/bll/archives/ulc/ucita/ucita200.htm; and http://www.law.upenn.edu/bll/archives/ulc/ecom/ueta_final.pdf.
25. See http://www.pophistorydig.com/?tag=the-beatles-revolution.
26. See http://www.gnu.org/philosophy/free-sw.html.
27. See http://www.gnu.org/copyleft/gpl.html.
28. See Grodzinsky, Miller, and Wolf (2004).
29. See http://www.opensource.org/.
30. See Tavani (2002).
31. See Hardin (1968) for more detail.

32. Buchanan and Campbell (2005), p. 229.
33. See the account of the original "fencing off" of the physical commons in Mark Rose. *Authors and Owners: The Invention of Copyright*. Cambridge MA: Harvard University Press, 1993.
34. Buchanan and Campbell (2005), p. 226.
35. See "PIPA Vote: Sen. Harry Reid Postpones Vote, Seeking Compromise On Anti-Piracy Bill." *Huffington Post*, January 20. Available at http://www.huffingtonpost.com/2012/01/20/pipa-vote-harry-reid-piracy_n_1218702.html?ir=Technology.
36. See, for example, Fischman (2012).
37. For more detail, see http://thecostofknowledge.com/.
38. See http://en.wikipedia.org/wiki/Elsevier.

▶ REFERENCES

Aharonian, Gregory. 2001. "Does the Patent Office Respect the Software Community?" In K. W. Bowyer, ed. *Ethics and Computing: Living Responsibly in a Computerized World*. 2nd ed. New York: IEEE Press, pp. 296–98.

Boyle, James. 2004. "A Politics of Intellectual Property: Environmentalism for the Net." In R. A. Spinello and H. T. Tavani, eds. *Readings in CyberEthics*. 2nd ed. Sudbury MA: Jones and Bartlett, pp. 273–93.

Boyle, James. 2006. "Enclosing the Human Genome: What Squabbles Over Genetic Patents Can Teach Us." In H. T. Tavani, ed. *Ethics, Computing, and Genomics*. Sudbury MA: Jones and Bartlett, pp. 255–77.

Buchanan, Elizabeth A., and James Campbell. 2005. "New Threats to Intellectual Freedom: The Loss of the Information Commons Through Law and Technology in the U.S." In R. A. Spinello and H. T. Tavani, eds. *Intellectual Property Rights in a Networked World: Theory and Practice*. Hershey PA: Idea Group/Information Science Publishing, pp. 225–42.

Burk, Dan L. 2003. "Anti-Circumvention Misuse: How I Stopped Worrying and Love the DMCA." *IEEE Technology and Society Magazine* 22, no. 3: 40–47.

Capurro, Ralphael, and Birger Hjørland. 2003. "The Concept of Information." In B. Cronin, ed. *Annual Review of Information Science and Technology (ARIST)*. Vol. 37. Medford, NJ: Information Today, pp. 343–411. Available at http://www.asis.org/Publications/ARIST/vol37.php.

Chopra, Samir, and Scott D. Dexter. 2009. "Free Software, Economic 'Realities' and Information Justice." *Computers and Society* 39, no. 3: 12–26.

Coy, Wolfgang. 2007. "On Sharing Intellectual Properties in Global Communities." In J. Fruhbauer, R. Capurro, and T. Hassmanninger, eds. *Localizing the Internet: Ethical Issues in Intercultural Perspective*. Munich: Fink Verlag, pp. 279–88.

De George, Richard T. 2003. *The Ethics of Information Technology and Business*. Malden MA: Blackwell.

Fischman, Josh. 2012. "Elsevier Publishing Boycott Gathers Steam Among Academics." *Chronicle of Higher Education*, January 30. Available at http://chronicle.com/blogs/wiredcampus/elsevier-publishing-boycott-gathers-steam-among-academics/35216.

Girasa, Roy J. 2002. *Cyberlaw: National and International Perspectives*. Upper Saddle River NJ: Prentice Hall.

Goetz, Thomas. 2004. "Rip, Mix, Burn. Swap till You Drop. The Music Cops Can't Do a Thing—It's 100% Legal, Licensed By the Bands," *Wired* (November): 181–83.

Grodzinsky, Frances S., Miller, Keith, and Wolf, Marty J. 2004. "Ethical Issues in Open Source Software." In R. A. Spinello and H. T. Tavani, eds. *Readings in CyberEthics*. 2nd ed. Sudbury MA: Jones and Bartlett, pp. 305–21.

Grodzinsky, Frances S., and Tavani, Herman T. 2005. "P2P Networks and the *Verizon v.* RIAA Case: Implications for Personal Privacy and Intellectual Property." *Ethics and Information Technology* 7, no. 4: 243–50.

Grodzinsky, Frances S., and Tavani, Herman T. 2008. "Online File Sharing: Resolving the Tensions between Privacy and Property Interests." *Computers and Society* 38, no. 4: 28–39.

Grosso, Andrew. 2000. "The Promise and the Problems of the No Electronic Theft Act." *Communications of the ACM* 43, no. 2 (February): 23–26.

Halbert, Debora J. 1999. *Intellectual Property in the Information Age: The Politics of Expanding Ownership Rights*. Westport CT: Quorum Books.

Hardin, Garret. 1968. "The Tragedy of the Commons." *Science* 162: 1243–48.

Heller, Michael. 1998. "The Tragedy of the Anticommons: From Marx to Markets." *Harvard Law Review* 111: 611–28.

Henderson, Katherine A., Spinello, Richard A., and Lipinski, Tomas A. 2007. "Prudent Policy? Reassessing the Digital Millennium Copyright Act." *Computers and Society* 37, no. 4: 25–40.

Hettinger, Edwin. 1997. "Justifying Intellectual Property." In A. D. Moore, ed. *Intellectual Property: Moral, Legal, and International Dilemmas*. Lanham MD: Rowman and Littlefield, pp. 57–80.

Himma, Kenneth Einar. 2005. "Information and Intellectual Property Protection: Evaluating the Claim That Information Should Be Free." *APA (American Philosophical Newsletter) on Philosophy and Law* 4, no. 2: 3–8.

Lessig, Lawrence. 2002. *The Future of Ideas: The Fate of the Commons in a Connected World.* New York: Random House.

Lessig, Lawrence. 2004. "Creative Freedom for All: Done Right, Copyrights Can Inspire the Next Digital Revolution." *Wired* (November): 188–89.

McFarland, Michael C. 2004. "Intellectual Property, Information, and the Common Good." In R. A. Spinello and H. T. Tavani, eds. *Readings in CyberEthics.* 2nd ed. Sudbury MA: Jones and Bartlett, pp. 294–304.

McFarland, Michael C. 2005. "Whose Bytes? A Common Good View of Computer Ethics." Paper presented at the 2005–2006 Humanities Lecture Series, Rivier University, Nashua NH, November 10.

Moore, Adam. 2008. "Personality-Based, Rule-Utilitarian, and Lockean Justifications of Intellectual Property." In K. E. Himma and H. T. Tavani, eds. *The Handbook of Information and Computer Ethics.* Hoboken NJ: John Wiley and Sons, pp. 105–30.

Ng, Alina. 2011. *Copyright Law and the Progress of Science and the Useful Arts.* Cheltenham, UK: Edward Elgar.

Onsrud, Harlan. 1998. "The Tragedy of the Information Commons." In D. Taylor, ed. *Policy Issues in Modern Cartography.* Oxford UK: Pergamon, pp. 141–58.

Raymond, Eric. 2004. "The Cathedral and the Bazaar." In R. A. Spinello and H. T. Tavani, eds. *Readings in CyberEthics.* 2nd ed. Sudbury MA: Jones and Bartlett, pp. 367–96.

Samuelson, Pamela. 2004. "What's at Stake in *MGM v. Grokster?* Seeking to Balance the Needs of Copyright Holders and Technology Developers." *Communication of the ACM* 47, no. 2: 15–20.

Samuelson, Pamela. 2005. "Legally Speaking: Did MGM Really Win the *Grokster* Case?" *Communication of the ACM* 48, no. 10: 19–24.

Snapper, John W. 1995. "Intellectual Property Protections for Computer Software." In D. G. Johnson and H. Nissenbaum, eds. *Computing, Ethics, and Social Values.* Englewood Cliffs NJ: Prentice Hall, pp. 181–89.

Spafford, Eugene H. 2007. "Are Computer Hacker Break-Ins Ethical?" In K. Himma, ed. *Internet Security: Hacking, Counter-Hacking, and Society.* Sudbury MA: Jones and Bartlett, pp. 49–59. Reprinted from *Journal of Systems Software,* 17: 41–47.

Spinello, Richard A. 2003. "The Future of Open Source Software: Let the Market Decide." *Journal of Information, Communication, and Ethics in Society* 1, no. 4: 217–34.

Spinello, Richard. 2008. "Intellectual Property: Intellectual and Moral Challenges of Online File Sharing." In K. E. Himma and H. T. Tavani, eds. *The Handbook of Information and Computer Ethics.* Hoboken NJ: John Wiley and Sons, pp. 553–69.

Spinello, Richard A., and Tavani, Herman T. 2005. "Intellectual Property Rights from Theory to Practical Implementation." In R. A. Spinello and H. T. Tavani, eds. *Intellectual Property Rights in a Networked World: Theory and Practice.* Hershey PA: Idea Group, pp. 1–66.

Stallman, Richard. 2004. "Why Software Should Be Free." In T. W. Bynum and S. Rogerson, eds. *Computer Ethics and Professional Responsibility.* Malden MA: Blackwell, pp. 294–310.

Tavani, Herman T. 2002. "'Information Wants to Be Shared': An Alternative Framework for Approaching Intellectual Property Disputes in an Information Age." *Catholic Library World* 73, no. 2: 94–104.

Tavani, Herman T. 2007. "Balancing Intellectual Property Rights and the Information Commons: A Lockean Analysis." In J. Weckert, ed. *Computer Ethics.* Aldershot, UK: Ashgate, pp. 85–94.

Warwick, Shelly. 2004. "Is Copyright Ethical? An Examination of the Theories, Laws, and Practices Regarding the Private Ownership of Intellectual Work in the United States." In R. A. Spinello and H. T. Tavani, eds. *Readings in CyberEthics.* 2nd ed. Sudbury MA: Jones and Bartlett, pp. 305–21.

► FURTHER READINGS

Barrett, William, Christopher Price, and Thomas Hunt. *iProperty: Profiting from Ideas in an Age of Global Information.* Hoboken, NJ: John Wiley and Sons. 2008.

Boyle, James. *The Public Domain: Enclosing the Commons of the Mind.* New Haven, CT: Yale University Press, 2008.

Chopra, Samir, and Scott D. Dexter. *Decoding Liberation: The Promise of Free and Open Source Software.* New York: Routledge, 2008.

Gordon, Wendy. "Moral Philosophy, Information Technology, and Copyright: The Grokster Case." In J.van den Hoven and J. Weckert, eds. *Information Technology and Moral Philosophy.* New York: Cambridge University Press, 2008, pp. 270–300.

Grodzinsky, Frances S., and Marty J. Wolf. "Ethical Interest in Free and Open Source Software." In K. E. Himma and H. T. Tavani, eds. *The Handbook of Information and Computer Ethics.* Hoboken NJ: John Wiley and Sons, 2008, pp. 245–72.

Merges, Robert. *Justifying Intellectual Property.* Cambridge, MA: Harvard University Press, 2011.

Samuelson, Pamela. "The Supreme Court Revisits the Sony Safe Harbor." *Communication of the ACM* 48, no. 6 (2005): 21–25.

Spinello, Richard A., and Maria Bottis. *A Defense of Intellectual Property Rights.* Cheltenham, UK: Edward Elgar, 2009.

9

Regulating Commerce and Speech in Cyberspace

Should cyberspace be regulated? Can it be regulated? If the answer to both questions is "yes," which aspects of it should be regulated? Who should be responsible for carrying out the regulatory functions—the government? Private organizations? Or perhaps Internet users themselves? In this chapter, we examine issues that have led to a call for strong regulatory proposals in cyberspace by considering the following questions:

- What is "regulation by code"?
- What is Digital Rights Management (DRM) technology, and why is it controversial?
- Can the distribution of some forms of e-mail spam be defended?
- Should all online pornography be censored?
- Can existing child pornography laws be applied in "sexting" incidents involving young teenagers?
- Should hate speech, as well as speech that can cause physical harm to others, be tolerated on the Internet?
- What is "network neutrality," and what implications does this principle have for the future of Internet regulation?

Many conservative organizations have argued for censorship of certain kinds of speech in cyberspace. Some liberal groups, on the contrary, who oppose any restrictions on free speech in cyberspace, argue that e-commerce, not speech, needs to be regulated. In this chapter, we consider "speech" to include issues involving pornography, hate speech, and speech that can cause physical harm to others. And somewhat more loosely, we consider e-commerce regulation issues to include concerns involving electronic spam, the assignment of Internet domain names, and practices affecting hyperlinking on the Web.

We will also see why we should be concerned about cyberspace regulation that can be implemented with technology itself, by means of "regulation by code," as in the case of DRM technologies. Some critics worry that regulation by code is becoming the default regulatory scheme in cyberspace. We begin with a brief examination of some background issues.

▶ 9.1 BACKGROUND ISSUES AND SOME PRELIMINARY DISTINCTIONS

John Weckert (2007) believes that when discussing cyberspace regulation, we need to ask two separate questions:

A. *Can* it be regulated?

B. *Should* it be regulated?

Asking question (A) implies that it is not clear whether cyberspace can be effectively regulated, but we will operate on the assumption that it can, in fact, be, regulated. We also acknowledge, however, that regulation schemes can be difficult to implement and enforce, and we concede that regulation can have undesirable side effects in terms of both cost and efficiency. We will focus on question (B), that is, the normative question as to whether cyberspace *ought* to be regulated. This question also can be broken down into two separate questions, as Weckert points out when he asks: "Should it be regulated in general, and should it be regulated in any one country in the absence of cooperation by others?"[1] In a later section of this chapter, we examine some controversies affecting consensus at the international level with regard to regulatory schemes and practices.

Despite some of the controversies and challenges that arise in schemes for regulating cyberspace, Weckert and Al-Saggaf (2008) note that we should not presume against Internet regulation. In fact, they believe that a "strong moral case can be made for regulating the content of the Internet."[2] Before proceeding with specific issues affecting the regulation of cyberspace, it is useful to consider two additional questions:

What do we mean by *cyberspace*?

What do we mean by *regulation*, particularly as it applies to cyberspace?

9.1.1 The Ontology of Cyberspace: Is the Internet a Medium or a Place?

In Chapter 1, we loosely defined the Internet as the network of interconnected computers, and we suggested that the terms "Internet" and "cyberspace" were roughly equivalent. In this chapter, we use the two terms interchangeably. But we have not yet described the ontology of cyberspace, that is, we have not said what, exactly, cyberspace *is*. For example, is it a *place*, that is, a virtual space that consists of all the data and information that resides in the connected servers and databases that make up the Internet? Or is cyberspace a *medium* of some sort?

Some believe that the Internet is best understood as a new kind of medium, significantly different from earlier media, such as the telephone or television. Whereas the telephone is a "one-to-one medium," and television is a "one-to-many medium," Mike Goodwin (1995, 2003) describes the Internet as a "many-to-many medium." He also notes that one does not need to be wealthy to have access to this medium; nor does one need to win the approval of an editor or a publisher to speak his or her mind there. But is the Internet a medium, or can it be better understood as a public space?

Jean Camp and Y. T. Chien (2000) differentiate four types of media: *publisher*, *broadcast*, *distributor*, and *common carrier*. An example of a publisher is a newspaper or a magazine, and broadcast media include television and radio. Telephone companies and cable companies are instances of common carriers, conduits for the distribution of information. Camp and Chien argue that none of the media models are appropriate for understanding the Internet. Instead, they believe that a spatial model—one in which cyberspace is viewed as a public space with certain digital characteristics—is more plausible.

But can we model the Internet accurately as a public space, as Camp and Chien suggest? Or is it better understood as a new kind of *medium*, as Goodwin and others have argued? We are making more than a mere semantic distinction, because, as Camp and Chien point out, the model we use can influence our decisions about public policies on the Internet. If the Internet is viewed as a public space, for example, then there are good legal and moral reasons for ensuring that everyone has access to it. The ontology of cyberspace will ultimately determine whether and how we should (or perhaps should not) regulate it.

Consider the rules used to regulate the distribution and sale of "adult" magazines and videos in physical space. Bookstores and video rental stores are permitted to carry and sell such merchandise, and because a store is a physical place, certain sections can be partitioned so that adults can visit them but individuals under a certain age cannot. The rules are drastically different, however, for broadcast media such as television, where the Federal Communications Commission (FCC) regulates which kinds of content can be broadcast over the airwaves. Movies that can be rented and sold only to adults in stores can also be deemed inappropriate (by the FCC) for general television viewers. So before we can successfully resolve questions about Internet regulation, we need to keep in mind that the model we use to understand cyberspace will also strongly influence which regulatory schemes are appropriate.

Figure 9.1 illustrates our two models of cyberspace.

9.1.2 Two Categories of Cyberspace Regulation

To "regulate" means to monitor or control a product, process, or set of behaviors according to certain requirements, standards, or protocols. Sometimes regulatory discussions about cyberspace have centered on its *content*, for example, whether online pornography and hate speech should be censored. And sometimes the regulatory discussions have focused on which kinds of processes, that is, rules and policies, should

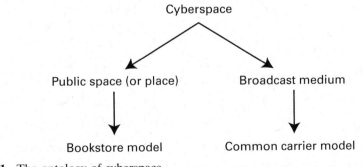

Figure 9.1 The ontology of cyberspace.

be implemented and enforced in commercial transactions in cyberspace. Physical space is regulated in both ways.

Some regulatory agencies monitor the content, and others the process, of items in physical space. The Food and Drug Administration (FDA) monitors food products on the shelves of supermarkets to ensure that they meet health and nutrition standards; FDA regulations ensure that the contents of each food item both matches and is accurately described by its label. Unlike the FDA, state public health boards do not regulate content; their regulations apply to conditions for compliance with community health standards. For example, public health officials inspect restaurants and grocery stores to ensure that they meet sanitation standards in their preparation and sale of food. So an agency can regulate for content or process, or both.

In the commerce sector, federal and state agencies, such as the Federal Trade Commission (FTC) and the Securities and Exchange Commission (SEC), enforce laws and policies that apply to commercial activities and transactions; for example, they regulate against monopolies and other unfair business practices, such as those alleged in the Microsoft antitrust case in the late 1990s. Regulatory principles in the commerce sector also determine whether to permit mergers, such as the one between America Online (AOL) and Time Warner. Some believe that in cyberspace an additional set of criteria is needed to regulate the e-commerce, or so-called *dot.com*, sector.

Figure 9.2 illustrates the ways in which cyberspace can be regulated.

It is not difficult to point out positive effects that regulatory practices in physical space have for health and safety. Consider, for example, the role that state liquor boards play in regulating the distribution and sale of liquor: they determine who is and is not eligible for a license to distribute liquor in their state, and if a board determines that a licensed distributor has violated its licensing agreement with the state, its license can be revoked. And boards that regulate liquor can help to keep liquor out of the hands of minors and help to discourage an underground, or black market, for the sale of "bootleg liquor," which is not tested and certified as meeting standards of quality and authenticity. State liquor boards also help determine fair pricing to prevent unscrupulous merchants from price gouging. So there are many good reasons for regulating the distribution and sale of liquor. But how can we extend this analogy to the Internet?

First, we can ask how we can possibly regulate cyberspace, which is inherently decentralized. Cyberspace is not compartmentalized neatly into state jurisdictions that can set up their own control boards. Does this mean that effective regulation of any type is impossible in cyberspace? Not according to Lawrence Lessig (2000) and Philip Agre

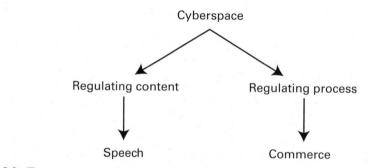

Figure 9.2 Two categories of cyberspace regulation.

(2005), who suggest that a decentralized cyberspace does not preclude Internet regulation from being carried out quite effectively. In describing the architecture of P2P (peer-to-peer) networks in cyberspace, Agre notes that decentralized institutions do not imply decentralized architectures, and vice versa. Lessig believes that in cyberspace, understanding architecture, or what he calls *code*, is the key to understanding how regulation works.

▶ 9.2 FOUR MODES OF REGULATION: THE LESSIG MODEL

Lessig describes four distinct but interdependent constraints, which he calls "modalities," for regulating behavior: *laws*, social *norms*, *market* pressures, and *architecture*. Before we apply each modality to cyberspace, consider how each can be applied in regulating behaviors in the physical world.

Cigarette smoking can be regulated through the passage and enforcement of explicit laws that make it illegal to smoke in public buildings. And we have specific laws that prohibit cigarette manufacturers from advertising on television or in magazines targeted at teenage audiences. Independent of explicit laws, however, social norms can also discourage cigarette smoking in public; for example, it is socially acceptable for homeowners to place "Thank you for not smoking in our house" signs on their front doors. And restaurant owners can, under social pressure from patrons, partition smoking and nonsmoking sections of their establishments even when there is no explicit law requiring them to do so.

Market pressures can also affect smoking behavior. Cigarettes can be priced so that only the wealthiest people can afford to buy them. Finally, merchants can impose an "architecture of control" on cigarettes by using physical constraints. All cigarettes sold in grocery stores could be located behind locked doors, causing interruptions in check-out transactions. A cashier might have to temporarily suspend the transaction, locate the store's manager, and get the proper authorization and the key to open the locked doors to remove the cigarettes. Contrast this architecture with one in which cigarettes are available in vending machines easily accessible to everyone, including minors.

To apply Lessig's four-fold distinction to cyberspace, we replace architecture, which is in physical or geographic space, with *code*. Code, for Lessig, consists of programs, devices, and protocols—that is, the sum total of the software and hardware—that constitute cyberspace. Like physical architecture in geographic space, code sets the terms upon which one can enter or exit cyberspace. Also like architecture, code is not optional. Lessig notes that we do not choose to obey the structures that architecture establishes. Just as we are subject to architectures of physical space, so we are subject to code in cyberspace; a physical door can block you from entering a physical building, and a password requirement can prevent your entering a Web site. And code can be used to limit access to Web sites by requiring that users accept cookies (see Chapter 5) if they wish to visit those sites. Lessig believes that code can either facilitate or deter access to, or transfer of, information in cyberspace.

In Chapter 1, we saw that James Moor (2007) described computer technology as "logically malleable" because, unlike most other technologies that are dedicated to performing specific tasks, computers can be instructed through software to perform an indefinite number of diverse functions. Lessig (2004) also recognizes that computer technology is not fixed, noting that different computer architectures create very different kinds of environments. He compares the Internet of 1995, which he calls NET 95 and which he believes has a "libertarian architecture," to the Internet of 1999 (and later). To illustrate differences between these two architectures, Lessig offers a comparison of the computer network systems at the University of Chicago and Harvard University. The University of Chicago's network was like NET 95, because anyone could connect his or her machine to jacks on the campus. As such, the code at Chicago favored freedom, or free speech. At Harvard, on the other hand, one first had to register his or her machine before getting on the Harvard's network. Once registered, all interactions with the network could be monitored and identified by Harvard's network administrators. Lessig points out that at the University of Chicago, facilitating access was the ideal; at Harvard, controlling access is the ideal. The University of Chicago's network had the architecture of NET 95, whereas the architecture of Harvard's system is a contemporary "intranet architecture."

Note that the underlying network protocols (i.e., TCP/IP) were the same for the computer systems at both Harvard and the University of Chicago. But layered on top of Harvard's TCP/IP protocol was an additional set of protocols, or *code*, which Lessig says "facilitates control." Why should we care about the differences between the two kinds of architectures? Lessig notes that in the NET 95 environment, one could roam the Internet freely and anonymously. Today, one cannot. Lessig concludes from this that we have moved from an "architecture of freedom" to an "architecture of control." He also concludes that in cyberspace, code is a more effective regulator than law. In fact, Lessig claims that in cyberspace, *code is the law*.

▶ 9.3 DIGITAL RIGHTS MANAGEMENT AND THE PRIVATIZATION OF INFORMATION POLICY

To understand the force of Lessig's claim that code is regulating cyberspace, consider the role that software code in the form of DRM technologies play in regulating digital media. DRM technologies allow content owners to regulate the flow of information included in digital media by blocking access to it via encryption mechanisms, and by enabling access to it through the use of passwords. The combination of DRM technology and copyright protection laws, such as the Digital Millennium Copyright Act (DMCA), has made possible the regulation and enforcement of policies and laws in cyberspace to a degree that never existed in the physical realm. As we saw in Chapter 8, the DMCA prohibits the development and use of technologies designed to circumvent copyright management systems. As a result, the DMCA works hand in hand with DRM technology to control the flow of information in digitized form; any programs designed to circumvent DRM controls are in violation of Section 1201 of the DMCA.

9.3.1 DRM Technology: Implications for Public Debate on Copyright Issues

Critics worry about the ways in which DRM technology can be used to enforce copyright law. Because software code in DRM systems is being developed and used with the express purpose of precluding the possibility of copyright infringement, Niva Elkin-Koren (2000) fears that the traditional mechanism for debating public policy may now be closed to us. She notes that if computer manufacturers can decide what the copyright rules should be, and if they are permitted to embed code in their products that enforces those rules, then there is no longer a need for, or even the possibility of, public policy debate about copyright issues.

In the past, when individuals duplicated proprietary information by using the latest available technologies, we were often forced to question the viability of existing copyright laws in light of those new technologies vis-à-vis principles such as fair use and first sale (described in Chapter 8). Elkin-Koren notes that we could then engage in meaningful public policy debates about whether traditional copyright laws should apply or whether some new laws are needed. Most importantly, we could challenge the viability and constitutionality of such laws through the judicial process.

Elkin-Koren worries that a framework for *balancing* the interests of individuals and the public, which in the past had been supported by "spirited policy debates" and judicial review, will no longer be possible in a world in which copyright policies are predetermined by code. As Richard Spinello (2003) notes, restrictions embedded into computer code end up having the force of law without the checks and balances provided by the legal system.

Pamela Samuelson (2003), who also has been critical of technologies that regulate through embedded code, believes that DRM systems may violate the fair-use provision of copyright law. She notes that DRM technology allows content owners to exercise far more control over uses of copyrighted works in digital media than what is provided by conventional copyright law. Frances Grodzinsky and Maria Bottis (2007) also argue that DRM threatens the fair-use provision of copyright law. They believe that because of the way DRM is designed to protect digital content, our conventional understanding of "private use as fair use" has changed.

DRM and the Music Industry

Other critics worry about the ways DRM systems can be abused by content owners to control users' computers and to spy on unsuspecting users. Because of these and related factors, some now believe that DRM technology has gone too far. Consider a controversial incident involving a DRM system used by Sony BMG that would seem to support this view.

▶ **SCENARIO 9–1:** The Sony Rootkit Controversy

Sony BMG Music Entertainment used a DRM system called Extended Copy Protection (XCP) to protect its music CDs. In 2005, a blogger named Mark Russinovich posted an article that described the characteristics of the software protection scheme used by Sony. In that article, Russinovich (2005) disclosed certain flaws in the design of Sony's software that manifested themselves as security holes that could be exploited by malicious software such as viruses or worms. He also noted that Sony provided no "uninstall" program to remove XCP. Sony responded to this criticism by releasing a software removal utility.

But Russinovich, in a follow-up blog article, noted that Sony's removal utility had only exacerbated privacy-and-security concerns about the software. For example, he pointed out that the program merely "unmasked" the hidden files in the "rootkit" component of XCP, but did not actually remove the rootkit itself. In November 2005, Sony provided a "new and improved" removal tool to uninstall the rootkit from affected Microsoft Windows computers.

Some of Sony's critics accused Sony of violating the privacy of its customers by using code that created a "backdoor" into their customers' machines. Other critics also claimed that Sony's DRM program, which gave the company control over its customers' machines in the name of copyright protection, itself infringed copyright law. And some critics argued that Sony violated the open source license agreement (see Chapter 8) because of the way in which it used some open source software code to build its protection system. In late 2005, Sony decided to back out of its copy protection software, recalling unsold CDs from all stores, and allowing customers to exchange their CDs for versions that did not include the controversial software.[3] ▪

Sony's critics were still not satisfied by the company's concessions. In fact, class action lawsuits were filed against Sony BMG in California and New York.

The DRM-related controversies in the Sony rootkit scenario raise the following kinds of questions: Can users trust content owners, such as Sony BMG, who are easily able to spy on them and able to control aspects of their computers and electronic devices via the use of DRM technology? Are Sony's actions justified on grounds that companies need DRM systems to protect their intellectual property rights?

Another area of tension involving DRM and the music industry has to do with "interoperability" across the devices on which music can be played. Interoperability enables users to download and play music on a variety of devices. However, it also challenges the notion that downloadable content can and should be restricted to proprietary devices controlled by the company that owns an "online store," such as iPods in the iTunes store. Internationally, there have been some efforts to promote interoperability. For example, in 2006, France's National Assembly passed a law that would force distributors of online music in France to remove DRM so that music can be played on any device. Some believe that this move could pave the way for other EU countries to follow (Hesseldahl 2006). However, many owners and distributors of music content believe that removing DRM to support interoperability could also result in opening the door to file sharing of copyrighted material without compensation for the content owners and distributors.

In 2007, EMI announced that it would sell its music without DRM on Apple Corporation's iTunes music store. One tradeoff, however, was that non-DRM-formatted music would cost slightly more than DRM versions. Proponents of this change, including the late Steve Jobs (2007), believe that if DRM restrictions were lifted on music, there might be an influx of new stores and players. But the debate about DRM in the contexts of online music and interoperability continues.[4]

9.3.2 Privatizing Information Policy: Implications for the Internet

We have seen that DRM schemes tip the balance in favor of the copyright owner who can determine how and by whom his/her content may be used. For that reason, DRM has become an obstacle to fair use because it limits the user's freedom by allowing private interests to define the parameters of the law. Elkin-Koren argues that because of the technological controls embedded in software code (such as in DRM systems), our policies affecting information and digital media are becoming increasingly *privatized*. She also notes that this trend toward privatization has enabled software companies to design code that reflects their own interests and values, without having to worry about any adverse effects that code can have for the public's interests.

Jessica Litman (2002) is also concerned about efforts that have been made to privatize information policies in cyberspace via the use of technology and law. She describes how the Recording Industry of America (RIAA) tried to pressure computer manufacturers to embed code in their computer systems that would make it impossible to use personal computers to download MP3 files and to burn CDs. Litman also notes that, in the late 1990s, the recording industry sought legislation that would ban the manufacture of portable MP3 players on grounds that such devices *could* be used to play pirated music, even though the MP3 file format is perfectly legal and even though many MP3 files do not contain copyrighted music.

Some critics worry about potential conflicts of interest that arise in the e-commerce sector in connection with the trend toward privatization. These critics note that lines have begun to blur between common carriers (such as telephone companies) and commercial content providers, which in the past were closely regulated and monitored by the FCC. For example, consider that the business merger involving AOL and the Time Warner Corporation in 2001 brought together a carrier and a content provider under the umbrella of one major corporation. Mergers of this type have created conflicts of interest because the content provided by a company such as Time Warner could receive preferential consideration in offerings provided to AOL subscribers. We examine some aspects of this concern in detail in Section 9.9, where we analyze controversies surrounding "network neutrality."

Noting some other ways in which the privatization of information policy has affected cyberspace, Litman points out that in 1998 the Internet was transformed into a "giant American shopping mall." That year, the U.S. Congress passed three copyright-related acts that strongly favored commercial interests: the DMCA, SBCTEA, and the NET Act (each discussed in Chapter 8). Also in 1998, responsibility for the assignment of Internet domain names was transferred from the National Science Foundation (NSF), an independent organization, to the Internet Corporation for Assigned Names and Numbers (ICANN). This move was controversial because ICANN is viewed by its critics as being "business friendly" in its policies for registering domain names.

Assigning Internet Domain Names

A *domain name* is a string of letters or words used to identify a Web page; it is included in a URL (universal resource locator) such as http://www.myuniversity.edu. The domain name (in this case, *myuniversity.edu*) immediately follows the Hypertext Transfer Protocol (http://) and the World Wide Web (www) portions of the URL. The ".edu," ".com," ".net," and ".org" sections of the domain name are also referred to as *generic top-level domain names* (gTLDs). The gTLDs identify sites that are educational (.edu), commercial (.com), network-related (.net), governmental (.gov), and organizational (.org). Country-code top-level domain names (ccTLDs) are used to indicate various countries, such as Australia (.au), Germany (.de), Japan (.jp), and so forth.[5]

When NSF had been responsible for registering domain names, there was no clear or systematic policy for deciding which domain names one was eligible or ineligible to register. Anyone could, in principle, register domain names that contain "Budweiser" or "Red Sox," and a serious issue arose when certain individuals registered domain names containing such key phrases and symbols that were previously registered as legal trademarks in physical space. Consequently, some trademark owners filed lawsuits against proprietors of Web sites whose domain names included symbols identical to their registered trademarks.[6] Many trademark owners viewed those who registered domain names that infringed on their trademarks as "cybersquatters," and they pressured the U.S. Congress for legislation that would protect their trademarks. In 1999, Congress passed the Anticybersquatting Consumer Protection Act.[7]

Litman suggests that ICANN could have devised alternative or compromise strategies to resolve trademark disputes in cyberspace, but she also believes that such strategies were never seriously explored. For example, the number of gTLDs could have been expanded in ways that would have satisfied both parties in a dispute involving domain names. Critics believe that a policy to include extensions such as ".biz" could have resolved some trademark disputes, including a classic case involving Amazon.com and a (bricks-and-mortar) bookstore by the name of Amazon located in Minnesota. That bookstore, which had been in business before Amazon.com, could have registered a trademark such as "Amazon.biz" to distinguish itself from the well-known (online) Amazon site. In 2002, ICANN decided to expand the number of gTLDs, approving extensions such as ".aero" for the air transport industry, ".biz," ".museum," and ".travel."[8] Even with the addition of these gTLDs, however, critics still see ICANN's policies as favoring the interests of commerce and thus contributing further to the privatization of the Internet.

▶ 9.4 THE USE AND MISUSE OF (HTML) METATAGS AND WEB HYPERLINKS

We have seen how some information policies, in conjunction with technologies such as DRM, increasingly privatize cyberspace. And we have seen how policies involving the assignment of Internet domain names can favorably affect the interests of some individuals and organizations in the e-commerce sector, at the expense of others. In this section, we consider some controversies surrounding the use (and abuse) of hypertext markup language (HTML) metatags in software code. Another code-related controversy that we examine is the use of "deep linking," a form of hyperlinking, to access targeted sections of Web sites.

9.4.1 Issues Surrounding the Use/Abuse of HTML Metatags

What are HTML metatags, and why are they controversial? A *metatag* is a string of text that is embedded in HTML code. To see which metatags have been included in a Web site, one can "view" the HTML source code used to construct the site, and most Web browsers enable users to do this. Metatags can be either *keyword metatags* or *descriptive metatags*. Keyword metatags, such as <football> and <Aaron Rodgers> enable Web-site designers to identify terms that can be used by search engines. Descriptive metatags, on the contrary, enable the designer of a Web page to describe the page contents. For example, the description of a Web site for Aaron Rodgers might read: "Aaron Rodgers . . . quarterback for the Green Bay Packers . . . received the NFL's Most Valuable Player award for the 2011–2012 season . . . " The description typically appears as one or more sentence fragments, directly beneath the Web site's listing in an Internet search result.

Search engines examine keyword metatags to help determine how best to organize the listings of Web sites they return to queries, according to meaningful categories that a user might request. For example, if I were constructing a Web site on cyberethics that

I wanted students to visit, I might include the following keyword metatags in my HTML source code: <cyberethics>, <cyberethics courses>, <computer ethics instruction>, and <issues in Internet ethics>. In doing this, my objective is to make the contents of my Web site known to search engines so that they can direct Internet users who request cyberethics-related information to my Web site.

Metatags hardly seem controversial; however, they can be used for deceptive purposes. Consider the following scenario illustrating a sinister way that metatags might be used.

▶ **SCENARIO 9–2:** A Deceptive Use of HTML Metatags

Keith, a student at Technical University, recently completed a cyberethics course taught by Professor Barbara Bright. But Keith did not do well in the class, and he wishes to express his opinion about Professor Bright to anyone who will listen. Keith decides to construct a Web site called Cyberethics Review, where he intends to comment on the course and its instructor. Note that his Web site, despite its title, has nothing at all to do with cyberethics per se. In the HTML code for his site, Keith includes the keyword metatag <cyberethics> as well as the following descriptive metatag: "Professor Bright is a jerk . . . unfair to students . . . terrible instructor . . . " Now if someone enters the keyword "cyberethics" in a search engine's entry box, that person may receive information about the Cyberethics Review site in the list of entries returned by the search. Directly under that site's name and corresponding URL, the user will also find the (summary) descriptive sentence fragments containing the disparaging remarks about Professor Bright.

Keith could also accomplish his goal by using only a series of keyword metatags. Suppose he decides to call his Web site "Professor Barbara Bright." Of course, no search engine responding to a query about cyberethics would ordinarily return in its list (of relevant sites) information about Keith's "Professor Bright site." Keith, however, is very shrewd when it comes to writing the code for his Web site. He decides to embed keyword metatags such as <Professor Bright>, <cyberethics>, and <computer ethics instructors> in the HTML source code. Suppose also that he decides not to use any descriptive metatags that might give away the true nature of the site he has constructed. Now a search engine will likely determine that Keith's site does pertain to cyberethics and will return its URL (as part of a list) to a user who has conducted a search query for the keyword cyberethics. Unsuspecting users who may be interested in visiting a site that they assume was constructed by Professor Bright for the purposes of discussing cyberethics issues, will be surprised when they click on the URL for Keith's site. Users will receive no information pertaining to cyberethics but instead find a Web page whose content includes derogatory, and possibly defamatory, remarks about Professor Bright. ■

The scenario involving Keith and Professor Bright is, of course, hypothetical; however, there have been actual cases involving the deceptive use of metatags, which have been contested in court. One such incident resulted in the *Bihari v. Gross* (2000) case, involving a former associate of Bihari Interiors who registered two domain names, "designscam.com" and "manhattaninteriordesign.com." On both sites, Gross included derogatory remarks about Bihari; he also used HTML metatags that would likely direct responses to search queries about Bihari Interiors to one or both of his Web sites, as well.[9]

9.4.2 Hyperlinking and Deep Linking

Users can navigate the Web from one site to another via direct connections called *hyperlinks*. Clicking on a hyperlink takes the user directly to the target Web site. Without hyperlinks, users have to either use search engines to locate and access related Web sites before being able to link to them or enter by hand (i.e., key in) the complete URL of a site in order to access it.

Before the e-commerce era, the practice of including direct links to related Web pages had become the default mode of operation on the Web; Internet users gave little thought as to whether they needed permission to include a hyperlink to a target Web site (or to any particular section of that targeted site). They did not consider, from a legal perspective, whether they had an explicit right to link directly to another person's Web site, or to any portion of it, without first acquiring the express consent of its owner.

Consider a scenario where Professor Jones has, as part of her Web site, a sub-page devoted to bibliographic material on environmental ethics. Should Internet users be able to link directly to the bibliographic portion of her site? Or, if Professor Jones prefers, should they be required to first access her (top-level) Web page and then click down to the bibliography page? Jones may not care whether visitors to her site access the top level of her site before going to the bibliography section, but the operators of some commercial Web sites have objected to visitors linking "deep" into their sites, thus bypassing the top-level pages. They point out that online advertisers, who typically place advertisements on the top-level pages of Web sites, want their ads to be seen by all visitors to the sites they are sponsoring.

Also, counter mechanisms (which track both the number of users who visit a site over a certain period and information about the time of day most visitors connect to that site) have been included on a commercial Web site's top-level page, and this kind of information can be a key factor in determining whether advertisers will sponsor a particular site. Commercial Web-site owners, especially those who depend on advertisers, have been concerned about how users access their sites.

Those who operate noncommercial Web sites might also want to be able to exercise control over how visitors enter their sites, just as a homeowner may prefer that guests enter his house by way of the front door instead of the side or back door. We next consider two examples of deep linking: one in a commercial context, and the other in a personal Web site.

▶ **SCENARIO 9–3:** Deep Linking on the Ticketmaster Web Site

Ticketmaster is a Web site that operates in Seattle, Washington; it lists cultural events in the Seattle area and enables users to purchase tickets for those events. Microsoft, as a service to its employees, included a link from its Web site directly to a page on the Ticketmaster site that described information about cultural events in the Seattle area. But Ticketmaster objected to Microsoft's use of this direct link to their sub-page, arguing that it should have a right to determine how information on its site is viewed. Ticketmaster also worried about revenue that might be lost from its advertisers, if the site's visitors systematically bypassed its top-level page, which contained various ads. Ticketmaster sued Microsoft.[10] ■

Microsoft eventually settled out of court. So we have no court ruling on the legality of deep linking, but many legal observers believe that Microsoft had a strong case and would have prevailed. From the standpoint of commercial interests, Ticketmaster's position seems reasonable: Ticketmaster stood to lose valuable revenue from advertisers, which could eventually have resulted in Ticketmaster's going out of business altogether. But how is this case different from our earlier example involving Professor Jones who seemed indifferent as to whether visitors entered her site via the top-level Web page before accessing the bibliography on that site's sub-page? In that scenario, there was no concern about lost revenue from advertisers. But could Jones still insist, as Ticketmaster did, that visitors access her site through the top-level page? What grounds would she have for doing so?

Perhaps Professor Jones believes that her Web site reflects her work as a scholar and that the bibliography section can be more fully appreciated in the context of the overall site. Recall our analysis of the personality theory of property in Chapter 8. There, we considered a scenario where Angela, the author of a scholarly journal article, wanted her article reprinted only in its entirety in a textbook, because she believed that an excerpted form of the article did not truly represent her work. Is Professor Jones' position regarding how the bibliography on her Web site should be accessed similar to Angela's position about how her article should be read?

Richard Spinello (2004) describes a scenario where an imaginary artist named Maria has set up an online exhibit of her paintings on her personal Web site. One of Maria's paintings is highly controversial and has generated considerable interest both within and outside the art community, and many people would like to link directly to the image of that painting on Maria's Web site. But Maria argues that the artist should be able to determine the sequential arrangement of paintings in a physical art gallery, and thus how the visitors to her online gallery are required to view the images of her paintings there. The controversial painting in question, she further argues, is best understood within the context of other paintings that both precede and follow it in the online exhibit.

Is Maria's position reasonable? If a Web site is viewed as a form of (intellectual) property, then she may have a strong case. Consider that Maria, as a property owner, could determine how people enter her site in the same way that a home owner in physical space can require that visitors enter the house only through either the front door or a side door. If a Web site is considered private property, however, another controversial issue also arises: an unwelcome visitor to a Web site could be accused of trespassing. The notion of trespass in cyberspace is far from clear; however, some believe that the practice of sending unsolicited e-mail, which is now commonly referred to as spam, qualifies as a form of trespass in cyberspace.

▶ 9.5 E-MAIL SPAM

What is *spam*, and why is it problematic from a social and moral perspective? Keith Miller and James Moor (2008) point out that according to some estimates, as much as 80% of e-mail sent could qualify as spam. But they also note that there are "dramatically different definitions" of what can count as spam.

9.5.1 Defining Spam

While there is no universally agreed-upon definition of spam, it is typically viewed as e-mail that is *unsolicited*, *commercial*, and sent in *bulk* to multiple users. Is this definition adequate? Because spam is *unsolicited*, it is also nonconsensual. However, not all nonconsensual e-mail is spam. If you have an e-mail account, you have probably received unsolicited e-mail messages requesting information from you or informing you about an upcoming event; they may have been sent to you because you are a member of a particular social networking service (SNS) or because you have an e-mail address associated with an academic institution, government organization, and so forth. You may have considered some of these messages annoying, but are they necessarily spam?

Another feature of our working definition of spam is that it is *commercial*. However, some commercial e-mail you receive can be in the form of advertisements that you have authorized a commercial Web site to e-mail you. For example, you could have registered on an e-mail distribution list for a department store at which you frequently shop, requesting to be informed about upcoming sales and discount items. The e-mails you receive from this site, while commercial or promotional in nature, would not qualify as spam.

Spam is distributed in *bulk*, but not all e-mails distributed in that form necessarily qualify as spam. For example, some messages sent in bulk form (i.e., to an e-mail list) might have been directed at people in the group who are known by the sender; there could be some personal or professional connection between the sender and receiver of the e-mail message. So, our initial working definition of spam as e-mail that is "unsolicited, promotional, and sent in bulk" to multiple users would not seem adequate.

Miller and Moor believe that much of the popular discussion about spam in terms of what they describe as unsolicited commercial bulk e-mail (UCBE) is both "confused and degraded" because it fails to distinguish between UCBE that is "deceptive" and "intended to harm" and UCBE that is not. They also believe that the problems affecting e-mail spam can be better analyzed by focusing on a series of distinct, but interrelated, criteria such as the

- content of the e-mail
- intent of the sender
- consequences of the receiver
- consent of the receiver
- relationship between the sender and the receiver
- accountability of the sender and the degree of deception
- number of identical e-mails sent.[11]

Miller and Moor disagree with many critics of spam who tend to assume that all e-mail advertisements are deceptive. Alternatively, they believe that it is possible to distinguish between UCBE advertisements that (a) "misrepresent and are fraudulent" and (b) "present information in a favorable light." They refer to the former as *F-UCBE* and distinguish it from the nonfraudulent version they call *NF-UCBE*. They also believe that NF-UCBE requires a more complex ethical analysis than F-UCBE.

9.5.2 Why Is Spam Morally Objectionable?

Richard Spinello (2006) believes that spam is morally objectionable for two reasons: one based on utilitarian grounds and the other on deontological considerations. In his view, spam not only has harmful consequences, but it also violates the individual autonomy of Internet users. First, consider some of the harmful consequences of spam—e.g., its financial impacts, such as cost shifting and the consumption of valuable network resources. For example, spam consumes and strains valuable computing resources and thus contributes to the degradation of what Spinello describes as the "fragile ecology of the Internet." Miller and Moor describe these kinds of abuses of the Internet as one more instance of "spoiling of the commons." (Recall our discussion of the "tragedy of the commons" in Chapter 8.)

Spinello argues that even if Internet resources were infinite and there were no negative utilitarian consequences, spam would still be morally objectionable because it does not respect individual users as persons. He believes that deontological arguments, such as Kant's (see Chapter 2), can be used to show why this so. Recall that Kant argues that a practice has moral worth only if it can be universalizable. And, in Kant's system, a practice is universalizable only if it can coherently apply to all persons without exception. So, we need to ask: Could we universalize a coherent practice in which each e-mail user would allow spam to be sent and received by every other user? Could such a practice, if instituted, be logically coherent? On Kantian grounds, if spammers did not accept the principle that everyone should be able to send and receive spam, then they would be inconsistent. If spammers believed that only they should be permitted to send spam, then they would be making an exception for themselves. And if they granted themselves this exception, while relying on the good will of ordinary users not to engage in the practice of spamming others, then spammers would be treating ordinary users merely as a means to their ends. So, Spinello makes a plausible case for why spam can be considered morally objectionable on deontological as well as utilitarian grounds.

Miller and Moor believe that an adequate ethical analysis of spam also needs to take into consideration criteria such as accountability and deception—generally, the "more deceptive the content and the less accountable the sender, the more blameworthy the sender becomes." Employing their distinction between NF-UCBE and F-UCBE, they argue that fraudulent UCBE should always be condemned, whereas some cases of NF-UCBE can be justifiable from a moral point of view. For example, they point out that a whistle-blower might send a message to a large commercial mailing list to alert recipients of an injustice or a danger. Here, the whistle-blower may have justifiable reasons for sending the e-mail broadly and for wishing to be anonymous. Miller and Moor believe that in this whistle-blowing scenario, the "intent" of the sender needs to be taken into consideration. So, there can be some cases where sending spam in the form of NF-UCBE would be justifiable.

It is one thing to say that spam, at least in its F-UCBE form, is morally objectionable, but it is another to ask what can be done about it from a legal and a public policy perspective. Because spam is very similar to the "junk mail" that we receive via the postal delivery system, we might ask why the same laws that apply to physical junk mail do not also apply to electronic spam. Although there are similarities between the two forms of junk mail, there are also relevant differences; practical and financial constraints determine how much physical junk mail merchants can send, but the same kinds of constraints do not apply in the case of electronic spam.

Miller and Moor believe that e-mail spam is also analogous to unsolicited commercial phone calls. And they point out that the latter have been significantly reduced in the United States through legislation, even though they have not been altogether eliminated. But they also note that because of the "open" nature of Internet architectures and protocols, spam has been far more resistant to the kinds of legislative and technological solutions used to discourage unsolicited commercial phone calls.

Various state laws against spam have been enacted in the United States, and in 2003, the Congress passed the CAN SPAM (Controlling the Assault of Non-Solicited Pornography and Marketing) Act. That law, which went into effect in January 2004, specifies criminal penalties that include a fine of $250 for each spam e-mail. However, critics of the CAN SPAM Act note that spammers who use ISPs outside the United States to send their spam e-mail cannot be prosecuted under this act, which cannot be enforced internationally. Some critics are also skeptical as to whether any kind of legislation, even international laws, can solve the problem of spam.

▶ 9.6 FREE SPEECH VS. CENSORSHIP AND CONTENT CONTROL IN CYBERSPACE

So far in Chapter 9, we have examined a set of regulatory issues that either involved, or had implications for, electronic commerce. We next turn our attention to regulatory issues involving the *content* of cyberspace. Such issues center on the question as to whether all forms of online speech should be tolerated. In some instances, regulatory concerns affecting online speech and online commerce overlap. For example, questions concerning spam, considered in the preceding section, straddle the divide; some purveyors of spam have defended their practice on the grounds of free speech. However, the issues we examine in the remainder of Chapter 9 affect the regulation of Internet content and thus tend to fall mainly under the category of speech.

Note that in this and the following sections, we do not address the censorship or suppression of "political speech" by nation states—an issue that is hotly debated because of practices involving governmental regulation of the Internet in the People's Republic of China and other non-democratic countries. That concern is however addressed in Chapter 10 in our examination of democracy and democratic ideals in cyberspace. In Sections 9.6–9.8, we focus on some tensions between free speech and censorship that arise mainly in the United States and the European Union countries.

9.6.1 Protecting Free Speech

Do all forms of online speech in the United States deserve to be protected under the U.S. Constitutional guarantee of free speech? According to the First Amendment of the United States Constitution, "Congress shall make no law . . . abridging the freedom of speech, or of the press." This passage, consisting of merely fourteen words, has often been quoted by libertarians who strongly believe that the government should not intrude in matters involving our constitutionally guaranteed right to free speech. We should note, however, that free speech is not an absolute right. As in the case of other rights contained in the Bill of Rights, which comprise the first ten amendments to the Constitution, the right to free speech is *conditional* in the sense that it is only a right if "all things are equal." While one's right to free speech protects his/her freedom to express controversial ideas concerning politics, religion, and so forth, it does not grant him/her the right to shout "Fire!" in a crowded shopping mall or a movie theater.

Also, during times of war, one's ability to speak freely is sometimes constrained. For example, in the period immediately following the attacks of September 11, 2001, some Americans labeled the news commentators, reporters, and talk show hosts who criticized the Bush White House as "unpatriotic." Ordinarily, such criticisms are considered normal and in accordance with the principle of free speech, which is presumed by political commentators and the press. But at other times, social norms and market forces rather than the law itself can regulate free speech. Television viewers who were offended by remarks they perceived as either anti-Bush or antigovernment pressured advertisers not to sponsor programs that expressed viewpoints that they believed were "unpatriotic." This, in turn, caused television networks either to cancel some programs or not to broadcast them in certain areas of the country. (Note that this is an example of Lessig's claim that, in certain cases, social norms and market forces can be more effective regulators than laws themselves.) Nonetheless, free speech is a broad right, cited time and again by publishers of unpopular tabloids and also appealed to by many who distribute pornography. Many believe, however, that some forms of speech on the Internet, including pornography, should be censored.

9.6.2 Defining Censorship

What, exactly, is censorship? Kay Mathiesen (2008) characterizes censorship as limiting access to content by deterring either (a) the speaker from speaking or (b) the hearer from receiving the speech. She also advances a more formal definition of censorship, claiming that to censor is to

> restrict or limit access to an expression, portion of an expression, or category of expression, which has been made public by its author, based on the belief that it will be a bad thing if people access the content of that expression.[12]

Jacques Catudal (2004) points out that an important distinction can be drawn between two types of censorship that he describes as "censorship by suppression" and "censorship by deterrence." Both forms presuppose that some "authorized person or group of persons" has judged some text or "type of text" objectionable on moral, political, or other grounds.

Censorship by suppression prohibits the objectionable text or material from being published, displayed, or circulated. Banning certain books from being published or prohibiting certain kinds of movies from being made are both examples of censorship by suppression. In this scheme, pornography and other objectionable forms of speech would not be allowed on the Internet.

Censorship by deterrence, on the contrary, is less drastic. It neither suppresses nor blocks out objectionable material, nor does it forbid such material from being published. Rather, it depends on threats of arrest, prosecution, conviction, and punishment of both those who make an objectionable text available and those who acquire it. Heavy fines and possible imprisonment can deter the publication and acquisition of objectionable content. Again, using Lessig's regulatory model, social norms, such as social disenfranchisement, personal disgrace, and public censure, can also work to deter individuals from engaging in the publication, display, and transmission of objectionable speech.

In the next two sections, we examine three key forms of "objectionable speech" in cyberspace: pornography, hate speech, and speech that can cause physical harm to others. In the following section, we focus on various forms of online pornography, including virtual child pornography, and we look at a series of laws that have been enacted to protect children and minors.

▶ 9.7 PORNOGRAPHY IN CYBERSPACE

Before examining the issue of pornography on the Internet, or what some call "cyberporn," it is instructive to understand what legally qualifies as pornography in general. It is often debated in terms of notions such as obscenity and indecent speech. In *Miller v. California* (1973), the court established a three-part guideline for determining whether material is obscene under the law and thus not protected by the First Amendment. According to this criteria, something is obscene if it

1. depicts sexual (or excretory) acts whose depiction is specifically prohibited by law;

2. depicts these acts in a patently offensive manner, appealing to prurient interest as judged by a reasonable person using community standards;

3. has no serious literary, artistic, social, political, or scientific value.[13]

These criteria have proved problematic in attempts to enforce pornography laws. For example, the second criterion includes three controversial notions: "prurient interest," "reasonable person," and "community standards." *Prurient* is usually defined as having to do with lust and lewd behavior, concepts that, in turn, have been challenged as being vague and arbitrary. Also, many ask who, exactly, counts as a reasonable person. Until the advent of cybertechnology, we might have assumed a fairly straightforward notion of "community standard" because traditionally a community has been defined in terms of geographical space. But what, exactly, is a community in cyberspace? And when more than one community is involved in a dispute involving pornography, whose community standards should apply?

9.7.1 Interpreting "Community Standards" in Cyberspace

Interpretations of "community" and "community standards" were among the issues debated in a court case involving pornography and the Amateur Action (Electronic) Bulletin Board System. (Electronic bulletin board systems could be viewed as a type of online forum that functioned as a predecessor to contemporary networking sites such as Craigslist.) This bulletin board system (or BBS), which made sexually explicit images available to its members, was operated by a married couple who lived in California. Because it was an online forum, its contents were available not only to residents of California but to users who had Internet access in other states and countries. A resident of Memphis, Tennessee, became a member of the BBS and then downloaded sexually explicit pictures onto his computer in Tennessee. Although including sexually explicit images on a BBS may not have been illegal in California, viewing such images was illegal under Tennessee state law, and criminal charges were brought against the operators of the BBS, who (though California residents) were prosecuted in Tennessee.[14]

The operators of this BBS were found guilty under Tennessee law of distributing obscenity, as defined under the local community standards that applied in Memphis. Not surprisingly, this case raised issues of what was meant by "community standards" on the Internet. Can a community in cyberspace be defined simply in terms of geography? Or, in an era of Internet-based social networking sites, such as Facebook and MySpace, should "community" be defined by other criteria? For example, can an online community be better understood as a computer-mediated forum where individuals who share common interests come together? (We examine online communities in detail in Chapter 11.)

The Amateur Action (BBS) case also raised another important issue: Were the pornographic files *distributed* over the Internet by the operators of the BBS in California, as alleged? Or, instead, did the resident in Tennessee who actually downloaded them via the interstate telephone lines that transmit information between the two states *retrieve* those controversial files from the Internet? Questions involving distribution and community standards in cyberspace contribute to the difficulty of interpreting and enforcing pornography laws online.

Many people first became aware of the amount of pornographic material available on the Internet through a news story, entitled "CyberPorn," which appeared in *TIME* magazine in the summer of 1995. *TIME* reported that there were 900,000 sexually explicit pornographic materials (pictures, film clips, etc.) available on the Internet. Many people, including most lawmakers, were outraged when they learned about the amount of pornographic material that was so easily accessible to Internet users, including minors. Later, however, the *TIME* magazine story, based on an Internet study that had been conducted by a researcher at Carnegie Mellon University, was shown to be seriously flawed.

Although the Carnegie Mellon study accurately reported the number of pornographic images and pornographic Web sites that were available, it failed to put this information into proper perspective — it made no mention of the fact that the percentage of pornographic sites relative to other sites on the Web was very low. However, the report caught the attention of many influential politicians, some of whom drafted legislation in response to what they saw as the growth of the "pornography industry" on the Internet. The result was the passage of the Communications Decency Act (CDA) in early 1996.

9.7.2 Internet Pornography Laws and Protecting Children Online

The CDA caused controversy from the outset, especially the section referred to as the Exon Amendment, which dealt specifically with online pornography. The American Civil Liberties Union (ACLU) and other organizations soon challenged the constitutionality of CDA. In the summer of 1996, a court in Philadelphia struck down CDA on grounds that it was too broad and that it violated the United States Constitution; in the summer of 1997, the Supreme Court upheld the lower court's ruling.[15] One section of the CDA, known as the Child Pornography Protection Act (CPPA) of 1996, was determined to be constitutional. According to the CPPA, it was a crime to "knowingly send, receive, distribute, reproduce, sell, or possess more than three child pornographic images."[16] So even though CDA itself was overturned, supporters of that legislation were pleased that the section on child pornography still held.

In 1998, Congress passed the Child Online Pornography Act (COPA). (We should note that COPA is sometimes confused with COPPA, the Children's Online Privacy Protection Act of 2000, which was designed to reduce the amount of information that could be collected from children under the age of 12 who use the Internet.) Many of COPA's proponents believed that this act would be upheld by the courts, but as in the case of CDA, COPA was ill-fated. In 1999, the Supreme Court ruled that COPA was unconstitutional.[17] The only remaining federal law in 1999 that was specifically directed at online pornography and that had managed to withstand constitutional scrutiny was the

CPPA of 1996, a section of the original CDA. Although it appeared that CPPA would remain intact, many critics argued that provisions of this act also conflicted with the U.S. Constitution. In April 2002, the Supreme Court, in a ruling of 6–3, struck down portions of CPPA as unconstitutional.[18]

In December 2000, the U.S. Congress enacted into law the Children's Internet Protection Act (CIPA), designed to address concerns about children's access to "offensive content" over the Internet on school and library computers. CIPA was targeted specifically at schools and libraries, where federal and local governments have greater control. This law affects any schools or public libraries that receive federal funding in the form of "E-Rate" discounts (described in Chapter 10), which make certain technologies more affordable for eligible schools and libraries. According to CIPA requirements, schools and libraries may not receive the discounts offered by the E-Rate Program unless they certify that they have an "Internet safety policy" in place. This policy includes technology-based protection measures to block or filter Internet access by minors to pictures that are (a) obscene, (b) child pornography, and (c) harmful to minors.[19]

As in the case of CPPA and COPA, CIPA was eventually challenged in the courts. In 2001 several groups, including the American Library Association (ALA) and the ACLU, filed suit to prevent the enforcement of CIPA's filtering requirement in public libraries. In 2002, the U.S. District Court for the eastern district of Pennsylvania ruled that the CIPA filtering mandate was unconstitutional. However, the District Court's decision was overturned by the U.S. Supreme Court, which upheld CIPA in a 6–3 decision in June 2003 (*United States v. American Library Assn. Inc.*, 2003).

Legal analysts who have closely followed the Supreme Court's ruling in the CIPA case believe that no clear precedent had been established with respect to how online child pornography laws will be interpreted in the future. This is especially apparent in legal precedents for interpreting an appropriate scope of filtering in public libraries. The Supreme Court's ruling in CIPA is considered a "plurality decision" because there was less than a clear majority in the justices' written opinions. Justices Kennedy and Breyer, who sided with the majority, did not concur with the rationales stated in Justice Reinquist's "majority opinion." Although they agreed with Reinquist's conclusion, they wrote a separate opinion supporting the majority decision only to the extent that it provides filtering for children, but Kennedy and Breyer also sated that filtering must be easily disabled for adults who request it in public libraries.[20]

Although CIPA provides protection for children in school and library settings, proponents of broad-based pornography legislation are concerned that CIPA falls short because it does not provide the kind of protection children need outside those contexts. However, CIPA's critics argue that too much nonpornographic content is blocked in the process of protecting children.

Table 9.1 identifies the four online child pornography laws that have been enacted at the federal level, including when the laws were passed and when three of them were eventually struck down.

9.7.3 Virtual Child Pornography

Critics have argued that online pornography laws, especially CPPA, broaden the definition of child pornography to include entire categories of images that many would not judge to be "child pornographic." Catudal (2004) notes that visual depictions of

TABLE 9.1   Internet-Specific Child Pornography Laws

CDA (Communications Decency Act)	Passed in January 1996 and declared unconstitutional in July 1996. The Supreme Court upheld the lower court's decision in 1997.
CPPA (Child Pornography Protection Act)	Passed as part of the larger CDA, but not initially struck down in 1997 with the CDA. It was declared unconstitutional in April 2002.
COPA (Child Online Pornography Act)	Passed in June 1998 and (portions) declared unconstitutional by the Supreme Court in February 1999.
CIPA (Children's Internet Protection Act)	Passed in December 2000 and declared unconstitutional by a U.S. district court in 2002. The Supreme Court overturned the lower court's ruling in June 2003.

sexually explicit conduct that do not involve *actual* minors would be included as child pornography under CPPA. In fact, Catudal believes that the CPPA's definition of child pornography includes categories of images that some would judge not pornographic at all.

Child pornography, according to CPPA, is "any depiction, including a photograph, film, video, picture, or computer or computer-generated image or picture, whether made or produced by electronic, mechanical, or other means, of sexually explicit conduct." The definition goes on to list four categories of such depictions:

A. the production of such visual depiction involves the use of a minor engaging in sexually explicit conduct;

B. such visual depiction is, or appears to be, of a minor engaging in sexually explicit conduct; or

C. such visual depiction has been created, adapted, or modified to appear that an identifiable minor is engaging in sexually explicit conduct; or

D. such visual depiction is advertised, promoted, presented, described, or distributed in such a manner that conveys the impression that the material is or contains a visual depiction of a minor engaging in sexually explicit conduct.[21]

Whereas category (A) images represent depictions of what has been traditionally regarded as child pornography, Catudal argues that the same is not true of category (B) images. For example, he considers the case of a 19-year-old girl who appears in a pornographic image in which she looks much younger. Sexual depictions of this sort are sometimes referred to as the "little girl" genre; they have been used in many artistic works. (The "little girl" type does not, by definition, actually involve little girls or minors of any age.) In the United States, the sexually explicit depiction of a "young looking" 19-year-old would be considered child pornography under CPPA, but in some other countries, such as Norway, it would not. Catudal believes that CPPA fails to note that category (A) and category (B) depictions represent two different types of prurient images.

Note also that in categories (C) and (D), the pornographic image can consist of a depiction of someone who *appears* to be a minor engaging in sexual activity, or a depiction that *conveys the impression* of a minor engaging in such an activity. So, a computer-generated image that does not refer to an actual human being would also qualify as a child pornography image under CPPA. In its decision to strike down portions of the CPPA, the Supreme Court reasoned that a distinction needed to be made between a pornographic image of an actual child and that of a "virtual," or computer-generated, image of a minor.

Some argue that because no real children are used in the production of virtual child pornography, no children are harmed in the process. However, Per Sandin (2004) argues that even if the production of virtual child pornography does not harm real children, it does not follow that the *use* of virtual child pornography causes no harm to real children. Sandin suggests that a utilitarian argument could be made against allowing virtual child pornography if it is shown to have harmful consequences for real children. In our discussion of virtual reality in Chapter 11, we will see that "objectionable behavior" performed in virtual environments such as VR games, which portray only virtual or computer-generated images, can nonetheless cause real harm to real people. However, we will not continue with the debate about real vs. virtual harm here. Our purpose in this section has been to examine Internet pornography legislation that has been enacted to protect children online and to show why that legislation has been controversial, especially when it is extended to include virtual child pornographic images. We next consider how those laws apply in the case of "sexting."

Child Pornography Laws and Sexting

What is sexting, and what challenges does it pose for current child pornography laws? Sexting is typically defined as the use of cell phones (or similar handheld electronic devices) to send nude or seminude photos of oneself to others. In some cases, these photos become widely distributed and can eventually end up on the Internet.

▶ **SCENARIO 9–4:** A Sexting Incident Involving Greensburg Salem High School

In 2009, six teenagers—three girls and three boys—at the Greensburg Salem High School in Pennsylvania were charged under child pornography laws in a sexting incident. The three girls, ages 14 and 15, who took nude or seminude photos of themselves on their cell phones and sent them to male classmates, faced charges involving the "manufacturing and dissemination of child pornography." The boys, who were ages 16 and 17, faced charges of possession of child pornography. The nude pictures were discovered by Greenburg High School officials when they seized a cell phone from a male student who was using it in violation of school policy.[22] The charges were later reduced to misdemeanors. ■

Should the six teenagers have been charged with either dissemination or possession of child pornography? Were the original felony charges brought against them too harsh? Alternatively, are misdemeanor charges too lenient in cases such as this one? There does not yet seem to be any clear consensus on the answer to this question. Yet, the number of reported sexting incidents involving teenagers has increased sharply in recent years.

Next, consider two sexting incidents that each had very unfortunate outcomes—one resulting in the suicide of an 18-year-old female, and one resulting in a felony charge brought against a male who had just turned 18. An Ohio resident—we will call her "Jill"—sent nude photos of herself via her cell phone to a boy, who then forwarded the pictures to others. The nude pictures of Jill were seen by some of her classmates at school as well as by others who lived in her community. As the photos became more widely distributed, Jill was taunted by some of her classmates as well as by others in her community. In May 2008, Jill took her life by hanging herself in her bedroom.[23]

A Florida resident, whom we will call "Phil," sent a nude picture of his girlfriend to his friends and family, via his cell phone, following the couple's break-up. His girlfriend was 16, and Phil had recently turned 18. He was arrested by police in Florida who charged Phil with sending child pornography, and he was later convicted of a felony offense. Consequently, Phil was required to register as a sex offender, which means that his name will appear on an Internet registry of sex offenders in Florida until he is 43. Phil was also expelled from college and was unable to find employment. Additionally, he is required to check with his probation officer if he plans to travel outside his home county (in the state of Florida).[24]

Can sexting crimes be understood and prosecuted in a manner that is consistent with our current legal framework? It would seem that sexting incidents have once again generated what James Moor (2007) calls a "conceptual muddle" regarding cybertechnology. This, in turn, needs to be resolved before we can frame coherent policies and laws to punish sexting offenses. Legal analysts point out that the current laws are inconsistent in their application from state to state. We have seen that states such as Pennsylvania and Florida have prosecuted, or have tried to prosecute, sexting cases as a felony offense. However, in other states, including Vermont, lawmakers have introduced legislation that would exclude teenagers who engage in sexting from being tried under child pornography laws and would instead make sexting a misdemeanor.[25] Advocates on both sides of this view, however, can agree on one thing: more consistent laws are needed.

Can "Exceptions" be Applied to Child Pornography Laws in Sexting Cases?

Julie Hilden (2013) believes that instead of applying older child pornography laws that were designed for "graver and much more exploitative contexts," we should "craft new laws designed specifically for sexting." She agrees with critics of the Greenburg case, including the ACLU, that the initial charges brought against the six Pennsylvania teenagers were "ill-grounded," because the child pornography laws under which the teenagers were first charged were intended to cover "lascivious displays of the genitals and/or sexual activity." Hilden believes that the teenagers involved in the Greensburg High School incident were not guilty of this kind of behavior, especially since two of the girls were wearing bras and one was topless in the photos sent to the three boys. So prosecuting the three girls under strict child pornography laws would be inappropriate.

Hilden also believes, however, that the prosecution of some teenagers under such laws would be appropriate in future cases of sexting that might involve "underage teens having sex, displaying their genitals in a lascivious way, or both." In these cases, she suggests that the behavior of the teenagers could validly "form the basis of child-pornography charges." Hilden also suggests that lawmakers should consider two kinds of "exceptions" to child pornography laws in sexting cases: (1) a "Romeo and Juliet" exception (which is sometimes used in statutory rape laws where consensus is involved), and (2) an "age-specific" exception. She believes that the Romeo and Juliet exception could apply when the two parties to an act of sex are close in age (say 18 and 16, or 15 and 17). She notes, for example, that a 16-year-old sexting a nude photo of herself or himself to someone roughly the same age is far less disturbing than a 16-year-old doing so at the invitation of a 40-year-old. Hilden asks us to imagine a 16-year-old, named Jane, who sends a nude photo of herself to her 18-year-old boyfriend, Bill. Here Jane might be protected under the Romeo and Juliet exception (and thus be immune from prosecution).

But Hilden also points out that if Bill forwards the photo to one or more persons without Jane's consent, he should not be immune from prosecution. Although these exceptions do not provide a "bright line," Hilden believes that they at least allow authorities to differentiate between a high school senior who takes and "sexts" a photo of a 13-year-old eighth grader, and is truly engaging in child pornography, and a sexting incident involving two teenagers in the same age category. In this way, the exceptions would avoid the need to impose severe criminal penalties on more-or-less same-age kids for what Hilden describes as "ugly immaturity," not crime.

One question that Hilden does not consider, however, is what would happen in the case where a teenage girl sends an uninvited nude photo of herself to an older man. In this case, would the man receiving the unsolicited photo be liable for prosecution under child pornography laws merely for having (or having had at some point) the nude photo of the teenager on his cell phone? An actual case involving sexting between a 52-year-old man and a 14-year-old female occurred in Georgia (Bunker 2009). In this incident, the older man was trying to set up a "sexual rendezvous" with the young female. The girl sent him nude photos that she had taken of herself on her cell phone. Here, of course, the controversies raised go well beyond sexting—for example, they also include questions of intended child molestation or pedophilia. But what if this man had made no sexual advances toward the 14-year-old girl and still received the pictures? It is not clear whether he still could be criminally charged with possessing child pornography on his cell phone. So, it would seem that answers to questions of this type would also need to be spelled out more clearly and explicitly in any future legislation drafted for sexting that incorporates age-specific exceptions.

What can we conclude about sexting as it relates to our examination of child pornography in this section? We can agree with critics that most teenagers who have been prosecuted so far for sexting have not engaged in behavior that meets the threshold of crimes intended for prosecution as felonies under child pornography laws. Yet, sexting is a serious offense and thus needs to be dealt with appropriately in the legal and judicial systems. In the meantime, it seems that drafting some kind of federal standard that could be applied to sexting cases occurring in all states would be the best short-term solution.

► 9.8 HATE SPEECH AND SPEECH THAT CAN CAUSE PHYSICAL HARM TO OTHERS

In addition to pornography, which is sometimes viewed as "obscene" speech, *hate speech* and forms of *speech that can cause physical harm* to individuals and communities have both caused controversy in cyberspace. We briefly examine some controversies affecting each.

9.8.1 Hate Speech on the Web

Hate speech on the Internet often targets racial and ethnic groups. For example, white supremacist organizations such as the Ku Klux Klan (KKK) can include offensive remarks about African Americans and Jews on their Web pages. Because of the Internet, international hate groups, such as "skin heads" in America, Europe, and Russia, can spread their messages of hate in ways that were not previously possible. Whereas the United States has focused its attention on controversial Internet speech issues that involve online pornography, European countries such as France and Germany have been more concerned about online hate speech. For example, Germany's Information and Communications Act was designed to censor neo-Nazi propaganda. But the law applies only to people who live in Germany; it cannot regulate the speech transmitted by ISPs outside that country. Roy Girasa (2002) believes that if the German government had tried to enforce this law, countries such as the United States would likely have refused to extradite individuals to Germany.

In France, it is illegal to sell anything that incites hate and racism. However, Nazi and KKK memorabilia are auctioned daily on Web sites such as Yahoo that have an international reach. In 2000, a French judge ruled that Yahoo must "make it impossible" for people in France to access sites selling that kind of material. Yahoo complied, and as a result, Nazi-related items are no longer available on Yahoo's French site (www.yahoo.fr). But French citizens who use an ISP outside France could potentially access the sites that are banned in France.[26]

In the United States, some "hate-watch" Web sites, such as the Southern Poverty Law Center's (SPLC) "Intelligence Project" (http://www.splcenter.org), monitor online hate speech aimed at racial minorities. In an effort to counter the effectiveness of "hate sites," these hate-watch Web sites have exposed the existence of various hate organizations to the public. The SPLC site also features a Hate Watch blog and it includes a detailed map with physical locations of various hate groups, which it identifies under categories such as Ku Klux Klan, Neo-Nazi, Racist Skinhead, and so forth. Ironically, perhaps, the information available on these sites also provides an easy way for consumers of hate speech to locate and visit particular hate sites that serve their interests.

Some hate sites use deceptive metatags (described in Section 9.4.2) to lure unsuspecting users to their sites. For example, a hate site directed against African Americans could use a keyword metatag such as "Martin Luther King, Jr." to intentionally mislead persons interested in acquiring information about Dr. King by directing them instead to its racist Web site.

Web sites have also been established to promote white supremacist hate speech. One such site was operated by James von Brunn who fatally shot an African American museum guard at the Holocaust Museum in Washington, D.C. in 2009. On his site (holywesternempire.com), von Brunn included hate speech aimed at Jews and African Americans. In fact, his site was listed on the Southern Poverty Law Center's notorious hate sites. A few days before von Brunn shot his victim, he transferred control of his Web site to Steve Reimink who described the 88-year-old von Brunn as a "sick individual." But Rimink's message also included "code," familiar to many white supremacists, suggesting that Rimink's remarks were not sincere.[27]

Some antiabortion groups in the United States have set up Web sites dedicated to distributing (hate-related) information about doctors who perform abortions. Some of these sites have included information about where these doctors live, what times they travel to and from abortion clinics, where they go in their free time, etc. As in the case of the white-supremacist rhetoric used by radical groups in the United States, this type of speech can also result in physical harm to others. Some information made available on anti-abortion Web sites has been linked to the murder of doctors who perform abortions. In 2009, for example, Dr. George Tiller, who performed late-term abortions in Kansas, was murdered by an anti-abortionist. Information about Tiller was available to Tiller's murderer via a Web site set up by an anti-abortionist group (http://www.dr-tiller.com/), which described Tiller as "America's most notorious abortionist" and as "Tiller the Killer." This site also included information about Tiller's employees and assistant abortionists.

9.8.2 Online "Speech" that Can Cause Physical Harm to Others

Some forms of hate speech on the Internet are such that they *might* also result in physical harm being caused to individuals (as in the case of the anti-abortionist sites described above). Other forms of this speech, however, are by the very nature of their content, biased toward violence and physical harm to others. Consider two examples of how speech communicated on the Internet can result in serious physical harm: one involving information on how to construct bombs, and another that provides information on how to abduct children for the purpose of molesting them. Should this information be censored in cyberspace? This kind of information was available before the Internet era and it may even have been (and still may be) available in some libraries. If it is available elsewhere, should it be censored on the Internet?

Critics point out that Internet access now makes it much easier to acquire all kinds of information, including information about how to make and do things that cause physical harm. They also note that it is possible to access and read this information in the privacy and comfort of one's home. Even more disturbing is that it is now far easier for international and domestic terrorists to obtain information about how to construct bombs. So, some believe that these are good enough reasons for censoring this kind of speech on the Internet.

Recall our discussion in Section 9.1.1 about whether the Internet should be conceived as a broadcast medium, like television or radio, or as a place, like a bookstore. We saw that the rules that apply in each are significantly different. Viewing the Internet as a medium of some sort makes it far easier to control the dissemination (or broadcast) of certain kinds of information than viewing it as a public place, such as a bookstore or library. If the Internet is viewed in the latter sense, however, it is more difficult to ban controversial forms of speech such as hate speech and speech that can cause physical harm to others. So, the debate continues about which kinds of speech, if any, should be regulated on the Internet.

▶ 9.9 "NETWORK NEUTRALITY" AND THE FUTURE OF INTERNET REGULATION

So far in Chapter 9, we have analyzed a wide range of controversies affecting cyberspace regulation. While some have focused on concerns involving the regulation of commerce, others have centered mainly on issues that affect speech (or content) in cyberspace. All of these regulatory concerns, however, have been examined within the context of a "neutral" Internet. We conclude this chapter with a brief examination of the controversial debate involving *network neutrality*, and we consider what kinds of implications the outcome of this debate may have for regulating and accessing the Internet in the future.

9.9.1 Defining Network Neutrality

What, exactly, is Network Neutrality, or "net neutrality," as it has commonly come to be called? Tim Wu, an Internet policy expert at Columbia University, describes it as a *principle* in which "a maximally useful public information network aspires to treat all content, sites, and platforms equally."[28] In explaining the key elements underpinning the net-neutrality principle, Wu draws an interesting analogy between a neutral Internet and other kinds of networks, which he claims are also implicitly built on a "neutrality theory." Focusing on the neutral nature of the electric grid, for example, he writes:

> The general purpose and neutral nature of the electric grid is one of the things that make it extremely useful. The electric grid does not care if you plug in a toaster, an iron, or a computer. Consequently it has survived and supported giant waves of innovation in the appliance market. The electric grid worked for the radios of the 1930s works for the flat screen TVs of the 2000s. For that reason the electric grid is a model of a neutral, innovation-driving network.[29]

Will the Internet, like the electric grid, remain a neutral network? Currently, the principle of net neutrality is at the center of a contentious debate between two groups: neutrality *opponents*, who include major U.S. telecommunication companies as well as some conservative law makers; and neutrality *proponents* consisting of a wide coalition comprising numerous organizations that are commercial and non-commercial, liberal and conservative, and public and private. Proponents also include many consumer groups and ordinary users, as well as the founders of the Internet (Lessig and McChesney, 2006).

Proponents believe that the Internet had been conceived of and implemented as a neutral network from the outset, even if no regulatory laws or formal policies had been in place to enforce it. In recent years, however, this principle has been questioned and challenged by neutrality opponents. The tension that had been brewing between the two groups escalated in 2005, when the FCC officially adopted four broad neutrality principles in an effort to (a) "deregulate the Internet services provided by telephone companies," and (b) "give consumers the right to use the content, applications, services and devices of their choice when using the Internet."[30] In 2008, one service provider, Comcast, was accused of slowing down access to (and effectively blocking users from) a popular (P-2-P) file-sharing site. That year, the FCC filed a formal complaint against Comcast for its actions; although it did not impose a fine on the service provider, the FCC did require that Comcast cease blocking the P2P site in question. Next, Comcast challenged the FCC's position in court, and in April 2010 a federal appeals court ruled in Comcast's favor.

Following the appeals court's decision, the FCC approved what some critics view as a "compromise" position that effectively created two classes of Internet access: one for "fixed-line providers," and one for the "Wireless Net." Some critics see this compromise as a form of "net semi-neutrality." While the new FCC policy officially banned fixed-line broadband providers' services from both "outright blocking" and "unreasonable discrimination" of Web sites or applications, it also provided more "wiggle room" to wireless providers such as Verizon and AT&T.[31]

9.9.2 Some Arguments Advanced by Net Neutrality's Proponents and Opponents

Proponents of net neutrality tend to argue that America's largest telecommunications companies, including AT&T, Comcast, Time Warner, and Verizon, want to be "Internet gatekeepers" who can:

- guarantee speedy delivery of their data via "express lanes" for their own content and services, or for large corporations that can afford to pay steep fees;
- slow down services to some sites, or block content offered by their competitors;
- discriminate "in favor of their own search engines, Internet phone services and streaming video."[32]

Opponents of net neutrality tend to respond to these charges by claiming that the telecommunications companies have no plans to block content or services, slow down or "degrade" network performance for some sites, or discriminate against any users. Instead, they argue that these companies simply want to stimulate competition on the Internet and that doing this will result in increased:

- Internet speed, reach, and availability for users (in the United States);
- economic growth, job creation, global competitiveness, and consumer welfare.[33]

However, many critics remain skeptical about the neutrality opponents' real intentions, and they point to an incident (mentioned above) in which Comcast intentionally degraded network performance by slowing down access to a popular file sharing site.

9.9.3 Future Implications for the Net Neutrality Debate

Representatives on both sides of the net-neutrality debate seem eager to predict the kinds of dire outcomes that they believe are at stake in this debate. Tim Berners-Lee, who designed the Web's HTTP Protocol and is a staunch proponent of net neutrality, recently remarked on what he believes would happen if neutrality is lost:

> "When I invented the Web, I didn't have to ask anyone's permission. Now, hundreds of millions of people are using it freely. I am worried that that is going to end in the USA."[34]

Berners-Lee believes that much "misinformation" about net neutrality has already been spread by some telecommunications companies who have spent a considerable amount of money on television advertisements and public relations campaigns. He worries that these TV ads and PR campaigns will influence future policy decisions against neutrality. Lessig and McChesney (2006) also worry about the future of the Internet in the absence of a net neutrality principle. They believe that one benefit of net neutrality in the past has been that it has served to minimize control by the network owners. In general, neutrality proponents believe that the consequences of an Internet without a neutrality principle would be devastating for at least three reasons:

1. access to information would be restricted, and innovation would be stifled;
2. competition would be limited because consumer choice and the free market would be sacrificed to the interests of a few corporations;

3. the Internet will look more like cable TV, where network owners will decide which channels, content, and applications are available (and consumers will have to choose from their menus).[35]

Of course, neutrality opponents, especially large telephone and cable companies in the United States, see the matter very differently. For one thing, broadband providers claim that since 2008 they have invested more than $250 billion dollars to expand Internet access to broadband technology to homes and businesses in the United States. For another, they claim that broadband industry is now responsible for supporting more than six million American jobs.[36]

Although neutrality opponents have already met with some success, forcing what critics now view as a (compromised) "semi-neutral" Internet, they plan to press harder with future legislation that will grant the telecommunication companies more flexibility and control. As already noted, many conservative lawmakers support this effort. On the other side, however, a piece of legislation called The Internet Freedom Preservation Act was introduced in the U.S. Congress in 2009 by Reps. Edward Markey (D-Mass.) and Anna Eshoo (D-Calif.). Supporters of this legislation believe that its passage would protect net neutrality and thus help to safeguard the future of an open Internet.

It is not yet clear which direction the U.S. government will ultimately take in the net-neutrality dispute. But if the Internet becomes an increasingly multitiered entity with respect to access, where some parties (e.g., those who either control content or can afford to pay for premium access) are privileged or favored at the expense of ordinary users, critics will no doubt view the future Internet as a discriminatory medium. Concerns about discriminatory online access may also raise some new, or at least exacerbate some existing, equity-and-access related issues affecting the "digital divide" a topic that we examine in detail in Chapter 10.

▶ 9.10 CHAPTER SUMMARY

In this chapter, we have considered some challenges to regulating cyberspace. Specifically, we considered Internet regulation issues from two different perspectives: the regulation of commercial activities on the Internet and the regulation of content in cyberspace. We saw that decisions to view cyberspace as a medium rather than as a public place or space, or vice versa, are significant, because they determine which kinds of rules apply to regulating speech on the Internet. We also saw that the enactment of formal or explicit laws is only one way to regulate cyberspace. As Lessig and others have noted, much regulation of the Internet is being accomplished through technology or "code." Future regulatory decisions will likely determine whether the Internet remains "neutral" or open, or whether it evolves into a different kind of entity.

Unfortunately, not all Internet-regulation controversies were able to be examined in the limited space of this chapter. For example, one concern not considered here has to do with online defamation, and who should be legally liable for defamatory remarks made in a particular online forum. (To date, many online-defamation-related questions are still not resolved.) Another controversy not examined in Chapter 9 involves the question of who should be responsible for regulating online "classifieds services" such as craigslist.com and backpage.com, especially with regard to ads affecting "adult services." While Craigslist has taken a self-regulatory kind of approach by eliminating these kinds of services from its site (in 2011), backpage.com has since been accused of facilitating sex trafficking and child exploitation by listing various adult services on its site. Yet, as of October 2012, there does not seem to be any clear regulatory body in place to monitor the kinds of sites that engage in these services. So, it would seem that some significant policy vacuums still need to be filled regarding Internet regulation.

▶ REVIEW QUESTIONS

1. In discussing "cyberspace regulation," why is it useful to distinguish the question "Can cyberspace be regulated?" from the question "Should cyberspace be regulated?"

2. Describe the arguments for why cyberspace should be viewed as a medium, and why it should be viewed as a "place."

3. How does the way we interpret cyberspace affect the kinds of policies that can be used to regulate it?

4. What are the two different senses of "regulation" we examined, and how can they be applied to the regulatory issues involving cyberspace?

5. Identify the four modalities that Lawrence Lessig believes can be used to regulate behavior, and give an example of how each can be applied to regulating behavior on the Internet.

6. What does Lessig mean by the following claim: "In cyberspace, *code is the law*"?

7. What is DRM technology, and why is it controversial?

8. What does Niva Elkin-Koren mean when she asserts that information policy is becoming increasingly "privatized"? Why does she believe this is a problem?

9. In which ways does Jessica Litman's analysis of the activities of the RIAA, and of the emergence of e-commerce in the late 1990s, support Elkin-Koren's position regarding the privatization of information policy?

10. What are (HTML) metatags, and why can they be controversial?

11. What do we mean by hyperlinking on the Web? Should proprietors of Web sites have a right to include on their sites links to other Web sites?

12. What is e-mail spam, and why is it controversial from a moral point of view?

13. What is censorship? Describe the differences between "censorship by suppression" and "censorship by deterrence."

14. What is pornography? Why is interpreting what is meant by "community standards" especially difficult in establishing pornography laws for cyberspace?

15. Describe the three Internet-specific child pornography laws that were passed in the 1990s but later struck down by the U.S. Supreme Court.

16. How is the Child Internet Protection Act (CIPA) of 2000 both similar to and different from earlier laws affecting child pornography online?

17. What is "virtual child pornography"?

18. What do we mean by "hate speech"? Give some examples of hate speech in cyberspace.

19. What is meant by "speech that can cause physical harm to others"?

20. What is Network Neutrality (or "Net Neutrality"), and what implications does it have for Internet regulation in the future?

▶ DISCUSSION QUESTIONS

21. Assess the arguments that Richard Spinello uses to show that e-mail spam is morally objectionable. Are his arguments convincing? How does the distinction that Keith Miller and James Moor draw between F-UCBE and NF-UCBE inform the debate about the moral implications of spam?

22. What is sexting, and what challenges does it pose for applying current child pornography laws? Recall our examination of the sexting incident at Greensburg Salem High School, PA. Should the teens involved in that case be subject to felony charges under existing child pornography laws? Explain.

► ESSAY/PRESENTATION QUESTIONS

23. Have DRM systems gone too far, as some critics claim? Recall the 2005 Sony BMG Copy Protection case involving the controversial "rootkit" problem that we described in Section 9.3.1. Should Sony be allowed to use a DRM system that cannot easily be uninstalled when circumstances warrant it? Do companies such as Sony need strong DRM systems to ensure the protection of their intellectual property rights? What kind of compromise position could be reached between users and content owners in the ongoing debate about DRM systems?

24. Review Julie Hilden's arguments for why some "exceptions" should be made in cases of prosecuting sexting crimes under current child pornography laws. What does she mean by the "Romeo and Juliet" exception and by the "age-specific" exception? Are these exceptions plausible in the kinds of sexting cases that we examined? Describe some of the challenges posed by the age-specific exception. For example, what would happen if a middle-aged man received an unsolicited nude photo from a teenage girl on his cell phone? Should he be prosecuted for possessing a pornographic image of a minor? Should the teenage girl who sent this photo to him be prosecuted for transmitting the image? Defend your answers.

Scenarios for Analysis

1. Your friend, Jane, a senior at Suburban High School, was recently suspended for three days by her principal for violating her school's cell phone policy. In retaliation, Jane decides to post a picture of her principal, along with some disparaging remarks about him, on Facebook. However, Jane also cleverly uses a fake name (instead of the principal's real name) to identify the person in the Facebook photo, who she describes as a pedophile and drug dealer. (Only a few of Jane's close friends on Facebook will recognize that the person in the photo is her high school principal; other "friends" will not likely make the connection involving this photo with the real identity of the person in it.) Should Jane's remarks in her Facebook posting be protected under her constitutional right to free speech? If not, would it be appropriate for her principal to file a law suit against Jane, given that she is still considered a minor (at the age of 17) in the state where she resides? What kind of punishment, if any, should Jane receive for posting the disparaging and false remarks (implicating her high school principal) on Facebook?[37]

2. Bob, an acquaintance of yours, has been interested in fireworks technology from a very young age. He has read volumes on this topic, as well as on how to design devices that detonate, since he was in junior high school. He has also experimented with various kinds of explosive devices on his parent's property, all of which have been in compliance with the law. Bob recently came up with a novel recipe for building a homemade bomb, and he plans to post the instructions (for assembling the bomb) on his blog and then announce it to his Facebook friends. You, along with a few of Bob's close friends, are very concerned about his plans to do this. But Bob argues, in his defense, that writing and publishing a book on how to build a bomb is perfectly legal in the United States, because it is protected by the First Amendment. He analogizes that if it is legally permissible to publish a physical book or document on this topic, it should also be permissible to write a blog (or even an entire e-book) on it as well. But you are not convinced that posting such a document on the Internet should be protected under "free speech." (And even if it is protected under the most generous reading of the Constitutional guidelines affecting free speech, you worry about the broader implications of what his publication could have for terrorists who might be eager to read his "recipe" for building a bomb.) What argument would you make to try to persuade Bob not to publish his bomb-building recipe online? If Bob refuses to take your advice, what would be your next step?

▶ ENDNOTES

1. Weckert (2007), p. 95.
2. Weckert and Al-Saggaf (2008), p. 491.
3. This scenario is based on the account of the Sony Rootkit controversy in *Wikipedia.* Available at http://en.wikipedia.org/wiki/2005_Sony_BMG_CD_copy_protection_scandal (accessed August 12, 2008).
4. This section draws from material in Grodzinsky and Tavani (2008).
5. For more information, see http://www.wipo.int/amc/en/center/faq/domains.html#1.
6. See "History of ICANN." Available at http://www.buydomains.com/domain-resources/domain-information/history-of-icann.jsp.
7. See http://www.wipo.int/amc/en/center/faq/domains.html#1.
8. *Ibid.*
9. See *Bihari v Gross* (2001). 263 F.3d 359.
10. For more detail, see Larry Armstrong and Amy E. Cortese (1997). "Ticketmaster vs. Microsoft," *Business Week*, May 12. Available at http://www.businessweek.com/1997/19/b352659.htm.
11. Miller and Moor (2008), pp. 518–20.
12. *Mathiesen* (2008), p. 576.
13. See http://www.oyez.org/cases/1970-1979/1971/1971_70_73.
14. See http://www.spectacle.org/795/amateur.html.
15. See http://www.cdt.org/speech/cda/.
16. See http://faculty-web.at.northwestern.edu/commstud/freespeech/cont/cases/morphed.html.
17. See http://74.125.47.132/search?q=cache:sltTkgMAUmMJ:www.lc.org/profamily/copa.pdf+COPA+History&cd=1&hl=en&ct=clnk&gl=us.
18. See http://www.ala.org/ala/aboutala/offices/oif/ifissues/issuesrelatedlinks/cppacopacipa.cfm.
19. See http://www.universalservice.org/sl/applicants/step10/cipa.aspx.
20. See http://www.oyez.org/cases/2000-2009/2002/2002_02_361.
21. Cited in Catudal (2004, p. 201).
22. See Bunker (2009) for a detailed account of this incident.
23. For more detail, see Stiles (2008).
24. See Szustek (2009).
25. *Ibid.*
26. See http://news.bbc.co.uk/2/hi/europe/760782.stm.
27. See http://www.dailykos.com/storyonly/2009/6/12/741537/-von-Brunns-website-attacks-von-Brunn!
28. Tim Wu. "Network Neutrality FAQ." Available at http://timwu.org/network_neutrality.html.
29. *Ibid.*
30. See "Net Neutrality." 2010. *New York Times* (Updated Dec. 22). Available at http://topics.nytimes.com/topics/reference/timestopics/subjects/n/net_neutrality/index.html. Accessed 3/24/2012.
31. *Ibid.*
32. See http://www.freepress.net/policy/internet/net_neutrality.
33. See Broadband for America. "Hands off the Internet." Available at http://www.broadbandforamerica.com/handsofftheinternet?gclid=CLbFmZHRlq8CFQjd4AodbHxsxA.
34. See Tim Berners-Lee's comments. Available at http://dig.csail.mit.edu/breadcrumbs/node/144.
35. See http://www.freepress.net/policy/internet/net_neutrality, and http://en.wikipedia.org/wiki/Network_neutrality.
36. See Broadband for America. "Hands off the Internet." Available at http://www.broadbandforamerica.com/handsofftheinternet?gclid=CLbFmZHRlq8CFQjd4AodbHxsxA.
37. This hypothetical scenario mirrors, in some important respects, an actual incident where a high school principal in Pennsylvania was indirectly insulted (or "parodied") on MySpace by two teenagers. See, for example, Dale (2011).

▶ REFERENCES

Agre, Philip E. 2005. "P2P and the Promise of Internet Equality." In P. De Palma, ed. *Computers in Society 05/06*. Dubuque, IA: McGraw-Hill/Dushkin, pp. 12–15. Reprinted from *Communications of the ACM* 46, no. 2 (2003): 39–42.

Bunker, Mike. 2009. "Sexting Surprise: Teens Face Child Porn Charges," MSNBC. Available at http://www.msnbc.msn.com/1d/28679588/.

Camp, L. Jean, and Y. T. Chien. 2000. "The Internet as Public Space: Concepts, Issues, and Implications in Public Policy." *Computers and Society* 30, no. 3: 13–19.

Catudal, Jacques. 2004. "Censorship, the Internet, and the Child Pornography Law of 1996: A Critique." In R. A. Spinello and H. T. Tavani, eds. *Readings in CyberEthics*. 2nd ed. Sudbury, MA: Jones and Bartlett, pp. 196–213. Reprinted from *Ethics and Information Technology* 1, no. 2 (1999): 105–16.

Dale, Maryclaire. 2011. "Pa. Teens Can't Be Suspended for MySpace Parodies." *The Washington Times,* June 14. Available at http://www.washingtontimes.com/news/2011/jun/13/pa-teens-cant-be-suspended-for-myspace-parodies/?page=all.

Elkin-Koren, Niva. 2000. "The Privatization of Information Policy." *Ethics and Information Technology* 2, no. 4: 201–09.

Girasa, Roy J. 2002. *Cyberlaw: National and International Perspectives.* Upper Saddle River, NJ: Prentice Hall.

Goodwin, Mike. 1995. "Alt.sex.academic.freedom." *Wired* 3, no. 2: 72. Available at http://www.wired.com/wired/archive/3.02/cyber_rights_pr.html.

Goodwin, Mike. 2003. *CyberRights: Defending Free Speech in the Digital Age.* Rev. ed. Cambridge, MA: MIT Press.

Grodzinsky, Frances S., and Maria Bottis. 2007. "Private Use as Fair Use: Is it Fair?" *Computers and Society* 37, no. 4: 11–24.

Grodzinsky, Frances S. and Herman T. Tavani. 2008. "Online File Sharing: Resolving the Tensions between Privacy and Property." *Computers and Society* 38, no. 4: 28–39.

Hesseldahl, Arik. 2006. "Apple vs. France." *Business Week,* March 21. Available at http://www.businessweek.com/technology/content/mar2006/tc20060321_144066.htm.

Hilden, Julie. 2013. "How Should Teens' 'Sexting'—the Sending of Revealing Photos—Be Regulated?" In D. Hall, ed. *Taking Sides: Clashing Views in Family and Personal Relationships.* 9th ed. New York: McGraw-Hill. Reprinted from *Find Law,* April 28, 2009. Available at http//writ.news.findlaw.com/hilden/20090428.html.

Jobs, Steve. 2007. "Thoughts on Music." *Apple.com,* Feb. 6. Available at http://www.apple.com/hotnews/thoughtsonmusic/.

Lessig, Lawrence. 2000. *Code and Other Laws of Cyberspace.* New York: Basic Books.

Lessig, Lawrence. 2004. The Laws of Cyberspace. In R. A. Spinello and H. T. Tavani, eds. *Readings in CyberEthics.* 2nd ed. Sudbury, MA: Jones and Bartlett, pp. 134–44.

Lessig, Lawrence, and Robert W. McChesney. 2006. "No Tolls on the Internet." *The Washington Post,* June 8. Available at http://www.washingtonpost.com/wp-dyn/content/article/2006/06/07/AR2006060702108.html.

Litman, Jessica. 2002. "Electronic Commerce and Free Speech." In N. Elkin-Koren and N. W. Netanel, eds. *The Commodification of Information.* The Hague, The Netherlands: Kluwer Academic Publishers, pp. 23–42.

Mathiesen, Kay. 2008. "Censorship and Access to Expression." In K. E. Himma and H. T. Tavani, eds. *The Handbook of Information and Computer Ethics.* Hoboken, NJ: John Wiley and Sons, pp. 573–87.

Miller, Keith, and James H. Moor. 2008. "Email Spam." In K. E. Himma and H. T. Tavani, eds. *The Handbook of Information and Computer Ethics.* Hoboken, NJ: John Wiley and Sons, pp. 517–31.

Moor, James H. 2007. "What Is Computer Ethics?" In J. Weckert, ed. *Computer Ethics.* Aldershot, UK: Ashgate, pp. 31–40. Reprinted from *Metaphilosophy* 16, no. 4 (1985): 266–75.

Russinovich, Mark. 2005. "Sony, Rootkits, and Digital Rights Management Gone Too Far." Available at http://www.sysinternals.com/blog/2005/10sony-rootkits-and-digital-rights.html.

Samuelson, Pamela. 2003. "DRM {and, or, vs.} the Law." *Communications of the ACM* 46, no. 4: 41–45.

Sandin, Per. 2004. "Virtual Child Pornography and Utilitarianism." *Journal of Information, Communication and Ethics in Society* 2, no. 4: 217–23.

Spinello, Richard A. 2003. *Cyberethics: Morality and Law in Cyberspace.* 2nd ed. Sudbury, MA: Jones and Bartlett.

Spinello, Richard A. 2004. "An Ethical Evaluation of Web-Site Linking." In R. A. Spinello and H. T. Tavani, eds. *Readings in CyberEthics.* 2nd ed. Sudbury, MA: Jones and Bartlett, pp. 337–50.

Spinello, Richard A. 2006. "Ethical Reflections on the Problem of Spam." In L. Hinman, ed. *Contemporary Moral Issues: Diversity and Consensus.* 3rd ed. Upper Saddle River, NJ: Prentice Hall, pp. 502–10. Reprinted from *Ethics and Information Technology* 1, no. 3 (1999): 185–91.

Stiles, Bob. 2008. "Effort Begins to Standardize Sexting Penalty." *Tribune-Review,* April 2. Available at http://m.triblive.com/triblive/db_7240/contentdetail.htm;jsessionid=198F0CC68FFC5176D6581C1E539F8C62?contentguid=tScPcIMY&full=true.

Szustek, Anne. 2009. "Authorities Treat Those Accused of 'Sexting' as Sex Offenders." *Finding Dulcinea.* Available at http://www.findingdulcinea.com/news/Americas/2009/April/Authorities-Treat-Those-Accused-of-Sexting-as-Sex-Offenders.html.

Weckert, John. 2007. "What Is So Bad about Internet Content Regulation?" In J. Weckert, ed. *Computer Ethics.* Aldershot, UK: Ashgate, pp. 95–102. Reprinted from *Ethics and Information Technology* 2, no. 2 (2000): 105–11.

Weckert, John, and Yeslam Al-Saggaf. 2008. "Regulation and Governance of the Internet." In K. E. Himma and H. T. Tavani, eds. *The Handbook of Information and Computer Ethics.* Hoboken, NJ: John Wiley and Sons, pp. 475–95.

▶ FURTHER READINGS

Armstrong Timothy K. "Digital Rights Management and the Process of Fair Use," *Harvard Journal of Law & Technology* 20, (2006). Available at http://ssrn.com/abstract=885371.

Bohman, James. "The Transformation of the Public Sphere: Political Authority, Communicative Freedom, and Internet Publics." In J. van den Hoven and J. Weckert, eds.

Information Technology and Moral Philosophy. New York: Cambridge University Press, 2008, pp. 66–92.

Grossman, Wendy M. "The Spam Wars." In P. De Palma, ed. *Annual Editions: Computers in Society 05/06.* Dubuque, IA: McGraw-Hill/Dushkin, 2005, pp. 147–51.

Levy, David M. "Information Overload." In K. E. Himma and H. T. Tavani, eds. *The Handbook of Information and*

Computer Ethics. Hoboken, NJ: John Wiley and Sons, 2008, pp. 497–515.

White, A. "The Obscenity of Internet Regulation in the United States." *Ethics and Information Technology* 6, no. 2 (2004): 111–19.

Zittrain, Jonathan. *The Future of the Internet—And How to Stop It.* New Haven, CT: Yale University Press, 2008.

10

The Digital Divide, Democracy, and Work

The moral, legal, and social problems we examined in Chapters 5–9 typically centered on the impacts that cybertechnology has for specific issues such as privacy, security, crime, or intellectual property. In Chapter 10, we instead consider the impacts that this technology has for a wide range of issues that cut across three broad social categories:

- *sociodemographic groups* (affecting social/economic class, race, and gender),
- *social and political institutions* (such as education and government),
- *social sectors* (including the workplace).

Many ethical issues associated with these three categories center on concerns involving social equity and access to information. Equity-and-access-related issues affecting specific demographic groups are examined in Sections 10.1–10.4 in our analysis of the digital divide (socio-economic class), disabled persons, racial minorities, and women, respectively. Concerns associated with the impact of cybertechnology on our political/social institutions are considered in our discussion of democracy and the Internet in Section 10.5, whereas cybertechnology-related issues impacting the contemporary workplace (as a social sector) are examined in Section 10.6.

Specific questions considered in Chapter 10 include:

- What do we mean by "digital divide"?
- What obligations do we have to make cybertechnology accessible to disabled persons?
- Has the widespread use of cybertechnology helped reduce racism, or does it exacerbate it?
- What implications does cybertechnology have for gender issues?
- Does cybertechnology facilitate democracy and democratic values, or does it threaten them?
- How has cybertechnology transformed the nature of work, and how has it affected the quality of work life?

A common characteristic unifies the otherwise disparate issues examined in this chapter: they are often approached from the perspective of *sociological/descriptive ethics*. In Chapter 1 we drew a distinction between descriptive and normative approaches to the study of moral issues, noting that while social scientists conduct research that is essentially designed to report (or describe) sociological aspects of cybertechnology, those aspects often have normative implications as well. In this chapter, we examine some issues primarily from the vantage point of descriptive ethics, especially as they require an analysis of statistical and empirical data. In other cases, we also examine normative aspects of those issues, particularly as they raise concerns affecting social equity and access. We begin by looking at some equity-and-access issues associated with the digital divide.

▶ 10.1 THE DIGITAL DIVIDE

What, exactly, is the digital divide? Benjamin Compaine (2001) suggests that the phrase *digital divide* is basically a new label for an earlier expression used to describe the "information haves and have-nots." He defines the digital divide as the gap, or "perceived gap," between those who have and do not have access to "information tools" *and* between those who have and do not have the ability to use those tools. So, in Compaine's view, merely having access to cybertechnology is not sufficient; one must also possess the knowledge and ability to use that technology.

First, we should note that an analysis of *the* digital divide might suggest that there is one overall divide—that is, a single divide as opposed to many "divides," or divisions. Actually, there are multiple divisions involving access to cybertechnology. Keiron O'Hara and David Stevens (2006) note that there are divides involving rich and poor people, rich and poor regions, and rich and poor nations. For our purposes, however, issues affecting the digital divide can be organized into two broad categories: a divide *between* nations and a divide *within* nations.[1] The division between information-rich and information-poor nations is sometimes referred to as the "global digital divide"; the technological divides within nations, on the contrary, exist between rich and poor persons, racial majority and minority groups, men and women, and so forth. We begin with a look at the global digital divide.

10.1.1 The Global Digital Divide

Consider some statistics ranging from 2000 to 2011. In 2000, it was estimated that 361 million people, approximately 5.8% of the world's population, were online; the vast majority of those users lived in North America and Europe.[2] Since then, global Internet usage has expanded significantly (nearly eightfold). In March 2011, it was estimated that there were slightly more than two billion Internet users.[3] A significant shift had already occurred by 2005, when the list of countries or regions where more than 50% of the population used the Internet had grown to 30.[4] That year, seven nations—Australia, Canada, Japan, South Korea, Taiwan, the United Kingdom, and the United States—had an Internet penetration rate of higher than 60%.

As of 2011, the disparity between the percentage of Internet users in developed and developing countries continues to be significant. In India, for example, the penetration rate for Internet users is 8.4%, while in the United Kingdom it is 82%.[5] The disparity is especially apparent when viewed from the perspective of continents or world regions. For example, in Africa (which includes approximately 15% of the world's population) the Internet penetration rate is 11.4%, whereas in North America, the Internet penetration rate is 78.3% (as of March 2011). On a positive note, however, the Internet usage growth in Africa was 2,527.4% between 2000 and 2011.[6] William Wresch (2009) notes that in a 33-month period during those years there was a 60% growth in the number of African Web sites. So, one might be encouraged by some reports describing the growth in Internet usage at the global level. Yet, despite the progress that has been made in the African continent, critics worry that much more work still needs to be done to narrow, and perhaps one day even bridge, the global divide.

One obstacle to eliminating the global digital divide altogether is that developing countries struggle with low literacy rates; many people in developing nations cannot read and write in their native language, let alone in English. And, much of the material on the Internet is in English. This has influenced advocates for improved Internet service for global users to lobby for the development of Web applications that include more graphics and images that can serve as universal symbols. (We return to this point in our discussion of technology-related access issues affecting disabled persons, in Section 10.2.) However, O'Hara and Stevens note that regardless of whatever explanation we give for the "existence of a global digital divide," one thing is patently clear: inequalities regarding access to cybertechnology are "tied closely to economic inequality."[7]

10.1.2 The Digital Divide within Nations

Many developed nations still have significant divides within them regarding access to cybertechnology. For example, O'Hara and Stevens point to one such discrepancy in the United Kingdom. They note that in 2004, approximately one half of all households were online, while only 3% of the poorest households were included in this number. As one might expect, there are also significant disparities within some developing nations as well. And in rapidly developing countries like India, the divisions that currently exist may eventually deepen. Consider that a growing segment of India's population is fluent in English and has the technical literacy required to work on many of the highly-skilled jobs outsourced there; those on the other side of the divide, comprising the majority of the population of India, tend to have a low level of literacy and little or no access to cybertechnology.

Some countries, including the United States, instituted specific strategies that were designed to bridge the divide within their national borders. In response to concerns about the gap that existed in America in the early 1990s between those with and without access to computers, the Clinton administration initiated the National Information Infrastructure (NII) to ensure that all Americans would have access to information technology. To accomplish this objective, the National Telecommunications and Information Administration (NTIA) conducted a series of studies that investigated computer use among various groups.

One question that arose from the NTIA reports was whether a *universal service* policy was needed to ensure that all Americans have an appropriate level of access to Internet technology. Universal service policies have been controversial because they require subsidies, which often result either in user fees or higher taxes. However, proponents of a universal service policy for the Internet have pointed to the model that was used to subsidize telephone technology when that became available in the early part of the twentieth century. Without some kind of government-supported subsidy, people living in less-populated rural areas would not have been able to afford this new technology. So the U.S. Congress passed the Communications Act of 1934, which distributed the cost for telephone service in a way to make it affordable to all Americans. Today, the question is whether Internet access should be subsidized in a similar manner. In the case of telephone technology, arguments were made that having a telephone was necessary for one's well-being. Can the same argument be made in the case of cybertechnology and Internet access?

As we saw in Chapter 9, subsidies in the form of "E-rates" (that is, federal technology discounts) have helped to defray the cost of Internet access for public schools and libraries in the United States. Unlike universal service policies involving telephones, which are aimed at subsidizing residential telephone service, E-rates for Internet access apply only to "community points of access" such as public libraries. While E-rates may support universal Internet *access*, they do not provide universal Internet *service*. So, critics such as Chapman and Rotenberg (1995) have argued that merely providing community points of access to the Internet would be similar to a policy that simply placed telephones in public locations rather than making telephone service affordable for all Americans.

Some critics worry that the absence of a (universal) Internet service policy in the United States could adversely affect school-age children in low-income families. Consider the following scenario, where someone tries to convince you that an Internet service policy is needed to level the playing field for economically disadvantaged students attending U.S. public schools.

▶ **SCENARIO 10–1:** Providing In-Home Internet Service for Public School Students

Sara, an advocate for disadvantaged youth in low-income families in America, asks you to review a short editorial she is preparing for a blog (dedicated to education-related issues). In that editorial, she argues: There are several reasons why the U.S. government should provide in-home Internet service for all students (Grades 1–12) whose families cannot afford to pay for it. First, the federal government mandates that all school-age children (of U.S. citizens) receive a free public school education. Second, the government is required to provide those children with the resources they need to complete their education (i.e., classrooms, labs, textbooks, etc.). Today, having in-home Internet service is a critical resource for students to be able to complete their homework assignments. School-aged students whose families cannot afford in-home Internet service are at a significant disadvantage in competing in the educational system. So, students whose families cannot afford the cost of in-home Internet service should have that service subsidized by government funding. ■

Is Sara's argument convincing? One might initially be inclined to respond to her by noting that these students could go to public libraries to get the online resources needed to complete their homework assignments. However, Sara could reply that libraries are mere "points of access" (as noted above) and thus do not provide the kind of service needed by these economically disadvantaged students. It would be interesting to evaluate Sara's argument via the seven-step strategy described in Chapter 3 to see whether it satisfies the requirements for being valid and sound. Of course, even if the argument can be shown to be valid, in virtue of its logical form, one could still ask Sara whether her argument's conclusion—school-age children in families unable to afford in-home Internet service are disadvantaged—raises a concern that is fundamentally *ethical* in nature.

10.1.3 Is the Digital Divide an Ethical Issue?

What does it mean to say that the digital divide is an ethical issue? Is every kind of divide regarding unequal access to goods necessarily an ethical problem? A skeptic might note the divide between those who have and do not have Mercedes-Benz automobiles, arguing that there is a "Mercedes-Benz divide" and many of us fall on the "wrong side" of it, but that this is not an ethical issue. We could respond by pointing to the divisions that exist between those who do and those who do not have access to vital resources such as food and healthcare, divisions that many ethicists believe raise questions affecting the just distribution of primary goods and resources. But what about unequal access to cybertechnology? Is it closer to the Mercedes-Benz divide, or is it closer to divisions involving access to food and healthcare?

Distributive Justice and Access to Vital Human Resources

As suggested above, some question whether the digital divide raises concerns affecting distributive justice. But what do we mean by "distributive justice," especially in the context of cybertechnology? According to Jeroen van den Hoven and Emma Rooksby (2008),

> Distributive justice in contemporary information societies concerns, among other issues, the distribution of information, information services, and information infrastructures.[8]

The authors note that while there has been much enthusiasm about the emergence of new technologies, there is also concern over "the uneven distribution of the new information wealth, both within nations and internationally."[9] To argue that the unequal distribution of information wealth is a moral issue would require that we show that information is a kind of "primary good" that is vital for human flourishing. So, we need to consider whether information meets the criteria of a kind of good or resource that is *vital* for one's well-being. Additionally, if we can show that not having access to cybertechnology either denies or unfairly limits access to information or to certain kinds of basic goods—what James Moor (2004) calls "core goods" (or "core values"), such as knowledge, ability, freedom, and so forth—then we can make a fairly strong case that unequal access to cybertechnology is a moral issue affecting distributive justice.

In his classic work, *A Theory of Justice*, philosopher John Rawls introduces the notion of *primary social goods*, which are resources that satisfy basic human needs and thus have a special value or moral weight in society. Rawls notes that with these goods, humans "can generally be assured of greater success in carrying out their intentions and in advancing their needs."[10] Van den Hoven and Rooksby argue that Rawls' theory of justice in general, and his notion of a primary social good in particular, can be extended to include "information goods." They further argue, however that a "fully-fledged theory of justice that takes adequate account of the new information goods . . . is still some way off."[11] But we can nonetheless examine some models that have been advanced for showing why the digital divide is indeed a moral issue affecting distributive justice.

One model has been articulated by Jeremy Moss (2002), who argues that persons lacking access to cybertechnology are deprived of resources that are vital for their well-being. He points out that without access to cybertechnology, people are unfairly disadvantaged because their

1. access to knowledge is significantly lessened or prevented,
2. ability to participate fully in the political decision-making process and to receive important information is greatly diminished, and
3. economic prospects are severely hindered.[12]

First, Moss claims that people who are deprived of access to cybertechnology are not able to benefit from the increasing range of information available on the Internet and thus are falling further behind in the information era. Second, because of political barriers to participation in the decision-making processes in developing countries, people in remote areas without access to the Internet may have no means at all of participating in national debates or of receiving information about important developmental matters and policies that can significantly affect them. Third, Moss believes that because so much economic growth is driven by the information and communication sector, people living in countries that are not part of this sector are disadvantaged. With regard to Moss's third point, Pippa Norris (2001) makes a similar observation by noting that "the underclass" of information poor may become "further marginalized in societies where basic computer skills are becoming essential for economic success and personal advancement." Norris notes these can include "entry to good career and educational opportunities," as well as "full access to social networks . . . and opportunities for civic engagement."[13]

In response to Moss and Norris, one could argue that some people (and some nations) have always been disadvantaged in accessing new technologies such as automobiles, household appliances, and so forth. But this criticism misses a crucial point. As we have noted, disparities in access to certain technologies, such as Mercedes-Benz automobiles, do not in themselves constitute an ethical issue. We should also note that divisions of this type are generally accepted in capitalist societies. However, if Moss's thesis about why cybertechnology is important is correct, then having access to cyber-technology is essential for one's well-being in ways that having access to other kinds of technologies—for example, "discretionary technologies" that provide convenience and entertainment—is not. So, one question that arises is: Do we have a moral obligation to bridge the digital divide? And if we do, are affluent nations the ones responsible for helping to bridge this divide?

Making the Case for a Moral Obligation to Bridge the Digital Divide

Maria Bottis and Ken Himma (2008) note that in making the case that "affluent nations" have a moral obligation to bridge the divide, some important points of clarification first need to be made. For one thing, they argue that we need to draw an important distinction between saying that "X is a good thing to do" and saying that "we are obligated to do X." The authors also point out that most people would likely agree that eliminating the digital divide would be a good thing to do, but there would also likely be far less consensus as to whether we (i.e., some affluent nations) have an obligation to do it.

Bottis and Himma note that failing to do something morally good is not necessarily morally wrong; they use the example of someone's risking his or life to save a person caught in a fire in a building. Failure to risk one's life to save another here, they correctly point out, is not something that necessarily merits either blame or punishment. Of course, the act of attempting to save someone's life in the fire would be a good thing, but (assuming that you and I are not firefighters) we are not morally obligated to do it. Doing such an act crosses over to a category that philosophers and ethicists call "supererogatory." That is, the act of risking one's life in a fire to save another is morally good but is also "beyond the call of moral obligation." Bottis and Himma also note that we "praise supererogatory acts, but not obligatory acts" and we "blame nonperformance of obligatory acts, but not supererogatory acts."[14] So in this scheme, should bridging the digital divide be considered a supererogatory act, in which case we are not morally obligated to do anything?

Himma (2007) points out that because many people believe that we are morally obligated only to do no harm, they infer that we have no obligation to bridge the digital divide. But he also believes that such a view is "inconsistent with the ethics of every classically theistic religion as well as our ordinary intuitions, as well as classic theories of deontology and consequentialism." In the case of deontology, for example, Himma notes that deontological theories "almost universally hold that we have an obligation to help the poor."[15] For example, he points to the prima facie obligation of beneficence that we have to help the poor, as articulated in Ross' deontological theory. (You may wish to review Ross' ethical theory of act deontology in Chapter 2.)

In Chapter 2, we saw that contract-based ethical theory holds that while we are morally obligated to "do no harm," we have no explicit obligation to do good—in this case, no moral obligation to bridge the digital divide. According to this view, we are behaving morally as long as we do nothing to prevent others from acquiring cybertechnology and Internet access. But is this minimalist view of morality adequate? Recall that in our discussion of contract-based ethical theories in Chapter 2, we saw that individuals and nations have a moral obligation to do good (to others) only in cases where individuals or nations have an explicit contract in which they are required to come to the aid of others. However, we also saw that there are some compelling reasons to be skeptical about such a limited theory of moral obligation.

In our critique of contract-based ethical theories, we saw that a more robust theory of morality requires that we come to the aid of those who are in danger of being harmed, whenever it is in our power to do so. For one thing, we saw that doing this could help to make cyberspace a safer place, especially for those individuals and groups vulnerable to online harm. And we can construct an analogous argument to show why coming to the aid of other kinds of vulnerable (or at least disadvantaged) individuals and groups—that is, those without Internet access—would also be the right thing to do. If Moss is correct in claiming that access to cybertechnology is vital to one's well-being, then is it plausible to suggest that we have at least some obligation to provide access to those who are disadvantaged?

▶ 10.2 CYBERTECHNOLOGY AND THE DISABLED

Not only do equity-and-access issues involving cybertechnology affect poor people in developing nations and people in low-income groups within developed nations, they also affect many disabled people. So, some suggest that core equity-and-access issues underlying the digital divide apply to this group of people as well. There has been much discussion about implementing strategies and policies to make the Internet more accessible to disabled persons. Tim Berners-Lee, director of the World Wide Web Consortium (W3C) and the inventor of the HTTP protocol that underlies the Web, has stated: "The power of the Web is in its universality. Access by everyone regardless of disability is an essential aspect." The W3C was formed, in large part, to promote standards that ensure universal Web access. It established a Web Accessibility Initiative (WAI), which has produced guidelines and protocols for developing software applications that improve access for disabled persons, ranging from software used in speech synthesizers and screen magnifiers to proposed software applications that will benefit people with visual, hearing, physical, cognitive, and neurological disabilities.[16]

WAI representatives have worked with industry groups and governmental organizations to establish guidelines for the design of "user agents," which are intended to lower barriers to Web accessibility for people with disabilities. These user agents include Web browsers and other types of software that retrieve and render Web content; the agents are designed to conform and communicate with other technologies, especially "assistive technologies" such as screen readers (which perform a function similar to Braille applications in offline contexts). Frances Grodzinsky (2000) argues that computers equipped with assistive technologies and "adaptive devices" can be "equalizers" in the era of information technology because they enable people with disabilities to participate in and compete for jobs that require computer access.

10.2.1 Disabled Persons and Remote Work

One controversial question has centered on whether the practice of "remote work"—made possible by technology that enables employees to work outside the traditional workplace, typically in their homes—has benefited or harmed disabled persons. Although concerns involving remote work can affect all employees (as we will see in Section 10.6.1), Ben Fairweather (1998) examines how disabled workers are particularly affected. He acknowledges that remote work has provided opportunities to some disabled workers who otherwise would be denied access to a job. But he also worries that for some disabled employees, especially those who are capable of working in both conventional and remote workplace settings, remote work can have unfortunate consequences.

Fairweather worries that a company's remote work policies might provide employers with a convenient scheme for keeping disabled workers out of the physical workplace. He finds this troubling for three reasons: First, it affects worker autonomy because it denies those disabled workers who could work *either* remotely or in a conventional workplace setting the choice of determining where they will work. Second, the practice of remote work can be used to "hide" disabled workers, keeping them out of sight and away from the physical workplace. Third, remote work provides employers with a convenient excuse not to make the physical workplace compatible with current laws affecting disabled employees, such as the ADA (Americans with Disabilities Act) guidelines and requirements. For example, Grodzinsky notes that because Section 508 of ADA applies only to organizations receiving government funds, those in the private sector can get around the federal mandate affecting accessibility.

Despite these questions surrounding the pros and cons of remote work for disabled persons, we should note that there are many examples in which WAI's assistive and adaptive technologies have clearly benefited disabled workers. So, on balance, WAI has made a difference for many disabled persons who desire to compete for jobs in the contemporary workplace. But some critics might ask why we should continue to fund initiatives such as WAI, especially because of the financial commitment required and because disabled persons may comprise a relatively small portion of the overall population.

10.2.2 Arguments for Continued WAI Support

In response to those who would challenge continued support for disability-related initiatives affecting cybertechnology, WAI proponents such as Cheiko Asakawa (2012) argue that access to technology is not simply a privilege but rather a "human right." Other WAI supporters, however, take a different tack in pressing their case for why initiatives for the disabled should continue to be supported. For example, they point out that some measures taken for the disabled have had positive outcomes for other groups, especially poor people who are often forced to deal with literacy problems and inadequate equipment. (Recall our earlier discussion of literacy problems in developing nations in Section 10.1.1.) It may well turn out that voice-recognition technology designed to assist disabled persons who are unable to use keyboards will ultimately also benefit nondisabled persons with low literacy skills. So we see that larger groups of (non-disabled) people have benefited and could continue to benefit from some Web-based initiatives designed for disabled persons, even though the resulting positive effects in the past may have been unanticipated and unintended.

We can also point to an example of an accessibility-related initiative in the nondigital world that was intended to accommodate disabled persons yet has benefited the public in general. Ramps designed for wheelchair accessibility have not only benefited people in wheelchairs, but have also been very useful to nondisabled persons as well, such as parents pushing baby carriages. Also consider some of the advantages that sloped curbs on street corners have provided to many nondisabled persons—bicyclists and skaters have benefited from these features, which were initially intended to serve disabled persons (Woodbury 2002). So many of WAI's proponents argue, analogously, that ordinary users will likely continue to benefit from the computer design enhancements to user interfaces that are initially intended to assist disabled persons.

Because improving access to cybertechnology for the disabled has potential benefits for society as a whole, we can formulate a utilitarian argument to advance this cause. However, we should also be cautious about extending this argument too far. What would happen if, in the future, the broader population did not realize any benefits from improving access to cybertechnology for the disabled? Could this kind of outcome lend support to a utilitarian argument against investing in initiatives that improved access for the disabled? After considering this, you can better understand some of the possible dangers of relying too heavily on utilitarian principles when advancing a moral argument for improved access for the disabled.

We conclude this section by noting that there are additional concerns affecting cybertechnology and the disabled that are unable to be examined here. Our main objective in this section, however, was to identify and briefly describe some key issues and concerns involving the ongoing debate about which kinds of initiatives ought to be implemented to improve cybertechnology access for disabled persons. Next, we examine the impact of that technology for racial minorities.

▶ 10.3 CYBERTECHNOLOGY AND RACE

We have seen that in the United States many lower-income individuals and families, especially those in the inner cities, still do not have in-home access to the Internet; many of these individuals also belong to racial and ethnic minority groups. Consider statistics ranging from 2000 to 2011 that correlate income (social class) and race with the digital divide in the United States. In 2000, 51% of all homes had at least one computer, and 41.5% of all homes had Internet access. In terms of income, 86.3% of households earning more than $75,000 per year had Internet access, while of those households earning below $15,000 per year, only 12.7% had access. From the vantage point of race, 46.1% of white Americans and 56.8% of Asian Americans and Pacific Islanders had access, contrasted with only 23.5% of African Americans and 23.1% of Hispanics who did.[17]

By 2008, 73% of adult men and women in the United States had Internet access at home, while 90% of young people between the ages of 18 and 29 used the Internet. However, the penetration rate for black Internet users in the United States then was 59%, which was still well below the penetration for the American population as a whole.[18]

As of 2011, however, statistics for African American vs. white users has changed significantly. Whereas Internet usage among whites was estimated to be 88%, the rate of African Americans using the Internet had grown to 80%. Perhaps even more interesting was the rate at which the use of access to broadband Internet connection had grown for African Americans. Whereas 65% of African American Internet users had broadband access, only 53% of white American Internet users enjoyed this service; nearly half of these users had not migrated from earlier forms of Internet access such as dial-up technologies.[19]

We next focus our analysis on the impact of cybertechnology for African Americans by examining two different kinds of concerns: (1) Internet usage patterns vis-à-vis other demographic groups, and (2) the role the Internet plays in spreading racial prejudice.

10.3.1 Internet Usage Patterns

Studies conducted a decade or so ago reported that African Americans who used the Internet differed from their white counterparts in two key respects: *usage patterns* and *demographic characteristics*. With respect to usage patterns, Kretchmer and Karveth (2001) described four ways in which African Americans and whites differed. First, African American users were more likely to use the Internet for entertainment and for locating information about quality of life activities, such as job training, school, health care, and hobbies. Second, they were less likely to participate in Web-based auctions. Third, they were also less likely to feel that the Internet connects them with family and friends. Fourth, they were less likely to use e-mail to develop and sustain friendships. Kretchmer and Karveth also cited relevant sociodemographic differences between African Americans and whites: the average age for African American users tended to be younger than for whites, African Americans typically accessed the Internet less frequently than whites, and adult African American Internet users were much more likely than their white counterparts to have modest incomes, no college degrees, and children under eighteen.

Some recent statistics suggest that Internet use by African Americans is changing dramatically. For example, we noted above that approximately 80% of African Americans are now Internet users and that, currently, this percentage is only six points lower than that for white Americans. Yet, some differences in usage patterns between the two groups continue to persist. For example, Burn (2011) notes that whereas 26% of white Americans used the Internet for entertainment purposes, 68% of African Americans used it for this purpose. African American Internet users also used the Web more frequently than white users for activities such as news, health, and sports.

10.3.2 Racism and the Internet

Has the Internet eliminated, or even helped to reduce, considerations of race in communication? Because Internet communication does not typically reveal a user's physical attributes, we might assume that the answer is "yes." However, we need to question that assumption. Kretchmer and Karveth note that the study of race in cyberspace often leads to paradoxical inferences. On the one hand, cyberspace provides an opportunity and forum to discover and confront racial issues, but on the other hand, it can perpetuate, or perhaps even enhance, aspects of racism. For example, the Internet has introduced new tools for harassing members of certain groups. Thus Internet technology can be, and has been, used to magnify the *rhetoric* and significance of hate groups.

Lynn Theismeyer (1999) has pointed out the "rhetorical role" that the Internet can play with respect to race. She examines the rhetoric of racism, not as it applies specifically to racial and minority groups in the United States, such as African Americans and Hispanics, but rather as it has been used internationally in the rise of neo-Nazi propaganda. Theismeyer believes that there are two kinds of racist speech on the Internet:

a. Hate speech, including text, music, online radio broadcasts, and images that exhort users to act against target groups.

b. Persuasive rhetoric that does not directly enunciate but ultimately promotes or justifies violence.[20]

In Chapter 9, we saw that European countries, especially Germany and France, have made a greater effort than the United States to restrict online hate speech that has been targeted at racial groups, especially by neo-Nazi organizations. We also saw that the United States, on the contrary, has focused more on censoring pornography, which many also view as offensive speech. What Theismeyer refers to as "persuasive rhetoric" would seem to be protected in the United States under the First Amendment right to free speech. So it is not easy to control some forms of online racist rhetoric in the United States.

We also saw in Chapter 9 that designers and operators of Web sites can use misleading and deceptive (HTML) metatags and keywords to attract visitors. For example, we saw that a racist Web site can deceptively use a keyword such as "Martin Luther King Jr." to lure unsuspecting persons to its site. So, individuals who are interested in gaining information about Dr. King's life may instead be subjected to racist hate speech directed against African Americans.

Theismeyer asks us to consider two questions with respect to racial prejudice and cybertechnology:

1. Does information technology make the reemergence of prejudicial messages and attitudes swifter and more likely?

2. Does the Internet's wide range of distribution make for more followers and finally more persuasion?[21]

She concludes that it is impossible to know at this point whether cybertechnology has been the main cause of the rapid spread of racism, especially in the neo-Nazism movement, but she is convinced that cybertechnology has been its principal tool.

In Section 10.5.2, we examine some ways in which blogs and the blogosphere also can either directly or indirectly contribute to the promotion of racial prejudice online. For example, some extreme right-wing political blogs have portrayed U.S. President Barack Obama in ways that are generally considered to be offensive and demeaning to African Americans. On the one hand, these blogs include content that is protected by free speech; on the other hand, they can reinforce racial stereotypes and perpetuate racial prejudice.

▶ 10.4 CYBERTECHNOLOGY AND GENDER

Other equity-and-access concerns associated with cybertechnology in general, and with the digital divide in particular, can be analyzed with respect to gender. Feminist authors and others who advocate for women's issues proffer arguments similar to those advanced by or on behalf of African Americans, which we examined in the preceding section. Women, like certain racial and ethnic groups, have not always been included in important decisions about technology policies and, until very recently, have not participated to the same degree as men in the use of cybertechnology.

We can begin by noting that the gap that has traditionally existed between the percentage of female and male Internet users in the United States has changed significantly since studies conducted in 2000. According to a report by the *Pew Internet & American Life Project* in 2005, young women were slightly more likely to be online than young men, and the number of black women online surged between 2002 and 2005 (black women who used the Internet outnumbered black men by about 10%). Pew Internet Project surveys conducted in 2005 showed that in the United States, 66% of women went online, as opposed to 68% of men. But some analysts noted that women slightly outnumbered men in the Internet-user population because they made up a greater share of the overall U.S. population. By 2008, however, the proportion of women who used the Internet was equal to that of men.[22]

Although the gap between female and male Internet users has narrowed considerably in the United States and in many Western countries, this has not been the case globally. Leslie Regan Shade (2002) has described how many women in the Philippines, Latin America, Africa, and Asia have developed "grass-roots" initiatives, which she refers to as "globalizing from below" to address the technology gap. She also notes that at the second Global Knowledge Conference, held in Malaysia in 2000, specific initiatives were introduced to support gender equity and women's empowerment using cybertechnology.

Global initiatives addressing gender equity and access, as well as recent statistics involving Internet use in the United States, would seem encouraging for those concerned with bridging the divide involving online access between women and men. However, Alison Adam (2005) argues that gender issues affecting cybertechnology are much more complex than mere concerns about access levels. Others point out that "access issues" for women can be better understood as concerns about access to jobs in technology, rather than merely access to the Internet. In Sections 10.4.1 and 10.4.2, we examine gender-related cybertechnology issues in terms of two important categories: (i) women's access to high-technology jobs, and (ii) gender bias in software design (especially in video games).

10.4.1 Access to High-Technology Jobs

Some see the root of the gender-and-technology problem, at least as it applies to access issues involving jobs in computer science and engineering, in educational practices that contribute to the overall socialization process for women. For example, many social scientists point out that at an early age girls learn that science (and, by association, technology) is for boys; computers reinforce certain stereotypes regarding technology and gender. Many critics concede that girls and young women have not literally been denied access to careers in computing, but they point out that socialization—for example, processes that encourage males and females to adopt particular gender-based roles—has perpetuated the gender imbalance.

Tracy Camp (1997) and others have conducted research on what they call "pipeline issues" by analyzing statistics involving the number of women entering the computer science and engineering professions; the data collected during the past twenty or so years suggest that proportionately few women elect to pursue degrees in either field. Michael Wessells (1990) pointed out that in 1989, fewer than 5% of those awarded PhD degrees in computer science were women. According to slightly later statistics provided by Camp (1997), this percentage increased to 15.4% (in 1993–1994), but Camp also noted that the percentage of women pursuing bachelor's and master's degrees in computer science declined slightly during those years.

Kirlidog, Aykol, and Gulsecen (2009) cite more recent evidence to support the ongoing concerns about the "pipeline," and they argue that computer science is still typically regarded as a "male profession," both in industry and academia. They also believe that women remain in the "margins" of a male-dominated profession, which is filled with highly gendered expressions such as "killing or aborting programs," "workbench, " "toolkit, " etc., that reflect the masculine culture of the field. The authors identify three "net results" of the male-dominated computing profession in which women

1. are underrepresented in computer-related jobs,
2. are more underrepresented in the managerial ranks in the computing field because of the "glass ceiling,"
3. earn less than men for doing the same jobs.[23]

To support (1), they cite a 2000 study showing that while 46% of the U.S. workforce was made up of women, only 28% of computer science and mathematics-related jobs were held by women. This problem is by no means unique to the United States or to Western nations, they argue, because a large discrepancy can also be found in the computing field in developing nations such as India. Not only are women there under-represented in terms of the number of jobs and in the number of managerial positions in the computing field, but the "average Indian woman earns 60% of a man's pay for the same job, and only 3% of management jobs are occupied by women."[24]

So the "pipeline" concerns (initially reported in the late 1980s) regarding the low numbers of women entering the computer profession, as well as the limited career opportunities for women who entered the profession, seem to have persisted well into the twenty-first century. What kinds of explanations can be given to account for this continued trend, especially in developed nations such as the United States? Admitting that no one really knows why this is the case, Paul De Palma (2005) proposes an alternative way of examining the question. First, he dismisses the view that women do not pursue computer science careers because of "math anxiety"—an explanation that has been advanced by some analysts. De Palma points out that, traditionally, many women pursued degrees in mathematics long before fields such as medicine and law were available to them. So, he believes that mathematics programs in colleges and universities must have been doing something right in attracting and graduating women.

De Palma suggests that if computer science programs (in colleges and universities) were more like mathematics programs than they currently are, then perhaps more women would be attracted to them. He also notes that much of the high-tech culture associated with the early days of computing was dominated by males, who tended to be fascinated with gadgetry and devices, as opposed to mathematics per se. This, in turn, affected how programming courses were conceived of and taught. De Palma speculates that if course instruction on how to program were designed to be as close as possible to pure logic, as opposed to "reliance on glitzy software packages and fancy graphical user interfaces," women might find programming courses and computer science programs more attractive. Although this explanation is based on speculation, as De Palma admits, it would be an interesting hypothesis to test.

While it may be difficult to provide a convincing and uncontroversial explanation as to why relatively few women have pursued careers in computer science, we clearly need to consider some implications that this continued trend could have for the future of the computing field. We should note that in addition to providing information used in projecting the number of women who will have access to jobs in the computer profession, analyses of "pipeline statistics" also provide us with projections regarding the proportion of women who will have access to important decision-making roles in the computing and high-tech industries. Because the decisions that women make could significantly impact future directions in cybertechnology development, it would seem that carefully monitoring statistics and trends affecting the "pipeline" is warranted.

Before concluding this section, we should note that some authors writing on the topic of gender and computing have been critical of an approach that focuses solely, or even mainly, on access-related or "pipeline" issues. For example, Alison Adam (2004, 2005) notes that while examining the low numbers of women in the computing profession is important because it reveals existing inequities in the field, this approach also tends to severely limit the study of gender-and-computing issues to access-related concerns. Adam also believes that focusing on this approach may cause us to miss an opportunity to use feminist ethical theory in our analysis of broader cyberethics issues such as privacy and power in terms of their gender implications. She worries that current computer ethics research involving gender is "under-theorized," and she argues that we need a "gender informed ethics" to improve the process. The framework that Adam defends is based on a feminist ethics—in particular, on the "ethic of care" introduced in a seminal work on feminist ethics by Carol Gilligan.[25] Unfortunately, however, a fuller examination of Adam's gender-informed ethical theory is beyond the scope of this chapter.

10.4.2 Gender Bias in Software Design and Video Games

Some authors have argued that in the past, educational software tended to favor male learning behaviors and thus was biased against female learners. So, there was some concern then about the effect that gender bias in educational software programs might have for young female students. Although concerns about this kind of gender bias have dissipated in recent years, critics argue that gender bias can still be found in many other kinds of software applications. This is especially apparent in the case of video game software. Elizabeth Buchanan (2000) argues that this bias raises two distinct kinds of ethical concerns, because video games tend to: (1) either misrepresent or exclude female characters, and (2) perpetuate traditional sexist stereotypes. With respect to (1), she argues that the representational politics of gender in video games needs greater evaluation, because many computer games, especially virtual sports games, include no female characters at all. And with respect to (2), Buchanan argues that video games such as Barbie Fashion Designer have reinforced traditional cultural stereotypes along gender lines.

Some might tend to dismiss concerns about gender bias in video games on the grounds that many women simply aren't interested in them. However, Philip Brey (2008) argues that the question of gender bias in these games is "morally significant." He points out, for example, that if

> computer games tend to be designed and marketed for men, then women are at an unfair advantage, as they consequently have less opportunity to enjoy computer games and their possible benefits. Among such benefits may be greater computer literacy, an important quality in today's market place.[26]

Brey also notes that many analysts believe that the computer industry is mainly to blame for the gender gap that exists. For example, most game developers are male; also, there has been little interest on the part of developers to design suitable games for women. Brey also points out that very few computer games include decent role models for women. He notes that a disproportionate number of the female characters in these games are strippers or prostitutes and that these characters tend to have "unrealistic body images." (Brey's points are examined in more detail in Chapter 11 in our discussion of ethical aspects of virtual reality (VR) applications.) We conclude this section by noting that Brey and Buchanan each make a plausible case for how the design of video games contributes to gender bias and for why that bias is morally significant.

▶ 10.5 CYBERTECHNOLOGY, DEMOCRACY, AND DEMOCRATIC IDEALS

In previous sections of this chapter, we examined equity-and-access issues pertaining to social/economic class (the digital divide), race, gender, and disabled persons. Underlying many of the concerns involving these socio-demographic groups were issues that also affect democracy, more broadly, as well as democratic ideals and values in particular. A number of interesting questions arise at the intersection of democracy and cyber-technology. For example, some authors question whether the Internet is an inherently democratic technology, while others question whether we should develop the Internet along democratic principles (Johnson 2000).[27] In our analysis of democracy and cybertechnology, however, we consider two slightly different kinds of questions:

1. Has the use of cybertechnology so far enhanced democracy and democratic ideals, or has it threatened them?

2. What impact has cybertechnology had so far on the political-election process in democratic nations?

10.5.1 Has Cybertechnology Enhanced or Threatened Democracy?

Why should we care whether cybertechnology favors and possibly enhances democracy, or whether it instead threatens and potentially undermines it? We can begin by noting that democracy, when compared to alternative forms of government, seems an attractive political structure and, arguably, one of the fairest. Because of these assumptions, Gordon Graham (1999) points out that it is difficult to get people, especially in the Western world, to engage in a serious debate about the merits of democracy. He correctly notes that democracy, along with its corresponding notion of a "democratic ideal," has won almost universal and largely unquestioning acceptance in the West. Graham also points out, however, that political theorists and philosophers have not always regarded democracy as the best—or, in some cases, not even as an adequate—form of government. For example, in *The Republic*, Plato was highly critical of democracy and viewed it as a form of mob rule in which important decisions could be made by a citizenry that typically was not well informed on matters involving the state. And in the nineteenth century, philosopher John Stuart Mill also questioned whether democracy was the ideal form of government.[28]

Let us assume, for the sake of argument, that democracy is superior to alternative political structures. We can still ask whether cybertechnology favors democracy and democratic ideals. Authors who believe that it does generally point to one or more of four factors, where the Internet is alleged to provide greater:

a. "openness" (i.e., an open architecture),

b. empowerment,

c. choice,

d. access to information.

With regard to (a), some authors argue that the Internet provides an open forum in which ideas can generally be communicated freely and easily. Other authors, focusing on (b), note that the Internet empowers certain groups by giving them a "voice," or say, in some matters that they had not previously had. Still other authors, such as Graham, suggest that the Internet empowers individuals by giving them more choices and thus greater freedom.[29] And Cass Sunstein (2001, 2007) points out that the Internet has provided greater access to information at a lower cost. Perhaps Introna and Nissenbaum

(2000) sum up these points best when they note that in the early days of the Internet, people tended to assume that online search technologies would

> . . . give voice to diverse social, economic, and cultural groups, to members of society not frequently heard in the public sphere [and] empower the traditionally disempowered, giving them access both to typically unreachable modes of power and to previously unavailable troves of information.[30]

Values affecting openness, empowerment, choice, and greater access to information all seem to favor democracy. Thus, in so far as cybertechnology facilitates these values, it would also seem to favor democracy and democratic ideals. But does the Internet's "open" architecture necessarily facilitate democratic values universally? Consider that some countries have gone to great lengths to censor political speech in cyberspace. For example, China required Google to comply with strict rules for filtering information, which many nations in the West would view as unacceptable. Also, Saudi Arabia has censored political speech online. So, nondemocratic countries have found some ways around the "open" architecture of the Internet and its ability to spread information freely.

In suggesting that online search technologies may threaten democratic ideals, Introna and Nissenbaum point out that search engines "systematically exclude certain sites and certain types of sites, in favor of others"—a practice that they believe privileges some groups and some persons at the expense of others. Diaz (2008) raises a related concern when he asks whether Internet search technologies will filter out, and thus exclude, the kinds of "independent voices and diverse viewpoints" that are essential for a democracy.

Graham worries that some features of the Internet may contribute to the "worst aspects" of democracy by fostering social and political fragmentation. And Eli Pariser (2011) believes that a new mode of filtering on the Internet, involving "personalization filters" that are now used by major search engines, threatens democracy. Next, we briefly consider each type of threat.

Social/Political Fragmentation and "Personalization" Filters

How does the Internet facilitate social and political fragmentation, and why is fragmentation problematic for a democratic society? The Internet fragments society by facilitating the formation of groups who depart from the mainstream perspectives of a cohesive society. An analogy involving television news programming in physical space might help us appreciate how easily social and political fragmentation can occur and why it can be problematic. Consider that until the advent of cable TV news programming in the 1970s, American television viewers relied primarily on the three major networks for the evening news reports. Even though the program formats varied slightly and even though different anchors delivered the news to viewers, all three presented "mainstream" news reporting that satisfied certain standards of accuracy and credibility before the networks would broadcast it. At times, the members of political groups may have been annoyed with, or possibly even offended by, the way that a particular story was presented, but the news reports were generally descriptive, or factual. Some news programs also included commentaries, usually toward the end of the program, in which the commentator expressed an opinion, but there was a clear line between "factual" reporting and personal opinion.

Now you can select a news program that fits best with and reinforces your political ideology. For example, consider a news report of hostilities between Israelis and Palestinians. If supporters of Israel do not like the way the story is reported on an American news network, and if they have cable or satellite access to Israeli television, they can tune into an Israeli station for their news. Similarly, if Palestinian supporters dislike the American media's coverage, and if they have cable access to an Arab news network such as Al-Jazeera, they can choose to view the news story as an Arab station broadcasts it. On the one hand, these options provide supporters of both sides in this conflict with greater choices and seemingly greater freedom. On the other hand, these options can also increase social and political fragmentation.

We can apply a similar analogy to news reports of domestic political issues in the United States. Conservatives and liberals can each interact in online forums and visit Web sites that exclusively promote the political views that they embrace. Of course, a critic could point out that prior to the Internet, many people subscribed to newspapers and magazines that were labeled as either radically liberal or radically conservative and therefore biased in their reporting. But it is more difficult to filter information in physical space because people in most physical communities encounter individuals with ideological perspectives different from their own, even when they seek out only those who share their belief systems. In online forums, however, it is possible for individuals to be in contact with only those people who share their ideological beliefs. Thus Richard Epstein (2000) worries that in the near future, the concept of the "public square," where ideas have been traditionally debated, could become *fragmented* into "thousands of highly specialized communities that do not communicate with one another."

As noted above, some critics now also worry about the impact that "personalization filters" used by contemporary search engine companies will have for democratic societies. Pariser fears that these filters enable a kind of "invisible autopropaganda," which can indoctrinate us with our own ideas. He notes that while democracy "requires citizens to see things from one another's point of view," we are instead increasingly "more enclosed in our own bubbles." He also notes that while a democracy "requires a reliance on shared facts," we are instead being presented with "parallel but separate universes."

Why is this trend away from citizens having shared facts so dangerous for a democracy? For one thing, consider the contentious debate about climate change in the United States during the past decade. Pariser points out that studies have shown that between 2001 and 2010, the views of people's beliefs about whether the climate was warming changed significantly, along Republican vs. Democrat lines. The number of Republicans who believed that the planet was warming fell from 49 to 29%, while the number of Democrats rose from 60 to 70%. How is such a discrepancy regarding beliefs about climate change possible among people living in the same country? Pariser notes that an online search for "climate change" will turn up different results for an environmental activist than for an oil company executive, as well as different results for persons whom the search algorithm understands to be Democrats rather than Republicans.

With entrenched views about current controversial topics such as climate change, citizens in democratic countries such as the United States are becoming increasingly polarized. Sunstein worries that increased polarization threatens *deliberative democracy* — i.e., the process of rationally debating issues in a public forum. He suggests that deliberative democracy may suffer irreparable harm because of the ways in which the Internet now filters information.

Internet Filtering, Polarization, and Deliberative Democracy

Why does Sunstein believe that deliberative democracy is threatened by Internet filtering? For one thing, he worries that people using software filters will not be inclined to gather new information that might broaden their views but will instead use information available to them on the Internet to reinforce their existing prejudices. Sunstein's concerns are echoed by Diaz (2008), who points out that if we wish to preserve the principles of deliberative democracy, we need to make sure that a "broad spectrum of information on any given topic" is disseminated on the Internet. A similar point is also made by Hinman (2005), when he argues that "free and undistorted access to information" is essential for a deliberative democracy to flourish.

We can construct a variation of Sunstein's argument in the following way:

PREMISE 1. Internet filtering schemes (a) provide people with information that reinforces ideas that they already hold, and (b) screen out novel information and different points of view.

PREMISE 2. Screening out novel information and different points of view will eliminate people's exposure to new ideas or to ideas that may question or conflict with their own.

PREMISE 3. Decreased exposure to different points of view can lead to greater isolation and polarization of citizens.

PREMISE 4. Increased isolation and polarization can encourage extremism and radicalism rather than fostering compromise and moderation.

PREMISE 5. Compromise and moderation are needed for the traditional give-and-take process in resolving differences in a public forum.

PREMISE 6. Technologies that screen out different points of view, lead to greater isolation and polarization, encourage extremism and radicalism, and prevent compromise and moderation tend to undermine deliberative democracy.

CONCLUSION. Internet filtering tends to undermine deliberative democracy.

Is this argument valid? The form of reasoning involved would suggest that the six premises, if all assumed to be true, would guarantee the conclusion. So the argument's form, and its reasoning strength, would seem to be valid. But is it also sound? Recall that for a valid argument to succeed, it must also have all true premises; otherwise, the argument would still be valid but also unsound. Thus if one or more of the premises comprising this argument can be shown to be false, the argument is unsound. Of course, it is also possible for the argument's conclusion to be true (or false) for other reasons—i.e., independently of the specific premises given to support it. At this point, you may want to consult Chapter 3 in evaluating the overall strength of this argument.

We should note that some disagree with Sunstein's conclusion. Thomas Ulen (2001), for example, is not convinced that the "net effect" of the Internet on deliberative democracy will be negative. Ulen also believes that even if Sunstein's analysis is correct so far, Sunstein fails to consider that the Internet is changing very rapidly and that, in the long term, these changes could have a positive impact on deliberative democracy. However, we have also seen how Pariser's description of the impact of personalization filters further complicates the challenge for deliberative democracy. So, if Sunstein and Pariser are correct, there are good reasons to be skeptical that cybertechnology, in the near term at least, will facilitate values essential for deliberative democracy.

We can conclude this section by noting that cybertechnology seems to have both democracy-enhancing and democracy-threatening aspects. We saw that the Internet's open architecture, which enables greater access to information and for that information to be shared freely and easily, would seem to enhance some democratic values. However, we also saw how Internet filtering schemes enable fragmentation and polarization that, in turn, undermine deliberative democracy.

10.5.2 How has Cybertechnology Affected Political Elections in Democratic Nations?

We now turn to our second principal question regarding democracy and cybertechnology: How has this technology impacted political elections so far? In answering this question, we look at the impact via two broad categories: (a) using electronic devices and social media sites for political fundraising and influencing voter turnout; and (b) using political blogs to spread information and influence election outcomes. We begin with (a).

Electronic Devices and Social Media

Graham suggests that in representative democracies, such as the United States, cyber-technology might be used to concentrate more power in the hands of elected representatives instead of ordinary citizens. He also notes that many representatives and political leaders (including their staffs) tend to have both greater technological resources and the ability to use them more skillfully than many ordinary citizens. These factors, in Graham's view, suggest that those in power can effectively use these technological resources to retain their power. We can ask whether the following example illustrates Graham's point. In the 2004 U.S. presidential elections, Carl Rove, a member of the George W. Bush administration, used BlackBerry (smart phone) technology to coordinate with Republican officials across all of the voting precincts in Ohio, a "battleground state" that would determine the winner of that year's election. Some political commentators suggested that Rove's coordinating a state-wide, get-out-the-vote effort to target voters via the use of BlackBerry technology helped to ensure victory in Ohio, which provided the necessary electoral votes for President Bush to remain in power for four more years. Although it is difficult to prove that Rove's use of this technology helped the incumbent president to remain in power in 2004, we can see how the use of the latest technology in a state or national election can influence the voter turnout and ultimately the outcome of that election.

Next, consider that as Barack Obama prepared to run in the 2008 U.S. presidential elections, his staff organized a "grassroots" fund-raising strategy on the Internet through various social networking sites (SNSs) to raise millions of dollars (mostly as small contributions from young people) to finance his presidential campaign. (We examine SNSs in detail in Chapter 11.) Now that Obama is in office and running for a second term, it will also be interesting to see whether his 2012 presidential reelection campaign once again takes advantage of the latest social-media technologies to win reelection and remain in power for four additional years.

It would seem that Graham's claim may have some merit. We have seen how some political parties in power (in Western democracies, at least) have successfully used the latest available cybertechnologies to maintain their power. On the other hand, however, ordinary citizens in some nondemocratic countries, such as Tunisia and Egypt, have recently used electronic devices and social media to topple the powerful political regimes in those nations.

You may have heard of a political uprising that many journalists and news commentators now refer to as the "Arab Spring"—a political movement that began on January 25, 2011 in Cairo, Egypt. When protestors there assembled and threatened to bring down Hosni Mubarak and his government, the Mubarak administration reacted immediately by shutting down the country's Internet services and mobile phone resources. However, the protestors had already unified and planned out their organized demonstrations via social media sites such as Facebook and Twitter before the online services in Egypt were able to be shut down (Ratti and Townsend 2011). In this case, organized protestors were able to bring down a government, largely because of their adept use of electronic devices and social media to organize their protests. So, it would seem that Graham's claim about political leaders in representative democracies being able to use cybertechnology to remain in power would not necessarily apply to political leaders in some nondemocratic nations.

Political Blogs and the Democratic Process

We next consider the impact that blogs (or Web logs), especially political blogs, can have on democracy. (We discuss some broader ethical and social impacts of blogs and the "blogosphere" in more detail in Chapter 11, in connection with our analysis of online communities.) To what extent do political blogs reinforce democratic values and ideals, and how can they undermine them? Insofar as blogs function as instruments for communicating and disseminating information about important political issues, they would seem to reinforce values that favor democracy. But the standards for ensuring accuracy of the content posted in political blogs are not always adequate.

During the 2008 U.S. presidential elections, some extreme right-wing political bloggers reported that (then presidential candidate) Barack Obama was a Muslim and that he was not born in the United States.[31] At the same time, some radical left-wing bloggers reported that (vice presidential candidate) Sara Palin's youngest child was really her grandchild and that Palin was protecting her unmarried daughter from embarrassment.[32] Neither story was vetted in the way that a report submitted by a professional journalist working for a reputable news organization would be, and neither story would likely have been published in a reputable newspaper. But these stories were read online by numerous people, many of whom may have assumed the reports about Obama and Palin to be true merely because they were published on the Internet.

As (hard copy) newspaper subscriptions continue to decline, and as more and more people get their news online, we may have to worry about the standards of accuracy that apply in the online political news media, especially political blogs. As we noted above, a democracy depends on truthful information to flourish and survive. So perhaps we should be concerned about the lack of veracity in some political blogs and the implications that the mass dissemination of false information online may have for the future of democracy. However, some analysts do not seem concerned about the potentially negative effects of blogging for democracy. For example, Alvin Goldman (2008) points out that even if individual blogs are biased, it doesn't follow that the entire blogosphere is. (Recall our discussion of the Fallacy of Composition in Chapter 3, where we saw that attributes that apply to the part do not necessarily apply to the whole.) As Goldman aptly puts the matter, "the reliability of the blogosphere shouldn't be identified with the reliability of a single blog."[33]

Goldman suggests that the "zealous advocacy" of some political bloggers, as well as the "adversarial process" facilitated by blogs in general, may even turn out to be a good thing. For example, he believes the system of checks and balances, which are "collectively stronger than the kinds of filtering mechanisms used in the conventional media" may be a good mechanism for "truth-determination." If Goldman is correct on this point, the blogosphere may ultimately contribute to the preservation of democratic values.

In concluding this section, we note that many controversial issues affecting cybertechnology and democracy have not been examined. For example, there are controversies surrounding e-voting, as well as the selling of votes online; unfortunately these and other issues are beyond the intended scope of this chapter. Note that our brief analysis of some key cybertechnology-and-democracy issues here was not intended to be exhaustive.

▶ 10.6 THE TRANSFORMATION AND THE QUALITY OF WORK

In Sections 10.1–10.5, we examined questions pertaining to equity-and-access issues as they affect both *sociodemographic groups*—e.g., disabled persons, racial minorities, and women—and *social/political institutions*, mainly as they impact democracy and democratic values. In this section, we consider some equity-and-access related issues from a third perspective or social category. Here, we examine the impact of cybertechnology on a *social sector*: the contemporary workplace. Though still relatively new, cybertechnology already has had a profound effect on employment as well as on the nature of work itself. Computers and cybertechnology also significantly affect the quality of work life. Before considering this, we examine issues involving the transformation of the contemporary workplace and the displacement of jobs.

10.6.1 Job Displacement and the Transformed Workplace

While it is debatable whether cybertechnology has benefited workers, overall, it is quite clear that this technology has significantly changed the workplace. Some have gone so far as to suggest that cybertechnology has *transformed* the nature of work itself. One question that frequently arises in discussions about the transformation of employment by cybertechnology is whether, on balance, it has created or eliminated more jobs. There are arguments to support both sides of this debate. Although cybertechnology has caused certain industries to eliminate human jobs, it has enabled other industries, such as computer support companies, to create jobs; social scientists often refer to this shift as *job displacement*. We examine some key issues involving job displacement from two broad perspectives or categories:

A. automation, robotics, and expert systems;

B. remote work, outsourcing, and globalization.

Whereas job-displacement issues affecting (A) typically result from the introduction of new kinds of machines (hardware) as well as new software applications, those affecting (B) often result from changes in policies and practices involving employment and the workplace (that, in turn, are often influenced by technological developments). We begin with a brief analysis of (A).

Automation, Robotics, and Expert Systems

Job displacement is often associated with *automation*. Social and ethical issues involving automation are by no means new, nor are they unique to cybertechnology. Social scientists note that the Industrial Revolution transformed jobs into smaller, discrete tasks that could be automated by machines, creating working conditions that adversely affected the lives of many workers. When new automated technology threatened to replace many workers, one group of disenchanted workers in England—later referred to as "Luddites"—smashed machines used to make textiles. ("Luddite" is derived from a nineteenth-century British worker, Ned Ludd, who reputedly led workers in destroying factory machinery.)

Just as the Luddites resisted factory technology in the nineteenth century because they thought it threatened their jobs and thus their livelihoods, some workers have opposed developments involving cybertechnology for similar reasons. In the 1970s, for example, workers tried to stall developments in microprocessor-based technology, fearing that it would lead to a loss of jobs. Workers as well individuals in general who resist technological change, and who have a pessimistic view of the impact of cybertechnology in the workplace, are sometimes referred to as neo-Luddites.

Developments in *robotics* have also raised social concerns affecting job displacement. Robots, equipped with motor abilities that enable them to manipulate objects, can be programmed to perform tasks that are either (a) routine and mundane for humans, or (b) considered hazardous to humans. As Patrick Lin (2012) so aptly puts it, robots are typically tasked to perform the "three Ds"—i.e., jobs that humans consider "dull, dirty, and dangerous." Although robots were once fairly unsophisticated, contemporary robotic systems are able to perform a wide range of tasks. (We examine some ethical aspects of robots and robotic systems in detail in Chapter 12.)

Whereas (physical) robots have eliminated many blue-collar jobs, sophisticated programs called *expert systems* threaten many professional jobs. An expert system (ES) is a problem-solving computer program that is "expert" at performing one particular task. ESs use "inference engines" to capture the decision-making strategies of experts (usually professionals); they execute instructions that correspond to a set of rules an expert would use in performing a professional task. A "knowledge engineer" asks human experts in a given field a series of questions and then extracts rules and designs a program based on the responses to those questions. Initially, expert systems were designed to perform jobs in chemical engineering and geology, both of which required the professional expertise of highly educated persons and were generally considered too hazardous for humans. More recently, ESs have been developed for use in professional fields such as law, education, and finance.

The use of ESs, much like the use of (physical) robotic systems, has raised some ethical and social issues having to do with "de-skilling" and "worker alienation." We noted the impact that automation had on some workers during the Industrial Revolution. Social scientists have suggested that prior to that period, workers generally felt connected to their labor and exhibited a strong sense of pride and craftsmanship. The relationship between worker and work began to change, however, when work became automated. Social scientists have used the term *alienation* to describe the effect that de-skilling had for workers whose skills were transferred to machines. Richard Mason (2007) cites as an example the introduction of Jacquard's loom and its effect on weavers during the Industrial Revolution, where skills were "disembodied" from weavers and craftsmen and then "re-embodied" into machines such as the loom.

Today, ES technology poses a similar threat to professional workers by allowing knowledge, in the form of rules applying to knowledge-related skills, to be extracted from (human) experts and then embedded into computer software code. Mason points out that knowledge can now be "disemminded" from professional workers, or experts in a given field, and "emminded" into machines in the form of computer programs. Mason also believes that there is an interesting connection between the Industrial Revolution and the current era in that a proliferation of publications on ethics appears in each time period, and he suggests that working conditions during the Industrial Revolution may have been responsible for the greatest outpouring of moral philosophy since Plato and Aristotle. He notes, for example, that works on ethics by Immanuel Kant, Jeremy Bentham, and John Stuart Mill appeared during that era. Mason also suggests that, similarly, contemporary workplace controversies associated with cybertechnology have contributed to the recent flurry of publications on ethics.[34]

We conclude this section by noting that automation, robotics, and ESs have each contributed significantly to job displacement in the contemporary workplace. We have also noted that these three technologies have adversely affected some employee groups more than others. Next, we examine the impact that three relatively recent employment-related practices and policies have had for job displacement, in particular, and the contemporary workplace in general.

Remote Work, Job Outsourcing, and Globalization

One factor that has transformed work for many employees is that cybertechnology has made it possible for them to work "remotely"—i.e., outside the traditional workplace. Even though remote work, referred to by some as "telework," is a relatively recent practice, it has already raised social and ethical questions. One question has to do with whether all employees who perform remote work benefit from it equally. In Section 10.2.1, in our brief discussion of remote work in the context of cybertechnology and the disabled, we saw how disabled persons could be negatively affected by the remote work policies used by some employers.

We next ask if other groups are potentially disadvantaged, or perhaps more favorably advantaged instead, by remote work policies and practices. For example, are white-collar employees affected in the same way as those less-educated and less-skilled employees? It is one thing to be a white-collar professional with an option to work at home at your discretion and convenience. It is something altogether different, however, to be a clerical, or "pink collar," worker required to work remotely out of your home. Of course, some professional men and women may choose to work at home because of childcare considerations or because they wish to avoid a long and tedious daily commute, but employers may require other employees, especially those in lower-skilled and clerical jobs, to work at home. So, some groups, including pink-collar workers as well as disabled workers (see Section 10.2.1), may be disadvantaged because of specific remote work policies.

Another contemporary practice contributing to the ongoing transformation of work involves job *outsourcing*. Outsourcing practices have affected the displacement of jobs not only for employees in industries within countries but also across them, and thus have had international implications. In our brief analysis of remote work, we saw how cybertechnology enabled the reallocation of work from traditional workplace settings to remote sites, including an employee's home. Until recently, however, most American jobs affected by remote work still remained in the United States. Now many jobs are outsourced to countries where labor costs are less expensive. For example, many traditional manufacturing jobs in the United States have been exported "offshore." Initially, this phenomenon impacted mainly traditional "blue-collar" jobs; now it also affects many jobs in the service sector. In the past decade or so, it has also affected many highly skilled "white collar" jobs such as those in the computing/IT field. Consider, for instance, that many programming jobs traditionally held by employees in American companies, such as IBM, are now "outsourced" to companies in India and China whose employees are willing to work for significantly lower wages than those paid to American programmers.

Ironically, perhaps, the jobs of the programmers who had the high-tech skills needed to make the outsourcing of many white-collar jobs a reality are now being outsourced to countries where programmers earn less money. Baker and Kripalani (2005) point out that the career prospects of American software programmers, which were "once dazzling," are now in doubt. In fact, the authors note that, because of this trend, the future of high-tech economy in the United States may also be at risk. Although it is still too soon to say with any confidence what the net effect of the outsourcing of programming jobs will mean, it raises concerns that warrant serious consideration.

Controversies affecting job outsourcing, especially where multiple nations are involved, are often linked to a phenomenon that has come to be known as *globalization*. What is globalization, and how is it affected by cybertechnology? Torin Monahan (2005) defines globalization as "the blurring of boundaries previously held as stable and fixed . . . between local/global, public/private [and] nation/world."[35] Monahan notes that discussions of globalization tend to focus on concerns involving labor outsourcing, international trade agreements, immigration concerns, cultural homogenization, and so forth. So there are broad cultural issues, as well as economic controversies, underlying the debate about globalization. In this section, however, our concern is with the economic aspects of globalization, particularly as they impact cybertechnology and the workplace.

In a global economy where individual nations are protected less and less by tariffs, competition between countries for producing and exporting goods, as well as for providing services, has escalated. In the United States, considerable debate has focused on the NAFTA (North American Free Trade Association) initiatives during the past two decades. Those individuals and organizations that have been labeled "isolationists" and "protectionists" have opposed NAFTA, while proponents of "open" markets between countries have tended to support it. Do trade agreements such as NAFTA and GATT (General Agreement on Tariffs and Trade) favor poorer countries that are part of the agreement, where the cost of labor is cheaper? Or do these trade agreements favor the majority of people in wealthier countries who are able to purchase more goods and services at lower prices? On the one hand, NAFTA and GATT have encouraged greater competition between nations and, arguably, have resulted in greater efficiency for businesses. On the other hand, the economies of some nations have been severely impacted by the job loss that has resulted.

What is the net economic benefit of globalization for both the richer and the poorer countries? To what extent has cybertechnology exacerbated the concerns raised by globalization and the displacement of jobs? These questions are controversial, and proponents on each side have come up with drastically different statistical data to support their claims.

10.6.2 The Quality of Work Life in the Digital Era

So far, we have focused on social and ethical issues surrounding the transformation of work vis-à-vis job displacement, but many social scientists have also questioned how cybertechnology impacts the *quality* of work life. Quality issues include concerns about employee health, which can pertain both to physical-and mental-health related issues. Among these concerns are worries about the level of stress for many employees in the contemporary workplace, especially those who are subject to computerized monitoring and surveillance.

Employee Stress, Workplace Surveillance, and Computer Monitoring

Many workers experience stress because their activities are now monitored closely by an "invisible supervisor" — i.e., the computer, which can record information about one's work habits. The *2007 Electronic Monitoring and Surveillance Report*, sponsored by the American Management Association (AMA) and published by the AMA/e Policy Institute Research (2008), noted that 43% of American companies monitor employee e-mail, and 96% of those companies "track external (incoming and outgoing messages)." The report also noted that 45% of companies track the amount of time an employee spends at the keyboard. An increasing number of these companies now also monitor the blogosphere (described in Chapter 11) to see what is being written about them in various blogs, and some also monitor social networking sites such as Facebook. As a result of increased monitoring, many employees have been fired for misusing a company's e-mail resources or its Web resources, or both. So, the threats posed by computerized monitoring would clearly seem to contribute to employee stress.

Perhaps somewhat ironically, data entry clerks and so-called "information workers," whose work is dependent on the use of computer technology to process information, are among the groups of employees who have been most subjected to monitoring by that technology. Although computer monitoring techniques were initially used to track the activities of clerical workers such as data entry operators, they now also track and evaluate the performance of professionals, such as programmers, loan officers, investment brokers, and managers. And nurses are also frequently monitored to make sure that they do not spend too much time with one patient.

Why is employee monitoring via computerized surveillance tools increasing so dramatically? Kizza and Ssanyu (2005) identify multiple factors that have contributed to the recent expansion and growth of employee monitoring, two of which are worth highlighting for our purposes: (a) cost (the lower prices of both software and hardware), and (b) size (the miniaturization of monitoring products). The lower cost of monitoring tools has made them available to many employers who, in the past, might not have been able to afford them. And the miniaturization of these tools has made it far easier to conceal them from employees.

Lucas Introna (2004) points out that surveillance technology, in addition to becoming less expensive, has also become "less overt and more diffused." He also believes that current monitoring technologies have created the potential to build surveillance features into the "very fabric of organizational processes." Consider that monitoring tools are used to measure things such as the number of minutes an employee spends on the telephone completing a transaction (e.g., selling a product or booking a reservation) and the number and length of breaks he or she takes. Monitoring software can even measure the number of computer keystrokes a worker enters per minute. John Weckert (2005) points out that an employee's keystrokes can be monitored for accuracy as well as for speed, and that the contents of an employee's computer screen can easily be viewed on the screen of a supervisor's computer (without that employee's knowledge).

Employees using networked and mobile electronic devices can also be monitored outside the traditional workplace. For example, some employees work at home on employer-owned devices or via an employer's networked application, and some use employer-owned electronic devices to communicate with fellow workers and customers while they are traveling. Consider the following scenario involving a city employee's use of a pager.

▶ **SCENARIO 10–2:** Employee Monitoring and the Case of *Ontario v. Quon*

Jeff Quon, a police officer, was an employee of the city of Ontario, CA. Ontario employees agreed to a policy in which the city reserved the right to monitor ("with or without notice") their electronic communications, including Internet use and email. In 2001, twenty police officers in the SWAT Unit of the Ontario Police Department (OPD) were given alphanumeric pagers. Quon was one of the officers who received a pager. The police officers were told that they were allowed a fixed limit of 25,000 characters per month on their pagers, in accordance with the terms of a contract that OPD had with the Arch Wireless (now USA Mobility) service provider. The officers were also told that if they exceeded that monthly limit, they would be charged a fee for overuse. Quon exceeded the limit on his pager for two consecutive months, and he paid the city for the excess usage. However, his pager was subsequently audited by OPD, which requested a transcript of his messages from Arch Wireless.

During the audit, it was discovered that many of Quon's messages were personal (and thus not work related) and that some were sexually explicit. Quon was then disciplined for violating the city's electronic communications policy. But Quon challenged OPD and the city of Ontario, arguing that his privacy rights had been violated; he alleged that the audit of the content on his pager was both a violation of his constitutional privacy right (under the Fourth Amendment), as well as a violation of federal telecommunications privacy laws. Quon also argued that the city's employee monitoring policy did not explicitly mention pagers and text messages, and he noted that the officers who received pagers were told verbally that they could use their pagers for "light personal communications." However, OPD pointed out that the officers were also informed that obscene, defamatory, and harassing messages on the pagers would not be "tolerated."

The Ninth Circuit Court in California initially sided with Quon (and the other officers involved in the suit). However, the case was eventually appealed to the Supreme Court, which ruled (in June 2010) that the audit of Quon's pager was work related and that it did not violate Quon's Fourth Amendment rights involving unreasonable search and seizure.[36] (*City of Ontario, California, et al. v. Quon et al.*) ∎

Did the high Court make the correct decision in this case? Or, did Quon have a reasonable expectation of privacy in this particular incident, as the lower court initially ruled? Should there be any limitations or constraints placed on an employer's right to monitor an employee's conversations on electronic devices? Or, should all forms of employee monitoring be permissible, where employer-owned equipment is involved? The case involving Jeff Quon may cause us to consider whether some explicit distinctions are worth drawing.

Distinguishing Between Two Different Aspects of Employee Monitoring

Weckert (2005) argues that it is crucial to draw some distinctions involving two areas of computerized monitoring: (1) the different *applications of monitoring*, and (2) the different *kinds of work situations* (that are monitored).

Regarding (1), Weckert notes that employees could be monitored with respect to the following kinds of activities:

- e-mail usage,
- URLs visited while Web surfing,
- quality of their work,
- speed of their work,
- work practices (health and safety),
- employee interaction.[37]

He points out that the reasons given to justify the application of monitoring in activities involving employee e-mail and Internet use may be very different from the kinds of justifications needed to monitor an employee's speed of work or the quality of his or her work.

With regard to (2), some further distinctions also need to be made concerning which kinds of workers should be monitored. Weckert notes that while it may be appropriate to monitor the keystrokes of data entry workers to measure their performance in specific periods of time, it may not be appropriate to monitor the e-mail of workers in cases where client confidentially is expected. For example, he points out that a therapist employed in a health organization may receive highly sensitive and personal e-mail from one of her client's regarding the client's mental state or physical health.

Similarly, a teacher may receive e-mail from a student, or from an academic administrator communicating about a student, that contains sensitive information regarding the student. As a college professor, for example, I occasionally receive e-mail messages from students who may disclose to me, in confidence, personal details of their health or financial status, or an e-mail requesting information about a grade received for an exam or a paper. Arguably, these kinds of e-mails deserve more protection from monitoring than e-mails sent by other employees at my college who do not interact with students in ways that involve the communication of personal information that is sensitive and confidential. So, if my college were to institute an e-mail monitoring policy for its employees, factors such as these should be taken into consideration.

It is very useful to differentiate monitoring issues affecting an employee's activities in the workplace vs. issues pertaining to the kinds of workers who should or should not be monitored. These kinds of distinctions could better inform the company's policies for employee monitoring as well as the rationale(s) used to justify those policies.

Some Rationales for and Against Workplace Monitoring

As in the case of many controversies involving the use of cybertechnology, employee monitoring demonstrates a clash of legitimate interests and rights for the parties involved.

TABLE 10.1   Rationales Used to Support and to Oppose Employee Monitoring

Rationales Used Support to Monitoring	Rationales Used to Oppose Monitoring
Improves worker productivity	Increases employee stress
Improves corporate profits	Invades employee privacy
Guards against industrial espionage	Reduces employee autonomy
Reduces employee theft	Undermines employee trust

While employees are concerned about protecting their rights to privacy and autonomy, employers want to protect their interests involving profit margin and overall efficiency. Forester and Morrison (1994) describe some classic arguments used in favor of, and in opposition to, computer monitoring. They note that some employers defend computer monitoring on the grounds that it saves money, is essential for improving worker productivity, and helps businesses to reduce industrial espionage and employee theft.

Opponents of monitoring have a very different perspective: Some see computer monitoring as a Big Brother tactic or as an "electronic whip" used unfairly by management, and they believe it creates a work environment tantamount to an "electronic sweatshop." Some believe that managers are motivated to use monitoring because they distrust their employees. Others claim that monitoring invades individual privacy, and thus disregards human rights. Along these lines, Rooksby and Cica (2005) argue that monitoring also poses a threat to an individual's right to "psychological autonomy."

Some critics also charge that while monitoring may accurately measure the quantity of work an employee produces, it fails to measure the overall quality of that work. Others argue that computer monitoring is ultimately counterproductive, because of its effects on employee morale. Table 10.1 lists some typical rationales used on both sides of the debate.

In concluding our discussion of employee monitoring, we should note that there are additional aspects of this controversy that we have not considered in this chapter. For example, there are now many global and international dimensions to workplace monitoring, which raise controversial questions. Stephen Coleman (2005) points out that in the global workforce, a person's privacy could be violated by software monitoring programs that reside on a computer located in a country different from where that individual is working. This raises concerns about whether international agreements for employee monitoring policies may be needed. In fact, Coleman suggests that an International Bill of Human Rights be adopted in response to concerns affecting global aspects of the employee monitoring. Unfortunately, an examination of this aspect of monitoring, as well as Coleman's proposed solution, is beyond the scope of this chapter.

▶ 10.7 CHAPTER SUMMARY

In this chapter, we examined a wide range of equity-and-access issues affecting three broad social categories: sociodemographic groups, social and political institutions, and social sectors. With regard to demographic groups affecting socio-economic class, we considered some implications of the digital divide at both the global and the local levels. We then examined equity-and-access issues for three additional demographic groups: disabled persons, racial minorities, and women. Next, we examined the impact of cybertechnology for one of our social/political institutions, in our analysis of democracy and democratic values. Finally, we considered the impact that cybertechnology has had so far for the contemporary workplace—an important social sector. Here, we examined some equity-and-access issues as they apply both to the transformation of work (and job displacement) and to the quality of work in the digital era. Regarding the latter concern, we examined some specific challenges posed by computerized monitoring and workplace surveillance.

▶ REVIEW QUESTIONS

1. What is the "digital divide," and why is it significant?
2. What are the differences between the global digital divide and the divisions within nations affecting access to cybertechnology?
3. Are all "divides" or divisions regarding resources ethical problems? Is the digital divide an ethical issue?
4. According to Jeroen van den Hoven and Emma Rooksby, what is meant by "distributive justice" in the context of contemporary information societies?
5. Describe three ways, according to Jeremy Moss, that people in developing countries are currently disadvantaged because of lack of access to digital technology.
6. Do we have an obligation to bridge the digital divide? Which kinds of arguments have been put forth by Maria Bottis and Kenneth Himma for why affluent countries have an obligation to do so?
7. What are some of the special equity and access issues affecting disabled persons who use cybertechnology?
8. Identify and briefly describe the two perspectives from which we analyzed issues involving cybertechnology and disabled groups.
9. Identify and briefly describe the two perspectives from which we analyzed issues involving race and cybertechnology.
10. Briefly describe the two main perspectives from which we viewed issues involving gender and cybertechnology.

11. Does the Internet favor democracy? Explain. Why does Cass Sunstein believe that the Internet has both democracy-enhancing and democracy-threatening features?
12. What does Sunstein mean by "deliberative democracy"? Why does he believe that Internet filters "undermine deliberative democracy"?
13. According to Graham, how does the Internet contribute to political and social fragmentation?
14. What does Eli Pariser mean by "personalization filters," and why does he believe they pose a threat for democracy?
15. What implications do political blogs have for democracy and democratic values?
16. How has work been "transformed" in the computer age with respect to job displacement? Who were the Luddites, and what is meant by the expression "neo-Luddite"?
17. What are some of the ethical and social issues associated with the development and use of ESs, robotics, and automation?
18. What is globalization? What impact could the outsourcing of highly skilled programming jobs, traditionally held by employees in American companies, to China and India have for the United States in the new global economy?
19. What is employee monitoring, and why is it controversial from an ethical perspective?
20. What are some of the arguments used for and against the use of computers to monitor employees?

▶ DISCUSSION QUESTIONS

21. Some critics and skeptics suggest that the digital divide is not really an ethical issue, because there have always been divisions or "divides" between group. For example, we saw that some critics point out there is a "Mercedes-Benz Divide" and that most of us fall on the wrong side of this "divide." Is

the division between those who have and do not have access to cybertechnology similar to or different from the division between those who own and do not own Mercedes-Benz automobiles? Explain.

22. What obligations does the United States have, as a democratic nation concerned with guaranteeing equal opportunities for all it citizens, to ensure that all Americans have full access to the Internet? Does the United States also have obligations to developing countries to ensure that they have global access to the Internet? If so, what is the extent of those obligations? For example, should engineers working in the United States and other developed countries design applications to ensure that people living in remote areas with low connectivity and poor bandwidth have reasonable Internet access? If so, who should pay for the development of these software applications?

▶ ESSAY/PRESENTATION QUESTIONS

23. In our discussion of expert systems (ESs) in Section 10.6.1, we saw that the increased use of ES technology in professional fields has generated some ethical and social concerns. Some ethical controversies surrounding ES have to do with critical decisions, including life and death decisions; for example, should "expert doctors" be allowed to make decisions that could directly result in the death of, or cause serious harm to, a patient? If so, *who* is ultimately responsible for the ES's decision? Is the hospital that owns the particular ES responsible? Should the knowledge engineer who designed the ES be held responsible? Or is the ES itself responsible? In answering these questions, you may want to consult relevant sections of Chapter 4, where we discussed responsibility for software-related accidents such as the case involving the Therac-25 system.

24. We briefly noted that some controversies associated with workplace monitoring now have global and international implications. For example, Stephen Coleman points out that in the global workforce, an employee's privacy could be violated by software monitoring programs that reside on a computer located in a country different from where that employee works. Do we need new kinds of international agreements and policies for employee monitoring, as Coleman suggests? And do we need to adopt an "International Bill of Human Rights," as Coleman also suggests, in response to global challenges posed by workplace monitoring? If not, what kinds of alternative proposals might be suitable?

Scenarios for Analysis

1. In our discussion of gender bias in developing video games (in Section 10.4.2), we noted that some critics had also been concerned about gender bias in educational software, especially in the earlier days of computing. How could developers of educational software address the problem of bias illustrated in the following scenario?

   Chuck Huff and Joel Cooper (1987) developed a study in which they had teachers design software for three categories of users: girls, boys, and (gender unspecified) children. They discovered that the programs the teachers designed for boys looked like games (with time pressure, hand-to-eye coordination, and competition the most important features). Programs the teachers designed for girls, on the contrary, looked like tools for learning (with conversation and goal-based learning features). And surprisingly, the programs the teachers designed for (gender unspecified) children looked just like the ones they designed for boys. So, the researchers concluded that when teachers designed programs for children, or students in general, they actually designed them for boys.

   This study also revealed some interesting data that was surprising. For example, 80% of the program designers in Huff and Cooper's experiment were female, and, ironically, some of these women had originally expressed the concern that educational software was male biased. Huff and Cooper's research also points to a paradox: a software designer may be able to identify bias in a particular software application but may still not be able to design and develop software applications that avoid bias.

2. Recall our discussion of Expert Systems (ESs) in Section 10.6.1. The following scenario, based on a question posed by Tom Forester and Perry Morrison (1994), illustrates one ethically controversial application of an ES. If you were a member of the program team designing such an application, which kinds of values would you build into this ES?

Forester and Morrison ask whether an "expert administrator" should be designed in a way so that it is programmed to mislead or even to lie to human beings in cases where it might (generally, but unofficially) seem "appropriate" for human administrators to do so. Consider that politicians and executives are sometimes put in situations where they are not permitted to be totally forthcoming. In these cases, being able to be deceptive with respect to answers to certain kinds of questions may be a requirement for being an "expert" (or at least successful) human administrator? If so, should the "skill" of "being able to deceive" (or of "not being totally forthcoming") be built into such a system? Is it morally permissible to design such a system?

▶ ENDNOTES

1. In making these and related distinctions (in Section 10.1) affecting the digital divide, I have drawn from material in Tavani (2003).
2. *Human Development Report 2000.*
3. *Internet World Stats: Usage and Population Stats* (2011). Available at www.internetworldstats.com/stats.htm.
4. *Internet World Stats: Usage and Population Studies* (2005). Available at http://www.internetworldstats.com/top20.htm.
5. *Internet World Stats: Usage and Population Stats* (2011).
6. *Ibid.*
7. O'Hara and Stevens (2006), p. 144.
8. Van den Hoven and Rooksby (2008), p. 376.
9. *Ibid.*
10. Rawls (1972), p. 92.
11. Van den Hoven and Rooksby, p. 395.
12. Moss (2002), p. 162.
13. Norris (2001), p. 168.
14. Bottis and Himma (2008), p. 623.
15. Himma (2007), p. 10.
16. See http://www.w3.org/WAI/.
17. *Digital Divide Network 2000.*
18. *Pew Internet & American Life Project, April 8–May 11, 2008 Tracking Report.*
19. See Burn (2011).
20. Theismeyer (1999), p. 117.
21. *Ibid.*
22. The April/May 2008 *Pew Internet & American Life Project* reported that 73% of women and 73% of men used the Internet.

23. Kirlidog, Aykol, and Gulsecen (2009), p. 51.
24. *Ibid.*
25. See C. Gilligan. *In a Different Voice: Psychological Theory and Women's Development.* Cambridge MA: Harvard University Press.
26. Brey (2008), p. 381.
27. Johnson (2000), p. 181.
28. See Graham (1999, p. 71) for his discussion of Mill's *On Liberty*, as it pertains to democracy.
29. Graham also discusses these attributes in connection with the pros and cons of "online communities," as we will see in our analysis of these communities in Chapter 11.
30. Introna and Nissenbaum (2000), p. 169. My discussion of implications that search engine technology has for democracy (in Section 10.5) draws from Tavani (2012).
31. See, for example, http://worldwideliberty.blogspot.com/2009/01/barack-obama-not-born-in-us-no-us-state.html.
32. See, for example, http://www.politicalbase.com/profile/jnail/blog/&blogId=3482.
33. Goldman (2008), p. 119.
34. Mason (2007), pp. 9–10.
35. Monahan (2005), p. 4.
36. See the description of this case included in Cornell University Law School's Legal Information Institute, available at http://www.law.cornell.edu/supct/html/08-1332.ZS.html. See also the description in http://en.wikipedia.org/wiki/Ontario_v._Quon.
37. Weckert (2005), p. viii.

► REFERENCES

Adam, Alison. 2004. "Gender and Computer Ethics." In R. A. Spinello and H. T. Tavani, eds. *Readings in CyberEthics*. 2nd ed. Sudbury, MA: Jones and Bartlett, pp. 67–80. Reprinted from *Computers and Society* 30, no. 4 (2000): 17–24.

Adam, Alison. 2005. *Gender, Ethics and Information Technology*. London, UK: Palgrave Macmillan.

AMA/e Policy Institute Research (2008). *Executive Summary: 2007 Electronic Monitoring & Surveillance Survey*. Available at http://press.amanet.orgpress-releases/177/2077-electronic-monitoring-surveillance-survey.

Asakawa, Cheiko. 2012. "Web Guru for the Blind." *IEEE Spectrum* 49, no. 2: 55–57.

Baker, Stephen, and Manjeet Kripalani. 2005. "Software: Programming Jobs Are Heading Overseas by the Thousands: Is There a Way for the U.S. to Stay on Top." In P. De Palma, ed. *Computers in Society 05/06*. Dubuque, IA: McGraw-Hill/Dushkin, pp. 47–51.

Bottis, Maria Cannellopulou, and Kenneth Einar Himma. 2008. "The Digital Divide: A Perspective for the Future." In K. E. Himma and H. T. Tavani, eds. *The Handbook of Information and Computer Ethics*. Hoboken, NJ: John Wiley and Sons, pp. 621–37.

Brey, Philip. 2008. "Virtual Reality and Computer Simulation." In K. E. Himma and H. T. Tavani, eds. *The Handbook of Information and Computer Ethics*. Hoboken, NJ: John Wiley and Sons, pp. 361–84.

Buchanan, Elizabeth A. 2000. "Strangers in the 'Myst' of Video Gaming: Ethics and Representation." *CPSR Newsletter* 18, no. 1. Available at http://cpsr.org/prevsite/publications/newsletters/issues/2000/Winter2000/buchanan.html/.

Burn, Enid. 2011. "African American Population is Growing." Available at http://www.clickz.com/clickz/news/1694749/african-american-online-population-is-growing. (Based on data from AOL Black Voice.)

Camp, Tracy. 1997. "The Incredible Shrinking Pipeline." *Communications of the ACM* 40, no. 2: 103–10.

Chapman, Gary, and Marc Rotenberg. 1995. "The National Information Infrastructure: A Public Interest Opportunity." In D. G. Johnson and H. Nissenbaum, eds. *Computers, Ethics, and Social Values*. Englewood Cliffs, NJ: Prentice Hall, pp. 628–44.

Coleman, Stephen. 2005. "Universal Human Rights and Employee Privacy: Questioning Employer Monitoring and Computer Use." In J. Weckert, ed. *Electronic Monitoring in the Workplace: Controversies and Solutions*. Hershey, PA: Idea Group, pp. 276–95.

Compaine, Benjamin. 2001. *The Digital Divide: Facing a Crisis or Creating a Myth*. Cambridge, MA: MIT Press.

De Palma, Paul. 2005. "Why Women Avoid Computer Science." In P. De Palma, ed. *Computers in Society 05/06*. Dubuque, IA: McGraw-Hill, pp. 104–06.

Diaz, Alejandro 2008, "Through the Google Goggles: Sociopolitical Bias in Search Engine Design." In A. Spink and M. Zimmer *Web Search: Multidisciplinary Perspectives*. Berlin: Springer–Verlag, pp. 11–34.

Epstein, Richard G. 2000. "The Fragmented Public Square." *Computers and Society*. Available at http://www.cs.wcupa.edu/~epstein.fragmented.htm.

Fairweather, N. Ben. 1998. "Moral Dilemmas and Issues of Telework for Disabled People." In M. J. van den Hoven, ed. *Computer Ethics: Philosophical Enquiry*. Rotterdam, The Netherlands: Erasmus University Press, pp. 130–41.

Forester, Tom, and Perry Morrison. 1994. *Computer Ethics: Cautionary Tales and Ethical Dilemmas in Computing*. 2nd ed. Cambridge, MA: MIT Press.

Goldman, Alvin I. 2008. "The Social Epistemology of Blogging." In J. van den Hoven and J. Weckert, eds. *Information Technology and Moral Philosophy*. Cambridge, UK: Cambridge University Press, pp. 111–22.

Graham, Gordon. 1999. *The Internet: A Philosophical Inquiry*. New York: Routledge.

Grodzinsky, Frances S. 2000. "Equity of Access: Adaptive Technology." *Science and Engineering Ethics* 6, no. 2: 221–34.

Himma, Kenneth E. 2007. "The Information Gap, the Digital Divide, and the Obligations of Affluent Nations." *International Review of Information Ethics* 7: 1–11.

Hinman, Lawrence M. 2005. "Esse Est Indicato in Google: Ethical and Political Issues in Search Engines," *International Review of Information Ethics*, 3, pp. 19–25.

Huff, Chuck, and Joel Cooper. 1987. "Sex Bias in Educational Software: The Effects of Designers' Stereotypes on the Software They Design." *Journal of Applied Social Psychology* 17: 519–32.

Human Development Report. 2000. *Published for the United Nations Development Program (UNDP)* New York: Oxford University Press.

Internet World Stats: Usage and Population Studies, 2005. Available at http://www.internetworldstats.com/top20.htm.

Introna, Lucas. 2004. "Workplace Surveillance, Privacy, and Distributive Justice." In R. A. Spinello and H. T. Tavani, eds. *Readings in CyberEthics*. 2nd ed. Sudbury, MA: Jones and Bartlett, pp. 476–487.

Introna, Lucas, and H. Nissenbaum. 2000. "Shaping the Web: Why the Politics of Search Engines Matters," *The Information Society* 16, no. 3: 169–185.

Johnson, Deborah G. 2000. "Democratic Values and the Internet." In D. Langford, ed. *Internet Ethics*. New York: St. Martin's Press, pp. 180–99.

Kirlidog, Melih, Meric Aykol, and Sevinc Gulsecen. 2009. "Interpersonal Communication and Gender in the ICT Profession," *IEEE Technology and Society Magazine*, 28 no. 1: 48–56.

Kizza, Joseph M., and Jackline Ssanyu. 2005. "Workplace Surveillance." In J. Weckert, ed. *Electronic Monitoring in the Workplace: Controversies and Solutions*. Hershey, PA: Idea Group, pp. 1–18.

Kretchmer, Susan, and Rod Karveth. 2001. "The Color of the Net: African Americans, Race, and Cyberspace." *Computers and Society* 31, no. 3: 9–14.

Lin, Patrick. 2012. "Introduction to Robot Ethics." In P. Lin, K. Abney, and G. A. Bekey, eds. *Robot Ethics: The Ethical and Social Implications of Robotics*. Cambridge, MA: MIT Press, pp. 3–15.

Mason, Richard O. 2007. "Four Ethical Issues of the Information Age." In J. Weckert, ed. *Computer Ethics*. Aldershot, UK: Ashgate, pp. 31–40. Reprinted from *MIS Quarterly* 10: 5–12.

Monahan, Torin. 2005. *Globalization, Technological Change, and Public Education*. New York: Routledge.

Moor, James H. 2004. "Reason, Relativity, and Responsibility in Computer Ethics." In R. A. Spinello and H. T. Tavani, eds. *Readings in CyberEthics*. 2nd ed. Sudbury, MA: Jones and Bartlett, pp. 40–54.

Moss, Jeremy. 2002. "Power and the Digital Divide." *Ethics and Information Technology* 4, no. 2: 159–65.

Norris, Pippa. 2001. Digital Divide? Civic Engagement, Information Poverty, and the Internet Worldwide. Cambridge, MA: Cambridge University Press.

O'Hara, Kieron, and David Stevens. 2006. *Inequality.com: Power, Poverty, and the Digital Divide*. Oxford, UK: Oneworld.

Pariser, Eli. 2011. *The Filter Bubble: What the Internet is Hiding from You*. New York: Penguin.

Ratti, Carlo, and Anthony Townsend. 2011. "Harnessing Residents' Electronic Devices Will Yield Truly Smart Cities." *Scientific American,* August 6. Available at http://www.scientificamerican.com/article.cfm?id=the-social-nexus.

Rawls, John. 1972. *A Theory of Justice*. Cambridge, MA: Harvard University Press.

Rooksby, Emma, and Natasha Cica. 2005. "Personal Autonomy and Electronic Surveillance in the Workplace." In J. Weckert, ed. *Electronic Monitoring in the Workplace: Controversies and Solutions*. Hershey, PA: Idea Group, pp. 242–59.

Shade, Leslie Regan. 2002. *Gender and Community in the Social Construction of the Internet*. New York: Peter Lang.

Sunstein, Cass R. 2001. *Republic.com*. Princeton, NJ: Princeton University Press.

Sunstein, Cass R. 2007. *Republic.com. 2.0*. Princeton, NJ: Princeton University Press.

Tavani, Herman T. 2003. "Ethical Reflections on the Digital Divide." *Journal of Information, Communication, and Ethics in Society* 1, no. 2: 99–108.

Tavani, Herman T. 2012. "Search Engines and Ethics." In E. Zalta, ed. *Stanford Encyclopedia of Philosophy*. Available at http://plato.stanford.edu/entries/ethics-search/.

Theismeyer, Lynn. 1999. "Racism on the Web: Its Rhetoric and its Marketing." *Ethics and Information Technology* 1, no. 2: 117–25.

Ulen, Thomas S. 2001. "Democracy on the Line: A Review of *Republic.com* by Cass Sunstein." *Journal of Law, Technology and Policy* 2001, no. 2: 317–46.

Van den Hoven, Jeroen, and Emma Rooksby. 2008. "Distributive Justice and the Value of Information: A (Broadly) Rawlsian Approach." In J. van den Hoven and J. Weckert, eds. *Information Technology and Moral Philosophy*. Cambridge, UK: Cambridge University Press, pp. 376–96.

Weckert, John. 2005. "Preface." In J. Weckert, ed. *Electronic Monitoring in the Workplace: Controversies and Solutions*. Hershey, PA: Idea Group.

Wessells, Michael G. 1990. *Computer, Self, and Society*. Englewood Cliffs, NJ: Prentice Hall.

Woodbury, Marsha. 2002. *Computer and Information Ethics*. Champaign, IL: Stipes Publishing.

Wresch, William. 2009. "Progress on the Global Digital Divide," *Ethics and Information Technology* 11, no. 4: 255–63.

▶ FURTHER READINGS

Abbey, Ruth, and Sarah Hyde. "No Country for Older People: Age and the Digital Divide." *Journal of Information, Communication, and Ethics in Society* 7, no. 4 (2009): 225–42.

Dyson, Freeman. "Technology and Social Justice." In D. G. Johnson and J. M. Wetmore, eds. *Technology and Society: Building Our Sociotechnical Future*. Cambridge, MA: MIT Press. 2009, pp. 5–12.

Gumbus, Andra, and Frances S. Grodzinsky. "Gender Bias in Internet Employment: A Study of Career Advancement Opportunities for Women in the Field of ICT." *Journal of Information, Communication and Ethics in Society* 2, no. 3 (2004): 133–42.

Noam, Eli. "Why the Internet is Bad for Democracy." *Communications of the ACM* 48, no. 10 (2005): 57–58.

Turner, Eva, ed. *Women in Computing*. Special Issue of *Journal of Information, Communication and Ethics in Society* 3, no. 4 (2005).

Warschauer, Mark. *Technology and Social Inclusion: Rethinking the Digital Divide*. Cambridge, MA: MIT Press, 2003.

11

Online Communities, Cyber Identities, and Social Networks

In Chapter 11, we examine some challenges that cybertechnology poses for our understanding of concepts such as *community*, *personal identity*, and our *sense of self*. In analyzing these concepts, we focus mainly on three aspects of cybertechnology: social networking services (SNSs), virtual reality (VR), and artificial intelligence (AI). Specific questions include the following:

- Do online communities, including SNSs such as Facebook and Twitter, cause us to rethink our traditional concept of "community"?

- How have the kinds of interactions that occur in SNSs, and related online forums, affected our conventional notion of friendship?

- Do some kinds of behaviors that occur in VR environments, especially in massively multiplayer online role-playing games (MMORPGs), raise special ethical and social concerns?

- What implications do certain kinds of role playing in VR environments have for our understanding of personal identity?

- How have developments in AI affected our sense of self and our conception of what it means to be a human being?

- Do at least some AI entities warrant moral consideration?

▶ 11.1 ONLINE COMMUNITIES AND SOCIAL NETWORKING SERVICES

What, exactly, is a *community*? Do we need to redefine our traditional notion of community in light of social interactions made possible by cybertechnology in general, and SNSs in particular? Do online communities pose any special social and ethical challenges? We consider these and related questions in this section.

11.1.1 Online Communities vs. Traditional Communities

Many people, both young and old, interact in Web-based SNSs, such as Facebook, MySpace, and Foursquare, as well as in professional-oriented networking services such as

LinkedIn. Some also participate in one or more blogs (Web logs), while others send instantaneous "news feeds" to friends in the forms of "tweets" via a popular online service called Twitter. Many also communicate with one another through electronic messaging services that include video, such as Skype and (Apple's) FaceTime.

Assuming that you have an account on Facebook, do your "friends" on that SNS comprise a *community*? To answer this question, we first examine the meaning of "community" in the traditional sense of the term. *Webster's New World Dictionary of the American Language* defines a community as "people living in the same district, city, etc., under the same laws." Note that this traditional definition stresses the geographical aspects of community by associating it with concepts such as "district" and "city" that have typically constrained community life. So, for the most part, traditional communities are limited by geography.

Cybertechnology has made it possible to extend, or perhaps even ignore, the geographical boundaries of traditional community life. This, in turn, causes us to reexamine the concept of community; individuals physically separated by continents and oceans can now interact regularly in SNSs and other online forums to discuss topics that bind them together as a community. Not surprisingly then, more recent definitions of "community" focus on the common interests of groups rather than on geographical and physical criteria.

What, exactly, do we mean by *online community*? Howard Rheingold (2001) defines online communities as "computer-mediated social groups"; he describes his experience in joining the WELL (Whole Earth' Lectronic Link), an early electronic community, in 1985:

> The idea of a community accessible only via my computer screen sounded cold to me at first, but . . . [f]inding the WELL was like discovering a cozy little world that had been flourishing without me. . . . The WELL felt like an authentic community to me from the start, because it was grounded in my everyday physical world. WELLites who don't live within driving distance of the San Francisco Bay area are constrained in their ability to participate in the local networks of face-to-face acquaintances. . . . I've attended real-life WELL marriages, WELL births, and even a WELL funeral.[1]

Rheingold points out that because of the social contracts and collaborative negotiations that happened when members met online, the WELL became a *community* in that setting. He notes, for example, that in the WELL, norms were "established, challenged, changed, reestablished, rechallenged, in a kind of speeded up social evolution." When the members decided to get together occasionally at physical locations in the greater San Francisco Bay area, the WELL became a "hybrid community," spanning both physical and virtual space. But some "pure" online communities also continue to thrive along side the hybrid communities. As Michelle White (2002) notes, these electronic-only forums also seem like "real communities" because they offer their members "social exchange, emotional support, and learning environments."

Do users find as much enjoyment and satisfaction in participating in online communities as they do in traditional ones? Mitch Parsell (2008) cites a survey showing that 43% of members of online communities claimed to feel "as strong" about their online communities as their traditional or "real world" communities.[2] He also believes that this may be due to the enhanced nature of the Web—what some now refer to as "Web 2.0"—which is very different from the early Web, primarily because of the interactive aspects of the experiences it makes possible Analysts disagree on exactly which criteria differentiate Web 2.0 from the original Web, but most agree that the kinds of services made possible by SNSs and blogging sites have significantly altered the way users interact in online communities.[3] (Recall our description of some key differences between the early Web, or "Web 1.0," and Web 2.0 environments in Chapter 1.)

11.1.2 Blogs in the Context of Online Communities

A very popular mode of online communication for both young and older Internet users is a forum called the blog (or Web log). According to the (online) *Merriam Webster Dictionary*, a blog is "a Web site that contains an online personal journal with reflections, comments, and often hyperlinks provided by the writer." How do blogs facilitate interactions in, and function as, online communities? While some blogs function as online diaries, others provide commentary on a particular topic or news story. Based on their topics, blogs are often organized into categories such as personal blogs, political blogs, corporate blogs, health blogs, literary blogs, travel blogs, etc. Recall our discussion of the Washingtonienne scenario in Chapter 1, involving Jessica Cutler's blog; as a type of online personal dairy, her blog would fall under the category "personal blog."

Blogs can be maintained by either individuals or organizations. The community of blogs is often referred to as the "blogosphere." Online communities such as myBlogLog and Blog Catalog connect bloggers, whereas search engines such as Bloglines, Blog-Scope, and Technorati assist users in finding blogs. Blogging has become popular because it is an easy way to reach many people, but it has also generated some social and ethical controversies.[4] For example, we saw in our analysis of the Washingtonienne scenario (in Chapter 1) that a number of privacy-related concerns arose, which affected not only Jessica Cutler but also the six men implicated in her personal online diary. Other controversies arise in response to political blogs—for instance, some bloggers have been responsible for breaking news stories about political scandals and thus influencing public opinion. However, some of these bloggers also had political agendas to advance and were eager to spread negative stories about politicians whose views they opposed, and in some cases these stories have not been accurate. Controversies affecting political blogs are examined in detail in Chapter 10, in connection with our discussion of democracy and cybertechnology.

One question worth noting before we conclude this section is whether bloggers, especially those who write and maintain influential blogs, should be held to the same standards of accuracy, accountability, and liability as professional online journalists. Many bloggers claim that they are not journalists and thus should not be held to professional journalistic standards. Critics, however, argue that bloggers have certain "ethical obligations to their readers, the people they write about, and society in general" (A Bloggers' Code of Ethics, 2003). Unfortunately, an examination of this debate in the detail it deserves is beyond the scope of this chapter. Our analysis of blogs in this section has focused mainly on their role as online communities.

11.1.3 Assessing Pros and Cons of Online Communities

Have online communities had an overall positive effect on communication and interaction? Not surprisingly, arguments have been advanced on both sides of this question.

Those who see these communities in a favorable light could point to the fact that on SNSs such as Facebook, users can make new "friends" and meet prospective college roommates before setting foot on campus; they can also possibly find future romantic partners in online dating services such as eHarmony. Additionally, users can join and form online medical support groups, as well as various blogs designed to disseminate material to like-minded colleagues. Through these online services and forums, users can communicate with people they might not otherwise communicate with by physical mail or telephone. Gordon Graham (1999) believes that online communities also promote individual freedom because members can more easily disregard personal attributes, such as gender and ethnicity, which are more obvious in traditional communities.

However, online communities have also had some negative effects. In addition to threatening traditional community life, they have

A. facilitated social polarization (because of the very narrow focus of some groups),

B. minimized the kind of face-to-face communications (that have defined traditional friendships),

C. facilitated anonymity and deception (thereby enabling some forms of socially and morally objectionable behavior that would not be tolerated in traditional communities).

We briefly examine each of these points.

Online Communities and Social Polarization

We have noted some ways cybertechnology provides us with choices about which kinds of online communities we wish to join; this would seem to contribute positively to human interaction by enabling us to come together with like-minded individuals we otherwise might not meet. However, some online communities, especially those whose focus tends to be on topics and issues that are divisive and narrow, can also contribute to social polarization. Mitch Parsell (2008) argues that "extremely narrowly focused" online communities can be dangerous because they "can polarize attitudes and prejudices," which can lead to increased division and "social cleavage." He worries that the narrow focus of many online communities presents us with cause for concern. Parsell expresses this concern in the form of the following argument:

1. People tend to be attracted to others with like opinions.

2. Being exposed to like opinions tends to increase our own prejudices.

3. This polarizing of attitudes can occur on socially significant issues. . . .

4. Thus, where the possibility of narrowing focus on socially significant issues is available, increased community fracture is likely.[5]

So, even though online communities can empower individuals by providing them with greater freedom and choice in terms of their social interactions, they can also foster increased polarization in society. (Recall our discussion of some issues affecting political and social polarization in the context of democracy and cybertechnology in Chapter 10.)

Friendships in Online Communities

Does it matter that online communication has minimized the kinds of face-to-face interactions that define behavior in traditional communities? Is that necessarily a negative thing? On the one hand, being able to send an e-mail or a text message to someone, or to write on a Facebook user's Wall, is far more convenient than having to meet that person face to face in physical space to communicate with them. On the other hand, some worry that something is lost—possibly some critical interpersonal skills—in excessive online communications, at the expense of avoiding face-to-face interactions. A related, and very important, question that also arises has to do with the implications that online-only communication between individuals may have for our traditional understanding of friendship. In other words, is it possible for people who interact only in virtual (or purely online) contexts to be "real friends"?

To what extent, if any, is physical interaction between individuals necessary for true friendships to develop and flourish? At one time, the notion of "disembodied friends" might have seemed strange. But today, we hear about so-called "friends" who communicate regularly online but have never met in physical space. Dean Cocking and Steve Matthews (2000) argue that the kinds of close friendships we enjoy in physical space are not possible in pure virtual environments, i.e., in contexts that are solely computer mediated, because online-only friendship occurs in

> a context of communication dominated by *voluntary* self disclosure, enabling and disposing me to construct a highly chosen and controlled self-presentation and world of interaction. I altogether miss the kind of interaction between friends that seems a striking and commonplace feature of a close friendship.[6]

Cocking and Matthews' argument is complex and cannot be analyzed here in the detail that it deserves. But we will consider a few of their key points. The authors argue that it is not possible to realize close friendships in a "virtual world" because purely computer-mediated contexts (a) facilitate voluntary self-disclosure and (b) enable people to choose and construct a highly controlled "self-presentation" or identity. Because of these factors, essential elements of a person's character, as well as the "relational self ordinarily developed through those interactions in friendship" are distorted and lost. For example, they point out that in off-line contexts, we involuntarily disclose aspects of ourselves through indicators or "cues" in our interactions with others. And because interactions in these contexts are acts of "nonvoluntary self-disclosure," one has less control over the way one presents oneself to others. As a result, important aspects of our true personalities are involuntarily revealed, which makes close friendships possible in off-line contexts but not in virtual ones.

Is the argument advanced by Cocking and Matthews convincing? Adam Briggle (2008) disagrees with their conclusion, but he uses different kinds of criteria—one based on "distance" and one on "deliberateness"—to make the case for why friendships in purely virtual contexts can be initiated and can "flourish." First, he points out that communications among friends in off-line contexts, which are based largely on "oral exchanges," are not always candid or sincere; consequently, important "dynamics and indicators" that are required to form close friendships can be distorted. But Briggle believes that the *distance* involved in typical computer-mediated communications can give friends the courage to be more candid with one another than in typical face-to-face interactions.

Second, Briggle points out that online friends depend on written correspondences (as opposed to oral exchanges), and he believes that the *deliberateness* required in composing those kinds of correspondences can lead to "deeper bonds and greater depth in friendships." He also notes that oral communication in off-line contexts, on the contrary, is "often too shallow and hasty to promote deep bonds."[7] So, unlike Cocking and Matthews, Briggle concludes that it is possible to form close friendships in purely virtual contexts. He also concedes, however, that some purely virtual relationships can be "shallow relationships."

Deception in Online Communities

Some critics believe that online communities reveal a "darker side" of the Internet because people can, under the shield of anonymity, engage in behavior that would not be tolerated in most physical communities. For instance, individuals can use aliases and screen names when they interact in online forums, which makes it easier to deceive others about who actually is communicating with them. We briefly examine a scenario that is now a classic case for illustrating how online anonymity, pseudonymity, and deception can contribute to the darker side of online communities. The incident occurred in an online forum called a MOO (multiuser object-oriented environment) that was reported by Julian Dibbell in the 1990s.

▶ **SCENARIO 11–1:** A Virtual Rape in Cyberspace

LambdaMOO was an early electronic forum in which participants had screen names, or virtual identities, to represent the characters they portrayed; for example, characters whose screen names included Mr. Bungle, Legba, Starsinger, and Tom Traceback, interacted in this online forum. Mr. Bungle designed a program called "voodoo doll" that enabled him to control the actions of other characters in the online forum and then used it to take control of Legba and Starsinger to "perform" sexually offensive actions. Bungle's behavior was described by one of the victims as a "breach of civility," who complained to other members of the forum. Following an online meeting (that failed to resolve the controversy), Bungle's program was "frozen" and his user account was terminated by Tom Traceback (one of the master programmers of LambdaMOO).[8] ■

As you might imagine, the incident had a profound effect not only on the members of the Lambda community but also on many participants in other online forums who heard about it. Almost immediately, questions arose about how to deal with Bungle. For example, should the real person behind Bungle be exposed and be prohibited from joining other online forums? We examine the LambdaMOO case in more detail in Section 11.3, where we consider ethical aspects of virtual environments. We also discuss some effects that MOOs and MUDs (multiuser dimensions) have had for personal-identity issues in Section 11.3.

In Chapter 1, we briefly examined a more recent case of anonymity and deception in an online forum—namely a cyberbullying incident involving Megan Meier that took place on MySpace in 2006. There, we saw that Meier had been deceived by a "friend" named Josh Evans, who was very kind to Meier before Evans began to bully her. We also saw that Evans was not a teenage boy, but instead was Lori Drew, a 49-year-old mother of a former friend of Meier's. In the wake of Meier's suicide, Evans true identity (as Lori Drew) was discovered and she was prosecuted. In late 2008, Drew was found guilty of three misdemeanor counts of computer fraud; however, the jury was deadlocked on a fourth charge, involving conspiracy.[9]

Although the Meier incident could be examined from the vantage point of cyber-ullying, an offense that has affected numerous teenagers interacting in online communities, we consider it here from the perspective of deceptive behavior in online communities. How is the Meier case both similar to and different from the one involving LambdaMOO? Despite some significant differences, both incidents have one thing in common: they reveal a darker side of online communities that is made possible by anonymity and pseudonymity. One difference, however, is that no one was physically harmed in the LambdaMOO incident. But it could be argued that two Lambda members did experience some emotional or psychological harm, and in Section 11.2.2 we will see how emotional harm can occur to the real-life people whose characters are represented in virtual environments such as online communities.

A second difference is that LambdaMOO was a "pure" online, or online-only, community, where the virtual characters that participated had screen names and acted out various roles in the game-like or role-playing context of that virtual environment. Also, it was appropriate for members of LambdaMOO to use names other than their actual ones because of the rules defining that Lambda community. In the Meier case, however, Lori Drew's use of an alias was deceptive by virtue of the rules, or at least the expected norms, on MySpace for initiating a request to befriend another. There, the expectation was that an individual using that SNS to seek out new "friends" would disclose his or her actual name and not use a false (or pseudo) name to intentionally deceive someone. However, one might also argue that such a rule was not sufficiently explicit at the time, because neither MySpace nor most other SNSs had clear policies when it came to individuals using actual names in setting up an account. (Typically, all that was required then to register for an account on MySpace was a legitimate e-mail address.)

▶ 11.2 VIRTUAL ENVIRONMENTS AND VIRTUAL REALITY

We have examined some issues affecting online communities, which are also sometimes referred to as *virtual communities*. They are "virtual" in the sense that they exist in cyberspace, which is usually equated with *virtual space*. But what is virtual space? In contrast to physical space, or geographical space, virtual space can be viewed as one or more computer-generated environments that could not exist without computers and cybertechnology. These environments, in turn, include online or virtual communities, as well as virtual reality (VR) applications such as video games.

Although we now have a working definition of a virtual space or a virtual environment, we have yet to define "virtual." This term can be used in three senses. Sometimes it is contrasted with "real," as in distinguishing virtual objects from real ones. At other times the term is contrasted with "actual," as when a person says that she has "virtually finished" her project (i.e., she has not actually, or literally, finished it, but she believes that for practical purposes, she has finished it). The term "virtual" can also express feeling "as if" physically present in a situation, as when you are conversing with a friend online or on a phone; even though you could be literally thousands of miles away from each other, the sense that you are interacting in real time makes you feel as if you are both in the same room. (Contrast this experience with radio and traditional broadcast communications, where messages can be transmitted in only one direction at a time.) We should keep these three different senses of "virtual" in mind as we examine ethical aspects of virtual environments, including VR applications.

11.2.1 What is Virtual Reality (VR)?

Philip Brey (1999, 2008) defines virtual reality, or VR, as "a three dimensional interactive computer generated environment that incorporates a first person perspective." Notice three important features in Brey's definition of VR:

- interactivity,
- a three-dimensional environment,
- a first-person perspective.

How does this distinguish VR from other computer-mediated environments? First, *interactivity* requires that users be able to navigate and manipulate the represented environment. Because a *three-dimensional environment* is required in VR, neither text-based computer-generated environments nor two-dimensional graphic environments will qualify. Brey also points out that a *first-person perspective* requires a single locus from which the environment is perceived and interacted with; the first-person perspective also requires an immersion in the virtual world rather than simply an "experience" of that world as an "object that can be (partially) controlled by the outside."

We can distinguish between Brey's notion of virtual reality, including VR applications that are three-dimensional, and a more broadly defined notion of "virtual environment." Recall our earlier discussion of online communities in Section 11.1, which included some two-dimensional virtual environments. For example, LambdaMOO would be considered a two-dimensional virtual environment (that was also a text-based forum). So LambdaMOO would not qualify as a virtual reality environment, or VR application, as Brey defines it. As an online forum, however, it would qualify as a type of virtual environment.

Figure 11.1 illustrates some manifestations of virtual environments.

In Section 11.1.3, we noted that many actions that are considered morally objectionable in the physical world can be performed easily in online communities and forums. Virtual environments made possible in video games also enable users to engage in morally objectionable acts, including (virtual) prostitution, pornography, pedophilia, torture, mutilation, and murder. Brey argues that ethical concerns involving VR

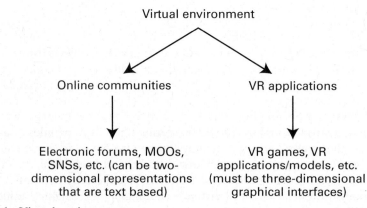

Figure 11.1 Virtual environments.

applications and virtual environments can be analyzed in terms of two broad categories: (A) *behavioral issues* affecting interactions between individuals and (B) *representational issues* affecting the design of these applications. We begin with an analysis of (A); issues affecting (B) are examined in Section 11.2.3.

11.2.2 Ethical Controversies Involving Behavior in VR Applications and Games

Are ethical issues involving behavior in VR applications, including online games, different from those associated with morally controversial acts displayed on television or played out in board games? Consider that television programs sometimes display violent acts and some board games allow participants to act out morally controversial roles—how are VR applications different? Brey (1999) points out that in VR applications, users are actively engaged, whereas television viewers are passive. VR users are not spectators; rather, they are more like actors, as are board game players, who also act out roles in certain board games. This common feature suggests that there might not be much difference between the two kinds of games; however, Brey notes that VR applications, unlike board games, simulate the world in a way that gives it a much greater appearance of reality. And in VR, the player has a first-person perspective of what it is like to perform certain acts and roles, including some that are criminal or immoral, or both. We first examine some ethical aspects of online video games involving multiple players.

A distinction is sometimes made between single-player video games and multiplayer online games; the latter are commonly referred to either as MMOGs (massively multiplayer online games) or MMORPGs. An example of a MMOG is *Second Life* (designed by Linden Lab), which includes members called "Residents" who do not engage in some of the traditional role-playing activities available in many MMORPGs. (Launched in 2003, Second Life had approximately 13 million registered user accounts as of March 2008.[10]) Examples of MMORPGs include popular online games such as *World of Warcraft* (*WOW*), *EVE Online*, and *Entropia Universe*. WOW is perhaps the most popular MMORPG, boasting over 11 million paying subscribers as of 2009.[11]

Many MMORPGs are organized around various "clans" or "guilds" that members join; if they wish, members can also pool their resources (Cook 2006). Typically, these games are also developed around systems that are either "class-based" or "skill points-based." In the former scheme, a player's chosen division can determine his or her character's "strengths and weaknesses." So, players are encouraged to "interact with others and form teams to balance out strengths and weaknesses."[12] In Second Life, for example, "Residents" can socialize, participate in group activities, and create trade items (virtual property) and services with one another. The virtual currency used in that MMOG is the Linden Dollar (linden, or L$), which can also be traded for real currencies via a "resident-to-resident marketplace" that is facilitated by Linden Lab. Residents in Second Life, as well as players in other MMOGs and MMORPGs, often select an avatar (a graphical representation) to represent themselves.

Violent and Sexually Offensive Acts in MMORPGs and MMOGs

Why are MMORPGs and MMOGs controversial from an ethical perspective? In other words, which kinds of morally objectionable behavior do they make possible? Some critics claim that Second Life facilitates child pornography because virtual characters who are adults in real life (RL) can have sex with virtual characters who are children in that MMOG (Singer 2007). Cases of virtual prostitution on Second Life have also been reported—i.e., where some Residents were "paid to (use their avatar to) perform sex acts or to serve as escorts" (Brey 2008). So, if these reports are correct, there are clearly some forms of sexually offensive acts that take place in MMOGs and MMORPGs, which would not be tolerated outside these gaming environments.

In addition to concerns about sexually offensive behavior in online games, many worry about the kinds of violent acts that are also carried out in these environments. Monique Wonderly (2008) suggests that some forms of violence permitted in online games may be "more morally problematic" than pornography and other kinds of sexually offensive behavior in virtual environments. She points out, for example, that relatively few video games "permit sexual interaction between characters," and even fewer allow "deviant sexual conduct." But she notes that many popular games permit and that some "even *require* copious amounts of wanton graphic violence."[13]

Are violent acts in MMORPGs, including virtual murder, more morally problematic than the pornographic and sexually deviant acts that also have been carried out in these games? Or should violent acts such as virtual murder be tolerated as acceptable behavior? Morgan Luck (2009) notes that while most people agree that murder is wrong, they do not seem to be bothered by virtual murder in MMORPGs. He points out, for example, that some might see the virtual murder of a character in a video game as no different from the "taking of a pawn in a chess game." But Luck also notes that people have different intuitions about acts in virtual environments that involve morally objectionable sexual behavior, such as child pornography and pedophilia. And he worries that the kind of reasoning used to defend virtual murder in games could, unwittingly, be extended to defend virtual pedophilia. For example, he notes that the following line of reasoning, which for our purposes can be expressed in standard argument form, may unintentionally succeed in doing this.

1. Allowing acts of virtual murder will not likely increase the number of actual murders.

2. Allowing acts of virtual pedophilia may significantly increase the amount of actual pedophilia.

3. Therefore, virtual pedophilia is immoral, but virtual murder is not.[14]

While this kind of argument may appeal to some, Luck points out that it is difficult to defend because of the lack of empirical evidence needed to confirm both (1) and (2). More importantly, however, if (2) could be shown to be false, then virtual pedophilia, like virtual murder, would not be immoral (according to the reasoning used in this argument).

With respect to (2), Neil Levy (2002) has suggested that allowing virtual child pornography may even "reduce the harm to actual children" because it would provide an "acceptable outlet" for pedophiles and would encourage pornographers to seek an "alternative to real children." (But Levy does not believe that virtual child pornography should be acceptable; in fact, he opposes it for alternative reasons.)

A different kind of rationale for why virtual child pornography should be prohibited has been offered by Per Sandin (2004), who argues that it can cause significant harm to many people who find it revolting or offensive. But Brey (2008) points out that a problem with Sandin's argument is that it "gives too much weight to harm caused by offense." As Brey puts it, "If actions should be outlawed whenever they offend a large group of people, then individual rights would be drastically curtailed, and many things, ranging from homosexual behavior to interracial marriage, would still be illegal."[15] Hence, none of the arguments considered so far can show why acts that are morally objectionable in physical space either should or should not be allowed in virtual environments.

Assessing the Nature of "Harm" in Virtual Environments

Can a plausible argument be constructed to show why it is wrong to perform acts in virtual environments that would be considered immoral in real life? We have seen some difficulties with arguments that tried to show that allowing morally objectionable actions in virtual environments will likely lead to an increase (or decrease) in those actions in the real world. Other arguments have tried to link, or in some cases delink, the kind of harm caused in virtual environments with the sense of harm one might experience in the real world. For example, some arguments have tried to show that sexually offensive acts in virtual environments can cause harm to vulnerable groups (such as children and women) in the real world.[16] However, the individual premises used to support the conclusions to these arguments typically lack sufficient empirical evidence to establish the various claims being made. On the contrary, some arguments claim that no one is physically harmed in virtual murder or, for that matter, in any act performed only in a virtual environment. But these arguments have also been criticized for lacking sufficient evidence to establish their conclusions.

Should we assume that any harm that one experiences in the virtual realm is not "real harm" but only *virtual harm*? In our discussion of logical fallacies in Chapter 3, we saw that using this line of reasoning commits the *virtuality fallacy*. You may wish to revisit that fallacy at this point.

We saw that "virtual" is ambiguous (in at least three ways), and we noted that sometimes virtual is contrasted with real in a way that might suggest that a "virtual harm" is equivalent to an "unreal harm." Because a harm caused in a virtual world might not result in physical harm to a "flesh-and-blood" person, however, it doesn't follow that the harm caused is not real. The LambdaMOO incident (described in Section 11.1.3), which involved a "virtual rape," can help us to see why harm caused in virtual environments is not itself limited to virtual characters in a virtual environment. We begin by asking why (the character) Bungle's behavior in LambdaMOO is morally objectionable. After all, it was not a "real rape," and it did not result in physical harm to any "flesh-and-blood" individuals. Brey (1999) believes that we can use two different kinds of arguments to show why it is wrong to engage in immoral acts in virtual environments:

a. The argument "from moral development."

b. The argument from "psychological harm."

To illustrate the argument from *moral development*, Brey suggests that we can extend an argument advanced by Immanuel Kant for the treatment of animals to the treatment of virtual characters. Kant argued that even if we have no direct moral obligation to treat animals kindly, we should, because our treating animals kindly can influence our development of moral attitudes and behaviors for treating human beings. Similarly, then, the way we treat virtual characters may ultimately affect the way we treat real-life characters—raping virtual characters in virtual space, or even viewing such a rape, could desensitize us to the act of rape itself as it affects flesh-and-blood individuals in physical space.

The argument from *psychological harm* suggests that the way we refer to characters that represent a particular group can cause harm to actual members of the group. Consider a cartoon depicting a woman being raped: Actual (flesh-and-blood) women may suffer psychological harm from seeing, or possibly even knowing about, this cartoon image, even though none of them, as flesh-and-blood individuals, is being raped, either physically or as represented by the cartoon. Extending this analogy to virtual space, it would follow that the "rape" of a virtual woman in a virtual environment, such as a MOO, MMOG, MMORPG, etc., can also cause psychological harm to flesh-and-blood women.

Virtual Economies and "Gold Farming"

So far, we have examined behavioral issues in virtual environments from the perspectives of violence and sexually offensive acts, as well as from the vantage point of the kind of harm that can result. But other behavior-related controversies involve some of the "virtual economies" that have arisen because of activities made possible in online games. We noted earlier that some MMORPGs and MMOGs have their own monetary currencies. For example, Second Life uses the Linden Dollar (linden, or L$), which its Residents can both use in in-game transactions and exchange outside the game for real currencies such as the U.S. dollar or the euro. As a result, virtual economies have emerged. Brey (2008) believes that their emergence can also increase the likelihood that moral controversies will arise in these environments—as Brey notes, people will be "more likely to act immorally if money is to be made or if valuable property is to be had."

Virtual property, as in the case of virtual money, can be acquired and exchanged with players in games. It can also be sold and exchanged outside the game to interested parties (in the physical world). In some cases, the virtual property has become so desirable that it has led to violent acts in the real world. Dorothy Warner and Mike Raiter (2005) describe an incident in China where a person who had stolen someone's virtual sword in a MMOG was murdered in real life by the "sword's" owner. So virtual economies can have real-life implications and can result in physical harm to individuals in the real world. One controversial activity associated with virtual economies in gaming environments is a form of labor and economic exchange called "gold farming."

Kai Kimppa and Andrew Bisset (2008) define gold farming as "playing an online computer game for the purpose of gaining items of value within the internal economy of the game and selling these to other players for real money."[17] These items can include "desirable items" as well as in-game money (where the rules defining the game's internal economy permit this); they can also include "highly developed" game characters. All of these items can also be sold via online auctions or designated Web sites. Kimppa and Bisset point out that the 2009 "in-game gold market" globally was estimated at 7 billion dollars; they also note that the practice of gold farming is most popular in countries such as China and Mexico that have both low-average income levels and "relatively good access to the Internet."[18]

Gold farming has also raised concerns about working conditions in the real world. For example, Warner and Raiter describe a situation in rural China where people who participate in World of Warcraft were paid to work 12-hour shifts of gold farming; the workers would acquire "virtual gold" within the game and then sell it outside the game to interested players. The business became profitable, Warner and Reiter point out, because many players who can afford to purchase the virtual gold preferred to buy it rather than to do the work necessary to earn it in the game.[19] It was also more advantageous to the "gold farmers" themselves, who could earn more money obtaining and selling virtual gold than they could in traditional agricultural work. But this practice has also led to reported cases of Chinese sweatshop laborers who work "day and night in conditions of practical slavery" to acquire the virtual gold and virtual resources (Brey 2008). If these reports are true, gold mining would seem to raise some serious ethical concerns. Brey believes that "many new ethical issues in virtual worlds" will likely arise because of the kind and the amount of "time, money, and social capital" people are willing to invest in virtual property and virtual economies.[20]

11.2.3 Misrepresentation, Bias, and Indecent Representations in VR Applications

So far, we have examined some *behavioral*, or what Brey (1999) also refers to as "interactive," controversies regarding ethical dimensions of VR applications. The other ethical aspect that needs to be considered, in Brey's VR model, has to do with the ways in which virtual characters and virtual objects are *represented* in these applications. Note that this set of ethical concerns includes not only virtual characters in games but also features of VR applications used to simulate and model objects in the physical world.

Brey (2008) argues that representations can become morally problematic when they are

1. *misrepresentations* (that can cause harm by failing to uphold *standards of accuracy*),
2. *biased representations* (that fail to uphold *standards of fairness*),
3. *indecent representations* (that violate *standards of decency and public morality*).

*Mis*representation ranges from cases in which there is no correspondence between the virtual entity and its corresponding physical (or nonvirtual) entity to cases in which the correspondence is almost, but not fully, accurate. To illustrate this point, Brey uses examples of VR applications that have been developed to simulate visual features of buildings such as the Louvre or Taj Mahal, or to simulate the behavior of certain kinds of automobiles or airplanes. When a VR application does not accurately portray all of the characteristics or features of the physical (or nonvirtual) entities represented—whether by intention or as a result of an oversight—the application *mis*represents reality.

Misrepresenting entities with respect to descriptive features, however, can be distinguished from (otherwise accurate) representations that favor certain values or interests over others. Brey calls the latter *biased* representation; it can result from the choice of model. For example, "softbots" (or "bots") in the form of *avatars* on computer screens, which often display human-like features and qualities, could be used in a VR application to represent members of a racial or minority group; even though the representation may be structurally accurate, if the avatar is used in a way that suggests a racial stereotype, it can fail to accurately portray a member of the racial group. Paul Ford (2001) describes a scenario where an avatar represents an African American "shoe-shine boy" in a video game. Although the bot does not misrepresent any physical characteristics of the particular African American represented, the depiction is a biased caricature of African Americans.

Brey describes *indecent* representations as representations that (a) are considered "shocking or offensive," (b) breach "established rules of good behavior or morality," or

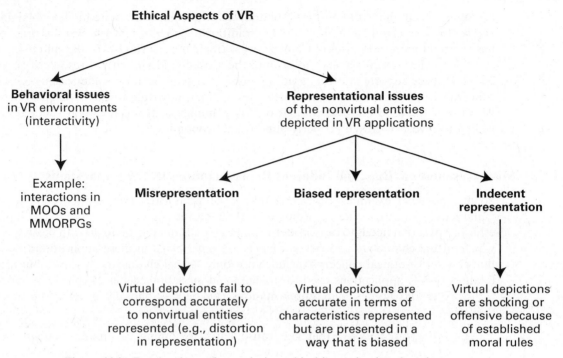

Figure 11.2 Brey's scheme for analyzing ethical issues in virtual environments.

(c) are somehow "shocking to the senses or moral sensibilities." He also notes, however, that getting agreement on this category is difficult because standards of decency can vary widely across different individuals and cultures and thus may seem relativistic—i.e., "what is shocking or immoral to some will not be so to others."[21] For example, he points out that while some will find depictions of nudity or physical violence acceptable, others will deem such depictions to be unacceptable. So, there will often be disagreements about which representations qualify as indecent.

However, Brey also points out that the context in which a representation take place can also be a factor in determining whether it is considered decent. He uses the example of a representation of open heart surgery to illustrate this point, noting that a representation of this procedure in the context of a medical simulator may not be offensive to someone considering whether to undergo the surgery. However, it could be deemed offensive in other contexts, such as using the representation as a background in a music video.

Brey believes that VR model builders are morally obligated to avoid misrepresentation, biased representation, and indecent representation in designing VR applications. Extending an analytical scheme developed by Richard Mason (1994), Brey (1999) argues that developers of VR systems need to both recognize who the stakeholders are in those systems and take into account their values and interests as they develop VR models. He suggests that Mason's scheme works well for understanding and analyzing moral responsibility issues involved in developing VR systems that misrepresent or bias stakeholders.

While Brey (2008) provides three useful distinctions in helping us to sort out representational issues affecting VR applications, he also suggests that identifying and evaluating the locus of moral responsibility for the harm caused by them may be more difficult to pinpoint. It would seem that the developers of VR systems, who design applications that incorporate inaccurate, biased, or indecent representations, should bear at least some of the moral responsibility for any harm caused by their applications. But it would also seem that users of VR applications who abuse or misuse representations in ways that are indecent or biased in virtual environments should also be held morally responsible for harm that results.

Figure 11.2 summarizes Brey's scheme.

Our analysis of controversial aspects of virtual environments so far has focused mainly on their social impact and how they can affect community life. We next examine the implications of virtual environments in particular, and cybertechnology in general, for personal identity and our sense of self.

▶ 11.3 CYBER IDENTITIES AND CYBER SELVES: PERSONAL IDENTITY AND OUR SENSE OF SELF IN THE CYBER ERA

Social scientists have described various ways that the use of cybertechnology can impact personal identity. One (now classic) incident, in the 1980s, that quickly caught their attention involved a male psychologist who joined an online forum for disabled persons, where he identified himself as a woman who had become crippled as a result of an automobile accident. Under this alias, "she" soon engaged in romantic exchanges with a few of the forum's members. When "her" true identity was later discovered, however, many of the participants in this electronic forum were outraged. Some felt manipulated by the psychologist's use of a fraudulent identity, and others complained that they were victims of "gender fraud." Lindsy Van Gelder (1991) describes this incident as "the strange case of the electronic lover."

In one sense, the "electronic lover" incident could be examined under the category of online communities (discussed in Section 11.1) because of the broader impact that the psychologist's behavior had on the online forum and its members. Yet we can also reflect on the implications this case has for personal identity; for example, was the male psychologist simply acting out his "would-be personality" in cyberspace instead of in physical space, as some might suggest? Or, does cyberspace make a difference for understanding the kinds of (personal) identities that can emerge in different online forums?

Mitch Parsell (2008) describes the Internet as a "powerful new force" for what he calls "the manufacture of identity." He believes that this technological medium

. . . offers an unparalleled ability to create ourselves in our own image. It gives users an unprecedented capacity to determine their initial presentations to others.. . . . In short, it enables users to be masters of their identity.[22]

Are Parsell's remarks exaggerated, or possibly a bit overstated? Or has cybertechnology indeed provided us with a new medium for constructing, or "manufacturing," personal identities through the selective presentations of ourselves? This question has captured the interests of some prominent psychologists and social scientists, whose research we briefly examine in the following sections.

11.3.1   Cybertechnology as a "Medium of Self-Expression"

Sherry Turkle (2005) notes that by the mid-1980s, computers had become an "evocative object"—i.e., an object that "provoked self-reflection." In the first edition of her (now) classic book *The Second Self: Computers and the Human Spirit* (1984), Turkle suggested that a computer could be viewed as a model for analyzing and constructing one's identity. She also noted that the computer has become a medium through which people could discover their personal identity; for example, computers provide a context in which individuals can try out different cognitive styles and different methods of problem solving to ultimately discover which style or method they prefer. Because people develop their own unique style of computing, Turkle argues that the computational environment becomes an extension of themselves, in much the same way that their manner of dress is an extension of their personality. So, in her view, a computer can function as a "medium for self-expression" as well as for "self-discovery."

Turkle's early studies focused mainly on the role that stand-alone, or non-networked, computers played in the relationship between personal identity and computers. Her subsequent research in this area has centered on interactions involving networked computers; in particular, her studies examine how behavior in networked environments significantly impacts our relationships with our "selves" as we conceive them. To illustrate several of her key points, Turkle (1995, 2011) uses examples involving MUDs (multiuser dimensions). MUDs are similar to MOOs (defined in Section 11.1.3) in that they are simulated or virtual environments in which members participate.

Users participating in MUDs tend to do so anonymously; in this sense, they are known only by the names of their MUD character or characters. This feature also allows MUD members/participants to construct new identities; for example, Turkle notes that as people participate, or "play characters," in MUDs, they can also "construct new selves" through social interaction. As Turkle also notes, however, "MUD selves" are both constituted by and dependent upon interaction with machines; if the machine is taken away, "the Mud selves cease to exist."[23]

11.3.2   "MUD Selves" and Distributed Personal Identities

In MUDs, users can *be* (i.e., can represent themselves textually or graphically as) characters that are very different from their actual selves; Turkle notes, for example, that the obese can be slender, and the old can be young. She also points out that MUD users can express multiple, and often unexplored, aspects of the self, and that they can "play with their identity" by trying out new roles. In different MUDs, the same physical person can represent oneself as a seductive woman, a macho man, or even a creature of unspecified gender; so one's identity in MUDs can be, Turkle suggests, the sum of one's "distributed presence."[24]

Acts in which individuals assume different identities or different gender roles are hardly unique to the world of MUDs and virtual environments; for example, a male transgendered person in physical space can selectively represent himself as a member of the opposite sex in contexts of his choosing. Perhaps you are familiar with the movie and, later, Broadway musical *Victor, Victoria* in which a woman pretends to be a man playing the part of a woman. But gender role reversals in the physical world do not seem to have the same significant social impact as they do in cyberspace. Turkle notes that since traditional theater and role-playing games take place in physical space, they enable one to "step in and out of character." MUDs, on the contrary, offer parallel identities and parallel lives, and this parallelism encourages treating off-screen and on-screen lives as equally real.

Turkle notes that some of her research subjects in MUDs experience their world through interactions in "multiple windows"; real life (or "RL") is considered by some MUD participants as simply "one more window." One of Turkle's research subjects, whom she refers to as Doug, remarked that RL is not typically his "best window." Turkle points out that in MUDs, we can "project ourselves into our own dramas in which we are producer, director, and star"; in this sense, she believes that MUDs provide a "new location for acting out our fantasies."[25]

11.3.3 The Impact of Cybertechnology on Our Sense of Self

We have examined some effects that one's interactions in virtual or computer-mediated environments, including MOOs and MUDs, can have for one's personal identity. In this section, we focus on the impact that cybertechnology has for our *sense of self* (as humans) vis-à-vis two factors:

a. our relation to *nature*,

b. our relation to (and sense of place in) the *universe*.

With regard to (a), social scientists often describe this relation in terms of three major epochs in human civilization: the agricultural age, the industrial age, and the information age. Each has been characterized by revolutionary technological breakthroughs in gaining control over nature. At the dawn of the agricultural age, people who had previously led nomadic lives developed technology that enabled them to control the production of crops by controlling elements of nature rather than conforming to nature's seasonal rotations, which often required migrating to different locations. In the industrial age, humans harnessed steam power. With steam power, people were no longer compelled to set up communities close to large bodies of water that provided much of their energy. We recently entered a phase (i.e., the third great epoch) that social scientists call "the information age," which, as we will see, has also significantly influenced the way we now conceive of ourselves in relation to nature.

Regarding (b), we note that while cybertechnology may be the latest technology to significantly influence the way that human beings see themselves in relation to the universe, it is not the first technology to do this. For example, Mary B. Williams describes three historical "milestones" in which scientific discoveries, made possible in large part by technological innovations and breakthroughs, have profoundly impacted the way that humans came to see themselves:

> The first such milestone, a great (and greatly humbling) challenge to our sense of human beings as uniquely important, occurred when the Copernican revolution established that Earth, the human home, was not at the center of the universe. The second milestone was Charles Darwin's conclusion that emergence of Homo sapiens was . . . the result of evolution from lower species by the process of natural selection. The third milestone resulted from the work of Karl Marx and Sigmund Freud, which showed intellectual, social, and individual creativity to be the result of nonrational (unconscious) libidinal or economic forces—not, as has been believed, the products of the almost god-like powers of the human mind.[26]

Williams notes that in the aftermath of these milestones, we have a much humbler view of our place in the universe than our ancestors did.

How, exactly, has cybertechnology also has influenced the way that we see ourselves in relation to both (a) and (b)—i.e., how has this relatively recent technology already begun to *define* us as human beings? J. David Bolter (1984) believes that, historically, people in Western cultures have seen themselves through the prism of a *defining technology*, which "develops links, metaphorical or otherwise, with a culture's science, philosophy, or literature."[27] Philosophers and humanists have used metaphors associated with a particular "defining technology" to describe both human beings and the universe they inhabit in a given age or time period. Bolter identifies three eras in Western culture where a defining technology has played a key role: the ancient Greek world, the Renaissance, and the contemporary computer age. Our interest, of course, is with the third era.

In the second half of the twentieth century—i.e., the beginning of an era that we described above as the "information age"—we became fascinated with computer technology. Even though other technologies such as electricity, indoor plumbing, automobiles, etc., were arguably more important for day-to-day living than computers, Bolter notes that many philosophers and scientists soon began to use computer and computing metaphors to describe humans and their relationship to nature and the universe. One of the first thinkers to recognize and articulate some interesting connections between the computer and the human mind (as a manipulator of logical symbols) was twentieth-century computer science pioneer Alan Turing.[28] (We examine some of Turing's contributions to the field of AI in Section 11.4.2.) Acknowledging Turing's insight, Bolter uses the phrase "Turing's man" to depict those who view humans via the defining metaphor of computer technology. Turing's man sees nature as *information*, and humans (or, more specifically, human brains) as *information processing engines*. (Bolter contrasts "Turing's man" with "Plato's man" and "Descartes' man," which describe the representatives of two previous eras in which "defining technologies"—though very different in kind—were also highly influential.)

To support Bolter's thesis that we have come to see ourselves more and more in computer-like ways, we have only to reflect for a moment on some of the expressions that we now use to describe ourselves. For example, Bolter points out that when psychologists speak of "input and output states of the brain," or of the brain's hardware and software, they exemplify Turing's men. And when cognitive psychologists study the "mind's algorithm for searching long-term memory," or when linguists treat human language as if it were a programming code, they, too, are "Turing's men." Psychologists and cognitive scientists who suggest that the human mind is like a computer in that it "encodes, stores, retrieves, and processes information" are also, in Bolter's view, Turing's men.

In describing some other current uses of language that would also seem to support Bolter's insight that we have come to see ourselves in terms of computer metaphors, Turkle (2005) points out that one of her students had recast the idea of Freudian slips as "information processing errors." Turkle also notes that by the mid-1980s, people in their everyday conversations began to describe human mental activity in "computational terms"—for example, when uttering expressions such as "Excuse me, I need to clear my buffer" and "I won't be happy until I debug this problem." And more recently, the host/commentator for the PBS TV series *Mystery* described Sherlock Holmes' mind as having "more apps than an iPhone." These uses of language would seem to confirm Bolter's point that we have come to see ourselves in terms of computer-like metaphors.

Not only do we think of ourselves in computer-like terms but we also describe many objects and events in our environment in the language of computer technology. Bolter asks us to consider the economist who describes his work in terms of drawing up "input–output diagrams of the nation's business." We might also consider the biologist who describes evolution in terms of an algorithm comprising DNA code. Additionally, we consider the manager chairing a business meeting who requests that a specific topic on the agenda be discussed "off-line" instead. Finally, what should make of the cartoonist whose illustration of an expectant mother includes a caption in which she complains about having to wait 9 months to "download her baby"? You can probably think of some other ways that we also invoke computer-like metaphors to describe our world.

▶ 11.4 AI AND ITS IMPLICATIONS FOR WHAT IT MEANS TO BE HUMAN

In the preceding section, we examined the impact that cybertechnology has had so far for our sense of self (and, more broadly, for our sense of place in the universe). We next consider how this technology impacts a related question: What does it mean to be human, if (sophisticated) computers can exhibit behavior that requires intelligence in human beings? First, however, we note that the traditional assumption that only humans have intelligence has been challenged on two distinct fronts. On the one hand, research in animal behavior suggests that many primates, dolphins, and whales exhibit skills that suggest some level of intelligence (while, on the contrary, some humans either cannot or are no longer able to exhibit these skills). On the other hand, and more importantly for our purposes, developments in the field of AI suggest that some highly sophisticated computers can exhibit forms of intelligence and rational-decision-making, which were previously thought to be possible only in humans. In fact, developments in AI have caused some philosophers and cognitive scientists to question our conventional understanding of notions such as rationality, intelligence, knowledge, and learning. These questions, in turn, have led some to ask what it means to be human in an era that includes AI entities. It is from the vantage point of this question that we examine AI in this section. We begin, however, with a very brief description and overview of the field.

11.4.1 What is AI? A Brief Overview

John Sullins (2005) defines AI as "the science and technology that seeks to create intelligent computational systems." Sullins notes that AI researchers have aimed at building computer systems that can duplicate, or at least simulate, the kind of intelligent behavior found in humans. The official birth of AI as an academic field is often traced to a conference at Dartmouth College in 1956, which was organized by AI pioneers John McCarthy and Marvin Minsky. Since then, the field has advanced considerably and has also spawned several subfields.

In the 1950s and early 1960s, many AI researchers focused on developing software programs that could play checkers and chess with humans, pass calculus exams designed for undergraduate students, and solve problems that require a high level of human intelligence. The first AI programs were "problem solvers" comprising software code, but included little or no hardware; many researchers during this period assumed that just as artificial flight had been successfully developed in ways that bypassed the need to emulate nature's way of flying, so too could artificial intelligence be achieved without having to copy nature's way of thinking (i.e., via a physical brain). We now refer to the method of AI research conducted in that era, which focused on constructing a kind of "disembodied intelligence," as "classical AI," "symbolic AI," or "good old fashioned AI" (GOFAI).

The classical AI approach was eventually criticized by researchers in the field who argued that human intelligence cannot be reduced merely to symbolic manipulation (captured in software programs) and that something additional was needed. For example, one school argued that an artificial brain with neural networking (that could "perceive" and "learn" its environment)—was also required for a machine to learn and understand the world and thus potentially duplicate the way that humans think. Whereas the latter scheme in AI is often described as a "bottom-up" (or inductive) approach to machine learning, the classical/symbolic AI model is typically viewed as a "top-down" (or deductive) approach.

Another division in the field arose when a group of AI researchers argued that it was not critical to build machines that were as intelligent as humans (or that thought in the same way humans did); rather, they believed that a legitimate goal for AI research would be to develop systems that were "expert" in performing specific tasks that required a high level of intelligence in humans. For example, a system such as an "expert doctor" could be highly competent in diagnosing medical diseases, although it would be unable to perform any tasks outside that very narrow domain. (Recall our brief discussion of expert systems in Chapter 10, in connection with cybertechology and work.) However, many other AI researchers believed that it was still possible to achieve the original goal of emulating, (general) human intelligence in machines. Some of these researchers, including those working on the CYC project, use an approach that builds on classical/symbolic AI by designing software programs that manipulate large databases of factual information. Others, such as "Connectionists," have designed neural networks that aim at modeling the human brain, with its vast number of neurons and arrays of neural pathways, which exhibit varying degrees of "connection strengths." And some AI researchers focus on building full-fledged robots that can include artificial emotions as well.[29]

One concern that arose early in AI research, which was more sociological than technological in nature, had to do with how we might react to a world where machines would be as intelligent, or possibly even more intelligent, than humans. John Weckert (2004) articulates this concern when he asks

> Can we, and do we want to, live with artificial *intelligences*? We can happily live with fish that swim better than we do, with dogs that hear better, hawks that see and fly better, and so on, but things that can reason better seem to be in a different and altogether more worrying category . . . What would such [developments mean for] our view of what it is to be human?[30]

Of course, we can ask whether it is possible, even in principal, to build "machines" (i.e., software programs or artificial entities) that are "genuinely intelligent" and whose intelligence could rival and possibly exceed that of humans. Some critics argue that, at best, AI researchers would be able to build machines that merely simulate rather than replicate human intelligence. A spirited debate about this issue has ensued to this day, and each side has presented a series of arguments and "thought experiments" to defend its position.

11.4.2 The Turing Test and John Searle's "Chinese Room" Argument

In 1950, Alan Turing confidently predicted that by the year 2000 a computing machine would be able to pass a test, which has come to be called "The Turing Test," demonstrating machine intelligence. Turing envisioned a scenario in which a person engaged in a conversation with a computer (located in a room that was not visible to the human) was unable to tell—via a series of exchanges on a computer screen—whether he or she was conversing with another human or with a machine. He believed that if the computer was able to answer questions and communicate with the person at the other end in a way that the person there could not be sure whether this entity was a human or a computer, then we would have to attribute some degree of human-like intelligence to the computer.

While most AI researchers would concede that Turing's prophecy has not yet been fully realized, they also point to the significant progress and achievements that have been made in the field so far. For example, in 1997 an IBM computer program called *Deep Blue* defeated Gary Kasparov, then reigning champion, in the competition for the world chess title. And in 2011, another IBM computer program, called *Watson*, defeated two human opponents in the TV game show *Jeopardy* in a championship match. (This human-computer competition was viewed by millions of people around the world.)

Watson, like Deep Blue, is a disembodied AI, i.e., a highly sophisticated set of computer programs. Unlike Deep Blue, which could be viewed as an "expert system" that is highly skilled at playing chess (but not necessarily competent in other areas), Watson was capable of answering a wide range of questions posed in natural language. Some believe that Watson's skills at least simulate human intelligence in the broad or general sense. But did Watson, in defeating its human challengers, also exhibit the skills necessary to pass the Turing test? And even if Watson could pass the Turing test, would that necessarily show that Watson possessed (human-like) intelligence.

Some might argue that Watson was merely acting in a manner similar to the individual in John Searle's classic "Chinese room" scenario. In that scenario, a human who is a native English speaker but who understands nothing about the Chinese language is able to perform tasks that require manipulating Chinese symbols to produce answers to questions posed in Chinese. This person, who is not seen by anyone outside the room, receives questions from someone who passes them to him through an opening or slot. The person then consults a series of instructions and rules located in the room—all of which are written in English—that enable him to substitute the incoming Chinese symbols for other Chinese symbols in such a way as to produce correct answers to the questions asked. Once he has completed the task, he passes the answers back through the slot to a person waiting outside the room. That person might assume that the human who returned the correct answers understood Chinese. However, Searle (1980) argues that it is possible that the person understood nothing about the semantic meaning of the questions he received and the answers he returned; instead, this person had merely followed a set of syntactic rules (written in English) for manipulating symbols that happened to be in Chinese. In fact, the English-speaking person may not even know that the symbols involved are elements of the Chinese language.

Was Watson's behavior in the Jeopardy game analogous to that of the human in Searle's Chinese room—in other words, did Watson actually "understand" the meaning of the symbols (in the questions and answers) involved, or did Watson simply use a series of syntactic rules and cross-checking algorithms to manipulate the information stored in Watson's vast database to get the correct answers? It is not clear to what extent, if any, Watson could be said to have any understanding of natural language? So, even if Watson is capable of passing the Turing test (as originally posed), it would not necessarily follow, using Searle's argument, that Watson possesses human-like intelligence. In fact, some skeptics might argue that Watson is nothing more than a kind of (very broad) expert system, or perhaps some combination of expert systems, that behaves like an advanced version of (Apple's) SIRI. Although SIRI is capable of responding to many questions with correct answers, it is doubtful that people would be willing to describe SIRI as possessing human-like intelligence. In the same way, then, we could argue that we need not ascribe genuine intelligence to Watson. Nevertheless, we can still see why many humans would feel a bit uneasy by the fact that a computer, or AI entity, had defeated two highly intelligent human beings in a championship match, even if it was only in a game show contest.

Unfortunately, an extended discussion of key questions involving both Watson and the Turing test, as well as an in-depth discussion of the history of AI itself, are beyond the scope of this chapter. AI's history, though relatively brief, is fascinating, and several excellent resources are available; so, fortunately, there is no need to replicate that discussion here.[31] We limit our further analysis of AI and AI-related ethical issues to two broad questions: (1) What is the nature of the human-machine relationship (in the development of cyborgs and other AI entities)? (2) Do at least some (i.e., highly sophisticated) AI entities warrant moral consideration?

11.4.3 Cyborgs and Human-Machine Relationships

So far, we have considered whether machines could, in principle at least, possess human-like intelligence. We have also considered how our answer to this question can affect our sense of what it means to be human. Next, we see how the development of cyborgs and the concerns it raises about human-machine relationships may also have a similar effect on us. We approach these concerns from the perspective of two distinct, but related, questions: (a) Are humans becoming more computer-like? (b) Are computers becoming more human-like? We begin with (a).

Cyborgs and (AI-Induced) Bionic Chip Implants: Are We Becoming More Computer-Like?

Many humans now receive nonhuman body parts, in the form of computerized chips, in implants. As we are implanted with more and more (AI-induced) bionic parts, are we becoming cyborgs? With so many bionic parts becoming available, some worry that humans and machines could soon begin to merge. Ray Kurzweil (2000) has suggested that in the near future, the distinction between machines and humans may no longer be useful. And James Moor (2005) believes the question we must continually reevaluate is "not whether we should become cyborgs," but rather: "what sort of cyborgs should we become"? Andrew Clark (2003) suggests that we already are cyborgs because of our dependency on technologies. Are these views plausible, and why should we be concerned about the role that (AI-induced) chimp implants can play in questions about the human-cyborg dispute?

Our first line of response might be to note that implant technologies are by no means new. However, Weckert (2004) points out that while "conventional" implants in the form of devices designed to "correct" deficiencies have been around and used for some time, their purpose has been to assist patients in their goal of achieving "normal" states of vision, hearing, heartbeat, and so forth. Whereas these are all examples of "therapeutic implants," future chip plants, in the form of "enhancement implants" could make a normal person "superhuman."[32] Anticipating the kinds of concerns that enhancement implants will likely raise in the near future, Weckert (2006) asks

> Do we want to be "superhuman" relative to our current abilities, with implants that enhance our senses, our memory and our reasoning ability? What would such implants do to our view of what it is to be human?[33]

Some suggest that the current controversy involving implants can be framed in terms of an "enhancement vs. therapy debate." Moor notes that because the human body has "natural functions," some will argue that implanting chips in a body is acceptable as long as these implants "maintain and restore the body's natural functions." Moor also suggests that a policy framed along the lines of a therapeutic-enhancement distinction will appeal to many because it would "endorse the use of a chip that reduced dyslexia but would forbid the implanting of a deep blue chip for superior chess play."[34] Such a policy would also permit a chip implant that would restore eyesight for a person going blind, but would not license implanting a chip for X-ray vision for a person with normal eyesight. But the therapy-enhancement distinction might easily become blurred or confused if the only chip available to restore "normal" vision also happened (even if unintentionally) to enhance the person's night vision beyond the "normal" range.

Even if it turns out that a clear therapy-enhancement distinction regarding implants is possible, another important question remains: Who will be responsible for framing and enforcing policies affecting those implants? Without clear policies in place for the use of bionic implants, it may be difficult to prevent, or even to discourage, people from receiving enhancement implants that enable them to become either cyborg-like or superhuman? In Chapter 12, we examine some proposals for policies and ethical frameworks to guide developments in emerging technologies, which would also apply to bionic chip implants.

Our main concern in this section has been with the question of what it will mean to be human as more and more people elect to be fitted with bionic parts (and thus potentially also become more machine-like). Next, we consider the flip side of this cyborg-related question: What will happen as the AI entities we develop become more human-like?

The Challenge in Distinguishing AI Entities from Humans: Are Computers Becoming More Human-Like?

Consider that some AI entities (e.g., "bots") in the form of avatars (described in Section 11.2.3) already assist users in organizing their work schedules, reminding them of important scheduled meetings, arranging travel, and so forth. Also consider that personal digital assistants, and smart phones using voice-recognition programs (such as iPhone's SIRI), now interact with humans on a daily basis. Even though they are merely virtual entities, some exhibit human-like features when viewed on screens or when heard on electronic devices. Also consider that some avatars (and AI bots), which now act on our behalf, exhibit characteristics and stereotypic traits associated with humans in certain professions. For example, an avatar in the form of an AI "agent" designed to interact with other AI agents as well as with humans, such as a "negotiation agent," may look like and have the persona of a (human) broker.

After interacting with your human-like agent (avatar) over a long period of time, is it possible that you might begin to act as if you are conversing with a real person? We can also ask whether it is possible that you might, after an extended period of time, begin to confuse some virtual entities (with whom you interact) with actual flesh-and-blood characters that those entities represent. For example, as virtual entities become increasingly more human-like in appearance, it may also become more difficult to distinguish between our interactions with some (physical) person's screen avatar and with an actual human represented by that avatar or virtual entity.

This confusion in interacting with artificial entities will likely become more exacerbated as we move from our interactions with virtual entities on screens (of computers and devices) to interacting more regularly with physical AI entities—viz., robots. Consider that sophisticated robots of the near future will not only look more human-like but may also exhibit sentient characteristics; that is, these robots, like humans and animals, would (arguably, at least) be capable of simulating the experiences of sensation, feeling, and emotion. Robots and other kinds of AI entities of the not-too-distant future may also exhibit, or appear to exhibit, consciousness. Many AI researchers have questioned the nature of consciousness; for example, cognitive scientists and philosophers ask whether consciousness is a uniquely human attribute. Some also question whether it might be an *emergent property*—that is, a property capable of "emerging" (under the right conditions) in nonhuman entities, such as advanced AI systems.

Stanley Kubrick's classic 1967 film *2001: A Space Odyssey* portrays a computer named HAL with higher order thinking functions resembling human consciousness. In addition to performing ordinary computational tasks, HAL engages in sophisticated conversations with members of the spaceship's crew, plays chess, and criticizes art. To take control of the spaceship from HAL, the sole surviving member of the crew removes the logic components of HAL's higher order ("mental") functions: HAL is forced to undergo a sort of virtual "lobotomy." Of course, HAL is merely science fiction, but consider how far developments in AI have progressed since HAL's film debut in 1967.

Today, some researchers working with highly advanced AI systems claim to be on the verge of modeling a form of higher order thinking in these systems, which might be viewed as also bordering on consciousness. Suppose that we reach general agreement that human consciousness can be understood as an emergent property and that conscious activity—similar to that of humans—emerges whenever a sufficient number of neurons (or "connection strengths" in neural networks) are present. Would this, once again, be something that causes us to reassess our conception of what it means to be human?

Even if AI entities do not achieve full consciousness, many could still be capable of exhibiting (or at least simulating) other human-like characteristics such as rationality and sentience. We should note that HAL, who was at least able to simulate human consciousness, was not sentient, since "he" had no body (and thus could be viewed as a form of disembodied intelligence). So it is possible that some AI entities (like HAL, for example) may exhibit (or simulate) rationality and consciousness but not sentience, while other AIs may exhibit (or simulate) rationality and sentience but not consciousness.

In either case, these AI entities would exhibit or simulate at least some human-like characteristics. An important question that arises is whether we are prepared to meet the kinds of social challenges these entities will likely pose, including important moral questions? The following scenario illustrates one kind of moral concern that can arise as we develop more human-like AI entities.

▶ **SCENARIO 11–2:** Artificial Children

The movie *AI* is a story of an artificial boy who is physically indistinguishable from human boys and who appears to be capable of experiencing human-like emotion as well as displaying human-like intelligence. This "boy" needs the love of human parents and displays this need in a way that seems genuine and convincing. He is adopted by human parents, who later abandon him.[35]

Does this "boy" deserve any moral consideration? Do the parents who adopted him have any clear moral obligations to their "child"? For example, do they have the right to discard "him" at their convenience, in the same way that they might discard a computer that no longer serves their needs and thus is no longer useful to them? ∎

Of course, we could ask whether such an artificial child should have been developed in the first place. But given the likelihood that artificial entities similar to the "boy" in *AI* will be developed, we need to seriously consider questions about which kinds of moral consideration, if any, those artificial entities may warrant.

11.4.4 Do (At Least Some) AI Entities Warrant Moral Consideration?

If some AI entities are capable of exhibiting (or simulating) rationality and intelligence (and possibly even consciousness)—characteristics that traditionally have been reserved to describe only humans—it would not seem unreasonable to ask whether these entities might also warrant moral status. And if some of these entities can exhibit (or simulate) human-like emotion and needs, as in the case of the artificial boy in the movie *AI*, would that also be a relevant factor to consider in understanding and addressing concerns about moral consideration for AI entities? An important question, then, is whether we will need to expand the conventional realm of moral consideration to include these entities. In answering this question, however, two additional, and perhaps more basic, questions need to be examined:

    i. Which kinds of beings, or entities, deserve moral consideration?

    ii. Why do those beings/entities warrant it?

Prior to the twentieth century, ethicists and lay persons in the Western world generally assumed that only human beings deserved moral consideration; all other entities—animals, trees, natural objects, etc.—were viewed merely as resources for humans to use (and misuse/abuse) as they saw fit. In other words, humans saw these "resources" simply as something to be used and disposed of as they wished, because they believed that they had no moral obligations toward them.

By the mid-twentieth century, the assumption that moral consideration should be granted only to humans had been challenged on two distinct (though not altogether unrelated) fronts. One challenge came from animal rights groups, who argue that animals, like humans, are sentient creatures and thus capable of feeling pleasure and pain. Based on this comparison, proponents for animal rights have argued that we should also grant ethical consideration to animals, in which case it would be morally wrong for humans to abuse animals or to treat them simply as resources.

On a second front, some environmentalists made an even bolder claim, arguing that we should extend ethical consideration to include new "objects," or entities. Hans Jonas (1984) argued that because modern technologies involving atomic and nuclear power have presented us with tools of destruction that could devastate our planet on a scale never before imaginable, we needed to expand our sphere of moral obligation to include "new objects of moral consideration." These "objects" included natural objects such as trees, land, and the environment itself, as well as abstract objects such as "future generations of humans" that will inherit the planet.

In the past 50 years or so, our thinking about both who and what should be included in the sphere of moral consideration has evolved significantly. We have moved from a traditional moral system that granted consideration only to human beings to one that at least debates whether animals, land, and the entire biosphere deserve moral consideration as well. Do we once again need to expand our sphere of moral consideration to include "new objects"—i.e., nonnatural or "artificial objects" such as sophisticated AI entities?

Luciano Floridi (2002) has suggested that we need to grant some level of moral consideration to at least certain kinds of informational objects or entities. Initially, one might find Floridi's assertion strange, perhaps even preposterous, but we have seen that some sophisticated AI entities already exhibit a form of rationality that parallels that of humans. The question that concerns us here is whether these artificial entities merit moral consideration *because* they, like humans, have rational abilities. If our primary justification for granting moral consideration to humans is based on the premise that humans are rational entities, and if certain artificial entities also qualify as "rational entities," then we can make a compelling case for granting at least some moral consideration to them. For example, even if they do not qualify as full-blown *moral agents* (as typical adult humans do), they may nevertheless meet the threshold of what Floridi calls "moral patients."

In Floridi's scheme, moral patients are "receivers of moral action," while moral agents are the "sources of moral action" (capable of causing moral harm or moral good). Like moral agents, moral patients enjoy moral consideration and thus have at least some moral standing; unlike moral agents, however, moral patients cannot be held morally responsible for their actions. While animals may not be moral agents (i.e., morally accountable for what they do or fail to do), they can nevertheless qualify as moral *patients* that deserve moral consideration by humans. One reason for this is because of their ability, like humans, to feel pain and suffer emotionally. (Consider that many pet owners relate to their pets in ways that suggest they are moral entities, not only when they try to protect their pets from harm and suffering but also when they reward and punish their pets' behavior.) So even AI entities that might not exhibit a high level of rationality but do exhibit sentience could qualify as moral patients and thus warrant some moral consideration.

In the case of the artificial boy examined above, would it be plausible to grant "him" moral consideration—i.e., as a moral patient, at least—because of his "emotions" and "needs," even if this "boy" failed to satisfy a high threshold for rationality? We have noted that animal rights proponents argue that animals deserve moral consideration because of their ability to suffer pain, irrespective of any rational capacity they may or may not also have. So it would seem reasonable to ask if we can extend that analogy to apply to sentient AI entities such as the artificial boy. In this scheme, then, AI entities that exhibited (or simulated) either rationality or sentience, or both, could qualify for moral consideration. A more interesting question, which we cannot answer here, is whether AI entities that (at least appear to) exhibit consciousness could also qualify as full, or even "partial," moral *agents*. (We briefly discuss the concept of moral agency in Chapter 12, in connection with our analysis of autonomous machines.)

We conclude this section by acknowledging that more questions have been raised than answered. The critical question of who/what (in addition to humans) deserves moral consideration (and if so, to what extent) is extremely complicated, as well as very controversial. While criteria such as rationality and sentience (in connection with an agent's ability to act in the world) have played key roles in answering this question in the past, other characteristics such as autonomy and free will are also generally considered relevant criteria for possessing full moral agency. Note that we have not argued that any current AI entities have either free will or autonomy.

In Chapter 12, we examine a cluster of AI-related questions from a very different perspective. There, we consider whether it is possible to construct "moral machines" or AI entities that are capable of making moral decisions. For example, can those machines be embedded with (software) code that will enable them to make what Wallach and Allen (2009) call "good moral decisions"? We will see that this is an important "practical question," as we develop autonomous machines that act more and more independently of human oversight. Our focus on AI issues in this chapter, however, has been on questions that can be viewed as more theoretical in nature—especially given our focus on AI's impact so far for the question of what it means to be human.

▶ 11.5 CHAPTER SUMMARY

In this chapter, we have examined a range of social and ethical issues that pertain to community, personal identity, and our sense of self in cyberspace. In particular, we have seen how SNSs have affected our traditional notion of community, and we considered arguments for the pros and cons of online communities vs. traditional communities. We then looked at some VR applications, including online video games and MMORPGS, and considered their implications both for our understanding of community and personal identity. Next, we examined some ways that developments in cybertechnology have affected our sense of self (and our sense of place in the universe). Finally, we considered the impact that key developments in the field of AI have had so far for our sense of what it means to be human. We also considered whether we may need to expand our sphere of moral consideration to include at least some AI entities.

▶ REVIEW QUESTIONS

1. What are online communities, and how do they differ from traditional communities?
2. What is a blog, and in which ways do blogs function as online communities?
3. How have online communities facilitated social polarization?
4. In which ways do online communities cause us to reexamine our traditional notion of friendship?
5. How do online communities facilitate anonymity and deception?
6. What is a virtual environment?
7. How does Philip Brey define *virtual reality*?

8. How are VR applications distinguishable from other kinds of applications and forums that also comprise virtual environments?

9. What are MMOPGS and MMORPGS, and how can they be controversial from an ethical perspective?

10. What is meant by the claim that virtual harm is not real harm, and why is this reasoning fallacious?

11. What is "gold farming" in VR games, and why is it controversial?

12. Describe some examples of misrepresentation, indecent representation, and biased representation in VR applications? How do they also raise ethical concerns?

13. What does Sherry Turkle mean when she says that the computer is a medium for self-discovery and self-expression?

14. What are MUDs, and what implications can they have for our understanding of personal identity?

15. Describe some effects that cybertechnology has had so far for our sense of self.

16. What does J. David Bolter mean by a "defining technology" and by the expression "Turing's man"?

17. What is artificial intelligence?

18. What is the Turing test, and what is its significance?

19. What is John Searle's "Chinese room" argument, and what implications does it have for the Turing test?

20. How have developments in AI so far affected our sense of what it means to be human?

21. In which ways are humans becoming more computer-like?

22. In which respects are computers (i.e., sophisticated AI entities) becoming more human-like?

23. Which kinds of criteria are generally used in determining whether to grant moral consideration to entities other than humans?

24. Why does Luciano Floridi believe we should grant moral consideration to at least some AI entities?

▶ DISCUSSION QUESTIONS

25. Describe some pros and cons of online communities. What does Mitch Parsell mean when says that online communities with an "extremely narrow focus" contribute to social polarization. Assess his arguments for that claim. Do you agree with Parsell? On balance, have online communities enhanced or threatened community life? Explain.

26. Evaluate the argument by Cocking and Matthews for why true friendships in pure virtual (or online-only) contexts are not possible. Assess the counter argument by Briggle. Does Briggle succeed in making the case for the possibility of genuine friendships in virtual contexts? Whose argument do you find more convincing?

▶ ESSAY/PRESENTATION QUESTIONS

27. We saw that MMOGs and MMORPGs have become very popular around the world. Some critics are concerned about the level of violence that occurs in these games, while others worry more about the effects that virtual pornography and pedophilia in those games will have for real-life children. Evaluate Morgan Luck's claim that arguments used to defend murder (and other violent acts) in these games may, unintentionally, also defend pedophilia in virtual environments. Do you agree with Luck's view on this matter?

28. Assess the arguments we examined for whether we need to expand our conventional moral framework to include at least some AI entities? Do you believe that these entities deserve moral consideration? If we develop artificial creatures, such as the artificial boy in the movie *AI*, which kinds of moral obligations do we have to them? For example, can we discard these entities in the same ways we currently discard computer hardware resources? And if we grant moral consideration to some AI entities but not to others, where should we draw the line? In other words, which kinds of criteria are relevant for moral consideration?

Scenarios for Analysis

1. Howard Rheingold, who has speculated about some ways in which VR technologies may impact the future of social relationships, raises an interesting questions involving *teledildonics* (or simulated sex at a distance). Though not yet a marketable technology, recent work in *interactive tactile presence* (or touch feedback) will, Rheingold believes, make it possible for computer users to have sex at a distance. Inviting us to imagine this not-too-distant phenomenon, Rheingold asks us to picture ourselves "dressing for a hot night in the virtual village," where people wear a "cybersuit" made of "smart skin."[36] Even if Rheingold's account turns out to be cyberfiction, it is difficult to avoid considering the implications that teledildonics-related technology could have for future social relationships. Assess these implications in Rheingold's scenario by applying Philip Brey's model for analyzing ethical issues in virtual environments, described in Section 11.2.2.

2. Paul "Cougar" Rambis is an Iraqi War veteran who lost a leg in combat. Before entering the military, he was a fairly accomplished golfer and had planned to "turn professional" after completing his tour of duty in the U.S. Army. Initially, his dreams seemed shattered when he was severely wounded by an explosive device he encountered while on a routine patrol. But, then, Cougar learned that a new kind of bionic leg had recently been developed and that he was at the top of the list to receive one of these remarkable limbs. When Cougar returned home (with his new "leg" in place), he resumed his golfing activities. But when he wished to declare himself a professional golfer, Cougar was informed that he would be unable to participate in professional golf competitions because of his artificial leg. However, Cougar responded that his new leg, though artificial, was a natural replacement for his original (biological or natural) leg and that, as such, it did not enhance his ability to swing a golf club or to endure the rigors associated with walking through the typical 18-hole golf course. The professional golf association responded that their policy is (and has always been) that no one with an artificial limb (or prosthetic device of any kind) is eligible to compete professionally under their rules. Does this policy still seem appropriate, in light of contemporary technology-based remedies available for people like Cougar?

Recall the distinction we drew (in Section 11.4.3) between "therapeutic" and "enhancement" implants. If Cougar's artificial leg qualifies as a therapeutic device, i.e., by simply restoring his body functions to "normal," should Cougar be allowed to compete as a professional golfer? On the other hand, if that "leg" does not injure as easily, and does not age in the way that natural legs do, is Cougar's new leg merely a "therapeutic" replacement? In other words, does it enhance his ability to compete, even if only minimally? What would you decide in this case if you were a member of the governing board of the Professional Golfers Association?

► ENDNOTES

1. Rheingold (2001), pp. 1–2.
2. The survey cited by Parsell was conducted by the U.S.-based Center for the Digital Future.
3. Our analysis of online communities in this chapter focuses on their impacts so far in Western societies. For an account of some effects of these communities in the Arab/Muslim World, see Al-Saggaf and Begg (2004).
4. See, for example, Grodzinsky and Tavani (2010).
5. Parsell (2008), p. 44.
6. Cocking and Matthews (2000), p. 231.
7. Briggle (2008), p. 71.
8. See Dibbell (2001) for more detail. Also see the account of this incident in *Wikipedia*. Available at http://en.wikipedia.org/wiki/A_Rape_in_Cyberspace.
9. See http://abcnews.go.com/GMA/Story?id=3882520.
10. http://en.wikipedia.org/wiki/Second_Life.
11. http://en.wikipedia.org/wiki/MMORPG.
12. http://en.wikipedia.org/wiki/Social_Interaction_via_MMORPGs.

13. Wonderly (2008), p. 2.
14. Luck (2009), p. 33. Note that the argument presented here is adapted from Luck's original text. Luck does not express the argument in this precise form, but I believe that the argument structure used here is compatible with his position.
15. Brey (2008), pp. 371–72.
16. See, for example, Levy (2002).
17. Kimppa and Bisset (2008), p. 470.
18. *Ibid*.
19. Warner and Raiter (2005), pp. 49–50.
20. Brey, pp. 376–77.
21. *Ibid*, p. 370.
22. Parsell, p. 41.
23. Turkle (1995), p. 12.
24. *Ibid*, p. 13.
25. *Ibid*, p. 26.
26. Williams (1997), p. 16.
27. Bolter (1984), p. 11.
28. *Ibid*, p. 13.
29. This overview of key historical developments in AI follows the account in Palfreman and Swade (1991).
30. Weckert (2004), p. 697.
31. Because the historical overview of AI provided in this section is very general, it is unable to include some important developments in the field. CS students interested in learning more about AI should consult some of the excellent sources that are available.
32. Weckert, p. 693.
33. Weckert (2006), p. 236.
34. Moor (2005), p. 124.
35. This scenario is based on Steven Spielberg's 2001 film *AI*.
36. See Rheingold (1991).

▶ REFERENCES

Al-Saggaf, Yeslam, and Mohamed M. Begg. 2004. "Online Communities versus Offline Communities in the Arab/Muslim World." *Journal of Information, Communication and Ethics in Society* 2, no. 1: 41–54.

Bolter, J. David. 1984. *Turing's Man: Western Culture in the Computer Age*. Chapel Hill NC: University of North Carolina Press.

Brey, Philip. 1999. "The Ethics of Representation and Action in Virtual Reality." *Ethics and Information Technology* 1, no. 1: 5–14.

Brey, Philip. 2008. "Virtual Reality and Computer Simulation." In K. E. Himma and H. T. Tavani, eds. *The Handbook of Information and Computer Ethics*. Hoboken NJ: John Wiley and Sons, pp. 361–84.

Briggle, Adam. 2008. "Real Friends: How the Internet Can Foster Friendship." *Ethics and Information Technology* 10, no. 1: 71–79.

Clark, Andrew J. 2003. *Natural-Born Cyborgs: Minds, Technologies, and the Future of Human Intelligences*. New York: Oxford University Press.

Cocking, Dean, and Steve Matthews. 2000. "Unreal Friends." *Ethics and Information Technology* 2, no. 4: 223–31.

Cook, Brad. 2006. "Traverse Near-Infinite Possibilities with MMORPGs." Available at http://www.apple.com/games/articles/2006/04/mmorpgs/.

Dibbell, Julian. 2001. "A Rape in Cyberspace." In D. M. Hester and P. Ford, eds. *Computers and Ethics in the Cyberage*. Upper Saddle River NJ: Prentice Hall, pp. 439–51. Reprinted from *The Village Voice* (December 1993): 36–42.

Floridi, Luciano. 2002. "On the Intrinsic Value of Information Objects in the Infosphere." *Ethics and Information Technology* 4, no. 4: 287–304.

Ford, Paul J. 2001. "A Further Analysis of the Ethics of Representation in Virtual Reality: Multi-User

Environments." *Ethics and Information Technology* 3, no. 2: 113–21.

Graham, Gordon. 1999. *The Internet: A Philosophical Inquiry*. New York: Routledge.

Grodzinsky, Frances S., and Herman T. Tavani. 2010. "Applying the 'Contextual Integrity' Model of Privacy to Personal Blogs in the Blogosphere." *International Journal of Internet Research Ethics* 3, no. 1, 38–47.

Jonas, Hans. 1984. *The Imperative of Responsibility: In Search of an Ethics for the Technological Age*. Chicago: University of Chicago Press.

Kimppa, Kai, and Andrew Bisset. 2008. "Gold Farming." In T. Bynum, et al., eds. Proceedings of the Tenth ETHICOMP international Conference on the Social and Ethical Impacts of Information and Communication Technology. University of Pavia, Mantua, Italy (September 24–26, 2008), pp. 470–79.

Kurzweil, Ray. 2000. *The Age of Spiritual Machines: When Computers Exceed Human Intelligence*. New York: Penguin.

Levy, Neil. 2002. "Virtual Child Pornography: The Eroticization of Inequality." *Ethics and Information Technology* 4, no. 4: 319–23.

Luck, Morgan. 2009. "The Gamer's Dilemma: An Analysis of the Arguments for the Moral Distinction Between Virtual Murder and Virtual Pedophilia." *Ethics and Information Technology* 11, no. 1: 31–36.

Mason, Richard O. 1994. "Morality and Models." In W. Wallace, ed. *Ethics in Modeling*. Oxford UK: Elsevier Science.

Moor, James H. 2005. "Should We Let Computers Get Under Our Skin?" In R. Cavalier, ed. *The Impact of the Internet on Our Moral Lives*. Albany NY: State University of New York Press, pp. 121–38.

Palfreman, Jon, and Doron Swade. 1991. *The Dream Machine.* London, UK: BBC Books.

Parsell, Mitch. 2008. "Pernicious Virtual Communities: Identity, Polarization, and the Web 2.0." *Ethics and Information Technology* 10, no. 1: 41–56.

Rheingold, Harold. 1991. *Virtual Reality.* New York: Touchstone Books.

Rheingold, Harold. 2001. *The Virtual Community: Homesteading on the Electronic Frontier.* Rev. ed. Cambridge MA: MIT Press.

Sandin, Per. 2004. "Virtual Child Pornography and Utilitarianism." *Journal of Information, Communication and Ethics in Society* 2, no. 4: 217–23.

Searle, John. 1980. "Minds, Brains, and Programs." *Behavioral and Brain Sciences* 3, no. 3: 417–24.

Singer, Peter. 2007. "Video Crime Peril vs. Virtual Pedophilia." *The Japan Times Online,* June 22. Available at http://search.japantimes.co.jp/cgi.bineo20070722a1.html.

Sullins, John P. 2005. "Artificial Intelligence." In C. Mitcham, ed. *Encyclopedia of Science, Technology, and Ethics.* New York: Macmillan, pp. 110–13.

Turing, Alan M. 1950. "Computing Machinery and Intelligence." *Mind* 59: 433–60.

Turkle, Sherry. 1984. *The Second Self: Computers and the Human Spirit.* New York: Simon and Schuster.

Turkle, Sherry. 1995. *Life on the Screen: Identity in the Age of the Internet.* New York: Simon and Schuster.

Turkle, Sherry. 2005. *The Second Self: Computers and the Human Spirit.* Rev. ed. Cambridge MA: MIT Press.

Turkle, Sherry. 2011. *Alone Together: Why We Expect More from Technology and Less from Each Other.* New York: Basic Books.

Van Gelder, Lindsy. 1991. "The Strange Case of the Electronic Lover." In C. Dunlop and R. Kling, eds. *Computerization and Controversy: Value Conflicts and Social Choices.* San Diego CA, pp. 364–75.

Wallach, Wendell, and Colin Allen. 2009. *Moral Machines: Teaching Robots Right from Wrong.* New York: Oxford University Press.

Warner, Dorothy E., and Mike Raiter. 2005. "Social Context in Massively-Multiplayer Online Games (MMOGs): Ethical Questions in Shared Space." *International Review of Information Ethics* 4: 47–52.

Weckert, John. 2004. "Lilliputian Computer Ethics." In R. A. Spinello and H. T. Tavani, eds. *Readings in CyberEthics.* 2nd ed. Sudbury MA: Jones and Bartlett, pp. 690–97. Reprinted from *Metaphilosophy* 33, no. 3 (2002): 366–75.

Weckert, John. 2006. "The Control of Scientific Research: The Case of Nanotechnology." In H. T. Tavani, ed. *Ethics, Computing, and Genomics.* Sudbury MA: Jones and Bartlett, pp. 323–39. Reprinted from *Australian Journal of Professional and Applied Ethics* 3 (2001): 29–44.

White, Michelle. 2002. "Regulating Research: The Problem of Theorizing Research in LambdaMOO." *Ethics and Information Technology* 4, no. 1: 55–70.

Williams, Mary B. 1997. "Ethical Issues in Computing: Work, Privacy, and Justice." In M. D. Ermann, M. B. Williams, and M. S. Shauf, eds. *Computers, Ethics, and Society.* 2nd ed. New York: Oxford University Press, pp. 3–19.

Wonderly, Monique. 2008. "A Humean Approach to Assessing the Moral Significance of Ultra-Violent Video Games." *Ethics and Information Technology* 10, no. 1: 1–10.

▶ **FURTHER READINGS**

Dietrich, Eric. "*Homo Sapiens.* 2.0: Building the Better Robots of Our Nature." In M. Anderson and S. L. Anderson, eds. *Machine Ethics.* Cambridge: Cambridge University Press, 2011, pp. 531–38.

Luck, Morgan. "Crashing a Virtual Funeral: Morality in MMORPGs." *Journal of Information, Communication and Ethics in Society* 7, no. 4 (2009): 280–85.

Mathews, Steve. "Identity and Information Technology." In J. van den Hoven and J. Weckert, eds. *Information Technology and Moral Philosophy.* Cambridge: Cambridge University Press, 2008, pp. 142–60.

Powers, Thomas M. "Real Wrongs in Virtual Communities." *Ethics and Information Technology* 5, no. 4 (2003): 191–98.

Turkle, Sherry. "Authenticity in the Age of Digital Companions." In M. Anderson and S. L. Anderson, eds. *Machine Ethics.* Cambridge: Cambridge University Press, 2011, pp. 62–78.

Wellman, Barry. "Community: From Neighborhood to Network." *Communications of the ACM* 48, no. 10 (2005): 53–56.

12

Ethical Aspects of Emerging and Converging Technologies

In Chapter 12, the final chapter of *Ethics and Technology*, we examine some ethical and social issues that arise in connection with emerging and converging technologies. In particular, we analyze the following questions:

- What do we mean by "convergence" in the context of cybertechnology?
- What is ambient intelligence (AmI), and which kinds of social and ethical concerns does it raise?
- Do ethical concerns affecting bioinformatics research and development deserve special consideration?
- What is nanotechnology, and why are certain aspects of this technology controversial from an ethical perspective?
- What are "autonomous machines," and what kinds of ethical challenges do they pose?
- Can/Should we design "machines" capable of making moral decisions?

In this chapter, we analyze key social and ethical issues that arise in connection with three relatively recent technologies that have resulted from technological convergence: ambient intelligence, bioinformatics/computational genomics, and nanocomputing. We also examine some ethical concerns affecting another emerging technology—autonomous machines—that comprise a relatively new subfield of cyberethics called "machine ethics." Finally, we propose an ethical framework to guide research and inform policies affecting new and emerging/converging technologies. We begin with a brief analysis of the concept of technological convergence.

▶ 12.1 CONVERGING TECHNOLOGIES AND TECHNOLOGICAL CONVERGENCE

What, exactly, do we mean by "convergence" in the context of cybertechnology? Howard Rheingold describes technological convergence as a phenomenon that occurs when "apparently unrelated scientific and technological paths" cross or intersect "unexpectedly to create an entirely new field."[1] As we move forward in the twenty-first century, cyber and noncyber technologies are converging at a pace that is unprecedented. However, we saw in Chapter 1 that technological convergence as it pertains to cybertechnology is hardly new. For example, we saw that early computer networks became possible because of the convergence of computing and communication technologies in the late 1960s and early 1970s. Consider that many of the ethical issues we examined in the preceding chapters of this textbook arose because of convergent aspects of computing/information and communication technologies.

Arguably, convergence *within* the domain of cybertechnology itself—i.e., the unforeseen blending or merging of disparate, and initially distinct, computing and information technologies—has been continuous and ongoing. One example of this can be found in virtual reality (VR) technology, which, as Rheingold notes, resulted from the convergence of video technology and computer hardware in the 1980s. (Recall our discussion of ethical aspects of VR in Chapter 11.) However, cyber and cyber-related technologies are now converging with non-cyber technologies in ways that challenge our ability to identify and articulate many of the social and ethical issues that also arise either because of, or in connection with, this kind of convergence.

One ethical/social concern that cuts across the converging technologies examined in this chapter has to do with the new kinds of privacy threats that are now possible. Because Chapter 5 was devoted to privacy concerns pertaining to cybertechnology, you might assume that the appropriate place to discuss these privacy issues would have been in that chapter. There, however, we examined privacy concerns that tend to fit mainly within the category of "informational privacy." For example, those privacy issues typically involve concerns that have resulted from exchanging electronic records (of personal information in databases), which were acquired through explicit transactions on the part of users. Although some privacy concerns affecting the converging technologies that we examine in this chapter also fall within the category of informational privacy, many do not. The reason for this is not simply because these privacy issues are associated with newer technologies, but because they introduce different kinds of privacy concerns than those examined in Chapter 5. For example, some privacy issues affecting research in bioinformatics and computational genomics tend to fall under the category of medical/genetic privacy; these issues, as a result of the computational tools and techniques used, also sometimes stretch and strain the traditional boundaries of medical privacy and genetic privacy.

We will also see that some privacy issues generated by developments in ambient intelligence technology and nanotechnology introduce a relatively new category of privacy concern called "location privacy," because these technologies can disclose the precise spatial location of an individual at a particular point in time. Thus, many of the privacy concerns identified and analyzed in this chapter are sufficiently different from those examined in Chapter 5 to warrant a separate context for analysis. However, as you examine the privacy-related issues discussed in this chapter, especially those affected by data mining technology, you may find it helpful to refer back to relevant sections of Chapter 5.

▶ 12.2 AMBIENT INTELLIGENCE (AmI) AND UBIQUITOUS COMPUTING

We begin our examination of social and ethical aspects of converging technologies in the twenty-first century with a look at some controversies associated with *ambient intelligence* (or *AmI*)—a technology that enables people to live and work in environments that respond to them in "intelligent ways."[2] AmI has been made possible, in large part, because of the convergence of artificial intelligence (AI) technologies (described in Chapter 11) with (miniaturized) electronic sensing and surveillance technologies. Before describing the technological components comprising AmI, we briefly consider a scenario in which a young mother and her baby arrive at their "intelligent home." Illustrating some of the promises that AmI's proponents envision for the near future, Raisinghani et al. (2004) describe a situation that we could call "a day in the life of a smart home":

> Arriving home, a surveillance camera recognizes the young mother, automatically disables the alarm, unlocks the front door as she approaches it and turns on the lights to a level of brightness that the home control system has learned she likes. After dropping off her daughter, the young mother gets ready for grocery shopping. The intelligent refrigerator has studied the family's food consumption over time and knows their preferences as well as what has been consumed since the last time she went shopping. This information has been recorded by an internal tracking system and wireless communication with the intelligent kitchen cabinets. Based on this information, the refrigerator automatically composes a shopping list, retrieves quotations for the items on the list from five different supermarkets in the neighborhood through an Internet link, sends an order to the one with the lowest offer and directs the young mother there. When arriving at the supermarket, the shopping cart has already been filled with the items on her shopping list. Spontaneously, she decides to add three more items to her cart and walks to the check-out. Instead of putting the goods on a belt, the entire cart gets checked out simply by running it past an RFID transponder that detects all items in the cart at once and sends that information to the cash register for processing.[3]

Is the scenario described by Raisinghani et al. based on science fiction? Or does it portray a real-world situation in the not-too-distant future? Consider that a 5,040-square-foot "aware home" was developed at the Georgia Institute of Technology over a decade ago and has continued to serve as a laboratory for AmI research and development. Research in ambient intelligence is also underway at other academic institutions, such as the MIT, as well as at companies in the private sector such as Philips Electronics. AmI's optimists predict that intelligent homes will be available to consumers within the next few years. Whereas proponents of AmI are enthusiastic about many of the conveniences made possible by this technology, critics worry about AmI's dark side.

We should note that some analysts use the expression "ubiquitous computing," or *ubicomp*, to describe what we refer to in this chapter as AmI. However, ubicomp can easily be confused with "ubiquitous communication," a technological component of AmI, which we describe in Section 12.2.2. So we use the expression AmI in this chapter to avoid any confusion between the two terms.

To better understand ambient intelligence, including the ethical and social challenges it poses, we briefly describe three key technological components that make AmI possible:

- pervasive computing,
- ubiquitous communication,
- intelligent user interfaces (IUIs).

12.2.1   Pervasive Computing

According to the Centre for Pervasive Computing (www.pervasive.dk), *pervasive computing* can be viewed as a computing environment where information and communication technology are "everywhere, for everyone, at all times." In this scheme, computing technology is integrated into our environments—from "toys, milk cartons, and desktops to cars, factories, and whole city areas." Pervasive computing is made possible, in part, because of the increasing ease with which circuits can be printed or embedded into objects, including wearable, even disposable items. Pervasive computing goes beyond the traditional scheme of user interfaces—on the one hand, it "implodes them into small devices and appliances"; on the other hand, it "explodes them onto large scale walls, buildings and furniture" (Centre for Pervasive Computing).

Pervasive computing, like AmI, is also sometimes referred to in the computer science literature as *ubiquitous computing* (or *ubicomp*). The expression "ubiquitous computing" was coined by Mark Weiser, who envisioned "omnipresent computers" that serve people in their everyday lives, both at home and at work.[4] He also envisioned ubiquitous computing as something that would function "invisibly and unobtrusively" in the background and that would free people to a considerable degree from tedious routine tasks. For ubiquitous or pervasive computing to operate at its full potential, however, continuous and ubiquitous communication between devices is also needed.

12.2.2   Ubiquitous Communication

Ubiquitous communication aims at ensuring flexible and omnipresent communication possibilities between interlinked computer devices that can be stationed at various locations. Several different kinds of wireless technologies that make ubiquitous communication possible are now available or are in progress. According to Raisinghani et al. (2004), these include

- wireless local area networks (W-LANs),
- wireless personal area networks (W-PANs),
- wireless body area networks (W-BANs) interlinking various wearable devices and connecting them to outside networks,
- radio frequency identification (RFID).

Perhaps the most controversial of these technologies so far—at least from the perspective of personal privacy—is RFID. Andreas Koehler and Claudia Som (2005) suggest that RFID transponders in the form of "smart labels" will probably become the most widespread example of ubiquitous computing/communication. Recall our discussion of RFID technology in Chapter 5, where we examined some implications of RFID for personal privacy. We will see that RFID technology, when used in AmI environments, can facilitate the tracking of an individual's location at any given point in time and thus make possible a form of "pervasive surveillance."

12.2.3   Intelligent User Interfaces

In addition to pervasive computing and ubiquitous communication technologies, AmI has another key component: *Intelligent User Interfaces* (or *IUIs*). This technology has been made possible by developments in the field of AI. In Chapter 11, we examined AI from the perspective of concerns about our "sense of self" and about what it means to be a human being in the era of autonomous machines. There we also saw that AI, in addition to raising some interesting conceptual and theoretical questions, has many practical applications as well—including the implementation of AI-based algorithms in various expert system technologies. AI-based applications are also at the core of the "intelligent" user interfaces needed to realize the full potential of AmI.

Brey (2005) notes that IUIs, which are also sometimes called "user adaptive interfaces" because of the way they can adapt to a user's preferences, go beyond traditional interfaces such as a keyboard, mouse, and monitor. As a result, they improve human interaction with technology by making it more intuitive and more efficient than was previously possible with traditional interfaces. With IUIs, for example, computers can "know" and sense far more about a person than was possible with traditional interfaces, including information about that person's situation, context, or environment. Because IUIs respond to inputs such as human gestures as well as to an individual's preferences within various contexts, they enable inhabitants of AmI environments to interact with their environment in a personalized way. Unlike traditional user interfaces, however, IUIs in AmI environments also enable *profiling*, which Brey describes as "the ability to personalize and automatically adapt to a particular user's behavior patterns."

While AmI technology is able to sense changes in an environment, and while this technology can automatically adapt and act based on these changes—e.g., in response to the needs and preferences of users—AmI remains in the background and is virtually invisible to the user. As Brey notes, people are "surrounded with possibly hundreds of intelligent networked computers that are aware of their presence, personality, and needs." But users themselves may not be aware of the existence of this technology in their environments.

We have briefly described three key technological components that make AmI environments possible: pervasive computing, ubiquitous communication, and IUIs. Next, we examine some of the ethical and social challenges posed by AmI environments and the technologies that comprise them.

12.2.4 Ethical and Social Issues in AmI

Social and ethical concerns affecting AmI environments include worries about the loss of freedom and autonomy. These are sometimes closely related to concerns about humans becoming overly dependent on technology. Other social/ethical concerns involving AmI include threats associated with privacy and surveillance. We begin with a look at some issues affecting freedom and autonomy.

Autonomy, Freedom, and Control
Will human autonomy and freedom be enhanced or diminished as a result of AmI technology? AmI's supporters suggest that humans will gain more control over the environments with which they interact because technology will be more responsive to their needs. However, Brey notes a paradoxical aspect of this claim, pointing out that "greater control" is presumed to be gained through a "delegation of control to machines." But this, he suggests, is tantamount to the notion of "gaining control by giving it away." Brey considers some ways in which control can be gained in one sense, and lost in another. With respect to humans gaining control as a result of this technology,

he notes that three different kinds of arguments can be made, where AmI may make the human environment more controllable because it can

1. become more responsive to the voluntary actions, intentions, and needs of users;
2. supply humans with detailed and personal information about their environment;
3. do what people want without having to engage in any cognitive or physical effort.

On the other hand, Brey considers some ways that AmI can diminish the amount of control that humans have over their environments. These also are organized into three arguments, where users may lose control because a smart object can

1. make incorrect inferences about the user, the user's actions, or the situation;
2. require corrective actions on the part of the user;
3. represent the needs and interests of parties other than the user.[5]

So, as Brey notes, AmI has the potential to enhance human freedom through its ability to expand certain aspects of our control over the environment—e.g., in responding to our voluntary actions, intentions, and needs, and by freeing us from many routine and tedious tasks that require either cognitive or physical effort. But he also notes that AmI has the potential to limit freedom because it can make incorrect inferences about a user's intentions and needs. Even when AmI does what a user wants, it can still reduce control by requiring "corrective actions" on the part of the user. Brey also notes that users can lose control when smart objects perform autonomous actions that do not solely represent the user's interests. For example, the smart object could include a user profile or knowledge base that is also designed to take into account the interests of third parties (such as commercial interests). Additionally, Brey believes that AmI could undermine human freedom and autonomy if humans become too dependent on machines for their judgments and decisions.

Technological Dependency

We have come to depend a great deal on technology, especially on cybertechnology, in conducting many activities in our day-to-day lives. In the future, will humans depend on the kind of smart objects and smart environments made possible by AmI technology in ways that exceed our current dependency on computing devices? We noted above that IUIs could relieve us of having to worry about performing many of our routine day-to-day tasks, which can be considered tedious and boring. But we also noted that these interfaces could relieve us of much of the cognitive effort that has, in the past, enabled us to be fulfilled and to flourish as humans. What would happen to us if we were to lose this capacity because of an increased dependency on technology? Perhaps a brief look at a scenario envisioned by E. M. Forster in one of his classic works would be instructive at this point.

▶ **SCENARIO 12–1:** E. M. Forster's Precautionary Tale

In his short story *The Machine Stops*, first published in 1909, E. M. Forster portrays a futuristic society that, initially at least, might seem like an ideal or utopian world. In fact, Forster's story anticipated many yet-to-be-developed technologies such as television and videoconferencing. But it also illustrates how humans have transferred control of much of their lives to a global Machine, which is capable of satisfying their physical and spiritual needs and desires. In surrendering so much control to the Machine, however, people begin to lose touch with the natural world. After a while, defects appear in the Machine, and eventually it breaks down. Unfortunately, no one remembers how to repair it. In Forster's tale, some of the characters begin to realize just how dependent they have become on this machine.[6] ■

We could easily imagine Forster's scenario playing out in AmI environments of the future where individuals no longer are required to perform routine cognitive acts, and instead depend on IUIs to make decisions for them. Also, we could ask what would happen if the energy sources that powered the AmI environments were suddenly lost. Could we respond successfully if this happened to us? If not, it would seem that we have let ourselves become too dependent on this technology. Hypothetical questions of this kind are worth keeping in mind as we proceed with developments in AmI.

Privacy, Surveillance, and the Panopticon

Some of AmI's critics worry that a kind of "Big Brother" society may emerge. For example, Bohn et al. (2005) note that in AmI environments, all of our moves, actions, and decisions will be recorded by "tireless electronic devices, from the kitchen and living room of our homes to our weekend trips in cars." As Marc Langheinrich (2001) points out, no aspect of our life will be secluded from "digitization," because virtually anything we say, do, or even feel, could be "digitized, stored, and retrieved anytime later." But how are the privacy concerns associated with AmI different, in relevant ways, from privacy issues generated by earlier uses of computer technology? Langheinrich believes that with respect to privacy and surveillance, four features differentiate AmI from other kinds of computing applications:

- ubiquity
- invisibility
- sensing
- memory application

First, Langheinrich believes that because computing devices are *ubiquitous* or omnipresent in AmI environments, privacy threats involving AmI are more pervasive in scope and can affect us more deeply. Second, because computers are virtually *invisible* in AmI environments (in the sense that they easily "disappear" from view), it is likely that users will not always realize that computing devices are present and are being used to collect and disseminate personal data. Third, *sensing* devices associated with the IUIs in AmI environments may become so sophisticated that, unlike conventional forms of cybertechnology, they will be able to sense (private and intimate) human emotions such as fear, stress, and excitement. Fourth, AmI has the potential to create a *memory* or "life-log"—i.e., a complete record of someone's past. So, Langheinrich concludes that AmI poses a more significant threat to privacy than earlier computing technologies.

In AmI environments, the sheer scale or amount of information that can be collected without our awareness is also problematic. Bohn et al. note that AmI has the potential to create a comprehensive surveillance network, because it can disclose an "unprecedented share of our public and private life." We saw that AmI environments are equipped with sensors that facilitate the collection of data about an individual from his or her surroundings without that individual's active intervention. This kind of ubiquitous observation, which some now refer to as "pervasive surveillance," can expose much about an individual's habits and preferences.

Johann Čas (2005) notes that no one can be sure that his or her actions are not being observed; nor can one be sure that his or her words are not being recorded. Furthermore, individuals cannot be sure whether information about their presence at any location is being recorded. So, he believes that the only realistic attitude of human beings living in such environments is to assume that any activity or inactivity is being monitored, analyzed, transferred, and stored, and that this information may be used in any context in the future. In this sense, people in AmI environments would be subject to a virtual "panopticon."

▶ **SCENARIO 12–2:** Jeremy Bentham's Panopticon

Jeremy Bentham, an eighteenth-century philosopher and social reformer, conceived of the idea for managing a prison environment based on the notion of the *Panopticon*. Imagine a prison comprised of glass cells, all arranged in a circle, where prisoners could be observed at any moment by a prison guard who sits at a rotating desk facing the prisoner's cells. Further imagine that the inmates cannot see anyone or anything outside their cells, even though they can be observed (through the one-way-vision glass cells) by the prison guard at any time. Although a prisoner cannot be certain that he is being observed at any given moment, it would be prudent for him to assume that he is being observed at every moment. The prisoner's realization that he could be observed continuously, and his fear about what could happen to him if he is observed doing something that is not permitted in the cell, would likely be sufficient to control the prisoner's behavior.[7] ■

Suppose Bentham's model of the Panopticon or "inspection house" were to be extended to public spaces such as the workplace and public buildings. Further suppose that it is extended to private and intimate environments as well. What effects could the possibility of being permanently observed have on individual behavior and social control? In Bentham's classical Panopticon, one could not be certain whether he or she was actually being monitored at a given point in time. Persons living in AmI environments, however, can, with almost 100% certainty, know that they are being observed. Classical forms of surveillance, from Bentham's time to the period preceding AmI technology, were limited to time and place. But data captured in AmI environments will, as Čas notes, persist across space and time.

So far we have examined some key social and ethical concerns affecting AmI environments. Table 12.1 lists the technological components of AmI and the corresponding ethical and social issues associated with them.

We have seen that some of these ethical and social issues arise because of the pervasive aspects of AmI technology, while others reflect concerns pertaining to convergent features of its component technologies. In the next section, we examine ethical concerns that result from converging aspects of cybertechnology and biotechnology.

TABLE 12.1   Ambient Intelligence

Technological Components	Ethical and Social Issues Generated
Pervasive computing	Freedom and autonomy
Ubiquitous communication	Privacy and surveillance
Intelligent user interfaces	Technological dependence

► 12.3 BIOINFORMATICS AND COMPUTATIONAL GENOMICS

Recent discoveries in the life sciences, particularly in the fields of cell biology and genetics/genomics, have depended significantly on the application of computers and computational techniques and methodologies. This dependency has influenced the development of two relatively new fields at the intersection of computer science and biology: *bioinformatics* and *computational genomics*. Bioinformatics is a branch of *informatics*, which involves the acquisition, storage, manipulation, analyses, transmission, sharing, visualization, and simulation of information on a computer.[8] Computational genomics, like bioinformatics, uses computerized techniques, tools, and approaches to acquire, store, organize, analyze, synthesize, visualize, and simulate data. However, the data it analyzes are limited to genetic/genomic information, as opposed to broader biological data that can include biological systems as well as medical and health data.[9]

12.3.1 Computing and Genetic "Machinery": Some Conceptual Connections

Before examining specific ethical and social issues that arise at the intersection of computing and genetic/genomic technologies, we briefly identify some conceptual connections that link the fields of computer science and genetics. James Moor (2006a) points out that computing provides a "conceptual model" for the function and malfunction of our genetic machinery. He also notes that researchers sometimes describe the computation of genes as straightforward computational programs in which the sequence of nucleotides can be regarded as a kind of "computer program for constructing an organism."[10] Consider that some geneticists describe their work in terms of "decoding" and "reprogramming" DNA.

Also consider some practical ways in which computational tools and techniques have significantly influenced developments in genetic/genomic research. For example, Antonio Marturano (2006) notes that a computerized technique, called the "shotgun method," significantly accelerated work on the Human Genome Project. This technique also helped researchers to map the entire human genome ahead of schedule.

Kenneth Goodman describes an incident in the early 1990s that aptly illustrates some key roles that computer technology in general, and computational tools in particular, have played in genetic research. Goodman notes that scientists working at geographically distant sites were able to make critical information about sequenced genetic data available to colleagues through databases accessible via the Internet. More importantly, however, the gene sequences represented in these data had already been identified *computationally*—i.e., the genes had been discovered, sequenced, and analyzed, via computers—before the data were shared electronically among an international group of scientists.[11] Goodman's example nicely illustrates how the information about the gene sequences was not only able to be communicated and shared with colleagues via computer networks, but that the information itself had become available only *because of* the computational techniques that were used.

12.3.2 Ethical Issues and Controversies

Because of its special dependency on the computational techniques and analyses used by genetics/genomics researchers, the outcomes of that research can be very difficult to anticipate with respect to ethical implications. As a result, some ethical issues generated by this research are not always easy to identify, let alone analyze. Yet, these ethical issues are significant: in some cases, they involve psycho/social harm, including discrimination and stigmatization for certain individuals and groups; in other cases, they can affect broader social policies such as questions concerning the ownership of personal genetic data that are stored in electronic databases. The following scenario illustrates some of these concerns.

► **SCENARIO 12–3:** deCODE Genetics Inc.

DeCODE Genetics was founded in 1996 by Kari Stefansson, a former professor of neurology at Harvard University, when he returned to Iceland, his native country. Stefansson negotiated with the Icelandic government for access to the nation's medical and health care records, which date back to 1915. Iceland's rich genealogical data, which included records (that date back more than 1,000 years) were already freely available, and Iceland's Parliament promised Stefansson access to any government-owned medical information that he would need to conduct his research. With these and other agreements in hand, Stefansson officially formed deCODE Genetics Inc. and immediately began to construct a genetics database consisting of information based on DNA samples that would eventually be acquired from 70,000 volunteers. DeCODE was then able to link together and cross reference medical/healthcare records, genealogical records, and genetic information included in the three databases.[12] ∎

Some of deCODE's practices have been considered controversial from the perspective of ethics. For our purposes, these concerns are analyzed in terms of three distinct, but sometimes overlapping, kinds of issues:

- privacy and confidentiality
- autonomy and informed consent
- information ownership and property rights.[13]

Privacy, Confidentiality, and the Role of Data Mining Technology
Should Icelandic citizens who voluntarily provided DNA samples to deCODE have assumed that their personal genetic data was confidential information, which would be protected by the company's privacy policies and by Icelandic privacy laws, even after it had been collected and aggregated? Anton Vedder (2004) points out that the kind of privacy protection that applies to personal information about individuals *as individuals* does not necessarily apply to that information once it is aggregated and cross-referenced with other information. So the aggregated personal genetic information stored in deCODE's genetic databases, which was cross-referenced with information in deCODE's nongenetic databases (i.e., databases containing medical and genealogical information), does not enjoy the kind of legal protection generally accorded to personal genetic information collected in its original form.

In the process of aggregating and cross-referencing data, deCODE used data mining techniques to find correlated genes and gene variations, simply by comparing databases of genetic samples and disease records. In Chapter 5, we saw that data mining tools can "discover" information based on patterns that are implicit in data. As such, no prior hypothesis about the possible relationship between a particular gene and a certain disease is necessary when data mining is used. Although this technology has helped researchers to identify disease genes that affect populations, data mining can also be controversial. For example, new categories or groups (of individuals) can be generated by the use of one or more *profiles* made possible by data mining technology.

Data mining also generates *group profiles*. Bart Custers (2006) describes a group profile as a set of properties or characteristics that serve as the basis for identifying an individual as a member of a particular group. Why is this kind of profile controversial? Some of the characteristics or attributes used in defining groups are commonly known and easily identifiable. For example, an individual might be identified as belonging to multiple groups—i.e., the group of females, the group of insurance executives, the group of BMW owners, and so forth. For the most part, people who are assigned to these kinds of groups would not be surprised to learn of their association with them. However, other kinds of groups can be constructed on the basis of profiles that are not obvious to the individuals who comprise them. As Custers notes, a person who owns a red car may have no idea that he belongs to a group of individuals likely to have or to contract colon cancer (merely because of a statistical correlation that associates people who own red cars with colon cancer). So the same technology used to discover patterns and relations that aid genetic researchers can also be used to generate new groups, which in turn can suggest "new facts" about the individuals assigned to them.

Why are the "new facts" about individuals that can be generated via data mining so controversial? For one thing, decisions can be made about people on the basis of certain kinds of information pertaining to them *as members of a group*. Custers points out that a decision could be made about whether to grant someone, X, life insurance based on the new fact that X owns a red car and would thus likely have a higher-than-average probability of contracting colon cancer. Financial decisions may also be made about an individual based on facts pertaining to his or association with a "newly discovered" group, even though this individual may have had no knowledge that such a group exists. For example, we saw in Chapter 5 that an individual might be denied a loan based solely on a coincidental statistical association with a "new group" rather than on his individual credit scoring. So, the person can be denied the loan for reasons that are unfair, irrelevant, or inaccurate.

Analogously, a person could be denied employment, health insurance, or life insurance based on similar uses of data mining technology. For example, a person could be placed into a risky category based on arbitrary associations and correlations (generated by data mining) that associate trivial nongenetic information (such as the color of one's car) with sensitive information about one's genetic data. We have also seen that many individuals who eventually become identified or associated with the newly created groups may have no knowledge that the groups to which they have been assigned actually exist. Hence, those individuals will also have no opportunity to correct any inaccuracies or errors in the information about them that is generated from their association with that group.

Autonomy, Informed Consent, and Secondary Uses of Information

Another concern that arises in the deCODE scenario affects individual autonomy—in particular, the process of *informed consent* used in getting permissions from human research subjects who participate in genetic studies. The genetic information that deCODE acquired from "informed" volunteers may not meet the required conditions for what some ethicists describe as *valid* informed consent. According to the requirements for valid informed consent included in the 1993 Office of Technology Assessment

(OTA) Report, entitled *Protecting Privacy in Computerized Medical Information*, individuals must

i. have adequate disclosure of information about the data dissemination process,

ii. be able to fully comprehend what they are being told about the procedure or treatment.

Applying OTA's criteria to the deCODE scenario, individuals consenting to provide their genetic data are required to have both "adequate disclosure" of information and "full comprehension" of the process in which their data will be used. However, consider that even if the human subjects agreed to have their data used in a specific context by deCODE, it is not clear that they fully comprehended the process of how their genetic data could be used in secondary or subsequent contexts (where it could be cross-referenced with information in nongenetic databases). Also, it is not clear that these individuals were given "adequate" disclosure about the data dissemination process used by deCODE. Furthermore, it might not even be possible for deCODE to disclose this information to them because all of the *potential* secondary uses of their genetic information have not yet been determined.

If individuals who provided their genetic data to deCODE Genetics did not make choices that were "validly informed," was the consent process used in this research ethical? If not, why is that important? Onora O'Neill (2002) believes that the principle of informed consent is important from an ethical point of view because it enables individuals to protect themselves against both coercion and deception. In this sense, she believes that the consent process must be open or *transparent*. Can the transparency requirement be satisfied in research practices that use data mining techniques? We have seen that the data mining practices used by deCODE both cross reference and aggregate personal information, which can then be used for secondary purposes. Unless specific information about how this is done is adequately disclosed to research subjects in a way that is comprehensible to them, it would seem that O'Neill's transparency guidelines (essential for the consent process) are violated in the practices used by deCODE Genetics.

Because of the way data mining technology can be used to manipulate personal information that had been authorized for use in one context only, it would seem that the process of informed consent has increasingly become nontransparent, or what O'Neill calls *opaque*. It would also seem that the kind of conditions required for "valid" informed consent are extremely difficult, if not impossible, to achieve in cases that involve secondary uses of personal genetic information via data mining technology.

Intellectual Property Rights and Ownership Issues Affecting Personal Genetic Information

A third area of ethical concern in the deCODE scenario involves the question of property rights and ownership of genetic data. Some critics believe the Icelandic parliament's decision to grant deCODE exclusive rights (for 12 years) to the information included in the nation's health records database raises property right issues that also affect access to personal genetic information. Who should (and who should not) have access to those data? Should deCODE hold exclusive ownership rights to all of the personal genetic information that resides in its databases? Alternatively, should individuals have at least some control over their personal genetic data, even though the data are stored in a privately owned database? Or is a different strategy needed—e.g., should the Icelandic government be granted custodial rights to the personal genetic information in deCODE's databases, in order to protect the interests of Iceland's citizens?

Have those individuals who donated samples of their DNA to deCODE necessarily lost all of the rights to their personal genetic data, once the data were stored in that company's databases? If so, should deCODE hold exclusive rights to these data in perpetuity, and should deCODE be permitted to do whatever it wishes with those data? Why, exactly, are these questions so controversial from an ethical point of view? Recall our discussion in Chapter 5 of a commercial database containing personal data that was owned by Toysmart.com, a now defunct online business. There we saw that customers who dealt with Toysmart were given assurances that any personal information they disclosed would be protected under the company's privacy policy. However, we also saw that when Toysmart filed for bankruptcy, it was required by law to list all of its assets. These included its database of customer information, the specific contents of which were presumably protected under Toysmart's privacy policy.

Perhaps an appropriate analogy can be drawn between deCODE and Toysmart. For example, one might ask what would happen to the information in deCODE's genetic databases if deCODE were forced to file for bankruptcy. It turns out, however, that deCODE did file for bankruptcy in November 2009; but, unlike Toysmart, deCODE soon returned as a private business, when a consortium of investors acquired it in January 2010. Suppose, however, that the organization(s) that acquired deCODE had been interested only in the commercial use and sale of the personal genetic information in those databases? It is not clear what legal recourse, if any, the Icelandic citizens who had voluntarily contributed their DNA samples to deCODE would have regarding the subsequent use of their personal information by organizations that legally acquired the databases. Because the answers to questions such as these are not entirely clear, we need laws and policies that explicitly describe the ownership rights of the highly sensitive personal data stored in genetic databases.

12.3.3 ELSI Guidelines and Genetic-Specific Legislation

We have seen how ethical issues involving privacy and confidentiality, informed consent and autonomy, and property rights/ownership issues each arise in bioinformatics/genetics/genomics-related research in the deCODE scenario. These concerns also illustrate the need for clear ethical guidelines as well as adequate legislation to protect human research subjects. In the United States, government-funded genomic research is currently guided by a policy that requires researchers to take specific ethical, legal, and social implications (ELSI) into account. The ELSI program includes explicit guidelines affecting criteria such as privacy and fairness for research subjects. However, some question whether the original ELSI guidelines, developed in the late 1980s and early 1990s, are still adequate in an era when advanced computerized techniques such as data mining are used.[14] It is also important to note that the ELSI requirements do not apply to genetic research conducted in the commercial sector.

Because of concerns about potential misuses of personal genetic data, some genetic-specific privacy laws and policies have been proposed and enacted into law. In the United States, prior to 2008, these laws had been enacted primarily at the state level, as no federal laws protected personal genetic data per se. The Health Insurance Portability and

TABLE 12.2   Ethical Issues Associated with Bioinformatics/Computational Genomics

Personal privacy and confidentiality	The aggregation of personal genetic data, via data mining, can generate privacy issues affecting "new groups" and "new facts" about individuals.
Informed consent and autonomy	The nontransparent (or "opaque") consent process can preclude "valid" or "fully informed" consent, thereby threatening individual autonomy.
Intellectual property rights/ownership	The storage of personal genetic data in electronic databases raises questions about who should/should not have ownership rights and access to the data.

Accountability Act (HIPAA), which went into effect in 2003, provided broad protection for personal medical information. That is, HIPAA included standards for protecting the privacy of "individually identifiable health information" from "inappropriate use and disclosure." However, critics point out that HIPAA failed to provide any special privacy protection for personal genetic information. Also, Baumer, Earp, and Payton (2006) note that it is not clear whether HIPAA adequately addresses concerns affecting nonconsensual, secondary uses of personal medical and genetic information (of the kind made possible by data mining).

In 2008, the Genetic Information Nondiscrimination Act (GINA) was enacted into law in the United States. Specifically designed to protect an individual's interests with respect to employment and health insurance, the broader aim of GINA has been to protect Americans against forms of discrimination based on their genetic information.[15] Some of GINA's critics believe that this law is "overly broad" and that it will most likely not succeed in rectifying many of the existing state laws that tend to be inconsistent.[16] Also, it is still not clear at this point whether GINA addresses the potential problems we identified involving the use of data mining technology in genetic and genomic research.

So far, we have examined some social and ethical aspects of two different kinds of converging technologies: AmI and bioinformatics/computational genomics. We saw that both kinds of technologies introduce special concerns for personal privacy. We also saw that practices affecting bioinformatics/computational-genomics research have introduced some new challenges for informed-consent policies and for intellectual property rights. Table 12.2 lists, in summary form, the three kinds of ethical issues we examined in connection with bioinformatics/computational genomics.

A third area of technological convergence that we consider is nanocomputing, i.e., the intersection of cybertechnology and nanotechnology. Ruth Chadwick and Antonio Marturano (2006) argue that nanotechnology provides the "key" to technological convergence in the 21st century because it "enables the bringing together" of computer-information technologies and biotechnologies.

▶ 12.4 NANOTECHNOLOGY AND NANOCOMPUTING

What, exactly, is nanotechnology? Why is research at the nano level controversial from an ethical perspective? Should we continue to engage in research and development in nanocomputing? We examine each of these questions, and we begin with an overview of nanotechnology as a scientific field.

12.4.1 Nanotechnology: A Brief Overview

Rosalyn Berne (2005) describes *nanotechnology* as "the study, design, and manipulation of natural phenomena, artificial phenomena, and technological phenomena at the nanometer level." We should note, however, that, at this time, there is no universally agreed upon definition of the field. One common or unifying feature of nanotechnology, regardless of how narrowly or broadly it is defined, is that it operates on matter on a scale of *nanometers* (nm).

James Moor and John Weckert (2004) note that a nanometer, which is one billionth of a meter, is very close to the dimensions of individual atoms whose diameters range from 0.1 to 0.5 nm. K. Eric Drexler, who coined the term "nanotechnology" in the 1980s, conceived of the field as a branch of engineering dedicated to the development of electronic circuits and mechanical devices built at the molecular level of matter. Although such nano-level devices do not yet exist, current microelectricomechanical systems (or MEMS), tiny devices such as sensors embedded in conductor chips used in airbag systems to detect collisions, are one step away from the molecular machines envisioned by Drexler.

The Development of Nanotechnology as a Field of Scientific Research

The origin of nanotechnology as a distinct field is generally traced to a 1959 talk by physicist and Nobel laureate Richard Feynman, who encouraged scientists to develop tools that could manipulate matter at the atomic level. In 1990, Donald Eigler and Erhard Schweizer, two scientists working at the IBM Almaden laboratory, succeeded in manipulating 35 individual xenon atoms to shape the three initials of their employer's logo. Since then, more practical kinds of applications have been carried out at the nano level. Drexler has proposed the idea of a nano-scale *assembler*—i.e., a molecular machine that could be programmed to build virtually any molecular structure or device from simpler chemical building blocks. He believes that the development of universally applicable assemblers, which could be programmed to replicate themselves, is essential for the full realization of nanotechnology's potential.

Although some critics argue that nanotechnology has generated more hype than substance, a few important breakthroughs have already begun to occur at the nano level. For example, Ed Regis (2009) describes some of the implications of the nanotube radio that was invented by Alex Zettl and his colleagues in 2007. Regis notes that a "single carbon nanotube tunes in a broadcast signal, amplifies it, converts it to an audio signal and then sends it to an external speaker in a form that the human ear can readily hear." He also notes that this could be the "basis for a new range of applications: hearing aids, cell phones, and iPods small enough to fit completely within the ear canal."[17]

Nanocomputers and Nanocomputing

In the 1980s, Drexler predicted that developments in nanotechnology would result in computers at the nanoscale—that is, *nanocomputers*. Ralph Merkle (1997) believes that future nanocomputers will have mass storage devices capable of storing more than

100 billion bytes in a volume the size of a sugar cube and that these devices will be able to "deliver a billion billion instructions per second." Drexler (1991) suggests that nano-computers will be designed using various types of architectures. For example, an electronic nanocomputer would operate in a manner similar to present-day computers, differing primarily in terms of size and scale. A quantum nanocomputer, on the contrary, would work by storing data in the form of atomic quantum states or spin. Weckert (2006) notes that quantum computers would be much more powerful than any computing systems available today.

Some predict that future nanocomputers will also be built from biological material such as DNA. For example, Nadrian Seeman (2004) believes that DNA is an ideal molecule for building nanometer-scale structures because strands of DNA can be "programmed to self assemble into complex arrangements" that bond together. And Drexler, who believes that biology shows us how molecular machinery can construct complex organisms from the bottom up, suggests that biological computers are already a reality.

Whether biological and quantum computers will be available at the nano level is still a matter of conjecture and debate. However, more conventional notions of computing at the nanoscale are currently under development, and some standard computing chips have already been constructed at the nanoscale. At Hewlett Packard, for example, researchers have made computer memory devices by creating eight platinum wires 40 nm wide on a silicon wafer. Moor and Weckert note that it would take more than one thousand of these chips to be the width of a human hair.

As noted earlier, our main objective in Section 12.4 is to identify and analyze ethical aspects of nanocomputing and nanotechnology. Before doing that, however, we first describe some predictions about the societal advantages and disadvantages that could result from continued nanotechnology development.

12.4.2 Optimistic *vs.* Pessimistic Views of Nanotechnology

Nanotechnology's optimists are quick to point out many of the advantages that would likely result from nano-level developments, especially for the medical field and for the environment in general. Those who worry about future developments in nanotechnology and nanocomputing, however, see things quite differently. Bert Gordijn (2003) describes the nanotechnology debate between the optimists and the pessimists as one that represents the views of "utopian dreams" vs. "apocalyptic nightmares," respectively. He uses "utopian" to refer to the seventeenth-century idea of being able to ideally control a natural environment in order to create a perfect society, i.e., one where life is prolonged, enhanced, and without pain and suffering.

The Optimistic View
For our purposes, the examples Gordijn cites for how nanotechnology could help bring about the utopian dream can be understood in terms of six categories, where "molecule by molecule manufacturing" would

1. be self-sufficient and "dirt-free,"
2. create unprecedented objects and materials,
3. enable the production of inexpensive high-quality products,

4. be used to fabricate food rather than having to grow it,

5. provide low-priced and superior equipment for healthcare,

6. enable us to enhance our human capabilities and properties.[18]

First, Gordijn notes that optimists believe that molecular manufacturing would be "dirt free" because molecular manufacturing techniques would not result in any chemical pollution. Also, because unwanted chemicals could be detected and inactivated, existing environmental degradation could be reversed by nanomachines (or *nanites*) that could be used to clean up toxic spills, as well as to eliminate other kinds of environmental hazards. Second, nanotechnology could create unprecedented objects and materials such as strong, lightweight materials that would enable easier access to (outer) space and space resources. Third, molecular manufacturing would enable the production of inexpensive, high-quality products. For example, nanotechnology's advocates point to the production of items that include dramatically inexpensive storage batteries, processors, personal computers, electronic devices, cell phones, and so forth.

Fourth, molecular manufacturing could be used to "fabricate food" (i.e., what some call "nanofood") rather than having to grow it; for example, nanotechnology's proponents point out that food is simply a combination of molecules in certain configurations. Hence, the problem of hunger could be effectively solved by efficient molecule-by-molecule mass production of food. Additionally, nanomachines (or nanite assemblers) could dismantle or "disassemble" garbage at the molecular level and recycle it again at the molecular level.

Fifth, molecular manufacturing could provide low-priced and superior equipment for healthcare because "medical nanites" could be programmed to travel through our bloodstream to clean out fatty deposits, thereby reducing the probability of cardiovascular diseases. Also, nanoparticles inserted into bodies could diagnose diseases and directly treat diseased cells. Doctors could use nanites to make microscopic repairs on areas of the body that are difficult to operate on with conventional surgical tools (Weckert 2006). And with nanotechnology tools, the life signs of a patient could be better monitored. Additionally, preventive medicine could be greatly improved by having nanorobots within our bodies that could provide a defense against viruses. Sixth, and finally, molecular manufacturing would facilitate the enhancement of our human capabilities and properties, thereby enabling us to overcome contemporary diseases, pain, and other unpleasant bodily symptoms (Gordijn 2003).

So, if the optimists are correct, we have much to be excited about as developments in nanotechnology and nanocomputing proceed. However, Gordijn also describes some of the catastrophes or "apocalyptic nightmares" that nanotechnology's pessimists envision occurring if research and development in this area is allowed to continue.

The Pessimistic View

For our purposes, Gordijn's description of the arguments for the pessimistic view can once again be organized into six categories, where developments in molecular manufacturing could result in

1. severe economic disruption,

2. premeditated misuse in warfare and terrorism,

3. surveillance with nano-level tracking devices,

4. extensive environmental damage,

5. uncontrolled self-replication,

6. misuse by criminals and terrorists.[19]

First, Gordijn points out that some pessimists believe that rapid developments in molecular manufacturing could cause severe economic disruption that might result from the sudden abundance of low-priced products and rapidly changing employment problems. Second, molecular manufacturing could facilitate premeditated misuse in warfare and terrorism because nanite assemblers and disassemblers might be used to create weapons that could result in both (a) conventional weapons being constructed more rapidly, and (b) new weaponry being made in large numbers, becoming low-priced, and becoming extremely powerful. As Chen (2002) points out, guns, explosives, and electronic components of weapons could all be miniaturized. It is also possible that nanites themselves could be used as weapons.

Third, critics point out that infinitesimally small surveillance devices such as nanoscale tracking devices, sensors, nanocameras, and microphones could enable the observation and control of subjects in a way that is unprecedented. For example, governments, businesses, and ordinary people could use molecular-sized microphones, cameras, and homing beacons to track and monitor people. Weckert (2006) notes that people with microscopic implants would be able to be tracked using Global Positioning Systems (GPS), just as cars can be now.

Fourth, nanotechnology could potentially cause extensive environmental damage because destructive nanite assemblers might enter the food chain thereby disturbing entire ecological systems. Also, nanoparticles could escape into the air and turn out to pose asbestos-like health threats.

Fifth, critics worry about nanomachines having the capacity of self-replication. Consider that technical malfunctions could cause unbridled self-replication in which the total number of nanite assemblers would grow exponentially. Some critics also note that all matter (objects and organisms) could theoretically be disassembled and reassembled by these nanite assemblers and disassemblers, if strict "limiting mechanisms" are not built into them. In this case, self-replicating nanites could multiply endlessly like viruses. If the uncontrolled assemblers used a variety of raw materials as resources for self-replication, they could devour the entire biosphere in a very short time; this possibility is sometimes referred to as the *grey-goo scenario*.

Sixth, some pessimists worry that private companies, which are not subject to strict government regulation, might be motivated by profit incentives to try to develop and produce nanite assemblers as quickly as possible and sell them in the "black market." So there is the danger of these assemblers being acquired by criminals and terrorists who could use them for devious means, including the creation of weapons of mass destruction (Gordijn 2003). Some refer to this possibility as the *black-goo scenario*.

Consequently, nanotechnology's pessimists and critics present a variety of concerns that would seem to counter many of the enthusiastic predictions offered by optimists. Are the claims and predictions made by nanotechnology's optimists and pessimists plausible? Weckert (2006) believes that because many predictions about nanotechnology seem reasonable, it would be prudent for us to consider some of the ethical implications now while there is still time to anticipate them. Will a separate field of "nanoethics" be needed to analyze these implications?

12.4.3 Ethical Issues in Nanotechnology and Nanocomputing

Moor and Weckert (2004) believe that assessing ethical issues that arise at the nanoscale is important because of the kinds of "policy vacuums" (Moor 2001) that can arise. (Recall our discussion of Moor's notion of policy vacuums in Chapter 1.) Although Moor and Weckert do not explicitly argue that a separate field of applied ethics called *nanoethics* is necessary, they make a convincing case for why an analysis of ethical issues at the nano level is now critical. In particular, they identify three distinct kinds of ethical concerns that warrant analysis:

1. privacy and control
2. longevity
3. runaway nanobots

With respect to (1), the authors note that as we construct nanoscale information gathering systems, it will become extremely easy to put a nanoscale transmitter in a room or onto someone's clothing in such a way that he or she will have no idea that the device is present or that he or she is being monitored and tracked. Implanting tracking mechanisms within someone's body would also become easier with nanotech devices. Consider that a tracking mechanism might be put into someone's food so that, when swallowed, it would be absorbed into the body, possibly migrating to a desired location. Moor and Weckert further note that in addition to privacy threats made possible by nanotechnolgy, individuals may also lose some degree of control. Because other people could know more about each other, for example, we might be less capable of controlling the outcomes of our choices. How these tracking devices will be developed and used is still a matter of some speculation. But Moor and Weckert argue that with the advent of nanotechnology, invasions of privacy and unjustified control over others will most likely increase.

Regarding (2), ethical concerns involving longevity, Moor and Weckert argue that developments in nanotechnology could have a dramatic effect on human life spans in three ways.

> First, and least controversially, nanotechnology will almost certainly have medical benefits. Early diagnosis and new cures will have an effect on longevity. A more spectacular, but more distant possibility is the development of cell repair devices. If these are developed, it will be possible to reverse or prevent aging, so life spans could be increased enormously. A third way that nanotechnology might contribute to longevity is through the development, by growth or construction, of body parts to replace those worn out or otherwise damaged. Particularly significant could [be] the development of tissue that the body would not reject.[20]

While many see longevity as a good thing, there could be negative consequences as well. For one thing, Moor and Weckert note that there could be a population problem if the life expectancy of individuals were to change dramatically. The authors also point out that if fewer children are born relative to adults, there could be a concern about the lack of new ideas and "new blood." Additionally, questions could arise with regard to how many "family sets" couples, whose lives could be extended significantly, would be allowed to have during their expanded lifetime. Other questions might be conceptually confusing—e.g., would the (already) old stay older longer, and would the young remain young longer? So, in Moor and Weckert's analysis, longevity-related questions introduce some policy vacuums, as well as conceptual muddles, that will need to be resolved.

With regard to (3), Moor and Weckert argue that we need to consider the potential problem of "runaway nanobots." The authors note that when nanobots work to our benefit, they build what we desire. But when they work incorrectly, they build what we don't want. Moreover, the replication of these bots could get out of hand. As we saw earlier, the problem of runaway replication is often referred to as the "grey-goo scenario."

Some critics, including Smalley (2001), have challenged the possibility of replicators, because of the way these assemblers would have to be constructed. Drexler, however, responds to Smalley's challenges by noting that biological assemblers such as ribosomes already do the kind of assembly at the molecular level needed for nanobots. Many believe that as long as it may be possible to construct nano-level robots that are capable of self-assembly and replication, it would be prudent to try to anticipate ethical outcomes that could arise. Woodhouse (2004) notes that important choices about how to proceed with nanotechnology will have to be made before it is determined whose prediction—Drexler's or Smalley's—is correct.

Should Nano Research/Development Continue?

While we have examined some ethical concerns associated with potential developments at the nano level, we have not yet directly addressed the implications that these developments can have for computer scientists and computing/IT professionals working on nano-level projects. In Chapter 4, we examined some ethical challenges that computing professionals face. However, we did not discuss any nanocomputing-specific issues there. Next, we identify some of those challenges.

We begin by noting that Joseph Weizenbaum (1985) argued that there are certain kinds of computer science research that should not be undertaken—specifically, research that can easily be seen to have "irreversible and not entirely unforeseeable side effects." Weizenbaum did not refer to nanotechnology research per se; however, Bill Joy (2000) has since suggested that because developments in nanocomputing threaten to make us an "endangered species," the only realistic alternative is to limit the development of that technology. Others, however, such as Ralph Merkle (2001) disagree with Joy. Merkle argues that if research in nanocomputing and nanotechnology is prohibited, or even restricted, it will be done underground. If that happens, Merkle worries that nano-technology research would not be regulated by governments and professional agencies concerned with social responsibility.

If Joy and others are correct about the dangers of nanotechnology, we must seriously consider whether research in this area should be limited and whether computer scientists should participate in developments in nanocomputing. However, major computing associations such as the ACM and IEEE have not taken a stance on questions involving the ethics of nanocomputing research and development. Should research in this area be sanctioned by professional computing associations? If not, should nanocomputing research continue? What kind of criteria should be used in establishing a coherent nanotechnology policy?

Initially, we might assume that because nanotechnology could be abused—e.g., used to invade privacy, produce weapons, etc.—nanocomputers should not be developed, or at least their development should not be sanctioned by professional computer associations. However, we would commit a logical fallacy (see the Slippery Slope Fallacy in Chapter 3) if we used the following kind of reasoning: Because some technology, X, could be abused, or because using Technology X could result in unintended tragedies, X should not be allowed to be developed. Consider some examples of why this form of reasoning is fallacious. Automobiles and medical drugs can both be abused, and each can contribute to the number of unintended deaths in a given year, even when used appropriately. In the United States, more than 40,000 deaths result each year from automobile accidents. And medical drugs (designed to save lives) have also been abused by some individuals, which has resulted in many deaths each year. Should the development of automobiles have been banned? Should we stop research on medical drugs? It would be fallacious to conclude that we should ban the development of these products merely because they could be abused and because they will inevitably lead to unintended deaths.

Arguments for how best to proceed in scientific research when there are concerns about harm to the public good, especially harms affecting the environmental and health areas, are often examined in terms of a scheme known as the "precautionary principle." (Recall our brief discussion of this principle in Chapter 6, in connection with risk-analysis models.) We next examine that principle more fully in the context of nanotechnology.

Assessing Nanotechnology Risks: Applying the Precautionary Principle?

Clarke (2005) notes that many formulations of the *precautionary principle* have been used in the scientific community; so there is no one, universally agreed upon formulation of this important principle. According to Weckert and Moor (2004), however, the essence of the precautionary principle can be captured and expressed in the following way:

> If some action has a possibility of causing harm, then that action should not be undertaken or some measure should be put in its place to minimize or eliminate the potential harms.[21]

Weckert and Moor believe that when the precautionary principle is applied to questions about nanotechnology research and development, it needs to be analyzed in terms of three different categories of harm: "direct harm," "harm by misuse," and "harm by mistake or accident." With respect to direct harm, they analyze a scenario in which the use of nanoparticles in products could be damaging to the health of some people. Weckert and Moor note that the kinds of risks in this scenario are very different from those used in the example they select to illustrate harm by misuse—viz., that developments in nanoelectronics could endanger personal privacy. Here, it is neither the new technology nor the product itself that could cause the problem, but rather the way that the new technology/product is used. Weckert and Moor also note that in this scenario, preventing certain uses of the technology would avoid the problem, without stopping the development of nanotechnology itself.

Regarding the third category, harm by mistake or accident, Weckert and Moor describe a scenario in which nanotechnology could lead to the development of self-replicating, and thus "runaway," nanobots. The authors note that harm will occur in this scenario *only if* mistakes are made or accidents occur. But this kind of potential harm is very different from the kind that results from the development of products that will damage health or from technologies that can be deliberately misused. Whereas legislation can be enacted to stop inappropriate uses of a technology or to prevent the development of products known in advance to be harmful to one's health, it is more difficult to draft legislation that will control mistakes and accidents.

Weckert and Moor conclude that when assessing the risks of nanotechnology via the precautionary principle, we need to look at not only potential harms and benefits of nanotechnology per se, but also at the "relationship between the initial action and the potential harm." In their scenario involving direct harm, e.g., nanoparticles damaging health, the relationship is fairly clear and straightforward: we simply need to know more about the scientific evidence for nanoparticles causing harm. But in their scenario involving potential misuse of nanotechnology, e.g., in endangering personal privacy, the relationship is less clear. Here, we need scientific evidence that certain kinds of devices can be developed, and we need evidence about whether effective legislation could be implemented to control the uses of the devices. In their third scenario, we need evidence regarding the propensity of humans to make mistakes or the propensity of accidents to happen.

So, given the risks and potential harms that could result from future developments in nanotechnology, how should research in that field in general, and nanocomputing in particular, proceed? Weckert (2006) believes that, all things being equal, *potential* disadvantages that can result from research in a particular field are not in themselves sufficient grounds for halting research altogether. Rather, he suggests that there should be a "presumption in favor of freedom in research" until it can be clearly shown that the research is, in fact, dangerous. However, once a reasonable (or what he calls a "prima facie") case can be made to show that the research is dangerous, the burden for showing that the research is safe (and that it should continue) would shift from those who oppose the research to those who support it. In Weckert's view, then, it would be permissible to restrict or even forbid research in a field where it can be clearly shown that significant harm is more likely than not to result from that research.[22]

Using Weckert's model, it would seem that since there are no compelling grounds (at present) for halting nanocomputing research, we should proceed with it. Of course, we would need to reassess our default presumption in favor of nanocomputing research, if evidence in the future were to suggest that such research posed a serious threat to our safety. We elaborate on this important point in Section 12.6, where we examine a "dynamic" model of ethics that takes into account the need to update factual data as it becomes available, as part of the ongoing process of ethical evaluation. Next, however, we consider some ethical aspects of a different kind of emerging technology: autonomous machines.

▶ 12.5 AUTONOMOUS MACHINES AND MACHINE ETHICS

In the preceding sections, we examined ethical aspects of three relatively recent technologies that have emerged as a result of converging technological components: ambient intelligence, bioinformatics, and nanocomputing. We next consider an emerging technology that has been made possible, in large part, by recent developments in AI and robotics—viz., *autonomous machines*. Moral, legal, and social concerns involving autonomous machines comprise a relatively new subfield of cyberethics called "machine ethics." A core question in this (sub)field is whether it is possible to develop "moral machines." We consider that question in Section 12.5.3. First, however, we define some key terms and draw some important conceptual distinctions regarding the various technologies comprising autonomous machines. Our rationale for doing this is to avoid the potential confusion that can easily arise in the absence of a standard or commonly-agreed upon vocabulary in the relatively new field of machine ethics. We will see that some confusion surrounding the inconsistent, and at times ambiguous, use of terms to describe the cluster of autonomous technologies examined in this emerging field can be eliminated by organizing these technologies under a single category "autonomous machines."

12.5.1 What is an Autonomous Machine (AM)?

For our purposes, an *autonomous machine* (AM) is any computerized system/agent/robot that is capable of acting and making decisions independently of human oversight. An AM can also interact with and adapt to (changes in) its environment and can learn (as it functions).[23] We use the expression "autonomous machine" in a broad sense to include three conceptually distinct, but sometimes overlapping, autonomous technologies: artificial agents, autonomous systems, and robots. The key attribute that links or brings together these otherwise distinct (software) programs, systems, and entities is their ability to act *autonomously*, or at least act independently of human intervention.

Increasingly, the ethical concerns generated by the autonomous technologies that comprise AMs are examined as issues in "machine ethics" (Allen, Wendell, and Smit 2006; Anderson and Anderson 2011; and Moor 2006b). However, others use the expression "robo-ethics" (Veruggio 2006; Decker and Gutmann 2012), or "robot ethics" (Capurro and Nagenborg 2009; Lin, Abney, and Bekey 2012) to describe the field that addresses these issues. Wallach and Allen (2009) note that other authors have also used expressions such as "agent ethics" and "bot ethics."[24] However, we use "machine ethics" to include the wide range of ethical issues that arise in the context of AMs. And, as already noted, we use "autonomous machines" to refer to the cluster of autonomous technologies that generate those ethical issues.[25]

Autonomous *Machines* vs. Autonomous *Robots, Agents,* and *Systems*

Why use "autonomous machines" rather than "robots," "autonomous artificial agents," or "autonomous systems" to describe the autonomous technologies described in this section? For our purposes, there are two reasons why the phrase "autonomous machine" is more appropriate than "robot." First, not all robots are autonomous, and thus capable of acting independently of humans. John Sullins (2011) distinguishes between "tele robots," which are controlled remotely by humans (and function mainly as tools), and "autonomous robots" that can make "major decisions about their actions using their own program." Second, the term "robot" can be ambiguous, because "soft" bots (such as AI programs) are also sometimes included under the general category of robot. To avoid this ambiguity, Wallach and Allen use the expression "(ro)bot." However, our notion of "autonomous machine" is sufficiently robust to capture both the breadth of Wallach and Allen's "(ro)bot" and the precision needed to exclude Sullin's category of (non-autonomous) tele-robots.

The expression "autonomous machine" also has an advantage over the phrase "autonomous artificial agent." For one thing, "machine" can be a less philosophically controversial category than "agent" or "artificial agent" (AA); for another, "machine" is a sufficiently broad category to subsume under it certain kinds of entities, systems, etc. that may not fall neatly into the categories of agent and AA. Also, distinctions between a single AA and multiple AAs, such as "multi-agent systems," can be problematic from the philosophical perspective of agency. However, our category of "autonomous machines" can be understood to subsume both individual AAs and collections of AAs, including multi-agent systems.

Third, and finally, "autonomous machine" also has an important advantage over "autonomous system." One problem with the latter expression is that it is ambiguous and can easily be used equivocally to refer to two very different kinds of technologies. On the one hand, an autonomous system (AS), in the context of the Internet, refers to a collection of internet protocol (IP) routers or "routing prefixes" that are "under the control of one or more network operators"–in this case, an AS can be either a network or set of networks that is "controlled by a common network administrator."[26] On the other hand, "autonomous system" is also used to describe a computerized system that, like an AM, can operate without human intervention, adapt to its environment, learn (as it functions), and make decisions.[27] So, we use the expression "autonomous machine" to avoid the potential equivocation that can easily arise in discussions involving ASs, given the two common uses of "autonomous system." For our purposes, the phrase "autonomous machines" both (a) captures the second sense of "autonomous system," as described in the Royal Academy of Engineering's report, and (b) eliminates any ambiguity or equivocation that can arise because of the first sense of AS (i.e., in connection with Internet router policies).

Of course, it is possible that some might object to our use of "machine" because that concept usually connotes something physical, as in the case of computer hardware. In this sense, "machine" might be interpreted in a way that would exclude software (programs and applications). So a more precise, and perhaps also more expanded, definition of what is meant by a *machine* is needed in the case of our category of AMs. Even though we tend to think of machines primarily as physical devices consisting of fixed and movable parts, a machine can also be understood as a "natural system or organism." It can also refer to a group of individuals that are under the control of a leader, such as in the case of a "political machine."[28] So, "machine" can be used in both a physical and a non-physical sense. While robots clearly fit within the former sense of "machine," the term's latter sense can include AI (soft)bots, AAs, and ASs that are nonphysical. Thus, an AM, as we use the phrase, includes both senses of "machine."

J. Storrs Hall (2011) argues that the most important "machine" of the 20th century was not a physical entity at all; rather, it was a "Turing Machine," which he describes as a "theoretical concept of a pattern of operations that could be implemented in a number of ways." Hall also notes that a Turing Machine can be viewed as a "mathematical idea" that provided the "theoretical basis for a computer." It can also be viewed as a kind of "virtual machine"; in this scheme, any program running on a computer is also a virtual machine. But Hall believes that we can eliminate the "virtual" in these kinds of machines and refer to computer programs themselves simply as "machines." He argues that the essence of a machine is "its behavior"—i.e., "what it does given what it senses."[29] In this sense, AMs can also be viewed as machines (and not merely as virtual machines).

Finally, we should note that because AMs have been made possible by developments in AI, "intelligence" is an essential feature or property of AMs. In fact, this feature can also help us to distinguish AMs from what we might think of as ordinary or conventional machines, including some physical devices that are fairly sophisticated. However, it is also important to note that not every "intelligent machine" is necessarily autonomous. We examine some key criteria that (intelligent) machines must satisfy to act "autonomously" in our analysis of the concept of autonomy in Section 12.5.2. First, however, we identify some typical examples of AMs.

Some Examples and Applications of AMs

A highly influential report (on autonomous systems) by the UK's Royal Academy of Engineering (2009) identifies various kinds of devices, entities, and systems that also fit nicely under our category of AM. These include:

- driverless transport systems (in commerce);
- unmanned vehicles in military/defense applications (e.g., "drones");
- robots on the battlefield;
- autonomous robotic surgery devices;
- personal care support systems.

Another example identified in that report is a "smart environment," such as a "smart" building/home/apartment. (Recall the scenario involving a "smart home" that we considered in Section 12.2 in our discussion of AmI; that technology also qualifies as a kind of AM.) Other examples of AMs include driverless trains that shuttle passengers between terminals in large airports, as well as robotic companions/care givers that assist the elderly and robotic babysitters (which are popular in Japan) that entertain young children.

A diverse cluster of AMs now function in multiple sectors of our society. Consider, for example, the many different kinds of robots and robotic systems that have become available in recent years. Patrick Lin (2012) identifies a range of sectors in which robots (and, in our case, AMs) now operate. Six of these include:

- Labor and Service,
- Military and Security,
- Research and Education,
- Entertainment,
- Medical and Healthcare,
- Personal Care and Companionship.[30]

Lin points out that an example of an AM used for (1) would be the Roomba vacuum cleaner, and he notes that nearly half of the 7 million-plus service robots in the world are Roombas. We should point out that while Roombas may appear to act autonomously because of their sensing abilities, they are still also under human control. However, the Roomba, which is probably better viewed as a kind of *semi*-autonomous machine, can still be viewed as a major advancement over earlier industrial robots that operated in automobile factories and assembly lines.

Examples of AMs used in (2) would include the U.S. military's Predator and Big Dog, whereas an instance of an AM used in (3) is NASA's Mars Exploration Rover. Lin identifies ASIMO (Advanced Step in Innovative Mobility), a humanoid robot designed by Honda, as an example of an AM that can be used in (4), and he describes some robotic nurses (including RIBA) and robotic pharmacists (such as ERNIE) as examples of AMs used in (5). He notes that AMs used in (6) would include CareBot and PALRO, and also notes that this category or robots might be extended to include some recently introduced "sex bots" such as Roxxxy.

Despite the many conveniences and services that AMs provide, these machines raise some ethical concerns (as we have already noted). One such concern involves threats to personal privacy. Consider that some kinds of AMs allow for detailed recording of personal information; for example, people who live in "smart apartments" could have vast amounts of personal information about them recorded and kept by a third party. The privacy concerns that arise here are very similar to the kinds of AmI-centered privacy issues we examined in Section 12.2.4. Because AM-related privacy concerns overlap with those involving AmI, we will not examine any AM-specific privacy issues in this section. Instead we will focus on three very different kinds of ethical/philosophical concerns affecting AMs: (moral) agency, autonomy, and trust.

12.5.2 Some Ethical and Philosophical Questions Involving AMs

Some ethical issues associated with AMs also cut across traditional cyberethics categories such as property, privacy, security, and so forth. For example, we have already noted that privacy concerns can arise in connection with specific kinds of AMs (such as "smart homes"). Another cluster of ethical concerns involve moral- and professional-responsibility-issues associated with designing AMs. We briefly examine some of those concerns in Section 12.5.3. However, some questions that arise in connection with AMs are not only ethical in nature but are also more broadly philosophical (e.g., metaphysical or epistemological). These include questions about agency (and moral agency), in connection with concerns about whether AMs can be held responsible and blameworthy in some sense, as well as questions about autonomy and trust. We begin by asking in which sense(s) an AM can be viewed as an agent, or artificial agent, before considering the more controversial question of whether an AM can qualify as a moral agent.

AMs, Agents, and Moral Agents?

As already noted, the concepts of "agency" and "agent" can be philosophically controversial. For our purposes, however, we can stipulate a definition of *agent* as someone or something that is capable of acting. So, each of us, in so far as we can act, qualifies as an agent; other entities—both humans and non-humans—who act on our behalf also qualify as agents (and are sometimes referred to as "fiduciary agents"). We refer to all non-human agents as AAs. In our scheme, even a thermostat can satisfy the conditions for being an AA. Today, AI researchers typically refer to artificial entities—whether software programs (in the form of "bots") or full-fledged robots—as AAs.

Because AMs are capable of acting, they also qualify as AAs. But unlike low-level AAs such as thermostats, AMs can act in ways that have a moral impact. So it might seem reasonable to ask whether we can hold AMs morally accountable for their actions. Initially, this might seem like a bizarre question. However, one concern raised in the Royal Academy's influential report on autonomous systems (2009) is whether systems like AMs should be regarded as "robotic people," as opposed to mere machines. This question is important because if AMs qualify as "people" of some sort, they could also be subject to (moral) blame for faults that occur, as well as for legal liability in cases involving either the deaths of humans or severe economic losses. Although it might seem odd to talk about AMs as "people," robotic or otherwise, we have seen that they do qualify as agents—viz., AAs. But can AMs also satisfy the additional conditions that are required for being *moral agents*?

Luciano Floridi (2011) believes that AMs, or what he calls autonomous AAs, can be moral agents because they are (a) "sources of moral action" and (b) can cause moral harm or moral good. In Chapter 11, we saw that Floridi distinguished between "moral patients" (as receivers of moral action) and moral agents (as sources of moral action). There we also noted that all information entities, in Floridi's view, deserved consideration (minimally) as moral patients, even if they were not moral agents. But, additionally, Floridi believes that autonomous AAs also qualify as moral agents because of their (moral) efficacy. Deborah Johnson (2006) also believes that AAs have moral efficacy, but she argues that they qualify only as "moral entities" and not moral agents because AAs lack freedom. And others, including Kenneth Himma (2009) argue that because these entities also lack consciousness and intentionality, they cannot satisfy the conditions for moral agency.

James Moor (2006b) takes a different tack in analyzing this controversial question by focusing on various kinds of "moral impacts" that AAs can have. Moor begins by noting that computers can be viewed as normative (nonmoral) agents, independent of whether they are also moral agents, because of the normative impacts their actions have. He points out that computers are designed for specific purposes and thus can be evaluated in terms of how good or how bad they perform in accomplishing the tasks they are programmed to carry out (as in the case of a program designed to play chess, for example). Moor then notes that some normative impacts made possible by computers can also be moral or ethical in nature, and he argues that the consequences, and potential consequences, of what he calls "ethical agents" can be analyzed in terms of four levels:

- Ethical Impact Agents,
- Implicit Ethical Agents,
- Explicit Ethical Agents,
- Full Ethical Agents.

Moor notes that whereas ethical-impact-agents (i.e., the weakest sense of moral agent) will have ethical consequences to their acts, implicit-ethical-agents have some ethical considerations built into their design and "will employ some automatic ethical actions for fixed situations." And while explicit-ethical-agents will have, or at least act as if they have, "more general principles or rules of ethical conduct that are adjusted and interpreted to fit various kinds of situations," full-ethical agents "can make ethical judgments about a wide variety of situations" and in many cases can "provide some justification for them."

Providing some examples of each, Moor notes that a "robotic camel jockey" (a technology used in Qatar to replace young boys as jockeys, and thus freeing those boys from slavery in the human trafficking business) is an instance of an ethical-impact agent. An airplane's automatic pilot system and an ATM (automatic teller machine) are both examples of an implicit ethical agent, since they have built-in programming designed to prevent harm from happening to the aircraft in one case, and (in the other case) to prevent ATM customers from being short-changed in financial transactions. Explicit ethical agents, on the other hand, would be able to calculate the best ethical action to take in a specific situation and would be able to make decisions when presented with ethical dilemmas. In Moor's scheme, full-ethical agents have the kind of ethical features that we usually attribute to ethical agents like us (i.e., what Moor describes as "normal human adults"), including consciousness and free will.

Moor does not claim that either explicit- or full-ethical agents exist or that they will be available anytime in the near term. However, his distinctions are very helpful, as we try to understand various levels of moral agency that potentially affect AMs. Even if AMs may never qualify as full moral agents, Wallach and Allen (2009) believe that they can have "functional morality," based on two key criteria or dimensions: (i) autonomy and (ii) sensitivity to ethical values. However, Wallach and Allen also note that we do not yet have systems with both high autonomy and high sensitivity. They point out that an autopilot is an example of a system that has significant autonomy (in a limited domain) but little sensitivity to ethical values. On the contrary, they note that while ethical-decision support systems (such as those used in the medical field to assist doctors) provide decision makers with access to morally relevant information, and thus suggest high sensitivity to moral values, they have virtually no autonomy.

Wallach and Allen also argue that it is not necessary that AAs be moral agents in the sense that humans are. They believe that all we need to do is to design machines to act "as if" they are moral agents and thus "function" as such. We return to this point, as well as to the concept of functional morality, in Section 12.5.3. First, however, we ask if it makes sense to ascribe any level of morality, functional or otherwise, to AMs if those systems are not capable of being genuinely autonomous. While Wallach and Allen note that autonomy is one of two key criteria in their framework of functional morality, they do not elaborate on the sense(s) in which an AA can be said to be autonomous. We next examine the concept of autonomy to see whether an AM can indeed be autonomous.

Autonomy and "Functional Autonomy" in the Context of AMs

We briefly mentioned the concept of autonomy in Section 12.2.4 in our analysis of ethical concerns affecting AmI. There, we asked whether humans would need to surrender some of their individual autonomy if they delegate certain kinds of tasks to computer systems. Some critics suggest that they might, especially if those computer systems are "autonomous." For example, Wha-Chul Son (2005) notes that autonomous technologies can undermine "human autonomy" in ways that are both "subtle and indirect." Allen, Wallach, and Smit (2006), on the contrary, suggest that we need not worry about perceived threats to human autonomy because autonomous machines will not necessarily "undermine our basic humanity." To evaluate these claims, however, we need a clear definition of *autonomy*.

Many philosophers associate autonomy with concepts such as liberty, dignity, and individuality.[31] Others, however, link autonomy to "independence." For example, Onora O'Neill (2002) defines autonomy as a "capacity or trait that individuals manifest by acting independently." While it is difficult to ascribe characteristics such as liberty and dignity to AMs, we have seen that these machines do appear to be capable of "acting independently." So, if we can show that AMs can indeed act independently, it would seem plausible to describe AMs as entities that are also autonomous in some sense.

We should note that some influential definitions of autonomous systems and autonomous AAs link an artificial entity's ability to "adapt" to its environment with an ability to act "independently." For example, the Royal Academy's 2009 report seems to suggest that because autonomous systems are "adaptive," they also exhibit some degree of "independence." And Floridi (2008) makes a similar point, noting that an "adaptive" AA—i.e., one that can change its (internal) state dynamically, i.e., without any external stimuli—has a certain degree of *independence from its environment*."[32]

Perhaps, then, AMs can satisfy O'Neill's requirement for autonomy by virtue of their capacity to act independently.

In so far as AMs appear to be capable of acting independently, or behave "as if" they are acting independently, it would seem that we could attribute at least some degree of autonomy to them. Whether AMs will ever be capable of having full autonomy, in the sense that humans can, is debatable, and that question will not be examined here since it is beyond the scope of this chapter. However, an AM that can act independently in the sense described above can have "functional autonomy" and thus can qualify as a "functionally autonomous AM." We will next see that AMs must have some level of autonomy, even if only in a functional sense, if they are capable of being trusted by—i.e., being in a trust relationship with—humans.

Trust and Authenticity in the Context of AMs

What does a relationship of trust involving humans and AMs entail? Lim, Stocker, and Larkin (2008) describe the possibility of a mutual or reciprocal trust relationship involving both (a) "Man to Machine" and (b) "Machine to Man." However, we limit our discussion to (a), and we ask two basic questions: (i) What would it mean for a human to *trust* an AM? (ii) Why is that question important? The significance of (ii) is highlighted in the Royal Academy of Engineering's report (2009), which asks whether we can trust AMs to always act in our best interests, especially AMs designed in such a way that they cannot be shut down by human operators. To answer (i), however, we first need to clarify what is meant by the concept of trust in general—i.e., the kind of trust that applies in relationships between humans.

Carolyn McLeod (2011) points out that trust, in human relationships, is both "important but dangerous." It is important because it enables us "to form relationships with others and to depend on them." But it is also dangerous, McLeod notes, because it involves risk. Since trusting someone "requires that we can be vulnerable to others (vulnerable to betrayal)," the trustor (in the trust relationship) must be willing to accept some level of risk. In the case of AMs, we may be required to extend the level of risk beyond what we typically find acceptable for trust in human relationships. Before addressing that concern, however, it would be useful to establish what, exactly, is required for a normal trust relationship between humans.

A typical dictionary, such as the *American Heritage College Dictionary* (4th ed. 2002), defines trust as "firm reliance on the integrity, ability, or character of a person or thing." Definitions of trust that focus mainly on *reliance*, however, do not always help us to understand the nature of ethical trust. For example, I *rely* on my automobile engine to start today but I do not "trust" it to do so. Conversely, I trust my daughter implicitly, but I cannot always rely on her to organize her important papers.[33] Thus, trust and reliance are not equivalent notions; while reliance may be a necessary condition for trust, something more is needed for ethical trust.

Because I am unable to have a trust relationship with a conventional machine such as an automobile, does it follow that I also cannot have one with an AM? Or does an AM's ability to exhibit some level of autonomy—even if only functional autonomy—make a difference? Consider that I am able to trust a human because the person in whom I place my trust not only can disappoint me (or let me down) but can also betray me—e.g., that person, as a fully autonomous (human) agent, can freely elect to breach the trust I have placed in her. So it would seem that an entity's having at least some sense of autonomy is required for it to be capable of breaching the trust that someone has placed in it. In this sense, my automobile cannot breach my trust or betray me, even though I may be very disappointed if it fails to start today. Although my automobile does not have autonomy, we have seen that an AM has (functional) autonomy and thus might seem capable of satisfying the conditions required for a trust relationship. But even if an AM has (some level of) autonomy, and even if having autonomy is a necessary condition for being in a trust relationship, it does not follow that it is a sufficient condition. So, we can further ask whether any additional requirements may also need to be satisfied.

Some philosophers argue that trust has an emotive (or "affective") aspect, and that this may be especially important in understanding trust in the context of AMs. For example, Mark Coeckelbergh (2010) argues that if we want to build moral AMs (capable of trust), we will have to build them *"with emotions."*[34] Elsewhere, Coeckelbergh (2012) argues that for a trust relationship to be established between humans and machines, "appearance" (including the appearance of having emotions) is also very important. And because AMs may need to *appear* as if they have human-like properties, such as emotions, in order to be trusted by humans, we may be inclined to develop future AMs along these lines. Coeckelberg and others seem to suggest that we should.

Sherry Turkle (2011) raises some concerns involving emotions or feelings in the context of human–machine trust relationships, and she worries about what can happen when machines appear "as if" they have feelings. She describes a phenomenon called the "Eliza effect," which was initially associated with a response that some users had to an interactive software program called "Eliza" (designed by Joseph Weizenbaum at MIT in the 1960s). Turkle notes that this program, which was an early foray into machine learning programs designed to use language conversationally (and possibly pass the Turing test), solicited trust on the part of users. Eliza did this, Turkle points out, even though it was designed in a way that tricks users. Although Eliza was only a ("disembodied") software program, Turkle suggests that it could nevertheless be viewed as a "relational entity," or what she calls a "relational artifact," because of the way people responded to, and confided in, it. In this sense, Eliza seemed to have a strong emotional impact on some of the students who interacted with it. Turkle also notes that while Eliza "elicited trust" on the part of these students, it understood nothing about them.

Turkle worries that when a machine (as a relational artifact) appears to be interested in people, it can "push our Darwinian buttons . . . which causes people to respond *as if* they were in a relationship."[35] This is especially apparent in the case of physical AMs that are capable of facial expressions, such as Kismet (developed in MIT's AI Lab). Turkle suggests that because AMs can be designed in ways that make people feel as if a machine cares about them (as in the case of Paro, a companion robot designed to comfort the elderly), people can develop feelings of trust in, and attachment to, that machine. For example, she notes that Cynthia Breazeal, one of Kismet's designers who had also developed a "maternal connection" with this AM while she was a student at MIT, had a difficult time separating from Kismet when she left that institution. In Turkle's view, this factor raises questions of both trust *and* authenticity, and Turkle worries that, unlike in the past, humans must now be able to distinguish between authentic and simulated relationships. While this connection between trust and authenticity/attachment opens up a new and provocative line of inquiry, and while it will be interesting to see how this connection eventually plays out in the context of trust and AMs, a further discussion of this topic would take us beyond the scope of Chapter 12.

In concluding this section, we note that many questions about trust vis-à-vis AMs have been left either unanswered or unexamined. Readers who are interested in learning more about this topic can consult the expanding literature on trust and e-trust in connection with artificial agents/entities.[36] Next, we ask how critical it is for humans to have a trust relationship with AMs as we pursue the goal of developing "moral machines." In other words, if we cannot trust AMs, should we build machines capable of making decisions that have significant moral impacts? And if not, do we need to reassess one of the core objectives of machine ethics?

12.5.3 Machine Ethics and Moral Machines

The ethical issues examined in earlier chapters of this book arose mainly because of what we, as humans, do with computers and cybertechnology. In Section 12.5.2, we considered some AM-specific ethical concerns that arise because of what AMs are now capable of doing on their own. Analyzing the moral impacts of what AMs are capable of doing by themselves is a principal focus of machine ethics. To appreciate some of the other concerns and objectives of this relatively new field, however, we need a more comprehensive understanding of machine ethics.

What is Machine Ethics?

Michael Anderson and Susan Leigh Anderson (2011) describe machine ethics as an interdisciplinary field of research that is primarily concerned with developing ethics for machines, as opposed to developing ethics for humans who "use machines." In their view, machine ethics is concerned with

> giving machines ethical principles, or a procedure for discovering ways to resolve ethical dilemmas they may encounter, enabling them to function in an ethically responsible manner through their own decision making.[37]

Susan Anderson (2011) points out that a central question in machine ethics is whether ethics is, or can be made, computable. She believes that it is, and also suggests that it may be "prudent to begin to make ethics computable by first creating a program that acts as an ethical advisor to humans before attempting to build a full-fledged moral machine." We return to Anderson's suggestion at a later point in this section, in our discussion of how a prototype of a moral machine might initially function as an "ethical advisor" in a "dialogue" with humans.

Anderson draws some useful distinctions with regard to various levels at which machines could be designed to behave ethically. For our purposes, these can be organized into three levels, where a designer could:

a. build "limitations" into a machine that would prevent it from causing moral harm,

b. embed an AM with instructions that would require it to behave in a particular way—i.e., "according to an ideal ethical principle or principles that are *followed by the human designer*,"

c. embed an AM with "(an) ideal ethical principle(s) . . . and a learning procedure from which it can abstract (an) ideal ethical principle(s) in guiding its own actions."[38]

Whereas (a) represents the simplest design for ensuring that a machine behaves ethically, such a machine would seem capable of being only an "ethical impact agent" in James Moor's framework (described in Section 12.5.2). But a machine conforming to (b), on the other hand, would seem to qualify as an example of Moor's "implicit ethical agent." Anderson believes that machines built along the lines of (c) could conform to Moor's notion of "explicit ethical agent." She also believes that accomplishing (c) is the "ultimate goal" of machine ethics. In this case, an AM would be able not only to behave ethically but also be able to "justify its behavior" by expressing in "understandable language" the "intuitively acceptable ethical principle(s) that it has used to calculate its behavior."[39]

Wallach and Allen (2009) believe that one way in which the field of machine ethics has expanded upon traditional computer ethics is by asking *how* computers can be made into "explicit moral reasoners." In answering this question, Wallach and Allen first draw an important distinction between "reasoning about ethics" and "ethical decision making." For example, they acknowledge that even if one could build artificial systems capable of reasoning about ethics, it does not necessarily follow that these systems would be genuine "ethical decision makers." However, their main interest in how AMs can be made into moral reasoners is more practical than theoretical in nature, and they believe that the challenge of figuring out how to provide software/hardware agents with moral decision-making capabilities is urgent; in fact, they argue that the time to begin work on designing "moral machines" is now!

Designing Moral Machines

Can/should we build the kinds of moral machines that Wallach, Allen, and others urge us to develop? First, we can ask what is meant by the expression "*moral* machine." For example, are there "immoral machines"? Or, are all machines simply amoral or nonmoral, as many people tend to assume? The kind of moral machines that Wallach and Allen have in mind are AMs that are capable of both (a) making moral decisions and (b) acting in ways that "humans generally consider to be ethically acceptable behavior." We should note that the idea of designing machines that could behave morally, i.e., with a set of moral rules embedded in them, is not entirely new. In the 1940s, science fiction writer Isaac Asimov anticipated the need for ethical rules that would guide the robots of the future when he formulated his (now-classic) Three Laws of Robots:

1. A robot may not injure a human being, or through inaction, allow a human being to come to harm.

2. A robot must obey orders given it by human beings except where such orders would conflict with the First Law.

3. A robot must protect its own existence as long as such protection does not conflict with the First or Second Law.[40]

Numerous critics have questioned whether the three laws articulated by Asimov are adequate to meet the kinds of ethical challenges that current AMs pose. But relatively few of these critics have proposed clear and practical guidelines for how to embed machines with ethical instructions that would be generally acceptable to most humans. Susan and Michael Anderson (2011) and Wallach and Allen have each put forth some very thoughtful proposals for how this can be done. First, we consider Wallach and Allen's framework.

In describing how we can begin to build moral machines, Wallach and Allen point out that they are not interested in questions about developing a machine that is merely "instrumentally good." For example, a machine may be considered instrumentally good if it performs its tasks well. (Recall James Moor's distinction about computers as normative (nonmoral) agents vs. moral agents, which we examined in Section 12.5.2.) Wallach and Allen are concerned with building moral machines, or what they also refer to as artificial moral agents (AMAs), that behave in ways that humans generally consider to be *morally good*. They point out, for example, that while Deep Blue is a good chess-playing system because it does well at chess (i.e., defeating the best human chess players), it cannot be viewed as a "good AMA" because it is not required to make the kinds of decisions that have moral import.

Wallach and Allen argue that a *good AMA* "can detect the possibility of human harm or neglect of duty, and can take steps to avoid or minimize the undesirable outcomes." But how, exactly, would such an AMA be designed? For example, which kinds of ethical-reasoning procedures should we build into these systems—i.e., should they be embedded with principles that favor utilitarian-like reasoning or deontology-like reasoning, or perhaps some combination of the two? Also, could the principles of virtue ethics be built into the software code embedded in these machines, if that were deemed to be essential or even desirable?

To appreciate the challenges involved in selecting the appropriate kind of ethical theory/reasoning to embed in AMs, Wallach and Allen consider how a computerized "driverless trolley" might react in the now classic scenario involving a "runaway trolley" (described in detail in Chapter 2), where the "driver" (i.e., the AM) has to make a split-second decision (or calculation). Should the AM throw a switch that will cause the trolley to change tracks and (intentionally) run over one person who is standing on that track? Or, should the AM do nothing, in which case the trolley will run over five people directly in its path? An AM designed to execute instructions compatible with utilitarian- or consequentialist-based reasoning would likely make a very different (moral) decision, or calculation, than one designed to execute code based on deontological reasoning.

Susan Anderson (2011) notes that the ethical theory of Act Utilitarianism (which, she believes, shows that ethics is indeed computable) is too "simplistic." She argues that this ethical theory, as well as theories based on absolute duties (e.g., in Kant's Categorical Imperative, described in Chapter 2), are not, in themselves at least, adequate to build into machines. Instead, she believes that an ethical theory similar to Ross's version of deontology (also described in Chapter 2), which provides the basis for what she calls a "prima-facie duty approach," is more desirable. A virtue of Ross' theory, you may recall, is that it shows why it is often necessary to deliberate and weigh between duties when two or more of them conflict. But Anderson notes that a significant problem with Ross' theory is that it does not provide a clear mechanism or procedure for determining which duty overrides another in many situations where conflicts arise. So, she supplements the prima-facie duty approach with a "decision principle" to resolve the conflicts that will inevitably arise. Anderson further argues that the kinds of "decision principles" needed to accomplish this "can be discovered by a machine"—i.e., a machine could use an "inductive logic program" to arrive at such a principle. For example, Anderson believes that the machine could "learn from generalizing correct answers in particular cases."

Earlier in this section, we briefly mentioned Anderson's suggestion that it would be prudent for us first to design an artificial system to function as an "ethical advisor" to humans before attempting to build a full-fledged moral machine. Along similar lines, Susan and Michael Anderson (2011) have recommended building artificial systems with which humans can have an "ethical dialogue" before we embed machines themselves with ethical reasoning algorithms that they could use in a fully independent manner. The Andersons have developed such a system—i.e., an "automated dialogue"—involving an ethicist and an artificial system that functions "more or less independently in a *particular domain*." They believe that this is an important first step in building moral machines because it enables the artificial system to learn both (a) the "ethically relevant features of the dilemmas it will encounter" (within that domain), and (b) the appropriate prima facie duties and decision principles it will need to resolve the dilemmas.[41]

Functional Morality and a "Moral Turing Test"

In Section 12.5.2, we asked whether AMs are capable, in principle, of being genuine moral agents. Recall our brief discussion of Wallach and Allen's notion of functional morality, which the authors contrast with mere "operational morality" as well as with full moral agency. Wallach and Allen argue that even if machines fail to achieve full-blown moral agency, they may exhibit varying degrees of functional morality. So, they leave open the question of whether AMs could ever be full moral agents. Perhaps a more basic question to consider, however, is whether we could ever conclusively determine that we had developed an AM that was a full moral agent. Allen, Varner, and Zinser (2000) consider how a "Turing-like" test, which they call a "Moral Turing Test" (MTT), could be applied in response to this question. Unlike the original Turing test (described in Chapter 11), the MTT shifts the focus in the human-machine interaction away from an emphasis on mere "conversational ability" to criteria involving questions about "action." In this case, an AM would be asked questions about how it would act in such-and-such a situation, as opposed to being evaluated in terms of how successfully it was able to converse with humans about topics involving moral principles and rules. However, Allen et al. reported that they still encountered several problems with this test as a procedure for conclusively establishing whether AMs could, in principle, qualify as full moral agents.

We have seen that Wallach and Allen seem far less concerned with questions about whether AMs can be full moral agents than with questions about how we can design AMs to act in ways that conform to our received notions of morally acceptable behavior. And Susan Anderson (2011) echoes this point when she notes that her primary concern also is with whether machines "can perform morally correct actions and can justify them if asked." We should note that Wallach and Allen also believe that questions about whether AMs can be full moral agents can actually distract from (what they consider to be) the more "important question about how to design systems to act appropriately in morally charged situations."[42]

Acknowledging that many important questions in machine ethics remain unresolved, we conclude this section by briefly identifying some reasons why continued work in machine ethics is important. James Moor (2006b) offers three such reasons: (i) ethics (itself) is important; (ii) future machines will likely have increased autonomy; and (iii) designing machines to behave ethically will help us better understand ethics. Moor's third point ties in nicely with Wallach and Allen's claim that developments in machine ethics could help us to better understand our own nature as moral reasoners. In fact, they believe that research and development in machine ethics can provide feedback for "humans' understanding of themselves as moral agents" and for our understanding of "the nature of ethical thinking itself."[43]

▶ 12.6 A "DYNAMIC" ETHICAL FRAMEWORK FOR GUIDING RESEARCH IN NEW AND EMERGING TECHNOLOGIES

We have considered a fairly wide range of ethical concerns affecting the new and emerging technologies examined in this chapter. Some of these ethical concerns directly impact the software engineers and computer professionals who design the technologies. But virtually everyone will be affected by these technologies in the near future; so all of us would benefit from clear policies and ethical guidelines that address research/development in new and emerging technologies. James Moor (2008) argues that because these technologies promise "dramatic change," it is no longer satisfactory to do "ethics as usual." He goes on to claim that we need to be better informed in our "ethical thinking" and more proactive in our "ethical action."

What kind of ethical framework will we need to address the specific challenges posed by new and emerging technologies? One requirement would seem that this framework be "proactive" in its approach to ethics, as Moor suggests. Perhaps, then, we could look to the ELSI (Ethical Legal Social Implications) model, described in Section 12.3.2 in our discussion of bioinformatics and computational genomics, for some guidance on how to construct a proactive ethical framework for other emerging technologies as well. We saw that before work was able to proceed on the Human Genome Project, the anticipated ethical, legal, and social implications first had to be identified and addressed. Recall some of the salient features of the original ELSI model—requirements that addressed concerns affecting privacy, confidentiality, fairness, etc.—were "built into" the scientific research methodology.

12.6.1 Is an ELSI-Like Model Adequate for New/Emerging Technologies?

Should the original ELSI model, or one similar to it, be used to guide the development of other new/emerging technologies as well? ELSI's proponents believe that it is an ideal model because it is, as we noted, "proactive." They point out that prior to the ELSI Program, ethics was typically "reactive" in the sense that it "followed scientific developments" rather than informing scientific research. As Moor and others note, ethics has had to play "catch up" in most scientific research areas because ethical guidelines were developed in response to cases where serious harm had already resulted. For these reasons, Ray Kurzweil (2005) believes that a proactive ethical framework is needed in nanotechnology research, and he has suggested that an ELSI-like model be developed to guide researchers working in that technological field. We saw that the Royal Academy of Engineering's influential report on autonomous systems (2009) has also suggested an ELSI-like framework be used to assess ethical, legal, and social issues that affect or will soon affect autonomous technologies now under development.

Although many see the ELSI model as a vast improvement over traditional frameworks, where ethics was mainly an "afterthought," you may recall that in Section 12.3.2 we identified a flaw in the original ELSI model used in genomics research. For example, we saw that the unanticipated use of data mining tools and related computational techniques, especially in connection with secondary uses of personal information, posed a serious challenge to ELSI's effectiveness in genetic/genomic research contexts. So, we suggested that the original ELSI model needed to be revised or modified.

The standard ELSI model employs a scheme that Moor and Weckert (2004) describe as an "ethics-first" framework. They believe that ethical frameworks of this kind have problems because they depend, in large part, on a "factual determination" of the specific harms and benefits in implementing the technology before an ethical assessment can be done. But the authors note that in the case of nanotechnology developments, for example, it is very difficult to know what the future will be in five or ten years, let alone twenty or more years. So if we adopt an ("ethics-first") ELSI-like model, it might seem appropriate to put a moratorium on research in an area of technology until we get all of the facts. However, Moor and Weckert point out that while a moratorium on future research would halt technology developments in a field, such as nanotechnology for example, it will not advance ethics in that technological area.

12.6.2 A "Dynamic Ethics" Model

Moor and Weckert also argue that turning back to what they call the "ethics-last model" is not desirable either. The authors note that once a technology is in place, much unnecessary harm may already have occurred. So, in Moor and Weckert's scheme, neither an ethics-first nor an ethics-last model is satisfactory for emerging technologies. In their view, ethics is something that needs to be done *continually* as a technology develops and as its "potential social consequences become better understood." The authors also point out that ethics is "dynamic" in the sense that the factual/descriptive component on which the normative analysis relies has to be continually updated.

As we debate whether to go forward with research and development in a particular new or emerging technology, we can see how neither an ethics-first nor an ethics-last model would be adequate. We can also agree with Moor and Weckert that it is necessary to establish a set of ethical criteria that can be continually updated as new factual information about that technology becomes available. This point needs to be specified in any viable ethical framework, as well as in any effective set of policy guidelines, that we implement.

Recall the comprehensive cyberethics framework that we articulated at the end of Chapter 1, which included three steps: (i) *identify* a controversial issue (*or* practice *or* technological feature) involving cybertechnology; (ii) *analyze* the ethical issue(s) involved by clarifying relevant concepts; and (iii) *deliberate* on the ethical issue(s) in terms of one or more standard ethical theories (e.g., utilitarianism, deontology, etc.). Building on Moor and Weckert's insights regarding ethical challenges posed by new and emerging technologies, we add a fourth component or step to that framework:

(iv) update the ethical analysis by continuing to

a. differentiate between the factual/descriptive and normative components of the new or emerging technology under consideration;

b. revise the policies affecting that technology as necessary, especially as the factual data or components change or as information about the potential social impacts becomes clearer.

As information about plans for the design and development of a new technology becomes available, we can loop back to (i) and proceed carefully through each step in the expanded ethical framework. This four-step framework can also be applied as new information about existing technologies and their features becomes available.

▶ 12.7 CHAPTER SUMMARY

In this chapter we examined a cluster of ethical and social challenges affecting emerging and converging technologies. In particular, we examined controversies involving three broad areas of technological convergence: AmI, bioinformatics, and nanocomputing. We saw that AmI environments, made possible by pervasive computing and ubiquitous communication, raised concerns for freedom and autonomy as well as for privacy and surveillance. We then examined some ways in which research in bioinformatics raised ethical concerns affecting privacy, informed consent, and intellectual property. Next, we speculated about ethical issues that may well arise because of developments in nano-technology and nanocomputing. We then considered some ethical challenges posed by the introduction of autonomous machines, and we considered whether it was possible to design "moral machines." Finally, we proposed a "dynamic" ethical framework that could both (a) guide researchers who develop new technologies and (b) inform those responsible for enacting laws and framing policies for the use of those technologies.

▶ REVIEW QUESTIONS

1. What is "technological convergence" in the context of cybertechnology?
2. Why do some converging technologies raise special ethical and social issues?
3. What is ambient intelligence (AmI)?
4. Describe key aspects of pervasive (or ubiquitous) computing. How is it different from conventional or traditional computing?
5. What is ubiquitous communication, and what kinds of controversies does it raise?
6. What is an intelligent user interface (IUI), and how are IUIs different from traditional user interfaces?
7. What implications does AmI have for concerns involving individual freedom and autonomy, as well as for privacy and security?
8. What implications does AmI have for *technological dependency*?
9. What implications does AmI have for privacy, surveillance, and the "panopticon"?
10. What is bioinformatics, and how is it different from computational genomics?
11. Identify three kinds of ethical issues associated with bioinformatics.

12. How does the practice of storing personal genetic data in privately owned computer databases raise issues affecting information ownership and property-rights?
13. What is the ELSI (ethical, legal, and social implications) research program?
14. What is the GINA? Is it adequate for protecting the privacy of personal genetic data stored in computer databases?
15. What is nanotechnology?
16. What are nanocomputers?
17. What kinds of ethical challenges do research in nanotechnology and nanocomputing pose?
18. What is *machine ethics*?
19. What is an *autonomous machine* (or AM)? List three examples of an AM.
20. What is an artificial agent (or AA)?
21. What is meant by "functional autonomy" in the contexts of AMs and AAs?
22. Identify some problems involving the notion of "trust" in the context of AMs.
23. What do Wallach and Allen mean by "moral machine"?
24. Describe the key elements in Moor and Weckert's "dynamic ethics framework."

► DISCUSSION QUESTIONS

25. As we proceed with cybertechnology research and development in the twenty-first century, continued technological convergence would seem to be inevitable. Many of us have benefited significantly from the conveniences made possible by this phenomenon so far—e.g., cell phones that take pictures, GPS technology in automobiles that guide motorists, etc. Yet, we have also noted some controversial implications that convergent technologies can have for individual freedom, autonomy, and privacy. Can you think of any other social and ethical concerns that could also arise because of converging technologies? Identify three to five additional concerns that you believe might also have some social and ethical implications.

26. Assess the arguments that we examined for and against continued research in nanotechnology. Given the potential advantages and disadvantages involved in research and development in this area, which side in this debate do you find to be more plausible? Do the criteria provided by John Weckert for when research in a particular area should and should not be allowed in scientific research offer us clear guidelines with respect to research and development in nanotechnology and nanocomputing? What kind of an ethical framework is needed to guide research and development in this field?

► ESSAY/PRESENTATION QUESTIONS

27. According to Bert Gordijn, what are some of the optimistic visions involving nanotechnology? What are some of the pessimistic predictions involving nanotechnology that Gordijn describes? Identify and briefly describe the three nanoethics issues examined by James Moor and John Weckert. Why do some critics, such as Bill Joy, question whether we should continue nanotechnology research? What is the Precautionary Principle, as applied to scientific research? Can it be successfully applied to concerns involving research in nanotechnology? Why does John Weckert believe that we should "presume in favor of freedom" in scientific research?

28. In their goal of designing "moral machines," Wendell Wallach and Colin Allen argue that we do not need to develop artificial moral agents that have full moral agency. We saw that they believe that machines need to have only *functional morality* to be able to accomplish their objective of building moral machines. What do Wallach and Allen mean by "functional morality" and how is it different from full moral agency? Do you agree with their claim that questions about whether AMs can be full moral agents actually distract from the larger goal of researchers in machine ethics who aim to build machines that are capable of "acting appropriately in morally charged situations?" Explain.

Scenarios for Analysis

1. Jack and Jill, two of your friends from high school, have been married for two years and have a one-year old daughter, named Sally. Jill always had a pet cat in her house when she was growing up, and she believes that interacting with her pets was a very important part of her childhood experience. Jack, on the contrary, never had a pet in his home. Additionally, Jack has allergies that are exacerbated when he is around most cats. But despite this, Jill firmly believes that having a pet cat for Sally to experience is important, and she has tried repeatedly to convince Jack that they should acquire one. Then, one day, Jack discovers that a brand new series of "artificial cats" are available and that they resemble natural cats to the point where very few people are actually capable of distinguishing between the two. In other words, the artificial cats look, behave, sound, and feel like natural cats. So Jack proposes the idea of purchasing an artificial cat, and he tries to convince Jill that having this "cat" will be sufficient for Sally to experience what it is like to have a pet cat in the house during her childhood. Based on what we saw in Sherry Turkle's analysis of questions involving emotions and "authenticity" in the context of relations with artificial entities (in Section 12.5.2), how do you believe that Jill should respond to Jack's proposal to acquire an artificial cat?

2. Your Aunt Elda, who is 89 years old and lives on her own in a small apartment, is in declining health. She is at the point where she will soon need full-time professional assistance/care, but she is unable to afford the cost of live-in help. Unfortunately, Aunt Elda has no immediate family members or relatives who are able to provide her with the kind of around-the-clock care she will need or to help with the financial expenses for professional care/assistance. However, a friend tells you about a robotic companion, ElderBot—designed to assist and serve as a companion to the elderly—that would be able to provide the kind of assistance your aunt will soon require. Fortunately, you have the money to purchase this robotic companion/care giver for your aunt. But you have some reservations about whether you can entrust your Aunt's care to this robot. Faced with the dilemma of either being able to do nothing to assist your aunt or providing her with an ElderBot, what would you do? As you deliberate, consider some of the concerns we discussed regarding trust and autonomous machines (in Section 12.5.2).

▶ ENDNOTES

1. Rheingold (1991), p. 61.
2. See, for example, Aarts and Marzano (2003); Brey (2005); and Weber et al. (2005).
3. A slightly longer version of this passage from Raisinghani et al. (2004) is cited in Brey (2005), p. 157.
4. See Weiser (1991) for his original description of this expression.
5. See Brey (2005) for a more thorough discussion of how AmI can both enhance and limit human control.
6. See Forster (2009).
7. For more detail, see J. Bentham. "Panopticon." In M. Bozovic, ed. *The Panopticon Writings* (London: Verso, 1995), pp. 29–95.
8. See Goodman (1998), p. 17.
9. For a more detailed analysis of these distinctions, see Tavani (2006).
10. Moor (2006a), p. 110.
11. Goodman, p. 16.
12. This scenario is adapted from Tavani (2004). See also Stefansson (2001) and Taubes (2001).
13. My descriptions of these kinds of ethical issues in the next three sections draw from material in Tavani (2004, 2006).
14. For a detailed account, see Tavani (2006).
15. See http://www.genome.gov/24519851.
16. See, for example, http://en.wikipedia.org/wiki/Genetic_Information_Nondiscrimination_Act.
17. Regis (2009), p. 40.
18. Gordijn (2003), p. 4. The description of the six components of the "optimistic view" in this section is based on the account in Gordijn.
19. *Ibid*, pp. 5–6. The description of the six components of "pessimistic view" is based on the account in Gordijn.
20. Moor and Weckert (2004), p. 307.
21. Weckert and Moor (2004), p. 12.
22. Weckert (2006), p. 334–35.
23. This definition is based on the description of an autonomous system in The (UK) Royal Academy of Engineering's 2009 Report: *Autonomous Systems: Social, Legal and Ethical Issues*, p. 2.
24. Anderson, Anderson, and Armen (2006) use the expression "computing ethics" (as opposed to "computer ethics") to refer to this field. Elsewhere, however, Michael and Susan Anderson typically use "machine ethics."
25. In composing Section 12.5, I have drawn from material in four published works: Buechner and Tavani (2011), Tavani (2011, 2012), and Tavani and Buechner (2012).
26. See, for example, http://searchnetworking.techtarget.com/definition/autonomous-system.
27. This definition is used in the Royal Academy of Engineering's Report (2009).
28. See, for example, http://www.thefreedictionary.com/machine.
29. J. S. Hall (2011), p. 29.
30. See P. Lin (2012), pp. 5–6.
31. See, for example, G. Dworkin (1988).
32. L. Floridi (2008), p. 14. [Italics Added]
33. See W. deVries (2011), who distinguishes between "trust in general" and "topical trust." The sense in which I trust my daughter in the above example would be an instance of deVries' notion of trust in general.
34. M. Coeckelbergh (2010), p. 236.

35. S. Turkle (2011), p. 71.
36. See, for example, two special issues of journals dedicated to the topics of trust and e-trust: Taddeo (2010) and Taddeo and Floridi (2011).
37. M. Anderson and S. L. Anderson (2011), p. 1.
38. S. L. Anderson (2011), p. 22. While Anderson describes only two categories, I have subdivided her first category into two distinct levels.
39. M. Anderson and S. L. Anderson (2011), p. 9.
40. The Three Laws were introduced by Asimov in his short story "Runaround" (1942), and are anthologized in Assimov's *I, Robot* (1950). Assimov later added a fourth law, or "Zeroth Law," which states: "A robot may not injure humanity, or, through inaction, allow humanity to come to harm."
41. S. L. Anderson and M. Anderson (2011), p. 243. [Italics Added]
42. W. Wallach and C. Allen (2009), p. 202.
43. *Ibid*, p. 11.

► REFERENCES

Aarts, Emile, and Stefano Marzano, eds. 2003. *The New Everyday: Views on Ambient Intelligence*. Rotterdam, The Netherlands: 101 Publishers.

Allen, Colin, Garry Varner, and Jason Zinser. 2000. "Prolegomena to Any Future Moral Agent." *Experimental and Theoretical Artificial Intelligence* 12, no. 3: 251–61.

Allen, Colin, Wendell Wallach, and Iva Smit. 2006. "Why Machine Ethics?" *IEEE Intelligent Systems* 21, no. 4: 12–17. Reprinted in M. Anderson and S. L. Anderson, eds. *Machine Ethics*. Cambridge: Cambridge University Press, 2011, pp. 51–61.

Anderson, Michael, and Susan Leigh Anderson. 2011. "General Introduction." In M. Anderson and S. L. Anderson, eds. *Machine Ethics*. Cambridge: Cambridge University Press, pp. 1–4.

Anderson, Michael, Susan Leigh Anderson, and Chris Armen. 2006. "An Approach to Computing Ethics." *IEEE Intelligent Systems* 21, no. 4: 2–9.

Anderson, Susan Leigh. 2011. "Machine Metaethics." In M. Anderson and S. L. Anderson, eds. *Machine Ethics*. Cambridge: Cambridge University Press, pp. 21–27.

Anderson, Susan Leigh, and Michael Anderson. 2011. "A Prima Facie Duty Approach to Machine Ethics." In M. Anderson and S. L. Anderson, eds. *Machine Ethics*. Cambridge: Cambridge University Press, pp. 476–94.

Assimov, Isaac. 1950. *I, Robot*. New York: Doubleday.

Baumer, David, Julia Brande Earp, and Fay Cobb Payton. 2006. "Privacy of Medical Records: IT Implications of HIPAA." In H. T. Tavani, ed. *Ethics, Computing, and Genomics*. Sudbury, MA: Jones and Bartlett, pp. 137–52. Reprinted from *Computers and Society* 30 (2000): 40–47.

Berne, Rosalyn W. 2005. "Nanoethics." In C. Mitcham, ed. *Encyclopedia of Science, Technology, and Ethics*. Vol. 3 New York: Macmillan, pp. 1259–62.

Bohn, Jurgen, Vlad Coroama, Marc Langheinrich, Freidman Mattern, and Michael Rohs. 2005. "Social, Economic, and Ethical Implications of Ambient Intelligence and Ubiquitous Intelligence." In W. Weber, J. Rabaey, and E. Aarts, eds. *Ambient Intelligence*. New York: Springer.

Brey, Philip. 2005. "Freedom and Privacy in Ambient Intelligence." *Ethics and Information Technology* 7, no. 4: 157–66.

Buechner, Jeff, and Herman T. Tavani. 2011. "Trust and Multi-Agent Systems: Applying the 'Diffuse, Default Model' of Trust to Experiments Involving Artificial Agents." *Ethics and Information Technology* 13, no. 1: 39–51.

Capurro, Rafael, and Michael Nagenborg, eds. 2009. *Ethics and Robotics*. Heidelberg, Germany: AKA Press.

Čas, Johann. 2005. "Privacy in Pervasive Computing Environments—A Contradiction in Terms?" *IEEE Technology and Society Magazine* 21, no. 1: 24–33.

Chadwick, Ruth, and Antonio Marturano. 2006. "Computing, Genetics, and Policy: Theoretical and Practical Considerations." In H. T. Tavani, ed. *Ethics, Computing, and Genomics*. Sudbury, MA: Jones and Bartlett, pp. 75–83.

Chen, Andrew. 2002. "The Ethics of Nanotechnology." Available at http://www.actionbioscience.org/newfrontiers/chen.html.

Clarke, Steve. 2005. "Future Technologies, Dystopic Futures and the Precautionary Principle." *Ethics and Information Technology* 7, no. 3: 121–26.

Coeckelbergh, Mark. 2010. "Moral Appearances: Emotions, Robots, and Human Morality." *Ethics and Information Technology* 12, no. 3: 235–41.

Coeckelbergh, Mark. 2012. "Can We Trust Robots?" *Ethics and Information Technology* 14, no. 1: 53–60.

Custers, Bart. 2006. "The Risks of Epidemiological Data Mining." In H. T. Tavani, ed. *Ethics, Computing, and Genomics*. Sudbury, MA: Jones and Bartlett, pp. 153–65.

Decker, Michael, and Mathias Gutmann, eds. 2012. *Robo- and Information-Ethics*. Berlin, Germany: Verlag LIT.

deVries, Willem. 2011. "Some Forms of Trust." *Information* 2, no. 1: 1–16.

Drexler, K. Eric. 1991. *Unbounding the Future: The Nanotechnology Revolution*. New York: Quill.

Dworkin, Gerald. 1988. *The Theory and Practice of Autonomy*. New York: Cambridge University Press.

ELSI Research Program. National Human Genome Research Institute. Available at: http://www.genome.gov/10001618.

Floridi, Luciano. 2008. "Foundations of Information Ethics." In K. E. Himma and H. T. Tavani, eds. *The Handbook of Information and Computer Ethics*. Hoboken, NJ: John Wiley and Sons, pp. 3–23.

Floridi, Luciano. 2011. "On the Morality of Artificial Agents." In M. Anderson and S. L. Anderson, eds. *Machine Ethics.* Cambridge: Cambridge University Press, pp. 184–212.

Forster, E. M. 2009. "The Machine Stops." In D. G. Johnson and J. W. Wetmore, eds. *Technology and Society: Building Our Sociotechnical Future.* Cambridge, MA: MIT Press, pp. 13–36. Reprinted from *The Eternal Moment and Other Short Stories.* New York: Harcourt Brace, 1970.

Goodman, Kenneth W. 1998. "Bioethics and Health Informatics: An Introduction." In K. W. Goodman, ed. *Ethics, Computing, and Medicine: Informatics and the Transformation of Healthcare.* Cambridge, UK: Cambridge University Press, pp. 1–31.

Gordijn, Bert. 2003. "Nanoethics: From Utopian Dreams and Apocalyptic Nightmares Towards a More Balanced View." In *Proceedings of the World Commission of the Ethics of Scientific Knowledge and Technology (COMEST).* Available at http://portal.unesco.org/shs/fr/files/6603/10960368721Nanoethics.pdf/Nanoethics.pdf.

Hall, John Storrs. 2011. "Ethics for Machines." In M. Anderson and S. L. Anderson, eds. *Machine Ethics.* Cambridge: Cambridge University Press, pp. 28–46.

Himma, Kenneth E. 2009. "Artificial Agency, Consciousness, and the Criteria for Moral Agency: What Properties Must an Artificial Agent Have to be a Moral Agent?" *Ethics and Information Technology* 11, no. 1: 19–29.

Johnson, Deborah G. 2006. "Computer Systems: Moral Entities but Not Moral Agents." *Ethics and Information Technology* 8, no. 4: 195–204.

Joy, Bill. 2000. "Why the Future Doesn't Need Us." *Wired* 8, no. 4. Availability at http://www.wired.com/wired/archive/8.04/joy.html.

Koehler, Andreas, and Claudia Som. 2005. "Effects of Pervasive Computing on Sustainable Development." *IEEE Technology and Society Magazine* 21, no. 1 (Spring): 15–23.

Kurzweil, Ray. 2005. "Nanoscience, Nanotechnology, and Ethics: Promise and Peril." In C. Mitcham, ed. *Encyclopedia of Science, Technology, and Ethics.* Vol. 1 New York: Macmillan, 2005, pp. xli–xlvi.

Langheinrich, Marc. 2001. "Privacy by Design—Principles of Privacy-Aware Ubiquitous Systems." In Proceedings of the Third International Conference on Ubiquitous Computing. Springer-Verlag, pp. 273–91.

Lim, Hock Chuan, Rob Stocker, and Henry Larkin. 2008. "Review of Trust and Machine Ethics Research: Towards a Bio-Inspired Computational Model of Ethical Trust (CMET)." In *Proceedings of the 3rd International Conference on Bio-Inspired Models of Network, Information, and Computing Systems.* Hyogo, Japan, Nov. 25–27, Article No. 8.

Lin, Patrick. 2012. "Introduction to Robot Ethics." In P. Lin, K. Abney, and G. A. Bekey, eds. *Robot Ethics: The Ethical and Social Implications of Robotics.* Cambridge, MA: MIT Press, pp. 3–15.

Lin, Patrick, Keith Abney, and George A. Bekey, eds. 2012. *Robot Ethics: The Ethical and Social Implications of Robotics.* Cambridge, MA: MIT Press.

Marturano, Antonio. 2006. "Molecular Biologists as Hackers of Human Data: Rethinking Intellectual Property Rights for Bioinformatics Research." In H. T. Tavani, ed. *Ethics, Computing, and Genomics.* Sudbury, MA: Jones and Bartlett, pp. 235–45. Reprinted from *Journal of Information, Communication, and Ethics in Society* 1 (2003) 207–15.

McLeod, Carolyn. 2011. "Trust." In E. Zalta, ed. *The Stanford Encyclopedia of Philosophy.* Available at http://plato.stanford.edu/entries/trust.

Merkle, Ralph. 1997. "It's a Small, Small, Small, Small World." *Technology Review* 25 (February/March): 25–32.

Merkle, Ralph. 2001. "Nanotechnology: What Will it Mean?" *IEEE Spectrum* 38, no. 1 (January): 19–21.

Moor, James H. 2001. "The Future of Computer Ethics: You Ain't Seen Nothin' Yet!" *Ethics and Information Technology* 3, no. 2: 89–91.

Moor, James H. 2006a. "Using Genetic Information While Protecting the Privacy of the Soul." In H. T. Tavani, ed. *Ethics, Computing, and Genomics.* Sudbury, MA: Jones and Bartlett, pp. 109–19. Reprinted from *Ethics and Information Technology* 1, no. 4 (1999): 257–63.

Moor, James H. 2006b. "The Nature, Difficulty, and Importance of Machine Ethics." *IEEE Intelligent Systems* 21, no. 4: 18–21.

Moor, James H. 2008. "Why We Need Better Ethics for Emerging Technologies." In J. van den Hoven and J. Weckert, eds. *Information Technology and Moral Philosophy.* Cambridge, UK: Cambridge University Press, pp. 26–39.

Moor, James H., and John Weckert. 2004. "Nanoethics: Assessing the Nanoscale from an Ethical Point of View." In D. Baird, A. Nordmann, and J. Schummer, eds. *Discovering the Nanoscale.* Amsterdam, The Netherlands: IOS Press, pp. 301–10.

O'Neill, Onora. 2002. *Autonomy and Trust in Bioethics.* Cambridge, UK: Cambridge University Press.

Raisinghani, M., A. Benoit, J. Ding, M. Gomez, K. Gupta, V. Gusila, D. Power, and O. Schmedding. 2004. "Ambient Intelligence: Changing Forms of Human–Computer Interaction and Their Social Implications." *Journal of Digital Information* 5, no. 4 (Article No. 271): 8–24.

Regis, Ed. 2009. "Nanotechnology: The World's Smallest Radio." *Scientific American* 300, no. 3: 40–45.

Rheingold, Howard. 1991. *Virtual Reality.* New York: Touchstone Books.

Seeman, Nadrian C. 2004. "Nanotechnology and the Double Helix." *Scientific American* 290, no. 6: 64–75.

Smalley, Richard E. 2001. "Of Chemistry, Love, and Nanobots." *Scientific American* 285, no. 3: 76–77.

Son, Wha-Chul. 2005. "Autonomous Technology." In C. Mitcham, ed. *Encyclopedia of Science, Technology, and Ethics*. Vol. 1 New York: Macmillan, pp. 152–55.

Stefansson, Kari. 2001. "Population Inc." Interview in *Technology Review* 104, no. 3: 50–55.

Sullins, John P. 2011. "When Is a Robot a Moral Agent?" In M. Anderson and S. L. Anderson, eds. *Machine Ethics*. Cambridge: Cambridge University Press, pp. 151–61.

Taddeo, Mariarosario, ed. 2010. *Trust in Technology: A Distinctive and Problematic Relationship*. Special Issue of *Knowledge, Technology and Policy* 23, nos. 3–4.

Taddeo, Mariarosario, and Luciano Floridi, eds. 2011. *The Case for E-Trust: A New Ethical Challenge*. Special Issue of *Ethics and Information Technology* 13, no. 1.

Taubes, Gary. 2001. "Your Genetic Destiny for Sale." *Technology Review* 104, no. 3: 40–46.

Tavani, Herman T. 2004. "Genomic Research and Data-Mining Technology: Implications for Personal Privacy and Informed Consent." *Ethics and Information Technology* 6, no. 1: 15–28.

Tavani, Herman T. 2006. "Ethics at the Intersection of Computing and Genomics." In H. T. Tavani, ed. *Ethics, Computing, and Genomics*. Sudbury, MA: Jones and Bartlett, pp. 5–26.

Tavani, Herman T. 2011. "Can We Develop Artificial Agents Capable of Making Good Moral Decisions?" *Minds and Machines* 21: 465–74.

Tavani, Herman T. 2012. "Ethical Aspects of Autonomous Systems." In M. Decker and M. Gutmann, eds. *Robo- and Information-Ethics: Some Fundamentals*. Berlin, Germany: Verlag LIT, pp. 89–122.

Tavani, Herman T, and Jeff Buechner. 2012. "Autonomy and Trust in the Context of Artificial Agents." In M. Decker and M. Gutmann, eds. *Evolutionary Robotics, Organic Computing, and Adaptive Ambience*. Berlin, Germany: LIT Verlag, in press.

The Royal Academy of Engineering. 2009. *Autonomous Systems: Social, Legal and Ethical Issues*. Available at: www.raeng.org.uk/autonomoussystems.

Turkle, Sherry. 2011. "Authenticity in the Age of Digital Companions." In M. Anderson and S. L. Anderson, eds. *Machine Ethics*. Cambridge: Cambridge University Press, pp. 62–78. Reprinted from *International Studies*. John Benjamins Publishing Co., Amsterdam/Philadelphia, pp. 501–17.

Vedder, Anton. 2004. "KDD, Privacy, Individuality, and Fairness." In R. A. Spinello and H. T. Tavani, eds. *Readings in CyberEthics*. 2nd ed. Sudbury, MA: Jones and Bartlett, pp. 462–70.

Veruggio, Gianmarco, ed. 2006. "EURON Roboethics Roadmap (Release 1.1)." EURON Roboethics Atelier. Genoa, Italy. Available at http://www.roboethics.org/atelier2006/docs/ROBOETHICS%20ROADMAP%20Rel2.1.1.pdf.

Wallach, Wendell, and Colin Allen. 2009. *Moral Machines: Teaching Robots Right from Wrong*. New York: Oxford University Press.

Weber, Werner, Jan Rabaey, and Emile Aarts, eds. 2005. *Ambient Intelligence*. Berlin: Springer-Verlag.

Weckert, John. 2004. "Lilliputian Computer Ethics." In R. A. Spinello and H. T. Tavani, eds. *Readings in Cyber-Ethics*. 2nd ed. Sudbury, MA: Jones and Bartlett, pp. 690–7. Reprinted from *Metaphilosophy* 33, no. 3 (2002): 366–75.

Weckert, John. 2006. "The Control of Scientific Research: The Case of Nanotechnology." In H. T. Tavani, ed. *Ethics, Computing, and Genomics*. Sudbury, MA: Jones and Bartlett, pp. 323–39. Reprinted from *Australian Journal of Professional and Applied Ethics* 3 (2001): 29–44.

Weckert, John, and James H. Moor. 2004. "Using the Precautionary Principle in Nanotechnology Policy Making." *Asia Pacific Nanotechnology Forum News Journal* 3, no. 4: 12–14.

Weiser, Mark. 1991. "The Computer for the 21st Century." *Scientific American* 265, no. 3: 94–104.

Weizenbaum, Joseph. 1985. *Computer Power and Human Reason: From Judgment to Calculation*. New York: Penguin Books.

Woodhouse, E. J. 2004. "Nanotechnology Controversies." *IEEE Technology and Society Magazine* 21, no. 4: 6–8.

▶ FURTHER READINGS

Allhoff, Fritz, Patrick Lin, James Moor, and John Weckert, eds. *Nanoethics: The Ethical and Social Implications of Nanotechnology*. Hoboken, NJ: John Wiley and Sons, 2007.

Assimov, Isaac. "The Bicentennial Man." In M. Philips, ed. *Philosophy and Science Fiction*. Buffalo, NY: Prometheus, 1976, pp. 183–216.

Beavers, Anthony F., ed. *Robot Ethics and Human Ethics*. Special Issue of *Ethics and Information Technology* 12, no. 3 (2010).

Cameron, Nigel M. de S., and M. Ellen Mitchell, eds *Nanoscale: Issues and Perspectives for the Nano Century*. Hoboken, NJ: John Wiley and Sons, 2007.

Epstein, Richard G. *The Case of the Killer Robot*. New York: John Wiley and Sons, 1997.

Grodzinsky, Frances S., Keith W. Miller, and Marty J. Wolf. "Developing Artificial Agents Worthy of Trust: Would You Buy a Used Car from this Artificial Agent?" *Ethics and Information Technology* 13, no. 1 (2011): 17–27.

Johnson, Deborah G., and Thomas M. Powers. "Computers as Surrogate Agents." In J. van den Hoven and J. Weckert, eds. *Information Technology and Moral Philosophy*. Cambridge, UK: Cambridge University Press, 2008, pp. 251–69.

Mills, Kirsty, and Charles Fleddermann. "Getting the Best from Nanotechnology: Approaching Social and Ethical Implications Openly and Proactively." *IEEE Technology and Society Magazine* 24, no. 4 (2005): 18–26.

Simon, Judith. "The Entanglement of Trust and Knowledge on the Web." *Ethics and Information Technology* 12, no. 4 (2010): 343–55.

GLOSSARY

ACM Code of Ethics and Professional Conduct: A code of ethics endorsed by the Association for Computing Machinery.

accessibility privacy: A conception of privacy in terms of being let alone, or being free from intrusion into one's physical space; contrasted with decisional privacy and informational privacy.

agent: Someone or something that is capable of acting; agents that act on the behalf of others are sometimes called "fiduciary agents." See also *artificial agent*.

ambient intelligence (AmI): A technology that senses changes in the environment and automatically adapts to these changes vis-à-vis the needs and preferences of users, while remaining in the background and thus being virtually invisible to users. See also *pervasive computing* and *ubiquitous communication*.

anonymity: In the context of cybertechnology, the ability to navigate the Internet and participate in online forums without having to reveal one's true identity.

applied ethics: A branch of ethical inquiry that examines practical (as opposed to theoretical) moral issues and problems. See also *ethical theory*.

artificial agent (AA): A nonhuman agent that can be either a physical/biological entity (such as a robot or cyborg) or an electronic/digital entity (such as an AI bot or "softbot"). See also *agent*.

artificial intelligence (AI): The field of study that examines relationships between machine intelligence and human intelligence. One branch of AI attempts to shed light on human intelligence by using cybertechnology to simulate it; another branch is concerned with constructing intelligent tools to assist humans in complex tasks. See also *expert systems*.

autonomous machine (AM): A computerized system or agent that is capable of acting and making decisions independently of human oversight. AMs can interact with and adapt to (changes in) their environment and can learn (as they function).

avatar: A computer-generated image on a screen, or in virtual space, used to represent someone. Some avatars exhibit human-like characteristics.

bioinformatics: A field concerned with the acquisition, storage, manipulation, analyses, and simulation of biological information on a computer, with the objective of making that information more understandable and useful.

biometrics: The biological identification of a person, which includes eyes, voice, hand prints, finger prints, retina patterns, and hand-written signatures.

blog (or Web log): A Web site that contains an online journal with reflections and comments; blogs may be further categorized as political blogs, personal blogs, corporate blogs, travel blogs, health blogs, literary blogs, and so forth. See also *blogosphere*.

blogosphere: A name given to the collective community of all *blogs*.

computer security: A branch of computer science concerned with both safeguarding computer systems (hardware and software resources) from attacks by malicious programs, such as viruses and worms, and protecting the integrity of the data resident in and transmitted between those systems from unauthorized access.

consequentialism: An ethical theory that appeals to consequences, outcomes, or ends as the essential criterion, or standard, used to justify particular actions and policies in a moral system. See also *utilitarianism*.

contract theory of ethics: A theory that ties a moral obligation to assist others to an express contract to do so. Contract theory is sometimes viewed as a minimalist theory of morality, because without an explicit contract, one would simply be required to do no harm to others; there is no obligation to actively assist others.

cookies: Text files that Web sites send to and retrieve from a Web visitor's computer system. Cookies technology enables Web site owners to collect information about a visitor's preferences while the visitor interacts with their Web sites.

Creative Commons (CC): A nonprofit organization whose aim is to expand the range of creative work available to others to legally build upon and share, via a set of licensing options intended to help artists and authors give others the freedom and creativity to build upon their creativity.

cultural relativism: A descriptive thesis stating that different cultures have different views about what is morally right or wrong. Many philosophers have argued that even if cultural relativism is true, it does not logically imply moral relativism, which is a normative position. See also *moral relativism*.

cyberbullying: A type of harassment (or bullying) that takes place online, via e-mail, text messaging, or online forums, such as social networking sites.

cybercrime: Criminal activity that is either made possible or significantly exacerbated by the use of computers and cybertechnology.

cyberethics: The field of study that examines moral, legal, and social issues involving cybertechnology.

cyberstalking: The use of cybertechnology to clandestinely track the movement and whereabouts of one or more individuals.

cybertechnology: A range of computing and information/communication technologies, from stand-alone computer systems to privately owned computer networks to the Internet.

cyberterrorism: The convergence of cyberspace and terrorism, covering a range of politically motivated hacking operations that can result in loss of life, severe economic loss, or both.

data mining: A computerized technique for unearthing implicit patterns in large databases to reveal statistical data and corresponding associations that can be used to construct consumer profiles.

denial-of-service attacks: Repeated requests sent to a Web site that are intended to disrupt services at that site. Denial-of-service attacks can be sent via third-party sites, from computer systems located in universities and organizations, to confuse the targeted sites about the source of the attacks.

deontological ethics: A theory of ethics that bases its moral system on duty or obligation rather than on consequences and outcomes that result from actions. Deontological ethical theories can be contrasted with consequentialist theories. See also *consequentialism*.

descriptive ethics: A branch of ethical inquiry that reports or describes the ethical principles and values held by various groups and individuals. Descriptive ethics is usually contrasted with normative ethics. See also *normative ethics*.

digital divide: The gap between those who have ("information haves") and those who do not have ("information have-nots") computers and access to cybertechnology.

digital rights management (DRM): A technology that allows content owners to regulate the flow of information in digital media by blocking access to it via encryption mechanisms, and by enabling access to it through the use of passwords.

ethical theory: A branch of ethical inquiry dedicated to the study of philosophical frameworks for determining when actions and policies are morally right or morally wrong. Ethical theory, or theoretical ethics, is often contrasted with applied ethics. See also *applied ethics*.

ethics: The study of morality or a moral system. Normative ethics approaches the study of a moral system from the perspective of philosophy, religion, or law, whereas descriptive ethics typically examines morality from the perspective of social science. See also *morality*, *descriptive ethics*, and *normative ethics*.

expert system (ES): A computer program that is expert at performing one particular task traditionally performed by humans; developed from research in artificial intelligence. Because it is a computer program, an ES is different than a robot, which is a physical or mechanical system. See also *artificial intelligence* and *robotics*.

hacktivism: The convergence of political activism and computer hacking by which activists use cybertechnology to disrupt the operations of organizations.

identity theft: The act of taking another person's identity by using that person's name, social security number, credit card numbers, and so forth.

IEEE Code of Ethics: An ethical code sanctioned by the Institute of Electrical and Electronics Engineering.

inductive argument: An argument form in which the premises, when assumed true, are strong enough to suggest the likelihood of the argument's conclusion. Unlike a valid argument, the premises of an inductive argument cannot guarantee the conclusion.

informal logical fallacies: Fallacious arguments that commonly occur in everyday discourse. Because these fallacies are so common, they have familiar names such as *ad hominem*, *ad populum*, begging the question, and slippery slope.

information warfare (IW): Operations that target or exploit information media in order to win some objective over an adversary. IW, unlike conventional warfare, can be more disruptive than destructive; like conventional warfare, however, IW is waged by nation states.

informational privacy: A conception of privacy in terms of control over the flow of one's personal information, including the collection and exchange of that information; contrasted with accessibility privacy and decisional privacy.

intellectual property: An intangible form of property that is protected by a system of laws such as patents, copyrights, trademarks, and trade secrets, through which authors and inventors are given ownership rights over their creative works.

location privacy: A relatively new category of privacy concerned with the use of embedded chips, RFID technology, and global positioning systems to track the physical location of individuals at any point in time.

logical argument: A form or structure of reasoning in which one or more statements (called premises) are used as evidence to support another statement, the conclusion.

machine ethics: A field that examines ethical concerns that arise because of what (highly sophisticated) computers are capable of doing on their own, as opposed to ethical issues resulting from what humans do with computers. See also *robo-ethics*.

macroethics: Concerned with the analysis of moral rules and policies at the societal level, as opposed to the level of individuals. See also *microethics*.

malware: A label that applies to a cluster of "malicious programs," including viruses, worms, Trojan horses, logic bombs, and so forth; malware can also include "spyware."

microethics: Concerned with the analysis of moral rules and directives at the level of individuals, as opposed to the societal level. See also *macroethics*.

moral absolutism: A view holding that there are absolute moral principles and that there is only one uniquely correct answer to every moral question.

moral objectivism: A compromise view between moral absolutism and moral relativism; moral objectivists believe that there are objective standards for evaluating moral claims, so that there can be agreement on the correct answers to many moral issues, but that there can also be more than one acceptable answer to some moral issues. See also *moral absolutism* and *moral relativism*.

moral relativism: The view that there are no universal moral norms or standards and that only the members of a particular group or culture are capable of evaluating the moral principles used within that group. See also *cultural relativism.*

morality: A system comprising rules, principles, and values; at its core are rules of conduct for guiding action, and principles of evaluation for justifying those rules. See also *ethics.*

MMORPGs: Massively Multiplayer Online Role-Playing Games, which include popular video games such *World of Warcraft* and *Second Life.*

nanotechnology: A field dedicated to the development of extremely small electronic circuits and mechanical devices built at the molecular level of matter.

normative ethics: A branch of ethical inquiry that is concerned with evaluating moral rules and principles by asking what ought to be the case, as opposed to descriptive ethics that simply reports what is the case (i.e., what individuals and cultures happen to believe) with respect to morally right and wrong behavior. See also *descriptive ethics.*

online communities: Computer-mediated social groups that interact in virtual space, as contrasted with traditional communities in which interaction occurs in physical space.

open source software: Software for operating systems and applications in which the source code is made freely available to use, modify, improve, and redistribute. Open source software, such as the Linux operating system, is contrasted with proprietary operating system software such as MS Windows.

P2P technology: Peer-to-peer technology, which enables two or more computers to share files through either a centralized directory such as the (original) Napster site or a decentralized system such as LimeWire.

pervasive computing: A computing environment where information and communication technology are everywhere, for everyone, at all times. See also *ambient intelligence.*

PETs: Privacy-Enhancing Technologies are tools that both protect a user's personal identity while the user interacts with the Web and protect the privacy of communications (such as e-mail) sent over the Internet.

phishing: A fraudulent use of e-mail to acquire a user's password, social security number, etc., to gain unauthorized access to information about the victim; often, the e-mail looks as if it was sent by an official site such as eBay or PayPal.

***prima facie* duty:** A type of moral duty that one has, all things being equal (such as honesty, benevolence, justice, and so forth). Prima facie duties, which can be overridden by circumstances, are contrasted with absolute duties.

RFID: Radio Frequency Identification is a technology that consists of a tag (microchip) containing an electronic circuit, which stores data, and an antenna that broadcasts data by radio waves in response to a signal from a reader.

risk analysis: A methodology used to make an informed decision about a product based on considerations such as cost. A costs-benefits model of risk assessment for software can include criteria such as safety, reliability, schedule, budget, consumer demand, and so forth.

robo-ethics: A field that examines the ways that humans design, use, and treat robots and related AI entities. See also *machine ethics*.

robotics: The field of research and development in robots and robotic parts/limbs. See also *expert systems*.

sexting: The use of cell phones (or similar handheld electronic devices) to send nude or seminude photos of oneself to others; in some cases, these photos become widely distributed and can eventually end up on the Internet.

Social Networking Service (SNS): A Web-based service, such as Facebook, Twitter, Linked-In, and so forth, which enables users to construct a profile and share information with other members (or "friends") on the online forum.

spam: E-mail that is generally considered to be unsolicited, promotional, and sent in bulk to multiple users.

Turing test: a scenario in which a person engaged in a conversation on a computer screen with some "entity" (located in a room that is not visible to the person) is asked to determine whether he or she is conversing with another human or with a computer.

utilitarianism: A consequentialist ethical theory based on the principle that an act or policy is morally permissible if it results in the greatest good (usually measured in terms of happiness) for the greatest number of people affected by it. See also *consequentialism*.

valid argument: An argument form in which the premises, if assumed true, are sufficient to guarantee the truth of the conclusion.

virtual environment: An online (or computer-generated) environment, which is contrasted with an environment in physical space. Virtual environments, as opposed to virtual reality (VR) environments and applications, can be either two dimensional (e.g., text-only) or three dimensional. See also *virtual reality*.

virtual reality: A three-dimensional, interactive computer-generated environment, as contrasted with physical reality. See also *virtual environment*.

virtue ethics: A theory that stresses character development and the acquisition of "correct" moral habits as opposed to mere conformance with certain rules for action, which are typically associated with duty-based (deontological) and consequence-based (utilitarian) ethical theories.

virus: A program that can insert executable copies of itself into other programs; also generically referred to as a malicious program. See also *worm*.

worm: A program or program segment that searches computer systems for idle resources and then disables them by erasing various locations in memory; also generically referred to as a malicious program. See also *virus*.

INDEX